Knowledge Management and Drivers of Innovation in Services Industries

Patricia Ordoñez de Pablos
The University of Oviedo, Spain

Miltiadis D. Lytras
American College of Greece, Greece

Information Science
REFERENCE

Managing Director: Lindsay Johnston
Senior Editorial Director: Heather A. Probst
Book Production Manager: Sean Woznicki
Development Manager: Joel Gamon
Development Editor: Myla Harty
Acquisitions Editor: Erika Gallagher
Typesetter: Nicole Sparano
Cover Design: Nick Newcomer, Lisandro Gonzalez

Published in the United States of America by
Information Science Reference (an imprint of IGI Global)
701 E. Chocolate Avenue
Hershey PA 17033
Tel: 717-533-8845
Fax: 717-533-8661
E-mail: cust@igi-global.com
Web site: http://www.igi-global.com

Library of Congress Cataloging-in-Publication Data

Knowledge management and drivers of innovation in services / Patricia Ordonez de Pablos and Miltiadis D. Lytras, editors.
p. cm.
Includes bibliographical references and index.
ISBN 978-1-4666-0948-8 (hbk.) -- ISBN 978-1-4666-0949-5 (ebook) -- ISBN 978-1-4666-0950-1 (print & perpetual access) 1. Knowledge management. 2. Organizational learning--Management. 3. Service industries--Management. I. Ordsqez de Pablos, Patricia, 1975- II. Lytras, Miltiadis D., 1973-
HD30.2.K6368423 2012
658.4'038--dc23
2011048477

British Cataloguing in Publication Data
A Cataloguing in Publication record for this book is available from the British Library.

List of Reviewers

Jingyuan Zhao, *Harbin Institute of Technology, China*
Patricia Ordóñez de Pablos, *The University of Oviedo, Spain*
Miltiadis D. Lytras, *American College in Greece, Greece*
Murat Çetin, *King Fahd University of Petroleum & Minerals, Saudi Arabia.*
Robert D. Tennyson, *University of Minnesota, USA*
W.B. Lee, *The Hong Kong Polytechnic University, Hong Kong*
Xi Li, *Macau University of Science and Technology, Macao SAR*

Table of Contents

Detailed Table of Contents

As firms lose skilled labour force through mass retirement, turnover and economic fluctuations, a pressing concern is how to ensure that the skills of the present-day masters are conveyed to the future professionals. This chapter examines the process of how the skills leading to professional performance are acquired in the context of on-the-job learning and identifies the key factors in this process. Based on an empirical examination of the on-the-job training periods of 20 Finnish vocational college students a model is built, suggesting that there are three different levels of professional performance on a junior's path towards professionalism. The results suggest that individual activity, critical observation, conscious doing and creativity are crucial in the learning process. The chapter contributes to the emerging discussion on knowledge sharing across generations in organisations.

In the knowledge economy, Knowledge Management (KM) has gained strategic importance in management agenda in many organizations, including those in the service industries. This chapter presents the case study of the Singapore Health Promotion Board (HPB), as a study of how KM can be harnessed to improve public sector performance in an area where bottom-line performance is hard to define. By analysing the development of the HPB's "Healthier Hawker Programme," the case study examines the HPB's journey in using increasingly sophisticated KM processes, tools, and techniques. The experiences and lessons learnt during the HPB's KM journey are analysed and presented using the Learning with Knowledge (LK) Cycle, a model that is useful to the formation of an ontology for analytic discussion and the implementation of KM.

This chapter develops a research protocol to identify a domain of organizational knowledge resources and assets within firms and provides the final main insights of a research project managed by the Intellectual Assets Center in Scotland in order to support the adoption of knowledge asset management initiatives for driving innovation and performance improvement of Small and Medium Enterprises (SMEs) operating in the renewable energy sector. The chapter first presents a methodology for valuing organizational knowledge assets within SMEs operating in the renewable energy industry. Then, an exploratory survey with a sample of 58 organizations from the Scottish renewable energy sector is introduced. Finally, the chapter analyses and discusses the main insights about SMEs' perception and orientation to identifying, measuring, and managing knowledge, and to qualitatively identify a feasible set of knowledge resources and assets potentially driving performance improvement.

Since the idea of "artificial intelligence with knowledge" had been introduced, so many thoughts, theories, and ideas in various fields of engineering, science, geology, social study, economics, and management methods have been proposed. Those things have been started as an extension of modern engineering control theories and practices. Firstly, expert system by using IF-Then rules came up to at a production spot in manufacturing, and then agent system method by using intelligent software programs for design, planning, scheduling, production, and management in manufacturing. And then after, the idea of "Knowledge" burst into the artificial intelligence field as a real aid for getting any purpose to be accomplished by having augmented the past key knowledge in terms of management (controlling). However, those augmented knowledge methods used to have usages only in a limited small area. In addition to this, lots of works have to be done before making the systems work for a target problem solving. And what is worse, lots of parts of systems have to be customized for a new application. This chapter introduces a new direction and a method in "Knowledge" by inaugurating the brand new idea of "Dynamics in Knowledge," which will behave more flexibly and intelligently in real usages.

This chapter presents a tool that distinguishes selects and supplies, among all products with similar characteristics that appear in the catalogue of a company, the product that better adapts to the necessities of the users. In order to achieve this, it uses a search system based on fuzzy logic techniques, being able to handle vague information or of difficult specification and thus making possible to administer to the tool by means of rules of "common sense," which talk about indefinite amounts. A fundamental aspect that provides great flexibility to the application is that the system can be modified and adjusted by the expert in real time. This allows changing quickly the output product set and without stopping the operation of the system based on the necessities of the company. The results are codified in XML format, facilitating the interoperability between systems and allowing the execution of the tool in multiple operative systems, as they only have to process the generated content. The possibility of displaying the clients the products that they are looking for, directly responding to their necessities, guiding and advising them in the purchase that are ready to make, is a competitive advantage that the company must not let escape.

Internet-based information, communication, and collaboration technologies are making it easier for organizations and knowledge workers to collaborate across organizational boundaries. However, it is necessary for organizations to monitor, regulate, and build appropriate security mechanisms in collaboration systems to prevent loss of strategic knowledge and competitive advantage. In this chapter, the authors synthesize literature on knowledge sharing and IS/IT risk assessment to present a risk assessment

Use of educational games during teaching process does not represent a new topic. However, the question "How to address the knowledge in educational games?" is still open. The purpose of this chapter is to propose a model that will attempt to establish the balance between knowledge integration into game on one side, and its reusability on other. The model driven approach presented in this chapter relies on the use of Learning Objects (LO) as constructing pieces of knowledge resources, which are specialized for educational game design purpose. Presented models contribute to methodology of educational games development in a way that they embrace principles of learning and knowledge management early in design process. The authors demonstrate applicability of their models in design case study, where they developed educational game editor where the educator can easily define new educational game utilizing existing knowledge, assessment, and multimedia from repository.

Preface

The reality is that there is very little research in service innovation. In the current economic environment, the service sector dominates the economies of the developed world. In this complex scenario, service is fast becoming the key driver of socio-economic, academic, and commercial research attention.

One of the main drivers that shape services and service companies, organizations, and governments is the increasing intensity of knowledge in services, and the impact of information and communication technologies on them. Because knowledge in knowledge-intensive services is typically located in product, service, or both, it is important to collect, store, modify, update, and distribute it in a way that would provide value for the clients.

Knowledge Management is concerned with all aspects of eliciting, acquiring, modelling, and managing knowledge, as well as its role in the construction of knowledge-intensive systems and services for the semantic web, knowledge management, e-business, natural language processing, intelligent information integration, and so on.

Application of knowledge resources successfully helps the organization to deliver creative products and services. Especially in service business, service job experience and information about the customer as well as the installed site equipment are key factors to deliver services efficiently and with high quality. In many cases supporting information is stored in different backend systems, and it needs to be retrieved, aggregated, and presented on demand. These requirements play a crucial role for contact centers, which have the first contacts with customers, as well as for the field service engineers, who have the closest contacts with the customers during executions of service jobs at the customers' sites.

The book's aim is to be an essential reference in the *subject areas* of a combination of knowledge management, innovation, information technologies and systems, and services industry.

Knowledge Management and Drivers of Innovation in Services Industries is organized into 19 chapters, which provide insight on knowledge management.

Chapter 1 (*ALSA CHINA: Knowledge Management and Drivers of Development and Innovation*) focuses on how ALSA began its operations in China in 1984, at the beginning of China´s policy of economic opening to the outside world. In order to become one of the companies of reference in the field of road passenger transport in China, ALSA has made a long process of adapting its business management to the characteristics of the country. This includes the establishment of a knowledge management system.

Chapter 2 (*Knowledge in Universities and Research Centres: Proposed Indicators for Measuring Relational Capital*) addresses how the knowledge economy and society is based on the creation, use, and dissemination of knowledge. It is clear that universities and research centres play a vital role in the knowledge creation, application and transfer processes. The current economic state, namely a financial crisis of international proportions, inhibits university and research and development program funding and the implementation of the Bologna Process, this strategic resource (knowledge) must be suitably managed. In order to achieve this, it is necessary to measure existing knowledge-based resources (intellectual capital) and draw up knowledge maps. This chapter proposes a conceptual framework for analysing relational capital in universities and research centres and presents indicators for measuring each of its components.

Chapter 3 (*Alternative Call Center Operational Indicators to Customer Satisfaction*) focuses on developing a set of alternative call center operational performance indicators, in order to enhance the relationship between call center performance and customer satisfaction. To achieve this, a methodological approach is taken using surveys, as well as stepwise multiple linear regressions, and is developed from 6,616 cases collected during three months from the telecommunication industry. Generally, it is concluded that a set of alternative call center indicators covering three dimensions, namely the call center ability to resolve a problem, the call center responsiveness and the prior customer satisfaction with the call center, together with traditional indicators, present a statistically significant relationship with customer satisfaction. The insights from this study can help managers to improve the customer satisfaction with call center, as well as to better sub-contract outsourcing call center operators.

Chapter 4 (*How Are Professional Skills Acquired? A Structured Process of on-the-Job Learning)* examines the process of how the skills leading to professional performance are acquired in the context of on-the-job learning and identifies the key factors in this process. These examinations are based on an empirical examination of the on-the-job training periods of 20 Finnish vocational college students. The chapter suggests that there are several key elements in the learning process, such as individual activity, critical observation, conscious doing, and creativity.

Chapter 5 *(Knowledge Management in the Public Service: The Case of the Singapore Health Promotion Board)* discusses how Knowledge Management (KM) in the knowledge economy has gained strategic importance in management agenda in many organizations, including those in the service industries. Specifically, this chapter presents a case study of the Singapore Health Promotion Board (HPB). It examines how KM can be harnessed to improve public sector performance in an area where bottom-line performance is hard to define. , the case study examines the HPB's journey in using increasingly sophisticated KM processes, tools and techniques by analysing the development of the HPB's "Healthier Hawker Programme". The experiences and lessons learned during the HPB's KM journey are analysed and presented using the Learning with Knowledge (LK) Cycle. This model is useful to the formation of ontology for analytic discussion and the implementation of KM.

Chapter 6 *(Assessing Knowledge Assets in Renewable Energy SMEs in Scotland: A Methodological Framework)* develops a research protocol to identify a domain of organizational knowledge resources and assets within firms. Also it provides the final main insights of a research project managed by the Intellectual Assets Center in Scotland in order to support the adoption of knowledge asset management initiatives for driving innovation and performance improvement of Small and Medium Enterprises (SMEs) operating in the renewable energy sector. First, the chapter presents a methodology for valuing organizational knowledge assets within SMEs operating in the renewable energy industry. Then, an exploratory survey with a sample of 58 organizations from the Scottish renewable energy sector is introduced. Finally, the chapter analyses and discusses the main insights about SMEs' perception and orientation to identifying, measuring, and managing knowledge, and to qualitatively identify a feasible set of knowledge resources and assets potentially driving performance improvement.

Chapter 7 (*Inside Entrepreneurship and Innovation Activities*) aims to investigate how entrepreneurship affects not only and innovation capabilities, but also the whole periphery and economy. Additionally, it examines how technological innovation is essential if companies - and countries - are to maintain their competitiveness in global markets. There are many underlying problems and questions regarding the measurement of entrepreneurship and innovation activities. In particular, this chapter attempts to analyze the whole framework of entrepreneurship and innovation activities, and in particular, to analyse the effects and implications to growth and competitiveness. Within this context, it is also aiming to emphasize and review the appropriate techniques, the most common methods, and the particular related problem.

Chapter 8 *(Achieving Competitive Advantage through Innovation: The Case of the Shanghai Supermarket)* examines innovation in the service/retail sector. Specifically, the authors look at how it has not been fully examined in the non-Western literature. This preliminary work presents a study that was conducted in Shanghai, China, and consults three sets of the literature: Porter's Generic Strategies Model, Hunt's Resource Advantage Theory (R-A), and previous studies in the service and retail sectors. Findings developed from six selected successful Chinese supermarket companies have identified three types of innovation adopted by Chinese retailers: Technology based, non-technology based, and resource based innovation. The study takes a qualitative approach by using the methods of documentation survey and in-depth interviews with a panel of ten supermarket experts. Some managerial implications are explicated, and the limitations of the study and directions for future studies are discussed.

Chapter 9 *(Adverse Events and Medical Errors in Greece: Knowledge Creation and Capture Methods)* analyzes the lack of standardized nomenclature and a universal taxonomy-classification for adverse events and medical errors that complicates the development of a response to these issues. Also, it reviews numerous methods of adverse events' and medical errors' knowledge management. Each of these has evolved over time and adapted to different contexts.

Chapter 10 *(Dynamics in Knowledge)* addresses the origins of "artificial intelligence with knowledge." Since the idea has been introduced, numerous thoughts, theories, and ideas in various fields of engineering, science, geology, social study, economics, and management methods in general have arisen. Those things would have been started as an extension of modern engineering control theories and practices. This chapter introduces a new direction and method in "knowledge" by inaugurating the brand new idea of "Dynamics in Knowledge," which will behave more flexibly and intelligently in real usages.

Chapter 11 *(Towards an Improved Hotel Reservation System: A Fuzzy Approach to Improve Service Industries)* develops a tool that distinguishes, selects, and supplies among products with similar characteristics that appear in company catalogues the product that better adapts to the necessities of the users. In order to achieve this, it uses a search system based on fuzzy logic techniques which is able to handle vague information or of difficult specification. As a result, it is possible to administer the tool by rules of "common sense" which talk about indefinite amounts.

Chapter 12 *(A Risk Assessment Framework for Inter-Organizational Knowledge Sharing)* summarises literature on knowledge sharing and IS/IT risk assessment. The goal is to present a risk assessment framework that can help organizations identify valuable knowledge assets exposed through collaboration technologies. Also, it aims to assess the risk of knowledge loss, intellectual property leakage, and the subsequent loss of competitive advantage so that appropriate security mechanism can be designed to prevent such a loss.

Chapter 13 *(Knowledge Management for Web-Based Learning Systems)* addresses how there is very little information available concerning how different users learn and retain information on websites. Web-based system characteristics may be an influencing factor which could positively or negatively impact a user's attitude. In this research, users' experience with information explains how different users derive the knowledge to use the systems that forms the basis of interaction with the system.

Chapter 14 (*A Predictive Modeling of Retail Satisfaction: A Data Mining Approach to Retail Service)* discusses how data mining allows managers to make more knowledgeable decisions by predicting future trends and behaviours. Marketing is one of the most widely used areas of data mining for the retail industry. Also, there are at least seven methods of analysis or statistical techniques that are commonly used in data mining. It is obvious that the approach to the data mining is the key determinant of the statistical technique to be used. Predictive modelling uses variety of techniques such as linear regression, logistic regression and their extensions can be used to identify patterns which can be used to predict the future. Specifically, this research focuses on the application of multiple regression technique a data mining tool in Indian retail industries to predict the retail satisfaction using store attributes as independent variables.

Chapter 15 *(Innovation for E-Services Management)* examines how over the last several years traditional services (face to face) have been transferred over to the electronic environment on the web also known as E-Services. There is very little knowledge to know how and why these services are used by consumers based on their knowledge and experience and motivation, ease of use and usefulness of e-services, acceptance and continued usage for e-services. This research explores the theoretical framework for developing e-services acceptance model (E-SAM).

Chapter 16 *(A Multi-Agent Knowledge Management System for Reactive and Proactive Knowledge Supply)* presents an agent-based architecture for integrating organizational knowledge repositories and business processes orchestrated by a workflow management system. This architecture proactively provides relevant knowledge to workflow tasks considering their context, and stores the information generated by its execution for future requirements. It describes components of the architecture, models a multi-agent system that enables the integration, presents a strategy to annotate and retrieval knowledge of non-structured information sources, and defines a new workflow pattern to be used in knowledge intensive tasks in order to make possible the knowledge provision. This architecture allows workers to count, in a proactive way, with all necessary information for the task executions without suspend their activities to retrieve information scattered in the organization. It reduces the wasted time in manual knowledge searches included in mostly knowledge management approaches.

Chapter 17 *(Framework of Knowledge and Intelligence Base: From Intelligence to Service)* introduces the concept of the "Intelligence Base." The Intelligence base was developed by the authors in a study on the information requirement of the management of a (military) organization. The purpose of the study was to conceive, for each level of an organization, an appropriate Decision Support System (DSS) and/or Knowledge and Information System. All systems would eventually have been integrated in an overall Enterprise Architecture (EA).

Chapter 18 *(Enhancing Information Retrieval Capabilities of Knowledge Management System)* addresses different dimensions of the major information retrieval techniques that can be used in a user services environment. Also, the chapter seeks to propose new models to enhance retrieval capabilities of KM systems. The basic elements that make up an information retrieval system including metadata, controlled and uncontrolled vocabularies are discussed. The chapter proposes three experimental search interfaces for enhancing information retrieval capabilities of a KM system.

Chapter 19 *(Knowledge Management in Educational Games)* proposes to answer the question "How should one address knowledge in educational games?" from the ongoing topic of using educational games during teaching process. A model is proposed that will attempt to establish the balance between knowledge integration into game on one side and its reusability on other. This model driven approach is relying on use of Learning Objects (LO) as constructing pieces of knowledge resources which are specialized for educational game design purpose. Presented models contribute to methodology of educational games development in a way that they embrace principles of learning and knowledge management early in design process. The applicability of the models is demonstrated in design case study, where educational game editors were created. This allows an educator to easily define new educational game utilizing existing knowledge, assessment, and multimedia from repository.

Patricia Ordóñez de Pablos
The University of Oviedo, Spain

Miltiadis D. Lytras
American College of Greece, Greece

Chapter 1
ALSA CHINA:
Knowledge Management and Drivers of Development and Innovation

Andrés Cosmen
ALSA CHINA, Hong Kong

ABSTRACT

ALSA began its operations in China in 1984, at the beginning of China's policy of economic opening to the outside world. In order to become one of the companies of reference in the field of road passenger transport in China, ALSA has made a long process of adaptation of its business management to the characteristics of the country, including the establishment of a knowledge management system.

INTRODUCTION

Regardless of previous stages of China's opening to the outside world, and if focusing only on the most recent years of economic development, China has changed dramatically, from being an isolated country, to being highly integrated into globalization that has led to China becoming the second economic world power.

This economic revolution over the three decades, has led to continuous changes in the framework of its economy and businesses, forcing all economic operators to adapt to a new environment in which they must develop and compete. For the Chinese enterprises these changes have resulted, not only in new opportunities for development, but also in great challenges, mainly arising from the lack of experience and knowledge of operating in a market economy. The need to adapt to the new situation, both in the local market motivated by the changes brought by the opening policy, as well as by the desire to participate and compete in markets abroad, where the rules of the game are different to those that they have been used to, makes knowledge management a priority for Chinese enterprises.

DOI: 10.4018/978-1-4666-0948-8.ch001

Knowledge Management to Chinese businesses is something new. Many foreign companies have tried to implement systems similar to those already used in their home as instruments for development and management of their knowledge. Despite this, for most Chinese companies it is still something new and highly abstract, more related to Western culture than to their own culture.

When we speak of economic changes such as those which have taken place in China, it seems clear that there are companies (both state-owned companies and private companies) who have already experienced the necessity to adapt to the new environment. All of them have been forced to evolve, starting with a change in both their philosophies and objectives. Those companies who were unable to adapt have been slowly disappearing. This has been far more evident for Chinese companies which have gone to compete abroad, where the lack of knowledge in the functioning of the market economy is further compounded by cultural differences. Whilst previously many had often enjoyed great competitive advantages derived from a cheap workforce, abundant supplies of natural resources with at low prices and strong protectionism from their Government. However, the lack of knowledge of those foreign markets and its own market mechanism has diminished their competitiveness.

For this reason, some large Chinese companies have begun to pay special attention to the development of knowledge management systems in order to improve their competences, to adapt to new markets and gain in competitiveness. With regard to State-owned enterprises, they are generally large corporations, with oversized management structures, where the economic objectives are not yet clearly defined. Despite this, in recent years there have been serious attempts of the Government to implement knowledge management systems in these companies. However, the limited technical training of many of its managers, many of whom possess more of a political profile than business orientation, combined with the weight of the Government itself, is making results unclear.

For the majority of companies whom were pioneers in China; like for example Alsa, were initially attracted by its local market and were willing to compete for a share of it. In general, these companies had great advantages of knowledge, both technically (more technologically advanced) in addition to superior management skills, (having a greater knowledge of management in a market economy, quality of service, etc.). However, with the passage of time, in many sectors of the economy, the Chinese companies are the ones who have developed more and have won a larger market share, while many foreign companies have failed in their objectives. Whilst the reasons for this are many and varied, in many cases ignorance, the failure of western companies and managers to understand the characteristics of the country and a lack of adaptation has proven decisive.

Generally speaking, many foreign companies imported their existing management techniques and working systems, assuming that what was good in their home markets will also work in China. The reality has been very different and the success of many of these companies has been a result of their ability to acquire knowledge of China and adapt to the Chinese business environment. Those companies who have failed to find the correct balance between their local knowledge and the new market have failed. It has been important for foreign companies to adapt their management systems to the characteristics of the country, but more importantly to identify which elements of their existing management systems could not be modified, despite local pressure to do so, to avoid the resulting losses of important competitive advantages.

ALSA IN CHINA

ALSA established its first company in China in 1984, to operate in domestic interurban road passenger transport. Like most of the companies that entered China during the early years of opening, Alsa tried to export its management and operation systems, thinking that if not all of them, most of them would be valid for China. ALSA relied on its human capital, people with experience in the company, who were able to transfer their knowledge to the new businesses in China, and to develop a flow of information between the head office and the branch offices in China, with the help of training programs for managers both in China and Spain.

Soon we realized that the situation in China was very different from expected. If we wanted to succeed here, we would need to know this new environment and adapt to it. The key was not to copy what already existed in China, since in the field of passenger transport management the local business situation was very precarious. Its performance was poor, both at the management level and in the service to customers. If we were to succeed we would need to change the transport industry and make it more profitable, whilst at the same time, changing and evolving to become a more local company. One very clear example of the level of service to passengers was that until our arrival, the buses did not have fixed departure times. Buses will depart for their destination only when they were full and all the seats were occupied.

During the early years of our business in the underdeveloped China market, Alsa focused on growth, acquiring and establishing business with local partners. At the same time we began to introduce and target changes in the sector, such as fixed schedules, quality of service, safety improvements and so forth, and then the business became profitable. We were competing in a market where the main players were State-owned enterprises, with oversized structures and low efficiencies, whom did not seem very interested in market competition.

Soon the market situation changed with the development of the economy and the construction of new expressways, which made passenger transportation businesses a very profitable industry. This, together with the ease in obtaining new transport operating licenses, multiplied the number of companies competing and it became a highly atomized market. The entry of these new actors, and the recent development of high-speed railways, has changed passenger road transportation in China into a highly competitive business sector.

ALSA CHINA AND KNOWLEDGE MANAGEMENT

The operations of Alsa China are based on joint venture companies, since Chinese law does not allow the establishment of wholly foreign owned enterprises to operate in the domestic road passenger transport. We normally choose our local partners from the transport industry, who bring business experience and knowledge of transport at the local level. These joint venture companies are located at important cities with a strategic position in transport, and each one of these companies is independent of the rest, since we have a different local partner for each. These are separate companies, with independent legal status, but with a common partner, Alsa, who is responsible for operations management under a unified system of rules and procedures. The local partners are the ones who manage the relationships with the local transport authorities in the areas where we operate.

At the end of the nineties, and through our corporate office in Beijing, we began to put in place a system to obtain, analyze, and store and use of the information received both from the companies and the environment where they operate. The task was to coordinate and improve the management systems of all our businesses and learn from the experiences of each one of them, sharing information, and establishing a strategy of knowledge management common to all Alsa companies in China.

We established as priority to obtain information from four main areas;

A. Company´s internal information. We should improve our information from all the company operation levels and from customers, and be able to use it to develop our own operating systems and improve them. The task was to control and coordinate the knowledge flow that was produced in connection with the activities at all the operation levels of the company, in order to create a set of key competences.
B. Information from the "country" that helps us understand more about the environment for greater cooperation where we operate. Further improving our understanding of cultural differences, and knowledge of the local environment, without limiting ourselves to the business level.
C. Market information. Understanding the local transportation market and anticipate its development.
D. Information from the transport sector. A greater understanding of Chinese companies in our industry, their policies, and to adopt more local forms of labor, so that we meet the key entities regulating the sector and learn how to interact with them.

To start we should design a data mining system, by selecting the sources where we would obtain the relevant information. We chose the companies themselves; the workers at all levels, from managers to drivers (who have a continuous contact with the customer), statistical systems of transport (by establishing new data reporting systems to our Beijing corporate office), financial systems and accounting systems (creating new systems to provide information to the management), public bus stations (to create systems to share information between different users of stations), management teams (developing relationships with local governments and transport Departments as well as other companies in the sector). We established regular meetings, seminars, courses, etc., destined not only to share information at all levels of the company, but also to obtain inputs in various departments. Service inspections to our own and additionally outside companies were scheduled.

Storage, Analysis, Use, and Distribution of Information

Some of this information came from statistical data, numerical data that is easy to encode and store. We have established a common database covering all areas of the company, and appointed data area managers who were in charge of obtaining the data, filtering and storage. Despite this, we have learned that most of the usable information, especially in the field of service operations and interactions with institutions and partners, was based on personal experiences and how workers are able to develop skills based on these experiences. This information is difficult to encode and store. We have tried to include much of this information within the system of rules and procedures, but some of it cannot be stored easily, and must be transferred by other means.

In the analysis of information we emphasized the need that data were evaluated from all perspectives, avoiding weighing one culture over the other. The case was not to only implement the views of Alsa as a company already developed in Europe, but from a local point of view, being necessary the participation in the process of local trained personnel from local companies and with a vision of the market different from our own. We had to consider the "Chinese characteristics" which affect our business operations.

We had to use this information in a useful manner, and to make the information transmission in a fluid way between workers in companies that are independent from each other whilst maintaining a margin of privacy. To do this, we created parallel databases with common areas and restricted areas. We set up "best practices" systems for internal processes. We created rules and procedures of operation, which were easy to implement because the Chinese labor culture is used to regulatory policy. We organized seminars for departments, meetings at all levels. Our aim was to put in practice a policy of information sharing within the company, through the use of technology tools, and encourage the participation of the employees.

Drivers of Development and Innovation

The main drivers of development and innovation were:

A. Regulatory framework. In the early years, almost all the actions leading to service innovations were banned, because China was a planned economy with very rigid policies, where companies had little freedom of action. As the country began the economic opening to the outside world, the regulatory framework was gradually liberalized, and we were able to put into practice services or activities that were previously prohibited.

B. Increase in the income levels of the population. The increasing income and higher education levels have led the population to be increasingly more sensitive to the problems of pollution and to demand better quality of life and improved public services. This means that customers demand services of a higher quality and are willing to pay a higher price. One example in ALSA China was the launch of the "Imperial Class" bus service, which is similar to the Business Class of airlines, which has a higher ticket price than the standard bus service.

C. Development of the Information Technologies. In the early stages we acquired Chinese companies in which there was not a single computer in the office. This circumstance was not extraordinary, but it represented the reality of the country from an information and technology point of view. Later on we jumped to acquire the latest technologies for management and control applied to transport, most of which was developed in China. Therefore, we have seen the development of new technology at very different pace from that in the West. We have moved quickly from a poorly evolved technology market and with few suppliers, to a market with excess supply and usually very competitive in price, although with some quality problems. Alsa China's companies have implemented these technological advances, using them to improve both the levels of management, safety, service of quality. We introduced digital tacographs systems capable of analyzing not only the behavior of the vehicle, but also that of the driver. We added to our fleet technological tracking via GPS to establish systems of safety and reliability. Onboard computer systems for real time traffic information were also added. We offer our passengers Wi-Fi service on board as a further improvement to the service quality. We equip our fleet and workshops with digital electronic test to know the status of them and thus improving safety. We created intelligent ticket sales channels and an internet ticket sales platform. All this technological revolution has helped us to maintain a leading position in the sector.

D. Development of transport infrastructure, in particular of the expressway network. China has gone from having only 300 kilometers of expressways in 1987 to over 74,000 kilometers at the end of the year 2010, becoming the second country in the world with more kilometers of expressways, only behind United States. This has meant a large reduction in traveling times, higher productivity of the fleet and personnel, and a more comfortable trip for passengers.

E. Increased competition. Competition has not only increased from other foreign companies that have established operations in the country, these are mainly from South and North Asia, but also from Chinese companies that have managed to adapt and develop to the new business environment and improve their services. New services are being continuously introduced.

F. Increase in population mobility. In our early days there were many restrictions to persons travelling from one province to another, and almost all of these restrictions have now disappeared. Currently it is easier for the population to travel and transportation services can be offered to many destinations without limitations for passengers.

G. Urbanization of society. The social transformation which is a result of the emigration of the population from the countryside to the cities has increased the size of our potential market. The urban population, with a higher level of income, travels more and demands more quality of service than the rural population, remains our market niche in China.

CONCLUSION

We believe that our experience in China has been highly positive. ALSA today enjoys a leading position at the forefront of the transportation industry, we are a reference and benchmark for transport institutions, as well as for both Chinese and foreign companies that have either already decided to or are considering establishing operations in the China transportation market.

In recent years we have been pioneers in the establishment of quality operational systems, control and safety systems, new ticket sale channels, agreements with large companies, loyalty cards and many other areas. Our objective is to remain innovative, marking and participating in the development of transport. Without doubt, to do so, we must continue to adapt new technologies and to develop an efficient strategy of knowledge management that results in the provision of an optimal service for our customers in the competitive China transport market.

Chapter 2
Knowledge in Universities and Research Centres:
Proposed Indicators for Measuring Relational Capital

Patricia Ordóñez de Pablos
The University of Oviedo, Spain

ABSTRACT

The knowledge economy and society is based on the creation, use, and dissemination of knowledge. There is no doubt universities and research centres play a vital role in the knowledge creation, application, and transfer processes. Against an economic backdrop such as the current one, namely a financial crisis of international proportions, cuts in university and research and development programme funding and the implementation of the Bologna Process, this strategic resource must be suitably managed. In order to achieve this, it is necessary to measure existing knowledge-based resources (intellectual capital) and draw up knowledge maps. This chapter proposes a conceptual framework for analysing relational capital in universities and research centres and presents indicators for measuring each of its components.

INTRODUCTION

In recent years we have we have witnessed an international crisis that is affecting, to a greater or lesser extent, the economies of every country on earth. The media is full of stories about important structural reforms being proposed by governments, the financial rescue of countries, falling stock market indexes, company closures and staff layoffs, etc. Companies and organisations are increasingly aware of the importance of people and what they know (their knowledge) for dealing with economic scenarios as complex as those we are seeing today and of individuals with a capacity for long-term vision and leadership. But knowledge is not only found in the individuals within companies and organisations, but also in the relationships these individuals develop

DOI: 10.4018/978-1-4666-0948-8.ch002

among themselves both inside and outside the company. There is also the knowledge present within the organisational structures and routines, in the company's policies and in its organisational culture, among others.

Intellectual Capital as a Strategic Knowledge Economy Resource

A fundamental question within the Strategic Management field is why do some companies gain a long-term competitive advantage and others do not. Strategic Management literature has made numerous efforts to construct coherent frameworks that synthesise the different contributions. Among these attempts at synthesis mention must be made of the resources and capacities theory. This theory integrates a set of contributions the focal or starting point of which is the heterogeneity of resources within the companies and their imperfect mobility, which helps to explain the sustained differences in the profitability observed. Intangible resources, such as knowledge, present these characteristics (Crook et al., 2008; Peteraf and Barney, 2003).

We can analyse the knowledge that exists within companies and organisations, in other words their intellectual capital, from a static perspective. This intangible resource corresponds to those knowledge-based resources which, despite contributing towards the creation of value within the company, are not reflected in its economic-financial statements. These include, for example, the knowledge of the employees or the value to the company of a relationship with a strategic partner.

At this point it is convenient to refer to the typology of intellectual capital most readily accepted in literature in order to study its components. This enables us to differentiate between human capital, relational capital and structural capital. The essential parts of human capital are the skills and knowledge of the company's employees. The scope of human capital is internal and resides in the mind of the employee, which makes it difficult to codify.

Relational capital refers to the flows of knowledge between individuals within a network and, therefore, includes the knowledge present in the relationships established with the environment, both internal and external. The first group would contain the relationships between company employees, managers and shareholders. The second group would consist of the relationships developed by the company with customers, suppliers, competitors, public administrations and other interest groups.

Finally, structural capital represents the knowledge that remains behind in the company when the employees have finished their working day, in other words it is that knowledge that does not depend on certain individuals or specific relationships but belongs to the company. An example of this knowledge would be organisational routines, strategies and organisational culture, among others.

Managers must know what knowledge types exist in their companies and organisations and where each of these is located. To ensure this it is necessary to measure the existing intellectual capital within companies, draw up organisational knowledge maps and compile intellectual capital reports.

Since its inception, intellectual capital literature has mainly focused on the study of intellectual capital within companies. However, the work being done on intellectual capital in universities and research centres is still negligible. In the following section we study the importance of universities and research centres as creators and disseminators of knowledge in the current economic environment.

The Role of Knowledge in Universities and Research Centres

The European Commission makes special mention (2006, 2008) of the strategic role played by the knowledge triangle (education, research and innovation) in regional economic and social development. Universities and research centres are, without doubt, an essential mainstay of the knowledge society.

The European Commission (2008) highlights a set of nine possible actions for responding to the challenges and overcoming the obstacles facing universities today, in a context of modernisation and international crisis, and for achieving the objectives of the Lisbon Agenda, identified by the European Commission in its Communication of 2006, "Delivering on the Modernization Agenda for Universities: Education, Research and Innovation". These reforms can be grouped into three principal areas: curricular reform, university governance and research and innovation. These nine actions are the following:

1. Break down the barriers around universities in Europe
2. Ensure real autonomy and accountability for universities
3. Provide incentives for agreements with the universities
4. Provide the right mix of skills and competencies for the labour market
5. Reduce the funding gap and make funding work more effectively in education and research
6. Enhance interdisciplinary and transdisciplinarity
7. Activate knowledge through interaction with society
8. Reward excellence
9. Make the European higher education area and the European research area more visible and attractive in the world

Four basic interdependent elements are present in the knowledge economy and society: (1) the production of new knowledge, (2) the transmission of knowledge through education and training, (3) the dissemination of knowledge via new information and communications technologies and, lastly, (4) the use of knowledge through new services or industrial processes. In all these actions the universities and research centres are key players with respect to achieving success.

Universities perform their activity within a globalised competitive environment and compete with each other to attract and retain the best possible human capital whilst at the same time competing for funding. They also face the risk of losing knowledge, for example, when a researcher with a solid international career decides to leave and go to another university because the remunerative conditions or career development opportunities do not fulfill expectations (Blackman and Kennedy, 2009; Wilkesmann and Würmseer, 2007).

A first step towards improved knowledge management in universities and research centres is being aware of the knowledge they have and where it is located and designing specific policies and programmes for the management of each type of knowledge.

KNOWLEDGE NETWORKS IN UNIVERSITIES AND RESEARCH CENTRES: RELATIONAL CAPITAL

Although when the term "knowledge" is mentioned we tend to think of people's knowledge, in other words individual knowledge, we must be aware of the existence of other forms of knowledge of a different origin and with different properties and potential. In this section we focus on a specific type of knowledge: relational capital.

The people who form part of companies and organisations form relationships with other people working in the same department or in other departments within the company. But they are also in contact, for reasons of work, with people from outside the company who work for other companies and institutions. New knowledge is generated as a result of these professional relationships with other individuals. When knowledge is a result of the interaction of people who work for the same company or organisation is called "internal relational capital". When knowledge emerges as a result of people within professional environments interacting with people from other companies it is known as "external relational capital".

Austrian universities represent a pioneering international example with respect to the compilation of intellectual capital reports. In response to the *Universities Act 2002* Austria became the first country in the world to promote the measurement of intellectual capital in universities. Since 2005 every Austrian university has been obliged by law to present a "Wissensbilanz" or intellectual capital report in order to contribute towards organisational transparency in the presentation of the results of the country's universities (Leitner, 2005; Leitner and Warden, 2004). This means institutions such as the Vienna University of Economics and Business and the University of Innsbruck have been presenting intellectual capital reports for a number of years.

In order to better study and analyse the relational capital of universities and research centres, we propose differentiating three types of relational capital: student relational capital, academic staff relational capital (teaching staff and researchers) and institutional relational capital (refer to Figure 1).

Let us now analyze each of these concepts. Student relational capital is the result of the interactions between students when performing practical studies and group projects, attending group tutorials imparted by the academic staff, group study sessions with other students during which doubts are voiced and everybody collaborates in resolving the doubts of colleagues, etc.

Academic staff relational capital is a consequence of the interaction between the teaching body of one institution and the professors of other universities and research centres both on a national and international level. By studying this concept in more depth, we could differentiate between teaching staff relational capital and research staff relational capital. In the first case the knowledge generated would be the result of participating in teacher training courses and exchanging experiences, academic staff meetings, guest professorships at other universities, among others. Research staff relational capital would be the result of group interaction on research projects, research seminars, guest research assignments, etc.

Institutional relational capital is the result of the agreements and partnerships with other universities, research centres and companies, of the university's reputation, of the evaluation of different groups of stakeholders, of the scores achieved in national and international rankings, of the awards for excellence received, etc.

Figure 1. Typology of relational capital in universities and research centres

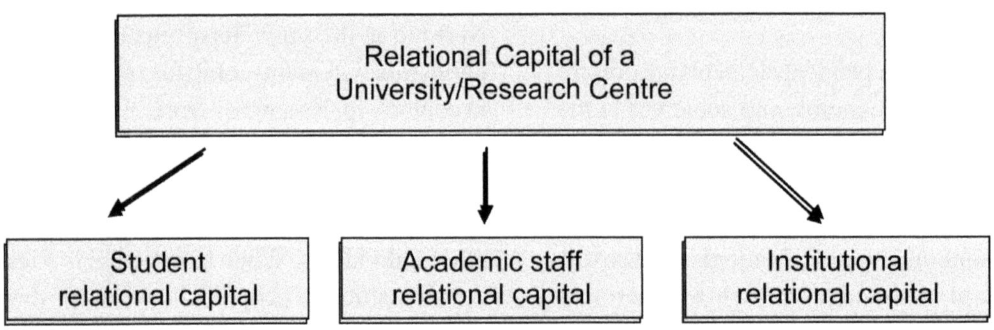

Indicators for Measuring the Relational Capital of Universities and Research Centres

In 1994 the Swedish company Skandia published the world's first ever intellectual capital report. This report captured the attention of academic researchers and companies who observed how this pioneering company was making the first international experiments in the measurement of intellectual capital and publishing reports containing the results of these measurements. Skandia was followed by Danish and Norwegian companies that also measured and compiled reports on knowledge-based intangible resources. A second wave of companies interested in measuring intellectual capital followed in 1997 centred mainly in Spain, Italy and Austria. Later still, interest in measuring intellectual capital reached Asia pioneered by Indian group Reliance and the company Shree Cement, also from India (Brüggen et al., 2009; Guthrie et al., 2006; Johansson et al, 2006; Ordóñez de Pablos, 2005)

In 2004, as a result of an international research project, the 3R Model was developed which provided a methodology for measuring in-company intellectual capital (Ordóñez de Pablos, 2004). This model, derived from an exhaustive study of intellectual capital reports published by pioneering international companies of the time, proposed that the measurement and publication of intellectual capital reports had to follow the steps listed below:

1. **Compiling the intellectual capital report:** On the one hand this report gathers information about the company's philosophy, mission and values as well as its business strategy. On the other it contains the intellectual capital measurements presented using tables, one for each intellectual capital component (human capital, relational capital and structural capital). These tables show the indicators and sub-indicators of each intellectual capital component together with their corresponding values.
2. **Compiling the intellectual capital flow report:** this is a report that shows the increases and decreases of intellectual capital and the short- and long-term objectives.
3. **Compiling the intellectual capital memorandum:** this is a report that includes information that complements the data presented in the intellectual capital and intellectual capital flow reports. It includes information about the company's activities, the norms used to evaluate the intangible resources as well as those events that may have occurred after the close of the previous reports and which, irrespective of their affect, contain information that is useful for the users of the intellectual capital reports.

Following this line of investigation, we analysed intellectual capital reports published internationally between 1994 and now (September 2011), participated in specialist international congresses at which the initial model and the subsequent models developed were presented, and also held interviews with managers and experts in measuring intellectual capital from different countries.

Next we proposed a list of indicators for quantifying the relational capital of universities and research centres. In accordance with the typology of relational capital described above, these indicators were divided into three categories: (1) academic staff relational capital, (2) student relational capital and (3) institutional relational capital. The following double entry table contains, by rows, the indicators for each category, while the columns show the value of these indicators in the current and previous financial year as well as the objective for each indicator (see Table 1).

Table 1. Relational capital indicators

RELATIONAL CAPITAL	Current Financial Year	Previous Financial Year	Objective
Academic staff relational capital • No. of the institution's researchers who spend time working at other universities: o Spanish universities o Overseas universities • No. of researchers from other universities who spend time at the university/research centre: o From Spanish universities o From overseas universities • Length of the research visits made by the institution's researchers: o Spanish universities: ▪ Less than 1 month ▪ Between 1 and 5 months ▪ Between 6 and 12 months o Overseas universities: ▪ Less than 1 month ▪ Between 1 and 5 months ▪ Between 6 and 12 months • Length of research visits made by researchers from other universities who spend time working at the university/research centre: o From Spanish universities: ▪ Less than 1 month ▪ Between 1 and 5 months ▪ Between 6 and 12 months o From overseas universities: ▪ Less than 1 month ▪ Between 1 and 5 months ▪ Between 6 and 12 months • No. of papers published: o By the institution's own researchers o Together with researchers from other Spanish institutions o Together with researchers from other overseas institutions • No. of research projects: o By the institution's own researchers o Together with researchers from other Spanish institutions o Together with researchers from other overseas institutions **Student relational capital** • No. of group tutorial hours imparted: o Spanish students only o Spanish and overseas students • No. of hours of group study sessions: o Spanish students only o Spanish and overseas students • No. of group projects implemented: o With Spanish students o With Spanish and overseas students • No. of group projects implemented that received prizes or recognition: o With Spanish students o With Spanish and overseas students			

continued on following page

Table 1. Continued

RELATIONAL CAPITAL	Current Financial Year	Previous Financial Year	Objective
Institutional relational capital • No. of student practical work experience agreements with companies: o Companies in Spain o Overseas companies • Length of student practical work experience agreements with companies: o Companies in Spain: ▪ Less than 1 year ▪ Between 1 year and 3 years ▪ More than 3 years o Overseas companies: ▪ Less than 1 year ▪ Between 1 year and 3 years ▪ More than 3 years • No. of student exchange agreements with universities/research centres: o Spanish centres o Overseas centres • Position in ranking of best universities/research centres: o Spanish ranking o Overseas ranking • No. of agreements with research centres: o Spanish centres o Overseas centres • No. of prizes received by the institution: • Appearances in the media for academic reasons: o Rector o Research project managers o Research groups o Individual researchers • No. of social assistance/social commitment programmes: o Same province o Country o Abroad			

CONCLUSIONAND FUTURE LINES OF RESEARCH

There is no doubt that to be able to efficiently manage a resource as special as the knowledge within an organisation it is necessary to draw up "knowledge maps" which show where this resource is located and the value it has. The knowledge present in the relationships between peoples –in other words relational capital- is a strategic resource that must be quantified. In the case of universities and research centres, it is necessary to show the university community and society in general the return obtained from the investments made in research and development, the assistance given to research projects and innovative educational projects and the collaborations between universities and research centres.

The construction of strategically valuable knowledge networks is not a simple task, but all the members of the academic community, both in Spain and abroad, must make an effort in their search for organisational excellence.

The relational capital indicators of the universities and research centres must serve to show the university community and society in general a part of the value created by the institution –we must not forget that the human capital and structural capital that should be measured also exists in universities. The periodic publication of this information will represent another step towards informative transparency in the annual reports compiled by universities and research centres.

A further step in the progress of this research would be to complete the knowledge map of the universities and research centres with human capital and structural capital indicators, namely the two other components of intellectual capital. Another step in this research would be to implement the measuring model and the compilation of intellectual capital reports in a university in line with the experience of the Austrian companies that have been compiling these reports since 2005.

REFERENCES

Blackman, D., & Kennedy, M. (2009). Knowledge management and effective university governance. *Journal of Knowledge Management*, *13*(6), 547–563. doi:10.1108/13673270910997187

Brüggen, A., Vergauwen, P., & Dao, M. (2009). Determinants of intellectual capital disclosure: Evidence from Australia. *Management Decision*, *47*(2), 233–245. doi:10.1108/00251740910938894

Communication from the Commission of February 5, 2003. (2003). *The role of the universities in the Europe of knowledge COM(2003) 58 final. The role of universities in the Europe of knowledge.*

Crook, R. T., Ketchen, D. J., Combs, J. G., & Todd, S. Y. (2008). Strategic resources and performance: A meta-analysis. *Strategic Management Journal*, *29*, 1141–1154. doi:10.1002/smj.703

Guthrie, J., Petty, R., & Ricceri, F. (2006). The voluntary reporting of intellectual capital. Comparing evidence from Hong Kong and Australia. *Journal of Intellectual Capital*, *7*(2), 254–271. doi:10.1108/14691930610661890

Johansson, U., Koga, C., Skoog, M., & Henningsson, J. (2006). The Japanese Government's intellectual capital reporting guideline. What are the challenges for firms and capital markets agents? *Journal of Intellectual Capital*, *7*(4), 474–491. doi:10.1108/14691930610709121

Leitner, K.-H. (2005). Managing and reporting intangible assets in research technology organisations. *R & D Management*, *35*(2), 125–136. doi:10.1111/j.1467-9310.2005.00378.x

Leitner, K.-H., & Warden, C. (2004). Managing and reporting knowledge-based resources and processes in research organisations: Specifics, lessons learned and perspectives. *Management Accounting Research*, *15*(1), 33–51. doi:10.1016/j.mar.2003.10.005

Observatory of the European University. (2006). *Methodological guide*. Final Report of the Observatory of the European University, PRIME Project. Retrieved from www.prime-noe.org

Ordóñez de Pablos, P. (2004). A guideline for building an intellectual capital statement: The 3R model. *International Journal of Learning and Intellectual Capital*, *1*(1), 3–18. doi:10.1504/IJLIC.2004.004420

Ordóñez de Pablos, P. (2005). Intellectual capital reports in India: Lessons from a case study. *Journal of Intellectual Capital*, *6*(1), 141–149. doi:10.1108/14691930510574717

Peteraf, M. A., & Barney, J. B. (2003). Unravelling the resource-based tangle. *Managerial & Decision. Economics*, *24*, 309–323.

Report from the Commission to the Council on the Council Resolution of 23 November 2007. (October 2008). *On modernising universities for Europe's competitiveness in a global knowledge economy.*

Wilkesmann, U., & Würmseer, G. (2007). Wissensmanagement an Universitäten. *Hochschulmanagement*, *1*, 1–6.

Chapter 3
Alternative Call Center Operational Indicators to Customer Satisfaction

Alexandre Ferreira Oliveira
Brazilian School of Public and Business Administration at Getulio Vargas Foundation, Brazil

Luiz Antonio Joia
Brazilian School of Public and Business Administration at Getulio Vargas Foundation, Brazil

ABSTRACT

The purpose of this chapter is to purport a set of alternative call center operational performance indicators, in order to enhance the relationship between call center performance and customer satisfaction. In order to do that, a methodological approach based on surveys, as well as stepwise multiple linear regressions, is developed from 6,616 cases collected during three months from the telecommunication industry. The general conclusion is that a set of alternative call center indicators covering three dimensions, namely the call center ability to resolve a problem, the call center responsiveness, and the prior customer satisfaction with the call center, together with traditional indicators, present a statistically significant relationship with customer satisfaction. The insights from this study can help managers to improve the customer satisfaction with call center, as well as to better sub-contract outsourcing call center operators.

INTRODUCTION

Despite the relevance of the call center industry, there is a lacuna in academic literature in correlating the relationship between operational performance indicators used by call centers and customer satisfaction.

DOI: 10.4018/978-1-4666-0948-8.ch003

In the United States, two studies conducted by Feinberg et al. in 2000 and 2002 attempted to pinpoint operational indicators which determine customer satisfaction. The results encountered were, however, divergent. In the first study in 2000, two indicators appeared to have some connection with the customer satisfaction level (Feinberg et al., 2000). In the second study, in

2002, with the focus of research directed at the call centers that served the financial market, no performance indicator showed any correlation to customer satisfaction (Feinberg et al., 2002).

Thus, this chapter aims to contribute to the technical literature, seeking to answer the following research question: What set of call center operational performance indicators have any bearing on customer satisfaction? This question is relevant as there is no consensus on this point in the academic world.

An attempt is also made to find empirical evidence to help company managers who either operate or hire the services of call center operations to develop strategies that improve customer satisfaction, thereby enhancing the competitiveness of these organizations, both in the domestic and international markets.

With this in mind, three operations of one of the leading companies in the Brazilian call center outsourcing market were analyzed. For reasons of confidentiality, this study will safeguard the identity of all the companies involved in the research.

BACKGROUND

Operational Performance Indicators

According to Black (1998), the efficiency of call centers is a critical aspect for the image of the organization. However, in the academic literature on call centers, there is no consensus on which operational performance indicators are related to customer satisfaction. Therefore, following the research stream adopted by Feinberg et al. (2000, 2002), a number of indicators considered fundamental to the achievement of excellence in operating a call center, according to the vision of Anton (2000), Cleveland and Mayben (1997), Evensen et al. (1999), Grimm (2001), Rosati (2001), Sparrow (1991) and Tom et al. (1997) will be adopted.

Thirteen indicators selected from the reference sources mentioned above, with their respective meanings, are listed below:

- **Service Level x Seconds (SL):** Attempts to measure the total number of calls handled within x seconds; usually 20 or 30 seconds. It is calculated by dividing the total number of calls answered within x seconds by the total number of calls.
- **Percentage of Call Block (PCB):** Attempts to measure the availability of the call center. It is calculated by dividing the total number of calls with busy tone by the total number of calls made.
- **Percentage of First-Call Resolution (FCR):** Attempts to measure the internal efficiency. It is calculated by dividing the total number of calls that are resolved on first contact by the total number of calls made.
- **Abandonment Rate (AbR)**: Attempts to measure the availability of the call center. It is calculated by dividing the total number of calls that were hanged up – or disconnected by the caller before being answered – by the total number of calls made.
- **Adherence (AD):** Attempts to measure the efficiency of the call center. It is calculated by dividing the total number of agents who were at the service post as scheduled by the total number of agents.
- **Time before Abandoning (TBA):** Attempts to measure the availability of the call center. It is calculated by dividing the total – in seconds – of calls that were abandoned before being attended, by the total of these calls.
- **Talk Time (TT)**: This is calculated by dividing the total – in seconds – of all calls that were answered by the total of all these calls.

- **Queue Time (QT)**: This is calculated by dividing the total – in seconds – of all the calls that remain on hold before being answered by the total of all these calls.
- **Average Work Time after the Call (WTC)**: This is calculated by dividing the total – in seconds – of the time spent after the close of a call attended by the total of all calls attended.
- **Average Training Time (TrT):** This is calculated by dividing the total days of training received by agents by the total number of agents.
- **Total Calls (ToC)**: This is the total of calls received or made by the agents.
- **Total of Calls Attended per Shift (TCS):** This is calculated by dividing the total number of calls received or made by the agents by the total number of agents per work shift.
- **Agent Turnover (Tu):** This is calculated by dividing the total number of agents who have left the company by the total number of workstation positions.

The data required for preparing these indicators are collected by the technological infrastructure that exists in the call centers. The data for the TrT (Average Training Time) are collected by ancillary systems.

Alternative Indicators

As presented by Parasuraman (2002), the concept of productivity, despite the vast amount of associated literature, favors the standpoint of the producer/provider due to the ease of data measurement that this approach affords. Thus, the set of alternative indicators of call center operations attempted to observe the customer perspective, subverting the dominant rationale and thereby following the opposite direction to that proposed by Parasuraman (2002).

The first of the dimensions chosen was the problem-solving capacity. This choice was made on the basis of the observation by Feinberg et al. (2000), which pointed to the First Call Resolution Capacity (FCR) indicator as being a significant factor for customer satisfaction. The choice of this dimension is also supported by the attribute of competence presented by Johnston (1995), as well as the reliability dimension postulated by Parasuraman et al. (1988).

The second dimension adopted was responsiveness, which finds support in Johnston (1995) and Parasuraman et al. (1988). Another point that motivated the choice of this dimension was the result obtained by Feinberg et al. (2000), which singled out the Abandonment Rate as also being one of the determinants of satisfaction with the call center, as this indicator is directly related to the waiting time online and/or total connection time (Feinberg et al. 2000; Anton, 2000).

The third dimension aimed to assess the customer's prior satisfaction *vis-à-vis* the company, insofar as this is a response to an evaluation process (Halstead et al.,1994; Fornell, 1992; Howard and Sheth, 1969; Westbrook, 1987; Oliver, 1992; Giese and Cote, 2000), also incorporating the importance of the image of the company (Grönroos, 1984) and quality of the process (Lehtinen, 1983) for its formation.

Customer Satisfaction

According to Babin and Griffin (1998) and Giese and Cote (2000), there is a lack of consistency in the conceptualization and measurement of the "customer satisfaction" construct (Babin and Griffin, 1998; Giese and Cote, 2000), even bearing in mind the economic impact that this aspect has on companies (Bitner et al., 1990, Cronin & Taylor, 1992; Fornell, 1992, Patterson, 1993). Thus, whereas quality and satisfaction are often treated as synonyms (Vandenberghe et al., 2004) in the context of services, for the purposes of this article it is necessary to clarify precisely what is meant by customer satisfaction.

One aspect that highlights the controversy surrounding this issue is the debate generated by Yi (1990), on the characteristic of satisfaction as a process or an output. Currently, the dominant approach considers satisfaction as a response to an evaluation process (Halstead et al., 1994; Fornell, 1992; Howard and Sheth, 1969; Westbrook, 1987, Oliver, 1992; Giese and Cote, 2000). An example that supports this approach is the position of Johnston (1995), whereby the customer's satisfaction with a particular service, occurring at a given moment, affects the satisfaction or dissatisfaction of the customer in relation to the service as a whole.

Based on an extensive review of the literature and validations by means of group and individual interviews, Giese and Cote (2000) argue that the "consumer satisfaction" construct has three essential components. Firstly, satisfaction consists of an affective response that varies in intensity in each situation. Subsequently, satisfaction relates to a product, service, purchase or consumption, depending on the situation. Finally, satisfaction has a limited duration period, which varies with each situation in question.

According to Dean (2002), there are few guidelines in the literature about the perception of the quality of a call center. Also, according to Bennington et al. (2000), the academic literature neglected the field of customer satisfaction in relation to the way in which the service provided by the call center is established.

In his study on the priority of service quality, Gilmore (2001) encountered different perceptions between managers and agents with respect to the degree of customer satisfaction. In this work, Gilmore (2001) showed how managers were more focused on more tangible aspects of the service, while the agents were concerned with intangible aspects of the delivery of services. Indeed, irrespective of the focus of each party, customer satisfaction is based on how the company will meet or even exceed the expectations of each customer in each interaction that occurs (Evensen et al., 1999).

In their work on the operational determinants of customer satisfaction with a call center, Feinberg et al. (2000 and 2002) sought to measure customer satisfaction by asking managers of the operation what their perception was regarding the satisfaction of their customers in relation to the services they provided. For the purposes of this article, this obstacle is circumvented because data gathered directly from the perception of each customer with respect to a given call will be used. This is done using secondary data derived from a survey conducted periodically together with different call center operations of the companies analyzed in this study.

RESEARCH METHOD

The research method adopted in this article is the cross-sectional survey (Malhotra, 2001), which involves information gathering from a one-time-only sample of representatives of a population.

Samples were collected from different groups of customers (business and corporate) of two different companies (Alpha and Beta). Alpha company is in the cell phone segment, whereas Beta company is an incumbent of the fixed-line segment, albeit both of them belong to the same controlling group. The company that operates the call centers (CC) of Alpha and Beta companies will be referred to as Gama company. Total Attendance Posts (AP) of each company is shown in Figure 1.

Considering the mono-method focus of Martin (1990), the research was of a quantitative nature, thereby ensuring objectivity, the possibility of causal relationships and generalizations (Vieira and Zouain, 2004, p.15).

In the sense of attempting to identify a relationship between a call center's operational performance indicators and customer satisfaction

Figure 1. Population researched

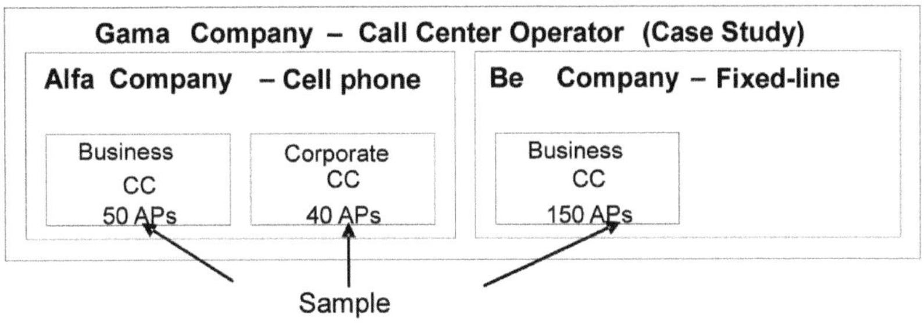

in operations of the Alpha and Beta companies in question, this study has explanatory characteristics. Explanatory or causal studies are useful to assess how given practices are working and why. They detect if there are problems and if changes are necessary and seek to explain the cause and effect relationships found. They also require more than one site for comparative analysis, which was done by means of the study of the three operations shown in Figure 1 (Morra and Friedlander, 1999).

In this study, the data regarding satisfaction were collected directly from customers in order to minimize the chances of misrepresentation.

Data Collection

Using the taxonomy of Matar (2002), primary data obtained from the electronic records of Gama company for the operations of Alpha and Beta companies were used for compilation of the thirteen operational performance indicators of call centers.

Additionally, internal secondary data (Malhotra, 2001) arising from a survey conducted by Alpha and Beta companies were used in order to assess the satisfaction of a customer with respect to a given call.

The research database was assembled between June and September 2008 and was culled from an automatic process, in which each agent in each of the different operations received a reminder at intervals ranging from 15 to 20 minutes to fill out the contact data for the customer that he/she was handling at that time.

All of the above contacts constituted a daily research database. Seven days after a call was made to the call center, customers to be contacted by telephone were chosen at random from this daily research database. The period of seven days was considered the minimum time required for extraction and compilation of data, as well as submission to the independent research institute for compilation of the research questionnaires. This process was repeated over the course of a month for each of the operations that were studied.

With respect to the reliability of the data, they were appraised and collected by an independent research institute, unrelated to Alpha, Beta and Gamma companies, which was responsible for the selection of the sample, final contact the general tabulation of the research form.

According to Giese and Cote (2000), the expressions 'customer satisfaction', 'consumer satisfaction', or even 'satisfaction' on its own, are used without the necessary precision. Therefore, for the purpose of this work, it is important to note that customer satisfaction refers to the response of an end user, who may or may not be the actual purchaser of this service. Considering that the universe of this research covers B2B (business-to-business) operations, this situation is common as the person who contacts a call center is not always the one who effectively has the purchasing power for that service.

Thus, the survey contained the question: "What is your level of overall satisfaction with the call center you contacted?" in which the customer could award a number from 1 to 10. This number was used as the dependent variable in the multiple linear regression that was structured in relation to the operational performance indicators of call centers. This was the Satisfaction with the Call Center variable (represented as the SAT_CC variable) and is thus aligned with the approach of Giese and Cote (2000). A total of 6.616 responses were recorded during the survey period.

During the survey preparation period between June and September 2008, primary data on operational performance indicators, based on the call details recorded in the databases of Gama company, were also collected.

The thirteen operational indicators were collected daily, which were the independent variables of the multiple linear regression used to verify the relationship between customer satisfaction and operational indicators. Daily collection was adopted as it is the shortest time interval possible to collect all thirteen indicators.

In terms of alternative call center indicator the problem-solving ability dimension was incorporated in the question: "What is the score (on a scale of 1 to 10) that you give to the Resolution/Forwarding of requests by the Call Center?

The responsiveness dimension was incorporated in the question: "What is the score (on a scale of 1 to 10) that you give to the Total Handle Time (from the beginning to the end of the connection to the call center)?"

The third dimension was incorporated through an evaluation on the part of the operator, with respect to the latter's perception in relation to the general satisfaction of the customer *vis-à-vis* the company. Using a Likert scale with 5 positions, where 1 means 'Very Dissatisfied' and 5 means 'Very Satisfied', at the end of each call the operator evaluated his/her perception on the level of the customer's satisfaction with the company.

Evaluations of the calls made by the agents were then associated with the answers to the survey taken by customers, to the extent that these evaluations were to be found in the same repository of data that formed the basis for the choice of sample researched, such that a biunivocal relationship could be created between them.

The Figure 2 schematically represents the various elements that were submitted to the multiple linear regression test in order to check the relationship between the operational and alternative performance indicators of call centers and customer satisfaction.

For this work, the Ho hypothesis sought to test the relationship between a given call center indicator and customer satisfaction. Thus, the Ho_i sub-hypothesis means Ho_i: There is a relationship between the I_i call center indicator and customer satisfaction.

To implement the linear regression, a daily Customer Satisfaction indicator was generated, represented by the average of the SAT_CC variable of all cases collected on a given day, in order to represent the dependent variable of regression in a consolidated manner. The sixteen independent variables were represented by their daily averages, so that the regression could be operationalized. In total, 145 Customer Satisfaction (dependent variable) daily averages were generated from the 6,616 cases collected in the survey, as well as the respective 145 daily averages for each of the thirteen operational performance indicators (independent variables).

Statistical Analysis

In order to verify the existence of a relationship between all of the indicators and customer satisfaction, multiple linear regression evaluation using the stepwise approach – with the thirteen traditional indicators plus three alternative indicators proposed earlier – was conducted, while also following the Field (2005) approach.

Figure 2. Research design

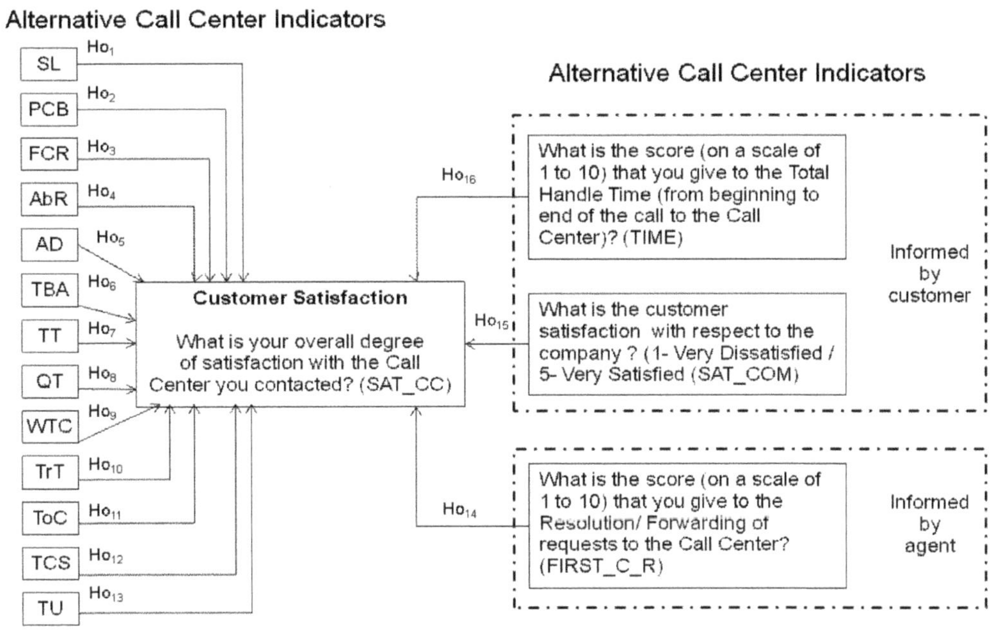

The summary of the model is presented in Table 1.

As can be seen, R^2 had a score of 75.5%. The dimension with the greatest impact on R^2 was Responsiveness (TIME), representing almost 67% of the total. The dimension related to the user's general satisfaction *vis-à-vis* the company from the operator's standpoint (SAT_COM) represented approximately 5%, the Abandonment Rate (AbR) about 3%, and the ability to resolve the problem from the customer's standpoint (FIRST_C_R) only 0.5% of R^2.

The Durbin-Watson statistical test produced a result close to 2, indicating that there were no problems with independence of error. VIF values met the conditions of Myers (1990), Bowerman and O'Connell (1990), Field (2005) and Menard (1995), suggesting no multicollinearity problems with the multiple regression. Cook's distance was less than 1, indicating no problems with influential cases (Field, 2005). The premises of normality, homoscedasticity, linearity and independence of error were tested and addressed using a graphical approach as suggested by Draper and Smith (1981) and Field (2005).

FINAL REMARKS

Firstly, the results of the adjusted R^2 of the regressions undertaken between all call center operational performance indicators and customer satisfaction are presented in a consolidated manner in Table 2. Based on this table, some conclusive remarks are presented.

An important aspect is that this study partially confirms the result obtained by Feinberg et al. (2000) with regard to the significance of the Abandonment Rate on customer satisfaction, as together with the alternative indicators it resulted in a far higher R^2 than previously found in his studies.

The alternative set of call center operational performance indicators had a quite satisfactory adjusted R^2 (75.5% - Table 2), thereby making it

Table 1. Regression model with the alternative call center operational performance indicators

Statistical Variations									
R	R^2	Adjusted R^2	Std. Error	R^2 Variation	F Variation	df1	df2	Sig F Variation	Durbin-Watson
0.819[a]	0.671	0.669	0.319	0.671	291.970	1	143	0.000	
0.846[b]	0.639	0.716	0.295	0.045	22.667	1	142	0.000	
0.869[c]	0.755	0.750	0.275	0.038	22.127	1	141	0.000	
0.873[d]	0.762	0.755	0.273	0.007	3.929	1	140	0.049	2.190

(a)-Predictor:(Constant),TIME, Dependent Variable: SAT_CC, (b)-Predictor:(Constant),TIME,SAT_COM, (c)-Predictor:(Constant),TIME,SAT_COM,AbR, (d)-Predictor:(Constant),TIME,SAT_COM,AbR,FIRST_C_R

Table 2. Consolidation of multiple linear regressions

		Adjusted R^2
AbR	Abandonment Rate	3.4%
TIME	Responsiveness	66.9%
SAT_COM	Satisfaction with the Company	4.7%
FIRST_C_R	Problem-Resolution Capacity	0.5%
Total Adjusted R^2		75.5%

an important proxy of the result of the customer satisfaction with the call center.

A point to be emphasized is the importance of the customer's perception of handle time, expressed in the TIME variable. As can be seen, it accounts for almost 67% of the explanation for the variation in customer satisfaction. This result may at first sight be considered contradictory, since the TT (Talk Time) was not identified as being significant, however, it should be stressed that in this case there is a clearly different situation between perceived time, operationalized by the TIME variable, and real time, operationalized by TT (Talk Time).

It also transpires that the perception of customer satisfaction *vis-à-vis* the company, on the part of the operator, is also significant. This is positive to the extent that preliminary information can be given to the call center managers at the end of a call, so that they can take some action to reverse a customer's negative perception about the company that was perceived by the agent.

Managerial Implications

This work presents a series of managerial implications for the call center outsourcing market in that it diverts the focus exclusively from the items traditionally accompanied such as Service Level and Talk Time. It reveals the importance of the perception on the part of the customer of the total call time, as well as the ability to resolve problems on the part of the agent.

Thus, the alternative call center operational performance indicators, due to the ease in obtaining them and their adequate explanation level, could be used to monitor call center performance in relation to customer satisfaction. These indicators could be used to establish remuneration brackets for the agents or even for the outsourced companies. In this way, if the level of satisfaction were to reach a given level, together with the ability to resolve problems (FIRST_C_R) and perception of time (TIME), the agents and outsourced companies would receive additional remuneration.

This practice, on an ongoing basis, would tend to reinforce the image attribute (Grönroos, 1984), thereby positively impacting the perception of quality of service of the company (Parasuraman et al., 1985, Bitner and Hubbert, 1994).

Currently, government regulatory agencies set quality targets for the provision of service in the call centers, which stipulate the level of service as an indicator that must be met. In line with this, the alternative indicators could be used by companies because, as seen above, they are far better parameters for assessing customer satisfaction with the call center.

With respect to future research, the application of a longitudinal study is recommended to analyze the impact of the various traditional and alternative call center operational performance indicators on customer satisfaction, in order to detect the existence or otherwise of changes in the relative importance among the various indicators over time.

REFERENCES

Anton, J. (1997). *Call center management by numbers*. Purdue University Press/Call Center Press.

Anton, J. (2000). The past, present and future of customer access centers. *International Journal of Service Industry Management, 11*(2). doi:10.1108/09564230010323534

Babin, B. J., & Griffin, M. (1998). The nature of satisfaction: An updated examination and analysis. *Journal of Business Research, 41*, 127–136. doi:10.1016/S0148-2963(97)00001-5

Bennigton, L., Cummane, J., & Con, P. (2000). Customer satisfaction and call centers: An Australian study. *International Journal of Service, 11*(2).

Bitner, M. J., Booms, B. H., & Tetreault, M. S. (1990). The service encounter: Diagnosing favorable and unfavorable incidents. *Journal of Marketing, 54*, 71–84. doi:10.2307/1252174

Bitner, M. J., & Hubbert, A. R. (1994). Encounter satisfaction versus overall satisfaction versus service quality: The consumer's voice. In Rust, R. T., & Oliver, R. L. (Eds.), *Service quality: New directions in theory and practice*. Thousand Oaks, CA: Sage.

Bowerman, B. L., & O'Connell, R. T. (1990). *Linear statistical models: An applied approach*. Belmont, CA: Duxbury.

Brown, L., Gans, N., Mandelbaum, A., Sakov, A., Shen, H., Zeltyn, S., & Zhao, L. (2002) *Statistical analysis of a telephone call center: A queuing-science perspective*. The Wharton School, The Wharton Financial Institutions Center. Retrieved December 3, 2006, from http://knowledge.wharton.upenn.edu /papers/1117.pdf

Cleveland, B., & Mayben, J. (1997). *Call center management on fast forward*. Annapolis, MD: Call Center Press.

Cronin, J. J., & Taylor, S. A. (1992). Measuring service quality: A reexamination and extension. *Journal of Marketing, 56*, 55–68. doi:10.2307/1252296

Dawson, K. (1999a). *The call center handbook: The complete guide to starting, running and improving your call center*. Gilroy, CA: Telecom Books.

Dawson, K. (1999b). *The call center savvy: How to position your call center for the business challenges*. Gilroy, CA: Telecom Books.

Dean, A. M. (2002). Service quality in call centres: Implications for customer loyalty. *Managing Service Quality, 12*(6). doi:10.1108/09604520210451894

Draper, N. R., & Smith, H. (1981). *Applied regression analysis* (2nd ed.). New York, NY: Wiley.

Evensen, A., Harker, P. T., & Frei, F. X. (1999). *Effective call center management: Evidence from Financial Services*. The Wharton School, The Wharton Financial Institutions Center. Retrieved December 3, 2008, from http://knowledge.wharton.upenn.edu /papers/50.pdf

Feinberg, R. A., Hokama, L., Rajesh, K., & Kim, I. (2002). Operational determinants of caller satisfaction in the banking/financial services call center. *International Journal of Bank Marketing*, *20*(4). doi:10.1108/02652320210432954

Feinberg, R. A., Kim, I., Hokama, L., Ruyter, K., & Keen, C. (2000). Operational determinants of caller satisfaction in the call center. *International Journal of Service Industry Management*, *11*(2). doi:10.1108/09564230010323633

Field, A. (2005). *Discovering statistics using SPSS for Windows*. London, UK: Sage.

Fornell, C. A. (1992). National customer satisfaction barometer: The Swedish experience. *Journal of Marketing*, *56*, 6–21. doi:10.2307/1252129

Gable, R. A. (1993). *Inbound call centers: Design, implementation and management*. Boston, MA: Artech House.

Giese, J. L., & Cote, J. A. (2000). Defining consumer satisfaction. *Academy of Marketing Science Review*, *1*. Retrieved December 20, 2008, from http://www.amsreview.org /articles/giese01-2000.pdf

Gilmore, A. (2001). Call centre management: Is service quality a priority? *Managing Service Quality*, *11*(3). doi:10.1108/09604520110391315

Grimm, C. (2001). Creating balanced measures in a multi-channel world. *Call Center Management Review*, *3*, 9–11.

Grönroos, C. (1984). A service quality model and its marketing implications. *European Journal of Marketing*, *18*(4), 36–44. doi:10.1108/EUM0000000004784

Halstead, D., Hartman, D., & Schmidt, S. L. (1994). Multisource effects on the satisfaction formation process. *Journal of the Academy of Marketing Science*, *22*, 114–129. doi:10.1177/0092070394222002

Howard, J. A., & Sheth, J. N. (1969). *The theory of buyer behavior*. New York, NY: John Wiley and Sons.

Johnston, R. (1995). The determinants of service quality: Satisfiers and dissatisfiers. *International Journal of Service Industry Management*, *6*(4), 53–71. doi:10.1108/09564239510101536

Lehtinen, J. R. (1983). *Customer oriented service system*. Service Management Institute Working Paper, Helsinki, Finland.

Malhotra, N. (2001). *Pesquisa acadêmica de marketing: Uma orientação aplicada*. Porto Alegre, Brazil: Bookman.

Mandelbaum, A., Koole, G., & Gans, N. (2003). *Call centers: Tutorial, review, and research prospects*. Retrieved December 4, 2008, from http://iew3.technion.ac.il /serveng/ References/CCReview.pdf

Martin, J. (1990). Breaking up the mono-method monopolies in organizational analysis. In Hassard, J., & Pym, D. (Eds.), *The theory and philosophy of organizations: Critical issues and new perspectives*. London, UK: Routledge.

Matter Neto, J. A. (2002). *Metodologia cientifica na era da informática*. São Paulo, Brazil: Saraiva.

Menard, S. W. (1995). *Applied logistic regression analysis* (2nd ed.). Thousand Oaks, CA: Sage.

Miciak, A., & Desmarais, M. (2001). Benchmarking service quality performance at business-to-business and business-to-consumer call centers. *Journal of Business and Industrial Marketing, 16*(5). doi:10.1108/08858620110400205

Morra, L., & Friedlander, A. C. (1999). *Case study evaluations*. Working Paper Series. OED (Operations Evaluation Department), World Bank, n. 2.

Myers, R. H. (1990). *Classical and modern regression with applications*. Boston, MA: Duxbury.

Oliver, R. L. (1992). An investigation of the attribute basis of emotion and related affects in consumption: Suggestions for a stage-specific satisfaction framework. In Sherry, J. F., & Sternthal, B. (Eds.), *Advances in consumer research* (pp. 237–244). Ann Arbor, MI: Association for Consumer Research.

Oliver, R. L. A. (1980). Cognitive model of the antecedents and consequences of satisfaction decisions. *JMR, Journal of Marketing Research, 17*, 460–469. doi:10.2307/3150499

Parasuraman, A. (2002). Service quality and productivity: A synergistic perspective. *Managing Service Quality, 12*(1). doi:10.1108/096045202104

Parasuraman, A., Zeithaml, V., & Berry, L. (1985). A conceptual model of service quality and its implications for future research. *Journal of Marketing*, 49.

Parasuraman, A., Zeithaml, V., & Berry, L. (1988). SERVQUAL: A multiple item scale for measuring customer perceptions of service quality. *Journal of Retailing, 64*(1), 1988.

Patterson, P. G. (1993). Expectations and product performance as determinants of satisfaction for a high-involvement purchase. *Psychology and Marketing, 10*(5), 449–465. doi:10.1002/mar.4220100507

Rosati, M. (2001). *Motivating call center agents with goals and measurements*. Credit & Collections World. Retrieved December 29, 2008, from http://www.collectionsworld.com/10papr01.htm

Sparrow, L. B. (1991). Managing the telephone enquiry bureau at British Gas West Midlands. In Littlechild, S. C., & Shutler, M. F. (Eds.), *Operations research in management* (pp. 167–173). London, UK: Prentice Hall International.

Vandenbergh, C., De Keyser, V., Vlerick, P., & D'Hoore, W. (2004). *Organizational changes, employee stress, and customer satisfaction: Emergence of the flexihealth concept*. Brussels: Belgian Science Policy.

Vieira, M. M. F., & Zouain, D. M. (2004). *Pesquisa qualitativa em administração*. Rio de Janeiro, Brazil: Editora FGV.

Westbrook, R. A. (1987). Product/consumption-based affective responses and postpurchase processes. *JMR, Journal of Marketing Research, 24*, 258–270. doi:10.2307/3151636

Yi, Y. (1990). A critical review of consumer satisfaction. In Zeithaml, V. A. (Ed.), *Review of marketing* (pp. 68–123). Chicago, IL: American Marketing Association.

Chapter 4
How Are Professional Skills Acquired?
A Structured Process of On-the-Job Learning

Sari Metso
Lappeenranta University of Technology, Finland

Aino Kianto
Lappeenranta University of Technology, Finland

ABSTRACT

As firms lose skilled labour force through mass retirement, turnover and economic fluctuations, a pressing concern is how to ensure that the skills of the present-day masters are conveyed to the future professionals. This chapter examines the process of how the skills leading to professional performance are acquired in the context of on-the-job learning and identifies the key factors in this process. Based on an empirical examination of the on-the-job training periods of 20 Finnish vocational college students a model is built, suggesting that there are three different levels of professional performance on a junior's path towards professionalism. The results suggest that individual activity, critical observation, conscious doing and creativity are crucial in the learning process. The chapter contributes to the emerging discussion on knowledge sharing across generations in organisations.

INTRODUCTION

Population ageing and shortage of skilled labour force are topical problems faced by many organizations. According to some recent studies the U.S. labour force participation rate is decreasing (DiCecio, Engemann, Owyang & Wheeler, 2008) and this trend is common for most developed countries. Governments are concerned since this phenomenon threatens the prevailing standard of living. Also, labour force quality related to education and experience is expected to decline in the future (Jorgenson, Goettle, Ho, Slesnick & Wilcoxen, 2008.)

DOI: 10.4018/978-1-4666-0948-8.ch004

The immediate challenge for organisations is to ensure that the essential skills of the present-day masters are conveyed forward to the future professionals. The article at hand contributes to solving this acute problem by presenting a structured process of acquiring the skills needed for professional performance in context of on-the-job learning. Thereby this study helps organizations to understand how professional performance is learnt and to recognize the most important phases in the learning process.

Interest towards learning at work has recently increased (Billett, 2001, 2004; Cheetham & Chivers, 2001a, 2001b; Collin & Tynjälä, 2003; Dymock & Gerber, 2002; Engeström, Engeström & Kärkkäinen, 1995; Eraut, 2004; Gherardi, 2001; Leslie, Kosmal Aring & Brand, 1998; Sauter, 1999). The emphasis of the recent literature has been on adult professional performance improvement at work. This type of learning is often called informal learning since it occurs outside classroom without curriculum and teachers. However, there is a shortage of research explaining how young students originally learn professional skills in authentic environments in the beginning stages of their careers. New perspectives on learning are needed since the nature of work and professions have changed rapidly and continue to do so. Hence, more research is needed in order to understand the process of the initial learning of professional performance.

It is relevant to study how young people become professionals since vocational qualification is mainly acquired through vocational college studies. While knowledge management literature has made many connections with the organizational learning literature, to the extent that knowledge management and organizational learning have been treated as synonyms (Argote & Ingram 2000), the literature on individual learning has received far less attention. However, we believe that for understanding how professional skills are transferred in an organization, it is useful also to examine this process from the perspective of the learning individual (Argote et al., 2000). Therefore our model is focused on understanding the individual-level issues connected with skills acquisition.

The chapter is organized as follows. First, we examine the basic theoretical tenets of understanding how individuals learn professional skills. We apply constructivist learning theory, which views learning in terms of active knowledge building, where concepts are constructed through personal interpretations of the meanings the learners attach to experiences (Bereiter, 2002; Vermunt, 1998). Secondly, we use empirical data collected from 20 third-year Finnish vocational college students and workplace instructors during the students' on-the-job periods to build a model of professional skills development. Finally, we discuss the wider theoretical and practical implications of the model.

THEORETICAL BACKGROUND

Individual Learning

This chapter examines the process of professional performance learning from individual point of view and hence, the central theoretical framework stems from individual learning theories. Organizational learning literature finds individual learning theories problematic since they do not explain learning in changing authentic situations which are characteristic for organizations. However, the role of individual learning in organizations has waked interest recently and several recent studies examine the interaction of individual and organizational learning (Bouty & Gomez, 2010; Driver, 2010; Nilsson & Eriksson, 2008; Yeo, 2005; Visser, 2007).

Three influential learning theories have dominated the discourse on individual learning, each in turn, from the beginning of the 20th century. Behaviorism flourished at the early 20th century while cognitivism became the most important topic at the 1960's. Constructivism entered the scene strongly at the 1980´s and still is the prevailing theory of individual learning. Behaviorism has its roots in behaviorist psychology and classical conditioning theory. Pavlov found that by pairing a conditioned stimulus with an unconditioned one leads to a response. By the same logic behaviorism suggests that learning is a result of stimulus and response that can be predicted as far as the stimulus is known. Conditioning occurs when a learner performs in a desired way. Reinforcement can be achieved through a reward. Behaviorism is based on positivistic ideas where knowledge is assumed to be fully observed and measured. In contrast, mental aspects are completely ignored (Boghossian, 2006). The learning process is strictly controlled by the teacher (Beatty & Nunan, 2004).

Cognitivism, which is based on cognitivist psychology, enlarged the viewpoint of behaviourism by arguing that mental processes do matter in the learning process. The emphasis is on what a learner knows and how she acquires knowledge (Ertmer & Newby, 1993). Learning is a process where a learner's knowledge structure alters quantitatively or qualitatively. It is essential for a learner to understand what she has learned and to actively participate in the learning process. Thus, learning includes problem solving, concept building, previous experiences and information gathering (McFadzean, 2001). As Ertmer and Newby (1993) state, memory is considered important in the learning process. Learning requires information storing in a learner's memory in a way that is both organized and meaningful. The teacher's role is to help the learner in this process.

The rise of constructivism at the 1980's was facilitated by rapid development of cognitive psychology, neuropsychology and artificial intelligence research. Constructivism includes several theories that share the common view of a learner's active role, knowledge acquisition as a construction process and the influence of prior knowledge and subjective experiences in learning. A teacher does not transfer knowledge to learners but encourages them to active knowledge construction and thinking. The work of psychologists Lev Vygotsky and Jean Piaget has affected the emergence of modern constructivism. Vygotsky (1979) recognizes the importance of an active role of an individual, the ability to affect one's existence, experiences, previous knowledge and social interaction in the learning process. In order to be meaningful for the individual, learning must be more than automation. Vygotsky (1979) states that learning must be "relevant to life" (pp. 117-118). According to Piaget (1978) knowledge cannot be constructed through experience alone. Neither is it a product of an individual's biological characteristics. In his retrospective comments on Vygotsky's criticism published in 2000, Piaget assumes that knowledge is a product of new structures that are successive and under constant development.

Constructivism

In this paper we argue that constructivism offers a suitable theoretical grounding for the examination of acquisition of professional skills. In context of professional skills acquisition through on-the-job learning the following characteristics of constructivism are emphasized. First, constructivist theories consider learning highly context-bound. Second, social interaction is seen as a crucial element in knowledge construction. Third, learning requires experiences that are meaningful for learner. Fourth, in a learning process where new knowledge is based on previous knowledge it is possible to detect and correct possible false insights, concepts, ideas and attitudes. This is crucial during the process of professional skills acquisition.

As discussed above constructivistic learning theories are partly built on the ideas of Vygotsky and Piaget (Bruner, 1986; Delanty, 1997; Spender 2006a). Constructivism emphasizes the internal learning process. Individuals learn by doing, not by studying theories (Spender, 2006b). A learner is an active constructor of her own knowledge.

The learning process involves creating meaning to individual experiences resulting in knowledge. These central ideas make constructivism a relevant theoretical framework for studying professional performance learning. Von Glasersfeld (1989) crystallizes the idea of constructivism as follows: "...*knowledge* refers to conceptual structures that epistemic agents, given the range of present experience within their tradition of thought and language, consider *viable*" (p. 124). Radical constructivism goes further and assumes that all knowledge is personal and subjective (Boghossian, 2006). Knowledge is always owned by an individual. It is constructed through subjective experiences and each individual carries this knowledge with her (von Glasersfeld, 1995). According to von Glasersfeld (1995) this does not exclude the effect of social interaction or the possibility to improve knowing through such interaction. Spender (2006a) continues by pointing out that knowledge based on individuals' experiences is always limited by the way they experience the reality.

Learning-by-Doing

Learning-by-doing provides a plausible perspective for learning when constructivism is taken as a theoretical framework. It includes active doing, social interaction, learning in authentic situations and experimenting. Learning professional skills is much about learning by doing in authentic environments. From the organizational perspective, learning-by-doing is assumed to generate experience in performing tasks which in turn reduces the costs through a learning curve (Reagans, Argote & Brooks, 2005). From the individual point of view learning-by-doing is based on constructivist ideas of learning. An individual learns thorough authentic situations and participation.

In context of on-the-job learning, the learning process is based on experiences. Discussion about learning-by-doing has been dominated by Kolb's (1984) influential but also increasingly criticized (Eraut, 2004; Jarvis, 2009; Miettinen, 2000; Vince, 1998) model of experiential learning. According to Kolb (1984), efficient adaptation of new knowledge or skills involves four phases: concrete experience, reflective observing, abstraction and active experimentation. Concrete experience is about personal experiences, feelings and creative orientation. Reflective observing includes the diverse reflection of experiences and situations. Abstraction involves systematic thinking and problem solving. Finally, active experimentation is about practical activities and affecting other individuals or different situations. Learning from experience requires respective abilities on the individual level. An individual is assumed to enter new situations consciously and with an open mind. She has to be able to reflect and observe experiences from different angles, to create concepts and to integrate the observations to logical theories. She also must use the theories in making decisions and solving problems.

On-the-job learning is a form of learning-by-doing. It is seen as learning from experience and it is created by collective activity in the basis of sharing (Dymock & Gerber, 2002). On-the-job learning includes learning of profession-related tasks in authentic environment by doing. In the Finnish literature, the concept of on-the-job learning is used in context of young people while the term on-the-job training refers to adult learning. In Finnish vocational colleges a certain minimum amount of on-the-job learning is obligatory. Hence, it is curriculum-based and guided. Many recent studies show the topicality of on-the-job or work-based learning (Bierema & Eraut, 2004; Billet, 2001, 2004; Collin & Tynjälä, 2003; Sauter, 1999). On-the-job learning is an efficient way to deepen the learning processes of professions. Young people learn relevant skills in authentic environment. The requirements of organizations regarding profession related skills can be taken into account. Firms are able to hire labor force that already knows their specific practices.

METHODS

Research Strategy

The aspect of how young people learn profession is important, since vocational college studies are the most common way to produce skilled labor force. However, there is a lack of research concentrating on this subject, and hence we adopt an inductive research approach for constructing a structured process description of acquiring professional skills. As explained above, theoretical considerations based on the constructivist individual learning theory provide the background for addressing this issue. However, they need to be complemented by qualitative data for building a structured process of acquiring professional skills. To examine how individuals learn the skills needed for professional performance, a qualitative empirical study was undertaken.

Specifically, we examined the on-the-job learning periods of 20 Finnish vocational college students as instances of learning professional skills. The typical duration of the on-job-learning period in Finland is eight weeks. The empirical research was conducted during six months and included students who were conducting their on-the-job learning periods in three professional fields: restaurant branch, security branch and business. The tasks met by the students were typical for respective professions. The tasks did not include knowledge work or managerial tasks.

The data provides a versatile description of authentic situations where acquisition of professional skills occurs. It makes possible to highlight the central factors from the viewpoint of learning. The data is enriched by discussions with students and workplace instructors together with observations in authentic environments and semi-structured interviews. This guarantees that the process of professional skills learning is examined from different angles. Furthermore, this study describes the learning process in two phases, at the beginning and at the end, which helps to create an insight of the entity.

Data Collection

Multiple types of data were collected at different points of the on-the-job learning period in order to obtain a wide and diversified idea of factors affecting learning of professional performance. The methods include observations during personal meetings, semi-structured interviews and free discussions. The course of the research material collection proceeded as follows. The researcher met each student twice at the workplace. The first meeting occurred at the beginning of the on-the-job learning period and the second one at the end of the period. Both meeting sessions included the student, the responsible teacher and the workplace instructor.

The first meeting began by discussing how the on-the-job learning period had started (the general assessment) proceeding to profession related issues. The second meeting concentrated on the vocational skills demonstration discussion. The course of the discussions during both meetings was entirely transcribed. The discussion sessions took typically one hour or at maximum two hours. Duration of the semi-structured and the free discussions varied from half an hour to one hour. Free discussions with the workplace instructors were typically short, less than half an hour meetings. The key point with these discussions was to collect the instructors' free comments on the students' performance. They also got an opportunity to express their thoughts about successful professional skills learning.

At the end of the meetings, the researcher conducted a semi-structured interview alone with the student. The semi-structured interview gives space for free discussion and new aspects especially when the research problem is not well understood (Ghauri & Gronhaug, 2002). First, the basic information about the student was asked: gender, age and vocational qualification studied. The themes included in the interview are (1) job experience from the studied profession, other job experience, type of tasks regarding the previous job experience and possible previous degree (2) the reason why the student chose the profession in the first place, (3) does the student still consider this choice correct, (4) what are the student's expectations regarding the on-the-job learning period, (5) what new skills / things the student can or want to learn during the period, (6) what are the most important factors facilitating learning of profession related skills during the period, (7) the student's opinion how the period has started. The first theme is about pre-knowledge. The second and the third ones reflect the student's motivation. The aim of the fourth, the fifth and the sixth theme is to examine the student's expectations, learning targets and ideas of core factors in learning profession related skills. The seventh theme gives an opportunity to reveal positive and/or negative thoughts regarding the on-the-job period and working place including e.g. the given tasks, colleagues and the organizational climate. At the end of the interview the student had an opportunity to comment freely on any other subject felt important at the moment. After this, the workplace instructor was interviewed alone in order to document his point of view concerning the student's performance. This was the first step in observing the learning process of the profession relate skills in authentic situations.

At the end of the on-the-job learning period the student, the workplace instructor, the responsible teacher and the researcher participated in the vocational skills demonstration grade discussion. Usually the student began by assessing individual performance, successes and problems. The workplace instructor and the teacher expressed their points of view regarding the demonstration. Each party justified the given grade. If the grades deviated from each other the discussion and justifying continued until all three parties agreed. The assessment discussions provided a valuable insight of the requirements needed in learning professional performance.

The second semi-structured student interview took place at the end of the second meeting. The themes are as follows: (1) pros and cons of the on-the-job period, (2) did the reality meet the expectations, (3) new things and skills learned,(4) the highlights of the period and (5) free comments. These themes were constructed to reflect and to complement the themes of the first semi-structured interview. The first theme facilitates the general analyze of the on-the-job learning period from the student's point of view. It also suggests factors that enhance or prevent learning of the skills related performance. The second theme helps to understand whether the deviations in expectations are student-based or depending on the conditions at the work place, thus complementing the first theme. The third theme defines the range of the learning of new skills. It also helps to examine whether the new skills learned are actually those required from the professionals. The fourth theme reveals the most inspiring experience for the student. This also helps to understand the process of learning and to identify the most important factors in the process.

Finally, the workplace instructor was able to comment freely (alone with the researcher) on the student's performance from the professional's point of view. The most interesting results from these discussions are considerations about the factors facilitating the successful learning of professional performance. Unfortunately, some of the workplace instructors were too busy for two private discussions. In addition, some workplace instructors were responsible for more than one student at the same time. However, it was possible to discuss with each instructor at least once during the on-the-job learning period.

The above described types of method were chosen. Discussions in authentic environment in the middle of the work offer more valuable observations than questionnaires or telephone calls. The workplace instructors gave feedback and suggestions how the junior may improve her professional performance. Discussions provided an excellent device to observe the progression of the student's professional skills. The methods above provided a rich data set to examine the process of learning professional performance.

Data Analysis

The data gathered through semi-structured interviews at the beginning of the on-the-job learning period was typed and classified in Excel by themes into three categories according to the vocational skills demonstration grade (excellent = 3, good = 2 and satisfactory =1 or failed=0). The data obtained from the second semi-structured interviews was classified in the same way. This helps to compare the similarities and differences between students that succeeded excellently and students with moderate or modest results. This type of classification and comparison is useful in order to detect the most important factors that affect the process of acquiring professional skills. Highlights of the on-the-job learning period, students' free comments and free discussions together with workplace instructors' comments provide valuable aspects about the organizational requirements with respect to successful learning on the job. The workplace instructors' free comments were typed in Excel for comparison and in order to detect the common features. The notes from authentic situation observations were utilized to perceive and construct the structured process of professional skills learning. Furthermore, the notes gave further and more detailed information about factors that are crucial for learning. The notes were read carefully many times. Factors common to several workplaces were highlighted. Also subjects that a student, a workplace instructor or a teacher considered important were highlighted. Conclusions were achieved by combining data classification and comparisons described above to observation notes and free discussions with the students and the workplace instructors. Data collected from various sources and points of time resulted in rich and integrated insight of the entire learning process.

FINDINGS: THE CRUCIAL PHASES IN THE PROCESS OF LEARNING PROFESSIONAL PERFORMANCE

The analysis based on the data reveals a process of professional performance learning including a prerequisite and three successive levels. Each phase is necessary in order to enter the subsequent level. To successfully reach the main goal of this process, i.e. professional performance, a number of critical factors must be considered. These factors concern both juniors and organizations. The phases are discussed more detailed below. Figure 1 presents relationships between the phases of the process of professional performance learning and related critical factors.

Prior Knowledge

In this study the third year vocational college students enter the on-the-job learning period with prior knowledge. In general, prior knowledge consists of formal learning (e.g. concepts and ideas), theoretical knowledge and personal experiences (e.g. job experience) and attitudes. This study considers job experience and attitudes. According to the data the scope and the depth of prior knowledge vary among the students. Learning a profession at the vocational college level is not about preparing students for simple tasks but to acquire skills required from firms. Prior knowledge is a prerequisite to be able to successfully perform basic level tasks in authentic situations during the third-year on-the-job learning period and to be able to construct advanced profession-related skills. This data revealed that workplace instructors expect the third-year students entering the on-the-job learning period to have some profession-related prior knowledge acquired through theoretical studies at the college and through previous on-the-job learning periods or work experience. They require knowledge of the very basic professional skills and knowledge of the general working life rules. Prior knowledge

Figure 1. The process of learning professional performance and the related critical factors

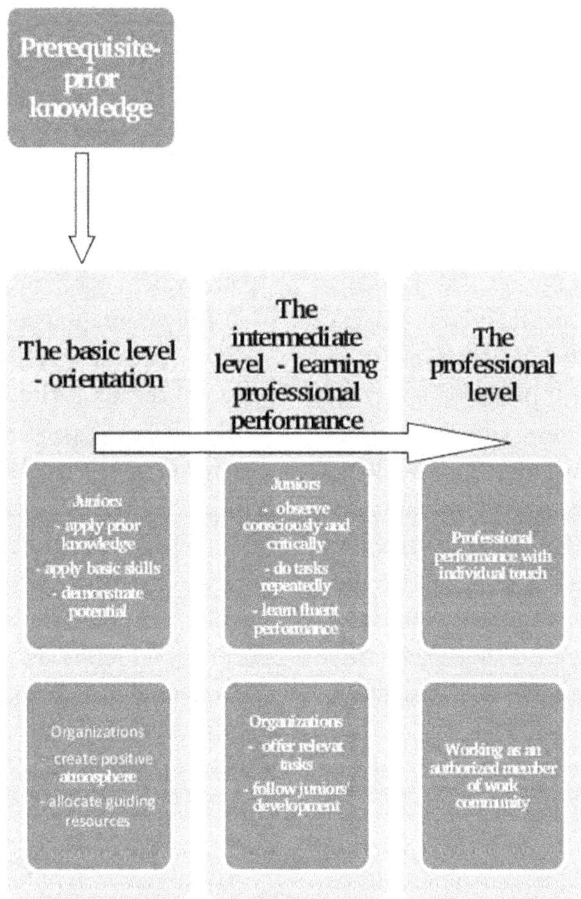

is also needed to expand skills beyond the basic level. As a workplace instructor stated, prior knowledge is always good but in some cases it may require learning away from old habits or patterns of thinking. Organizations even at the same branch have their own ways of performing tasks, special working environments and equipments not to mention differences in organizational cultures, not always explicitly expressed. Hence, a student's ability to apply prior knowledge in different situations is important. Discussions with the workplace instructors together with the observations revealed that prior knowledge should be applied in all performance, not just in executing a specific task.

According to some workplace instructors, a student can learn to perform at a basic level meeting the minimum requirements or she may learn to perform like a professional during the third year on-the-job learning period. Beside prior knowledge there are general factors that may affect a student's performance and ability to success as a professional in a specific branch. Certain personal characteristics e.g. problems with motor coordination or difficulties of perceiving may prevent a person from becoming a professional.

It seems natural to assume that interest towards own profession creates motivation resulting in professional performance. On the one hand, this study finds that some students are able to obtain excellent results regarding the vocational skills demonstrations even when they do not consider the chosen field of vocational education and training the best possible. These hesitations were revealed in private discussions at the beginning of the on-the-job learning period. The students explained later during the second private discussions that they wanted to do their best even when they were not sure they will be working at that particular branch in the future. This may reflect these juniors' overall mature attitude and realistic view about professions. Despite of hesitations it is possible to show activeness and independency. On the other hand, the data suggests that interest towards the chosen studies and willingness to work at the branch in the future do not necessarily imply an excellent result in the vocational skills demonstration.

Orientation Period

This study shows that the organizations have introduced a practice of an orientation period for the students at the beginning of the on-the-job learning period. It is usually an informal but a well established practice. During approximately one week or at most two weeks the students familiarize themselves with the workplace by doing basic tasks. Students should recognize and fully utilize this phase. As a workplace instructor stated: "Some students remain trainees while others become team members". The juniors are expected to show initiative, observe how the professionals act and learn from it. One the one hand workplace instructors expect the students to assess own skills against skills needed in the organization and alter them when needed. On the other hand they wanted the juniors to demonstrate their potential. The orientation period is the basis for further learning in a specific environment.

As discussed earlier, the third-year student is expected to master the very basic skills, i.e. the common rules of working life and the basics of a particular profession. Hence, the orientation period is more about applying prior knowledge and basic skills to the specific working environment rather than learning them. By doing the basic tasks and observing the environment the student is supposed to detect the possible deficiencies in her working patterns and alter her performance accordingly.

The orientation period is crucial for the future of the student's on-the-job learning period for several reasons. The data shows that the workplace instructors observe closely how the students perform. The instructors form their opinion about the students and assess what they are capable of doing from the professional point of view. An active student with the "right attitude" is more likely to receive interesting tasks and to be accepted as a fellow worker. Achieving this shows that people at the work place trust the student's ability to develop professionally. Hence, she has better opportunities for deep understanding and for acquiring profession related skills. In this study the best acknowledgment a junior can receive is that she performs "like one of us". The term "right attitude" came up frequently in the discussions with the workplace instructors. The concept of "right attitude" was described as activity, ability to receive instructions, willingness to learn, to be open to new things, flexibility, ability to interact with other personal, trustworthy and ability to take responsibility. These are the basic elements in any profession reflecting a mature professional attitude.

The students' free comments and the observation notes suggest a number of organization-based factors related to successful orientation period. First, organizations must create a positive atmosphere among personal towards juniors. Juniors are welcomed from the beginning and they are considered as team members. Second, a junior requires own workplace instructor who has the main responsibility for giving orientation in the organization- specific practices. Third, a workplace instructor must be aware of the goals of the on-the-job learning period and the requirements of the vocational skills demonstration. It is important to discuss these factors with students and thus to ensure mutual understanding.

Learning Professional Performance

This study suggests that a student needs structured personal experience through independent and guided doing in order to learn professional performance. Many workplace instructors stated in different situations that the only way of learning to master a specific task or a working process is to do it oneself repeatedly. A junior should not give up if she does not success with a particular task at once. However, repeating as a mechanical procedure does not result in professional performance. A workplace instructor and other seniors give advice in authentic situations when necessary. It is not about separate reflection sessions but situation-related spontaneous guiding. The data shows that professionals pay attention to how a junior reacts to guidance. Both development in performance and ignoring guidance are noticed by workplace instructors. Challenging and more advanced tasks are given to alert students. At the beginning of the on-the-job learning period a junior works both under guidance of professionals and independently. With increased skills she works more as a team player and independently according to the situation. The data suggests that the ability of working independently and being a team member at the same time require advanced professional skills. Being able to work fluently in authentic situations requires professional skills and the ability to understand the entire work process. A junior with excellent grade in vocational skills assessment got positive feedback from the workplace instructor: "When we worked together I didn't even have to say aloud what should be done". This suggests that professional performance requires both independent working and team work. It also suggests tacit dimension being present in these situations because team members, their working patterns and reactions vary in different situations.

The workplace instructors value courage to get down to work. On the one hand, when the rush reaches its peak it is important for a junior to act accordingly. In case she has enough experience to participate demanding tasks the seniors expect activity from the student. If the student's skills are not sufficient the seniors accept that she stays out of the activity or just assists. However, this is not idle time for the student. She has an excellent opportunity to observe how seniors handle a demanding situation. As the observations during the workplace visits suggest workplace instructors recommend critical observation: What did the seniors do? Was it successful? Would I do the same? If not, how would I do it? Was the senior's performance in line with the workplace rules? When the hectic period is over it is a proper moment for a student to try demanding and new tasks. In general, it is important for a junior to critically observe the professionals' working. A task can successfully be done in several different ways. It is important for the junior to see the outcomes of different working habits. On the other hand, exceptional quiet periods are a good measure for a student's professional attitude. The workplace instructors appreciate students who are willing to get down to minor or "dull" tasks by own initiative.

Both students and workplace instructors considered very important that a junior is taken as a member of the team, as "one of us". A student feels to be accepted, respected and trusted. She has a better opportunity to learn to understand the entity: why she does a particular task, what impact it has, what is the significance of own performance and the role of it. Implicitly this means that the students get diversified and relevant tasks with guidance and feedback. The organization has to provide them with an opportunity to learn. The data shows that workplace instructors must have enough time to guide juniors. It is important to plan e.g. working schedules so that workplace instructors are working the same shifts with juniors. In planning shifts it is also crucial to take into account what are the best moments for juniors to learn. Discussions and observations revealed that workplace instructors tend to ensure sufficiently demanding opportunities to learn by planning shifts carefully. Furthermore, judging by the juniors' free comments and observations workplace instructors must have time to observe how juniors succeed in building up skills. Workplace instructors should notice when juniors are capable for more demanding and new tasks. In this delicate phase workplace instructors must use encouraging measures in guidance. A striking character for the workplaces in this study was hurry. Despite of hectic environment it is important to pay attention to the quality of the tasks given to juniors. Juniors cannot acquire advanced skills by concentrating mainly on routine tasks. A good insight of the entity requires diverse and advanced tasks. It is also important to provide juniors with sufficient opportunities for repeating tasks. The data shows that repeating is needed to remove juniors' insecurity and hence, to enable professional growth. As a workplace instructor said: "Vocational competence requires time and doing, it can be achieved through repetition".

Performing Professionally in Authentic Situations

According to our interpretation, independent working together with taking into account the entity implies that junior has reached a new level of professional performance. A junior performs successfully without copying methods or patterns from others. She has created her own personal touch regarding professional performance. She recognizes how her individual performance affects the entity and the co-workers. In this data the juniors with excellent grades described new things they have learned during on-the-job learning period in terms of processes and large entities. The juniors with good and satisfactory grades tended to answer the same theme by describing more details and specific tasks. Workplace instructors notice this type of performance and they describe it as perceptible sureness and fluency. In this study workplace instructors seem to relate professional performance to potential labor force. In private discussions workplace instructors expressed this spontaneously by assessing juniors' possibilities to get a job in their organization.

In sum, the active role of the junior is emphasized during the on-the-job learning period underpinning the chosen theoretical basis of individual, constructive and experiential learning. Learning professional skills includes continuous and critical observing of how seniors work. Applying this to own performance through serious training in authentic situations is necessary. This study shows that the students mostly received feedback and advice in the middle of daily working instead of profound discussions between the seniors and the juniors. In some cases, feedback came directly from customers. The data showed that the seniors discussed the given feedback with each other. From the organization's side it is required that the seniors are prepared and willing to guide the juniors. They have to have enough time for guidance and feedback. The organization has to create an atmosphere where the junior feels welcome. Some planning regarding the orientation period and the diversity of the tasks given to the junior are required.

The process of learning professional performance discussed above can be divided into three different levels described in the table above. First, the junior enters the orientation period with prior knowledge which is a prerequisite for successful on-the-job learning period. She applies prior knowledge by working at the basic level and by managing the routine tasks in the work place. She learns to know the company rules, context-based procedures and other workers. The junior demonstrates her present skills and professional attitude. She recognizes the expectations she is supposed to fulfill. It can be said that the orientation period offers, in terms of Ausubel (1960), a sort of subsuming concepts to the junior for further learning of professional skills. It is the first step to achieve the general view of the professional skills to be learnt. All this emphasizes the importance of the orientation period in the learning process.

Second, at the intermediate level juniors learn professional performance by experiencing varying authentic situations. Students must repeat different tasks sufficiently in order to obtain self-confidence and sureness in their performance. They put their new skills in practice thus constructing further professional skills. Third, when successfully learned required skills at the intermediate level through conscious repeating of relevant tasks juniors may enter the professional level. At this point an individual is able to perform flexibly and sensibly in varying authentic situations. She applies professional skills creatively in changing situations. A toolkit of a professional includes interaction skills needed in a work community, workplace-specific skills and strong professional skills. It is important to note that according to the data in this study all these skills are bound to the specific work environment, i.e. they are context-bound.

CONCLUSION

There is a shortage of theoretical models explaining how individual learning of professional performance in the early stages of one's career occurs in practice. Understanding this process is relevant since many organizations are increasingly suffering from shortage of skilled labor force. Furthermore, the majority of skilled workers entering the job market come from vocational colleges. This study contributes by presenting a process of professional performance learning. Specifically, it examines how juniors learn professional skills by interacting with seniors in context of on-the-job learning. Juniors are expected to have basic skills that they construct towards professional performance in changing authentic situations. The process helps organizations to understand the most important factors in learning professional performance. The theoretical framework for the model stems from the individual learning theories, constructivism, experiential learning and the perspective of learning-by-doing emphasizing the important role of an active individual, pre-knowledge and knowledge construction through sharing and interaction. Although this study argues strongly for individual activity it also recognizes the role of organization in the successful learning process.

The process identifies the central phases in learning professional performance. These phases form three subsequent and interrelated levels describing the state of professional performance: the basic level, the intermediate level and the professional level. Pre-knowledge is the starting point in learning professional performance. Many studies consider previous knowledge important in adapting new knowledge (Sutherland, 1999). In context of this study, previous knowledge guarantees some basic knowledge about the profession and about the general rules of working life. Despite of formal vocational education the third-year juniors are on different stage regarding their pre-knowledge due to differences in e.g. job experience and attitude. The data shows that the orientation period i.e. the basic level is crucial for the future learning of professional skills. During this period the junior needs to apply and adjust her pre-knowledge according to the workplace. Seniors are monitoring the junior's (basic) skills and attitude. The junior adopts the common rules of the organization and learns how the seniors work.

The organization has to be prepared for the junior's coming. An orientation plan including resources, time table, the central goals and tasks should exist to facilitate successful learning. On-the-job learning periods require that the juniors are taken into account in planning everyday work, e.g. in making shift lists. Pre-knowledge and orientation period are needed in order to get to the core of professional performance on the intermediate level. It requires an authentic environment and interaction with colleagues. Alert existence in authentic situations and a professional attitude form the starting point. This study suggests that critical observation of performance of professionals is the key function for the junior. She has an opportunity to see how the professionals handle changing authentic situations and to observe the outcome. Hence, it is possible to learn different operation modes.

Finally, a junior finds her own way to perform professionally suggesting that the level of professionalism has been reached. Professional performance includes deep knowledge of the profession, flexible using of seamless teamwork and individual work according to the situation, individual operation modes and a clear idea of the entity of the work process. Professional performance is dynamic, context-based and varying with the changing authentic situations. The process described in this study can be applied in any situation where an individual possessing the basic skills of profession enters an organization.

As discussed above pre-knowledge is necessary for the learning process of professional performance. It is out of the scope of this study to examine the exact contents of pre-knowledge and the exact effect of it on learning professional performance. Studying how e.g. profession related theoretical knowledge and work experience affect the learning process (both together and separate) would help to understand the process more detailed. Another subject for future research is to examine factors that separate the juniors with an excellent success in learning professional performance from the less successful ones. This would help to understand better the individual and organizational responsibilities in the learning process.

REFERENCES

Argote, L., & Ingram, P. (2000). Knowledge transfer: A basis for competitive advantage in firms. *Organizational Behavior and Human Decision Processes*, *82*(1), 150–169. doi:10.1006/obhd.2000.2893

Ausubel, D. P. (1960). The use of advance organizers in the learning and retention of meaningful verbal material. *Journal of Educational Psychology*, *51*(5), 267–272. doi:10.1037/h0046669

Beatty, K., & Nunan, D. (2004). Computer-mediated collaborative learning. *System*, *32*, 165–183. doi:10.1016/j.system.2003.11.006

Bereiter, C. (2002). *Education and mind in the knowledge age*. Mahwah, NJ: Lawrence Erlbaum Associates.

Bierema, L., & Eraut, M. (2004). Workplace-focused learning: Perspective on continuing professional education and human resource development. *Advances in Developing Human Resources*, *6*(1), 52–58. doi:10.1177/1523422303260859

Billett, S. (2001). Learning through work: workplace affordances and individual engagement. *Journal of Workplace Learning*, *13*(5), 209–214. doi:10.1108/EUM0000000005548

Billett, S. (2004). Workplace participatory practices. Conceptualising workplaces as learning environments. *Journal of Workplace Learning*, *16*(6), 312–324. doi:10.1108/13665620410550295

Boghossian, P. (2006). Behaviorism, constructivism, and socratic pedagogy. *Educational Philosophy and Theory*, *38*(6), 713–722. doi:10.1111/j.1469-5812.2006.00226.x

Bouty, I., & Gomez, M.-L. (2010). Dishing up individual and collective dimensions in organizational knowing. *Management Learning*, *41*(5), 545–559. doi:10.1177/1350507610377584

Bruner, J. (1986). *Actual minds, possible words.* Cambridge, MA: Harvard University Press.

Cheetham, G., & Chivers, G. (2001a). Part I – How professionals learn – The theory! *Journal of European Industrial Training, 25*(5), 250–269.

Cheetham, G., & Chivers, G. (2001b). Part II – How professionals learn – the practice! What the empirical research found. *Journal of European Industrial Training, 25*(5), 270–292.

Collin, K., & Tynjälä, P. (2003). Integrating theory and practice? Employees' and students' experiences of learning at work. *Journal of Workplace Learning, 15*(7/8), 338–344. doi:10.1108/13665620310504828

Delanty, G. (1997). *Social science, beyond constructivism and realism.* Suffolk, UK: St. Edmundsbury Press Ltd.

DiCecio, R., Engemann, K., Owyang, M. T., & Wheeler, C. H. (2008). Changing trends in the labor force: A survey. *Federal Reserve Bank of St. Louis Review, 90*(1), 47–62.

Driver, M. (2010). Learning as lack: Individual learning it organizations as an empowering encounter with failed imaginary constructions of the self. *Management Learning, 41*(5), 561–574. doi:10.1177/1350507610374427

Dymock, D., & Gerber, R. (2002). Unintegrated training? Exploring links between off- and on-the-job learning. *Education + Training, 44*(1), 23-30.

Engeström, Y., Engeström, R., & Kärkkäinen, M. (1995). Polycontextuality and boundary crossing in expert cognition: Learning and problem solving in complex work activities. *Learning and Instruction, 5*, 319–336. doi:10.1016/0959-4752(95)00021-6

Eraut, M. (2004). Informal learning in the workplace. *Studies in Continuing Education, 26*(2), 247–273. doi:10.1080/158037042000225245

Ertmer, P. A., & Newby, T. J. (1993). Behaviorism, cognitivism, constructivism: Comparing critical features from an instructional design perspective. *Performance Improvement Quarterly, 6*(4), 50–70. doi:10.1111/j.1937-8327.1993.tb00605.x

Ghauri, P., & Gronhaug, K. (2002). *Research methods in business studies. A practical guide.* Harlow, UK: Pearson Education Limited.

Gherardi, S. (2001). From organizational learning to practice-based knowing. *Human Relations, 54*(1), 131–139. doi:10.1177/0018726701541016

Glasersfeld von, E. (1989). Cognition, construction of knowledge, and teaching. *Synthese, 80*(1), 121–140. doi:10.1007/BF00869951

Glasersfeld von. E. (1995). *Radical constructivism. A way of knowing and learning.* London, UK: The Falmer Press.

Jarvis, P. (2009). Learning to be a person in society. Learning to be me. In Illeris, K. (Ed.), *Contemporary theories of learning. Learning theorists...in their own words* (pp. 21–34). New York, NY: Routledge.

Jorgenson, D. W., Goettle, R. J., Ho, M., Slesnick, D. T., & Wilcoxen, P. J. (2008). U.S. labor supply and demand in the long run. *Journal of Policy Modeling, 30*(4), 603–618. doi:10.1016/j.jpolmod.2008.04.008

Kolb, D. A. (1984). *Experiential learning. Experience as the source of learning and development.* New Jersey: Prentice-Hall P T R.

Leslie, B. H., Koshmal Aring, M., & Brand, B. (1998). Informal learning: The new frontier of employee & organizational development. *Economic Development Review (Schiller Park, Ill.), 15*(4), 12–18.

McFadzean, E. (2001). Supporting virtual learning groups. Part 1: A pedagogical perspective. *Team Performance Management*, *7*(3/4), 53–62. doi:10.1108/13527590110395658

Miettinen, R. (2000). The concept of experiential learning and John Dewey's theory of reflective thought and action. *International Journal of Lifelong Education*, *19*(1), 54–72. doi:10.1080/026013700293458

Nilsson, J., & Eriksson, K. (2008). The role of the Individual – A key to learning in preparedness organizations. *Journal of Contingencies and Crisis Management*, *16*(3), 135–142. doi:10.1111/j.1468-5973.2008.00542.x

Piaget, J. (1978). *The development of thought. Equilibration of cognitive structures*. Oxford, UK: Basil Blackwell.

Piaget, J. (2000). Commentary on Vygotsky's criticisms on language and thought of the child and Judgement and reasoning in the child. *New Ideas in Psychology*, *18*(2-3), 241–259. doi:10.1016/S0732-118X(00)00012-X

Reagans, R., Argote, L., & Brooks, D. (2005). Individual experience and experience working together: Predicting learning rates from knowing who knows what and knowing how to work together. *Management Science*, *51*(6), 869–881. doi:10.1287/mnsc.1050.0366

Sauter, E. (1999). The risks and opportunities of learning on the job. *European Journal of Vocational Training*, *17*(2), 14–24.

Spender, J.-C. (2006a). Method, philosophy and empirics in KM and IC. *Journal of Intellectual Capital*, *7*(1), 12–28. doi:10.1108/14691930610639741

Spender, J.-C. (2006b). Getting value from knowledge management. *The TQM Magazine*, *18*(3), 238–254. doi:10.1108/09544780610659970

Sutherland, P. (1999). The application of Piagetian and Neo-Piagetian ideas to further and higher education. *International Journal of Lifelong Education*, *18*(4), 286–294. doi:10.1080/026013799293702

Vermunt, J. D. (1998). The regulation of constructive learning process. *The British Journal of Educational Psychology*, *68*, 149–171. doi:10.1111/j.2044-8279.1998.tb01281.x

Vince, R. (1998). Behind and beyond Kolb's learning cycle. *Journal of Management Education*, *22*(3), 304–319. doi:10.1177/105256299802200304

Visser, M. (2007). Deutero-learning in organizations: A review and a reformulation. *Academy of Management Review*, *32*(2), 659–667. doi:10.5465/AMR.2007.24351883

Vygotsky, L. S. (1979). Mind in society. In Cole, M., John-Steiner, V., Scribner, S., & Souberman, E. (Eds.), *The development of higher psychological processes*. Cambridge, MA: Harvard University Press.

Yeo, R. K. (2005). Revisiting the roots of learning organization. *The Learning Organization*, *12*(4), 368–382. doi:10.1108/09696470510599145

Chapter 5
Knowledge Management in the Public Service: The Case of the Singapore Health Promotion Board

Hak Seng Ang
Health Promotion Board, Republic of Singapore

Pak Tee Ng
National Institute of Education, Nanyang Technological University, Republic of Singapore

ABSTRACT

In the knowledge economy, Knowledge Management (KM) has gained strategic importance in management agenda in many organizations, including those in the service industries. This chapter presents the case study of the Singapore Health Promotion Board (HPB), as a study of how KM can be harnessed to improve public sector performance in an area where bottom-line performance is hard to define. By analysing the development of the HPB's "Healthier Hawker Programme," the case study examines the HPB's journey in using increasingly sophisticated KM processes, tools, and techniques. The experiences and lessons learnt during the HPB's KM journey are analysed and presented using the Learning with Knowledge (LK) Cycle, a model that is useful to the formation of an ontology for analytic discussion and the implementation of KM.

INTRODUCTION: KM IN THE PUBLIC SERVICE

With the emergence of the knowledge economy, many organizations now recognize knowledge as a critical resource to achieve sustainable competitive advantage (Davenport and Prusak, 2000; Drucker, 1988; Hertog and Huizenga, 2000). Knowledge Management (KM) has gained strategic importance in management agenda and there are formal KM programmes in many organizations. According to Nonaka (1991), knowledge creating companies constantly encourage the process whereby personal knowledge is made available

DOI: 10.4018/978-1-4666-0948-8.ch005

to others (articulation) for them to use to extend their own tacit knowledge base (internalisation). Nonaka (1991) further argues that the key to competitive advantage lies latent within the organisation and the role of management is to provide a conceptual framework that helps employees to manage this knowledge. According to Chait (1999), knowledge management seeks to ensure that the right information is available to the right people, in the right places, at the right time, and that the individual knowledge elements are leveraged and multiplied in value. Most literature will argue that KM affects bottom-line performance in manufacturing industries, in enhancing production efficiency and increasing profits. However, in service industries, KM is harder to quantify but still can be measured by its effects on profitability. However, what is interesting is KM in the *public* service, in an area like health promotion where bottom-line performance is hard to define.

Global trends in public sector administration have reflected a shift from the bureaucratic stereotype, to one with an increased focus on citizen as customer in an effort to improve its efficiency and effectiveness. Singapore has been part of this trend and 1995 marked the launch of PS21 (or Public Service for the 21st Century), the umbrella movement for the transformation of its public service. This is a movement that urges the public service to embrace change, innovate and seek constant improvement (Ong, 2010). PS21 is designed to institutionalise processes, structures and a culture for organisational excellence and learning. Under the PS21 banner are several initiatives that promote service excellence, productivity, knowledge sharing, and innovation (Neo and Chen, 2007).

The PS21 movement seeks to bring about fundamental changes required of both the Singapore economy and public sector. It reflects the economic strategy to move Singapore towards the new knowledge driven economy. Evolving the public sector is seen as integral to reshaping the economy. One clear shift has been the steady movement away from a system of rules and compliance to one in which principles and common values guide behaviour. This has helped to create and unlock new public value.

To allow for greater autonomy and flexibility in the implementation of policy, Singapore has historically set up Statutory Boards as autonomous entities with separate governance frameworks and the freedom to operate more like the private sector. While the day-to-day management and operations of a Statutory Board remain independent of the government, the ethos and philosophies remain that of the public service. One such Statutory Board is the Health Promotion Board (HPB). HPB was set up in 2001 as the national coordinating body to oversee all health promotion and ill health prevention efforts. The philosophy behind HPB is to promote a healthy lifestyle among Singaporeans, such as regular physical activities, a healthy diet, non-smoking lifestyle, good mental wellbeing, and the early detection of diseases through screening. The business of Health Promotion involves harnessing ideas, implementing them through collaborations and partnerships, and the marketing and selling of a healthy lifestyle as a product to citizens. The business model of HPB thus relies heavily on human capital and knowledge as key resources.

KM has been embedded as a key enabler of the organisation since HPB's formation. From the start, the principles and values of health promotion placed a heavy emphasis on evidence-based practice, reflecting its roots in epidemiology and the close links to medical practice and healthcare. This mindset is evident in the use of systematic literature reviews, data analysis and research to form the basis of programme design. As part of health promotion practice, officers routinely incorporate learning frameworks and evaluation methods to understand project success or areas for improvement.

As a study of how KM can be harnessed to improve public sector performance, a case study is now presented on the development of HPB's

Table 1. Evolution of KM as part of Healthier Hawker Programme development

KM Processes, Tools, and Techniques	Evolution of Healthier Hawker Programme		
	Version 1	Version 2	Version 3
Data Analysis	Data used to justify the programme. Pre- and post- survey of knowledge, attitudes and behaviours	Data analysis used to guide the programme. Analysis of nutrient profile of Singaporeans, with basic simulation and projections of impact post campaign	Data analytics used to prescribe programme development. Detailed profiling of food items and ingredient composition feeding into a systems analysis Use of Data and Analytics as part of the programme solution via Nutrient Information
After Action Review	Unplanned AAR triggered by recruitment challenges and hawkers raising prices	AAR was designed as part of the programme, but only conducted at the end	Living AAR practice: learning and review before, during and after a programme
Knowledge Creation, Transfer and Reuse.	Knowledge remained tacit. It is locked within the project team, with no plans on how knowledge learnt will be applied to future programme.	Knowledge was created using "plan-to-do" philosophy with heavy reliance on data analysis, especially at the early phase of programme development. Knowledge does not get transferred and reused effectively at actual implementation and policy implementation cycle.	At the centre of knowledge creation was "do-to-plan" philosophy that used rapid prototyping as learning and planning mechanism. In rapid prototyping, we draw the current corporate knowledge and transfer it across units in the organisation – best practices are extracted and applied rapidly to the implementation process Knowledge was created through learning from outside the organisation, especially the food industry and hawkers.
Knowledge Repository	Knowledge is stored in staff personal drive.	Knowledge is stored in the department's shared drive. However, to retrieve the knowledge, one needs to know the folder in which the document is stored, as the document is not tagged.	Knowledge is stored in the organisation's knowledge portal (C.L.I.C.K.). C.L.I.C.K. has corporate taxonomy and metadata that allows knowledge to be easily searched and retrieved – and thus increases knowledge reusability.

"Healthier Hawker Programme". The case study (overview in Table 1) serves to showcase 4 keys areas of HPB's KM journey, reflecting the use of increasingly sophisticated processes, tools and techniques.

THE SINGAPORE HAWKER CENTRE

The hawker centre (or food centre) is an integral part of Singapore culture and life, offering a diverse menu befitting the multi-cultural mix in the country. Originally set up along the streets without any licenses or regulation, hawker vendors were in the 1950s and 60s moved into centralised open air structures to have greater control over their hygiene practices. Usually paired with a market, there are now more than 100 hawker centres spread throughout the island of Singapore. A 1998 study found that 75% of Singaporeans ate at the hawker centre at least twice a week.

Hawker food is predicated on good taste at the lowest possible price. A typical dish at the hawker centre costs about S$3.00 (about US$2.70) and is the food of choice for almost all segments of the population, particularly the middle and lower income groups. However, hawker food is often unhealthy. Many of the hawker dishes evolved from traditions that are not informed by modern knowledge of healthy nutrition. Most are heavily dependent on the use of oil, seasonings, and are thus high in fat, salt and calories, while at the same time low in vegetables and fibre. The impact on the health of the population (in terms of health indicators such as obesity rates) is compounded by the evolving lifestyles in Singapore to a more sedentary one as residents embrace a knowledge economy.

Healthier Hawker Centre: Version 1.0

The "Ask For" Campaign

The hawker centre has thus long been a logical and obvious target for changing the nutritional practices of Singaporeans. One of the earliest attempts was a campaign to encourage individuals to ask for healthier modifications to their hawker fare. The entire campaign was centred on the concept of "Ask for...," with point of sale labels placed at hawker stalls to remind customers that they could request for healthier modifications to their dishes. A slew of different variations were created including:

- Ask for Less Oil
- Ask for Less Gravy/Sauce
- Ask for Less Sugar/Syrup
- Ask for More Vegetables
- Ask for Skin to be Removed (from poultry)

Each variation came with its own coloured label that was placed visibly at the front of the stall. The entire effort was coupled with a media campaign to raise consumer awareness.

The philosophy behind the "Ask for" campaign was to create the demand for healthier options that would drive changes in the hawker food. This was derived from a dialogue with hawkers. Their initial concern was that it was difficult for them to change their food preparation without consumers complaining that they were being short-changed. Hawkers were also unsure whether customers would actually prefer the healthier options. The onus was thus placed on the consumer to request for the healthier modification. The design of the different "Ask for..." messages also allowed as many hawkers as possible to be part of the programme, with each adjusting their menus according to their means. Thus dessert or beverage stalls would put up the "Ask for Less Sugar" sign, while the chicken rice stall would have the "Ask for Skin to be Removed" sign.

The "Ask for" campaign was a moderate success, with an increase in people asking for healthier food options in the hawker centres between 2002 and 2004. However, the project team found that:

A. It was increasingly difficult to recruit hawkers to the programme after the initial numbers, as it was very much left up to the hawkers to voluntarily join the programme. After the initial drive, several hawkers also dropped out of the programme due to the lack of incentive to remain in it.
B. There was also a social barrier for consumers to actually "Ask for" a modification in the food. It was part of the Asian culture. Some customers found it embarrassing to make such requests which were perceived to bring inconvenience to the hawker and other customers who were behind them in the queue.
C. The "Ask for more Vegetables" sign had created unhappiness among consumers as reports emerged in the newspapers that some hawkers were charging customers more (10 - 50 cents) for the extra ingredients.

Because of these challenges, it was difficult to raise the participation rate of the programme beyond 40%. Furthermore as the "Ask for" signs were varied and dependent on the willingness of each stall-holder to modify his menu, the programme could not achieve the desired reach and impact on overall eating habits of Singaporeans.

KM at this point could be described as follows:

- Data was collected through a simple pre-implementation and post-implementation survey to examine changes in knowledge, attitude, and behaviours resulting from the "Ask for" campaign. Data was utilised to 'justify' the programme implementation.
- After Action Review (AAR) was not an institutionalised learning process. Instead, it was conducted only when the team found it increasingly difficult to recruit hawkers to the programme and when complaints about rising prices emerged.
- Knowledge remained tacit and locked within the project team.
- The knowledge repository infrastructure was weak. Programme documents were stored within personal computer drives of HPB officers, making it difficult for them to be found and accessed. Thus, the knowledge gleaned from the project remained within individuals and the project team.

Healthier Hawker Centre: Version 2.0

National Nutrition Survey

In 2004, HPB mounted the 2nd National Nutrition Survey (NNS) to inform nutrition policies. Among the many findings, it revealed that between 1998 and 2004 total energy (calories) and total fat intake had increased, with 85% of the population consuming more than their dietary limits for saturated fat. This was of particular concern as excess saturated fat contributed to cardiovascular illness and obesity. The hawker centre programme and other nutrition strategies were not having their desired impact (Health Promotion Board, 2004).

In addition the NNS revealed that a major contributor to fat intake was fried dishes, such as fried rice, noodles and vegetables. Many of these dishes were common in hawker centres (leading one local artiste to muse that "Singapore is my Fried Rice Paradise"). The NNS also showed again that more than half of Singaporeans ate out, reflecting a culture that was increasingly reliant on the convenience of hawker food.

Improving the Campaign Approach

Based on the knowledge gleaned from the latest NNS statistics and analysis, as well as the tacit knowledge and experience gained from the previous campaign, the team went about redesigning the healthier hawker programme. Two key changes were made in the approach. Firstly, rather than depend on consumer-led demand to "Ask for" modifications, the team made a decision to focus on the development of healthier ingredients. Given the high usage of oil in hawker fare, cooking oil was targeted. The team worked with the local industry to develop healthier blended cooking oil which would reduce saturated fat content by a third. By replacing cooking oil in hawker centres with the healthier version, the mean saturated fat intake of the population would be reduced from 30 g to 26 g per day. A simple simulation estimated that this would lower the risk of cardiovascular diseases by 20%. The new approach was thus a supplier-induced model that aimed to change the nutrition profile of Singaporeans without even their personal intervention.

Secondly, the way hawkers were recruited was changed. The HPB collaborated with its sister agency the National Environment Agency (NEA), to leverage on NEA's legislative influence over the hawkers. The NEA is in charge of hawker hygiene, and issues licenses and labels to reflect the hygiene practices of each hawker. The HPB negotiated to ride on the hygiene labels, issuing hawkers who came on board the healthier hawker scheme an additional recognition of HPB's Healthier Choice Symbol. Furthermore, learning from the experience of engaging the hawkers during the "Ask For" campaign, and through dialogue with the more experienced NEA officers, HPB modified the approach of recruiting the hawkers. Instead of getting hawkers to gather at a central office for briefing sessions, which disrupted their business and led to a poor turn-out, hawkers were visited one by one at their stalls. NEA officers would accompany HPB staff on their rounds to lend weight to the effort of convincing the hawkers to come on board the programme.

Challenges

This time as part of a planned review of the programme, several key findings emerged.

A. One significant challenge that emerged was the higher cost of the new blended oil. Compared to the normal oil used by hawkers in the market, the healthier oil cost an additional S$1.50 per tin, with an average of 10 tins consumed per hawker per month. For an industry that was heavily dependent on keeping costs low to achieve the margins required, this was a large disincentive.

B. Also as consumers were largely left out of the loop, there was little increase in demand that the hawkers could look forward to. Thus using the healthier oil was not seen as a competitive factor, despite the presence of the healthier choice logo on the NEA hygiene sign. This reduced the motivation for the hawkers to take part in the programme.

In sum, while the programme was moderately successful in changing the ingredients, and thus the nutrition of the population, concerns were raised on how the programme could be made sustainable.

KM at this point was more developed than the earlier version and could be described as follows:

- Data analysis was utilised at the start to guide the programme design. Analyses of the major nutrient categories were performed to identify appropriate interventions and simple simulations used to project the expected benefits.
- The AAR was pre-planned and drew from a wider source of data, including that from the industry. However, the AAR was only conducted at the end of the programme, rather than throughout the project lifecycle.
- There was a conscious effort to create knowledge, using data analyses. However, knowledge gained was not sufficiently applied during policy formulation and project implementation to improve the results.
- Knowledge still remained tacit – locked within the project team. Knowledge was stored in the department's shared computer drive and thus was only searchable by staff in the department. The documents were also untagged – making it difficult for them to be retrieved and reused.

Healthier Hawker Centre: Version 3.0

Charting the Energy Pathway

Drawing from the lessons learnt from the previous two healthier hawker centre models, the programme improved again and made several changes in version 3. A more sophisticated system analysis of the energy intake pathway in Singapore was introduced (Figure 1). Briefly, the systems analysis identified hawker centres as a key lever in the national health strategy given the high volume of food sales through them. Changes made at the hawker centres would thus benefit the citizens, who were drawn to the lower cost food options compared to the restaurants. While the import of food seemed a promising lever, Singapore being a small market would find it difficult to mandate changes to food composition. However a two-pronged strategy was developed, working closely with local enterprises (which though smaller, was easier to influence) to produce local solutions, and targeting major multinational food companies (such as Nestle and Unilever) to influence their global portfolio of products.

Analysing the consumption habits of Singaporeans also supported the strategy of modifying food ingredients as the leverage for changing diets. Whole-grain was identified as a gap in the Singaporean diet, with only 14% of the population meeting the recommended guideline of at least ½ a serving per day. Scientific studies show that whole-grain consumption can reduce the risk for diabetes, hypertension, obesity and cardiovascular disease. Rice as a staple was an obvious target and brown rice was selected as a healthier choice.

The NNS was further analysed to reveal that 9 out of 10 Singaporeans ate noodles at least once a week. The average Singaporean ate 1 bowl of noodles every day. The noodle thus became a key target of efforts to address the nutritional needs of Singaporeans. However, there were no ready healthier noodles in the market. The experience of working with the industry on the healthier oil proved to be a useful model. By collaborating with a local food manufacturer, HPB developed a special formulation of noodles that incorporated ground brown rice to make a product that could fulfil half the daily requirements of whole-grains to the Singaporean diet. The development of the noodles in itself was an interesting experience as it required several modifications that tapped on the nutritional knowledge of HPB staff, and the industrial preparation techniques of the partner firm. The initial version of the healthier noodle used whole-grain wheat, and was coarse and unpalatable. HPB suggested using ground brown rice in place of wheat, which after experimentation by the industry, led to the creation of the innovative product. During the development, samples were tested with the hawkers and the knowledge gained was very useful (for example, the healthier noodle required a modification to the cooking time as it was slightly more brittle than the typical noodles).

Figure 1. Simplified systems flow of energy intake pathway

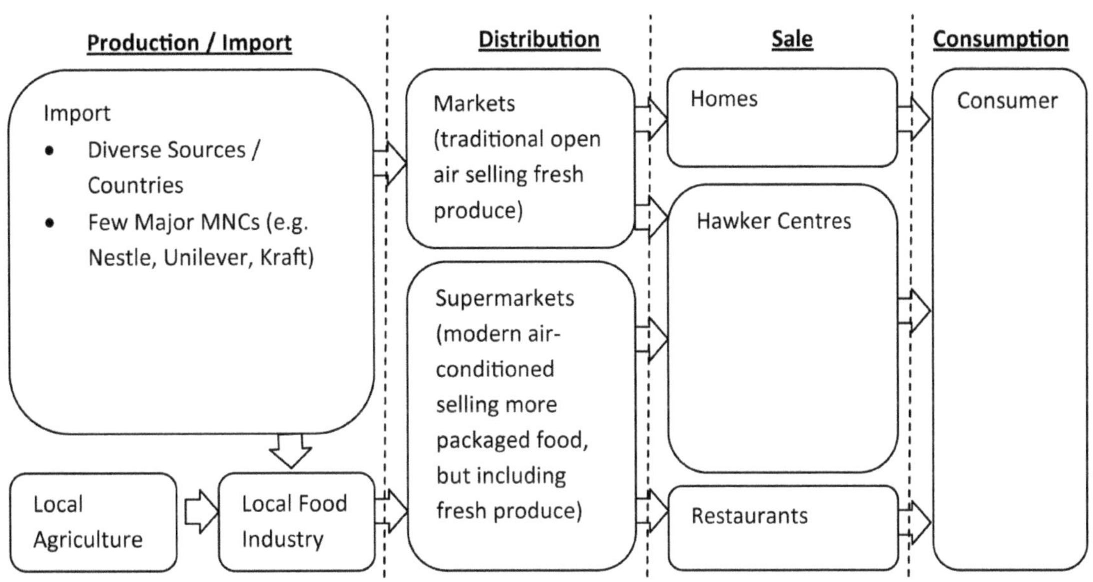

Mobilising the Community

To sustain the project, the experience from the first version was reviewed and the action plan improved upon. The local community centre and community groups near hawker centres were engaged to educate local citizens about the choices available to them, and to inform them about the proximity of hawker stalls selling healthier modifications. The HPB also worked with the community to organise activities (e.g. cooking competition) to promote traffic to the hawker centres with healthier food options.

Food Composition Systems Singapore

Concurrently, the development of a new analytics capability brought enhancement to the programme. The FOCOS (Food Composition System Singapore) was developed with the aim of providing nutrient information about different food dishes in the local context. It not only had information about unique local dishes, but also information that was customised to the local serving sizes and preparation. The FOCOS could also create an improved information menu that allowed consumers to make informed decisions about their purchases. Menu boards could now contain the caloric content of the dish, and together with the healthier choice symbol, allow consumers to make informed choices about their orders. Rather than having to request for modifications to items in the menu, consumers could now just choose dishes that satisfied their caloric requirements.

The FOCOS system also enabled more sophisticated analyses. Beyond simple projections based on changes to individual nutrient categories, the HPB could now project how changes in specific ingredients would impact on the nutrition composition and caloric profile of Singaporeans. This allowed the HPB to set a target of reducing 25 billion calories within 3 years as part of a broader strategy of arresting the rising rate of obesity in the country.

Health as a Premium

The HPB also engaged the private sector to support the health programme by absorbing the cost difference. The HPB worked with suppliers and put forward a business case for selling healthier ingredients. Coupled with the promotional efforts to create demand, a case was made for suppliers to lower the cost of the healthier ingredients as a way to brand their products. The strategy was to eventually reap an economy of scale when consumers shifted to the healthier items. Thus one supplier chose to sell brown rice at the same price as normal rice, while another offered to sell healthier choice canned drinks (with less sugar) at a lower cost than normal drinks. The local community hawker association also helped to market the healthier ingredients.

The result was a healthier hawker centre, where supply, demand and market interventions came together in an integrated ecosystem (Figure 2). The ecosystem pulled together resources from the different sectors: people (local community), private enterprises (industry, hawkers), and public organisations (HPB, NEA).

KM in the HPB has evolved considerably. A critical development was the adoption of a rapid prototyping approach, where the various components were quickly tested in a single hawker centre. Enhancements to the learning and evaluation frameworks were also being introduced as part of the evolution of KM in the organisation. Prototype evaluation processes were developed to quickly extract best practices, and to modify and improve the hawker centre model as it was incrementally rolled out to the rest of Singapore. Knowledge sharing platforms were also developed to facilitate the sharing of experiences and lessons across the organisation. A framework for project learning focusing on 'before, during and after' project learning was developed to support the "Do-to-Plan" philosophy. Knowledge transfer and sharing platforms such as an online knowledge portal were developed with the aim to enhance

Figure 2. Healthier Hawker Centre ecosystem

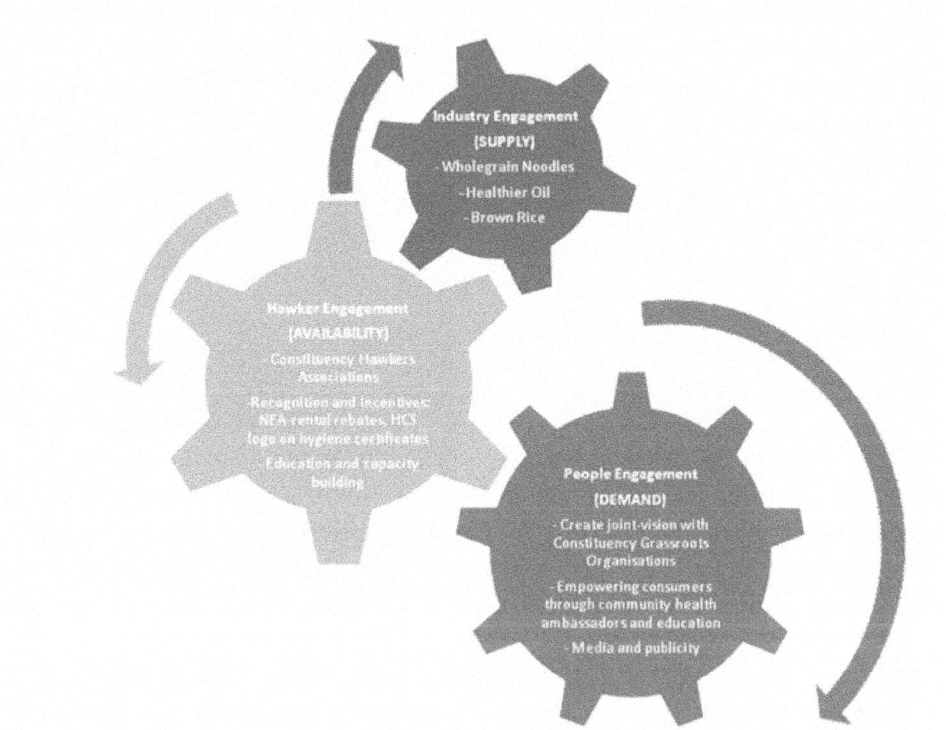

knowledge sharing and collaboration, through online workspaces complete with document libraries, wikis and discussion forums.

KM at this point, was deliberate and used to enable the project team to meet the programme objectives. It could be described as follows:

- Data analyses were utilised to facilitate programme development. The results of the analyses were used to produce detailed profiling of food composition and applied to systems analysis. Nutrient information was integrated with programme solutions.
- AARs were planned for, and conducted at critical phase of the project: before, during, and after the programme. Rapid prototyping was used to create, transfer, and reuse knowledge. It enabled the organisation to reuse its internal knowledge to create prototypes. Once the prototypes worked, the organisation would create, transfer and re-use new knowledge (experience/insights gained during prototype testing) in similar environments.
- Knowledge was drawn from outside the organisation (industry, hawkers) and harnessed during programme design.
- Knowledge was stored in knowledge portal (C.L.I.C.K.) with advanced KM features such as knowledge taxonomies and metadata. These two features increased knowledge reusability and reduced knowledge silos in the organisation.

Lessons Learnt during HPB's KM Journey

The experiences and lessons learnt during HPB's KM journey can be analysed and presented using Rowley's (2001) Learning with Knowledge (LK)

Cycle, a model that is useful to the formation of an ontology for analytic discussion and the implementation of KM. The stages in the LK Cycle are:

- Knowledge creation and construction;
- Knowledge articulation and sharing;
- Knowledge repository updating;
- Knowledge diffusion, access and dissemination;
- Knowledge use; and
- Knowledge revision (loops back to knowledge creation and construction).

The LK Cycle represents the learning process within organisations and is applicable to both tacit and explicit knowledge.

Knowledge Creation and Construction

Throughout the journey for the Healthier Hawker Centre from version 1 to version 3, it is clear that the HPB progressed in an iterative manner; learning through experience; decision making and outcomes; and involving new people. These activities improve tacit knowledge creation and construction. Moreover, the HPB made efforts in improving their scientific, technical and market research. These activities improve explicit knowledge creation and construction. For example, the HPB had the strategic foresight to invest in customised analytical tools such as the FOCOS database to meet a niche business need, i.e. to gain insights on Singaporeans' Nutrition Needs. The FOCOS database not only provided information for research but also served as a tool for communication (caloric value of food on menu boards), and provided more powerful projections of the energy reductions required to reduce obesity rates. More importantly, knowledge creation and construction was driven by an awareness and commitment to develop a knowledge-based organisation. In the case of HPB, the top management acknowledged that decision-making in public policy, programme development and implementation all needed to be knowledge-driven. With the utilisation of the right tools at the right time (e.g. appropriate data analytics), the HPB was able to generate the required knowledge to prescribe its policy positions and target courses of action for the public good. This direction by the top management was essential in the context of the development of appropriate organizational culture for KM (Ribiere and Sitar, 2003; Ellis and Rumizen, 2002; Schein, 1996).

Knowledge Articulation and Sharing

The HPB also made sure that knowledge was increasingly articulated and shared. Increased team work and external scanning improved tacit knowledge articulation and sharing. Market research reports, strategy documents and communication documents with hawkers and customers enhanced explicit knowledge articulation and sharing. The HPB believed that knowledge was a key asset for all and should not remain tacit within a few staff members in the organisation. Knowledge articulation and sharing should also not be seen as limited to between units within the business. Many of the breakthroughs in this hawker centre experiments were developed through sharing of information with parties outside of the organisation. As exemplified by the development of the healthier noodles, information shared between HPB, the industry, and the community (hawkers) was important to the development of a viable product. Concerns about Intellectual Property were addressed and managed through MOUs or contracts. But the value to be unlocked through the tapping on knowledge outside the organisation could be powerful.

Here, the concept of networks that supports new approaches to HPB's core purpose of promoting a healthy lifestyle becomes increasingly apparent and important. Networks help organisations to become more agile, more responsive to customer needs, making better use of information and knowledge (Stewart, 2001). Such networks are dynamic syntheses of ICT networks with people networks. In knowledge organisations, networks become the main means by which information is conveyed and work gets done. Hierarchical considerations and organisational boundaries are broken for a common and higher value proposition. Networks work on the principles of cooperation and collaboration – not just internally but also cross-businesses (Stewart, 2001). Knowledge transfer and the predictor of successful transfer is the quality of relationship between operating units (Uzzi and Lancaster, 2003; Song, Almeida, and Wu, 2003). This is where the HPB has worked consciously on.

Knowledge Repository Updating

Knowledge repositories include both systems and people (Rowley, 2001). System repositories include archives, databases and filing protocols. People repositories are embodiments of knowledge within people's understanding, practices and awareness. Knowledge repositories need to respond to the dynamic nature of knowledge, keeping them relevant and archiving outdated or redundant knowledge. Throughout the journey, the HPB has made a conscious effort to update its knowledge repository. In explicit ways, databases were updated and documents collected. In implicit ways, through working in project teams, experiences were shared and values, stories, practice and other cultural artefacts exchanged.

Here, it is worthwhile to mention that technology can be an effective KM enabler. By investing in a knowledge portal (C.L.I.C.K.) that had corporate taxonomy and metadata, there was less risk of knowledge loss and greater conversion of tacit knowledge residing in individuals into a corporate asset beneficial to all. Lessons learnt from the earlier versions of the programme showed that information stored in personal drives made it difficult for others who wanted to make use of the organisation's knowledge to access the information. With C.L.I.C.K., however, any project team in HPB would be able to access relevant knowledge within the organisation. It enhanced knowledge dissemination across the organisation. This agrees well with the view that organisations can learn but that they cannot do so in their own right without infrastructural support and enablers such as information systems (Baxter, Connolly and Stansfield, 2009). C.L.I.C.K. also drove knowledge repository updating because peoplewere are always using it and the top management had an interest in keeping it useful because it was a huge investment.

Knowledge Diffusion, Access, and Dissemination

Knowledge access may be initiated by the potential recipient when an individual seeks knowledge, either by searching a system, or by contacting others, or it may be initiated by some other agency, as when knowledge is disseminated to an individual or group. Targeted dissemination can be viewed as a means of influencing the behaviour of a group of people because of the knowledge input. In the case of the HPB, it has enhanced its knowledge diffusion, access and dissemination, not just internally but also externally. In the case of Healthier Hawker Centre from version 1 to version 3, there was an increase in the knowledge diffusion, access and dissemination through its project teams, working sessions and enhanced relationships between working units. Externally, through working with the local community centre, community groups and local grassroots, knowledge diffusion, access and dissemination took place with local citizens about healthier choices of hawker food available to them.

Knowledge Use

This part of the cycle is significant in terms of measurable outputs. Knowledge may be used as the basis for developing new knowledge through integration, creation, innovation and extension of existing knowledge and/or it may be used as the basis for actions or decisions. These actions or decisions impact on business performance. They not only justify organisational learning, but also form a basis for measuring the effectiveness of the organisational learning process and the knowledge management activities that contribute to that process.

In the case of the HPB, new knowledge generation and usage, coupled with the use of rapid prototyping (Brown, 2009), led to the development of public policies and programmes with higher effectiveness. The policy problems faced by the HPB were complex and had multiple layers and levers that had to be analysed to focus limited resources for action. Furthermore, the interconnected network of cause and effect relationships had to be studied for unintended effects. However, inaction could often be as detrimental to the public good. This was where prototyping complements systems analysis for the HPB. Prototypes enabled knowledge creation, transfer and reuse on the fly. Once the prototype worked, the HPB officers could extract the knowledge embedded in the prototype, and turn it into good practices – which were transferred and reused within the organisation.

Knowledge Revision

Knowledge revision takes place as a result of knowledge use and reflection on the decisions and actions taken. Such reflection drives learning which forms the basis of the creation of new knowledge to supplement or substitute existing knowledge. This stage is crucial to individual development and organisational learning. One of the most important ways to achieve knowledge revision in the HPB was to institutionalise the After Action Review (AAR). The HPB lost some critical knowledge from the earlier versions of Healthier Hawker Programme, because AARs were only conducted at the end of the programme. Important details of programme development had been lost by then due to time lag and staff turnover. Today, in the HPB, AARs are integrated as part of the implementation process of any initiative and conducted at critical junctures. The AAR is no longer used on an ad-hoc basis, or conducted only at the end of a programme. The AAR is now part of any programme management process and the organisation proactively conducts it at critical junctures of their programmes. This is also where the prototyping and "Do-to-plan" approach adopted in version 3 become very important, as knowledge is constantly being updated through experiences garnered during implementation and immediately fed back into the implementation process.

CONCLUSION: THE NEXT LAP FOR HPB

Perhaps most importantly, the HPB journey shows the importance of a KM culture within an organisation. Within the HPB, knowledge sharing and collaboration is increasingly embedded as part of its organisational culture, with the leadership team playing a pivotal role to drive its direction and operationalization. Top leadership at the HPB guides strategic directions and the development of enabling systems, structures and governance while operational leadership drives key processes, promotes the use of relevant tools and builds KM capacity. Recognition and incentives to foster a culture of knowledge sharing and collaboration is a key feature of the HPB's KM strategies with various formal and informal mechanisms put in place to encourage desired behaviour. These include recognition at Board level platforms, Employee of the Year Award, clear knowledge sharing and collaboration behaviours articulated and measured as a part of HPB staff performance appraisal and incentives from participation in various knowledge sharing platforms.

The application of rapid prototyping also reflects a further change in the organisational culture of the HPB. Managing knowledge (create, transfer, and reuse knowledge) is only possible when there is a means to quickly recover from unsatisfactory programme implementation. To create, transfer, and reuse its knowledge the organisation's mindset needs to change from "prevent failure" to "quickly recover from failure". Prototyping thus liberates the staff to experiment, collaborate, and innovate.

The experience of the HPB is in harmony with KM literature which suggests that organizational culture should be the focal point of KM programmes (e.g. Davenport and Prusak, 2000; Bock, 1999; Krogh et al., 2000; Nonaka and Takeuchi, 1995; Rastogi, 2000). Some organizations that have proven to be more successful than others in their KM efforts have often cited their inherent culture as the central aspect behind their success (Hackett, 2000).

This case study of the Healthier Hawker Programme at the HPB showcases several layers of KM in support of the development of public policies. Moving forward, the HPB is developing new capabilities in its KM journey. Given HPB's deep engagement of the community, one need is to develop a database to manage our customer engagement. At the basic level, the HPB is reviewing the internal processes to standardise the engagement of customers. Overlaid on this will be a Customer Relationship Management (CRM) system that will empower health promotion officers on the ground as they engage the community (e.g. hawkers). HPB is also planning to develop a Centre of Excellence for Nutrition, harnessing on the fruitful knowledge sharing relationship borne from this healthier hawker centre experience. By harnessing on the expertise residing the private sector, coupling it with HPB's own knowledge about local diets and nutritional needs, the HPB plans to encourage the development of commercially viable food products that will make both public health and business sense.

REFERENCES

Baxter, G. J., Connolly, T. M., & Stansfield, M. (2009). How can organisations learn: An information systems development perspective. *Learning Inquiry*, *3*(1), 25–46. doi:10.1007/s11519-009-0038-8

Bock, F. (1999). The intelligent approach to knowledge management: Viewing KM in terms of content, culture, process, and infrastructure. *Knowledge Management Review*, *7*, 22–25.

Brown, T. (2009). *Change by design: How design thinking transforms organizations and inspires innovation*. New York, NY: HarperBusiness.

Chait, L. P. (1999). Creating a successful knowledge management system. *The Journal of Business Strategy*, *20*(2), 23–26. doi:10.1108/eb039991

Davenport, H. T., & Prusak, L. (2000). *Working knowledge: How organizations manage what they know*. Boston, MA: Harvard Business School Press.

De Long, D. W., & Fahey, L. (2000). Diagnosing cultural barriers to knowledge management. *The Academy of Management Executive*, *14*(4), 113–127. doi:10.5465/AME.2000.3979820

Drucker, P. F. (1988). The coming of the new organization. *Harvard Business Review*, *66*(1), 45–53.

Drucker, P. F. (1999). Knowledge worker productivity: The biggest challenge. *California Management Review*, *41*(2), 79–94.

Ellis, M. S., & Rumizen, M. (2002). The evolution of KM at Buckman Laboratories: How its KM program has developed with the new leadership. *Knowledge Management Review*, *5*(1), 12–15.

Hackett, B. (2000). *Beyond knowledge management: New ways to work and learn*. New York, NY: The Conference Board.

Health Promotion Board. (2004). *Report of the National Nutrition Survey 2004*. Singapore: Health Promotion Board.

Hertog, J. F. D., & Huizenga, E. (2000). *The knowledge enterprise: Implementation of intelligent business strategies*. London, UK: Imperial College Press.

Krogh, G. V., Ichijo, K., & Nonaka, I. (2000). *Enabling knowledge creation: How to unlock the mystery of tacit knowledge and release the power of innovation*. New York, NY: Oxford University Press.

Neo, B. S., & Chen, G. (2007). *Dynamic governance: Embedding culture, capabilities and change in Singapore*. Singapore: World Scientific Publishing. doi:10.1142/9789812771919

Nonaka, I. (1991). The knowledge creating company. *Harvard Business Review*, *69*(November–December), 96–104.

Nonaka, I., & Konno, N. (1998). The concept of 'ba': Building a foundation for knowledge creation. *California Management Review*, *40*(3), 1–15.

Nonaka, I., & Takeuchi, H. (1995). *The knowledge-creating company: How Japanese companies create the dynamics of innovation*. New York, NY: Oxford University Press.

Ong, P (2010). *Role of PS21 and leadership in supporting public service productivity*. Opening address by Mr Peter Ong, Head of Singapore Civil Service at the PS21 ExCEL Convention forum and award ceremony, 2 November.

Rastogi, P. N. (2000). Knowledge management and intellectual capital: the new virtuous reality of competitiveness. *Human Systems Management*, *19*(4), 39–49.

Ribiere, V., & Sitar, A. (2003). Critical role of leadership in nurturing knowledge supporting culture. *Knowledge Management Research and Practice*, *1*(1), 39–48. doi:10.1057/palgrave.kmrp.8500004

Rowley, J. (2001). Knowledge management in pursuit of learning: The learning with knowledge cycle. *Journal of Information Science*, *27*(4), 227–237. doi:10.1177/016555150102700406

Schein, E. H. (1996). Three cultures of management: The key to organizational learning. *Sloan Management Review*, *38*(1), 9–20.

Schein, E. H. (1999). *The corporate culture survival guide*. San Francisco, CA: Jossey-Bass.

Song, J., Almeida, P., & Wu, G. (2003). Learning by hiring: When is mobility more likely to facilitate interfirm knowledge transfer? *Management Science*, *49*(4), 351–365. doi:10.1287/mnsc.49.4.351.14429

Stewart, T. A. (2001). *The wealth of knowledge*. London, UK: Nicholas Brealy Publishing.

Uzzi, B., & Lancaster, R. (2003). The role of relationships in interfirm knowledge transfer and learning: The case of corporate debt markets. *Management Science*, *49*(4), 383–399. doi:10.1287/mnsc.49.4.383.14427

Chapter 6
Assessing Knowledge Assets in Renewable Energy SMEs in Scotland:
A Methodological Framework

Antonio Lerro
University of Basilicata, Italy

Giovanni Schiuma
University of Basilicata, Italy

Robert Huggins
University of Wales Institute Cardiff (UWIC), UK

Daniel Prokop
University of Wales Institute Cardiff (UWIC), UK

Maria Weir
Intellectual Assets Centre, UK

ABSTRACT

This chapter develops a research protocol to identify a domain of organizational knowledge resources and assets within firms and provides the final main insights of a research project managed by the Intellectual Assets Center in Scotland in order to support the adoption of knowledge asset management initiatives for driving innovation and performance improvement of Small and Medium Enterprises (SMEs) operating in the renewable energy sector. The chapter first presents a methodology for valuing organizational knowledge assets within SMEs operating in the renewable energy industry. Then, an exploratory survey with a sample of 58 organizations from the Scottish renewable energy sector is introduced. Finally, the chapter analyses and discusses the main insights about SMEs' perception and orientation to identifying, measuring, and managing knowledge, and to qualitatively identify a feasible set of knowledge resources and assets potentially driving performance improvement.

DOI: 10.4018/978-1-4666-0948-8.ch006

1. INTRODUCTION

Great attention has increasingly been placed on the role and relevance of the Knowledge Asset Management (KAM) to support and drive the improvement of organizational performance in the energy industry (Edwards, 2007; Foxon et al., 2005). However, most of the interest has been developed by big oil companies searching for improvements in their efficiency (Etkind et al., 2003; Nelson, 1997; Smith and Farquhar, 2000). On the other hand, SMEs operating in the energy industry, and particularly in the renewables sector, are increasingly recognizing the relevance of KAM, even if they still do not have formal KAM initiatives in place within the organization. Indeed, SMEs' knowledge and intangible assets are fundamentally managed implicitly, i.e. without the use of formal approaches and tools (Franco and Haase, 2009; Weir et al., 2009). Moreover, although knowledge–based resources and assets are recognized as being fundamental to organizational success (Carlucci et al., 2004; Kelliher and Rainl, 2009; Schiuma and Lerro, 2008; Schiuma et al., 2008), the tools for valuing organizational knowledge in renewable energy industry are still crude and often inadequate. In this paper we suggest a process for valuing organizational knowledge that can be effectively applied in the energy industry and specifically in renewable sector. On the basis of a literature review (Wilcox King and Zeithaml, 2003), using a sample of 58 organizations from the Scottish Small and Medium Enterprises (SMEs) in the renewable energy sector, we draw main insights about their perceptions and orientations to identifying, measuring and managing knowledge.

2. A METHODOLOGY FOR VALUING ORGANIZATIONAL KNOWLEDGE ASSETS

To achieve a more fine-grained insight into knowledge resources and assets, we present a four-step methodology for valuing organizational knowledge in renewable energy industry constructed from practicing owners and managers' perspectives. We test it with 8 Scottish organizations. Then, an exploratory survey was administered on 58 Scottish SMEs organizations operating in renewables.

2.1 Step 1: Defining Scope: Industry and Organization Selection

Industry and organization selection was driven by the aims of a research project managed by the Intellectual Assets Center in Scotland, in order to support the adoption of knowledge asset management initiatives for driving the improvement of value creation mechanisms of SMEs operating in the renewable energy sector. In particular, we selected established SME companies having well-defined boundaries and operating in: *solar energy*, i.e. the energy of the sun's rays that can be converted into other forms of energy, such as heat or electricity; *wind power (onshore and offshore)*, i.e. the harnessing of wind by turbines that convert the energy into electricity; *hydrogen*, as potential use in the operation of hydrogen-powered automobiles; *biomass*, which includes plants grown for the production of fuels; and *hydro-power (wave and tidal),* harnessing of the sea or river water by turbines that convert the water energy into electricity.

We solicited more than one hundred renewable energy industry companies and drew together a complementary cohort. We sent letters to these companies describing the project, requesting a participation in the research project and an interview with the owners or top-managers as well as inviting them to participate in a series of Workshops and Masterclasses about the project. Out of the population, 58 agreed to participate in studies. The involved companies had different core-business but by comparing key-variables for the sample of organizations we recognized no significant differences. These organizations include those shown in Table 1.

Table 1. Sector of activities of companies interviewed

Sector of activities of companies interviewed
Architect
Civil Engineering
Civil Engineering / Wind Farms
Commercialization of Science and Technology
Community Estate - owns wind farms
Design
Diving - Commercial and Scientific
Economic Development - Wave and Tidal
Energy Efficiency
Energy Efficiency Design
Energy Services
Engineering
Environmental
Environmental Science
Forestry - New Trees
Forestry & Rural Development
General marine and diving contractor & marine consultant providing project management
Hydro Engineering
Logistics
Manufacturing
Marine
Marine Energy
Marine Services
Micro Renewable Service Provider and Macro Renewable Consultancy
Nuclear/Public Sector/Oil & Gas
Oil & Gas
Oil& Gas, Nuclear, Alternative Energy, Marine op's
Renewable Energy
Renewable Energy / Wind Farms
Renewable Energy and Carbon Energy
Renewable Energy Consultancy
Renewable Energy Projects
Renewable Energy Services
Renewable Services
Research Institute Marine and Environmental Research
Strategic Development and Regeneration
Tidal Power
Wave Energy
Wind Energy
Wind Energy R&D
Wind Farms Engineering Consultancy
Wind Turbine, Installers & Distributors

continued in following column

Table 1. Continued

2.2 Step 2: Research and Protocol Design: Building Scholars Knowledge

The next step began with in-depth research. On the basis of insights from a literature review (Weir et al., 2009), we improved our familiarity with industry-specific issues and terminology. This understanding enhanced our credibility and enabled us to investigate richer and more probing questions when conducting the interviews. To structure the interviews with the owners or top managers, we developed a protocol that included an overview letter and a broad outline of questions. The protocol was pre-tested on a panel of academics and experts ofknowledge management, performance management and energy industry, soliciting feedback regarding clarity, overall impressions and terminology to be used to improve organizations' participation. Based on their feedback, we decided to use the label "*knowledge*" as broadly consisting of research and development, ideas, skills, expertise and other information that is, or potentially can be, used to make the operation of a company more effective, "*knowledge management*" (KM) as the group of approaches, methodologies and tools used in an organisation to identify, create, represent and exploit knowledge to improve organisational performance and value creation, and "*knowledge assets*" as any resource made of, or incorporating, knowledge which provides an ability to carry out a process or an activity aimed to create and/or deliver value.

2.3 Step 3: Data Collection: Survey of Owners and Top Management to Identify Organizational Knowledge Resources and Assets

To identify an inventory of organizational knowledge resources and assets we interviewed a range of renewable energy companies' owners and top-managers. Prior to each interview, we faxed and emailed the overview to the owners and top-managers to establish expectations for the meeting and provide initial guidance in scoping the knowledge resources and assets. During each interview, we asked respondents to identify the "knowledge or skills that may provide competitiveness" at their organization and in the industry. The interview involved an iterative process as the respondents talked through the sources of competitive advantage at the company and worked to articulate organizational knowledge on an appropriate scale, specific enough to clearly relate to ways organizational knowledge can add value in the industry, and general enough to allow for reapplication to support value in future endeavours. Interviewers used a line-by-line open coding method to generate a list of the knowledge resources and assets discussed during that interview (Strauss and Corbin, 1990). For each organization, we then compared our lists and our notes for content, tone and accuracy and, following a discussion, determined a final company-specific list. Based on these interviews, we identified 15 knowledge assets, 5 dimensions of knowledge assets, and 7 knowledge management processes in the renewable energy industry. We made every effort to describe knowledge-based factors that were simple, not ambiguous and not "double-barreled" (DeVellis, 1991). External readers familiar with the issues reviewed the final list of knowledge assets, dimensions and processes to confirm their clarity and comprehensiveness. These insights were incorporated into an explorative survey.

2.4 Step 4: Data Collection: Explorative Survey of Owners and Top Managers to Value Organizational Knowledge Resources and Assets

In order to value organizational knowledge resources and assets, a questionnaire was administered *vis a vi*, by phone and by email with owners and managers of 58 companies. These teams completed surveys appraising the knowledge factors generated through the interviews. The questionnaire was divided in four main sections for a total of 13 questions, mainly rated using a 5-point Likert scale. The aim of the first section (Q1-Q3) was to investigate the level of awareness of the importance to effectively manage knowledge within the organizations, identifying the ways by which knowledge is important to the renewables SME companies as well as the most important knowledge dimensions for maintaining or improving the competitiveness of the organization. The second section (Q4-Q7) was finalized to better understand the state-of-the art about the possession and the exploitation of knowledge assets by companies and the knowledge management processes organizations consider most important for their competitiveness. Specific attention was paid to investigate the knowledge sources that organizations use to undertake their innovation dynamics.

The third section (Q8-Q11) aimed to explore the knowledge flows and the relationships system in the renewable energy industry, in terms of collaboration engaged with universities or research centres around specific activities, relationships with the big energy companies, emergence of supply-chains among renewable energy industry companies, nature and characteristics of these relationships. Finally, the fourth section (Q12-Q13) was aimed to investigate the issue of the new products or services or adaptations to existing products and services made by the companies in the last three years as well as the most important constraints that the companies face in acquiring or creating the knowledge required to maintain or improve innovation dynamics and competitiveness. The questionnaires were treated confidentially. A total of 58 usable surveys were returned. Additionally, the data on companies was supported by the qualitative information.

3. MAIN EVIDENCES AND IMPLICATIONS OF ORGANIZATIONAL KNOWLEDGE IN SCOTTISH RENEWABLE ENERGY INDUSTRY SMES

Energy industry companies, and in particular SMEs in the renewable energy sector, are increasingly asked to create and support competitive advantages, especially in situations of rapid and unpredictable market and normative change, pressures about environmental issues, and increase of energy demand from developing nations. The knowledge asset management represents a fundamental way to improve and develop organizational value creation capacity. This methodology for valuing owners and managers' perceptions of knowledge assets makes a novel and important contributions to the Knowledge Management research streams.

The level of awareness of the importance to effectively manage knowledge within the organizations is relatively high, scoring 4.32 on a 5-point Likert scale as indicated by companies. However, the identification of the ways by which knowledge is important to the renewable energy SMEs shows that companies still do not address some specific mechanisms enhancing their performance dimensions. In particular, SMEs do not recognize specific stronger impact of knowledge assets in terms of innovation, organizational value creation, and strategic planning but attribute about the same importance to all of these.

Regarding the most important knowledge dimensions for maintaining or improving the competitiveness of the organization, as shown in Figure 1, it emerges that SMEs pay particular attention to the Human Capital (HC), i.e. competences, skills, abilities, know-how and leadership of their employees and Relational Capital (RC), i.e. relationships with customers, suppliers, community, regulators and other stakeholders However, competitive factors linked to Technological Capital (TC) and Organizational Capital (OC)

Figure 1. Importance of the organizational factors for competitiveness

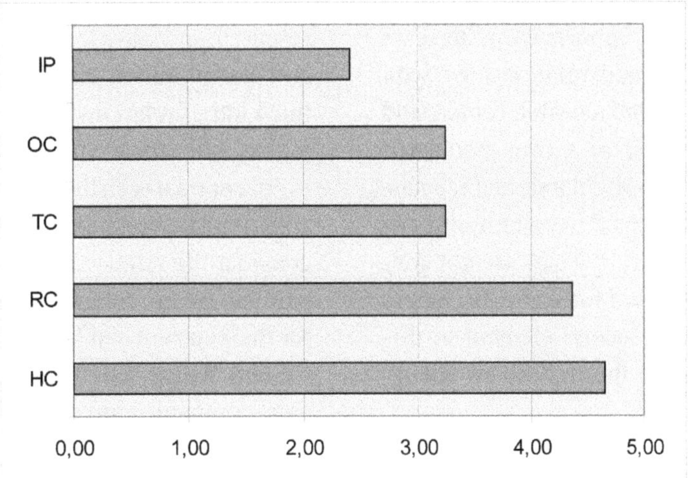

have good relevance, while Intellectual Property has the lower level.

Moreover, at an aggregate level, renewable energy SMEs consider to possess a good endowment of knowledge assets, particularly in terms of reputation of the organization, organization's customers databases, organization name and logo, processes and technological know-how, relationships and quality of the human capital.

However, most of the organizations from the sample are aware that for majority of these assets they have not taken steps to fully exploit or manage them and recognize the wide space for improvement in these areas in order to gain new sustainable competitive advantages in their industry.

Figure 2a and Figure 2b depicts the levels of possession and exploitation of knowledge assets from Scottish renewable energy companies, taking into account that the respondents had the opportunity to select multiple choices in the questionnaire.

In terms of the importance of knowledge management processes for organizational competitiveness, as shown in Figure 3, renewable energy SMEs pay particular attention to the knowledge sharing within the organization. In addition, knowledge transfer to the organization and codification of know-how are also significant knowledge management processes.

Regarding the process of knowledge creation through learning mechanisms (Figure 3a), most of the SMEs underline the importance of the team working, specialization and relationships with other firms, universities and research centers and institutions, as in the case of a firm associated with the University of the Highlands and Islands, while limited attention is paid to communities of practice. Decision Support Systems are not considered particularly relevant for competitiveness and this aspect can be a second element of differentiation in respect to the traditional energy industry companies.

Regarding the sources of knowledge for undertaking innovation, as shown in Figure 4, at the aggregate level, SMEs effectively use a wide spectrum of modalities. In particular, strong relevance is assigned to the internal dimension of sourcing knowledge, but also traditional external sources in terms of analysis of the competitors, conference, trade fairs and exhibitions, scientific journals and suppliers and customers show a good perception. However, according to the traditional SMEs approaches, even if internal sources are still important at the same level as the external ones, potentialities still not fully exploited stand in building better collaborations with commercial laboratories, institutions, research centers and universities as well as with consultants highly-skilled in KM in renewables. Moreover, it emerges that SMEs source knowledge mainly from organizations and companies located in Scotland, and then in UK, while contacts overseas are very limited. This insight highlights the need of a stronger internationalization of the SMEs and alliances to search new inspiring sources of knowledge driving their value creation dynamics.

These latter evidences are supported by the evidences emerging from the engagement of the companies with universities and research centers in the past three years. The main collaboration activities are mostly concentrated on the recruitment of highly-skilled people, while other activities, such as patents development, collaborative research, and knowledge transfer partnerships are still in exploration stage (Figure 5). Nevertheless, this kind of relationship is not considered strategically relevant for the SMEs.

In contrast with the importance of the relationships with universities and research centers, SMEs consider the relationships with big and/or multinational energy companies strategically important for their current and future competitiveness (Carrol and Wagar, 2010). In particular, the big energy companies are a mean for SMEs to access

Figure 2. Within Figures a) and b) possession (in blue) and exploitation (in red) of knowledge assets

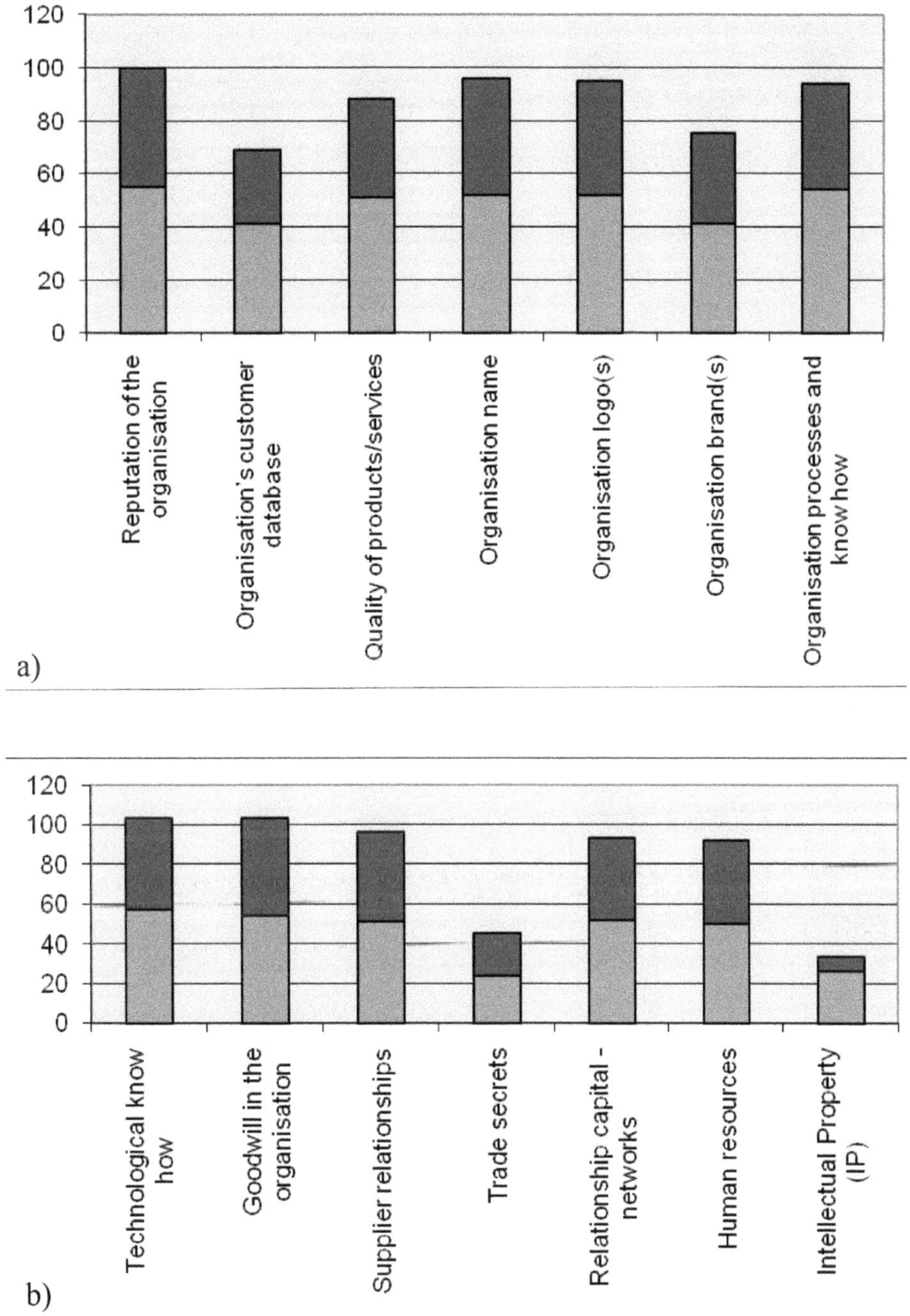

Figure 3. a) Importance of the knowledge management processes for competitiveness b) Knowledge Creation through learning mechanism – Cross-section

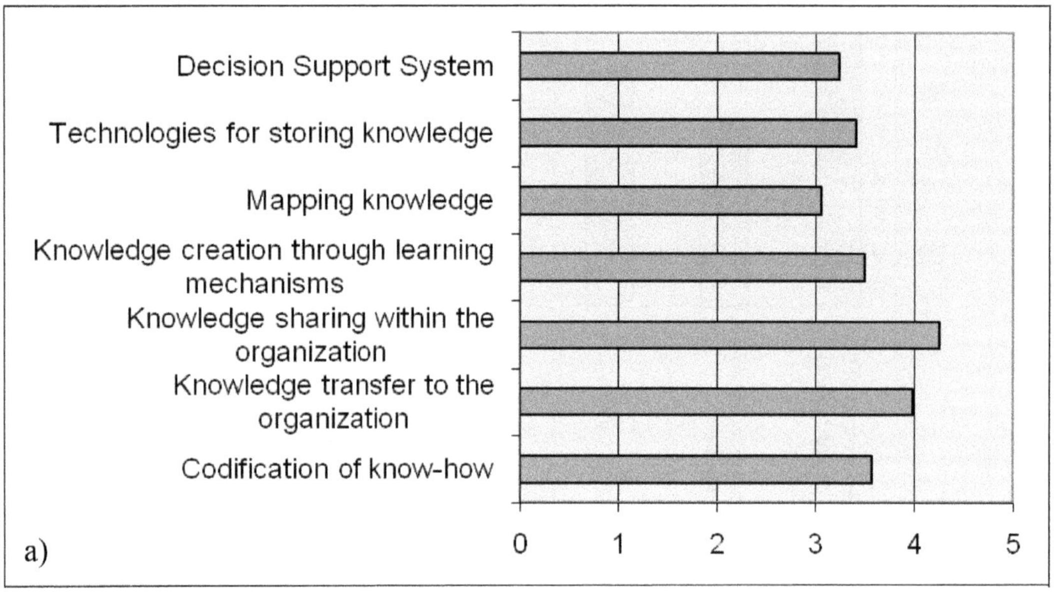

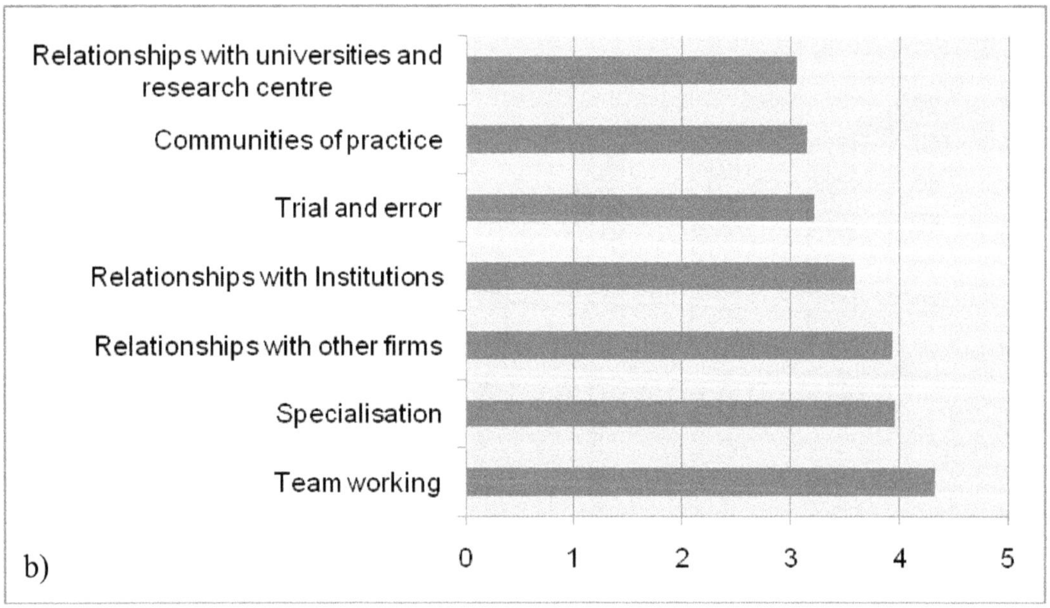

Figure 4. Sources of knowledge for undertaking innovation

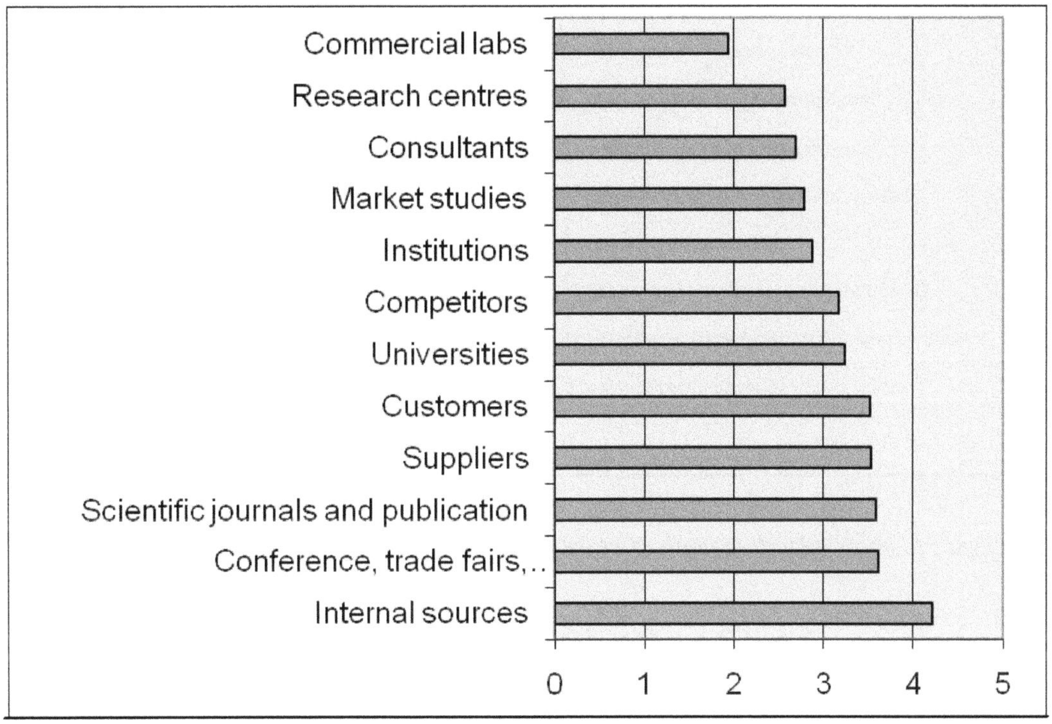

market or competitor intelligence, professional information, skills and expertise, and results of research and development activities (Fig.6). Nevertheless, this evidence could strongly drive a better definition and implementation of the policies aimed to support the growth of the renewable energy industry in Scotland in terms of enhancing collaborative dynamics and investments attractions from big energy companies.

Moreover, it emerges that the supply chains of the renewable energy industry companies are still evolving, and that the nature of the relationships is mainly based on competitive dynamics. Finally, as shown in Figure 7, it emerges that the most important barriers that the SMEs face in acquiring or creating the knowledge they require to maintain or improve competitiveness are mainly linked to the inability to access suitable finance and skilled labour, to the quality or applicability of available business support or advice, as well as to issues related to training and education (Burger-Helmchen, 2009).

4. CLOSING REMARKS

In this chapter we have presented a research protocol to identify a domain of organizational knowledge resources and assets within SMEs operating in the renewable energy industry. Using a sample of 58 organizations from the Scottish renewable energy sector SMEs, we draw main insights about their perceptions and orientations to identifying, measuring and managing knowledge, and to qualitatively identify a feasible set of knowledge resources and assets potentially driving performance improvement. This evidence shows an increasing awareness of the relevance of the knowledge-based factors. Generally, firms possess a good endowment of knowledge assets and perceive their organizational competitiveness to be attributed typically to the knowledge management of relational and human dimensions.

The highly significant knowledge management processes are considered to be internal, i.e. knowledge sharing within the organization, but

Figure 5. Activities of engagement of SMEs with universities and research centers

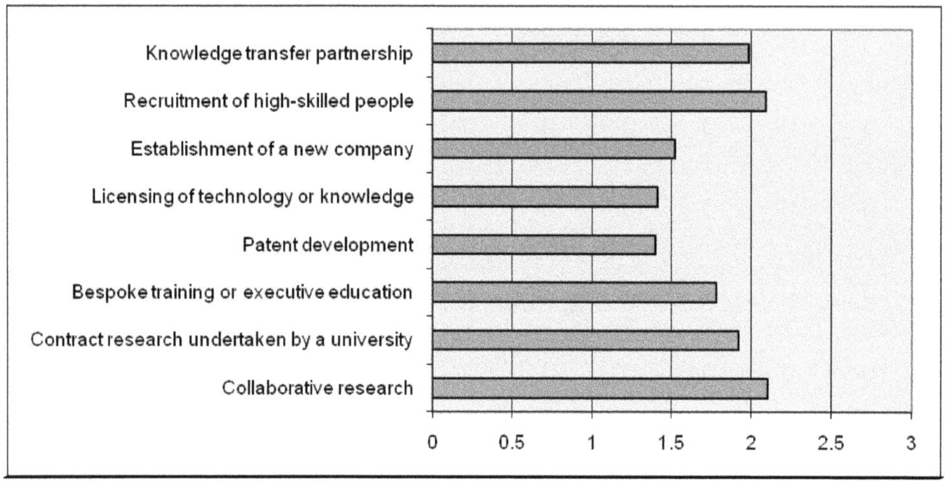

Figure 6. Types of knowledge frequently accessed from big energy companies

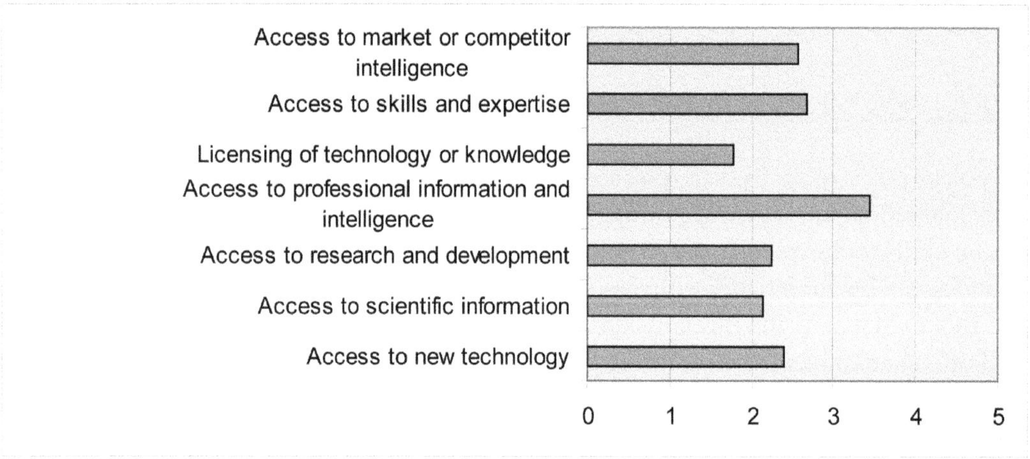

Figure 7. Barriers for acquiring or creating knowledge in renewable

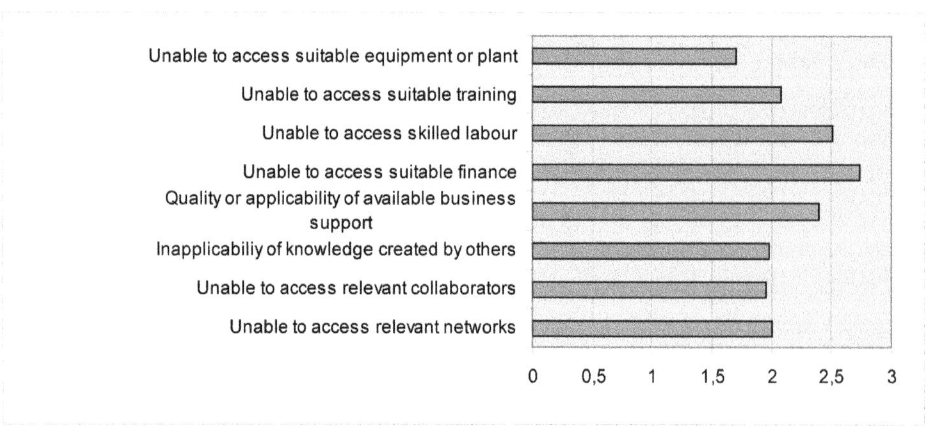

also a knowledge flow from external agents has emerged as important, and is mainly attributed to relationships with other firms and education or research institutions. Furthermore, this exploratory study has shown that firms access a wide range of knowledge sources for undertaking innovation activities. Nevertheless, there are apparent deficiencies in the exploitation of knowledge assets and knowledge management processes, as well as a limited access to suitable finance and skilled labor, which suggests the need for efforts to better address the development requirements of renewable energy sector SMEs.

On the basis of these insights, we have outlined some key research and policy issues which could drive the design and implementation of a more extended research and policy projects for fully exploit both at micro and macro level the main organizational knowledge asset grounding organizational performance improvement and value creation dynamics (Yosuf, 2010).

REFERENCES

Burger-Helmchen, T. (2009). Capabilities is small high-tech firms: A case of plural-entrepreneurship. *Journal of Small Business and Enterprise Development*, *16*(3), 391–405. doi:10.1108/14626000910977125

Carlucci, D., Marr, B., & Schiuma, G. (2004). The knowledge value chain – How intellectual capital impacts business performance. *International Journal of Technology Management*, *27*(6/7), 575–590. doi:10.1504/IJTM.2004.004903

Carrol, W. R., & Wagar, T. H. (2010). Is there a relationship between information technology adoption and human resource management? *Journal of Small Business and Enterprise Development*, *17*(2), 218–229. doi:10.1108/14626001011041229

DeVellis, R. F. (1991). Applied Social Research Methods Series: *Vol. 26. Scale development: Theory and application*. Newbury Park, CA: Sage.

Edwards, J. (2007). Knowledge management in the energy sector: Review and future directions. *International Journal of Energy Sector Management*, *2*(2), 197–217. doi:10.1108/17506220810883216

Etkind, J., Bennaceur, K., Dmec, M., & Luppens, C. (2003). Knowledge portals support widely distributed oil fields projects. *Proceedings of IEEE International Professional Communication Conference IEEE*, Orlando, FL, (pp. 189-200).

Foxon, T. J., Gross, R., Chase, A., Howes, J., Arnall, A., & Anderson, D. (2005). UK innovation systems for new and renewable energy technologies: drivers, barriers and systems failures. *Energy Policy*, *33*, 2123–2137. doi:10.1016/j.enpol.2004.04.011

Franco, M., & Haase, H. (2009). Entrepreneurship: An organizational learning approach. *Journal of Small Business and Enterprise Development*, *16*(4), 628–641. doi:10.1108/14626000911000965

Graeff, C. L. (1980). Some methodological issues concerning comparative hospital studies. *Academy of Management Review*, *5*, 539–548.

Kelliher, F., & Rainl, L. (2009). A resource-based view of micro-firms management practice. *Journal of Small Business and Enterprise Development*, *16*(3), 521–532. doi:10.1108/14626000910977206

Mehra, A. (1996). Resource and market based determinants of performance in the U.S. banking industry. *Strategic Management Journal*, *3*, 307–322. doi:10.1002/(SICI)1097-0266(199604)17:4<307::AID-SMJ820>3.0.CO;2-2

Nelson, H. R. (1997). Virtual seminars. *Computers & Geosciences*, *23*(5), 601–606. doi:10.1016/S0098-3004(97)00029-0

Porac, J. F., Thomas, H., & Baden Fuller, C. (1989). Competitive groups as cognitive communities: The case of Scottish knitwear manufacturers. *Journal of Management Studies*, *26*(4), 397–416. doi:10.1111/j.1467-6486.1989.tb00736.x

Porac, J. F., Thomas, H., Wilson, F., Paton, D., & Kanfer, A. (1995). Rivalry and the industry model of Scottish knitwear producers. *Administrative Science Quarterly*, *40*(2), 203–227. doi:10.2307/2393636

Schiuma, G., & Lerro, A. (2008). Foreword: Intellectual capital and company's performance improvement. *Measuring Business Excellence*, *12*(9), 3–9. doi:10.1108/13683040810881153

Schiuma, G., Lerro, A., & Sanitate, D. (2008). Intellectual capital dimensions of Ducati's turnaround – Exploring knowledge assets grounding a change management program. *International Journal of Innovation Management*, *12*(2), 161–193. doi:10.1142/S1363919608001935

Smith, R. G., & Farquhar, A. (2000). The road ahead for knowledge management - An AI perspective. *AI Magazine*, *21*(4), 17–40.

Strauss, A., & Corbin, J. (1990). *Basics of qualitative research: Grounded theory procedures and techniques*. Newbury Park, CA: Sage.

Weir, M., Huggins, R., Schiuma, G., Lerro, A., & Prokop, D. (2009). Managing knowledge assets in renewable energy industry: Defining a research agenda for Scotland's SMEs. *Proceedings of the 5th EIASM Workshop on Visualing, Measuring and Managing and Intangibles and Intellectual Capital*, 7-8 October, Dresden, Germany.

Wilcox King, A., & Zeithaml, C. P. (2003). Measuring organizational knowledge: A conceptual and methodological framework. *Strategic Management Journal*, *24*, 763–772. doi:10.1002/smj.333

Chapter 7
Inside Entrepreneurship and Innovation Activities

George M. Korres
University of Newcastle, UK & University of Aegean, Greece

ABSTRACT

The growing importance of entrepreneurship and innovation activities in world production and employment is one of the characteristics of the last four decades. Entrepreneurship is not only a determinant of growth, but also affects the international competition and the modernization of a country. This chapter analyses the entrepreneurship and innovation activities and the way they contribute essentially to growth and competitiveness. The chapter aims to investigate how entrepreneurship affects not only and innovation capabilities, but also the whole periphery and economy, as well as how technological innovation is essential if companies - and countries - are to maintain their competitiveness in global markets. There are a lot of underlying problems and questions regarding the measurement of entrepreneurship and innovation activities. In particular, this chapter attempts to analyze the whole framework of entrepreneurship and innovation activities and in particular to analyse the effects and implications to growth and competitiveness. Within this context, it also aims to emphasize and review the appropriate techniques, the most common methods, and the particular related problems.

INTRODUCTION

Entrepreneurship and the relevant policies have played an important role for socio-economic and regional growth. Indeed, facilitating increasing rates of enterprise creation is an almost universal concern for local authorities who seek to accelerate development or reverse decline in localities, whether disadvantaged or prosperous. New enterprises can procure a range of benefits that contribute to local development, including: rises in employment and incomes; enhanced provision of services for consumers and businesses; and possibly, demonstration and motivational effects. Foreign direct investment contributed substantially to the transfer of new technologies and consequently to the modernisation and reorientation of the structure of the economies. The main bulk of technology transfer took place either through foreign direct investments (FDIs)

DOI: 10.4018/978-1-4666-0948-8.ch007

(mainly through multinationals MNEs) or through *technological agreements* (for instance, licensing and joint ventures).

Innovation is now recognized as a major source of competitiveness of firms and innovation systems. It is recognized as highly relevant to economic performance and sustainability and thus has been gaining more support and attention. This does not mean that innovation policy is immune from pressures for regulatory reform, shared with other policy areas. Innovation policy also needs to draw on evidence, be evaluated to be based on the best available knowledge and to become a learning process.

Archibugi and Michie (1997) concur: "To understand technological change it is crucial to identify the economic, social, political and geographical context in which innovation is generated and disseminated. This space may be local, national or global. Or, more likely, it will involve a complex and evolving integration at different levels of local, national and global forces".

Hommen and Doloreux (2004) conclude: "To develop a more comprehensive approach to understanding RIS, it will be necessary to consider failures as well as successes, non-localized as well as localized learning, and different modes of integration, both locally and globally. One possible line of inquiry might centre on the precise nature and the relative importance of localized and non-localized learning, relating these to the forms of knowledge accumulation that sustain the globalization of firms and the competitiveness of regions. On this basis, it would be possible to develop a more discriminating account of the conditions that enable some regions to adapt and generate certain forms of knowledge, more successfully than others".

Furthermore, innovation is a phenomenon that is relevant to a wide range of policies. For example, policies areas -such as education, environment, and Intellectual Property- have implications for innovation. Still policies whose fundamental concern is not innovation, have effects on innovation processes. These interrelations are often poorly understood, and this may have resulted in policy designs that are sub-optimal. Interactions between regulatory reform in all policy areas, the changing nature of innovation processes and the changing content of innovation policies need to be continually explored.

Government policies in new technologies and innovations aims exactly to this point: to reinforce technological capabilities in order to enhance productivity, competitiveness and economic growth of their countries. Government support is usually taken under the form of "direct" and "indirect" measures that is, different grant, loans, tax concessions, and equity capital.

This Chapter attempts to examine the structure and role of technological policy, the national and the regional systems of innovations and their implications on sustainable development and social change. This Chapter also deals with the entrepreneurship activities, the Foreign Direct Investments (FDIs), the transfer of technology and innovation activities.

ENTREPRENEURSHIP, FDIs, AND INNOVATION ACTIVITIES

Entrepreneurship is a complex subject of study and its characteristics, dynamics, determinants and manifestations differ across countries. The overall level of economic development is an important contextual distinction for the research on entrepreneurship, as it can take very different forms. Entrepreneurship in a Schumpeterian view is defined as an attitude of helping innovative ideas become reality by establishing new business models and at the same time replacing conventional business systems by making them obsolete ("creative destruction", Schumpeter).

The entrepreneur is the innovator who implements change within markets through the carrying out of new combinations. The carrying out of new combinations can take several forms;

- The introduction of a new good or quality thereof
- The introduction of a new method of production
- The opening of a new market
- The conquest of a new source of supply of new materials or parts
- The carrying out of the new organization of any industry

The entrepreneurship research has identified a number of factors affecting the emergence and success of new enterprises. Many of these factors, at least indirectly, also relate to the attractiveness and image of entrepreneurship. Factors can be divided into personality and environmental characteristics. Personality factors presented in the literature include:

- Risk-Taking propensity to gain profits
- Locus of control
- Need for autonomy and independence
- Initiative
- Innovativeness and creativity
- Self-confidence and self-determination
- Tolerance for failure
- Tolerance for ambiguity
- Need for achievement
- Previous employment
- Ability to learn

Entrepreneurship plays a crucial role in innovative activity by serving as the mechanism by which knowledge spills over from the organization producing that knowledge, to the (new) organization commercializing it. While the conventional wisdom is derived from the Schumpeterian Hypothesis and assumption that scale economies exist in R&D effort, more recent theories and empirical evidence suggests that scale economies bestowed through the geographic proximity facilitated by spatial clusters seems to be more important than those for large enterprises in producing innovative output.

Contemporary theories of entrepreneurship generally focus on the decision-making context of the individual. Thus, while the entrepreneurship literature considers opportunities to exist exogenously, in the economics literature they are systematically and endogenously created through the purposeful investments in new knowledge. Of course, that the former is focusing on the cognitive context of the individual while the latter is concerned with the decision-making of the firm provides at least some reconciliation between these two different views.

Entrepreneurship for empirical measurement is a difficult task and the degree of difficulty involved increases exponentially when cross-country comparisons are involved. There is a vast literature and many studies attempt to measures entrepreneurship, such as:

- Audretsch, Carree, van Stel and Thurik (2002) use a measure of business ownership rates to reflect the degree of entrepreneurial activity. This measure is defined as the number of business owners, in all sectors excluding agriculture, divided by the total labour force.
- Other measures of entrepreneurship focus more on change that corresponds to innovative activity for an industry. Such measures include indicators of R&TD activity, the numbers of patented inventions, and new product innovations introduced into the market (Audretsch, 1995).
- Similarly, other measures of entrepreneurial activity focus solely on the criterion of growth. Firms exhibiting exceptionally high growth over a prolonged duration are classified as gazelles. For example, Holmes et al (1990) measures the number of gazelles to reflect entrepreneurship. Such measures of entrepreneurship must also be qualified for their narrow focus not only on a single unit of observation – enterprises – but also on a single measure of change – growth.

Figure 1. Integration between entrepreneurship and innovation policy

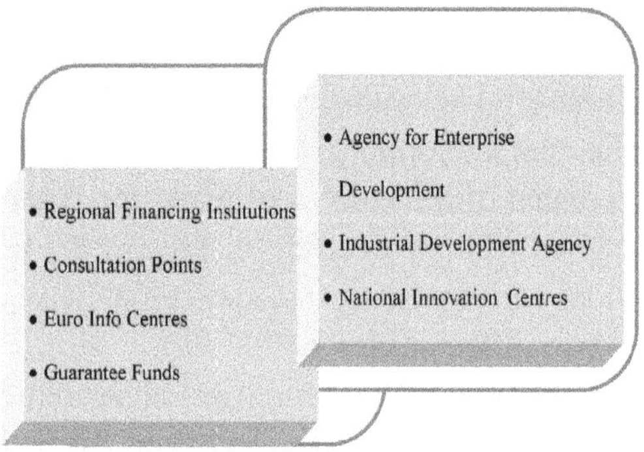

- Lundstrom and Stevenson (2001) followed the precedent of the Global Entrepreneurship Monitor (GEM) study (Reynolds et al., 2000) by defining and measuring entrepreneurship as "mainly people in the pre-startup, startup and early phases of business" (Lundstrom and Stevenson, 2001, p. 19).

Enterprise is at the heart of successful innovation, and not just in the private sector. Entrepreneurial attitudes - even if not precisely identical motivations – underpin much innovation in public sector organisations. Support for such enterprising attitudes in general should be fostered. Small and medium sized enterprises (SMEs) will continue to remain an important focus of innovative effort, and of policy interest. The two should be brought together: innovation support facilities can be built into systems that aim at supporting SMEs in general (European Commission, 2002). Figure 1 illustrates the main domain of entrepreneurship and innovation and also the integration between entrepreneurship and innovation policy.

Investment motives refer to economic advantages provided to foreign enterprises by a government, so that they are encouraged to locate in the specific potential host country. The motives of location choice can be categorized in four general categories:

- Motives related to the expected demand in a certain region
- Motives related to the factors of cost
- Motives related to the agglomeration effects
- The motives related to the public policies of attracting investment capital

Table 1 illustrates the main categories and the types of motives for FDIs. Efforts in the areas of FDIs and research activities have been associated in the economic literature with higher growth rates, increases in exports and trade, gains in productivity, growth in income and output, bigger business profits and lower inflation, international competitiveness. We can also distinguish among *technology transfer*, *technology capacity* (that is, the flow of *knowledge* and the *stock of knowledge*, respectively), and *technology of innovation* (which indicates the type of technology that gives the capacity to the recipients country's to establish a new infrastructure or to upgrade obsolete technologies).

Figure 2 illustrates FDI, innovation and the growth process. There is a huge literature on the effects of innovation activities. However, only a small part of these studies their effects on a regional level. Most innovation results from intentional efforts to develop new varieties of products, higher quality levels of existing products, or lower cost methods of production (process improvements). The development of technological capabilities is the outcome of a complex interaction of inventive structure with human resources, technology efforts and institutional factors. The incentive structure includes macroeconomic incentives, incentives from competition and factor markets; and the institutions includes market and non-market institutions such as legal framework,

Table 1. Categories and type of motives for FDIs

Motive categories	Type of motives
Motives related to expected demand	Market size or market potential
	Gross Domestic Product
	Population density
	Access to national and regional markets
	Barriers to international activity
Motives related to the factors of production cost	Tenure of natural resources
	Access to low-cost labour
	Wage costs adjusted for Quality of human capital or labour productivity,
	Labour market conditions
	Production costs
	Specialized working force.
	Level of infrastructure
	Productivity rates
Motives related to the agglomeration effects	Distance
	Availability and quality of infrastructure
	Economies of agglomeration
	Economic openness
	Capital market integration
	Peripheral or central location of the region
	Cost of transport
	Geographic degree of concentration
Motives related to public policies	Policy liberalisation
	Policy toward FDI
	Political, economic and legal environment
	Institutional quality of the host country
	Macroeconomic stability
	Institutional stability
	Political stability
	General investment dangers

industrial institutions, and training and technology institutions.

FDIs contributes to regional innovation in the following ways (Korres, 2011):

- R&D and other forms of innovation generated by foreign firms and R&D labs of MNEs increases the innovation outputs in the region directly
- Spillovers emanated from foreign innovation activities may affect the innovation performance in the region they locate
- FDI may affect regional innovation capacity through competition effect

Figures 3-6 illustrates the entry rate for the average period 2000-07 for a number of newly registered corporations as a percentage of all regis-

Figure 2. FDI, innovation, and growth process

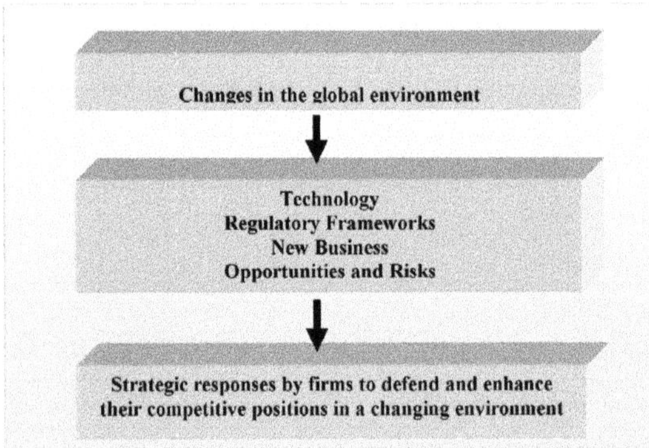

tered corporations (as entry Rate is defined as the number of newly registered corporations divided by the number of total registered corporations), the days needed to start a business and also the foreign inventions owned by countries, 2005-07: Relative to country shares in patent applications (data refers to counts of patent applications filed through the Patent Co-operation Treaty, at international phase, by applicant's residence country and priority date. Foreign inventions owned by countries refer to the share of patents owned by a country's resident with no inventors residing in the country over total patents owned by the same country. Only economies having applied for more than 100 patent applications over the period are included in the chart.)

In summary, FDI impacts regional innovation capabilities in several ways.

- FDIs may contribute to the overall regional innovation performance directly due to the greater innovation intensity in MNEs
- FDIs may contribute to regional innovation performance through greater innovation efficiency in MNEs
- FDIs may affect innovation capability of local indigenous firms through technological and managerial knowledge spillovers

Figure 3. Domestic absorptive capacity and external flows

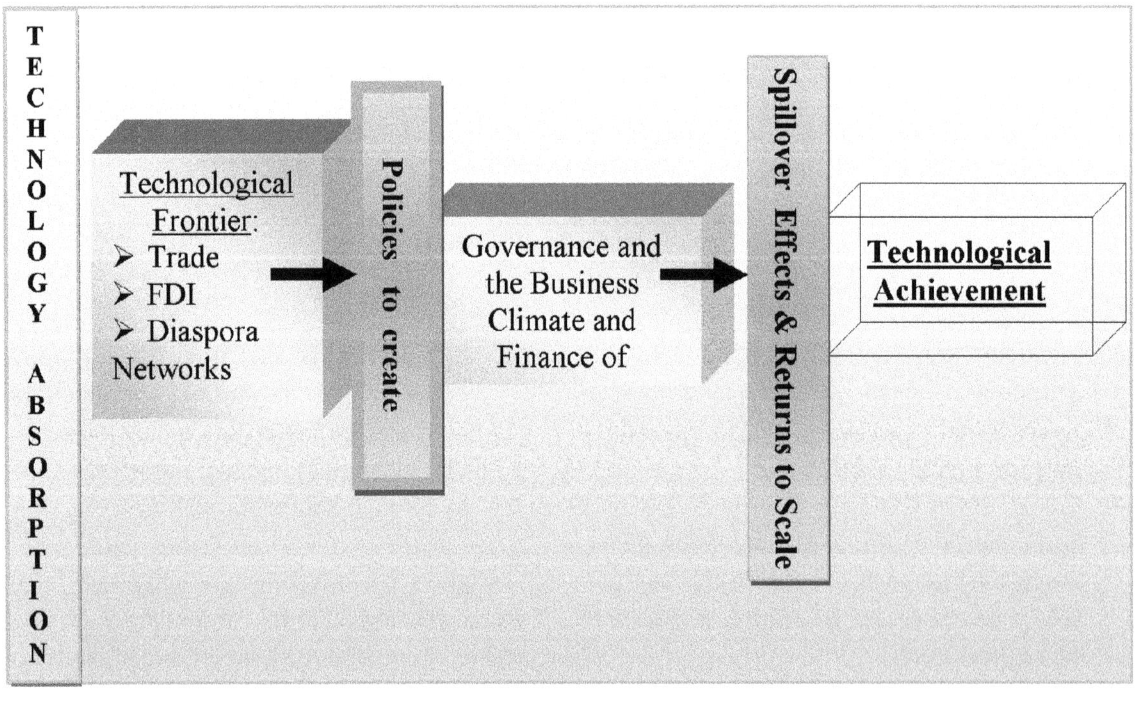

Figure 4. Entry rate, average 2000-07: Number of newly registered corporations as a percentage of all registered corporations

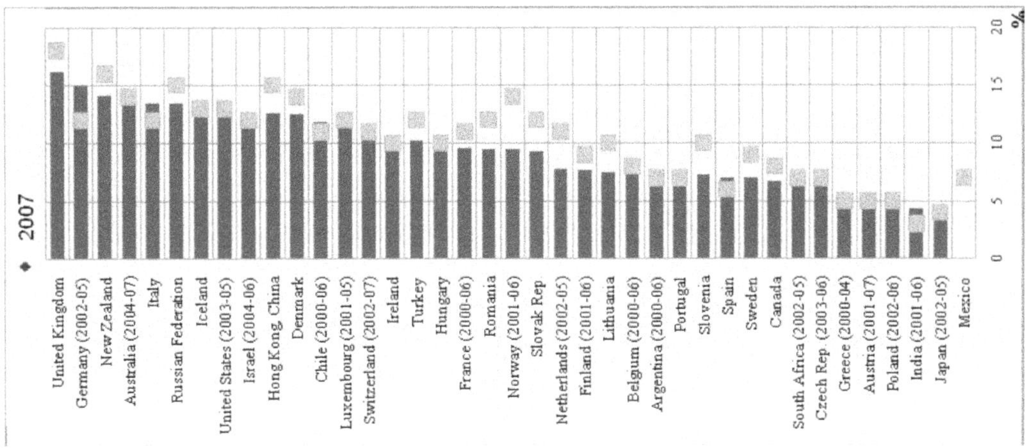

- The strength of the FDI effect on regional innovation capabilities depends upon the absorptive capacity of and the complementary assets in the domestic sector, the linkages between the foreign and the domestic sectors, and the technology content of the FDI

SUMMARY CONCLUSION

Technology transfer through FDI is an important factor on the process of economic development and economic performance. MNEs and FDIs are the main policy tools for the international technology transfer and the development of innovation activities in many countries. Multinationals also produce and control most of the world's advanced technology. There is a number of characteristics of innovation systems in less advance regions which make them less efficient, that is:

- Firms may not be capable of identifying their innovation needs or maybe unaware of the existence of a technical solution
- There may be poorly developed financial systems in the area with few funds available for risk or seed capital, which are specifically adapted to the terms and risks of the innovation process in firms
- There may be a lack of technological intermediaries capable of identifying and "federating" local business demand for innovation R&TD and channelling it towards sources of innovation R&TD which may be able to respond to these demands
- Co-operation between the public and private sectors may be weak, and the area may lack an entrepreneurial culture which is open to inter-firm co-operation, leading to an absence of economies of scale and business critical mass which may make certain local innovation efforts profitable
- Traditional industries and small family firms which have little inclination towards innovation may dominate. There may be a low level of participation in international R&TD networks and a low incidence of large, multinational firms

In setting different priorities, we should take into account different conditions of each country and each regions as well as different elements and objectives of other sectors. The various objectives of entrepreneurship and innovation policies may be subsumed under following headings:

Figure 5. Days needed to start a business, 2010

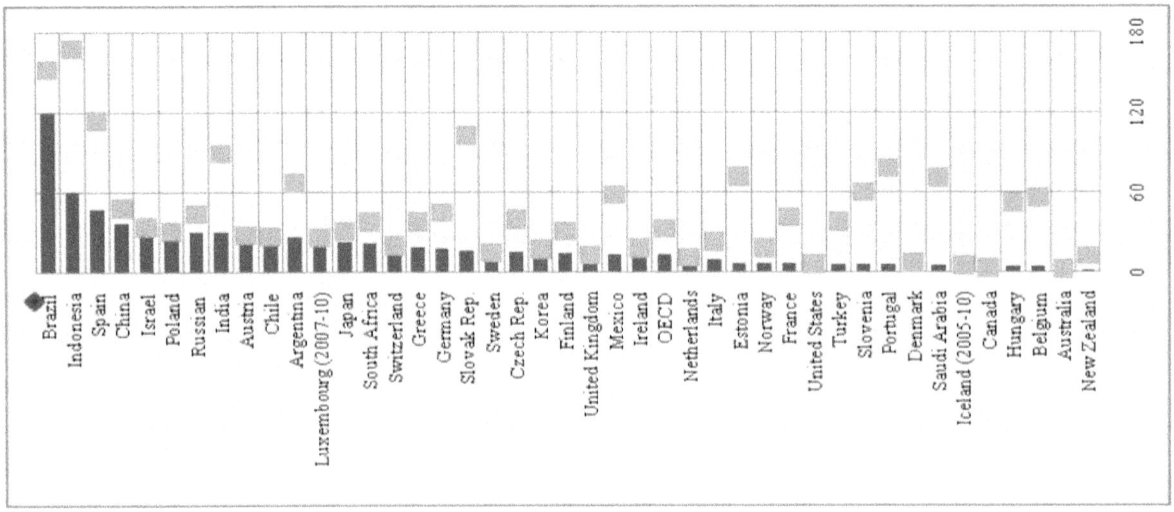

- To improve the efficiency of the transfer of technology from foreign suppliers to the local users
- Increase the efficiency of operation of technology
- Strengthen the industrial base
- Develop the indigenous technological capability
- Smooth adjustment forced by new technologies

Figure 6. Foreign inventions owned by countries, 2005-07: Relative to country shares in patent applications

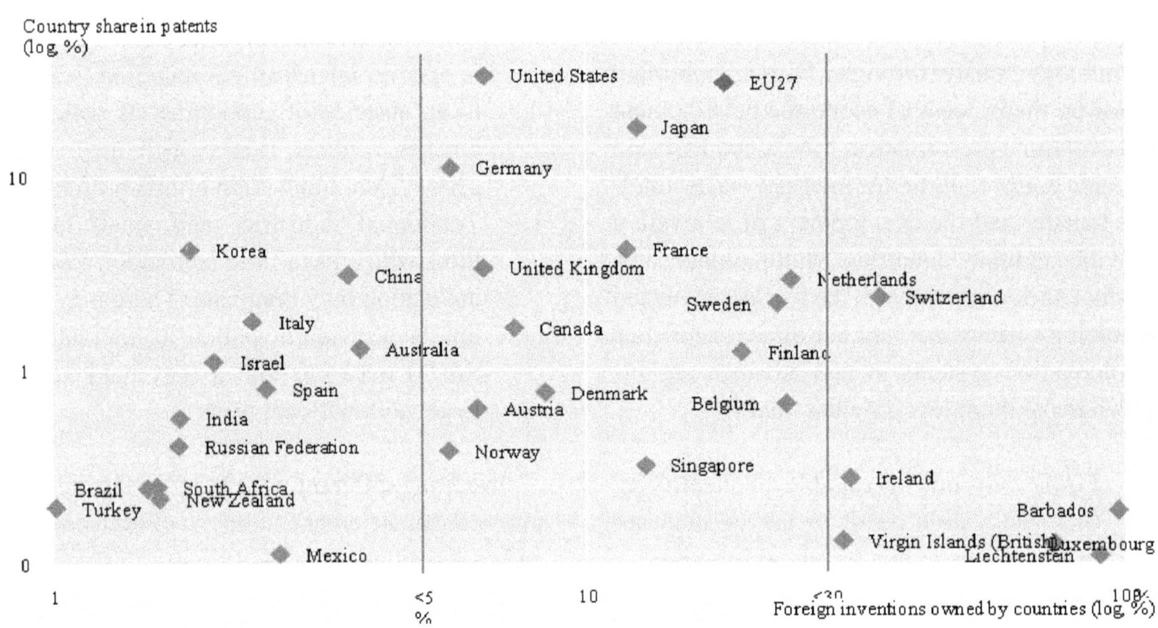

- To assess the possibilities and needs of private and public enterprises with respect to research and technological activities
- Choose those priority objectives that can delineate government technological action
- Strength the links between enterprise and the knowledge base, through, for instance, R&D grants, spinout and licensing assistance
- Support networks, skills initiatives and tailored business support packages, focused on needs and issues of certain sectors
- Participate in the inter-regional initiatives, where there are sector synergies with other regions
- Ensure stable macroeconomic and framework conditions to underpin the entrepreneurial business environment;
- Promote an entrepreneurial society and entrepreneurial culture, in particular through education and training
- Integrate the local development dimension into the promotion of entrepreneurship
- Ensure that programmes in support of SMEs and entrepreneurship are realistic in terms of cost and are designed to deliver measurable results
- Strengthen the factual and analytical basis for policymaking so that policy makers can take decisions in an informed manner based on empirical evidence
- Increase the ability of women to participate in the labour force by ensuring the availability of affordable child care and equal treatment in the workplace
- Support the emergence and maintenance of innovative clusters
- Promote policy coherence at regional, national and international level.

REFERENCES

Archibugi, D., & Michie, J. (1997). *Innovation policy in a global economy*. Cambridge, UK: Cambridge University Press.

Audretsch, D. B. (1995). *Innovation and industry evolution*. Cambridge, MA: MIT Press.

Audretsch, D. B., Carree, M. A., van Stel, A. J., & Thurik, A. R. (2002). Impeded industrial restructuring: The growth penalty. *Kyklos*, *55*(1), 81–98. doi:10.1111/1467-6435.00178

Brush, C. G. (1992). Research of women business owners: Past trends, a new perspective and future directions. *Entrepreneur Theory and Practice*, *16*(4), 5–30.

European Commission. (2002b). *Innovation tomorrow: Innovation policy and the regulatory framework: Making innovation an integral part of the broader structural agenda*. Louis Lengrand & Associés, Innovation Papers, No: 28, Luxembourg.

Holmes, T. J., & Schmitz, J. A. Jr. (1990). A theory of entrepreneurship and its application to the study of business transfers. *The Journal of Political Economy*, *98*(4), 265–294. doi:10.1086/261678

Hommen, L., & Doloreux, D. (2004). Bring back labour in: A 'new' point of departure for the regional innovation approach. In Flensburg, P., Hörte, S. A., & Karlsson, K. (Eds.), *Knowledge spillovers and knowledge management in industrial clusters and industrial networks*. London, UK: Edward Elgar Publisher.

IFC and World Bank. (2009). *Doing business 2010*. London, UK: Palgrave Macmillan.

Korres, G. (2011). *A Handbook of innovation economics*. New York, NY: Nova Publishers.

Lundstrom, A., & Stevenson, L. (2001). *Entrepreneurship policy for the future*. Stockholm, Sweden: Swedish Foundation for Small Business Research.

OECD. (2010). *Patent database*. Paris, France: OECD.

Reynolds, P. D., Hay, M., Bygrave, W. M., Camp, S. M., & Autio, E. (2000). *Global entrepreneurship monitor*. Kansas City, MO: Kaufman Center for Entrepreneurial Leadership.

World Bank. (2008) *Entrepreneurship database.* WBGES08, Washington DC.

Chapter 8
Achieving Competitive Advantage through Innovation:
The Case of the Shanghai Supermarket

Wei Song
Thompson Rivers University, Canada

ABSTRACT

Innovation in the service/retail sector has not been fully examined in the non-Western literature. This preliminary work presents a study that was conducted in Shanghai, China. Three sets of the literature are consulted: Porter's Generic Strategies Model, Hunt's Resource Advantage Theory (R-A), and previous studies in the service and retail sectors. Findings developed from six selected successful Chinese supermarket companies have identified three types of innovation adopted by Chinese retailers: Technology based, non-technology based, and resource based innovation. The study takes a qualitative approach by using the methods of documentation survey and in-depth interviews with a panel of ten supermarket experts. Some managerial implications are explicated, and the limitations of the study and directions for future studies are discussed.

INTRODUCTION

It has been recognized that innovation is the key to firms' success by promoting long term growth. Traditionally, most innovation studies focus on the manufacturing industries while the service/retail sectors are less investigated. This is likely because the former is knowledge intensive (KIS) while the latter is less-knowledge intensive as the service/retailing sectors are regarded as innovation process "laggards" or "later adopters" (OECD, 2009). However, the significant developments in service/retailing sectors and related advancements in information technology innovation in

DOI: 10.4018/978-1-4666-0948-8.ch008

these non-manufacturing sectors have triggered recent studies by academicians and professionals. Most of these studies have addressed three main issues: the differences in innovation processes between manufacturing industries and service or retail sectors; the effect of innovation on economic performance, such as financial inputs and outputs; and the relevance in adapting technology and non-technology innovations to different sectors, i.e., manufacturing and service/retailing sectors. However, this third area of innovation, especially from emerging countries, has not been fully explored. This study discusses the issue related to the third area by using the case of the Chinese supermarket sector in Shanghai.

The research findings vary; some hold that technology innovation is crucial for the hi-tech industries while the non-technology innovation is more relevant to service sectors. Also, some studies believe there is not a direct correlation between the innovation and financial performance. For example, the research and development (R & D) inputs are not necessarily positively correlated to financial outputs, such as sales and productivities regardless of implementation of technology and non-technology innovation. However, the research has not specifically addressed which type of innovation would be the most relevant to the service/retail sector which is the important research question directly affecting a firm's business strategy and management execution. Moreover, resource based innovation which uses a firm's internal resources to advance the financial performance in the service/retail sector has not been well addressed. Finally, extant empirical investigations are gleaned mainly from the developed countries, but the research from emerging countries, such as China and India, remains scarce. This preliminary study empirically identifies the types of innovation in supermarket sectors and reports the preferred approach associated with implementation of innovation undertaken by the Chinese supermarket enterprise.

With the foreign retailers' entries and the rapid growth of the Chinese supermarkets, as well as the information technology advancement, adapting innovation is becoming crucial for Chinese retailers to gain a sustainable competitive advantage. The purpose of adapting innovation in the retail sector is twofold: reducing the marginal costs and generating added values to its customers for higher financial returns. Therefore, innovation enables the firm to exploit its resources and create differentiation. The structure for the remainder of this paper is as follows: a literature review of Porter's competitive advantage model, Hunt's resource advantage theory, and the research work on innovation. The main data sources were from both documentation survey and semi-structured in-depth interviews with a panel of supermarket experts. The findings and discussion of the investigation are analyzed. The management implication is discussed. The limitation and the direction of the study are also presented.

LITERATURE REVIEW

The very purpose of innovation is to enable firms to create differentiation in order to gain a competitive advantage. With the relevance of this study, two sets of the literature have been consulted: three schools of study in competitive advantage and the studies regarding the innovation in the service/retailing sector.

Previous Work on Competitive Advantage

A body of previous work on competitive advantage creates the core theoretical background to the research in the areas of differentiation, generic strategies, and resource advantage. Differentiation advantage is the key element of competitive advantage as competition is for differentiation (Alderson, 1957, p.101). The key to success in the competition is to gain a differential advantage, which would provide a firm with strength over its competitors (Alderson, 1957, p.102). The essential process of the competition is to gain a differentiation advantage because it provides the value that a firm is able to create for its customers. This can be either differentiation on price or on quality (Alderson, 1957, pp.122-125). Differentiation is a basic but fundamental advantage in competition, which constitutes the possibility of achieving a competitive advantage.

Porter has further clarified the nature of competitive advantage and how to achieve this advantage. His model highlights that superior financial performance is the main indicator for a firm being in a competitive position, and that this is affected largely by external factors. It holds that environmental forces determine the intensity of competition and profitability. These forces shape the structure of the industry (Porter, 1980, pp.4-6) and determine the collective strength of the company to achieve a competitive advantage (Porter, 1985, p.4). Moreover, Porter stresses that in order to achieve a sustainable competitive advantage, a firm must either implement a low cost leadership or differentiation defined by Porter as a generic strategy (Porter, 1980), while a firm 'stuck in the middle' would gain no advantage. Porter's generic strategy has only addressed the issue of what competitive advantage is and how to achieve it. It does not explain completely the source of achieving such an advantage.

Resource Advantage Theory

Resource Advantage Theory (Hunt, 2000), as a general theory, has amended these deficiencies by advocating the new concept of competition, that is, comparative advantage in resources. The theory has drawn on 11 research traditions from three major arenas: Economics (p.17), Differential Advantage (p.39), and Competitive Advantage (p.67). Under this theory, competition is defined as an evolutionary and dynamic process; therefore, environmental factors only affect the strategies which must be diversified based on the resources, which will "yield" a competitive advantage (Hunt and Derozier, 2004, p.4). The theory confirms that comparative advantage means achieving a superior performance that exhibits cost efficiency or value effectiveness or both. It can achieve the comparative advantage in innovation, including pro-innovation and reactive-innovation. Hunt has endeavored to explain what firm-specific resources would be available for the companies in achieving a competitive advantage through innovation (Hunt, 2000, 2002; Hunt and Derozier, 2004). The theory emphasizes the significance of resources in the role of competition. It states that within each firm, resources play a major role in gaining a competitive advantage. Each firm has its unique resources that contribute and construct a stronger position over its competitors. The more unique resources that a company possesses, the better chance it has to beat the competition. The resources controlled, not owned, by a company make it possible for a firm to implement the strategies which increase both efficiency and effectiveness (Barney, 1991; Autry, Griffis, Goldsby, and Bobbitt, 2005), while a management role in the process of achieving a competitive advantage is to develop and deploy such resources (Hunt, 2000, 2002; Hunt and Derozier, 2004).

Retailing Competition under Resource Advantage Theory

Resource Advantage Theory maintains the following assertions: (a) the competitive advantage is a dynamic and ongoing process, (b) each firm possesses some resources unique to it, (c) comparative advantage in resources leads to a competitive advantage. Resource Advantage Theory explains the retailing competition from the resource aspects. Due to the nature of the dynamic and ongoing process of competitive advantage, retailers can achieve their superior financial performance by using their own resources to implement the innovation (Gatignon and Soberman, 2002; Cooper, 2003; Lowson, 2003). For example, Tesco, Sainsbury, and ASDA all have achieved resource advantage via innovation. These retailers use their firm-specific resources, such as a heterogeneous market demand (Christopher, 1997; Lowson; 2003), imperfect consumer information (Kotler and Keller, 2004), and diversified consumers' taste and preference to sustain their competitive position in a marketplace (Dawson, 2001). Each of these retailers has its own identities (Devlin, Birtwistle and Macedo, 2003), its own loyal customers (Corstjens and Lal, 2000; De Wulf, Odekerken-Schroder, Goedertier, and Van Ossel, 2005), and its own brands in its own market segment (Collins-Dodd and Lindley, 2002). Although these firms are in the same industry and in a similar environment, they still have won over the competition by constantly finding and identifying new resources (Colla and Dupuis, 2002; Uusitalo, 2004). These firm-specific resources have become the source of innovation

Research Work on Innovation

Extensive research on innovation has been undertaken by various experts, e.g., Hargadon, and Sutton, 1997, 2000; Kim, 1997; Boone, 2001; Malerba, 2004; Niosi, 2010. Innovation is not a new concept, especially for the manufacturing industries, and it is the common approach that firms undertake. Innovation in the service/retail sectors has become one of the strategies to gain competitive advantage (Hill, 1999; Hipp and Grupp, 2005; Cainelli, Evangelista and Savona, 2006; Dahlander and Gann, 2010). Based on current studies, there are two types of innovation: technology based and non-technology based innovation (Bonanno and Haworth, 1998; Boone, 2001; Ofek and Sarvary, 2001). The former involves the technology advancement and new creation of knowledge. This type of innovation has been extensively utilized by the hi-tech industries or knowledge intensive service/retailing sectors The latter is more related to process and system innovation which is frequently adopted in service and retailing sectors (Musolesi and Huiban, 2010). A special type of non-technology based innovation is resource based innovation which is very relevant in the retail sector. This type of innovation uses firm-specific resources which are unique and non-imitated as well as sustainable in nature (Wernerfelt, 1984; Mcgrath, Tsai, Venkataraman and Macmillan, 1996; Hunt and Derozier, 2004).

Innovation generates three main advantages. First, it advances the quality of products and services (Hlavacka, 2001; Ofek and Sarvary, 2001; Powers and Hahn, 2004; Musolesi and Huiban, 2010). By accelerating the intensity of the competition, through a shortened product life cycle, changing environments, as well as rigorous customer demand (Beal and Lockmay, 1999), differentiation has become crucial to all firms as the cost leadership strategy is challenged (Hill, 1995; Passemard and Kleiner, 2000; Krieg, 2004). Many companies have employed innovation in products, systems, and processes as a main strategy for achieving world-class performance levels (Adam, 1992). Through innovation, quality differentiation has demonstrated its significance in a company's overall performance (Beal and Lockamy III, 1999; Krieg, 2004).

Second, innovation insulates the competitors via differentiation. This creates brand loyalty, which causes customers to prefer the products of one brand to the products of the competition. This effectively reduces the sensitivity to the lower price while differentiated products or services offer extra value to the customers who want to pay more against the competitors with a lower price (Hlavacka, 2001; Powers and Hahn, 2004; Pappu, Quester, and Cooksey, 2006; Gallouj and Savona, 2009; Masso and Vahter, 2011).

Third, innovation can reduce the cost from the supplier side and provide added value to the customers from the demand side (Ofek and Sar-

Table 1. The development of China's chain stores, 1996-1999

Items/Years	1996	1997	1998	1999
Sales (billion yuan)	30	42	100	150
Increased by (%)	----	40	138	50
Firms	700	1000	1100	1800
Increased by (%)	----	43	10	64
Stores	10,000	15,000	21,000	26,000
Increased by (%)	----	50	40	24

Source: Adapted from Chen, 2004, p.22

was very small. Each chain store company had less than 10 stores, but the development was evident. Some modern, full-service supermarkets have rapidly developed since the early 1990s. Although the growth of China's supermarkets exponentially increased in the early 1990s, due to the haphazard opening of new stores and inappropriate locations with higher operating costs, development of supermarkets "cooled off" around 1993 (Yu and Li 1995). However, the temporary slow pace provided the opportunity for the Chinese to rethink and to relearn how to manage the new retail format in ways that would best fit Chinese consumers' needs in order to fulfill future development. In the second period, China's retailing modernization in supermarkets was still in the early stage of the process.

The Third Period of Chinese Supermarket Development

The third period, from the middle 1990s to the late 1990s, retailers started to adopt various formats in the supermarket sector. It was a growing period. In addition to the existing format, i.e., the standard supermarket, the new formats, such as hypermarkets, warehouse clubs, convenience stores, and discounters, entered China's retail market. Then international retailers moved into China's retail market. In 1996, both Carrefour and Metro opened their first stores in Shanghai, which became one of the early movers in the supermarket/hypermarket sector of China. The growth of China's supermarket sector was much quicker than that of many countries. Towards the end of 1999, there were approximately 1800 chain store companies with 26,000 units (Chen, 2004, p.22). Based on the survey conducted by Shanghai Commercial Net, the increase of the store units was very strong over the four-year period from 1996 to 1999 as is shown in Table 1.

The Fourth Period of Chinese Supermarket Development

The fourth period started in 2000 and continues to the present. Geping Guo, the director of the Chinese Chain Store Association, stated that China's supermarket sector has entered the fourth period, as it has completed the transition from the single format to the multi-formats in the supermarket sector. Both major domestic and international retailers have begun new ventures by expanding their businesses to other provinces and cities, including some less developed inland provinces and cities. In 2003, there were 74,000 supermarket outlets nationally with sales -totaling approximately 460 billion yuan (China National Committee, 2005[1]). The development of this period continues.

METHODOLOGY

The objective of this study is to examine the perceptions from supermarket experts on Chinese supermarket innovation strategy which is the key to success of Chinese supermarket enterprises. The research questions sought were: What types of innovation did successful Chinese supermarket companies adopt? and How were these types of innovation implemented?

Shanghai was selected for this study due to four factors: various types of retailing systems with nearly a half of the national chain stores' turnover volumes[2] ; a diverse population from 50 provinces and over 100 countries; the researcher's good connection with the people in Shanghai; and a cost-effective approach because of the single case design.

This study has been undertaken using a qualitative method (Blaikie, 2000) or paradigm (Creswell, 1994) based on three sets of considerations: an "exploratory" inquiry, the experts' opinions, and previous researchers' reports. Two types of research methods were employed: documentation survey and semi-structured in-depth interviews. The documentation survey provided the background and information on the entry point of the interviews. In addition, it can also verify and validate the interviews. Two aspects of the documentation were reviewed: journal articles, including professional magazines and trade publications; and companies' documents, such as internal reports and memorandums. Journal articles were identified via two major Chinese search engines: Chinese National Science Digital Library (CSDL) and China Knowledge Information Net (CNKI). The former was used to search the articles related to information technology innovation while the latter was employed to locate the papers regarding supermarket and retailing strategies. All of these articles were written in Chinese. The authors from these articles are scholars, consultants, managers, and professionals. The key words of "innovation"," retail", "supermarket", "technology" and " resources" were used to match the articles' titles and abstracts. A total of 45 pieces of academic and trade journal articles were collected. These articles are non-empirical papers and the main readership is academicians, practitioners, and managers. Companies' internal documents were collected from firms' Web pages, Internet, trade associations, and the managers and consultants interviewed.

Another set of data source for this study is the semi-structured interviews with a total of ten retail experts from six major supermarket companies in Shanghai, China. The list of the six supermarket companies and ten interviewees was recommended by the Shanghai Chain Store Association. These supermarket companies have been very successful in reference to the reputation of the companies and their financial performance. The types of retailers included standard supermarkets, hypermarkets, convenience stores, discount stores, and one wholesale club. Ownership represented domestic and international companies. The main language employed during the interviews was Mandarin, the official language in China.

Data analyses were performed based on thematic analysis (Boyatzis, 1998): First, the themes were developed from the raw data of the informants by taking an inductive approach, categorizing the codes in comparison to the prior research findings; i.e., technology based and non-technology based innovation adapted from Western literature. Second, new categories of the codes were created, which were not matched with the existing themes; i.e., resource based innovation. Third, the internal validity and external validity of coding was examined.

In order to ensure the quality of the field-note translation, a back-translation method was implemented via language software translation and consultation with an English professor in Shanghai. It must be mentioned that anonymity was required by all the interviewees, which made it difficult to use direct quotations in this study.

FINDING AND DISCUSSION

Our research has revealed that three types of innovation adopted by six well performed Chinese supermarket companies have been identified: Technology innovation, non-technology innovation, and resource based innovation.

Technology Based Innovation

Technology innovation has been implemented by all the major supermarket companies in China. The most noticeable changes under technology innovation endeavors are in the areas of logistic system changes and customer information database development.

Logistic System Changes

Since mid 1990s, Chinese supermarket enterprises started to adopt information technology systems. Some major supermarket chains have made aggressive technology innovations, making large financial investments to insure their success. For example, Lianhua, one of the largest supermarket companies in China, invested 6 billion yuan in 2005 to build its first class distribution center[3]. Technology innovation has been undertaken in three areas: logistic system, performance evaluation system, and the customer database network. There are two routes for Chinese retailers to replenish their merchandise: directly to the store or through a distribution center. Both methods have been employed, and the selection of the delivery method is based on the requirements of the store and the nature of the delivery, such as the time constrains, facility capability, and the frequency of the ordering. The high turnover merchandise and the perishable goods may use a direct delivery system via the arrangement with the suppliers who monitor the stock level with the Point of Sale (POS) terminal.

With the advanced technology implementation logistic system, the overall operational performance has significantly improved. First, the stock ordering system is well controlled. The major supermarkets in Shanghai have implemented Electronic Data Interchange system (EDI) with suppliers who can automatically fill the goods for the retailers. The EDI process is more efficient and accurate than the previous system. The adoption of EDI has decreased the firm's logistic costs and increased employees' productivity. One of the benefits for implementing this system is that the shortage of "A" and "B" class products is greatly reduced in comparison to the time prior to the introduction of the IT system.

Second, the introduction of the IT enhanced logistic system could keep the food products fresh and reduce the spoilage of the perishable goods due to real time delivery and technology enhanced facilities in the distribution center. The computer system can send a signal that food products are approaching the expiration date or it can effectively eliminate the food that has passed the expiration date; therefore, additional action can be taken, such as reducing the price of the food close to the expiration date. The freshness and food safety issues are always crucial to the customers, while the implementation of technology innovation in logistics has significantly improved the overall quality of the food products in the supermarkets.

Third, the IT technology innovation efforts make the relationship between retailers and suppliers closer and enhance the collaboration for both parties. Suppliers can obtain first hand information from the retailers through digital transmission and develop new products that meet customers' preferences. In addition, store managers can send their orders from their offices to the suppliers, and suppliers can accurately meet their requirements due to IT technology innovations.

Cost reduction can also be achieved with the introduction of IT systems. Three types of cost reduction are associated with IT technology innovation in the Chinese supermarket sector: (a) delivery cost reduction by calculating the optimal distance between the store and distribution center with the computer data mapping techniques; (b) labor cost reduction by installing an advanced container system which enables the firm to perform the delivery by automation rather than laborers. Before the technology was introduced, each delivery used at least three employees to process the goods, but now with the automation system, the machine can fulfill all the tasks without delivery workers; (c) store location search cost reduction. With the assistance of the computer program, the store location selection becomes more effective, thereby preventing cannibalization issues by defining how many stores should be opened and where the stores should be located when a firm expands its operation.

Customer Information Database Development

Collecting customers' information is one of the Chinese supermarket database marketing strategies. In the mid 1990s, Chinese supermarket companies started to systematically develop customer databases. For example, HuaLian invested more than 8 billion yuan to update its information technology system from the basic system, Novell, to a more advanced IT system.

A series of data collection methods were used by Chinese grocers, e.g., phone surveys, responses from advertisements, and information gleaned through customers' purchases. Running a store promotion was also used to solicit customers' opinions and suggestions about their shopping experiences. Not many customers were willing to participate in the data collection process during the 1990s. Database marketing was not prevalent in the Chinese market during that time. Chinese retailers were not familiar with the data collection process which directly affected the retailers' use of the customers' information effectively.

With the information and communication technology advancement, customer loyalty programs stated to emerge among the Chinese supermarket companies. Almost every major supermarket company developed a loyalty membership program. The program has had a positive effect on customer retention and lowering the customer switch rate. In China, customer privacy law is not enacted which permits the retailers to use the data without the restriction. However, lacking effective database management, consumer data have not been well utilized. Customers cannot receive the customized service, such as the individual customer's purchasing preference. Therefore, store loyalty programs have not gained their full potential as they have in the West.

The recent development of using social media has enabled Chinese retailers to have other venues to gain a better understanding of their customers. Some major supermarket companies have created websites which allow existing and potential customers to make comments on the assortments, prices, and customer services, etc. The firms also regularly check the customers' online review boards from the relevant websites, such as MicroBlog and Taobao Net. These web-based customer feedback channels provide real time information which contains valuable customer knowledge. However, the data are still raw materials which need to be further analyzed. It is a very challenging task to explore the knowledge value from customers. Using social medium as a marketing tool to understand customers is a good approach, but the outcome by taking such an approach is based on both the levels of IT database management and marketing education, such as upgraded information management systems and the marketing personnel training. More importantly, measurement and evaluation on the web-based information need to be incorporated into the routine reporting system.

In addition to the store offerings, Chinese supermarket companies have successfully launched their online operations via online stores. The E-commerce approach offers many ways for retailers to reach consumers and conduct business without the need of a storefront. The virtual environment provides consumers a shopping experience distinct from the physical-based market in terms of convenience, search cost, delivery, and price. Our investigation reveals that a positive association exists between online store image and store loyalty in the Chinese supermarket sector.

One of the senior managers commented that technology based innovation advances the supermarket companies' information technology level which enables the firm to stay abreast of the modernization. We do not have the specific data to support that initial investment to R&D has generated a significant return, but we do know in the long run that the benefits from technology innovation are immense. However, technology based innovation is most vulnerable to be replaced or imitated by other competitors who can take the free ride of R & D investment (Interviewee #2).

NON-TECHNOLOGY INNOVATION

Non-technology innovation includes the process and system innovation. Chinese supermarket companies underwent significant non-technology innovation with two routes: format and structure innovation. These two sets of the innovation were the result of supermarket competition in China.

Competition among the Supermarket Companies

In addition to major Chinese supermarkets, several international retailers have entered China since 1992 (Chen, 2004). Major retailers, e.g., Metro, Carrefour, Wal-Mart, Lotus, etc., established their businesses in China during the period of the mid-1990s and mid-2000s. These international retailers have attained a strong financial position by developing large stores and offering a wide range of products with lower prices. Therefore, usually they can attract more customers. For example, the estimates for each store in Carrefour of Shanghai had a daily average of 12,000 customer visits (Yuan, 2000)[4]. After December 11, 2004, the Chinese retail sector was fully opened to international retailers[5], and the entry of international retailers has pushed the competition into a higher level. The Chinese retailers view the entry of international retailers as a challenge. There are three tiers of competition: the competition between domestic and international supermarkets, the competition among domestic supermarkets, and the competition among international supermarkets. In order to respond to the fierce competition, supermarket companies, including domestic and international supermarkets, significantly underwent the format and structure innovation. The former was completed by employing various store formats while the latter was undertaken by massively opening new stores.

Format and Structure Innovation

Retail format varies based on the price range and the service level. Chinese supermarkets underwent format innovation by operating several different types of retail stores concurrently in order to differentiate themselves from other retailers. The rationale behind this type of innovation was to serve different segments of customers and employ various strategies. See Table 2.

Multiple retail formats provide different advantages. The advantage of the hypermarket is to provide a comfortable shopping environment and a variety of products and services, as well as an every-day-low price sales policy. Standard supermarkets stress their convenient locations and reasonable prices. Some standard supermarkets place strong emphasis on perishable foods; for example, Lianhua and Shanghai Nonggongshang Shengxian[6] goods have been well received by the consumers. Convenience stores emphasize convenient locations, well-selected products, and longer business hours.

In addition to the format innovation, supermarket retailers also completed the structure innovation by opening new stores. Domestic supermarket companies expanded their stores' units significantly. The peak of the supermarket expansion was from 2000 to 2005. Based

Table 2. Supermarket innovation via operating multiple formats (2005)

Retailer	Sales (million yuan)	Unit	Format
Lianhua	30,681	3,123	Super/Hypermarket /conveniences
Hualian	21,518	1,693	Super/Hypermarket /conveniences
Carrefour China	16,241	62	Hypermarket
Beijing Hualian	16,000	70	Hypermarket
Suguo	13,880	1,345	Supermarket/Conveniences
Nonggongshang	13,703	1,232	Super/Hypermarket/conveniences
Trust Mart	12,000	88	Hypermarket
RT-Mart	9,500	40	Hypermarket
Wal-Mart	7,635	43	Hypermarket
Lotus	7,394	41	Hypermarket
Hymall/Tesco	7,000	31	Hypermarket
Metro	6,459	23	Warehouse club

Source: Adapted from GAIN Report, 2006

on the survey of top retail chains conducted by China Chain Enterprise and Franchise Association in 2006, eight out of the top ten retailers were domestic-owned enterprises and they all opened new store units over a short period of time. Up to 2005, sales from the top 100 chains increased to 707.6 billion yuan, which was 42.4% higher than that of 2004, and the store units increased to 38,260 which was 25.8% in comparison to 2004. Data from the top 100 chains provide a snapshot for the overall growth of supermarkets over the last five years in China's market. See Tables 3.

More significant expansion of Chinese supermarkets was taking place in Shanghai. Table 4 illustrates the structure innovation by store expansion in the last five years.

Non-technology based innovation has enabled firms to gain a competitive advantage, but this advantage is not sustainable. Like technology based innovation, the format innovation and the structure innovation, by opening new stores, can also be easily imitated and copied by other firms.

Resource Based Innovation

Recourse based innovation refers to using a firm's specific resource to create the differentiation which is harder to be imitated by competitors. The best practice under this category of innovation is the development of retailer brands which is one of the most effective strategies to gain the differentiation advantage. Three types of resources have been used by Chinese supermarket companies. These resources are organizational, relational, and country or region of origin.

Organizational Resources

This type of resources is generated from the firms' own facilities; for example, the firms either own a farm or a factory. The retailer is involved in the entire end-to-end process of making retailer brands, starting from the beginning design and specification phases to the final production and packaging phases. The products are usually of good value or are differentiated from those of other retailers' brands. These special featured and value-added products are unique to the market

Table 3. Sales and store units of top 100 retail chains (2001-2005)

Year	Sales (billion yuan)	Increase %	Stores (units)	Increase %
2001	162	0	13,117	0
2002	246.5	52.2	16,986	29.5
2003	358	45.2	20,424	20.2
2004	496.8	38.8	30,416	48.9
2005	707.6	42.4	38,260	25.8

Source: Li & Fung Research Center: China Trading and Distribution, Issue 33, 2006

Table 4. Major Shanghai supermarket expansion (2005-2009)

Company/year	2 005	2 006	2 007	2 008	2 009
Lianhua Supermarket Company	3 786	3 928	3 774	3 932	5 599
Carrefour	8	11	12	19	19
RT-Mart Supermarket Company	32	36	36	50	63
Nonggongshang Supermarket Company	1 572	1 872	3 217	3 354	3 322
Metro Cash % Carry Co Ltd.	27	33	37	38	42

Source: Source: the data complied is based on Shanghai Statistical Yearbook (2006-2010). Accessed on January 25, 2011 http://www.stats-sh.gov.cn/2003shtj/tjnj/nj10.htm?d1=2010tjnj/C1419.htm. **These selected Shanghai supermarkets also have their outlets in other provinces.*

which enables the firm to create a retailer-specific, value-added product.

Relational Resources

This type of resource is generated from firms' association with other companies. For example, a retailer has a strong connection with the national branded manufacturers who have well established reputations in the product lines to make the first type of products. The retailers who have a close relationship with these national brand manufacturers usually can negotiate a favorable own brand contract with the manufacturers. The own brand quality is higher because own brand suppliers are actually national brand manufacturers. The cost is reduced by cutting channel expenses and shortening the process of the production, or by eliminating some ingredients.

The third type of resource is related to a specific country or region. This type can be further divided into two sub-classes: a) those products with ingredients or formulas that originate from a specific area, creating a unique product that differentiates itself from similar products made in other locations; e.g., Chinese Longjin Tea. and b) products manufactured from a country or region known for good quality; e.g., French wine and Belgian chocolate. In addition, some major cities in China, such as Shanghai and Beijing, have a good reputation for quality. Therefore, the products originating in these two cities have a higher perceived value in the consumers' minds. Resource based innovation is sustainable, but the challenge is how to continually explore the new resources within the firm and use them effectively.

Our studies have identified a unique pattern that successful supermarket enterprises in China all have adopted these three types of innovation simultaneously rather than separately. The interconnection among these three kinds of innovation is the key to success for these Chinese supermarket firms. Technology based innovation provides the solid foundation for the firms' reaching at a higher level which represents the vertical development. Non-technology based innovation further enhances the firms' management system which demonstrates the horizontal development. Resource based innovation enables the firm to gain its full potential which leads the firm to achieving the sustainable advantage. The study result reveals that three types of innovation should be implemented concurrently in order to achieve the competitive advantage. The managers further indicate that the resource based innovation would be the enhancement of the technology and non-technology based innovation. It is still unclear if there are other factors contributing to the success of Chinese supermarket enterprises in addition to adopting three types of innovation simultaneously.

CONCLUSION

The study has identified three types of innovation, i.e., technology based, non-technology based, and resource based innovation, undertaken by the major Chinese supermarket companies with good reputations and sound financial performance. We have found there is a link between the implementation of innovation and the firms' economic performance, as the firms undertaking these three types of innovation simultaneously have achieved financial success. The study suggests that innovation has significant impact on supermarket economic performance and achievement of competitive advantage.

The findings suggest a number of managerial implications that Western and Chinese retailers might consider when developing Chinese supermarket strategies. First, since innovation has a significant impact on the retail sector from both Western and non-Western countries, it implies that the ultimate competition is not the marketing mix, such as price, quality and service, etc., but rather innovation. In other words, the firms with the most successful innovation progress outperform the ones without implementing successful innovation programs.

Second, retail innovation creates a competitive advantage for the supermarket companies but it may be easily imitated. Retailers may consider developing a unique innovation formula with the firms' resources.

Third, the technology and non-technology based innovations play a major role in Western service and retail sectors, while many successful innovation practices in China are resource-based, which supports the theory that competitive advantage can be achieved through a firm's resources (Hunt, 2000).

Fourth, resource based innovation is more relevant for retailers in order to create differentiation advantage in China's market than that of the West; therefore, this approach may be appropriate in the emerging market where technology and non-technology based innovation levels are still in the developing stage while the resource based innovation can be another source for strengthening the technology and non-technology based innovations.

Finally, the resource based innovation examined in this study is very China-specific; therefore, it could be the case that the innovation types in non-Western markets may be country-specific. The localization model may be appropriate versus the globalization model in taking an innovation approach for the non-Western retailers.

A single case design from one market, document reviews from only Chinese articles and reports, and the interviewees chosen limited to Chinese retail experts are the main limitations of this study which may produce incomplete results as the non-Western countries have diverse markets. Due to the time and information access constraints, we have not been able to investigate the relationship among these three types of innovation thoroughly. We do not know if these types of innovation equally contribute to the success of firms' financial performance or one type of innovation is more relevant than another. We have not explored if other factors other than innovation are also the drivers of a firm's economic growth. Therefore, further studies in these areas are highly recommended. These include the research in other non-Western countries, the investigation by taking a quantitative method with a larger sample size, as well as the comparative studies from both developed and developing markets. The further study is necessary to complete the research portfolio on innovation in service and retail sectors.

ACKNOWLEDGMENT

This research has been partially funded by the research grant from the School of Business and Economics, Thompson Rivers University.

REFERENCES

Adam, E. E. (1992). Quality improvement as an operations strategy. *Industrial Management & Data Systems*, *4*, 3–12. doi:10.1108/02635579210012223

Alderson, W. (1957). *Marketing behavior and executive action: A functionalist approach to marketing theory*. Homewood, IL: Richard D. Irwin, Inc.

Autry, C. W., Griffis, S. E., Goldsby, T. J., & Bobbitt, L. M. (2005). Warehouse management systems: An initial assessment, empirical analysis, and research agenda. *Journal of Business Logistics*, *26*(2), 165–183. doi:10.1002/j.2158-1592.2005.tb00210.x

Barney, J. (1991). Firm resources and sustained competitive advantage. *Journal of Management*, *17*(1), 99–120. doi:10.1177/014920639101700108

Beal, R. M., & Lockamy, A. III. (1999). Quality differentiation for competitive advantage: A contingency approach. *European Journal of Innovation Management*, *2*(2), 71–81. doi:10.1108/14601069910269781

Blaikie, N. (2000). *Designing social research: The logic of anticipation*. Cambridge, UK: Polity Press.

Bonanno, G., & Haworth, B. (1998). Intensity of competition and the choice between product and process innovation. *International Journal of Industrial Organization*, *16*(4), 495–510. doi:10.1016/S0167-7187(97)00003-9

Boone, J. (2001). Intensity of competition and the incentive to innovate. *International Journal of Industrial Organization*, *19*, 705–726. doi:10.1016/S0167-7187(00)00090-4

Boyatzis, R. E. (1998). *Transforming qualitative information: Thematic analysis and code development*. London, UK: Sage.

Cainelli, G., Evangelista, R., & Savona, M. (2006). Innovation and economic performance in services. *Cambridge Journal of Economics*, *30*, 435–458. doi:10.1093/cje/bei067

Chen, X. K. (2004). The evolution of Chinese commerce revolution: Format innovation, in chain store. *Conference Proceedings: Shanghai Chain Association 10th Anniversary*, (pp. 17-27). Shanghai, China (In Chinese).

Clark, J. M. (1961). *Competition as a dynamic process*. Washington, DC: Brookings Institution.

Colla, E., & Dupuis, M. (2002). Research and managerial issues on global retail competition: Carrefour/Wal-Mart. *International Journal of Retail & Distribution Management*, *30*(2/3), 103–111. doi:10.1108/09590550210418128

Collins-Dodd, C., & Lindley, T. (2003). Store brands and retail differentiation: The influence of store image and store brand attitude on store own brand perceptions. *Journal of Retailing and Consumer Services*, *10*(6), 345–352. doi:10.1016/S0969-6989(02)00054-1

Cooper, D. (2003). Findings from the competition commission's inquiry into supermarkets. *Journal of Agricultural Economics*, *54*(1), 127–143. doi:10.1111/j.1477-9552.2003.tb00054.x

Corstjens, M., & Lal, R. (2000). Building store loyalty through store brands. *JMR, Journal of Marketing Research*, *37*, 281–291. doi:10.1509/jmkr.37.3.281.18781

Creswell, J. W. (1994). *Research design: Qualitative & quantitative approaches*. London, UK: Sage.

Dahlander, L., & Gann, D. M. (2010). How open is innovation? *Research Policy*, *39*, 699–709. doi:10.1016/j.respol.2010.01.013

Dawson, J. (2001). Is there a new commerce in Europe? *International Review of Retail, Distribution and Consumer Research*, *11*(3), 287–299.

De Wulf, K., Odekerken-Schroder, G., Goedertier, F., & Van Ossel, G. (2005). Consumer perceptions of store brands versus national brands. *Journal of Consumer Marketing*, *22*(4), 223–232. doi:10.1108/07363760510605335

Devlin, D., Birtwistle, G., & Macedo, N. (2003). Food retail positioning strategy: a means-end chain analysis. *British Food Journal*, *105*(9), 653–670. doi:10.1108/00070700310497372

Gatignon, H., & Soberman, D. (2000). Competitive response and market evolution. In Weitz, B., & Wensley, R. (Eds.), *Handbook of marketing* (pp. 126–147). London, UK: Sage.

Goldman, A. (2000). Supermarkets in China: The case of Shanghai. *International Review of Retail, Distribution and Consumer Research*, *10*(1), 1–21. doi:10.1080/095939600342370

Hargadon, A., & Sutton, R. I. (1997). Technology brokering and innovation in a product development firm. *Administrative Science Quarterly*, *42*, 716–749. doi:10.2307/2393655

Hargadon, A., & Sutton, R. I. (2000). Building an innovation factory. *Harvard Business Review*, (3): 157–166.

Helms, M. M., Dibrell, C., & Wright, P. (1997). Competitive strategies and business performance: Evidence from the adhesives and sealants industry. *Management Decision*, *35*(9), 689–703. doi:10.1108/00251749710186531

Hill, P. (1999). Tangibles, intangibles and services: A new taxonomy for the classification of output. *The Canadian Journal of Economics. Revue Canadienne d'Economique*, *32*, 426–446. doi:10.2307/136430

Hipp, C., & Grupp, H. (2005). Innovation in service sector: The demand for service-specific measurement concepts and typologies. *Research Policy*, *34*, 517–535. doi:10.1016/j.respol.2005.03.002

Hlavacka, S., Bacharova, L., Rusnakova, V., & Wagner, R. (2001). Performance implications of porter's generic strategies in Slovak hospital. *Journal of Management in Medicine*, *15*(1), 33–66. doi:10.1108/02689230110386489

Hu, Y. L., & Xiao, X. L. (2003). *Supermarket marketing*. China: Business Administration Publication. (In Chinese)

Hunt, S. D. (2000). *A general theory of competition: Resources, competence, productivity, economic growth.* London, UK: Sage.

Hunt, S. D. (2002). Marketing and a general theory of competition. *Journal of Marketing Management, 18*(1/2), 239–247. doi:10.1362/0267257022775909

Hunt, S. D., & Derozier, C. (2004). The normative imperatives of business and marketing strategy: grounding strategy in resource advantage theory. *Journal of Business and Industrial Marketing, 19*(1), 5–22. doi:10.1108/08858620410516709

Kim, L. (1997). *Imitation to innovation: The dynamics of Korean technological learning*. Boston, MA: Harvard Business School Press.

Kotler, P., & Keller, K. L. (2004). *Marketing management* (12th ed.). Upper Saddle River, NJ: Prentice-Hall.

Krieg, R. (2004). Impact of structured product definition on market success. *International Journal of Quality & Reliability Management, 21*(9), 991–1002. doi:10.1108/02656710410561808

Lowson, R. H. (2003). The nature of an operations strategy: Combining strategic decisions from the resource-based and market-driven viewpoints. *Management Decision, 41*(6), 538–549. doi:10.1108/00251740310485181

Malerba, F. (Ed.). (2004). *Sectoral systems of innovation*. Cambridge, UK: Cambridge University Press. doi:10.1017/CBO9780511493270

Masso, J., & Vahter, P. (2011). The link between innovation and productivity in Estonia's service sectors. *University of Tartu - Faculty of Economics & Business Administration Working Paper Series, 80*, 3-34.

Mcgrath, R. G., Tsai, M. H., Venkataraman, S., & Macmillan, I. C. (1996). Innovation, competitive advantage and rent: A model and test. *Management Science, 42*, 389–403. doi:10.1287/mnsc.42.3.389

Musolesi, A., & Huiban, J. P. (2010). Innovation and productivity in knowledge intensive business services. *Journal of Productivity Analysis, 34*, 63–81. doi:10.1007/s11123-009-0163-5

Niosi, J. (2010). Rethinking science, technology and innovation (STI) institutions in developing countries. *Innovation: Management. Policy & Practice, 12*(3), 250–268. doi:10.5172/impp.12.3.250

Nissen, M. E. (2005). Experimental assessment of an innovation knowledge system for decision support. *Business Process Management Journal, 11*(5), 444–475. doi:10.1108/14637150510619821

OECD. (2009). *Innovation in firms. A microeconomic perspective*. Paris, France: OECD.

Ofek, E., & Sarvary, M. (2001). Leveraging the customer base: creating competitive advantage through knowledge management. *Management Science, 47*(11), 1441–1456. doi:10.1287/mnsc.47.11.1441.10249

Pappu, R., Quester, P., & Cooksey, R. (2006). Consumer-based brand equity and country-of-origin relationships: Some empirical evidence. *European Journal of Marketing, 15*(5/6), 696–717. doi:10.1108/03090560610657903

Passemard, D., & Kleiner, B. H. (2000). Competitive advantage in global industries. *Management Research News, 23*(7/8), 111–117. doi:10.1108/01409170010782307

Porter, M. E. (1980). *Competitive strategy: Techniques for analyzing industries and competitors*. New York, NY: The Free Press.

Porter, M. E. (1985). *Competitive advantage: Creating and sustaining superior performance*. New York, NY: The Free Press.

Powers, T. L., & Hahn, W. (2004). Critical competitive methods, generic strategies, and firm performance. *International Journal of Bank Marketing, 22*(1), 43–64. doi:10.1108/02652320410514924

Qiang, G., & Harris, R. P. (1990). Retailing reform and trends in China. *International Journal of Retail and Distribution Management*, *18*(5), 31–39.

Uusitalo, U. (2004). Competitive reactions to market entry: The case of the Finnish grocery retailing industry. *British Food Journal*, *106*(9), 663–672. doi:10.1108/00070700410558193

Wernerfelt, B. (1984). A resource-based view of the firm. *Strategic Management Journal*, *5*(2), 171–180. doi:10.1002/smj.4250050207

Yiu, H. L. (2003). The check point of retailers' own brand development. [In Chinese]. *Journal of Xinjiang*, *11*(1), 24–26.

Yu, S. H., & Li, C. F. (1995). The status and suggestions of Shanghai supermarket development. [In Chinese]. *Market Modernization*, *5*, 20–23.

Yuan, W. H. (2000). Commercial Chain management and analysis of its issues. [In Chinese]. *Financial and Trade Research*, *3*, 29–30.

ENDNOTES

[1] China National Committee for Pacific Economic Cooperation: http://www.pecc-china.org/Article_Show.asp?ArticleID=155 Retrieved on March 12, 2011.

[2] http://www.fiducia-china.com/info/library/smktsha.pdf

[3] Lianhua Supermarket http://baike.baidu.com/view/1249782.html

[4] One customer entering the store counts as one visit.

[5] Based on WTO regulation, the Chinese retail sector could have three years of 'preparation', which limited the entry of international retailers. After December 11, 2004, the restriction was lifted and all international retailers could do business in China's market.

[6] Shengxian are perishable foods, e.g., meat, vegetable, and seafood, etc.

Chapter 9
Adverse Events and Medical Errors in Greece:
Knowledge Creation and Capture Methods

Athanassios Vozikis
University of Piraeus, Greece

ABSTRACT

For years, experts have recognized that medical errors exist and compromise healthcare quality. Much has been written worldwide about medical errors and improvements in their reporting and handling, with the proposals ranging from the implementation of nationwide mandatory reporting with public release of performance data to voluntary reporting and quality-assurance efforts that protect the confidentiality of error-related data. In the present chapter, the author first points out the lack of standardized nomenclature and a universal taxonomy-classification for adverse events and medical errors, which complicates the development of a response to these issues. The chapter also reviews a number of methods of and adverse events' and medical errors' knowledge management, each of which has evolved over time and been adapted to different contexts. Finally, the author assesses each of these methods, unveiling their particular strengths and advantages, and also weaknesses and limitations.

INTRODUCTION

For years, experts have recognized that medical errors exist and compromise health care quality, but the response to the November 30, 1999, release of the Institute of Medicine's (IOM) report, "*To Err is Human: Building a Safer Health System*", brought medical errors to the forefront of public attention *(IOM, 1999)*. In March 2001, the second IOM report, "*Crossing the Quality Chasm: A New Health System for the 21st Century*", was published *(IOM, 2001)*. The 'chasm' report extends the findings of the 'error' report to other important dimensions of healthcare quality.

DOI: 10.4018/978-1-4666-0948-8.ch009

The reports concluded that the majority of these errors were the result of systemic problems rather than poor performance by individual providers, and outlined a four-pronged approach to prevent medical mistakes and improve patient safety.

Much has been written worldwide about medical errors and improvements in their reporting and handling since then.

Recently, the Eurobarometer survey, which was released by the European Commission *(E.C., 2005)* found that almost half of those surveyed said that hospital patients should be worried about being victims of medical errors.

In this paper we first point out the lack of standardized nomenclature and a universal taxonomy-classification for adverse events and medical errors, that complicates the development of a response to these issues and we also review a number of methods of studying errors and adverse events, each of which has evolved over time and been adapted to different contexts. Moreover, we assess each of these methods unveiling their particular strengths and advantages, and also weaknesses and limitations.

In detailed, in sections 1 and 2, the definitions, context and the most accepted classifications of characteristics and consequences of *adverse events* and *medical errors* are given.

In sections 3 and 4, the framework for identifying medical errors, as well as the methods of medical errors' knowledge creation and capture, are presented.

Finally, in section 5, conclusions are drawn for medical errors and adverse events in Greece.

1. DEFINITIONS AND CONTEXT

The lack of standardized nomenclature and a universal taxonomy for adverse events and medical errors complicates the development of a response to the issues outlined in this paper. A number of definitions have been applied to medical errors and patient safety.

The World Health Organization (WHO) Collaborating Centres for International Drug Monitoring defines an adverse drug event as follows (WHO, 1984):

- *Noxious and unintended and occurs at doses used in man for prophylaxis, diagnosis, therapy, or modification of physiologic functions.*

In *To Err is Human*, the IOM adopted the following definitions:

- An error is defined as the failure of a planned action to be completed as intended or the use of a wrong plan to achieve an aim.
- An adverse event is defined as an injury caused by medical management rather than by the underlying disease or condition of the patient

In an effort to thoroughly consider all of the relevant issues related to medical errors, the QuIC expanded of the IOM definition, as follows *(QuIC, 2000)*:

- An error is defined as the failure of a planned action to be completed as intended or the use of a wrong plan to achieve an aim. Errors can include problems in practice, products, procedures, and systems.

2. CLASSIFICATIONS

Most people believe that medical errors usually involve drugs, such as a patient getting the wrong prescription or dosage, or mishandled surgeries, such as amputation of the wrong limb. However, there are many types of medical errors. The following seven categories summarize types of medical errors that can occur (Bates et al., 2003):

- **Medication Errors**: Such as a patient receiving the wrong drug
- **Surgical Error**: Such as amputating the wrong limb.
- **Diagnostic error**: Such as misdiagnosis leading to an incorrect choice of therapy, failure to use an indicated diagnostic test, misinterpretation of test results, and failure to act on abnormal results.
- **Equipment failure:** Such as defibrillators with dead batteries or intravenous pumps whose valves are easily dislodged or bumped, causing increased doses of medication over too short a period.
- **Infections:** Such as nosocomial and post-surgical wound infections.
- **Blood transfusion-related injuries**: Such as a patient receiving an incorrect blood type.
- **Misinterpretation of other medical orders**: Such as failing to give a patient a salt-free meal, as ordered by a physician.

There are many possible ways to categorize medical errors, but no universally accepted taxonomy. Various proposed classifications have included (Thomas et al., 2000), (Bates et al, 1995), (Dickinson, 2000), (Null et al, 2007), (Lazarou, Pomeranz & Corey, 1998):

- Type of health care service provided (e.g., classification of medication errors by the National Coordinating Council for Medication Error Reporting and Prevention).
- Severity of the resulting injury (e.g., sentinel events, defined as "any unexpected occurrence involving death or serious physical or psychological injury" by the Joint Commission on Accreditation of Healthcare Organizations (JCAHO, 2006).
- Legal definition (e.g., errors resulting from negligence *(IOM, 1999)*).
- Type of setting (e.g., outpatient clinic, intensive care unit), and
- Type of individual involved (e.g., physician, nurse, patient).

Leape *(1993)*, proposed a classification of medical errors' types as presented in Table 1.

Finally, the National Coordinating Council for Medication Error Reporting and Prevention Index for Categorizing Errors, proposes the following categories of *Adverse Events* severity (Rozich, Haraden, Resar, 2003):

Category A: Circumstances or events that have the capacity to cause error
Category B: An error that did not reach the patient
Category C: An error that reached the patient but did not cause harm
Category D: An error that reached the patient and required monitoring or intervention to confirm that it resulted in no harm to the patient.
Category E: Temporary harm to the patient and required intervention
Category F: Temporary harm to the patient and required initial or prolonged hospitalization
Category G: Permanent patient harm
Category H: Intervention required to sustain life
Category I: Patient death

Categories A, B, C and D describe medication errors that do not cause harm, while categories E, F, G, H, and I of the NCC MERP Index describe errors that do cause harm.

3. FRAMEWORK FOR IDENTIFYING MEDICAL ERRORS

The overall goal of improved safety in health care is to reduce patient injury or harm, which underscores the importance of distinguishing between errors and harm. Although detection and analysis of errors is important in understanding failure-

Table 1. Types of medical errors

Medical errors	
Diagnostic	• Error or delay in diagnosis • Failure to employ indicated tests • Use of outmoded tests or therapy • Failure to act on results of monitoring or testing
Treatment	• Error in the performance of an operation, procedure, or test • Error in administering the treatment • Error in the dose or method of using a drug • Avoidable delay in treatment or in responding to an abnormal test • Inappropriate (not indicated) care
Preventive	• Failure to provide prophylactic treatment • Inadequate monitoring or follow up of treatment
Other	• Failure of communication • Equipment failure • Other system failure

prone aspects of health care delivery systems and designing strategies to prevent and mitigate these failures, there is special value in quantifying actual harm. Medical errors are failures in processes of care and, while they have the potential to be harmful, numerous reports have shown they are often not linked to the injury of the patient. Because events of harm are clear clinical outcomes, they are particularly likely to engage both clinicians and administrators in a thorough review of the system factors that led to the adverse event, with a clear focus on improving patient outcomes. By concentrating on the events actually experienced by patients, a hospital can begin to foster a culture of safety that shifts from individual blame for errors to comprehensive system redesign that reduces patient suffering. To address the clear need to quantify adverse patient outcomes, this paper focuses on the identification of harm or injury to the patient, as shown in Figure 1.

4. METHODS FOR KNOWLEDGE CREATION AND CAPTURE

There are a number of methods of studying errors and adverse events, each of which has evolved over time and been adapted to different contexts. Each of the methods has particular strengths and advantages, and also weaknesses and limitations.

Table 2 illustrates a general framework to help select error and adverse event measurement methods (Thomas, 2003):

Although these methods can provide important and actionable information about systems, they also have weaknesses. They are incapable of providing error or adverse event rates because they are imprecise, primarily because of the various factors that influence whether an error or adverse event leads to a claim, incident report, or autopsy.

In the error reporting systems method, errors witnessed or committed by health care providers may be reported via structured data collection systems. Analysis of error reports may provide rich details about latent errors that lead to active errors and adverse events. But error reporting systems alone cannot reliably measure incidence and prevalence rates of errors and adverse events because numerous factors may affect whether errors and adverse events are reported. Providers may not report errors because they are too busy, afraid of lawsuits, or worried about their reputation. High reporting rates may indicate an organizational culture committed to identifying and reducing errors and adverse events rather than a truly high rate (Vincent, Stanhope & Crowley-Murphy, 1999), (Wald & Shojania, 2001). Despite these limitations, error reporting systems can identify errors and adverse events not found by other means, such as chart reviews, and can thereby be used in efforts to improve patient safety.

Figure 1. Framework for identifying medical errors

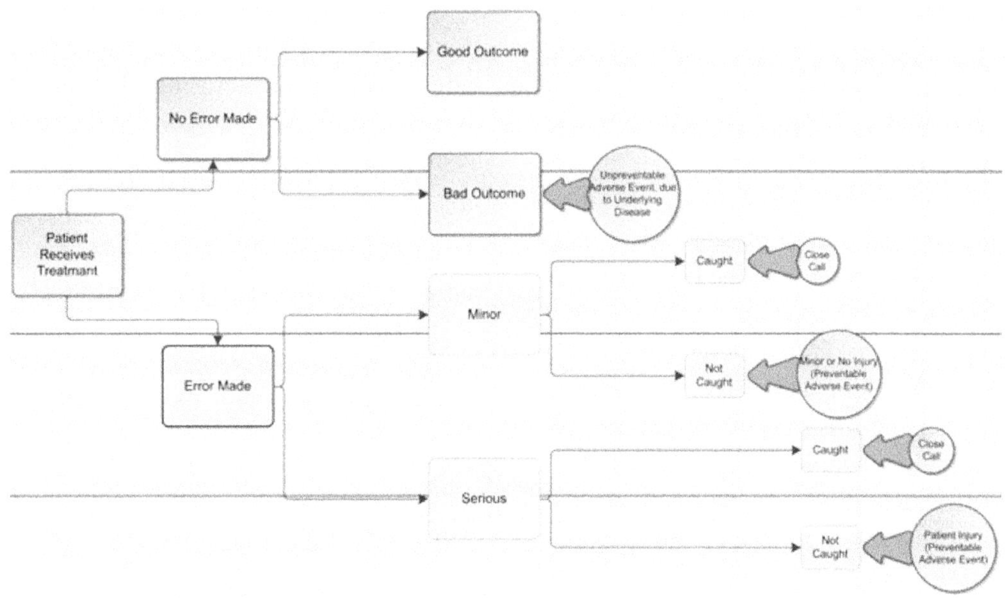

Table 2. Advantages and disadvantages of methods used to create and capture knowledge about medical errors

Study method	Advantages	Disadvantages
Morbidity and mortality conferences and autopsy	Can suggest contributory factors Familiar to healthcare providers	Hindsight bias Reporting bias Focused on diagnostic errors Infrequently used
Case analysis/root cause analysis	Can suggest contributory Factors Structured systems approach Includes recent data from interviews	Hindsight bias Tends to focus on severe events Insufficiently standardized in practice
Claims analysis	Provides multiple perspectives (patients, providers, lawyers)	Hindsight bias Reporting bias Non-standardized source of data
Error reporting systems	Provide multiple perspectives over time Can be a part of routine operations	Reporting bias Hindsight bias
Administrative data analysis	Uses readily available data Inexpensive	Might rely on incomplete and inaccurate data The data are divorced from clinical context
Record review/ chart review	Uses readily available data Commonly used	Judgments about adverse events not reliable Medical records are incomplete Hindsight bias
Review of electronic medical record	Inexpensive after initial investment Monitors in real time Integrates multiple data sources	Susceptible to programming and/or data entry errors Expensive to implement
Observation of patient care	Potentially accurate and precise Provides data otherwise unavailable Detects more active errors than other methods	Time consuming and expensive Difficult to train reliable observers Potential concerns about confidentiality Possible to be overwhelmed with information
Active clinical surveillance	Potentially accurate and precise for adverse events	Time consuming and expensive

5. CONCLUSION

It is clear that a systematic effort to understand and reduce medical errors will be the cornerstone of health care providers' professional responsibility in coming years.

There isn't a widely accepted classification system of various characteristics and properties of the adverse events and medical errors, in international level. An absence of an acceptable classification system obstructs any attempt of a standardized recording and analysis of adverse events and medical errors in Greece, leading to a lack of relative data concerning their causes, characteristics, frequency, severity and consequences.

In the present paper, we present different approaches concerning the content and suggestions related to the characteristics of the adverse events and medical errors, with the aim of the reflection and elaboration of stakeholders with this issue. Our scope is to trigger off the implementation of reporting and analysis systems of adverse events and medical errors, in Greece.

Of course, the key task for the future effectiveness of any medical errors' reduction strategy and policy will be to identify quality assurance practices that could respond effectively to system data. We must not forget, that even countries with a long history of error reporting, have not yet implemented comprehensive programs to correct problems once they are identified.

Also, information about new medical technologies should be included in programs to reduce the incidence of medical errors (*Vozikis, Riga, 2008)*, (*Vozikis, 2009*). Although the medical literature has focused primarily on medication- and procedure-related errors, there is little information on the potential benefits and hazards associated with the use of new medical technologies.

REFERENCES

Bates, D. W. (2003). Policy and the future of adverse event detection using information technology. *Journal of the American Medical Informatics Association, 10*(2).

Bates, D. W., Cullen, D. J., & Laird, N. (1995). Incidence of adverse drug events and potential adverse drug events. Implications for prevention. ADE Prevention Study Group. *Journal of the American Medical Association, 274*(1), 29–34. doi:10.1001/jama.1995.03530010043033

Dickinson, J. G. (2000). FDA seeks to double effort on confusing drug names. *Dickinson 's FDA Review, 7*(3), 13-4.

European Commission. (2005). *Special Eurobarometer*.

Institute of Medicine. (1999). *To err is human: Building a safer health system*. Washington, DC: National Academy Press.

Institute of Medicine. (2001). *Crossing the quality chasm: A New health system for the 21st century*. Washington, DC: National Academy Press.

JCAHO. (2006). *Reporting of medical/health care errors: A policy statement*. Joint Commission on Accreditation of Healthcare Organizations.

Lazarou, J., Pomeranz, B. H., & Corey, P. N. (1998). Incidence of adverse drug reactions in hospitalized patients: A meta-analysis of prospective studies. *Journal of the American Medical Association, 279*(15), 1200–1205. doi:10.1001/jama.279.15.1200

Leape, L. L. (1993). Preventing medical injury. *Quality Review Bulletin, 19*(5), 144–149.

NQF. (2007). *Serious reportable events in healthcare—2006 update*. ISBN 1-933875-08-9

Null, G., et al. (2007). *Death by medicine.* Life Extension Foundation, 2007.

Quality Interagency Coordination Task Force (QuIC). (2000). *Report to the President, doing what counts for patient safety: Federal actions to reduce medical errors and their impact*. Retrieved September 7, 2003, from http://www.quic.gov / report/mederr4.htm#evidence

Rozich, J. D., Haraden, C. R., & Resar, R. K. (2003). Adverse drug event trigger tool: A practical methodology for measuring medication related harm. *Quality & Safety in Health Care*, *12*, 194–200. doi:10.1136/qhc.12.3.194

Thomas, E. J., & Petersen, L. A. (2003). Measuring errors and adverse events in health care. *Journal of General Internal Medicine*, *18*(1), 61–67. doi:10.1046/j.1525-1497.2003.20147.x

Thomas, E. J., Studdert, D. M., & Runciman, W. B. (2000). A comparison of iatrogenic injury hospital characteristics. *International Journal for Quality in Health Care*, *12*, 371–378. doi:10.1093/intqhc/12.5.371

Vincent, C., Stanhope, N., & Crowley-Murphy, M. (1999). Reasons for not reporting adverse incidents: An empirical study. *Journal of Evaluation in Clinical Practice*, *5*(1), 13–21. doi:10.1046/j.1365-2753.1999.00147.x

Vozikis, A. (2009). Information management of medical errors in Greece: The MERIS proposal. *International Journal of Information Management*, *29*, 15–26. doi:10.1016/j.ijinfomgt.2008.04.012

Vozikis, A., & Riga, M. (2008). M.E.R.I.S: Information system for the identification, collection, analysis and reporting of medical errors. *2nd International Scientific Conference e R A-2 Proceedings,* (pp. 423-437).

Wald, H., & Shojania, K. G. (2001). Incident reporting. In Shojania, K. G., Duncan, B. W., & McDonald, K. M. (Eds.), *Making health care safer: A critical analysis of patient safety practices*. Rockville, MD: Agency for Healthcare Research and Quality.

World Health Organization. (1984). *Publication DEM/NC/84.153(E), June 1984.*

Chapter 10
Dynamics in Knowledge

Shigeki Sugiyama
University of Gifu, Japan

ABSTRACT

Since the idea of "artificial intelligence with knowledge" had been introduced, so many thoughts, theories, and ideas in various fields of engineering, science, geology, social study, economics, and management methods have been proposed. Those things have been started as an extension of modern engineering control theories and practices. Firstly, expert system by using IF-Then rules came up to at a production spot in manufacturing, and then agent system method by using intelligent software programs for design, planning, scheduling, production, and management in manufacturing. And then after, the idea of "Knowledge" burst into the artificial intelligence field as a real aid for getting any purpose to be accomplished by having augmented the past key knowledge in terms of management (controlling). However, those augmented knowledge methods used to have usages only in a limited small area. In addition to this, lots of works have to be done before making the systems work for a target problem solving. And what is worse, lots of parts of systems have to be customized for a new application. This chapter introduces a new direction and a method in "Knowledge" by inaugurating the brand new idea of "Dynamics in Knowledge," which will behave more flexibly and intelligently in real usages.

INTRODUCTION

As an introduction, here briefly touches upon the conventional methods for engineering controls, an expert system, an agent method in term of management, which will be related with the future advancements.

DOI: 10.4018/978-1-4666-0948-8.ch010

History of Management Method in Control

One of the earliest open-loop control systems was seen by Hero's device for opening and closing the doors of a temple in the first century at Greece. The opening and closing required inputs to the system were by lighting and extinguishing of the fire of the altar. By the expanding the hot air under the fire made the water transfer from the container into the bucket. As the result of this, the bucket became heavier because of the incremented and fulfilled water, so that the bucket naturally caused to descend because of its gravity. And so its movement made the door spindles turn by means of a rope, and which could open the door. On the other hand, the door could be closed by moving the water of the bucket back to the container again by cooling the container with extinguishing the fire of the altar so as the pressure was being reduced. Thus the bucket became lighter, and then the bucket was moved down so as the door was closing.

The first significant work in automatic control was James Watt's centrifugal governor for the speed control of a steam engine by controlling the vapor pressure of the tank in stable.

And the frequency-response method made it possible for engineers to design linear feedback control systems that could satisfy lots of the engineering requirements. And then, the root-locus method in control system design was developed, which was working more intimately.

These methods are the major control methods. And then, because of necessity to treat many inputs and outputs, these methods became less significant. And then modern control theories have been developed. In modern control theories, linear control method, non-linear control method, and discrete control method have been developed by using a computer more and more even for complex systems.

After the classical control methods had been developed, the application of modern control theories expanded quite rapidly even in the fields of geology, economics, medicine, and sociology, etc. What is more, with developing of the micro processors process speeds and those software, it has become possible to have a discrete control and an expert system which is able to mimic human skills in manufacturing and management (thought of thinking).

Almost in the same period, Petri Net, Neural Networks, Fuzzy Logic by L.A. Zadeh, GA, Immune Control Method, Chaos, Complexity theory, and others have come up to the world as Intelligent Management Methods. And nowadays these methods are tried to be used in more complex and huge systems as a total management system.

PAST, PRESENT, AND FUTURE SITUATIONS IN PRODUCTION AND MANAGEMENT

Technologically Speaking, It has the Following History and the Future

1. One skilled person production
2. Power assisted by the nature (water) that helped a skilled person production
3. Power aided by artifacts that promoted a skilled person's production
4. Jobs Distributed System for Production
5. Worker Assisted by Mechanics Production for a tiny spot
6. Worker Assisted by Mechanics Production for a spot
7. Worker Assisted by Mechanics Production for an area
8. Worker Assisted by Machine Production
9. Worker Assisted by Mechatronics Production
10. Worker Assisted by Semi-Automatic Machine Production
11. Worker Assisted by Automatic Machine Production
12. Worker Assisted by Robot Production
13. Worker Assisted by Expert System
14. Manager/Worker Assisted by Artificial Intelligent System, (at present.)
15. Manager Assisted by Information Technology and Artificial Intelligent Management System, (in the future.)
16. Manager Assisted by Artificial Intelligent and Information Technology Management System

17. Manager Assisted by Dynamic Knowledge Base System
18. Semi-Autonomous Artificial Intelligence Management System
19. Autonomous Artificial Intelligence and Knowledge Management System
20. Management System assisted by Autonomous Artificial Intelligence

In these thirty years, especially, we had the drastic change in production and management. That is to say, the assisted parts in production have shifted from Power to Human Knowledge as shown below.

Power Assisted Skill → Replace Part of Skill by Knowledge → Replace Part of Job by Knowledge → Job Assisted by Knowledge → Human Assisted by Knowledge.

These phenomenon are observed by the facilities that we have been using now as shown below.

1. Exclusive Use of Computer Assisted Machine
2. Group Controlled Machine System
3. Semi-Automatic Machine and Automatic Machine
4. AGV
5. Robot
6. CIM
7. Process Control by GA, Fuzzy Logic, Neural Network, and Artificial Intelligence
8. Total Control and Management System
9. Knowledge Base
10. Management System in Complexity
11. Data Mining (Sort)
12. Total Management System for various fields

Through observing these developments in production (management) and in facilities, it is obvious to say that many kinds of production and management systems and facilities including computer have been developed in order to assist a manager/worker, physically, in an effective way. And now it is a small and tiny phenomenon, but Human Assisted System by using Knowledge Base or Artificial Intelligence with Knowledge is beginning to come up for real use.

Problems in General

Here, the general phenomenons in the management systems are discussed in terms of problems.

Because of the social needs/changes or because of the restrictions in the production and the management methods, we have the major four key difficulties and problems as mentioned below.

1. **Agile Production/Management (AP):** Firstly, in general, the most important thing for industries to be existed is to offer desired production goods at the places wanted, on the time desired with the highest quality and the necessary quantity. This is the only way to satisfy Need (Desire) in a society (Sugiyama (Ed) et al. 2002c). There are many kinds of facilities and many kinds of management systems that will facilitate these kinds of productions and managements quite easily, but these are the things that money can buy. So under this situation, those can be bought from anywhere in the world if there is a greedy person to do so. This means that those management systems can be constructed if there is a person to do so with money. In another words, once a good system is invented, there must be someone who is going to use the same system for lowering a cost production at somewhere in the world. So the companies will have been always facing this kind of the problem (Sugiyama (Ed) et al. 2002c) that is never ignored.
2. **Huge and Complex System (HC):** Secondly, in order to improve productivity and efficiency in a total production and management, the control areas of fields have been expanding more and more from a tiny spot of a machine to a whole company. So

the system to be treated will become so huge and complex. After all, the conventional methods in a production and management system will have become less effective in sense of getting the profits.

3. **Networking Allover (NA):** Thirdly, management in production and in sales, the globalization comes up, so that the functions of a company have been distributed at various places in the world geologically, but those distributed places always need very intimate and close relationships one another in order to create the most profitable output. So they need to behave as if they are very close and near geologically, in another words, they need to behave as if they are one unit of function.
4. **Intelligence like Human (IH):** Fourthly, it is quite important to watch the system closely whether it goes well or wrong even though a system is controlled automatically. Because a system easily goes wrong by a disturbance or by miss usage of systems. And to get it back to the normal situation it usually needs the proficiency of human to do. But ideally it would be the best if a system can do them intelligently. So in order to reduce this burden by human, the system needs a kind of intelligence to do this autonomously in replace of human.

RELATED WORK AND DIFFICULTY

Here examines how the today's methods including the conventional methods work and are working in order to reduce the problems (AP, HC, NA, IH) mentioned above. And also if today's methods do not work well, here shows what sort of difficulties they are facing.

Conventional Method

For controlling a motor, a machine, a transportation, etc., we have a method of continuous control method. But as every behavior of the control targets has to be written mathematically in detail, it is not easy and tough thing to do. As the result of this difficulty, the control areas are very limited within the special fields. If it is failed to express the target system mathematically in detail, lots of optimization have to be made. And as the result of this, it may cause to loose the accurate control.

In the early days of controlling and management, we have the following types of control methods, which are Open-loop control system and Closed-loop system. Open-loop control system (Bertalanffy 1950) is the one in which the control action is not influenced by the results of that action. Some desired or reference input is sensed and amplified and then operate on by the controller.

So this control method has a difficulty in that Open-loop control can be used in practice only if the relationship between the input and output is known and if internal and external disturbances are not much concerned.

A closed-loop control system (Saucedo et al. 1968) is the one in which the output quantity is in feedback for comparison with the input, and the difference, or the error quantity, is applied to the amplifier in order to reduce the error and it cause to bring the output of the system to a expected value. This is better off than the open-loop control system in terms of the accuracy, and what is more, this system is more robust under the disturbance.

Mathematically, generally speaking, the above two control methods can be shown in the simplest expression as shown below.

$$[O] = [G] \times [I] \quad (1),$$

where,

[O]: Output,
[I]: Input,
[G]: Transfer Function.

So as the results of these discussions, it is quite obvious to say that, for applying these methods, the target object of the whole system needs to be defined mathematically with continuous functions (linear or non-linear functions). That is to say, however large and complex the target system is, it should be clearly defined mathematically all through the system. And once the system has been defined, it should keep the system structure whatever happens. What is more, the variable numbers to Input are limited to certain values, that is to say, we cannot input arbitrarily number of variables.

As the results of these, we face the following difficulties;

1. It is hard to apply these methods in an excessively complex and huge system.
2. It is quite hard to use an irrational function.
3. It is impossible to use a graphically and experimentally expressed data.
4. It is hard to put an intelligence into the system.
5. It is quite hard to modify the system to the continuous change of the conditions.

So the problems of (AP), (HC), (NA), and (IH) are left as the difficulties.

Discrete Control Method

Discrete-time systems, or sampled-data systems (Saucedo et al. 1968), are dynamic systems in which one or more variables can change only at discrete instants of time. These instants may be the performing time at which some physical measurement is performed or the time at which the memory of a digital computer is read out, etc. The time interval between two discrete instants is taken to be sufficiently short so that the data for the time between these discrete instants can be approximated by simple interpolation. Discrete-time systems differ from continuous-time ones in that the signals for a discrete-time are in sampled-data form, so that the basic idea is almost the same as the methods mentioned above section, but only the mathematical expression is different.

Mathematically, generally speaking, the above control method can be shown in the simplest expression as shown in the equation below.

$$[O]^* = [G]^* \times [I]^* \qquad (2),$$

where,

[O]*: Discrete Output,
[I]*: Discrete Input,
[G]*: Discrete Transfer Function.

Some of the advantages of digital method comparing with very conventional analogue ones may be summarized as follows.

1. Digital method is able to perform complex computing with a constant accuracy at high speed.
2. Digital method makes possible to use a larger system compared with the analogue method.
3. Digital method is very flexible in applications.

So as the results of these, this method is better than the conventional methods in a sense of treatment in the system operation, however there are almost all the problems of (AP), (HC), and (IH) that the other conventional methods have.

BACKGROUND

Artificial Intelligence Method

Artificial intelligence is a growing field that covers many disciplines as stated by Nick Cercone and Gordon MacCalla in the paper "Artificial Intelligence."

Artificial intelligence is an interdisciplinary field. It is related with Artificial Intelligence derives, including contributions from psychology, philosophy, linguistics, electrical engineering, and computer science. The intersection between psychology and Artificial Intelligence centers on the sub areas known as cognitive psychology and psycholinguistics. Philosophy and Artificial Intelligence come together in the areas of logic, philosophy of language, and philosophy of mind. Intersections with linguistics include computational linguistics, psycho-linguistic. Philosophy and Artificial Intelligence come together in the areas of logic, philosophy of language, and philosophy of mind. Intersections with linguistics, include computational linguistics, psycholinguistics, and socio-linguistics. Mutual concentrations between electrical engineering and Artificial Intelligence include image processing, pattern recognition, and robotics. Computer science overlaps Artificial Intelligence proper and the related field of adaptive system.

So there are so many ways to define the field of Artificial Intelligence as Nick Cercone and Gordon MacCalla are mentioning. That is to say, as a science, it will be essentially part of cognitive Science, and the goal of Artificial Intelligence is to understand principles that will make intelligence possible to work. As a technology and as a part of computer science, the goal of Artificial Intelligence will be to design intelligent computer systems that will show the characteristics associated with intelligence in human behaviour; that is to say, understanding language, environment, behaviour, learning, reasoning, solving problems, and so on. Especially Artificial Intelligence including knowledge representations, problem solving, learning, natural-language understanding, computer vision, robotics, Artificial Intelligence languages, expert systems, and several others is for studies. Many of these areas are related to one another theoretically and technically.

Knowledge Representation and a fundamental element of Artificial Intelligence were how to express information of a target object, a treatment in action, and processes into data structures and procedures. The most popular current approaches are rules, definitions, and basic logics without inferring, and production mechanisms. Knowledge representation schemes can be classified into declarative and procedural ones. In a case of a declarative one, it generally requires wasteful searching of data. And a procedural one base is relevant with programming methods.

From here on it is described a little bit more in detail about the typical areas of researches related with Artificial Intelligence.

Natural Language

Unit of "word" is not difficult to treat and to understand for various usages. But "sentence" cannot be treated like "word" as mentioned. And what is more, if it is treated in a context, we have much difficulty in some cases. So an ultimate purpose of natural language study is to learn "understanding of any sentence." It is said that studies of natural language in understanding has three categories: syntactic, semantic, and pragmatic. Syntactic is to structure and to make the grammatical relationships between words in sentences. Semantics is termed with assigning meaning within various syntactic contexts. Pragmatic is to relate individual sentences one another in the whole context category. So the problems of (HC), (NA), and (IH) are still left as the difficulties.

Computer Vision

The purpose of computer vision is to find and to understand a target object in the surroundings. This is initiated in a production spot in order to find a target object and to treat (examine, grasp, fixing, etc.) purposely. And this study comes further to understand an environment by recognizing objects by edging of the objects individually in order to recognize an individual object. And this tendency goes beyond further up to recognition of environment itself including road, tree, moving objects, etc.

So the problems of (HC), (NA), and (IH) are still left as the difficulties.

Expert System

Expert systems is initiated by an idea of imitation a professional expertise behaviour of management and production. A professional behaviour of expertise is ruled out of examining their behaviour one by one in detail. And then those behaviour are programmed in a computer in order to use by anyone needed. But to rule out of behaviour is not an easy task to do at all and the core problem is to understand a professional expertise behaviour by another. So the problems of (HC), (AN), and (IH) are still left as the difficulties.

Theorem Proving and Logic Programming

Theorem proving refers to the process of making logical deductions starting from a non-contradictory set of axioms specified in the predicate calculus. Robinson (Robinson 1995) showed how it was possible to totally automate this process by using a method called resolution. The idea and principle of resolution method is based upon theorem-proving research. And he says further on: "Any assertion that is to be proved using resolution theorem-proving techniques is first represented as a formula in the predicate calculus and then its negation is added to the set of axioms. A purely mechanical set of transformations can then be carried out by the theorem-proving program to put the axioms and negated assertion into so-called 'clause' form. Any pair of these clauses can be 'resolved' against one another in a matching process that results in the creation of a third clause that logically follows from the previous two clause. The resolution method automatically performs a series of such resolutions, eventually building a tree of clause, resolute, resolute of resolute, and so on. If eventually two clauses resolve to 'nil', then the two clauses are contradictory which, in turn, implies that the initial set of clauses is contradictory and this implies, finally, that the assertion has been proved since its negation caused a non-contradictory set of clauses to become contradictory." So the problems of (HC), (NA), and (IH) are still left as the difficulties.

Knowledge Representation

For a system to be able to behave intelligently it must have knowledge of expertise as mentioned in Expert System in the above. In a sense, Knowledge Representation is a process before ruling out of behaviour in terms of logical steps that are related with semantic networks by nodes and combinations. One of a common nodes and combinations in semantic networks is "ISA" link which is able to make facts to be attached to classes of objects and then inherited by specific objects in the class.

So the problems of (HC), (AN), and (IH) are still left as the difficulties.

Learning

At first, learning had not been a major concern for Artificial Intelligence and Knowledge Base. Most Artificial Intelligence researchers seemed to even ignore this kind of study. But after an idea of autonomous behaviour in artificial intelligence came up to as a current issue, leaning has begun to take on ever increasing significance in Artificial Intelligence. So the problems of (HC), (NA), and (IH) are still left as the difficulties.

Dynamic Knowledge Base

Simply to make an artifact like a certain kind of human knowledge which is able to understand a matter, a knowledge, and a figure is being done with various methods. For example Sugiyama (Sugiyama 2004, 2006, 2008) is introducing, the ideas that some kinds of human knowledge are able to be represented and be stored into a computer by using the back propagation neural networks (BPNN). And he proved that these kinds of the knowledge include "Remembering," "Retrieving," "Deducing," and some kind of logical "Thinking-out." However, the abilities achieved by those methods are quite different from the human knowledge that is able to Think-Out dynamically. But this is the main and the most important issue for getting the mechanisms of Artificial Intelligence by using a computer. So this will be the one of the key field in Artificial Intelligence studies.

However, the study itself is under way and no direction for study has been even acquired yet. So the problems of (HC), (NA), and (IH) are still left as the difficulties.

Distributed Computing Method

Distributed computing creates the foundation for manufacturing mediated via intranets of the Internet. In its simplest form, distributed computing having tens and thousands or more computers connected by a network that is working to solve the same problem. Real manufacturing is more complicated, that is to say, machines at a factory have got each computer and the machines should be coordinated/collaborated. The coordination collaboration pattern is not unique but it depends on the type of manufacturing and the company. So usually it is hard to manage the whole system. However, the Internet and intranets are used for getting them work together.

So the problems of (AP), (HC), and (IH) are left as the difficulties.

Agent Method

The Agents are intelligent knowledge bases that can be connected through intranets or the Internet to gather information on purchasing, designing, planning, production, marketing, planning, etc. But it is quite hard to make a proper agent that is able to satisfy the demands and needs because an agent is expected to behave like human. And it seemed that there would not have clear picture and clear definition to an agent logically.

So the problems of (AP), (HC), and (IH) are left as the difficulties.

Holonic Method

The word "HOLON" is firstly used in the book called "The Ghost in the Machine" by Auther Keostler. And he introduced the idea of "Self-regulating Open Hierarchic Order (SOHO)." This can be expressed as "YANUS."

And it says that SOHO has characteristics as;

1. The same as the living creature, it consists of sets of parts and does not consist of uni-motivated chains.
2. The whole of each creatures is branched into sub-wholes one after another autonomously and itself has a hierarchy of multi-levels.
3. It has Self-regulating Open Hierarchic Order; YANUS.
4. It has an autonomy and an integrality.
5. It has hierarchy and networking.
6. It has regulation and it is targeted.
7. The hierarchy has its own ordering regulations.

The studies have started first in Europe, and then Australia, then USA, and in Japan. HOLON is defined in the Consortium in Europe as follows.

HOLON: An autonomous and co-operative building block of a manufacturing system for transforming, storing and/or validating information and physical objects. The HOLON consists of an information processing part and often a physical processing part. HOLON can be a part of another HOLON.

Autonomy: the capability of an entity to create and control the execution of its own plans and/or strategies.

Co-operation: A process whereby a set of entities develops mutually acceptable plans and executes these plans.

Holarchy: A system of HOLONs that can co-operate to achieve a goal or objectives. The holarchy defines the basic rules for co-operation of the HOLONs and thereby limits their autonomy.

Holonic Manufacturing System (HMS): a holarchy that integrates the entire range of manufacturing activities from order booking through design, production, and marketing to realize an agile manufacturing enterprise.

Holonic attributes: attributes of an entity that make it HOLON. The minimum set is autonomy and co-operativeness.

In Europe this is still under the development and study for the aim of application in industrial companies. They have a prototype model of idea of HOLON, but it is that only the idea of HOLON is taken philosophically and the model behaves holonically under only a few conditions. That is today, it does not have a mathematical expression at all. In Australia, US, and Japan, the situation is almost the same as Europe, which means that the philosophical ideas have been implemented in systems, and there have not been introduced usual way of control methods.

By using the idea of HOLON, any complex system or organism is able to be expressed and so this idea can be applied to an engineering control field for a huge and very complex system. But this idea is still in need of a mathematical investigation and study in order to treat it logically and systematically. And the problems of (AP), (HC), (NA), and (IH) are still left for refinement and for constructing a basic idea for real usages.

Chaos; Complexity Theory

"Chaos" by James Gleick became a best seller in 1987. Since then, this world seemed to be caught up by this idea. And many kinds of the phenomenon in this world have been explained or expressed or described by this idea. Since then, mathematical explanations have been given to this idea, but it is still under-going theme to solve as Stuart Daw who is a researcher at the Oak Ridge National Laboratory in Oak Ridge said at the fifth annual conference on "Chaos in Manufacturing" in Santa Fe, N.M., 1997.

"No one can yet define complexity or say exactly how to manage a company in accordance with its principles. But computer tools exist to predict explosions and metal fatigue where once the timing of such a failure was anybody's guess...."

Now we have got the general algorithm (the typical steps) in building a simulation model of Chaos.

Simplify the problem as much as possible while keeping what is essential.

1. The program which simulates many components following simple rules with specified interactions and randomizing elements.
2. Run program many times with different random number seeds, collecting data and statistics from the different runs. Attempt to understand how the simple rules gave rise to the observed behaviour.
3. Perform parameter changes and "lesions" on the program to locate the sources of behaviour and the effects of different parameters.
4. Simplify the simulation even further if possible, or add additional elements that were found to be a necessary.

But this idea is still in need of a mathematical investigation and study in order to treat it logically and systematically. And the problems of (AP), (HC), (NA), and (IH) are still left for refinement and for constructing a basic idea for real usages.

As seeing from the above discussions on an expert system, an agent method, a knowledge base, and an intelligence system in a management system, and as we can easily notice from the focused problems in the above discussions, it is quite important thing to use "Knowledge" for solving the problems (AP, HC, NA, and IH).

MAIN FOCUS OF THE CHAPTER

Here discusses on the main issue of the problems' (AP, HC, NA, and IH) solving by giving some definitions about Knowledge, Knowledge Base, and Artificial Intelligence (Sugiyama 2004e, 2005g, 2006h, 2008i, 2009k). Especially the discussion will be focused on the dynamic behaviour (Dynamics in Knowledge) in processing of Knowledge by using a neural networking (Sugiyama 2008j, 2009k) in order to solve the problem facing.

Firstly here discusses on Artificial Intelligence, Knowledge, and Knowledge Base in General.

Even though in the above Sections there explained and discussed on Artificial Intelligence, Knowledge and Knowledge Base, they are very ambiguous "words" to explain and to define in detail. It may be related with abilities for actions; knowing, understanding, thinking, familiarity gained by experience, and doing things, or it may be related with a behaviour for actions. And also Artificial Intelligence, Knowledge, and Knowledge Base have a very ambiguous "structures" to explain and to define in detail although there are some explanations for those. These facts will show that the present techniques can only be applied to an individual target in certain limited areas within nonflexible technical and system limitations although those system and technique sometimes work such and such individually in very limited usages.

So at present, we may conclude to say that we do not know yet and do not have yet a clear picture of it although it has been challenged to make Artificial Intelligence, Knowledge, or Knowledge Base by using a computer for many years.

So, it is very important and necessary to know more about what Artificial Intelligence, Knowledge, and Knowledge Base are meant to mean. And also it is quite important to find a description method of Artificial Intelligence, Knowledge, and Knowledge Base as a system.

Core Factors and Definitions of Dynamics in Knowledge

As we can easily notice from the above discussions, it is quite important to use Artificial Intelligence, Knowledge, and Knowledge Base for solving the problem (AP, HC, NA, and IH). Because the direction of the behaviour for those is to behave like human. So here further discusses on this key matter in detail.

Artificial Intelligence, Knowledge, and Knowledge Base

All the knowledge of human intelligence has not been fully studied yet, but those have been rationally applied in many fields to bring about an intelligent artificial creature for solving a problem. This clearly shows that the researchers know the limit of an artificial intelligence as a narrow sense of intelligence. And there is small doubt among some researchers that an artificial intelligence will be capable of creating an intelligent thought even in the near future.

At this stage we can say that there are many different approaches to Artificial Intelligence, Knowledge, and Knowledge Base, and that none of which are either completely right or wrong. Some are obviously more suited than the others in some cases, but the others do not.

In the past, Artificial Intelligence research has mostly been focused on solving specific problems. And this phenomenon makes the field of Artificial Intelligence split into many branches; from a pattern recognition to an artificial Life, including Evolutionary Computation, Soft Computing, Fuzzy Logic, and Neural Networking.

Here, we look at Artificial Intelligence, Knowledge, and Knowledge Base from a point of meanings.

A dictionary briefly says about Knowledge/ Intelligence as follows.

1. Understanding.
2. Familiarity gained by experience.
3. Within a range of information.

So, in another words, we can interpret the above expression such that "Knowledge" or "Artificial Intelligence" means to understand what is going to do, is doing, and has done for a purpose to be accomplished in a range of information.

However, this is a knowledge statement for Humankind, we need to restate and to redefine for Artificial Intelligence, Knowledge, and Knowledge Base as follows.

"Artificial Intelligence, Knowledge, or Knowledge Base is a mechanism for accomplishing a desired purpose to be done by getting a necessary information one by one from an environment facing through the sensors or by communicating among entities (Artificial Intelligence, Knowledge, Knowledge Base, Data, Objects, etc.) within a range of information."

At this stage, we can easily understand about the Artificial Intelligence, the Knowledge and the Knowledge Base as the same kind of entity because of the behaviour. So from now on, Artificial Intelligence, Knowledge and Knowledge Base will be written just as "Knowledge."

Next, we will look at this matter from a point of view in "structure."

Generally speaking, as it is mentioned in the above, we have a problem in a structural uncertainty. And they are as follows.

1. Not easy to describe and to control a whole system (Environmental Uncertainty; (EU)).
2. Many pre-processes are needed before inputting data onto Knowledge (Data Uncertainty; (DU)).
3. Not easy to understand a rough environment (Functional Uncertainty; (FU)).
4. Poor for a system to understand what Knowledge is doing (Knowledge Uncertainty; (KU)).
5. Not easy to communicate among agents (Communicational Uncertainty; (CU)).
6. No way to re-examine an output quality (Self Recognition Uncertainty; (SU)).

If we look at the uncertainties above (EU, DU, FU, KU, CU, and SU) more closely, they will be focused onto a rigidity of Knowledge. Because we are able to have a nice Knowledge that will behave nicely for solving a problem only if we have a usage within a very limited condition with a very stable environment. That is to say, on the contrary, "Dynamics" in Knowledge is the key matter in order to let Knowledge work appropriately. And so, here gives some discussions and studies on Dynamic Behaviour in Knowledge.

Piaget (Piaget 1999) has given us two views about 'Knowledge Acquisition' from a psychological stand point of view. And they are as follows.

Assimilation → "Passive Modification"

1. The modification of an incoming stimulus by the activity of a pre-existent mental structure. Such structures are denoted 'schemes', and represent the regular structure of an action.

Example. The general method involved in catching a ball: The ball catching scheme, producing 'the catching action', assimilates the unique circumstances in which the person and the ball may start moving within a very limited behaviour.

Accommodation → "Active Modification"

2. The active modification of the structure – scheme – itself, so as to adapt to the situation.

Example. Catching the ball from different directions: An initial attempt is made to assimilate the object into a general ball catching scheme. If this fails – the object cannot be caught by the method of assimilation – then an accommodation takes place. The catching scheme is adapted, for instance, by adjusting an arm form by twisting the arm for the glove to face the ball, and then re-applied and happily could get the ball. It may be retried again if it does not go well by collecting another scheme of catching the ball.

So from the facts about the human knowledge acquisition mechanisms from Piaget, we can conclude to have the following views about Knowledge.

1. Passive Modification would cause a problem when Knowledge faces an unexpected situation.
2. Active Modification would be better off in behaviour for Knowledge to overcome an unexpected situation.

Here looks at the case of living creatures what will happen for problem solving as behaviour in action. The following shows about functions of brain what to do in action. In general, a living creature's brain will be functioned as follows.

1. At first stage, there is stimulation from the world to the five senses of a living creature, or from an internal brain itself.
2. Next, capturing the stimulation through the senses or by the frontal cortex. The stimulation will be transformed into 'a semantic form' in a sense of words or a real image or an abstraction in order to understand what it will be.
3. Taking an action according to this understanding.
4. If the input (the requirement) is satisfied by the action, it completes the process and ceases to activate the group of neurons.
5. If it is not satisfied, taking a next action for the input accomplishment by introducing a next related group of neurons or a next related knowledge within the numbers of co-related group of knowledge. This process will be able to go on and on until it reaches to some limitation that makes the process cease to act as "Active Modification" in a case of satisfaction to the input, or in a case of the nature of neurons.

In the above events, there are several events ((2), (3), (4), (5)) that are not good at processing for the present "Knowledge" system.

From the weak processing events shown above, we can extract Core Properties existed to show below.

A. A General Expression in Description of Knowledge.
    1. System - Knowledge - Action - Event - Core Factors - Group of Processing.
B. Forming Co-related Group of Knowledge with a semantic form.
C. A method of Active Modification within the co-related groups.

Solutions

In the above section, we look at the core factors of "Active Modification" in Knowledge, which will assist and solve a problem facing.

Here shows the core factors for solving the problems [(AP, HC, NA, and IH), (EU, DU, FU, KU, CU), (a, b, c)], and SU by introducing "Knowledge" as "Notion."

Notion 1: (Primitive Element)

As we know about human brain mechanism, input information to eye, ear, etc. are broken (transformed) into pieces at one mediator to another in brain in order to get very primitive elements of those. With those very primitive transformed elements, human brains can recognize and understand things from outer world.

We can use this mechanism of human brain (primitive element) in order to make a system communicate with others (entities).

Notion 2: (Hierarchy of Multi-levels)

Hierarchy of multi-levels (a finite set of whole U, finite sets of parts $\{\sum Pi\}$ and finites sets of subparts $\{\sum SP1j\}$,..., finites sets of sub-subparts, ... $\{\sum SPnk\}$) of system of organization) is defined mathematically. And the structure of the system's elements' connection at each layer is defined by $\{U \supseteq \sum Pi \supseteq \sum SP1j \supseteq ... \supseteq \sum SPnk\}$. And these U, Pi, SP1j,...., SPnk are correspond to each layer; Layer-1, Layer-,2 Layer-3,..., Layer-(n+2) in the system of organization, where $i \in [0, m0]$, $j \in [0, m1]$, $k \in [0, m2]$, $n \in [0, m3]$, m0, m1, m2, m3 are positive integers. Hierarchy of multi-levels is made arbitrarily by grouping in terms of a function's mechanism, a function's attribute, and a function's physical figure together.

We can use this mechanism of Hierarchy of Multi-levels in order to make a system transformed into very primitive stages.

Notion 3: (Networking, Regulation, Targeted)

The system of organization that has Networking, Regulation, and Targeted factors of being themselves networked with one another in a regulated way. For targeted has a characteristic of independent itself as well as dependent to another.

We can use these functions of Networking, Regulation, and Targeted in order to make a system combine one another in elements of all over the system and multi-levels.

Notion 4: (SOHO)

Self-regulating Open Hierarchic Order (SOHO) is defined by a property that each of U, Pi, SP1j,...., or SPnk has its own independent system of organization. And those of U, Pi, SP1j, ..., SPnk are independent themselves and also dependent one another as well. And each of those is self-regulating.

We can use this mechanism of SOHO in order to make a system flexible to changes.

Notion 5: (Interchange of Whole and Part)

Every factor of U, Pi, SP1j,...., or SPnk in a system has a moment to be the whole of it and at another instance the whole may become a part of it. This topological interchange of the whole and a part can occur when $U \cap Pi \cap SP1j \cap ... \cap SPnk = \Phi$. When the interchange between the whole $\{U\}$old and an arbitrarily $\Psi \subseteq \{U\}$old is made, the topological transformation from the old hierarchy $\{U \supseteq \sum Pi \supseteq \sum SP1j \supseteq ... \supseteq \sum SPnk\}$old to the new hierarchy $\{Unew \supseteq \{\Psi, \sum Pi \cap \Psi\}$new occurs.

We can use this function of Interchange in order to make a system simple and targeted.

Notion 6: (Mathematical Expression for Knowledge)

Let X denote the set of arbitrary primitive data through the preprocessor from the outside world and assume there are (m x n) real valued functions. X is mapped into R, which is the set of relevant knowledge. It is defined as below.

$\Phi ij(x): X \rightarrow R$, i=1,...,m,

$\Omega j(r): X \rightarrow R$, j=1,...,n.

Each element of X is producing a primitive data through the preprocessor for each pattern and each element of R is producing an output to X.

Writing $\Phi j(x)$ to denote the value of the ith primitive data of pattern x, the vector $\Phi j(x)$ is shown as follows,

$\Phi j(x)=[\Phi 1j(x),..., \Phi mj(x)]T.$

Writing $\Omega(r)$ to denote the value of jth knowledge base of entity r related with $\Phi j(x)$, vector $\Omega(r)$ is shown as follows,

$\Omega(r) =[\Omega 1(r),..., \Omega n(r)]T.$

The above are feature vectors description of x and r.

There are no restrictions on the forms of the functions Φij; they can be linear or non-linear functions of X.

This makes possible to express the above Notions mathematically and logically in order to treat Knowledge as an entity that will be implemented in a computer system.

Notion 7: (Select Any Part)

Let the whole universe {U} consists of

$$\Psi=\{\Psi 1,\ldots,\Psi n\}$$

as shown below.

$$U\supseteq\Psi.$$

$\Omega(r)$ is correspond to Ψ each other as shown below.

$$\Omega 1(r)\rightarrow\Psi 1,$$

$$\Omega n(r)\rightarrow\Psi n.$$

The Reflex Transformation is defined as,

$$U\rightarrow\Psi k\supseteq\{U\cap\Psi\cap\Psi k=\varphi\}.$$

This also makes possible to express the above Notions mathematically and logically in order to treat Knowledge as an entity that will be implemented in a computer system.

Notion 8: (Dynamics in Knowledge)

It was possible to organize "Knowledge" in a conventional method within a very limited behaviour and actions with very much rigidity by using Back Propagation Neural Networking (BPNN). And by adding the ideas of "Dynamics in Knowledge" (Sugiyama 1994a, 2001b, 2002d, 2004e, 2005g), we can make "Knowledge" that will behave dynamically in order to select a related knowledge out of the related group of Knowledge.

This is shown by using a simple example by using BPNN as shown below.

Firstly, "Knowledge" in conventional sense is shown. That is to say, whenever a complex Knowledge is made, the behaviour is simply to produce the output even though the output is not an expected one as illustrated in Figure 1.

This Knowledge does not behave properly when unexpected event occurs. As mentioned in the previous sections, the reason is that this Knowledge is lack of flexibility in change.

But the Knowledge shown in Figure 2 below has a flexibility to select desired and related group of Knowledge in a category by Linker from the content related database of accumulated Knowledge, which is able to search and to form a related kinds Knowledge as a group. The group is selected by the value of Co-Relational Factor, which is given by BPNN output value.

By using the group of related Knowledge, a system can select the most appropriate Knowledge from time to time. That is to say, if there is a problem that goes good in a certain situation, the system tries to find another most appropriate Knowledge for this situation as shown in Figure 3 below.

This example showed that this Knowledge could behave like in a case of living creatures what will happen for problem solving as in action. That is to say, the system is able to select a proper Knowledge from a group of the related Knowledge in order to face to a problem solving.

Notion 9: (General Behaviour)

By using these Notions, "Knowledge" is able to have a hierarchical structure and is also able to reconstruct for targeted, so that a necessary

Figure 1. Conventional knowledge presentation in general

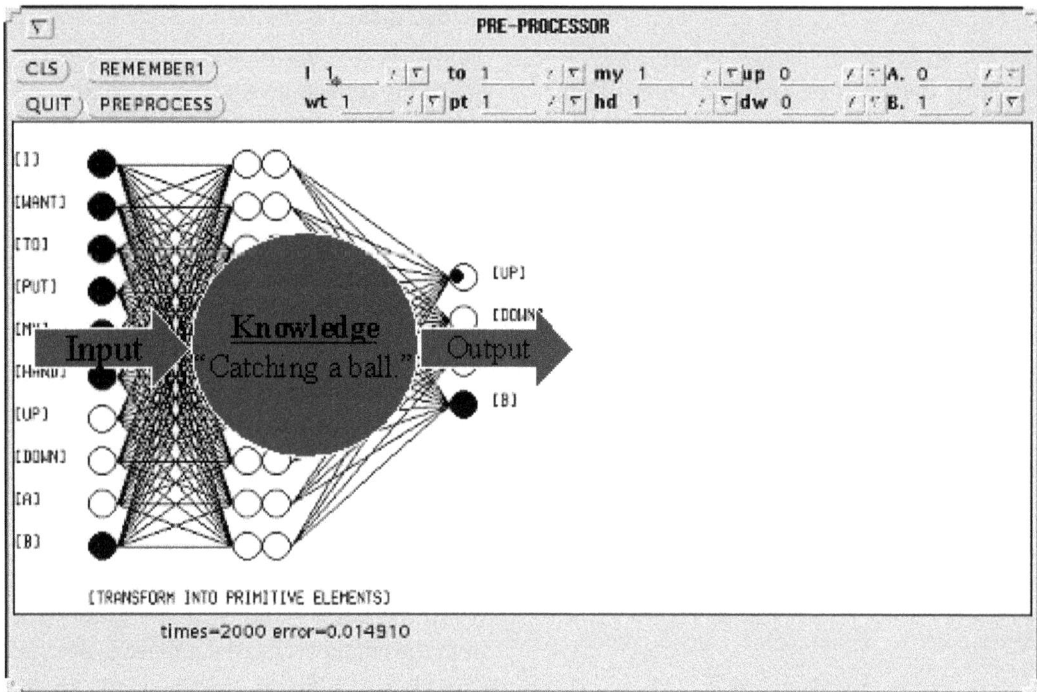

Figure 2. A group of related knowledge

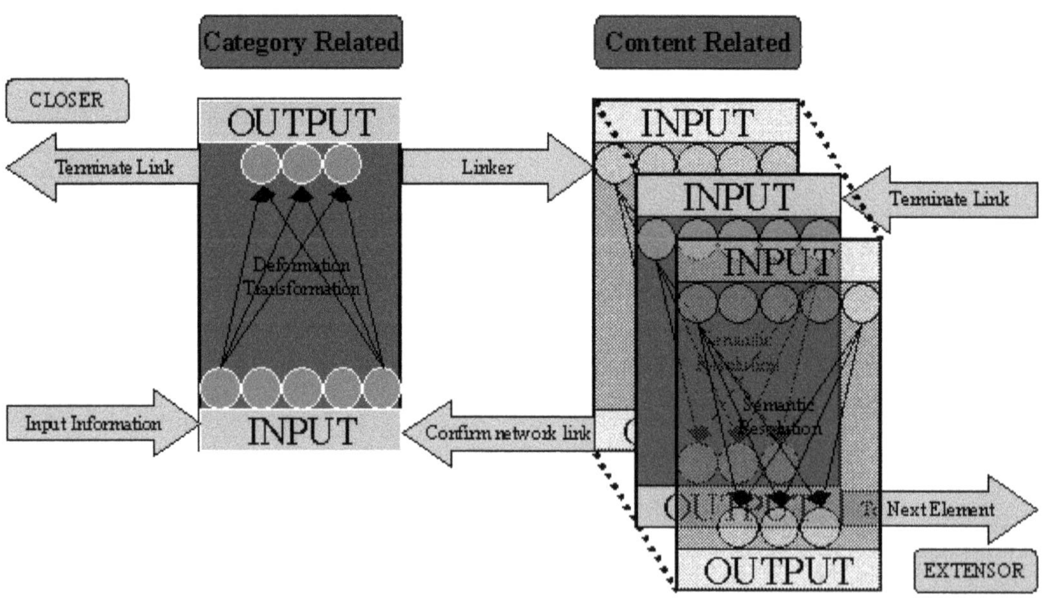

Figure 3. Active modification for new knowledge

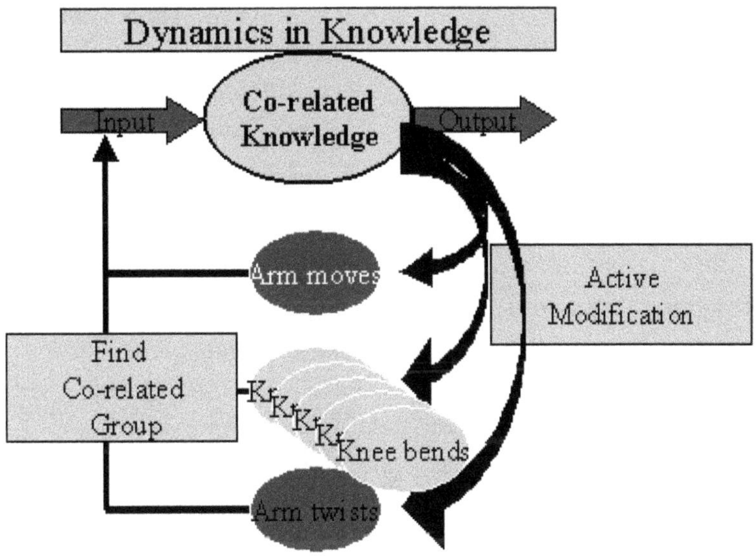

knowledge is able to be given one after another for re-processing in order to get an improved output through communication.

This says that any necessary knowledge Ψk can be extracted, can be targeted, and can be concentrated in order to get the desired output.

So by using Notions 1 to 9 stated above, we can expand any system (system, agent, organization, etc.) hierarchically with multi-levels of layers, linked and networked. And also each element at each layer can easily communicate with another because of its primitively hierarchical structure.

FUTURE RESEARCH DIRECTIONS

Here shows issues left for studies on Dynamics in Knowledge in order to get further developments.

A flexibility of Knowledge is given by the ideas shown above sections. But it goes better in the behaviour of Knowledge if Knowledge can communicate each other like human. The Knowledge studied here consists of primitive elements by BPNN, so that some kind of communication between Knowledge is capable to make but it is quite a primitive level of communication in the behaviour. One tip for solving this issue is to make a general Knowledge for each category that will understand a whole context of each category.

The flexibility for each primitive Knowledge (atomic Knowledge) in a sense of structure is also important matter. That is to say, each Knowledge that will be able to change its structure as describe in the Notion 5 is also very important matter to have. Because it is quite easy to get a proper output if Knowledge is transformed into the figure of Knowledge that is most suitable one. For example, if there is the Knowledge of searching an object, it would be better to transform the figure for a particular object. Because "Searching a pen" and "Searching the meaning of Pen" is different from each other.

And it is strongly expected to study on data structure for Knowledge. That is to say, whether or not it would be better to have data for each Knowledge or for the whole Knowledge or to be unified?

CONCLUSION

Through the examinations and discussions in this paper on Knowledge related matters and Knowledge itself, the following results have been given as shown below by touching upon a basic level of control, management, knowledge base, and artificial intelligence.

1. Basic idea of the Hierarchical Multiple Knowledge method has been introduced.
2. General mechanism of dynamic behavior of Knowledge through communication that behaves more intelligently than before has been introduced.
3. Overall system description method in complexity and hugeness by using the idea of Hierarchical Multiple Knowledge has been introduced.
4. A new direction and a method in "Knowledge" is logically expressed by inaugurating the brad new idea of "Dynamics in Knowledge," which will behave more flexibly and intelligently in real usages.

REFERENCES

Sugiyama, S. (1994a). *Semantic and logic theories in neuron networks*. IEEE International Conference on system, Man and Cybernetics.

Sugiyama, S. (2001b). *Reflex transformation of consciousness: Toward a science of consciousness*.

Sugiyama, S. (2002c). *Basic model for muscle control in primitive neural sets with reflection*. First World Congress on Biomimetics. CDROM version.

Sugiyama, S. (Ed.). Imai, S., Kobayashi, T., Takeuchi, A., Hirayu, H., Miwa, S. (2002d). *Investigational research report: Studies on next generation industry and company system*. Tokai Techno Highland.

Sugiyama, S. (2004e). *Augmented agent for multi-purposes*. World Congress Biomimetics, Artificial Muscles & Nano-Bio 2004.

Sugiyama, S. (2004f). *Agent talk in neural networks*. ANNIE.

Sugiyama, S. (2005g). Multiple layer control method. In J. A. Meech & Y. Yoshiyuki Kawazoe (Eds.), *Intelligence in a Small Materials World: Selected Papers from LPMM-2003*, (pp. 286-298). ISBN1932078193

Sugiyama, S. (2006h). *Tele diagnostic by Web*. SPIE2006 Medical Imaging, CA.

Sugiyama, S. (2008i). *Fundamental behaviour in communication method*. IEEE/INFORMS International Conference on Service Operations and Logistics, and Informatics (IEEE/SOLI'2008).

Sugiyama, S. (2008j). *Ubiquitous framework in service science. The 2008 Logic and Science of Service*. The New Wealth and Wellbeing of Nations.

Sugiyama, S. (2009k). *Feature extraction in system*. INFORMS International Conference on Service Science (ICSS'2009). Hong Kong.

Sugiyama, S., & Burgess, L. (2011). Advanced design approaches to emerging software system: Principles, methodology, and tools. In Liu, X., & Li, Y. (Eds.), *Principle for engineering service based system by swirl computing*. Hershey, PA: IGI Global.

ADDITIONAL READING

Anderson, J. A. (1989). *Introduction to neural networks*. Cambridge, MA: MIT Press.

Arbib, M. A. (1989). *The brain as network of neurons. The metaphorical brain*. New York, NY: Wiley-Interscience.

Barth, D. (2004). *Mammalian neurophysiology: Sensorimotor system I*.

Bertalanffy, L. (1950). The theory of open systems in physics and biology. *Science*. (n.d)., 111.

Bloom, C. A., & Lazerson, A. (2008). *Moving brain mind and behavior*.

Bloom, F. E., Lazerson, A., & Hofstadter, L. (1985). *Brain, Mind, and Behavior*. Educational Broadcasting Corp.

Elman, J. L. (1993). *Learning and development in neural networks: The importance of stating small, cognition*.

Piaget, J. (1999). *The MIT encyclopedia of the cognitive sciences*. MIT.

Robinson, J. A. (1995). *A machine-oriented logic based on the resolution principle* (pp. 23–43). ACM.

Chapter 11
Towards an Improved Hotel Reservation System:
A Fuzzy Approach to Improve Service Industries

Israel González-Carrasco
Universidad Carlos III de Madrid, Spain

José Luis López-Cuadrado
Universidad Carlos III de Madrid, Spain

Ángel García-Crespo
Universidad Carlos III de Madrid, Spain

Ricardo Colomo-Palacios
Universidad Carlos III de Madrid, Spain

Belén Ruiz-Mezcua
Universidad Carlos III de Madrid, Spain

ABSTRACT

This chapter presents a tool that distinguishes selects and supplies, among all products with similar characteristics that appear in the catalogue of a company, the product that better adapts to the necessities of the users. In order to achieve this, it uses a search system based on fuzzy logic techniques, being able to handle vague information or of difficult specification and thus making possible to administer to the tool by means of rules of "common sense," which talk about indefinite amounts. A fundamental aspect that provides great flexibility to the application is that the system can be modified and adjusted by the expert in real time. This allows changing quickly the output product set and without stopping the operation of the system based on the necessities of the company. The results are codified in XML format, facilitating the interoperability between systems and allowing the execution of the tool in multiple operative systems, as they only have to process the generated content. The possibility of displaying the clients the products that they are looking for, directly responding to their necessities, guiding and advising them in the purchase that are ready to make, is a competitive advantage that the company must not let escape.

DOI: 10.4018/978-1-4666-0948-8.ch011

1. INTRODUCTION

Kenteris, Gavalas and Economou (2009) stated that the convergence of IT and communications technologies and the rapid evolution of the Internet have been some of the most influential factors in tourism that have changed travelers' behavior. The hotel industry is one of the leading stakeholders in the tourism sector. This industry has been influenced by the internet in a deep way. Normally, hotels that have a purchase site online where they offer a catalogue, requires that the client searches the whole site looking for the service he or she desires. This forces the client to know some concrete aspects of the service to make successive searches in the different categories in which the products or services supplied by the company are included. How to deliver relevant information to both potential and existing customers has become an important task for the hospitality industry (Xiang et al. 2007), which, in many cases, is based on artificial intelligence techniques (Schiaffino & Amandi, 2009).

On the other hand, in order to model human logic in a mathematical way within computer environment, we resort to the so-called fuzzy logic, which allows expressing different values or levels of truth for a certain concept. This means that it is not codified in the binary form false/true, but in a similar way to the human reasoning, with rules like "if...., then...", using the theory of fuzzy logic and sets. The fuzzy or diffuse logic transforms inputs into outputs, a fuzzy set into another one. The rules of a fuzzy set define a set of zones that are overlapped, relating a complete series of inputs to another complete series of outputs.

Taking full advantage of fuzzy logic theories and expert systems, in this work authors present an architecture that support hotel reservation systems. The computer application of these theories is shaped in the denominated Expert Systems based on fuzzy knowledge, which use previously the information provided by experts in each concrete field. This way, the system works with flexibility responding to hotel reservation systems. Thanks to these systems we can model the knowledge of an expert in a certain field and construct therefore the necessary rules to respond to the concrete necessities of a client. In the following section we introduce the theory of fuzzy logic and sets and its application within the denominated expert systems.

2. KNOWLEDGE-BASED SYSTEMS

2.1. Fuzzy Logic

The fuzzy logic, or rather, the fuzzy logics, are basically multivalued logics that amplify the statements of the classic logics. The classic logics impose the values false or true to their statements and this way they model satisfactorily a great part of "the natural" reasoning. But the human reasoning really uses values that they do not have to be necessarily "so determinist". By means of the fuzzy logic, we can formulate mathematically slight knowledge like "a little cold" or "very hot", so that they are processed by computers quantifying vague human expressions, such as "very high" or "shining light". This way, the way the human being thinks can be applied to the programming of computers, sensors, Chips, etc. (Lee, 1990; Hájek & Godó, 1997).

This logic allows to thus quantify the imprecise descriptions that are used in the language and the gradual transitions in the household-electric devices like going from "dirty water" to "clean water" in a washing machine, being able to adjust the washing cycles through sensors. The ability of the fuzzy logic to process partial values really has been helpful for engineering.

In conclusion, fuzzy logic create mathematical approaches in the resolution of certain kinds of problems, producing exact results from vague data, being for that reason specially useful in electronic and computer applications.

The application of the "diffuse" or "fuzzy" adjective is due to the fact that the values that are really used in the fuzzy logics mainly have an uncertainty connotation. Therefore the uncertainty is compared to the diffusivity, that is to say, with the indeterminism property. An element, therefore, can be full of uncertainty that is to say, of diffusivity. That does not mean that the values of truth assumed by nondeterministic statements, are known. In fact, the diffuse can be understood like the possibility of assigning more values of truth to the statements than "false" or "true" and even in certain areas of knowledge, these statements really go associated to values that are degrees of veracity or falsification.

Therefore, the fuzzy logics are considered a special type of multivalued logic that can redefine the degrees of veracity of the output statements as they refine the input ones (Zadeh, 1988, Zadeh, 1989).

2.2. Fuzzy Sets

The main motivation of the Theory of Fuzzy Sets is the construction of a formal frame that allows treating and manipulating the uncertainty that is present in numerous scopes of the human knowledge (Zadeh, 1965).

The classic theory of sets establishes if the different elements of a universe do belong to a set or not. Thus, for example, if we consider the universe of positive natural numbers:

U={1, 2, 3, 4, 5...}

it is possible to say that 3 belongs to the set of uneven numbers, whereas 8 does not. Also, 9 belongs to the set of the numbers greater than 5, whereas 3 does not. The ownership to a set of different elements is usually represented graphically by means of the so-called function of ownership, as it is in Figure 1. In the function of ownership, the value of those elements that belong to the set take is 1, whereas the value of those who do not belong is 0.

The theory of fuzzy sets proposes the extension of the concept of ownership so that it admits graduation between the non ownership and the total ownership to the set (Kaufmann & Gupta, 1985). Thus, if we choose the set of the elder people, we could say that a person in his 30's belongs to this set with degree 0 (that is to say, he does not belong), a person in his 50's belongs with some degree (for example, 0.4) and a person of 78 years would belong with degree 1 (that is to say, he belongs completely). Using the idea of function of ownership of this fuzzy set we would obtain, for this example, the representation that is indicated in Figure 2.

The fuzzy sets provide a way to define sets for which the ownership is a question of degree, or for which it is not completely defined. They establish a gradual border between the no ownership and the ownership, and therefore they conform a tool for modelling the imprecision or the uncertainty.

The modelling of the imprecision by means of fuzzy sets has allowed the treatment of numerous problems whose resolution according to schemes and/or classic techniques is not completely sat isfactory. Some of the environments where the imprecision or the vagueness is an intrinsic part of the knowledge are the following (Dubois & Prade, 1980; Dubois & Prade, 1991; Dubois & Prade, 2000):

- Problems of classification
- Recognition of patterns
- Signal processing
- Data Bases
- Knowledge-Based Systems (also known as Expert Systems)
- Temporary Reasoning

Figure 1. Belonging function of the set of numbers greater than 5

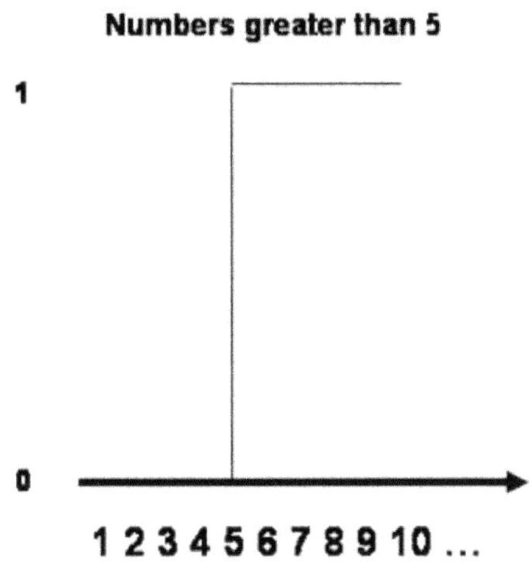

Figure 2. Graphical representation of the belonging function of the fuzzy set "older person"

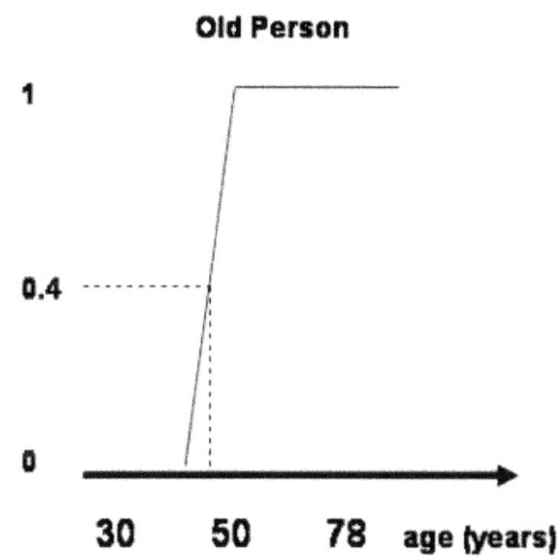

2.3. Fuzzy Knowledge-Based Systems

The application that is presented here uses the theory of fuzzy sets within the scope of the expert systems, allowing to emulate the reasoning of the expert within multiple operative surroundings thanks to the fuzzy logic.

Knowledge based systems help the creation, transfer and application of knowledge in companies (Alavi & Leidner, 2001). An expert system based on fuzzy knowledge can be defined as a computer system (hardware and software) that simulates the human experts in an area of specific specialization (Durkin, 1994).

Therefore the expert systems not only think and reason as an expert would in a certain specialty or field, making the traditional functions to handle great amounts of data, but that also manipulating that data so that the result is intelligible and has the necessary meaning required to answer questions that are not completely specified (Stevens, 1994).

A decisive characteristic of the Expert Systems is the separation between knowledge (rules, facts) and its processing. In addition, there is an user interface and an explanatory component. Here is a brief description of each component (Durkin, 1994):

1. The *Knowledge Base* of an Expert System contains the knowledge about the facts and the experiences of the experts in a certain field.
2. The I*nference* Engine of an Expert System can simulate the strategy of solution of the expert.
3. The *Explanation Component* explains the user the strategy of found solution and why the decisions where taken.
4. The *User Interface* is used for making the request in a language that is the most natural possible.
5. The *Acquisition Component* offers help when structuring and implementation of the knowledge in the knowledge base.
6. The *Data Base* lodges the necessary information for the correct operation of the system.

According to Gomez et al. (1997), in Figure 3 the existing relations between the different components that compose the expert system can be observed.

A number of studies have analyzed the success factors of expert systems in several fields like manufacturing (Metaxiotis, Askounis and Psarras 2002) or engineering (Nurminen et al. 2003). Examples of methodologies and applications of expert systems in the past years can be found in Liao (2005).

Pham and Pham (1999) state that fuzzy logic is one of the common techniques applied in the industry. The expert systems can work on a vague knowledge, resorting to the denominated fuzzy controllers, which allow inferring the suitable control of a specific process based on a set of "linguistic" rules, defined in advance after the observation of the output and the rules of operation of this process. In Figure 4 the general scheme that follows the fuzzy controllers is shown. In this way a number of recent works on knowledge based systems allow the integration of fuzzy logic as García-Crespo et al. (2011).

It is important to point out that, whereas it is usual that the process of reasoning on the variables is made handling fuzzy values, the actions of control on the system as much as the input values of the variables of state are usually clear values. For that reason, it is necessary that stages of transformation between the fuzzy dominion and the numerical dominion exist, that act as an interphase between the system under control and the own controller.

The interphase of "fuzzyfication" works on these values in order to obtain the associated linguistic variables. It is necessary to resort to the fuzzy sets since we cannot affirm resoundingly if the price is cheap or not. The problem could be solved partly considering that a price is cheap when its value surpasses certain threshold fixed in advance. But this does not solve the problem completely since a part the mentioned threshold is established in an arbitrary way, and on the other hand it could happen that two prices with very different values were both considered as cheap. Evidently, if the concept "cheap" is defined like this, it would give a very poor information on the price of a hotel. In short, this interphase transforms the precise input values into fuzzy sets, who act as inputs to the set of rules in charge of making the reasoning process.

The fuzzy knowledge base synthesizes the concepts that the human controller handles mentally whose expert behaviour we wished to model. It consists of fuzzy proposals (variables and values) that conform rules like *IF condition THEN control action*. The objective of the Fuzzy Knowledge Base is to obtain fuzzy values for the variables of control, once made the reasoning applying all the rules that are relevant for the present values of the variables of state.

Finally, the "defuzzyfication" process turns the inferred fuzzy values for the variables of control into numerical values that constitute the final action of control to make on the system.

3. DESCRIPTION OF THE DESIGNED SYSTEM

We have developed a tool that allows to distinguish, to select and to supply, among all the similar products of a company, the one that better adapts to the necessities of the users. In order to achieve this, we use the techniques, models and procedures that the fuzzy logic provides to capture the vague knowledge of the human experts of each field and to construct the necessary rules so that valid conclusions are obtained.

The complete process appears in Figure 5, in the first place the client, through an iterative process, must answer several questions designed by the expert of the field. These questions allow gathering the necessities of the client with regard to the product portfolio available, once that this process has ended the front-end application returns the answers to the designed Fuzzy Logic System (FLS). This system obtains as well an ordered product list based on a score that reflects the degree of approach to the desires of the client.

Figure 3. Expert system components

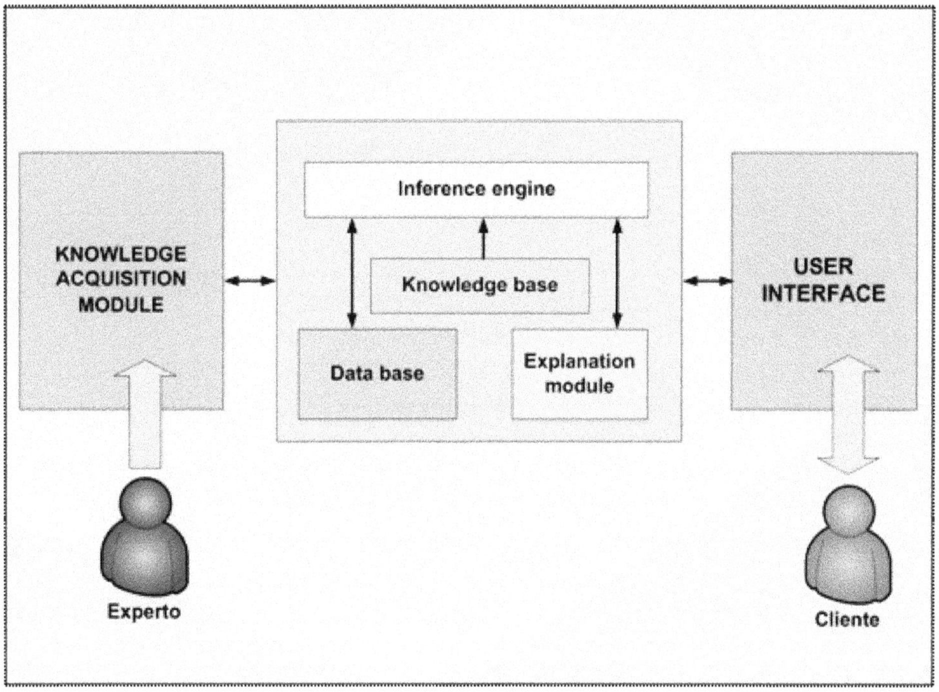

Therefore, the developed application is a really powerful tool to model the knowledge that the human expert have on a concrete field, in processes that are badly defined, when there is not an appropriate model of the system or this one is very complex and, in general, when it is easier to model to the knowledge and/or the behaviour of the expert than the own process. The application is divided in two different modules:

1. **Administration Module:** The objective of this module is to maintain the application ready for its operation, managing and maintaining the data base of the system.
2. **Search Module:** The search process and selection of the products that are finally presented to the user are elaborated based on the answers that the user has given to the system and on the information stored in the data base.

There are two different types of users when working with the tool, in the first place the expert or administrator of the tool that is in charge of adjust the relations user-product so that the system responds correctly at any moment. On the other hand, the client or end user, who is the one in charge of interacting with the system in order to obtain the recommendations that better adjust to his requests.

3.1. System Performance

In the first place the client must answer a series of questions designed by the expert of the dominion. This phase is denominates phase or process of advising and the set of answers that the client facilitates to the system forms the user characteristics, whereas on the other hand the set of characteristics that define products or services of the dominion forms the denominated product characteristics.

Figure 4. Diffuse controller

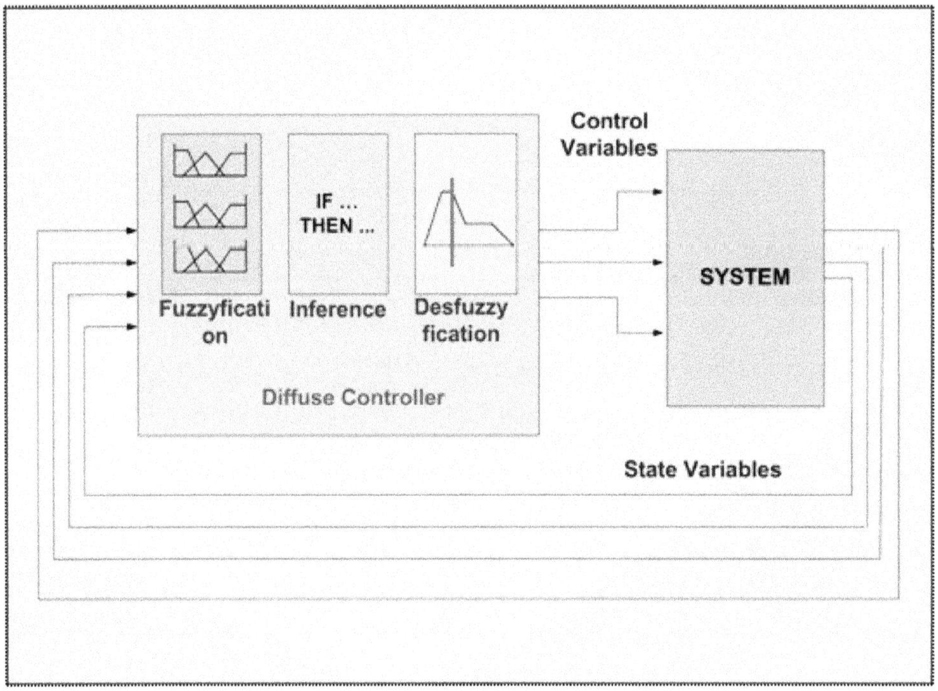

Based on the answers gathered during the advising process, the system distinguishes between all the product stocks with similar characteristics, those that satisfy more accurately what the client demands. For it the system receives the characteristics that the user has marked like interesting, and it links them to the characteristics of the products introduced in the system through a data base. These relations user-product are created and refined by the administrator of the tool, assigning a specify weight to each one of these relations based on the present necessities.

The product and user characteristics, as well as the relations between both must be created and optimized by the expert, since this he is the one in charge to reflect his knowledge on a certain dominion in the system.

The search module that allow to find the products and/or services that better adjust to the necessities of the client, are based on techniques of fuzzy logic, allowing the system to handle vague information or of difficult specification. This makes possible to manage the tool using rules of "*common sense*" related to undefined amounts.

These capabilities are based upon fuzzy sets and a rule - based inference system of the type "*IF...THEN.....*", where the "premise" linguistic values and "consequence" are defined in fuzzy sets. By this way the rules always turn a fuzzy set in another one.

In Figure 6 is shown the complete system that has been designed. The core of the same one is the fuzzy system which communicates with the front-end application that allows to the client and the administrator to communicate with the system.

Unlike a classic control system, that it tries to model the process in himself, this implementation using control fuzzy rules return, of a direct form, the experience of the expert on the process, and it does through a set of proposals next to the vague form of expressing of this human expert.

Thanks to the theory of the diffuse sets the tool is able by itself to catch the linguistic vagueness of words and commonly accepted sentences, like

Figure 5. Designed system interaction process

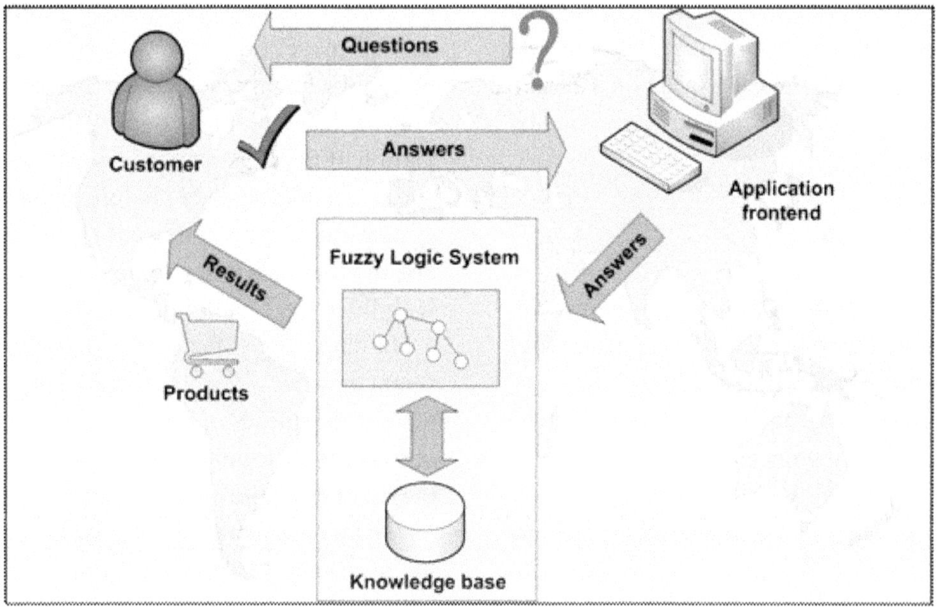

"cheap hotel" or "slight change". A Linguistic variable is that variable whose values are words or sentences that are going to frame themselves in a predetermined language. For these linguistic variables it will be used a name and a linguistic value on a Universe of Speech.

These diffuse sets can be used to represent expressions such as (Höhle & Rodabaugh, 1999):

The hotel is CHEAP.
The beach is NEAR.

From this previous expressions the system can manage others more complex and with more linguistic like:

The hotel is not CHEAP.
The beach is NEAR but is not very CLEAN.

These linguistics variables of the type a little, much or nothing are used later in the zone of premises or condition of the rules.

These expressions are the entrances of the system and are provided by the client to the application through an iterative process of questions and answers designed by the expert. These answers express the preferences of the same one in a certain dominion.

Therefore the application is able to work directly with these preferences, to make it the system extracted of these expressions the fuzzy values through the linguistic variables. The fuzzyfication phase is solely in charge to redirect these variables to the set of rules of the FLS.

This set of rules, is based on fuzzy proposals of the type *IF condition THEN action control*, created by the expert of the dominion. Thanks to these rules can be formed *schemes of approximated reasoning*, which allow reproducing the mental schemes of the human brain in the reasoning process. These rules act over the set of fuzzy inputs obtaining a series of fuzzy outputs expressed by linguistic variables.

Finally these fuzzy outputs are transformed into manageable numerical values by the application thanks to the desfuzzyfication phase. These numerical outputs allow the FLS to find products or services that better adjust to the necessities expressed by the client through the application.

Therefore thanks to the system, the client receives a set of products or services. This set obtained is similar to which the expert would obtain after applying his knowledge on a certain dominion, based on the necessities expressed by the client.

3.2. User Interface

This component is the one in charge to present/display the tool to the user. The main requirements or characteristics of the interface that have considered when making the development of the tool are the following ones:

1. **The learning of the application manage must be fast:** As much for the expert or administrator of the system like for the final client of the tool. In the case of the client thanks to that the system can be integrated in Web environments it obtains a comfortable and simple operating of the same one.
2. **The mistaken input of data must be avoided as far as possible:** For make it possible the tool guides the user during the advising process reducing the possibilities of making some type of error during the introduction of the answers.
3. **The results must appear in a clear form for the user:** Logically the system created pay special attention to the form that the data is shown to the user thus avoiding confusions between the different products that are recommended.

3.3. Knowledge Base

The knowledge base designed contains all the facts, the rules and the procedures of the application dominion that are important for the solution of the problem.

This knowledge base allows storing all the information relative to the different product portfolios of a company, which allows making an integrated manage of several products lines from the same tool. Each one of the portfolios is formed as well by several products which have a series of qualities or characteristics that define them.

In order to be able to treat all the relative information of the products, we have been developed and integrated a specify module. Thanks to this the system can manage different product catalogues and the products that compose each one of them with their corresponding qualities.

In our case the facts correspond with the different *product characteristics* that specify the technical qualities of products and the *user characteristics* that gather the answers provided by the user before the questions made by the system.

The tool also allows of simple way to create the necessary set of product and user characteristics for each dominion, which are made up of the following fields:

- Product that the characteristic qualifies
- Name assigned to this quality
- Measurement unit, which specifies how this characteristic is quantified. For example the hotel category it is measure with stars
- Set of values this quality can obtain. These values can be a list of themselves or individual values. In both cases, it is admitted the use of logic operators of the kind <ó>. For example, the list of possible prices of a product can be indicated by means of ranges of values. (<40€, 40-80€, >80€)

Joined to these facts, the knowledge base has rules that allow to link the two types of existing characteristics. These rules denominate relations user-product are links that the expert establish between a user characteristic and a product characteristic.

These links can have different importance degrees, since the fuzzy logic systems allow a set of defined possible values by means of the fuzzy sets. Our tool takes advantage of this possibility

Figure 6. Interaction of the complete system

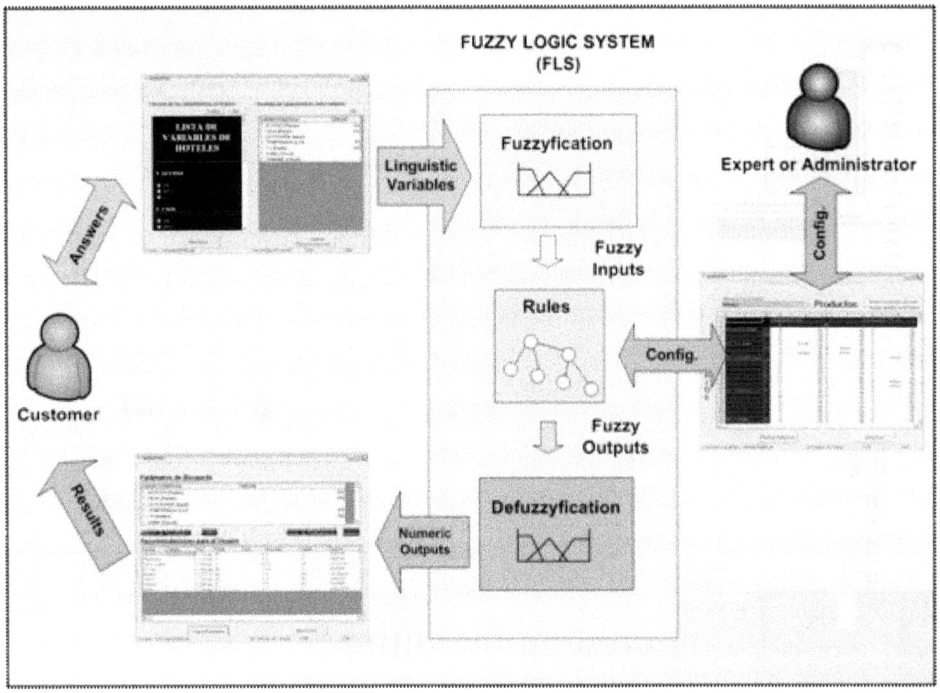

and allows the representation of concepts defined with precise and vague limits, allowing the use of qualifiers like: much, little, several.

The created rules or links can be of two types, simple or complex, and have the following format:

If **premise(s)** Then **Conclusion**

The premises zone includes logic links referring to the products qualities, whereas a conclusion is not more than the deduction of a fact from the premises of the rule.

In order to be able to create these relations in a coherent way within the system, it is necessary that a clear relation exists between the characteristics of user introduced and the product characteristics. The premises zone is formed by product characteristics that can be related by means of logic operators AND/OR, a rule example is the following one:

If **category(hotel$_i$)=5 stars** AND **zone(hotel$_i$)=Madrid** Then **Conclusión**

where *hotel$_i$* indicates the instance of the product that is being evaluated then in the inference engine. On the other hand, the conclusion zone indicates the result of the activation of the rule, and introduces in the knowledge base a new fact associated to the instance of the product.

3.3.1. User- Product Relations

The rules involved in this fuzzy system recreate the behaviour of the people implicated in the shopping process, turning the input into output in agreement with the logic hypotheses analysed. For the induced reasoning to obtain optimal results, it is necessary that a human expert refines and calibrates the rules introduced.

These propositions form the core of our user-product relations, because they relate directly to the specific characteristics of the stored products in the database, achieving, once the products are incorporated, that the system reaches a great power and approaches reality.

To carry this out, the tool includes a module called relations editor, in which the user characteristics that the system is going to gather, the product characteristics that define the products and the relations between them can be created.

As it has been commented in the former section, the area of premises of a rule is formed by user characteristics that can relate by means of logic operators AND / OR. This allows building complex rules to gather common necessities of the clients and is known inside the tool as product guidelines.

In an analogous way, different necessities expressed by the client can be grouped in user characteristics by means of user guidelines, which allows to create more compact and powerful user-product relations. These relations can be related to characteristics or guidelines of the product by associating them to a specific weight or importance to the relation.

In Table 1 is shown the structure of the relations codified in the system. It can be seen that each of the values that a user characteristic can obtain can be linked to a user characteristic with a specific weight. This gives the system a great flexibility as the system can be optimized just by changing these relations and its associated weights.

Figure 7 shows the matrix of the user-product relations designed in the too, where the columns compose the product's characteristics or guidelines, whilst the rows compose the user's. Each of the crossings between these two characteristics should have an associated weight, what determines the importance of the relation inside the scope according to the expert's knowledge.

3.4. Inference Engine

The inference mechanism is the logic unit with whom conclusions of the knowledge base are extracted, by means of a fixed method of problem solution which is configured imitating the human process of the experts to solve problems.

A conclusion is produced by means of the rules application on the current facts. Example:

A rule is: If p and q then r

P and q are just those facts that are mentioned in the "if" clause of the rule, that is to say, the conditions for the rule applicability. Apply the rule is: deduce from the facts p and q the fact r.

In the System designed, a fact exists only when it is contained in the knowledge base. The facts which figure in the "if" clause are called *premises*, and the content in the "then" clause is called *conclusion*. When a rule is applied on some facts whichever, then it is said it is activated. The shot of a rule causes the insertion of the new fact in the knowledge base.

Therefore, the inference mechanism designed is in charge of determining the actions that will take place, the order in which they'll do it and how they will do it among the different parts of the Expert System. They will also have the responsibility of determining how and when the rules will be processed, and given the case, the election of which rules should be processed too.

The algorithm developed gathers the user characteristics selected by the client and looks for the user-product relations marked for each of the existing products. In other words, a relation is activated and generates a rule inside the inference engine, when there is an important crossing between the user characteristic and a product characteristic in the relation's matrix.

The importance of each user characteristic is determined by the weight that it has in the relation with the product characteristic, allowing the system to carry out different calculations with these weights depending on the degree of the optimization selected. These different degrees of optimization allow to sum or multiply these weights to calculate the final value of a product depending on the user characteristics specified.

Table 1. Structure of the user-product relations

		Product Charact / Guideline 1			Product Charact / Guideline 2		
		Value 1	...	Value n	Value 1	...	Value n
User Charact / Guideline 1	Value 1	X (Weight)					
	...						
	Value n			X (Weight)			X (Weight)
User Charact / Guideline 2	Value 1				X (Weight)		
	...						
	Value n				X (Weight)		

Another possibility quite useful in certain environments is to return those products that have any product characteristic activated during the searching process.

Finally, only the products which have the highest level of right values are presented. The number of products to be returned can be modified thanks to the parameter Maximum number of products, which is very useful if we do not want to saturate the client with a big number of answers.

This group of results depends on the relations created by the expert and logically it can occur that the tool returns suboptimum products. These are products that do not fulfil everything sought after by the client, but they have a score in the system depending on the weights assigned by the expert to each of the relations between the product and user characteristics. In this way, it is guaranteed that the tool is always going to return a result the closest to the client's necessities.

3.4.1. System Parameters

As it has been formerly commented, there are different parameters, which allow to configure the tool in order to obtain results more refined. The expert has in his disposal in the first place two general parameters which allow to delimit and optimise the results obtained by the tool.

The first parameter available is the degree of optimization. It refers to the algorithm used to calculate the total score that a product achieves during the searching process. The values it can obtain are the following: basic, sensitive and normal. The first one, basic optimization, marks like valid all of the products that fulfil some user characteristic, in other words, some of the relations is activated during the searching process.

The second option, sensitive optimization, multiplies the weight of all the relations that are fulfilled. That is to say, the total score if each of the products is calculated following Formula 1, where $P_{product}$ indicates the total score achieved by the evaluated product depending on the sum of the activated relations W_r. Formula 2 expresses the way to obtain the products to be returned once they have been evaluated, where $P_{product}$ reflects the set of selected products. This set is delimited depending on the parameter *number of products to return*, specified with *n* in the formula, in the case the value of n being zero, all the products evaluated would be returned.

Formula 1. Score calculation with sensitive optimization degree

Figure 7. Relations' editor

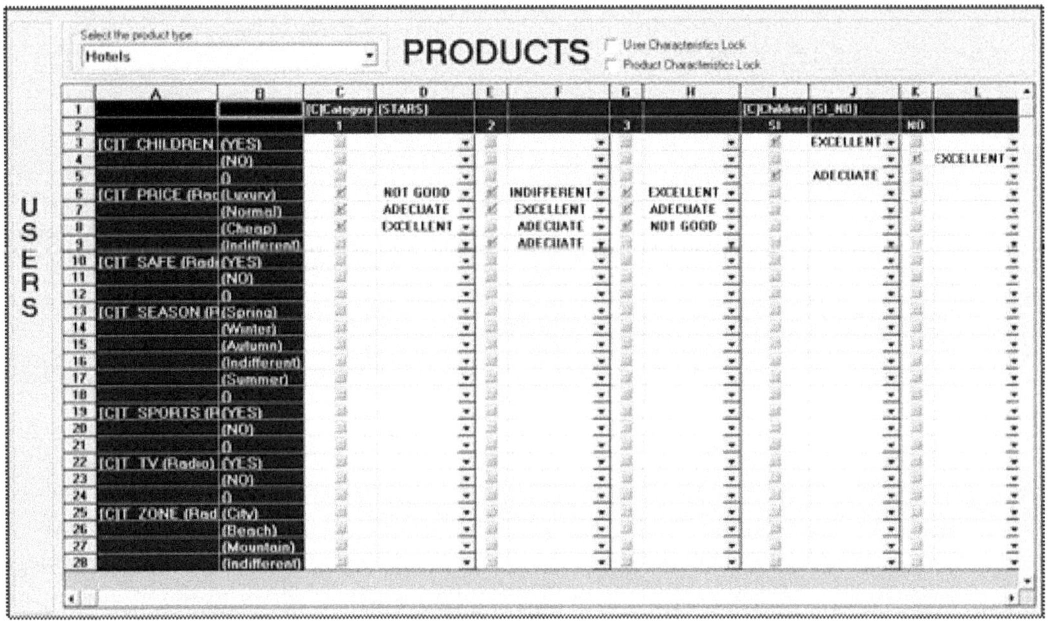

$$P_{product} = \prod(W_{relationzhip})$$

Formula 2. Returned products with normal and sensible optimization degree

$$P_{product} = Max_n([P_{product}])$$

The third option, *normal optimization*, adds the weight of all the relations that fulfil. In other words, the total score of each of the products is calculated following Formula 3. The products returned by the system are calculated by means of Formula 2.

Formula 3. Score calculation with normal optimization degree

$$P_{product} = \sum(W_{relationship})$$

The second parameter to configure is maximum number of products. It allows to delimit the number of products to be shown to the client after the searching process. This turns out to be very useful when the product's catalogue is very high and the products are very similar between them, as the system would not be able to differentiate between them as it would obtain a very similar score when it carries out the score calculations and it would return a high number of them.

On the other hand, the expert can modify the different weights that are associated with the user-product relations. In order to be easier to use, the tool allows both to modify the numeric values and to associate textual descriptions with these values.

Therefore, as each of these links can have a different degree of importance and the system allows to use different optimization degrees, the expert can change dynamically the results that are offered to the client depending on the necessities and availability in each moment.

3.5. Interaction with the Fuzzy Logic System

The global operation of FLS can be summarised in five basic steps: collection of necessities, fuzzyfication, inference, defuzzyfication, and result calculations. Thanks to this, the tool is capable of making decisions and of recognising concepts which are compatible with high levels of vagueness and ambiguity, for example:

- I like cheap hotels.
- I want a hotel close to the beach
- I'm looking for a room that costs less than 40€.

The system has been designed in such a way that in the fuzzyfication phase values expressed both in a fuzzy and numeric way can be collected. The latter are strengthened with logic operators. These values are stored in the so-called *user characteristics*.

Therefore, the FLS is capable of receiving this type of expressions and of obtaining from it the linguistic variables or numeric values associated. If we take as an example the fist sentence expressed by the client, we would obtain that user characteristic price has a value of cheap. For the second expression, the system obtains that the location variable is the same as beach. Last, the third expression is seen by the system like the price variable has a value <40€.

Thus the system is capable of receiving input of both types, fuzzy or of little specification, or values expressed numerically by means of logic operators and work directly with them.

Once all the linguistic variables and numeric values of input are extracted, the inference engine comes to work evaluating the set of rules activated for each of the products depending on each user characteristic.

For the user characteristic (price = cheap), a rule example would be the following:

If **category** $(\textbf{hotel}_i)$ **= 1 star** Then **ADEQUATE**

Whereas for the user characteristic (location = beach), a rule example would be the following:

If **location** $(\textbf{hotel}_i)$ **= beach** Then **ADEQUATE**

A great advantage of the designed tool is the so-called product and user guidelines which allow to group characteristics in a single rule promoting the FLS.

An example of product guideline would be that one that groups in a single rule two linguistic variables extracted before, whereas a user guideline is that one that groups in a single user characteristic these two linguistic variables. Therefore if user characteristic is (price = cheap and location = beach) the system could find rules of this type:

R1: If **category** $(\textbf{hotel}_i)$ **= 1 star** Then **ADEQUATE**
R2: If **location** $(\textbf{hotel}_i)$ **= beach** Then **ADEQUATE**
R3: If **category** $(\textbf{hotel}_i)$ **=1 star and location** $(\textbf{hotel}_i)$ **=beach** Then **VERY ADEQUATE**

As it can be observed, the last rule approaches much more to the wishes expressed by the client as it joins in the premises area his two necessities, cheap hotel and close to the beach. Thus the linguistic value returned indicates a degree of possession much bigger to the set, as the tool knows internally that the weight or the importance of the linguistic variable VERY ADEQUATE is bigger than the ADEQUATE one.

Each of the rules of the inference engine actualises the knowledge base, as the score associated with the fact of a specific product is modified depending on the conclusion area.

The last of the phases, the one corresponding to the defuzzyfication, corresponds to the conversion of these linguistic values to numeric values, what is easily carried out thanks to the fact that these labels have a weight of numeric value associated in the system.

A basic aspect that allows to obtain great flexibility in the tool, is that both the belonging function and the values associated to the weights are established in an arbitrary way. In this example, we could consider as adequate a value that in another scope would not be correct or, on the contrary, a change in the politics of the business could make necessary to return a series of products different to those obtained with the previous rules.

Lastly, the FLS must calculate the score that achieves each of the products depending on the rules activated and the associated weights. Each product therefore obtains a total score that depends directly on its characteristics and on the knowledge the expert has introduced in the system.

3.6. System's Compatibility

The great advantage of the system created is its possibility of encapsulation in dynamic links' libraries (DLL), what allows its use in different systems and operative environments. Any type of application, Windows or Web, can use the system just by calling the external communication functions defined in the library.

Moreover, the tool works internally with codified data in XML language (Extensible Markup Language). This is a extensible markup language or metalanguage, in other words, a language to define languages of text structuring based on explicit marks or tags, so its simultaneously human- and machine-readable format. Its primary purpose is to facilitate the sharing of data across different systems, particularly systems connected via the Internet

The answers facilitated by the client to the system compose the denominated input dataset, while that the products given back by the system are the output dataset. These two data types are codified internally in XML, what eases the interoperation between systems and allows the tool be executed in multiple operative environments, having to process only the content generated.

Figure 8 shows an example of input data codified with XML inside the application.

4. OPERATION EXAMPLE

As it has been commented in the former section, the system can be used in different environments thanks to the fact that it is encapsulated in dynamic links libraries (DLL) and to its total compatibility with XML data. These characteristics allow the incorporation of the proposed system in a web environment in order to explode the benefits of the integration of web and knowledge technologies (Duan et al. 2005).

To show an operation example, a Web environment has been chosen, being the system installed in a server which contains:

- A *server of applications*.
- The *dll libraries* where the developed system is encapsulated.
- The *database* where to save the necessary knowledge to make the system work.

Due to the fact that we are dealing with a Web system, any light client, typically a web browser can easily connect to the system through an Internet connection. In Figure 9 can be seen the sketch of the architecture chosen to carry out this example.

The example chosen shows how the tool advises a client to carry out the booking of a hotel depending on the necessities that the client expresses to the system and on the available products. In this case, the example shown is made in a Web platform in which both the questions that are made to the user and the answers provided by the system once the advising process is finished are executed in an Internet browser. Thanks to this, the interaction with the tool by the user is made easier, as the interface of this type of applications is highly spread. On the other hand, the possibilities of the system are highly increased as it is available any moment and from anywhere with Internet connection providing service to various users simultaneously.

In the first place, the expert must create a new database which will compose the knowledge base of the system. In this knowledge base the expert can save as many products' catalogues as he wants, being each of them stored in a database's table. In order to carry out this step, the system includes a module that allows to administrate the knowledge base, to manage the different product catalogues, and to create the products that compose each of them with their corresponding qualities. For this example, a group of hotels with the following qualities are included in the catalogue:

- Identification code
- Name
- Location
- Category
- Owns children's areas
- Owns sports areas
- Owns safe
- Owns via satellite television

Figure 10 shows the products introduced for the system's hotel catalogue.

Once the catalogue with its products is created, the expert must specify the characteristics of each product, which reflect in the system technical data that define their quality. The expert must clarify for each of these characteristics the set of possible values that it can adopt. In this case, the created characteristics of the product and its corresponding description are:

- **SPORT:** It indicates if the hotel owns sport areas (YES, NO).
- **SAFE:** It indicates if the hotel owns a safe (YES, NO).
- **CATEGORY:** It indicates the hotel's category (1,2,3,4,5).
- **SATELLITE:** It indicates if the hotel's room owns a via satellite television.
- **LOCATION:** It indicates the place where the hotel is situated (Madrid, Valencia, Mallorca, Tenerife, Barcelona).
- **CHILDREN:** It indicates if the hotel owns children's areas (YES/NO).

Figure 11 portraits one of the product's characteristics created, in this case the one that specifies the hotel's category (1, 2, 3, 4 and 5 stars).

Once the expert has created by means of the tool the product characteristics that describe the different catalogue's products, he must create *the user characteristics* which are going to collect within the system the answers provided by the user, specifying its profile in each of the advising sessions. The expert must specify for each of these characteristics the set of possible values that the client can answer to. In this case, the user characteristics created and its corresponding description are:

- **T_SPORT:** It indicates if the hotel owns sport areas (YES, NO or Empty).
- **T_SAFE:** It indicates if the hotel owns a safe (YES, NO or Empty).
- **T_PRICE:** It indicates the type of hotel the client wants depending on its price (Cheap, Normal, Luxury or Indifferent).
- **T_SEASON:** It indicates the season when the booking of the holidays is wanted. (Spring Summer, Autumn, Winter or Empty).
- **T_TV:** It indicates if the hotel owns via satellite television (YES, NO or Empty).
- **T_ZONE:** It indicates the preference of the client to the hotel's location (Mountain, Beach, City or Indifferent).
- **T_CHILDREN:** It indicates if the hotel boasts children's areas (YES or NO).

In Figure 12 is shown one of the user characteristics created, in this case the one that gathers the client's wishes about the hotel's price (Luxury, Normal, Cheap or Indifferent).

As it can be observed, there is a clear relation between the product characteristic *Category* and the user characteristic T_Price, the highest hotel's category the highest is its price. The former reflects the possible stars that a hotel has whereas the

Figure 8. Input data compatibility with XML

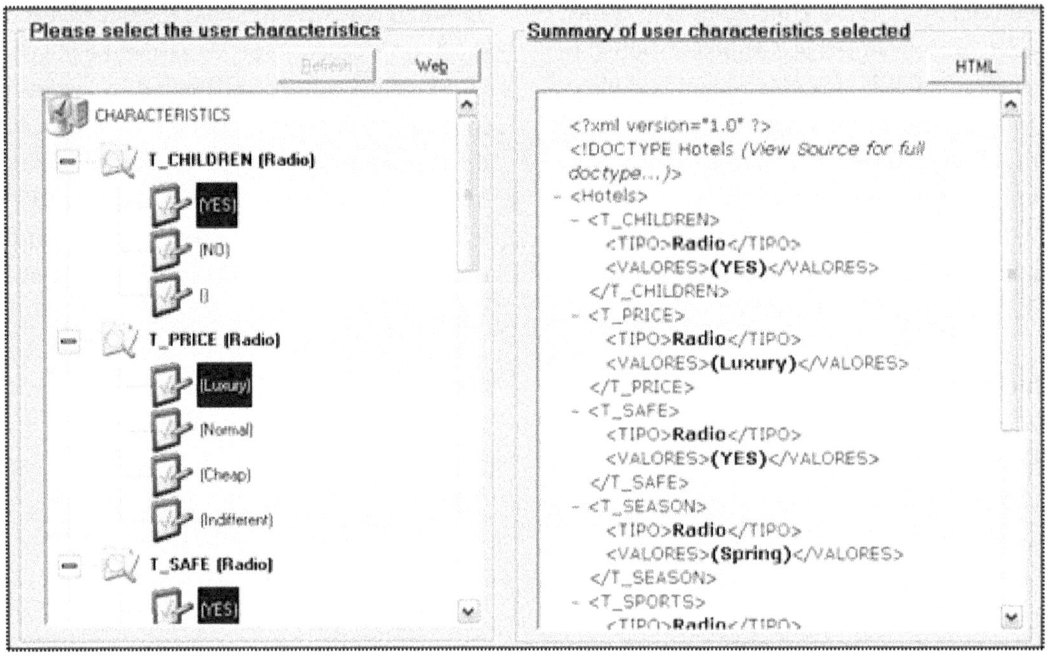

latter expresses the client's wishes as far as the maximum category to be wasted is considered.

Therefore the next step lies in the expert who creates the relations between the client's wishes and the possibilities offered by the hotel in a particular quality.

Before putting the system into action, it is necessary that the expert configures some of the general parameters that are going to permit an optimum system operation. In the first place, it must be indicated the *degree of optimization* for the product searches; in this case we use a *normal optimization*. Thanks to this optimization degree the total score of each of the products is calculated adding the weight values of each of the relations in which there is a right value between the user characteristics and the product characteristics. The other parameter to be configured specifies the *maximum number of products to return,* which allows to delimit the number of products to show to the client once the searching process is carried out. These results very useful when the product's catalogue is very high and the products are very similar between them as the system would not be able to differentiate between them and would return a high number of them.

Figure 13 portraits the window of parameter configuration with the values used in this example.

To conclude, through the relations' editor, the different links between the user and product characteristics have to be created. Each of the links can have a different *importance degree*, what added to the different optimization degrees that the system allows when searching the products, permits the expert to improve the results determining what products have to be offered in each of the cases

The relations between the product characteristics and the user characteristics can adopt different values, in order to make simpler the tool's use, it allows to associate textual descriptions with these numeric values. The values used and the different weight's description used in this example are depicted in Figure 14.

Once the general tool's parameters are configured, then we can start to create the relations

Figure 9. Sketch of the architecture chosen

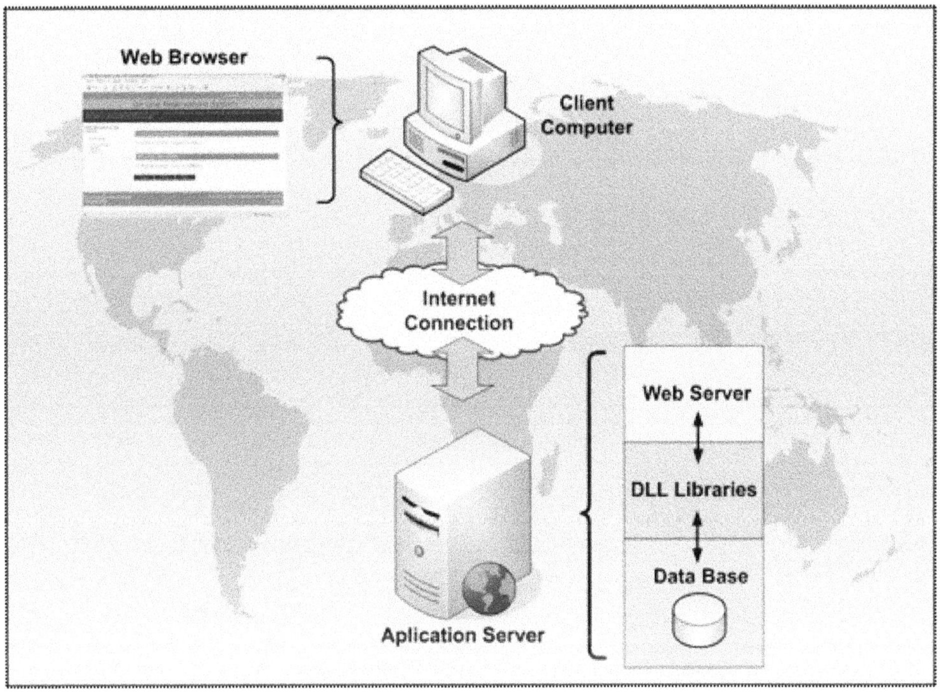

by means of the *relation's editor* incorporated. For the particular case of the user characteristic *T_Price* and the product characteristic *Category* of a hotel, the following relations have been created.

Client wants a Cheap hotel:

- *If **category (hotel)** = **1 star** Then **EXCELENT***
- *If **category (hotel)** = **2 star** Then **GOOD***
- *If **category (hotel)** = **3 star** Then **REGULAR***
- *If **category (hotel)** = **4 star** Then **NOT GOOD***
- *If **category (hotel)** = **5 star** Then **NOT GOOD***

Client wants a Normal hotel:

- *If **category (hotel)** = **1 star** Then **REGULAR***
- *If **category (hotel)** = **2 star** Then **NORMAL***
- *If **category (hotel)** = **3 star** Then **NORMAL***
- *If **category (hotel)** = **4 star** Then **REGULAR***
- *If **category (hotel)** = **5 star** Then **NOT GOOD***

Client wants a Luxury hotel:

- *If **category (hotel)** = **1 star** Then **REGULAR***
- *If **category (hotel)** = **2 star** Then **REGULAR***
- *If **category (hotel)** = **3 star** Then **NORMAL***
- *If **category (hotel)** = **4 star** Then **GOOD***
- *If **category (hotel)** = **5 star** Then **EXCELENT***

These rules and their associated weights are closely related to the selected optimization degree, due to the fact that the products returned are calculated depending on the weights of the relations that are activated and on the type of calculation

Figure 10. Administration of the knowledge base's module

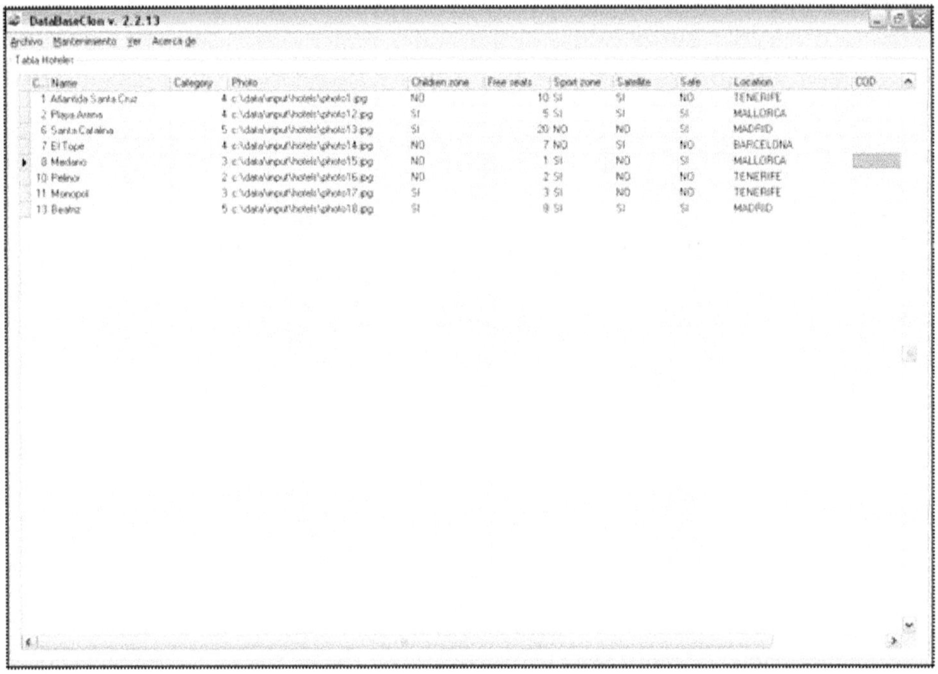

to be carried out with the weights. The expert can change the set of options as many times as he wants until achieving the optimum results.

Figure 15 shows in the tool these relations with the associated weights.

Another example of the rules created are the ones that relate the hotel's location to the client's wishes about its possible situation. In this case the expert must take into account where the hotel is situated (product characteristic LOCATION) and the possible answers that the client can provide (user characteristic T_ZONE), in other words, a hotel located in Madrid does not have beach but it is in a centrally situated city, whereas if the hotel is situated in Barcelona, the hotel boasts beach and is located in a big city.

The rest of the relations would be created following the same method. In any case these relations can be dynamically changed, allowing the expert to optimize continuously the results produced by the tool.

Once this step is fulfilled, the expert can now test the system to check that the results obtained are the ones expected. It is advisable to carry this out before putting into operation the system for the client. For this purpose, the tool's module *recommendation obtaining* can be resorted to.

Figure 16 portraits the system's screen in which the expert introduces the values that simulate the client's answers, in this case a luxury hotel that would owns sports areas and a via satellite television.

The results of this test are shown in Figure 17. As it can be observed, the first two hotels have a similar score due to the fact that they fulfil the same characteristics. In this case the tool returns them in order just as it obtains them from the database.

In the case the expert does not agree with the results obtained, he could redefine the relations or the general parameters. If, on the contrary, the results are correct he could already set the system to production providing access through Internet.

Figure 11. Creation of the product's characteristic "category"

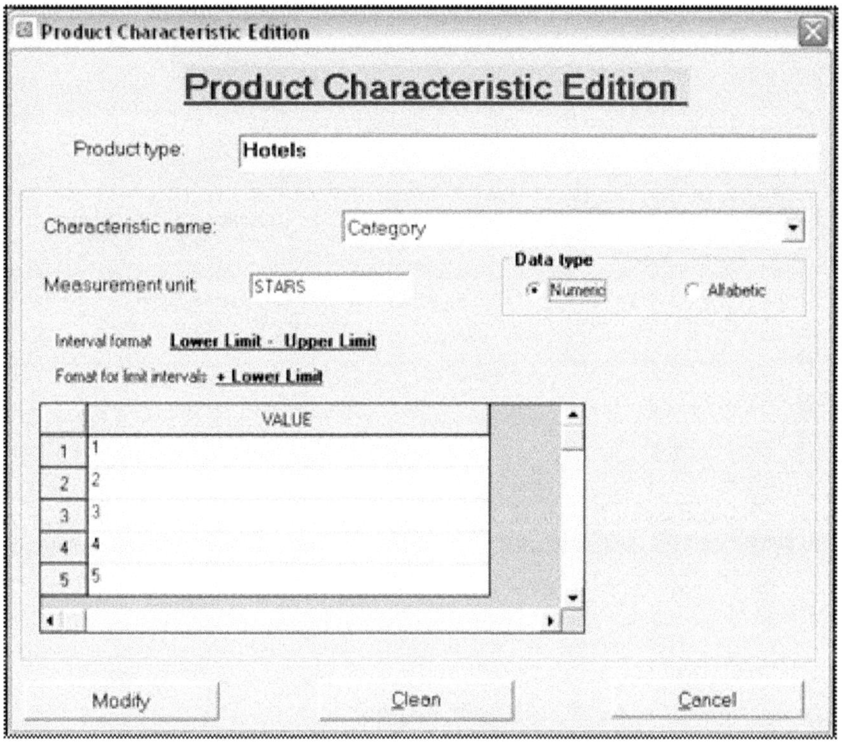

Figure 12. Creation of the user characteristic "T Price"

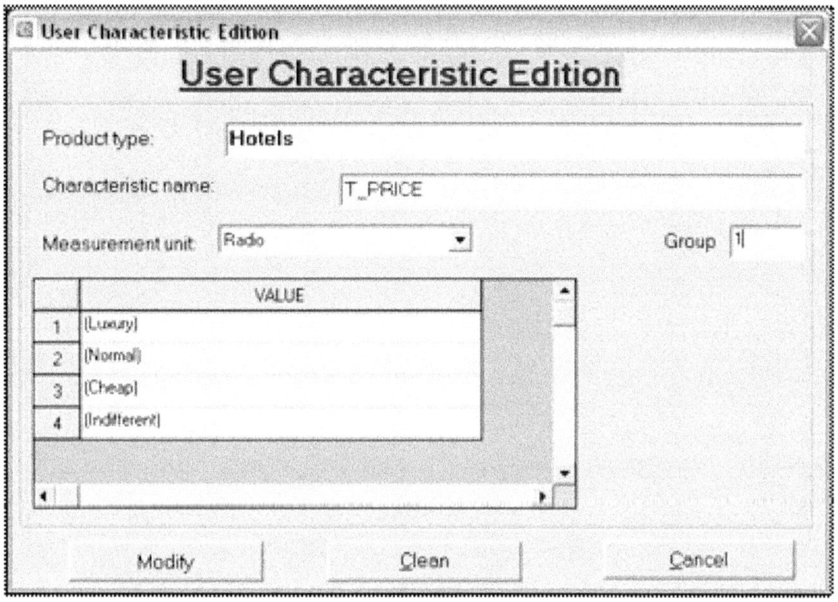

Figure 13. Configuration of the system's operation parameters

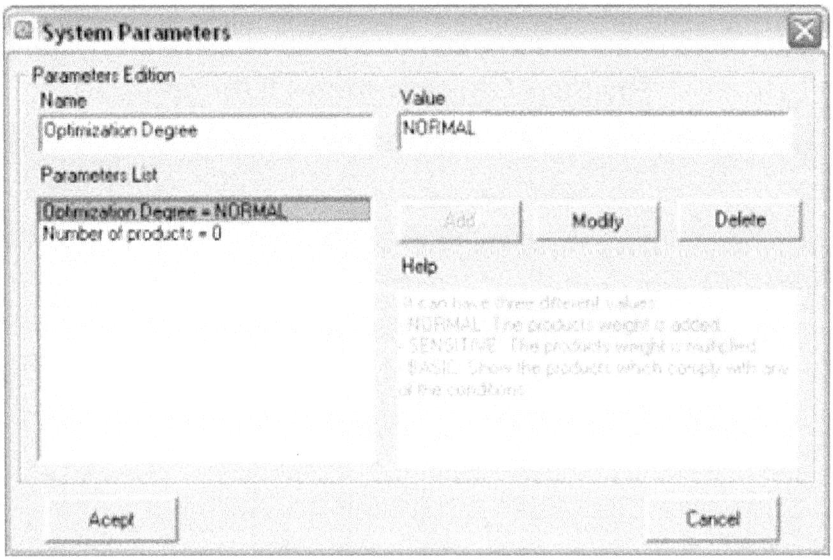

Figure 14. Values' configuration for the different weights

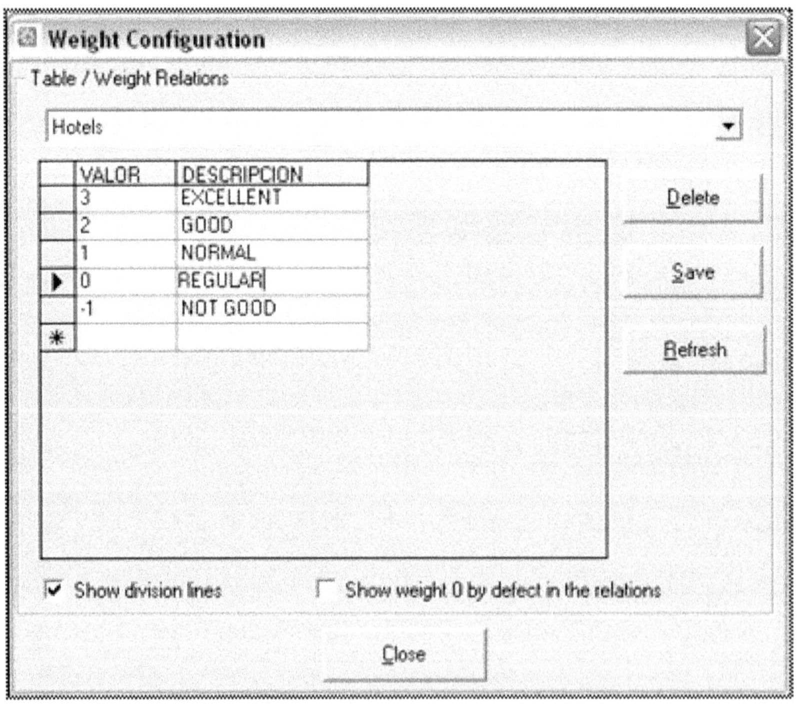

Figure 15. Detail of the relations for the hotel's category and price

		[C]Category (STARS)				
		1	2	3	4	5
[C]T_PRICE	(Luxury)	REGULAR	REGULAR	NORMAL	GOOD	EXCELLENT
	(Normal)	REGULAR	NORMAL	NORMAL	REGULAR	NOT GOOD
	(Cheap)	EXCELLENT	GOOD	REGULAR	NOT GOOD	NOT GOOD
	(Indifferent)				NORMAL	NORMAL

For this purpose, the expert has had to design previously the necessary Web pages to carry out the necessary advising process in order to collect the client's necessities depending on the products existing in the portfolio.

Next, the detailed example of the system's operation is commented from the client user's view. Figure 18 shows the first set of questions designed to the expert that are presented to the user. The client must choose the season for the hotel's booking and the area where it has to be located. The summer's season and nearness to the beach have been chosen for the example.

When the next button is pressed, the system leads the user to the following set of questions, Figure 19 portraits these questions. In this case, the client wants a luxury hotel, with no children's areas and he would like to practise sports during his stay and enjoy via satellite television in his room.

Based on the answers facilitated to the system, the system shows to the user a series of different Web pages. For example if the client wishes a hotel for the winter the supplied package will be different from the one from a summer hotel. Equal it happens when a hotel of low category is asked for, since the options available are smaller and therefore they will not be available. Figure 20 shows an example of cheap hotel and winter season.

When the next button is pressed, the system processes all the answers provided by the user, and turns them into understandable values for the fuzzy logic system created. By means of the inference engine and using the rules created, the system succeeds to deduce the results that adjust most to the necessities expressed by the client in his answers.

As it can be seen in Figure 21, the list of hotels appears arranged by the right value degree on the set of the client's preferences. The first hotel of the list is the one that approaches most or the one that suits best the necessities expressed by the system's user. In this case the client asked for a hotel with high category (luxury hotel) and owns sports areas and via satellite television, being the first hotel in the list the one to obtain the highest score. In case of equality in the score, the first three have obtained the same score, the system arranges the results just as it obtains them from the database.

Next, the client must select the hotel that interests him most, in this case he selects the "Atlántida Santa Cruz" hotel. Once this is done, the client is shown a breakdown of the price of each type of room and a description of the courses he's interested in. Figure 22 depicts a detail of this detach.

To finish, the client can choose between doing the booking for that hotel at a fixed time selecting the type of room, repeat the advising process in order to specify other preferences, or, on the contrary, finish to work with the system. Figure 23 shows the data requested by the system to do the booking.

Figure 16. System tests carried out by the expert

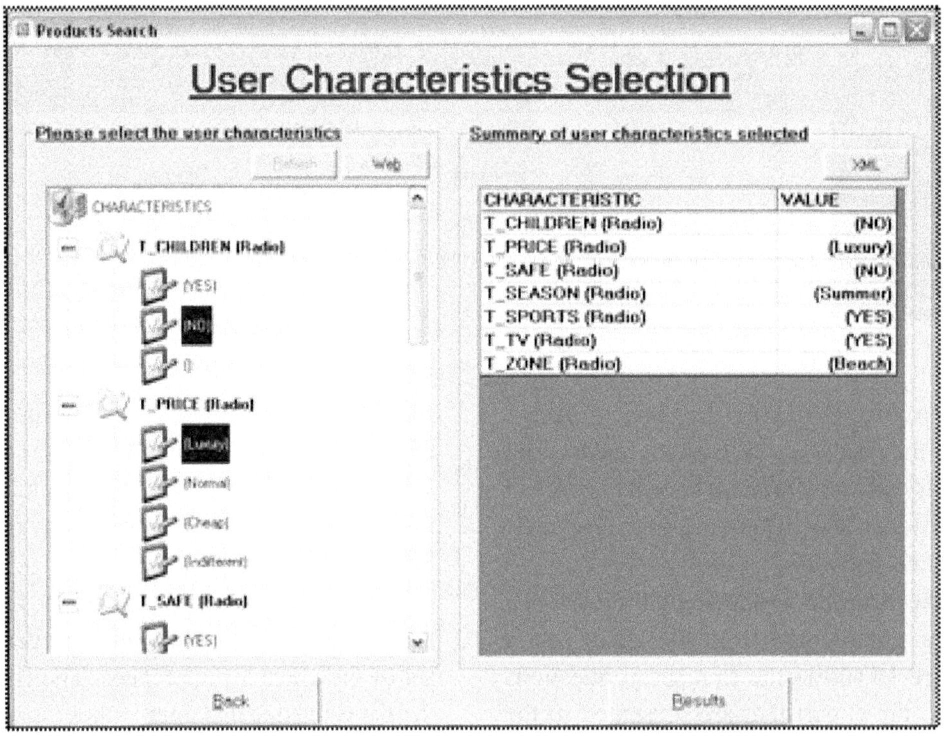

Figure 17. Results of the tests carried out by the expert

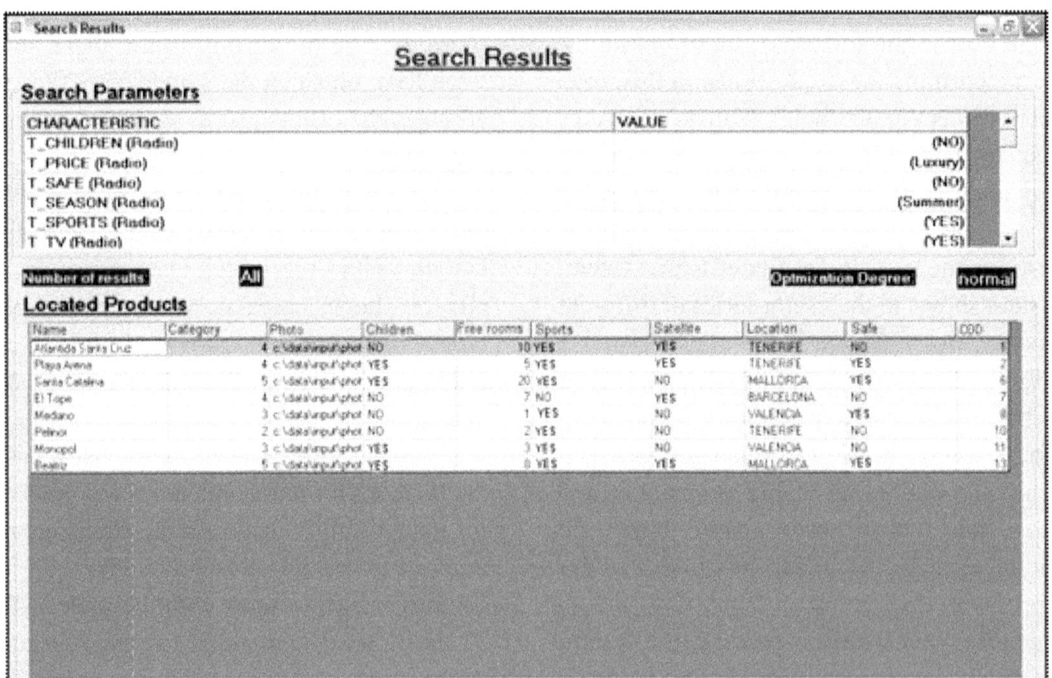

Figure 18. First step of the advising process

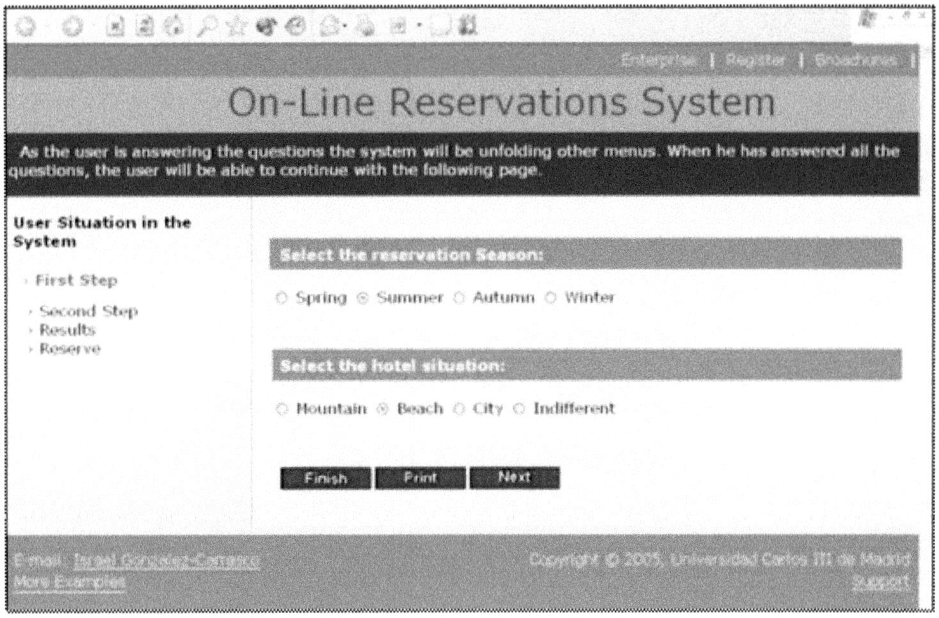

Figure 19. Second step of the advising process

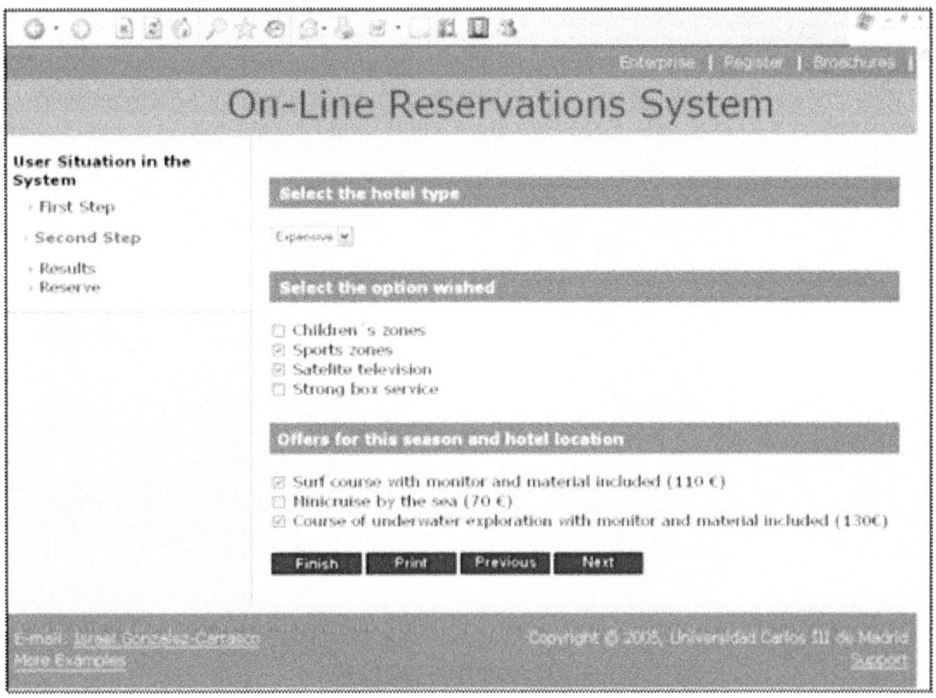

Figure 20. Continuation of the second step

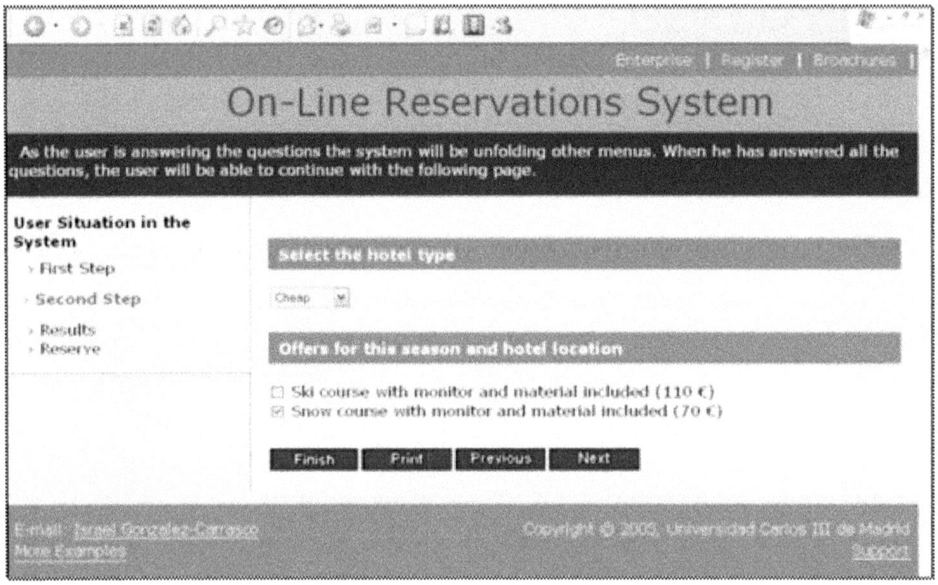

Figure 21. List with the advising process' results

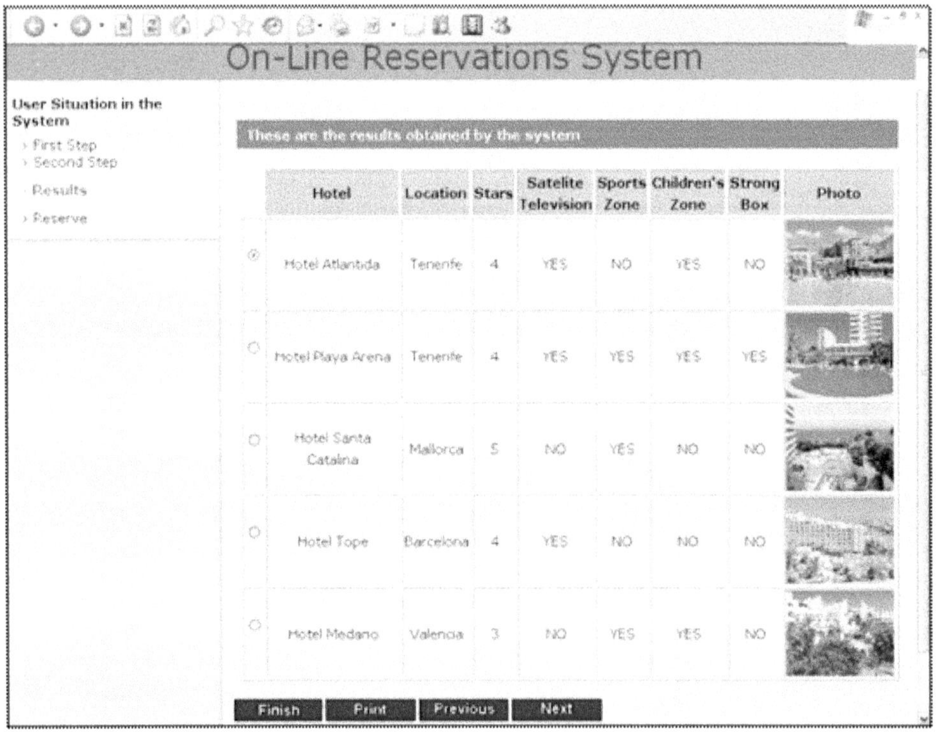

Figure 22. Hotel's detach and selected activities

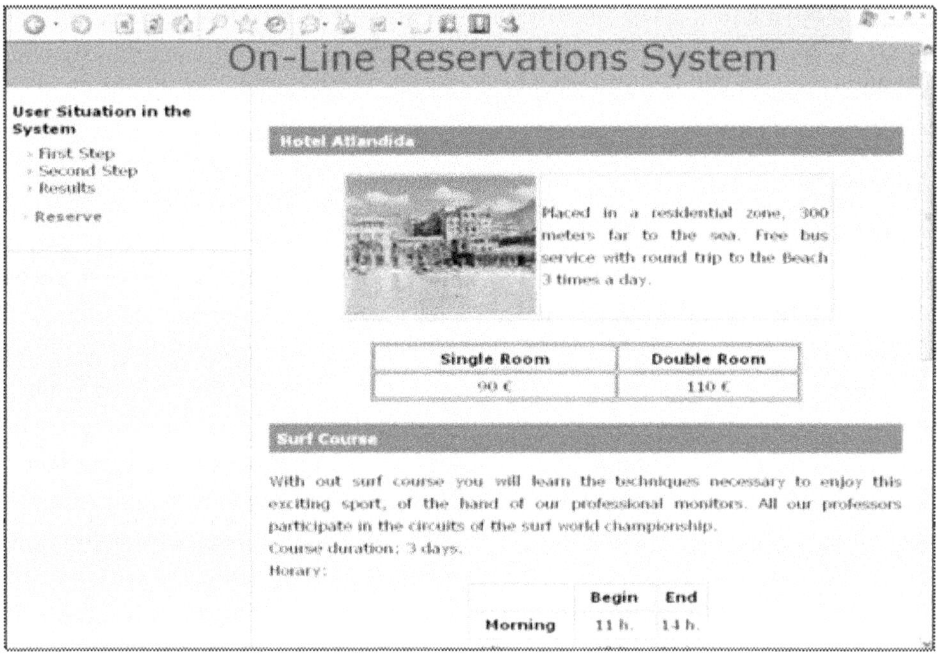

Figure 23. Room booking in the selected hotel

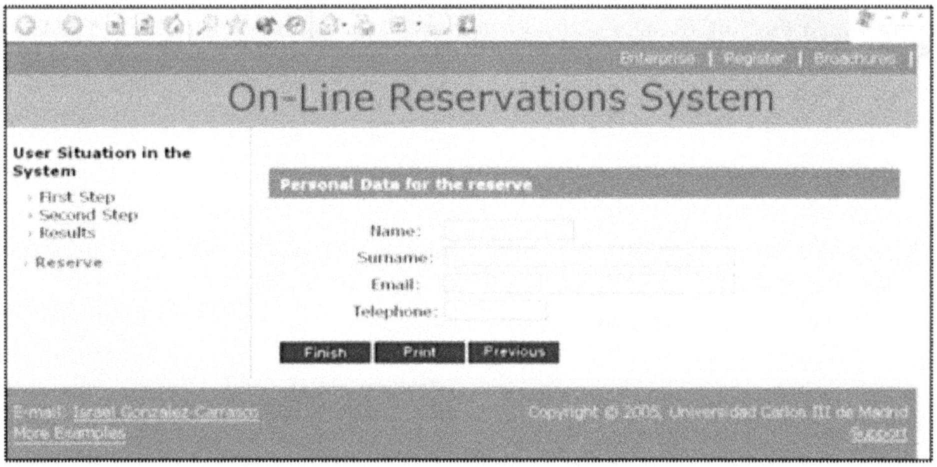

Therefore, the developed system allows guiding the client in the buying process of a specific product thanks to the processing of the preferences the client provides in a comfortable and simple way by means of the Web forms.

5. CONCLUSION

The fuzzy logic is a branch of artificial intelligence that is based on the concept "Everything is a degree question". This allows us to handle vague information or with difficult specification to govern a system by means of "common sense" rules, which refer to indefinite quantities. This set of rules, is based on fuzzy proposals of the type *IF condition THEN action control*, created by the expert of the dominion. Thanks to these rules it's possible to establish *schemes of approximated reasoning*, which allow to reproduce the mental schemes of the human brain in the reasoning process. These rules act over the set of fuzzy inputs obtaining a series of fuzzy outputs expressed by linguistic variables.

The developed system takes advantage of these possibilities and is based on the so–called fuzzy sets and on a fuzzy inference system. This inference system includes rules of the type "IF..... THEN.....", where the premises and results of the linguistic variables are defined by fuzzy sets. Thanks to the theory of the diffuse sets the tool is able by itself to catch the linguistic vagueness of words and commonly accepted sentences, like "cheap hotel" or "slight change".

Our proposal is the implementation of a tool that allows distinguishing, selecting and offering, among all the similar products in a business, the one that best suits the users' necessities. Depending on the answers that are provided to the system during the advising process, the system distinguishes among the whole product stock with similar characteristics, those ones that fulfil with the highest precision that the client demands. This process is completely interactive, and allows satisfying in an efficient and dynamic way the needs expressed by the client.

A basic aspect that allows obtaining great flexibility in the tool, is the fact that the system can be modified and improved in real time by the expert. This allows changing quickly and without stopping the system's operation, the product's set to return depending on the business' necessities. Because of that reason the system allows the expert to create diverse sales environments.

On the other hand, the maintenance of products portfolio, entrances of new products or modifications of the values, is quite simple, since the answers of the system are based on the rules created by the expert and not in each one of products.

Another of the great advantages of the developed system is the possibility of using it in different environments, Windows or Web application, increasing therefore its use possibilities.

Therefore the developed application is a really powerful tool to model the knowledge that the human expert has on a concrete dominion, especially when the products are similar among them and the product portfolio undergoes continuous modifications.

Finally, an example of the tool's operation in a real case of advising in a buying has been included. Thanks to this, the power and flexibility of the tool can be observed when responding to the necessities expressed by different system's clients.

REFERENCES

Alavi, M., & Leidner, D. (2001). Knowledge management and knowledge management systems: Conceptual foundations and research issues. *Management Information Systems Quarterly*, *25*(1), 107–136. doi:10.2307/3250961

Duan, Y., Edwards, J. S., & Xu, M. X. (2005). Web-based expert systems: Benefits and challenges. *Information & Management, 42*(6), 799–811. doi:10.1016/j.im.2004.08.005

Dubois, D., & Prade, H. (1980). *Fuzzy sets and systems: Theory and applications*. Academic Press.

Dubois, D., & Prade, H. (1991). Fuzzy sets in approximate reasoning II (Logical approaches). *Fuzzy Sets and Systems, 40*, 203–244. doi:10.1016/0165-0114(91)90051-Q

Dubois, D., & Prade, H. (2000). *Fundamentals of fuzzy sets*. Kluwer Academic.

Durkin, J. (1994). *Expert systems: Design and development*. Maxwell Macmillan.

Garcia-Crespo, A., Ruiz-Mezcua, B., López-Cuadrado, J. L., & González-Carrasco, I. (2011). Semantic model for knowledge representation in e-business. *Knowledge-Based Systems, 24*(2). doi:10.1016/j.knosys.2010.09.006

Gómez, A., Juristo, N., Montes, C., & Pazos, J. (1997). *Ingeniería del conocimiento*. Centro de Estudios Ramón Areces.

Hájek, P., & Godó, L. (1997). Deductive systems of fuzzy logic. In *Fuzzy Structures Current Trends*.

Höhle, U., & Rodabaugh, S. E. (1999). *Mathematics of fuzzy sets: Logic, topology, and measure theory*. Kluwer Academic.

Kaufmann, A., & Gupta, M. M. (1985). *Introduction to fuzzy arithmetic*. V.N. Reinhold.

Kenteris, M., Gavalas, D., & Economou, D. (2009). An innovative mobile electronic tourist guide application. *Personal and Ubiquitous Computing, 13*(2), 103–118. doi:10.1007/s00779-007-0191-y

Lee, C. C. (1990). Fuzzy logic in control systems: Fuzzy logic controller-parts 1 and 2. *IEEE Transactions on Systems, Man, and Cybernetics, 20*(2), 404–435. doi:10.1109/21.52551

Liao, S. H. (2005). Expert system methodologies and applications - a decade review from 1995 to 2004. *Expert Systems with Applications, 28*, 93–103. doi:10.1016/j.eswa.2004.08.003

Metaxiotis, K. S., Askounis, D., & Psarras, J. (2002). Expert systems in production planning and scheduling: a state-of-the-art survey. *Journal of Intelligent Manufacturing, 13*, 253–260. doi:10.1023/A:1016064126976

Nurminen, J. K., Karonen, O., & Hatonen, K. (2003). What makes expert systems survive over 10 years - Empirical evaluation of several engineering applications. *Expert Systems with Applications, 43*, 199–211. doi:10.1016/S0957-4174(02)00149-5

Pham, D., & Pham, P. (1999). Artificial intelligence in engineering. *International Journal of Machine Tools & Manufacture, 39*, 937–949. doi:10.1016/S0890-6955(98)00076-5

Schiaffino, S., & Amandi, A. (2009). Building an expert travel agent as a software agent. *Expert Systems with Applications, 36*(2), 1291–1299. doi:10.1016/j.eswa.2007.11.032

Stevens, L. (1985). *Artificial intelligence. The search for the perfect machine*. Hayden Book Company.

Xiang, Z., Kim, S. E., Hu, C., & Fesenmaier, D. R. (2007). Language representation of restaurants: Implications for developing online recommender systems. *Hospital Management, 26*(4), 1005–1018. doi:10.1016/j.ijhm.2006.12.007

Zadeh, L. A. (1965). Fuzzy sets. *IEEE Information & Control*, *8*, 338–353. doi:10.1016/S0019-9958(65)90241-X

Zadeh, L. A. (1988). Fuzzy logic. *Computer*, *1*(4), 83–93. doi:10.1109/2.53

Zadeh, L. A. (1989). Knowledge representation in fuzzy logic. *IEEE Transactions on Knowledge and Data Engineering*, *1*, 89–100. doi:10.1109/69.43406

Chapter 12
A Risk Assessment Framework for Inter-Organizational Knowledge Sharing

Ruba Aljafari
University of Nebraska at Omaha, USA

Surendra Sarnikar
Dakota State University, USA

ABSTRACT

Internet-based information, communication, and collaboration technologies are making it easier for organizations and knowledge workers to collaborate across organizational boundaries. However, it is necessary for organizations to monitor, regulate, and build appropriate security mechanisms in collaboration systems to prevent loss of strategic knowledge and competitive advantage. In this chapter, the authors synthesize literature on knowledge sharing and IS/IT risk assessment to present a risk assessment framework that can help organizations identify valuable knowledge assets exposed through collaboration technologies, and assess the risk of knowledge loss, intellectual property leakage, and the subsequent loss of competitive advantage so that appropriate security mechanism can be designed to prevent such a loss.

INTRODUCTION

Organizations are increasingly using collaboration technologies and systems to move towards collaborative inter-organizational network structures. Such network structures are being used to manage various business processes such as supply chain processes, joint product development, customer relationship management, development of industry standards, and for engaging in collaborative commerce. In addition to formalized inter-organizational collaboration mechanisms, organizations and their knowledge workers are also leveraging the powerful capabilities of Web 2.0 technologies such as Wiki's, blogs, discussion forums, social networks and online communities in serving their business needs. Examples of

DOI: 10.4018/978-1-4666-0948-8.ch012

use include interaction with customers in order to generate ideas and feedback as in cases like GM, Domino's Pizza, and Dove or to encourage employees to communicate ideas and experiences (Chui, Miller, & Roberts, 2009).

While knowledge workers continue to leverage such technologies to engage in ad hoc collaboration with customers, vendors, and professional colleagues to exchange knowledge and provide improved services, it is also necessary to ensure that they do not expose strategic organizational knowledge to threats (Fanning, 2007). Web 2.0 technologies are inherently difficult to secure, as they make organizational intelligence more accessible and searchable (Short, 2009). Several news reports and companies have reported cases of intellectual property leakage and loss due to insufficient protection of knowledge assets (Burrows, 2004; Hamm, 2006; Herbst, 2009; Zhen, 2005). Even as companies restrict the use of technologies by using tools such as e-mail monitoring or non-disclosure policies, data and IP leakage is still considered a major risk that is even ahead of viruses and Trojans (Oricchio, 2009; Probasco, 2009; Spring, 2008).

Benefits and risks associated with inter-organizational collaboration and knowledge sharing have been discussed in the literature from a very high level and strategic perspective. Significant work has also been done in the area of information security risk assessment and security mechanisms for inter-organizational collaboration systems. While there are several IT risk assessment models such as the Control Objectives for Information and related Technology COBIT (*COBIT*, 2001) the Information Technology Infrastructure Library ITIL (*Information Technology Infrastructure Library ITIL*, 2001) and the series of information security standards ISO/IEC 27000 (*The Information Security Management Systems Family of Standards*, 2000) their scope is limited to technology infrastructure and data and information assets and does not consider knowledge assets. In their study of identifying risks in e-commerce relationships, Sutton, Hampton, Khazanchi, and Arnold (2008) point that IT governance frameworks do not provide guidelines for assessing inter-organizational risks, as they seem to focus solely on technical issues. Moreover, most information assurance frameworks focus on data assets rather than knowledge. On the other hand, while there are several knowledge management frameworks that help identify and analyze knowledge assets, such frameworks are rarely integrated into existing risk assessment frameworks. There is limited literature that provides a structured process for identifying strategic knowledge assets exposed through collaboration systems, specific risks associated with sharing those assets in inter-organizational collaboration, and strategies for selecting techniques to minimize the knowledge sharing risk in inter-organizational collaboration.

In this chapter, we synthesize on research in knowledge sharing and Information Systems risk assessment and present a framework for identifying strategic knowledge assets and potential threats to the knowledge assets exposed by collaboration technologies. In this framework, we take an integrated approach to address the complexity of business networks or the extended enterprise (Dynes, Kolbe, & Schierholz, 2007). We define knowledge assets as tangible and "intangible assets that encompass the knowledge as well as the ability of an organization to leverage that knowledge. They can also be the technology that facilitates the interaction of the knowledge with the human capital" (Freeze and Kulkarni, 2005). The term risk is used in this study to refer to the potential damage, loss, or negative effect of sharing those knowledge assets. Bayer and Maier (2006) further elaborate on these negative effects by stating that "knowledge risk can be caused by the loss of, unsuccessful intended or unintended transfer of knowledge assets that result in loss or non-exclusivity of these assets".

The framework includes a systematic process through which organizations can identify, value knowledge assets and estimate potential strategic risks by sharing those assets. The framework consists of five essential components that focus on (1) identifying knowledge sharing practices, (2) identifying knowledge assets, (3) identifying collaboration technologies that expose these knowledge assets, (4) identifying the risk associated with the knowledge assets, and (5) a Dempster-Shaefer based model for quantifying the risks.

The rest of the chapter is organized as follows. Section 2 provides background and context on inter-organizational collaboration. Section 3 reviews relevant literature in inter-organizational collaboration and knowledge sharing and information technology risk assessment. Based on the findings from the literature review, we generate the requirements of the KM risk assessment framework in Section 4, and provide a detailed description of the framework in terms of the required steps and the objective, method and output of each step. Section 5 presents the design of a decision support system based on the framework. Finally, Section 6 concludes the chapter with a summary of contributions and opportunities for future research.

BACKGROUND

Previous research has suggested that firms are better off when they use and re-use mature internal as well as external ideas in different domains, because this is more cost effective than creating the same ideas from scratch (Hargadon & Sutton, 2000). Organizations are therefore increasingly exploring inter-organizational knowledge sharing arrangements within an environment that allows them to build valuable intellectual capital and knowledge assets (Das & Teng, 2001).

In Figure 1, we present a typical knowledge sharing scenario in inter-organization networks in the context of the value chain of a computer manufacturing organization, where inbound, manufacturing, and outbound logistics bring together suppliers, manufacturers, customers, retailers and other partners. The labeled arrows between different entities show the flow of different types of knowledge that may take place between the entities.

As can be noted from the figure, knowledge sharing can appear at any stage or sub-process within the value chain of a company. For example, component design knowledge can be transferred between a Semi-conductor chips manufacturer and the computer manufacturer. Best practices and benchmarking knowledge can be transferred between different computer manufacturers. Customer support agents may share product design knowledge with customers and receive customer requirements knowledge. While several knowledge sharing activities may have beneficial impacts on the company, harmful knowledge sharing activities are also possible. Inadvertent disclosure of sensitive business knowledge or information could be an example of such activities (Johnson & Dynes, 2007). Computer engineers and knowledge workers at the computer manufacturer, for instance, may share product design knowledge inadvertently with competitors through communities of practice or ad hoc collaborations. Such harmful transfer of knowledge may also occur through regular customer support interactions, or interactions with suppliers and vendors resulting in a strategic risk to the computer manufacturer.

Collaboration among organizations can take the form of strategic alliances, where knowledge sharing and acquisition are critical for creating customer value and improving competitive advantage (Marshall, Nguyen, & Bryant, 2005). However, knowledge sharing may be problematic in such systems since it involves diverse relationships and participants in this system may have conflicting interests. For example, risks pertaining to knowledge sharing may arise when knowledge is transferred to other projects that may benefit competitors of the firm that owns the original product or when the partner decides to move to innovating the basic product (Arakji & Lang, 2007). Thus, a more systematic approach is required to help

Figure 1. Knowledge sharing in the computer industry

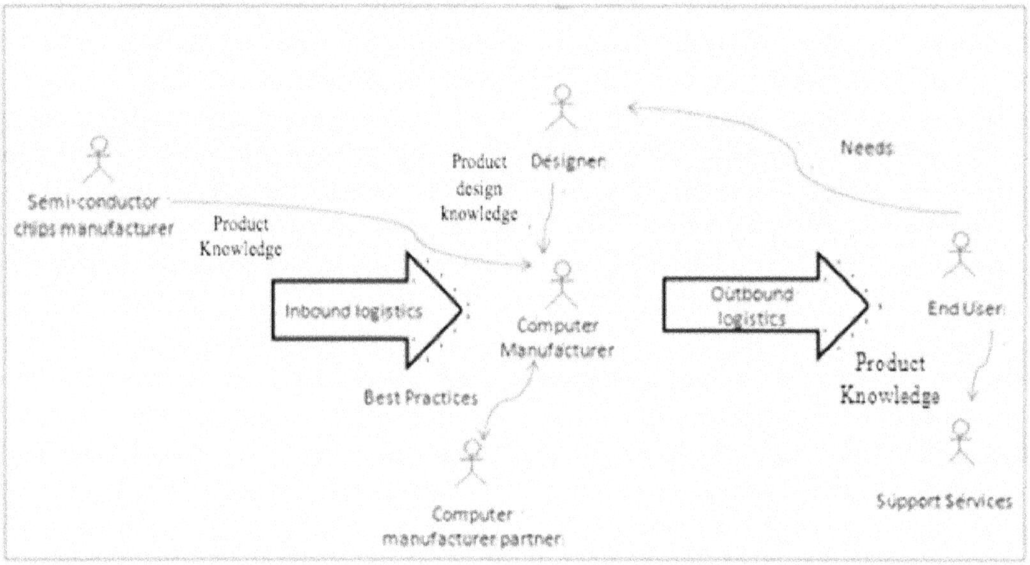

organizations in identifying and assessing risks and therefore be able to design the most effective security measures. Such a framework will enable organizations to take a more proactive approach in a given knowledge sharing scenario.

LITERATURE REVIEW

We classify relevant literature into two main categories that include inter-organizational collaboration and information technology risk assessment.

Inter-Organizational Collaboration and Knowledge Sharing

Inter-organizational knowledge sharing has been analyzed from three different perspectives, technical, behavioral and strategic. The technical perspective is mostly focused on designing and implementing secure systems and architectures for collaborative knowledge sharing. The behavioral perspective includes research that explores behavioral issues related to collaborative knowledge sharing, such as trust and social ties among participants in the same collaboration system. Finally, the strategic perspective analyzes inter-organizational knowledge sharing benefits and risks from a high level. We further explore the strategic perspective as it provides key insights necessary for the identification and assessment of knowledge sharing risks. The importance of the strategic perspective is risk management illustrated by Schlaak, Dynes, Kolbe, and Schierholz (2008) who develop an IS risk oriented outsourcing model based on the notion that the vocal point of risk management should be the business mission rather than focusing directly on IT security issues. The model integrates best practices in IS risk management and abstractions of the outsourcing process in order to identify and manage IS risks with outsourcing partners. In order to analyze the strategic impact of knowledge sharing, Levy, Leobbecke, and Powell (2003), proposed a game theoretic approach to analyze inter-organizational knowledge sharing among small and medium enterprises (SME). In an empirical investigation of their model, they find that SME's are good at knowledge creation but are poor at knowledge retention and need to recognize the value of knowledge shared to retain competitive advantage. Most firms depend on legal contracts and policies to control knowledge sharing. However, developing such policies to ensure high level of control and flexibility at the same time is a difficult problem (Behrend, 2006). Moreover, organizations may acquire and use knowledge that is beyond the boundaries of the legal agreement governing specific knowledge assets. For example, partners in a strategic alliances can learn from each other business and management skills that they were lacking individually (Medcof, 1997).

According to Das and Teng (2001) there can be two types of risks in strategic alliances, that include relational risk and the performance risk. Performance risk is basically related to the probability that alliance objectives may not be met despite good relations between partners (Das & Teng, 2001). Such risks may arise because of new entrants to the industry, demand fluctuations, changing government policies, and lack of competence of partner firms. In the context of supply chain management, Dynes, Brechbühl, and Johnson (2005) analyze information security in the extended enterprise by focusing on two types of risks. Those include, risks pertaining to internal IT systems and information as a result of integrating the supply chain and risks to a firm's ability to produce products as a result of supply chain disruptions caused by information infrastructure events. The relational risk arises because of the fact that partners may have their own individual interests that may conflict with those of other partners. This may result in opportunistic behavior, as described by (Das & Teng, 2001; Das & Teng, 1999), such as cheating, distorting information or knowledge and appropriating shared resources. In the supply chain, for instance, access to valuable logistics information can be used to seize control of cargo (Zhang & Li, 2006). Even in cases where legal agreements exist, partner organizations may acquire and use knowledge not covered by legal agreements for competing purposes. Other knowledge sharing risks may include diffusion of the firm's knowledge (Beeby & Booth, 2000), as the value of the shared knowledge diminishes, which results in a potential loss of competitive advantage (Pardo, Cresswell, & Zhang, 2007). In strategic alliances, predicting and managing conflicts, which may be important sources of risk, is usually overlooked (Panteli & Sockalingam, 2005). While there are many benefits to knowledge sharing, organizations need to weigh the benefits against risks pertaining to knowledge sharing. A summary of the risks related to knowledge sharing is illustrated in Table 1.

Information Technology Risk Assessment

In addition to literature on strategic risk in alliances and collaborations, another related area of literature includes the Information Technology risk assessment techniques. The main focus of Information Technology risk assessment literature is the securing of IT assets from external and internal threats. There are several IT risk assessment models proposed in literature (*COBIT*, 2001; *Information Technology Infrastructure Library ITIL*, 2001; Rees, Bandyopadhyay, & Spafford, 2003; Stoneburner, Goguen, & Feringa, 2001; Sun, Srivastava, & Mock, 2006; *The Information Security Management Systems Family of Standards*, 2000; *The OCTAVE approach*, 2003) A typical IT risk assessment process begins with identifying data, information and technology assets that might be exposed to risk and quantifying threats associated with them (Rees, et al., 2003).

Table 1. Risk factors

Risk factor
Unauthorized learning
Unauthorized sharing of sensitive knowledge
Unauthorized use of knowledge asset
Manipulation of knowledge asset
Appropriation of knowledge asset

This process can be challenging since evaluation in this domain can be highly subjective (F. Farahmand, Navathe, Sharp, & Enslow, 2003), as managers assign personal judgments on related risks. After identifying those vulnerable assets and determining risk, experts can design, select, apply the best protection mechanisms and evaluate them in an iterative manner (F. Farahmand, et al., 2003; F. Farahmand, Sharp, & Enslow, 2005). Examples of IT Risk Assessment models include the Policy Framework for Interpreting Risk in E-business Security (PFIRES) (Rees, et al., 2003), the Risk Management Guide for Information Technology Systems by (*The Information Security Management Systems Family of Standards*, 2000), OCTAVE (*The OCTAVE approach*, 2003), and COBIT (*COBIT*, 2001).

Although there are risk assessment frameworks for information technology assets, and literature on collaboration risk and strategic issues in inter-organizational knowledge sharing, currently there is no structured process that can help organizations analyze risks in inter-organizational knowledge sharing and Web 2.0 collaboration and sharing environments. Organization's knowledge assets, which may be tacit or explicit, are vulnerable to threats when exposed to external organizations through collaborative settings. Thus, organizations need to analyze different aspects related to knowledge sharing in these settings. For instance, is there a risk that partners can gain access to knowledge that the sharing firm uses in other business areas? What kind of knowledge is being diffused through employee blogs or employee participation in technical discussion forums? Is the knowledge diffused strategic to the company? What are the most appropriate protection mechanisms in such situations? Currently there exists no framework that can help managers address these aspects. In the next section, we build on past literature in Information Technology risk assessment to develop a framework that can help in assessing risks of knowledge sharing.

RISK ASSESSMENT FRAMEWORK

A firm must go through a systematic methodology to assess inter-organizational knowledge sharing risk. In this chapter, we extend previous risk assessment methodologies such as the NIST Risk Management Guide for Information Technology Systems (Stoneburner, et al., 2001) and the PFIRES by (Rees, et al., 2003) to develop a risk assessment framework that is suited for the inter-organizational knowledge sharing case. Since knowledge is often shared using information and communication technologies, we begin by building upon Information Technology risk assessment frameworks and extend them to incorporate knowledge assets and risks associated with knowledge sharing. In the next section, we present the requirements of the framework followed by a detailed description of the risk assessment process.

Requirements

The main objective of the framework is to provide a structured process for managers to identify and evaluate risks pertaining to knowledge sharing. We have identified three key factors from strategic knowledge sharing and risk management literature that influence the utility and success of the framework. The factors include identifying and recognizing the content that is shared, the context in which knowledge is shared, and the inherent subjectivity in valuing knowledge assets and assessing risks.

A key element of the risk assessment process is the systematic identification of the assets that need to be protected (F. Farahmand, et al., 2005; Rees, et al., 2003; Zhang & Li, 2006). As organizations increasingly engage in inter-organizational collaborative projects, it is important that they recognize the knowledge assets that are involved in the collaborative processes, their characteristics, and the strategic advantage provided by the knowledge asset to the organization (Behrend, 2006; Carlsson, 2003) Identification of knowledge assets as well as their strategic value is essential to retain strategic advantage as organizations balance benefits and risks of knowledge sharing in co-operation and competition situations (Levy & Powell, 2003).

In addition to identification of knowledge assets, the context in which the knowledge assets are shared has important implications for assessing knowledge sharing risks (Behrend, 2006). The knowledge sharing context includes the business processes in which knowledge is being shared, the entities involved, and the associated collaboration and communication technologies. Communication and Collaboration technologies are important conduits for knowledge transfer and different technology features can act as filters or enablers of knowledge transfer.

Mentzas and Apostolou (2006) for instance, emphasized the need for understanding the role of electronic media in analyzing inter-organizational knowledge transfer. Bayer and Maier (2006) consider the role of collaborative use of information systems in knowledge transfer. In their study of information sharing in supply chain management systems, Zhang and Li (2006) identify information technology solutions as important elements in ensuring the security of information sharing. Thus, identifying collaboration technologies through which potential knowledge transfer takes place is an important requirement of the risk assessment process.

The subjectivity in experts' judgments in estimating risks also needs to be reduced by deploying sufficient analytical capabilities. Since risk assessment involves judgment and decision making at some point in the process, a common problem associated with such situations is the subjective nature of those judgments. Subjective judgments could negatively affect the quality and the reliability of the risk assessment process as a whole (Goto, 2007; Sun, et al., 2006). Thus, there is a need for controlling this problem in order to generate "bias-free" risk estimates.

Risk Assessment Process

In this section, we describe tasks in the risk assessment process in terms of the objective, method, and output. An overview of the risk assessment framework is presented in Figure 2.

Identify Inter-Organizational Processes

Objective: The objective of this step is to identify organizational processes that may involve sharing of knowledge assets with external entities. This step is based on the notion that boundaries of the IT system must be defined in the early stages of the assessment process (Stoneburner, et al., 2001). An organization can identify the extent of knowledge sharing activities by identifying the business process that provide the context through which

Figure 2. Risk assessment process

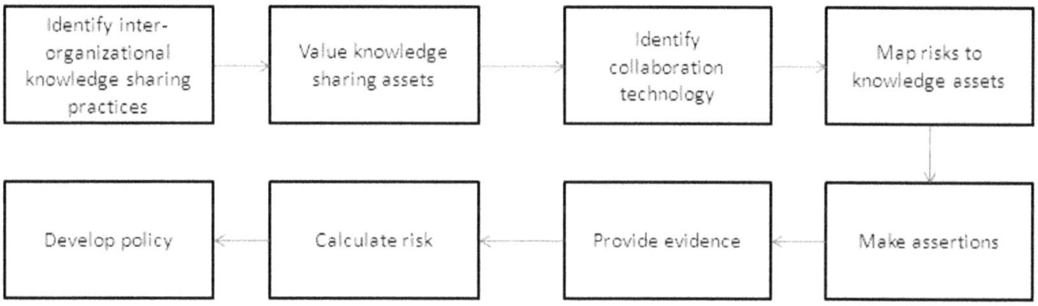

knowledge assets are shared. This step follows a top down approach that assists managers by starting with the main process and then narrows down the focus towards assets involved and their associated risks.

Method:

- Identify key business processes executed by organizational units using the value chain model, for instance, or any business model that clearly represents the firm's business processes and its relationships with suppliers, customers, and competitors.
- Identify organization's members and external partners involved in those business processes.

Output: The final output of this step would be a list of business processes and associated internal as well as external entities.

Value Knowledge Assets

Objective: The main objective of this step is to identify the most valuable knowledge assets that need to be protected. Organizational knowledge assets may reside in people, documents, or technology artifacts. In this step, managers begin by identifying and classifying knowledge assets. This is important because being specific about knowledge assets can help in identifying related threats and later in identifying securing policies.

Method:

- One approach that can be used to identify knowledge assets is to sketch a tree diagram with different types and repositories of knowledge resources, so that managers can clearly spot and identify knowledge assets (Becerra-Fernandez, Gonzalez, & Shabherwal, 2004). Knowledge can be stored in individual's or expert's mind as tacit knowledge or in groups as collective and synergistic (Becerra-Fernandez, et al., 2004). It can also be encapsulated in artifacts such as practices (e.g. procedures and rules), technologies and knowledge repositories.
- Identify strategic knowledge assets by assessing the (a) value, (b) rareness and (c) imitability of each knowledge asset. This approach is based on the resource-based view of knowledge and designed to measure the competitive advantage provided by the knowledge asset (Carlsson, 2003). The value of a knowledge asset is a measure of the extent to which the asset enables the firm to sense and respond to opportunities and threats in the business environment. The rareness of the knowledge asset measures the extent to which competing firms may possess similar knowledge and imitability refers to the difficulty of obtaining or imitating the knowledge resource by other organizations that do not own it. In this framework, a manager could value knowledge assets using these criteria on a scale from 1 to 5, with 5 indicating the highest value and 1 indicating the least value.

Output: The output of this step would be a ranked list of knowledge assets based on the previously discussed criteria. These assets will be used later on in the risk assessment process as the unit of focus.

Identify Collaboration Technologies

Objective: The objective of this task is to identify the medium or collaboration technology through which knowledge could be transferred to an external entity. Examples of such technologies include, but are not limited to, e-mail, Wiki's, blogs, and discussion boards.

Method: The method used to accomplish this task involves identification of collaboration technologies used to share a knowledge asset in the context of the previously identified processes, internal as well as external entities and strategic assets.

- The technology is identified in the context of a process. For example, the requirements collection template might be shared with customers via a consultant/customer portal, whereas, it is shared with vendors and affiliated developers via a project management website/code versioning system during the development process.

Output: The output of this step is a Process-Technology-Asset matrix that can help document the knowledge asset vulnerabilities. Questions evaluating risks will be generated later on based on elements in this matrix.

Map Risks to Knowledge Assets

Objective: The objective of this step is to identify potential threats to strategic knowledge assets in a given context. In this step, the manager identifies which of the risks factors previously identified in Section 3.1 apply to the knowledge assets used in a particular business process.

Method:

- List potential threats to the given knowledge assets. Threats arising due to knowledge sharing include unauthorized learning, unauthorized sharing, unauthorized use, manipulation, and appropriation of knowledge asset.

Output: The output of this step is a list of applicable threats to a given combination of processes, strategic knowledge assets, and collaboration technologies.

Make Assertions

Objective: The main objective of this process is to make assertions on the risks pertaining to sharing knowledge assets in the context that was generated by the previous steps.

Method:

- For each knowledge asset, make assertions, as per the evidential reasoning model of Dempster-Shafer theory (Dempster, 1968; Shafer, 1976), on the vulnerability of knowledge asset to the identified threats through the given technology. For example, best practices are not vulnerable to unauthorized sharing through employee blogs. The following step then estimates the extent to which this assertion holds true given the evidence.

Output: The final output of this step is a list of assertions for each knowledge asset that relates the knowledge asset to different technologies and potential threats.

Provide Evidence

Objective: The main objective of this step is to estimate the extent to which the assertions developed in the previous step hold true by evaluating the current measures, if any, in place to protect the knowledge assets from the identified threats. The steps required for achieving this objective are as follows.

Method:

- The manager identifies the different mechanisms in place to protect the knowledge assets from the different threats identified in the previous step and enters subjective judgments as to the extent to which the mechanisms reduce the risk of specific threats to the knowledge asset. For example, consider the threat of unauthorized sharing for a best practices knowledge asset through an extranet portal. In order to evaluate the assertion that "sharing best practices through extranet is not vulnerable to unauthorized sharing by the external entity", the manager may identify the mechanisms in place to protect the knowledge asset from unauthorized sharing as non disclosure agreements, access control mechanisms and digital rights management techniques.

- Then, the manager or an expert can input his/her own judgment about the effectiveness of the given techniques in protecting the knowledge asset from unauthorized sharing. Such judgments are captured on a 0-1 scale and are expressed as a degree of belief in support of the assertions, in support of the negation of the assertion and a degree of uncertainty. Delphi methods can be used to help achieve consensus among experts or analysts, and therefore, avoid the effect of subjective judgment when the values are assigned (Sun, et al., 2006).

Output: The output of this step is an evidential reasoning model that includes assertions and risk likelihood estimates from multiple experts combined in one model. This model will group these estimates in a hierarchical way in order to calculate the overall level of risk in the next step.

Calculate Risk

Objective: The main objective of this step is to calculate the overall level of risk by integrating estimates provided by experts in the previous step. This objective can be accomplished by following an analytical method that is based on the Dempster-Shafer theory to calculate risks (Dempster, 1968; Shafer, 1976).

Method:

- The Dempster-Shafer theory is based on the notion of combining separate pieces of evidence to calculate the probability of an event. It is a generalization of the Bayesian theory of subjective beliefs and is widely applied in diverse domains including information systems risk assessment (Sun, et al., 2006). The overall level of risk is calculated based on weights assigned for evidences within each assertion. The numbers associated with evidence and assertions such as the belief supporting the assertion and the belief negating the assertion can be assigned, as mentioned previously, by experienced managers and analysts.

Output: The output of this step would be the overall level of risk for each knowledge asset based on experts' estimates provided in the earlier step. Following the risk calculations, a ranking of knowledge assets based on the level of risk associated with sharing each knowledge assets through a particular technology is presented. For example, the risk of sharing a particular knowledge asset via technology X may be higher than sharing the same knowledge asset via technology Y.

Develop Policy

After the overall level of risk is calculated, the manager/s needs to develop a security policy in order to mitigate these risks. Mitigation efforts include technology solutions such as those described in (Becerra-Fernandez, et al., 2004), or policy and legal solutions. One way to mitigate risk, for example, is to focus on evaluating the reputation of potential partners, as explained in (Bayer & Maier, 2006), to help in anticipating opportunistic behavior.

A DECISION SUPPORT SYSTEMS FOR ASSESSING KNOWLEDGE SHARING RISKS

In this section, we present the design of a decision support system for knowledge sharing risks based on the risk assessment framework described earlier. The decision support system implements the risk assessment framework and includes analytical capabilities for ranking strategic knowledge assets, automatically developing a evidential reasoning model, and calculating risks based on the Dempster-Shaefer theory (Dempster, 1968; Shafer, 1976).

The basic components of the system, as shown in Figure 3, include an implementation of the risk assessment process, a knowledgebase of knowledge sharing risks for mapping knowledge assets to potential threats, multi-criteria decision algorithms to rank strategic knowledge assets and Dempster-Shaefer theory based algorithms for risk estimation. The design includes an interactive user interface to enable the manager to input information on knowledge assets and displays the evidential reasoning model as well as summary risk reports and recommendation. Figure 4 illustrates an activity diagram that highlights the risk assessment tasks.

As can be noted from the logic illustrated in the previous figure, the process starts by creating a profile for a particular business unit. The profile includes basic information such as the business unit name, number of companies and employees involved, and key processes. The next step would be to identify internal as well as external entities involved and the knowledge assets used in each of the processes followed by identification of technologies used to share those assets. The list of knowledge assets is then presented to the manager to elicit ratings on the value, imitability and rareness of the knowledge assets. The ratings are then processed by an AHP-based multi criteria decision algorithm (Saaty, 2008)that ranks the knowledge assets based on their strategic value. Using a pair-wise comparison matrix, the knowledge assets are compared to each other with respect to the value, imitability and rareness criteria and the overall score for a knowledge asset is determined by combining its priority scores for each criteria. The knowledge asset with the highest score is ranked as the most valuable asset.

Next, the system automatically develops an evidential reasoning model with assertions based on a knowledgebase of knowledge sharing risks, information on strategic knowledge assets, and the technologies through which they are shared. The process for generating the evidential reasoning model is shown in Figure 5. Specifically, it begins with a main assertion developed for each knowledge asset to represent the extent to which sharing the knowledge asset is secure. As in (Sun, et al., 2006), the formal representation of the main assertion can be given as: A_i (Sharing) = {(Secure, X), (Not Secure, Y)}

Where A_i (Sharing) denotes the assertion made on a particular Asset i, Secure and Not Secure denote the evaluation grades, X is the value or extent to which sharing A_i is secure, and Y is the value or the extent to which sharing A_i is not secure. The main assertion is then further decomposed into more detailed assertions that capture the risk of sharing the particular knowledge asset via a particular technology. Next, another level of sub-assertions is developed to decompose the knowledge sharing risks into the specific threats identified in Table 1. The manager then identifies mitigating measures currently in place to address the knowledge sharing risks and estimates the extent to which the mitigating measures address the knowledge sharing risks. Examples of mitigating measures include signing non-disclosure and non-compete agreements and using access control mechanisms. For each knowledge asset, a belief function is generated to assess risk factors by propagating across the model probability estimates on the extent to which the mitigating measures address the underlying risk factors. Finally, the system analyzes the information and outputs different reports that rank the assets based on their strategic value and overall risk to the knowledge asset, risk components and technology sources of the risk.

Figure 3. System components

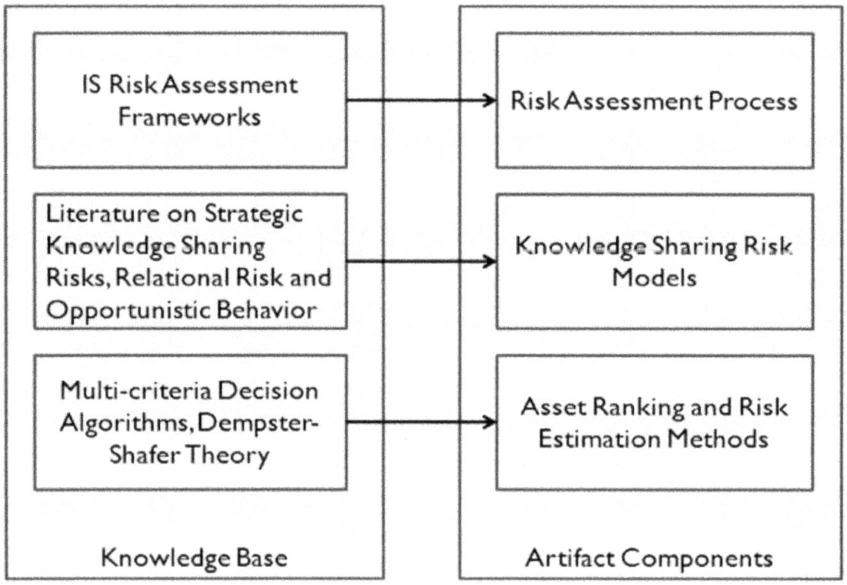

Figure 4. Activity flowchart

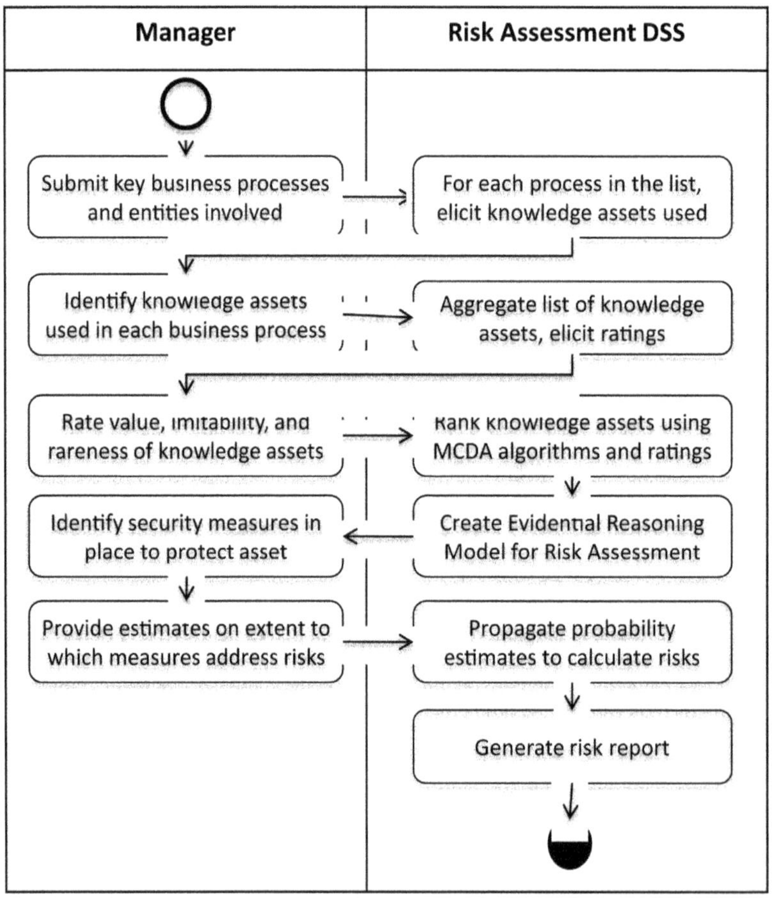

Figure 5. Process for building evidential reasoning model

1. **Identify the set of strategic knowledge assets**
2. **For each strategic knowledge asset A_i, create a main assertion regarding its overall security A_i (Sharing) = {(Secure, X), (Not Secure, Y)} where X and Y are unknown variables that represent the extent to which the knowledge asset is assumed to be secure or not secure.**
3. **For each main assertion about Ai, create a sub-assertion that identifies the technology through which the asset is shared and could be a sources of potential risks.**
4. **For each sub-assertion A_i (Sharing through Technology T), create a new sub-assertion that maps the parent sub-assertion to knowledge sharing risks identified Table 1.**
5. **For each sub-assertion of the form A_i (Sharing through Technology T is vulnerable to risk R), identify mitigating measures and elicit probabilities on the extent to which the mitigating measures prevent a particular threat, do not prevent a particular threat, and the level of uncertainty of the effect of the mitigating measure.**
6. **Propagate the probability estimates for each sub-assertion to the parent sub-assertions using Dempster-Shaefer rule and calculate the values for X and Y in Step 2.**

CONCLUSION

A critical dilemma that modern firms face in today's dynamic business environments is realizing the benefits of collaboration while maintaining competitive advantage, especially when collaboration involves sharing knowledge assets contributing to the firm's advantage. Incidents such as Intellectual Property (IP) leakage and failure of strategic alliances call for more research in this domain. While there is always a margin of error in predicting the success of inter-organizational relationships, organizations could benefit by following a more proactive approach in identifying potential vulnerabilities to strategic knowledge assets that are exposed in collaborative settings, which can help in the design of more efficient and dynamic securing policies.

In this chapter, we have reviewed, synthesized, and leveraged work in two relevant areas, knowledge management and risk assessment, in designing a potential approach for solving solving such dilemma. Specifically, our contributions in this chapter include (1) a risk assessment framework that assists project managers in identifying strategic knowledge assets that are shared through particular business processes using specific collaboration technologies. (2) a system design for a decision support system for knowledge sharing risks based on the knowledge risk assessment framework

To the best of our knowledge, our approach is among the first to present a structured framework for organizations to help identify strategic knowledge assets and their vulnerabilities. The knowledge sharing risk assessment framework can provide significant benefits to organizations in identifying and protecting their strategic knowledge assets and competitive advantage.

REFERENCES

Arakji, R. Y., & Lang, K. R. (2007). Digital consumer networks and producer–consumer collaboration: Innovation and product development in the video game industry. *Journal of Management Information Systems*, *24*(2), 195–219. doi:10.2753/MIS0742-1222240208

Bayer, F., & Maier, R. (2006, September). *Knowledge risks in inter-organizational knowledge transfer.* Paper presented at the the 6th International Conference on Knowledge Management, Austria.

Becerra-Fernandez, I., Gonzalez, A., & Shabherwal, R. (2004). *Knowledge management and KM software packages*. New Jersey: Prentice Hall.

Beeby, M., & Booth, C. (2000). Networks and inter-organizational learning: A critical review. *The Learning Organization*, *7*(2), 75–88. doi:10.1108/09696470010316260

Behrend, F. (2006). Collaborate today, compete tomorrow. *Knowledge Management Review*, *6*(5), 24–27.

Burrows, B. A. (2004, November, 10). A little less swagger at Cisco. *Business Week*. Retrived from http://www.businessweek.com/technology/content/nov2004/tc20041110_9788_tc024.htm

Carlsson, S. (2003). Strategic knowledge managing within the context of networks. In *Handbook on knowledge management: Knowledge matters*. New York, NY: Springer-Verlag.

Chui, M., Miller, A., & Roberts, R. (2009). Six ways to make Web 2.0 work. *The McKinsey Quarterly,* February.

COBIT. (2001). *IT governance institute*. Retrieved from http://www.ITgovernance.org

Cooper, S. (2009, June). Making sense of Web 2.0. *Small Business Edge*. Retrieved from http://www.smallbusinessedge.com/article/Technology/Making_Sense_of_Web_2.0_

Das, T. K., & Teng, B. (2001). Trust, control, and risk in strategic alliances: An integrated framework. *Organization Studies*, *22*(2), 251–284. doi:10.1177/0170840601222004

Das, T. K., & Teng, B. S. (1999). Managing risks in strategic alliances. *The Academy of Management 13*(4).

Dempster, A. P. (1968). A generalization of the Baysian inference. *Journal of the Royal Statistical Society. Series A (General)*, *30*, 205–447.

Dynes, S., Brechbühl, H., & Johnson, E. (2005). (2005). *Information security in the extended enterprise: Some initial results from a field study of an industrial firm.* Paper presented at the Workshop on the Economics of Information Security WEIS05, Boston, MA.

Dynes, S., Kolbe, L., & Schierholz, R. (2007, August). *Information security in the extended enterprise: A research agenda.* Paper presented at the the 13th Americas Conference on Information Systems AMCIS07, Denver, Colorado.

Fanning, E. (2007, March 19). Editor's note: Security for Web 2.0. *Computer World*. Retrieved from http://www.computerworld.com/s/article/283283/Security_for_Web_2.0

Farahmand, F., Navathe, S., Sharp, G., & Enslow, P. (2003, September). *Managing vulnerabilities of information systems to security incidents.* Paper presented at the the 5th International Conference on Electronic Commerce, Pittsburgh, Pennsylvania

Farahmand, F., Sharp, G., & Enslow, P. (2005). A management perspective on security threats to information systems. *Information Technology Management*, *6*, 203–225. doi:10.1007/s10799-005-5880-5

Freeze, R., & Kulkarni, U. (2005, January 3-6). *Knowledge management capability assessment: Validating a knowledge assets measurement instrument.* Paper presented at the the 38th Hawaii International Conference on Systems Sciences, Waikoloa, Hawaii

Goto, S. (2007). The bounds of classical risk management and the importance of a behavioral approach. *Risk Management & Insurance Review*, *10*(2). doi:10.1111/j.1540-6296.2007.00118.x

Hamm, S. (2006, October 23). IBM Takes on Amazon. *Business Week.* Retrieved from http://www.businessweek.com/technology/content/oct2006/tc20061023_158174.htm?chan=top+news_top+news+index_businessweek+exclusives,

Hargadon, A., & Sutton, R. (2000). Building innovation factory. *Harvard Business Review*, 157-166.

Herbst, M. (2009, January 9). Satyam's U.S clients face tough choices. *Business Week.* Retrieved from http://www.businessweek.com/bwdaily/dnflash/content/jan2009/db2009019_127597.htm?chan=technology_technology%20index%20page_computers

Information Technology Infrastructure Library ITIL. (2001). *The office of governement commerce.* Retrieved from http://www.itil-officialsite.com

Johnson, E., & Dynes, S. (2007, June 7-8). *Inadvertent disclosure: Information leaks in the extended enterprise.* Paper presented at the the 6th Workshop on the Economics of Information Security, Pittsburgh, PA.

Levy, M., & Powell, P. (2003). SMEs, co-opetition and knowledge sharing: The role of information systems. *European Journal of Information Systems*, *12*, 3–17. doi:10.1057/palgrave.ejis.3000439

Marshall, R. S., Nguyen, T., & Bryant, S. E. (2005). A dynamic model for trust development and knowledge sharing in strategic alliances. *Journal of General Management*, *31*(1), 41–57.

Medcof, J. W. (1997). Why too many alliances end in divorce. *Long Range Planning*, *30*(5). doi:10.1016/S0024-6301(97)00050-2

Mentzas, G., Apostolou, D., Kafentzis, K., & Georgolios, P. (2006). Inter-organizational networks for knowledge sharing and trading. *Information Technology Management*, *7*(4), 259–276. doi:10.1007/s10799-006-0276-8

Panteli, N., & Sockalingam, S. (2005). Trust and conflict within virtual inter-organizational alliances: A framework for facilitating knowledge sharing. *Decision Support Systems*, *39*(4), 599–617. doi:10.1016/j.dss.2004.03.003

Pardo, A. T., Cresswell, A., & Zhang, T. F. (2007). Knowledge sharing in cross-boundary information system development in the public sector. *Information Technology Management*, *7*, 293–313. doi:10.1007/s10799-006-0278-6

Probasco, M. (2009, July 20). *Workers flood blogs with company secrets.* Retrieved from http://www.newser.com/story/64791/workers-flood-blogs-with-company-secrets.html

Rees, J., Bandyopadhyay, S., & Spafford, E. (2003). PFIRES: A policy framework for information security. *Communications of the ACM*, *46*(7). doi:10.1145/792704.792706

Saaty, T. (2008). Decision making with the analytic hierarchy process. *International Journal of Services Sciences*, *1*(1), 83–89. doi:10.1504/IJSSCI.2008.017590

Schlaak, B., Dynes, S., Kolbe, L., & Schierholz, R. (2008, August 14-17). *Managing of information systems risks in extended enterprises-The case of outsourcing*. Paper presented at the the 14th Americas Conference on Information Systems, Toronto, Canada.

Shafer, G. (1976). *A mathematical theory of evidence*. Princeton, NJ: Princeton University Press.

Short, J. (2009, June). Risks in a web 2.0 world. *Risk Management*. Retrieved from http://www.rmmagazine.com/MGTemplate.cfm?Section=RMMagazine&NavMenuID=128&template=/Magazine/DisplayMagazines.cfm&IssueID=328&AID=3760&Volume=55&ShowArticle=1

Spring, T. (2008, May 23). Work for a big company? Odds are good your boss is reading your e-mail: Study. *PC World*. Retrieved from http://blogs.pcworld.com/staffblog/archives/007005.html

Stoneburner, G., Goguen, A., & Feringa, A. (2001). *Risk management guide for information technology systems: Recommendations of the National Institute of Standards and Technology*. NIST.

Sun, L., Srivastava, R., & Mock, T. (2006). An information systems security risk assessment model under the Dempster-Shafer theory of belief functions. *Journal of Management Information Systems*, *22*(4), 109–142. doi:10.2753/MIS0742-1222220405

Sutton, S., Hampton, C., Khazanchi, D., & Arnold, V. (2008). Risk analysis in extended enterprise environments: Identification of critical risk factors in B2B e-Commerce relationships. *Journal of the Association for Information Systems*, *9*(3/4).

(2000). *The Information Security Management Systems Family of Standards*. The International Organization for Standardization.

The OCTAVE Approach. (2003). *CERT Coordination Center*. Retrieved from http://www.cert.org/

Zhang, C., & Li, S. (2006). Secure information sharing in internet-based supply chain management systems. *Journal of Computer Information Systems*, *46*(4), 18–24.

2. RESEARCH METHODOLOGY

The aim of the study is to investigate the adoption of web-based learning amongst users. This led to the development of converging lines of inquiry, a process of triangulation (Yin 1994). In the first instance discussions were held together with three senior staff members involved in implementing the web-based learning project. They included the executive director, IT Manager, and an outside Consultant. In the second round separate individual interviews are conducted with these participants.

The third round of interviews was conducted with the admissions manager and separate individual interviews with two other staff members. Altogether six separate interviews with participants were held. Though the participant's gender is not a major factor for introspection, it coincided to balance, three males and three females. In the first round interviews the data collected were compared with the second round and third round interview data, for consistency, clarity and accuracy of the information.

Interview data were also compared to test for the factors having effect on users with high and low performance in learning how to use the web-based system. This provided the advantage of not duplicating the data with just one set of evidence. The discussions and interviews were open-ended (Yin 1994), the researcher in the beginning provided the topic, and the respondents are probed of their opinion about the events.

The questions are directed towards user's learning experience with the web-based system. This led the users in reflecting their recent learning experiences with the system and demonstrating its effectiveness in the web-based task. It provides the opportunity of capturing rich information that is fresh and part of the user-learning interface within the web-based system. It not only provides information about the user's learning experience, but also demonstrates the boundaries of the web-based learning system, in other words the scope of the system in providing enhanced learning is clearly reflected from the data the user's provided to what the system was capable of doing within the parameters. This approach took into consideration the users and the system context in understanding the web-based learning process. It provides important information from the user's perspective in the terms of the learning process available in the web-based system.

3. CASE ANALYSIS

The case study examines the web-based framework of the University of Australia (not the real name). International students have the option to lodge an admission application through either of: web-based e-service on the Internet, phone, fax, or in person. On receiving the application a decision is made by the staff on the admission status. Within this process the department is implementing an electronic delivery of its services on the website. Web-based e-service has been in use for the last two and half years. The complete process involves students making the application and the staff processing applications on the website. The staff is currently using the web-based e-service and the paper-based system in conducting the tasks. Transition from paper-based to web-based e-service is believed by the department to be a significant step in the direction of moving the complete student admission process over the website and gradually removing the paper-based system. The users learning experience in adopting the web-based system is focus of attention in the study.

4. EXPLORING USER'S INFORMATION EXPERIENCE ON WEBSITES

Specific expertise needed for conducting the task was lacking. Different task requires different skills when done on paper, doing it electronically requires different experience with information and knowing what was happening beyond the user's computer screen. In the paper-based system, it was known to the user how different process of a task and where information was stored and retained when needed, such as the filing, organizing, storing of documentation was systematically interconnected, in case of electronic service little was known by way what constituted as web-based e-service task process beyond the computer screen. Proper documentation providing information to the user's for referencing were either missing or unknown. The users didn't have learning experience in how to operate the system. One participant mentioned:

User's had no confidence in the system and decision making.

The user perception of web electronic service is a burden and acted as a barrier to their work. The users learnt that it increased the workload, slowed the work process, and brought in complexity to the task. The department did not implement electronic services or introduce technology into jobs at the same time. The effect on user learning experience in using the e-service is not estimated when the system was being developed. Understanding the task sequence from start to finish, and integrating those functions into web-based learning process is missing. It lacks coherence. Individual users did not have consistent skills in learning how to use the system because of differing levels of expertise (i.e., user category).

The users were asked to enter all information directly to the web. To expect a user to start using an electronic service without prior learning the user's experience is not perceive to be appropriate. Despite providing regular training the user resistance to use the electronic system increased. The following quote support this notion:

There are quite a few fields where we can't use the web-based e-services.

Martin (1991) suggest that user learning experience evolves, or ranges, from naïve (no system knowledge) through inexperienced to competent and finally to expert. On such basis user's can be divided into following categories: novice, intermediate, and experienced. It is important to remember that different categories of user's learning experience vary at different stages in performing the task. It is anticipated the user's are in a learning process and shift from one mode to another, with experience sliding up or down on the learning swing and the user experience varies, till they reach a point (see Figure 1, point A) where the learning experience flow is at the optimum level in doing the task.

The assimilation and dissimulation of learning experience in conducting the web-based e-service task may provide the user an option in retaining that experience which can be remembered easily. A participant claimed:

Need to rely on paper documents and another database to complete the task... have to use all...

The information disclosed by the participant point to the fact that the web-based system was short from offering the user a learning process which if available would have gradually build on user's prior information experience, rather the user's were juggling with multiple sources to collect the information that was needed in completing the web-based task.

The experience attained in online or offline environment is likely to direct the user in retaining the most recent learning experience because this would be much easier to recall, provided that the information is relevant to the current context. Zemke and Connellan (2001) posit that each learning experience, regardless of whether it's online or offline, sets the stage of expectations for future interactions. The user tends to focus on ease of use (more than the usefulness), familiarity, skills needed, website-to-website learning comparison, and on the task complexity. The task complexi-

Figure1. Learning-experience swing

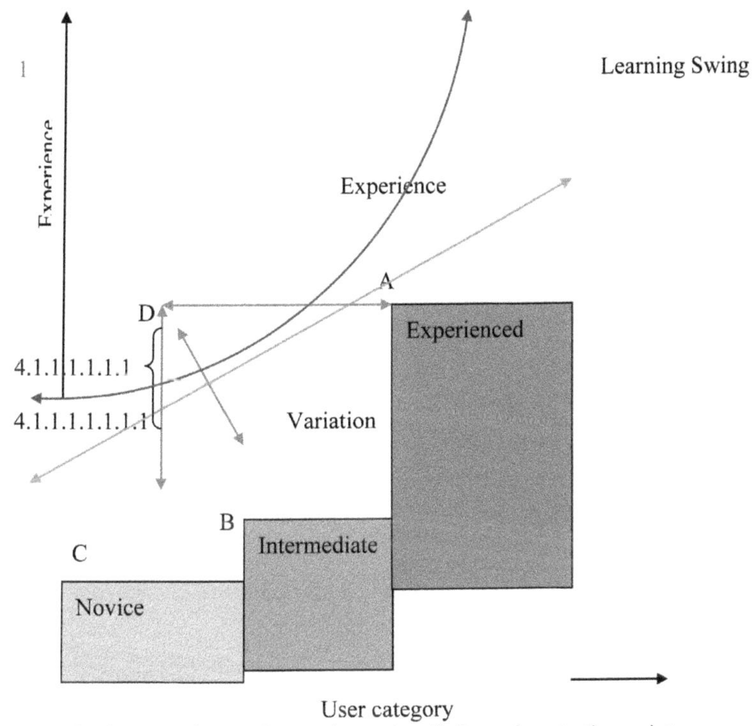

A- Optimum point; B- Improving point; C- Learning starting point;
Experience variation point

ties can be defined in terms of navigation on the website, information search, transaction processing, and online support (i.e., help). A participant related this in terms of the web-based system as:

System is not intelligent to check simple errors like spell checks, grammar checks...

The statement referred to the user's learning expectation of the systems capabilities in terms of their prior experience. The user's had used this functionality in another system and expected to match with their prior information experience in the web-based system. The user's perceived experience about the current system being below its standard and not helpful in doing the task. It did not meet the user's information requirement for the task.

Similarly if the user's needs are met on one dimension and unmet on another, they are actively searching for an alternative on another website or in offline environment. This is supported in our study; the participants reported switching to the paper-based system, as the learning process and its outcome was easier to understand and follow. Zemke and Connellan (2001) suggest that to succeed on the website, it is important to consistently manage the total user learning experience (i.e. information experience) in the categories in upper three (black) boxes (see Figure 2). They claim to have successfully used the model at Dell Computers in understanding the total user's interaction. However, there is no quantitative data and analysis of the model that suggest how well the model works across web-based e-learning.

Zemke and Connellan (2001) developed a model (Customer Experience Grid, see Figure 2) to capture the sum total of a user learning experiences. The vertical axis of the user experience grid is the outcome the user receives, and offered on a website. On the horizontal axis the user's goes through the learning process to obtain the outcome, such as navigating the website, printing out information, looking for pricing, ordering a product etc. User compares similar outcomes on other website or in an offline environment in user transaction process. Zemke and Connellan (2001) claim that the process – the way they are served – is what makes it into learning experience, positively or negatively for users. If the user's needs are not met on the process and outcome axes, they tend to go elsewhere, and hence called defectors.

The user's interaction in computer mediated environment is an intense flow being a continuous variable ranging from none to intense (Berthon and Davies 1999; Foulkes 1994; Hasher and Zacks 1984; Chea and Lou 2008; and Chellappan 2008). The user's purpose of visit to the website may be perceived as more encouraging of exploratory behaviors than others (Trevino and Webster 1992). If the website meets the primary information need of the user, it may positively affect the user in further progressing with the activity leading to a state of intense flow. It is likely that user's developing a high flow will visit those websites more regularly and for longer duration (Berthon et al. 1996; and Berthon and Davies 1999). The state of intense learning flow was either missing or faced obstacles. The users weren't able to proceed with the task in the electronic environment. User may tend to reflect on the past experience for future interaction. A participant reflected this in a statement:

The system is not 100% ready...Adds on to the task...increases our task load.

It was believed that the users were loosing learning interest in the web-based system due to continuously being put down. To retain interest

Figure 2. User experience grid

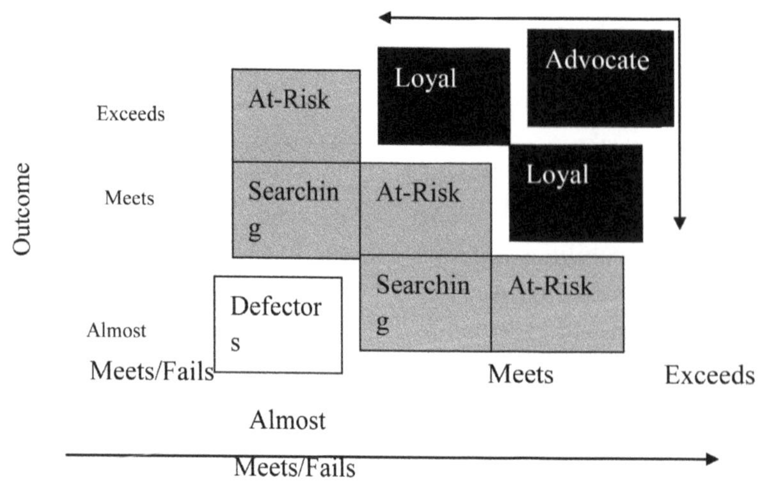

in a site, there should be enjoyment on the part of the user during the interaction of the site. A participant statement highlights this concern:

If the system can be fixed it can be fixed, otherwise we will continue using it as it is.

It was known to the users that if the web-based system didn't work they could depend on an alternative system (i.e., paper-bases system) in doing the task. The shifting of learning experience between the paper-based and web-based emerged as a continuum on which the user viewed the web-based system effectiveness before proceeding with the task, which was based on an understanding from past experience. If the user felt the task could be (not only) performed and also completed they went ahead with the web-based system; otherwise they opted for the paper-based system. Any adverse feelings were filtered towards learning the web-based system at that time affecting the decision making to use the web-based system. Those claims were supported by participant statements:

Verifying information on the Internet is not possible; we still have to check student's education credential in paper form

Site needs to be improved with better features and functionality that will make it easier for us to use.

In the flow state, the user's focus or attention is narrowed to a limited stimulus field, and irrelevant thoughts are filtered out. Csikszentmihalyi (1975) suggest that in a flow state the person becomes absorbed in the activity, while increasing his awareness of his own mental processes in the interaction with the web, the computer screen can serve as the limited stimulus field, focusing the individual's attention (Trevino and Webster 1992). The user faced hurdles during the flow state affecting their learning in doing the task. A participant expressed this:

Due to time out period that disconnect, the user has to reenter all the information once again... this creates duplicity of information for us...as the same user is reapplying again and it is hard to differentiate between the same application.

As users become more frequent users they place more reliance on learning from internal sources (memory) than external sources (advertisements, word of mouth, etc) (Johnson and Mathews 1997). Many researchers have noted the ways in which memory is biased (Foulkes 1994). Frequent events are easier to recall than infrequent ones (Hasher and Zacks 1984). Therefore remembering an event is biased by the availability of information within memory (Johnson and Mathews 1997). The mechanical process of conducting the task with the available tools on the website forms a basis of interactivity for the user and is similar to recalling frequent and infrequent events. Prior research suggests the application of tools to vary across different users from novice to advance (see Martin 1991).

The development of intelligent agents guiding the user in conducting the task from start to completion tends to improve the user learning interface and reduce uncertainty in learning and problematic experience. This has led to smart software taking over the task, reducing and limiting user's interactivity with the task, and completion of task within a few ticks and clicks of a mouse. The whole process tends to be reduced, removing the intricacies the user can encounter, and at the same time standardizing the users web-based learning across all domain and user developing a positive experience.

The intelligent agent capability in storing and remembering user's transaction details, and displaying on revisits has also reduced the user's need to keep paper record of transaction, making it easier for the user in conducting the task with the availability of past, current and future information records available online. This has an effect on the user learning experience in using the traditional service where the information available is not swift and quick. A reliance on internal search means that the user's memory will have considerable influence on the formation of "learning expectancies" (Foulkes 1994). Hasher and Zacks (1984) argue that the accuracy with which people encode information increases with the frequency of encoding. Although their research focuses on consumers' exposure to advertising, a parallel can be drawn with consumers' exposure to web-based e-learning. Similarly, Zeithaml et al. (1993;2000) in their study pointed to information gap on the basis of users learning experience with website that leads to providing incomplete or in accurate information to the users. It is anticipated that the application of intelligent agents in user interactivity will further enhance and integrate into the user learning experience with information, and become part of the user guidance in conducting web-based task. A participant directed the claim:

If any information is missed, there is no way to check, there are no compulsory fields to inform of missing information.

Meuter et al. (2000) report that 80% of the customer complaints are made in person to the company, either by phone or by visiting a service facility. This suggests that the when the user is effected with a problematic experience on websites, and to resolve the issue, the user adopts the traditional approach of face-to-face interaction, rather than online approach. The participant in the study evaluated the web-based task, and weighted its effectiveness by comparing it to the paper-based service.

We can't offer admission letters to higher degree research students on the web-based system, as letter templates not there; we have to offer it on paper.

The degree of tolerance for web-based system may be intense due to the competitor's service being a click away (Zeithaml et al 2000). The users are quick in changing over to paper-based service, which is believed competing with the web-based system. Thus user's tolerance level for web-based system, their immediate reactions to the service failure and their consecutive behavior, are interrelated and forms part of the user learning experience. A participant expressed:

If the system can be fixed it can be fixed, otherwise we will continue using as it is.

When the web-based system fails it has fallen outside the user's zone of tolerance (Zeithaml et al. 1993). So far nothing is known about user's tolerance levels of web-based systems, or the user's propensity to complain about online service failures (Riel et al. 2001), and user's reaction to it. Zeithaml et al. (2000) claim that customers have no expectations, customers have been found to compare web-based service to competitor's services and to brick and mortar stores (Meuter et al. 2000 and Szymanski and Hise 2000). The degree of user's tolerance is not known. Another participant states;

They are frightened for asking help if needed... rather they ask for help than provide wrong information.

It seemed there are considerable obstacles the user's developed in their learning experience to use web-based system.

5. CONCLUSION

In understanding the new set of implications, initial research revealed that though uptake and use of this new innovation has been positive, its acceptance and continued use has been limited.

The available research though identifies some main issues it lacks in understanding the impact of the critical success factors. Further research will attempt to explore a more structured understanding to web-based systems user learning within a referenced theoretical construct.

From the preceding discussion it has been clear that web-based system adoption is not a simple and straightforward process. Rapid development in technology delivery is gradually shaping the consumer learning in uptake and usage of this new innovation. The level of interaction from traditional services to web-based services and simultaneous use of both has laid a new set of implications for the universities, organizations, government, consumers, practitioners, and researchers.

In line with the preceding discussion it is suggested that web-based systems adoption takes into account the user learning experience that develops with user interaction with the system. Though prior studies even adopted the general technology user models like the TAM model (Davis 1989; Davis et al. 1989; and Davis 1993), which is of significance, they do not take into account the user context issues on a commercial situation basis.

To study web-based system from a user learning perspective centered context and combining it with adoption and acceptance models may enhance that understanding. To explore the context further, issues related to situation specific personalization of individual user learning needs in online and offline environment may be used to produce evaluation guidelines that would facilitate the adoption and continuation process.

Earlier studies investigated the adoption of web-based system in different contexts, but not provide insight into acceptance and continued use by users. Though a consumer may use a web-based system for the first time, its continued use relates to the success. The user's web-based learning experience may form an impression of the system in terms of how easy or how difficult it is to operate the system.

REFERENCES

Berthon, P., & Davies, T. (1999). Going with the flow: Websites and customer involvement. *Internet Research: Electronic Networking Applications and Policy*, *9*(2), 109–116. doi:10.1108/10662249910264873

Berthon, P., Pitt, L., & Watson, R. T. (1996). The World Wide Web as an advertising medium: Toward an understanding of conversion efficiency. *Journal of Advertising Research*, *36*, 43–45.

Csikszentmihalyi, M. (1975). *Beyond boredom and anxiety*. San Francisco, CA: Jossey-Bass.

Csikszentmihalyi, M., & LeFevre, J. (1989). Optimal experience in work and leisure. *Journal of Personality and Social Psychology*, *56*(5), 815–822. doi:10.1037/0022-3514.56.5.815

D'Ambra, J., & Rice, R. E. (2001). Emerging factors in user evaluation of the world wide web. *Information & Management*, *38*, 373–384. doi:10.1016/S0378-7206(00)00077-X

Davidow, W. H., & Uttal, B. (1989). Service companies: Focus or falter. *Harvard Business Review*, (4): 17–34.

Davis, F. D. (1989). Perceived usefulness, perceived ease of use, and user acceptance of information technology. *Management Information Systems Quarterly*, *13*(2), 319–340. doi:10.2307/249008

Davis, F. D. (1993). User acceptance of information technology: Systems characteristics, user perceptions and behavioral impacts. *International Journal of Man-Machine Studies*, *38*(3), 475–487. doi:10.1006/imms.1993.1022

Davis, F. D., Bagozzi, R. P., & Warshaw, P. R. (1989). User acceptance of computer technology: A comparison of two theoretical models. *Management Science*, *34*(8), 982–1002. doi:10.1287/mnsc.35.8.982

Foulkes, V. S. (1994). How consumers predict service quality: What do they expect? In Oliver, R. L. (Ed.), *Service quality, New directions in theory and practice*. Beverly Hills, CA: Sage Publication.

Hasher, L., & Zacks, R. T. (1984). Automatic processing of fundamental information: The case of frequency of occurrence. *The American Psychologist, 39*, 1372–1388. doi:10.1037/0003-066X.39.12.1372

Hoffman, D. L., & Novak, T. P. (1996). Marketing in hypermedia computer-mediated environments: Conceptual foundations. *JMR, Journal of Marketing Research, 60*(7), 50–68.

Johnson, C., & Mathews, B. P. (1997). The influence of experience on service expectations. *International Journal of Service Industry Management, 8*(4), 290–305. doi:10.1108/09564239710174381

Karahanna, E., Straub, D. W., & Chervany, N. L. (1999). Information technology adoption across time: A cross sectional comparison of pre-adoption and post-adoption beliefs. *Management Information Systems Quarterly, 23*(2), 183–213. doi:10.2307/249751

Martin, M. P. (1991). *Analysis and design of business information systems*. New York, NY: Macmillan Publishing Company.

Meuter, M. L., Ostrom, A. L., Roundtree, R. I., & Bitner, M. J. (2000). Self-service technologies: Understanding customer satisfaction with technology-based service encounters. *Journal of Marketing, 64*, 50–64. doi:10.1509/jmkg.64.3.50.18024

Oliver, R. L. (1993). *Service quality, new directions in theory and practice*. Beverly Hills, CA: Sage Publication.

Riel, A. C. R., Liljander, V., & Jurriens, P. (2001). Exploring consumer evaluations of e-services: A portal site. *International Journal of Service Industry Management, 12*(4), 359–377. doi:10.1108/09564230110405280

Sandhu, K., & Corbitt, B. (2002). *Exploring an understanding of electronic service end-user adoption*. The International Federation for Information Processing, WG8.6, Sydney.

Szymanski, D. M., & Hise, R. T. (2000). E-satisfaction: An initial examination. *Journal of Retailing, 76*(3), 309–322. doi:10.1016/S0022-4359(00)00035-X

Trevino, L. K., & Webster, J. (1992). Flow in computer-mediated communication: Electronic mail and voice evaluation. *Communication Research, 19*(2), 539–573. doi:10.1177/009365092019005001

Yin, R. K. (1994). *Case study research: Design and methods* (2nd ed.). Sage Publications.

Zeithaml, V. A., Berry, L., & Parasuraman, A. (1993). The nature and determinants of customer expectations of service. *Journal of the Academy of Marketing Science, 21*(1), 1–12. doi:10.1177/0092070393211001

Zeithaml, V. A., Parasuraman, A., & Malhotra, A. (2000). *A conceptual framework for understanding e-service quality: Implications for future research and managerial practice*. Marketing Science Institute, Working paper, Report no: 00-115.

Zemke, R., & Connellan, T. (2001). *E-service: 24 ways to keep your customers when the competition is just a click away*. American Management Association.

Chapter 14
A Predictive Modeling of Retail Satisfaction:
A Data Mining Approach to Retail Service Industry

M. Hemalatha
M.A.M. College of Engineering, India

ABSTRACT

Data mining allows managers to make more knowledgeable decisions by predicting future trends and behaviors. One of the most widely used areas of data mining for the retail industry is in marketing. There are also at least seven methods of analysis or statistical techniques that are commonly used in data mining. It is obvious that the approach to the data mining is the key determinant of the statistical technique to be used. Predictive modeling uses variety of techniques such as linear regression, logistic regression, and their extensions can be used to identify patterns, which can be used to predict the future. This research specifically focuses on the application of multiple regression technique a data mining tool in Indian retail industries to predict the retail satisfaction using store attributes as independent variables.

1. INTRODUCTION

Data analysis, especially statistics, has been used in the social life of human beings for more than two hundred years. Data analysis could not widely affect our daily life until the creation of computer in 1950s. Using computational and storage power of computer, people gradually developed database, database management system, and data warehouse in the last 40 years. These computing environments provided the bases for us to efficiently use a number of mathematical tools, such as statistics, artificial intelligence, machine learning, and so on to solve larger-scale data analysis problems. Now, here comes data mining, the interface of some of the approaches. Strictly speaking, data mining discovers the hidden patterns of data from a large-scale data warehouse by precise mathematical means (Cheng *et al.*, 2006).

DOI: 10.4018/978-1-4666-0948-8.ch014

Loosely speaking, data mining may refer to the analysis of the large quantities of data that were stored in computers. It can be viewed from three different angles: process, methodology, and mathematical methods. From the aspect of the process, data mining consists of four stages: (1) selecting, (2) transforming, (3) mining, and (4) interpreting. While stages (1) and (4) are mainly business-related problems, stages (2) and (3) involve mathematical modeling and computer algorithms. From the aspect of methodology, the functions of data mining can be classified as association, classification, clustering, predictions, sequential patterns, and similar time sequences. Each function can be applied to different nature of the problems. From the aspect of mathematical methods, the functions of data mining can be implemented through statistics decision tree, neural networks, rough set, fuzzy logic and mathematical programming (Cheng *et al.,* 2006).

Data mining has become a widely accepted process for organizations to enhance their organizational performance and gain a competitive advantage. Because the data mining process is a relatively new concept, it has been defined in various ways by various authors in the recent past. The definitions of data mining given by these authors are somewhat different but all have the same idea: to extract important information from existing data and enable better decision making throughout an organization. Not only data mining can improve decision making by searching for relationships and patterns from the extensive data collected by organizations, but it can also reduce information overload (Zhu *et al.*, 2001). Data mining enables an organization to focus on the most important information in the database, which allows managers to make more knowledgeable decisions by predicting future trends and behaviors. Before data mining was utilized, managers were not as capable of making such informed decisions because searching through large amounts of data was too expensive and time-consuming.

One of the most widely used areas of data mining for the retail industry is in marketing. Market basket analysis is a marketing method used by many retailers to determine the optimal locations to promote products. Another marketing tactic employed by many retail stores is the use of loyalty cards. There are an increasing number of retail companies utilizing data mining for marketing purposes and benefiting from its use. Risk management is another area where data mining is used in the retail industry; however, there has not been as much research done in this area. Retail industries must also be aware that fraud detection is necessary. Fraud occurring at POS terminals is a concern for retailers, but can be reduced using data mining (Hormozi and Giles, 2004).

In marketing, data mining enables an organization to sort through vast amounts of customer data to target the right customers. In risk management, data mining helps an organization predict the number of customers who are likely to be lost to competitors, so that the business can be better prepared. Data mining is useful for fraud detection because, by detecting these fraudulent actions, an organization can keep from losing substantial amounts of money. Data mining is also important for customer acquisition and retention, enabling an organization to target new customers and retain the customers it already has. Those industries that effectively utilize data mining have the ability to develop or enhance a competitive advantage (Hormozi and Giles, 2004).

Throughout the literature, data mining operations are also classified in different ways. The following are a few categorizations of data mining operations, including (1) clustering/segmentation, (2) visualization, (3) predictive modeling, (4) link analysis, (5) deviation detection, (6) dependency modeling, and (7) summarization (Hormozi and Giles, 2004). This study made an attempt to identify the dimensions of retail satisfaction based on the retail strategy mix which influences the shopper's shopping behaviour using predictive modeling (multiple regression) technique.

First we developed a scale for measuring the retail satisfaction by literature review and focus group interview. Then we checked the reliability and validity of the instrument developed. Finally we developed a multiple regression model for the retail satisfaction measurement which will help the retailers to decide their retail strategy mix for planning retail events. The multiple regression model has been built based on the factors which influences the shopping behaviour of apparel shoppers during the clearance sale. The result of multiple regression analysis of the retail satisfaction depicts that higher the level of merchandise, discount, employee service and retail operation will lead to higher clearance sales store satisfaction. Similarly price, promotion, retail services and store atmosphere have an insignificant effect on clearance sales store satisfaction.

2. A SNAPSHOT ON INDIAN RETAIL INDUSTRY

Anything involved in direct selling to a consumer at any point of time can be termed as retailing. This retailing can be done in a shopping mall, in a departmental store or in a basic mom-and-pop store. A retailer has to identify a good location for his operations, and attract consumers using advertising and promotional schemes. Retailers succeed in forming a bond with the consumer through personalised attention via face-to-face interaction and convenient geographical location (Sharma, 2008). Organised retail in India has seen remarkable growth in the last decade. In addition to the blossoming economy, one of the major drivers of this strong growth trajectory can be attributed to the rapid mall development in the country (Kuruvilla and Ganguli, 2008).

According to AT kearney's report, India is the world's 4th largest economy in terms of purchasing power parity after USA, China and Japan. It is expected to move to the third position in the future. India is rated ahead of China on the foreign direct investment index making it an attractive retail market among other emerging economies in the world. Indian retail sector is experiencing highest growth in the world. The potential growth is so vast that the Indian market just cannot be ignored. India's retail market which currently stands at USD 350 billion is expected to grow to further. The organized retail sector, currently pegged at USD 8 billion is also expected to grow further (Shivani and Usha, 2008).

As western markets become saturated, global retailers are seeing the developing world as the new frontier. India in particular has become a place to be: Marks and Spencer, Wal-Mart and Carrefour are joining domestic brands Reliance, Bharti Enterprises, Aditya Birla and Pantaloon in announcing ambitious expansion plans, indicate their intention to capitalise on the tremendous growth of the retail sector. But, as on any new frontier, many challenges accompany the potential gains. Organised retailing on a corporate scale has grown significantly in India over the past three years (Jindal, 2008).

India is the ninth-largest retail market in the world. It is expected to grow to further in the coming years. At present, organised retailing comprises only six per cent of the market, but its share is expected to rise to 15 per cent within two years. This growth is being driven by several factors. Retail demand in India is being fuelled by country's huge middle class, a large young working population which is less burdened than previous generations with educating children and providing healthcare for elderly parents, while retirement is still a long way off, Meanwhile, India's economy is increasing rapidly (Jindal, 2008).

This would create opportunities for organized retail, as an increase in purchasing power would mean a higher demand for better shopping ambience, superior quality products, and improved service. Improved access to education and exposure to the latest trends through various media have also led to an increase in demand for lifestyle goods. Indian consumers, like their international counterparts, are becoming increasingly demanding and knowledgeable. They are tough critics, savvy purchasers, value-driven spenders and practical thinkers when it comes to shopping. The demand for their time at work and home has made them extremely selective about how they would want to spend their limited and precious leisure hours. Shopping today is much more than just buying; it is an experience in itself. To best utilize the available time, Indian consumer is on the look-out for avenues that would give him the maximum value for his money and time spent (Parikh, 2006).

In emerging markets around the world, the spending power of consumers is rapidly changing the retail industry, both globally and locally. Multinational retailers seeking new sources of growth are watching the mass markets of Brazil, China, and India, whose large populations and strong economic growth have made them nearly irresistible. As consumers have greater disposable income, they increasingly spend their money on items beyond the basic necessities (Bharadwaj *et al*., 2005). It has been well documented in the marketing literature that customer satisfaction is critical to any businesses' success. However, it is far less clear as on how marketers comprehend customer differences in customer satisfaction evaluations, and leverage such understanding in forming their marketing strategies. Recently researchers have begun to explore the notion of individual or segment differences in the formation of overall satisfaction judgments (Jianan and DeSarbo, 2005).

Data mining can also help in acquiring and retaining customers in the retail industry. The retail industry must deal with an enormous amount of competition and can use data mining to better understand what their customers' needs are. A retailer can study customers' past purchasing histories and know with what kinds of promotions and incentives to target customers. Also, if a store has seen a number of people leave the store and go to competitors, data mining can be used to study the customers' past purchasing histories and then use this information to keep other customers from going to a competitor store (Hormozi and Giles, 2004).

In business, firms are shifting their marketing approach from mass marketing to relationship based marketing leading to an era of customer relationship management. CRM requires sustainable long term relationship with customers and allocation of resources to maintain these relationships (Aeron *et al.,* 2010). Customer Relationship Management systems are adopted by the organisations in order to achieve success in the business and also to formulate business strategies, which can be formulated based on the predictions given by the data mining tools. Basically three major areas of data mining research are identified: implementation of CRM systems, evaluation criteria for data mining software and CRM systems and methods to improve data quality for data mining (Sharma *et al*., 2008). In this paper, multiple regression approach is presented and discussed with respect to Indian retail market.

3. APPLICATION OF DATA MINING IN RETAIL SECTOR

Sharing of data among multiple organisations is required in many situations. The shared data may contain sensitive information about individuals which if shared may lead to privacy breach. Thus, maintaining the individual privacy is a great challenge. In order to overcome the challenges involved in data mining, when data needs to be shared, privacy preserving data mining has evolved as a solution (Kumar *et al*., 2011). Similarly computational and digital advancements with the advent of relationship marketing have changed the land signs of business. Digital revolution led to generation and collection of data in companies and extracting knowledge from this data through knowledge discovery in databases (KDD) process. KDD involves many steps, of which an important step is data mining. Data mining is a process of extracting patterns in data through statistical and other techniques and algorithms (Aeron *et al.,* 2010).

Managing the growing problem of computer fraud within organisations has led researchers and practitioners to emphasise the need to take into account the 'social' aspects of information security. In addition, wider organisational issues such as lack of communication have been associated with computer fraud. In trying to minimise 'opportunities' for computer fraud, Shalini (2008) argues that managers' awareness and knowledge of how an organisation functions can significantly affect the effectiveness of management information security. This is because managers can send 'cues' to other employees, which influence how the latter perceive and abide by information security and other policies and procedures in their daily activities. Such perception and application are examples of tacit knowledge development. Data mining is a new technology that helps businesses to predict future trends and behaviours, allowing them to make proactive, knowledge-driven decisions. When data mining tools and techniques are applied on the data warehouse based on customer records, they search for the hidden patterns and trends. These can be further used to improve customer understanding and acquisition (Sharma *et al.*, 2008).

Today, organizations are realizing the advantages that come with the utilization of data mining. Data mining is proving to be a valuable tool, by identifying potentially useful information from the large amounts of data collected, and enabling an organization to gain an advantage over its competitors. Marketing is one of the foremost areas where data mining techniques can be applied. Data mining enables an organization to sort through vast amounts of customer data to target the right customers. This is of vital importance to the marketing department of any organization. Substantial amounts of time and money can be saved if an organization knows who their customers are and are able to predict what their spending patterns will be. By better understanding customers, an organization is able to target those customers who have a higher chance of responding favorably (Hormozi and Giles, 2004).

Data mining also represents a step in the process of knowledge discovery in databases (KDD). The recent rapid increase in KDD tools and techniques for a growing variety of applications needs to follow a consistent process. The business requirement that any KDD solution must be seamlessly integrated into an existing environment makes it imperative that vendors, researchers, and practitioners all adhere to the technical standards that make their solutions interoperable, efficient, and effective. Providing a realistic view of this field, these articles should help identify the opportunities for applying data mining tools and techniques in any area of research or practice, now and in the future. They also reflect the beginning of a still new science and the foundation for what will become a theory of effective inference from and exploitation of all those massive databases (Fayyad and Uthurusamy, 2002).

There are at least six data mining approaches. Most of these are well known in the marketing literature. However, a brief review is in order. Classification - Assigning data to unique classes such as regular buyers and occasional buyers, Regression - Establishing a relationship between series of items, such as that upper income customers buy more from us, Time Series - Establishing a relationship between properties of timed information, such as our customers income have increased two fold during the past ten years, Clustering - Simplifying large number of observations by creating a set of generalizations such as 60 percent of our sales are from two groups of people professionals and skilled white collar workers, Association - Identifying what customers buy in a shopping visit, such as beer and potato chips and Sequential Analyzers - Analysis of sequential events such as car sales, then battery sales (Samli *et al.*, 2002).

There are also at least seven methods of analysis or statistical techniques that are commonly used in data mining. It is obvious that the approach to the data mining is the key determinant of the statistical technique to be used. If for example, there is a need for clustering of certain market segments, it is not generic algorithms but k-nearest neighbor technique needs to be employed. Decision Trees - These tree-shaped structures describe a set of rules that facilitate a decision such as to purchase a product. They may be used to generate customer databases, Genetic Algorithms - These are optimization techniques. They provide the opportunity to determine the best model to be used for a given set of data. They facilitate identification of hidden patterns. They are not good for segmentation and clustering applications, Neural Networks - These are non-linear predictive models leads to detecting patterns in regard to clustering, sequencing and predictions, Predictive Modeling - A variety of techniques such as linear regression, logistic regression and their extensions can be used to identify patterns which can be used to predict the future, Rule Induction - This is a process of extracting if.then.rules from data based on statistical significance, Fuzzy Logic - This technique handles imprecise concepts (like small, big, young etc.) and is more flexible than other techniques. It generates the notion of a fuzzy set rather than clear demarcation boundaries such as .9 or .64. and K-nearest neighbor (K-NN) - it places an object of interest into a class or group by examining its attributes and grouping it with others whose attributes are closest to it. It enables discovery of associations and sequences (Samli *et al.*, 2002).

In today's competitive environment, rapid advances in economic globalization and information technology have forced many organizations to anticipate and respond to increasing volatility and competitive pressures. Numerous researches have focused on developing techniques on the analysis, design and management of whole business in particular in the domain of data mining, data analysis and data classification. While the data mining techniques and computational intelligence techniques are good independently for solving specific tasks, they can be synergized through the formation of an integrated and unified model (Ho *et al.*, 2004).

The traditional approach to data analysis for decision support has been to couple domain expertise with statistical modeling techniques to develop handcrafted solutions for specific problems. More recently, several trends have emerged to challenge this approach. One is the increasing availability of large volumes of high-dimensional data occupying database tables with millions of rows and thousands of columns. Another is the competitive demand for the rapid construction and deployment of data-driven analytics. A third is the need to give end users analysis results in a form they readily understand and assimilate, helping them gain the insights they need to make critical business decisions (Apte *et al.*, 2002).

During the past few years, recognition of the strategic value of business analytics has led to significant developments in business applications that analyze customer data. Newer applications analyze the data to provide insights about the performance of suppliers and partners, material expenditures, accuracy of sales forecasts for controlling materials inventory, accuracy of production plans, and accuracy of plans for order delivery. The massive databases requiring a mix of automated analysis techniques and human effort to give business users strategic insight about the activity on their sites, as well as about the characteristics of the sites' visitors and customers. With many millions of click streani records generated every day, aggregated to customer focused records with hundreds of attributes, there is a clear need for automated techniques for finding patterns in the data (Kohavi *et al.*, 2002).

Business users, while expert in their particular areas, are still unlikely to be expert in data analysis and statistics. To make decisions based on the data collected by and about their organizations, they must either rely on data analysts to extract information from the data or employ analytic applications that blend data analysis technologies with task-specific knowledge. In the former, business users impart domain knowledge to the analyst, then wait for the analyst to organize and analyze it and communicate back the results. These results typically raise further questions, hence several iterations are necessary before business users can actually act on the analysis. In the latter, analytic applications incorporate not only a variety of data mining techniques but provide recommendations to business users as to how to best analyze the data and present the extracted information (Kohavi *et al*, 2002).

Moreover, knowledge discovery in databases (KDD) techniques emphasizing scalable, reliable, fully automated, explanatory structures have shown that in data analysis, such structures supplement, and sometimes supplant, existing human-expert-intensive analytical techniques for improving decision quality. KDD applications deliver measurable benefits, including reduced cost of doing business, improved profitability, and enhanced quality of service. Industries in which such benefits have been demonstrated include insurance, direct-mail marketing, telecommunications, retail, and health care. Insurance and direct mail are two industries that rely on data analysis to make profitable business decisions. Effective data analysis leading to the creation of accurate predictive models is essential for addressing these issues (Apte *et al.*, 2002). This article is concerned with identifying the impact of store attribute on retail satisfaction of Indian shoppers using multiple regression technique to support knowledge discovery.

4. REVIEW OF SHOPPING SATISFACTION LITERATURE

Rajagopal (2008) analysed the consumer responses to clearance sales, both in terms of consumer satisfaction with the decision process and in terms of subsequent store-choice behaviour. The results suggest that the consumer response to clearance sales is driven to a large extent by two factors: the effect of a clearance sale on the available options of goods and the degree of store loyalty. Overall, the discussion of results demonstrates that the consumer response to clearance sales, both in terms of decision-satisfaction levels and of attractiveness of retail stores, is strongly influenced by the variables of price sensitivity, attractiveness of products, loyalty and perceived value of available brands.

Leela-Rani (2008) empirically examined the impact of situational, consumer, store and product characteristic variables on consumers' behavioural reactions in out-of-stock situations in retail. A survey method for data collection was used with a sample of 1,207 retail customers in India's unorganised retail sector across five product categories in Varanasi, India. Results showed that 11 out of 13 independent variables had a significant impact on at least one of the three behavioural responses considered. Empirical research like this helps to develop an understanding about the consumer behaviour which differs widely across settings. It is one of the first studies in an unorganised retail in India.

There has been little investigation into the impact on share of wallet. Using data from the Canadian banking industry, Cooil et al. (2007) aims to provide the first longitudinal examination of the impact of changes in customer satisfaction on changes in share of wallet and to determine the moderating effects of customer age, income, education, expertise, and length of relationship. Data from 4319 households indicate a positive relationship between changes in satisfaction and share of wallet. In particular, the initial satisfaction level and the conditional percentile of change in satisfaction significantly correspond to changes in share of wallet. Two variables, income and length of the relationship, negatively moderate this relationship.

To examine the relative roles played by cognition and emotion in the development of customer satisfaction in a retail setting. Burns and Neisner (2006) employed an experimental design and the participants were asked to complete scales measuring their cognitive evaluation of the perceived performance and their emotional reaction to the perceived performance. They found out that both cognitive evaluation and emotional reaction were found to explain the level of satisfaction experienced in a retail setting.

Froehle (2006) conducted an exploratory research to examine the interaction of media richness, represented by three different technology contexts, with six customer service representative characteristics and their influences on customer satisfaction. Using a large-sample customer survey data set, the article develops a multigroup structural equation model to analyze these interactions. Results suggest that customer service representative characteristics influence customer service satisfaction.

The Positive effect of positive emotions on consumers' satisfaction was significantly higher in traditional retailing than in shopping centres. It is possible that other unobserve) elements in the shopping experience (for example, interactions between salespeople and shoppers) might be more significant in the traditional retailing environment (Andreu et al., 2006).

To boost online sales, the online store managers need to give their best effort to enhance their customers' perceived satisfaction because satisfied customers have a greater chance of purchasing merchandise. Kijoo and Kim (2006) examined what features of online stores possibly influence the perceived satisfaction of online retail shoppers. The findings imply that the online retailers may need to emphasize on providing contact information company information more clearly to convince the customers that the online store is trustworthy. It is also important to guarantee delivery of correct merchandise at low prices and clearly specify all related costs to merchandise at the time of purchase.

Terblanche and Boshoff (2006) made an attempt to develop a generic instrument that could be used to measure customer satisfaction with the controllable elements of the in-store shopping experience. By closely following the most contemporary guidelines for scale development, and involving 11,063 respondents in four different surveys, the authors emerge with a 22 item instrument to measure satisfaction with the in-store shopping experience.

Eroglu *et al.* (2005) conducted two studies to examine whether shopping values are affected by perceived retail crowding, and whether shopping values mediate the relationship between perceived retail crowding and shopping satisfaction. Results of the first study show that perceived retail crowding affects shopping values, albeit not very strongly. However, the effects appear to be moderated by factors such as personal tolerance for crowding, time spent shopping, shopping intention, and whether a purchase was made. Study 2 indicates that the impact of perceived crowding on shopping value is mediated by emotions experienced by the shopper. The emotions and shopping value reactions, in turn, mediate the effect of spatial crowding on shopping satisfaction. Interestingly, the results show that when these mediating variables are accounted for, human crowding positively affects shopping satisfaction.

Martinez-Tur *et al.* (2005) tested the links of social and technical situational constraints to customer satisfaction with services. To this end, a field survey study was conducted using a sample of 57 managers and 835 customers of organisations. The results also showed that the unique contribution of technical constraints to customer satisfaction was greater than that of social constraints.

In the past several years, the Taiwan marketing channel environment has replaced product supplier dominance situation by the marketing channel terminal of the retailer industry. Chang and Tu (2005) attempted to explore the store image, customer satisfaction and customer loyalty relationship, and examined whether have significant influence among them in the Taiwan hypermarket industry. The conclusions were as follows: First, the study divided store image dimension into four operational variables "facilities, store service, store activities and convenience". These variables can effectively predicted customer satisfaction and the customer are loyalty. Finally, this paper also found out that the hypermarket industry customer satisfaction acted an intermediation role between store image and customer loyalty.

Majority of scholars consider the relationship between quality attributes and customer satisfaction to be linear. However, Ting and Chen (2002) carried out an investigative study on hypermarket customers and it was found that the relationship between most quality attributes and customer satisfaction is asymmetrical and non-linear.

Terblanche and Boshoff (2001) examined the influence of three dimensions of consumer's total retail experience on their satisfaction levels. They considered personal interaction between employees and consumers, physical cue and product variety and assortment are the three components of the total retail experience. Finally confirmed that personal interaction between employees and consumers, and the physical cue impact strongly on customer satisfaction.

Increase in perceived crowding in a retail store created from either human or spatial density can decrease the level of satisfaction that shoppers have with the store. Several potential moderating and mediating influences the relationship between retail crowding and customer satisfaction. The decrease in shopping satisfaction due to crowding is moderated by expectations of crowding and personal tolerance for crowding; the relationship is partially mediated by the emotions (Machleit *et al.*, 2000).

Based on prior research in the field of retail attributes, McDonald (1991) investigates the influence of the of the supermarket store attribute on the Chinese customer satisfaction. The results indicate that the store attributes of distance and speed check out were significant for age and that delivery service and price reduction were significant by income. Total independent variable ranking indicated store location, price and product variety were the most important store attributes influencing satisfaction.

With respect to retailing establishments, Westbrook (1981) developed a conceptualization of retail satisfaction and reports an empirical study for a large conventional department store. Results relative to the components of retail satisfaction and its relationship to product satisfaction are presented. Previous research on retail shopping satisfaction imply that important determinants of shopping satisfaction with respect to retail event have been left out in the previous attribute based models. So in this study, we have developed a model to measure the retail event satisfaction.

5. RESEARCH DESIGN AND DATA ANALYSIS

We have selected clearance sales event celebrated in Tamilnadu, India to develop regression model. We have chosen the shopping of clothing and apparels activity which is a common task associated with the clearance sales event. clearance sales are mainly celebrated by clothing and apparel, electronics and gold selling retailers of Tamilnadu, India. Since clothing and apparel is a product purchased by all the segments, we wish to study the clearance sales shoppers' preference based on clothing and apparel shopping activity.

A preliminary qualitative study has been performed based on focus group interview with customers who are frequently visiting the stores during clearance sales. Each focus group consists of 10 shoppers were focused on their clearance sales shopping experience and their opinion about the retail offerings during the clearance sales is collected. Each focus group interview lasted for 60 minutes. Finally, store attributes of clearance sales were formulated and listed in the questionnaire items. However, a number of variables are modified in order to match the vocabulary of the customers. All items related to the clearance sales store attributes were measured using a 5-point Likert scale. All statements were phrased positively, which is preferable for developing scale-items for investigating store attributes of the clearance sales shoppers. We have tested the questionnaire using a pilot study with 352 clearance sales shoppers and finally modified the questionnaire based on the consumer suggestions.

Mall intercept method is widely used in studies related to the shopping behavior of the respondents. The typical mall intercept respondent is a more frequent user of shopping centers. This type of respondent may be more knowledgeable about shopping and able to supply the survey researcher with more store-oriented information. Additionally, this more knowledgeable shopper may be easier to reach. So we have used mall intercept method for data collection during the clearance sales event. Likewise we have used systematic sampling technique for data collection in three major cities of Tamilnadu, India. These cities are Chennai, Coimbatore and Tiruchirappalli.

We have collected data during the clearance sales event that is Aadi clearance sales which is celebrated in these cities of Tamilnadu, India. The reason for including three different shopping areas was to reduce the effect of differences in competitive intensity across the different regions and to increase the external validity of our results. Under systematic sampling technique the first sample is selected randomly and then every 5th clearance sales shopper is selected for the inclusion in the sample. Therefore Data collection is made through the mall intercept method using questionnaires within the geographical area where the apparel and clothing stores are located. Finally a total of 664 clearance sales shoppers are surveyed during clearance sales event.

First, we have checked the missing values prior to data analysis. We have used a somewhat larger sample size of 664 respondents. Normality was tested based on the skewness and kurtosis of the observed variables. Finally, we tested for the existence of outliers. Our analyses revealed there is no observation that might be considered as outliers. The statistical software SPSS 15.0 is used for the analysis. The data analysis techniques multiple regression technique is used in the analysis phase.

First reliability and validity of the constructs are evaluated. Reliability is the extent to which a measurement is free of variable errors. In particular we are looking for consistency among the scales used to evaluate clearance sales store attributes. The most popular measure of reliability is cronbach's coefficient alpha, which should be routinely calculated to assess the store attributes of measure. In this study Cronbach's alpha is used to assess the reliability of measurement scales with 5-point items relating to the components of the clearance sales store attributes. The coefficient alpha based on the standardised items is above 0.7 which indicates satisfactory internal consistency reliability among the items of all dimensions. The construct validity of the items is systematically evaluated by a team of academic and retail industry practitioners.

Then the store attributes were subjected to multiple regression analysis to construct a model for the clearance sales store satisfaction measurement. The multiple regression model on clearance sales satisfaction is significant with R square value 0.656 ($F=156.346$ and $p<0.01$). R square is an indication of total variation of the model, and it is interpreted as the portion of variation of the observed shopper's satisfaction that can be explained by the linear regression model. A high

R square would mean the model fits the data well, and there is high degree of linear association between variables. Taking this into account, the R square value for the model can be considered very reliable considering the multitude of factors that satisfy the clearance sales shoppers. The result of F-test signifies that the explained variation was statistically significant at one per cent level.

It is observed from the multiple regression model that the overall store satisfaction from the clearance sales = 2.277 + 0.617 (Merchandise) + 0.030 (Price) + 0.255 (Discount) + 0.023 (Promotion) + 0.096 (Employee service) + 0.084 (Retail operation) - 0.004 (Retail services) - 0.049 (Store atmosphere). The Table 1 exhibits the impact of various clearance sales store attributes on the store satisfaction. The above equation describes that, on an average if the score of merchandise increases by one unit, there will be 0.617 unit increase in the clearance sales store satisfaction. Similarly when the price increases by one unit, there will be 0.030 unit increase in the clearance sales store satisfaction. In the same way if the discount factor increases by one unit, there will be 0.255 unit increase in the clearance sales store satisfaction. Similarly, if the promotion factor increases by one unit, there will be 0.023 unit increase in the clearance sales store satisfaction.

The equation also describes that, on an average if the score of employee service increases by one unit, there will be 0.096 unit increase in the clearance sales store satisfaction. Similarly when the retail operation increases by one unit, there will be 0.084 unit increase in the clearance sales store satisfaction. In the same way if the retail services factor increases by one unit, there will be 0.004 unit decrease in the clearance sales store satisfaction. Similarly, if the store atmosphere factor increases by one unit, there will be 0.049 unit decrease in the clearance sales store satisfaction.

The result of multiple regression analysis of the clearance sales depict that the merchandise has the greatest impact on the clearance sales store satisfaction. The result showed that the shoppers shop at clearance sales season mainly for the best merchandise. Our clearance sales store satisfaction model confirms that discount is the second most important element driving clearance sales store satisfaction. Employee service and retail operation is the third and fourth element driving clearance sales store satisfaction. Finally the store attributes such as price, promotion, retail services and store

Table 1. Impact of store attributes on store satisfaction

Independent Variable	Unstandardized Multiple regression Coefficients	Standard Error	Standardized Multiple regression Coefficients	t -value	Sig.
Constant	2.277	0.276	-	8.251	0.000
Merchandise	0.617	0.033	0.564	18.792	0.000
Price	0.030	0.038	0.018	0.788	0.431
Discount	0.255	0.027	0.288	9.547	0.000
Promotion	0.023	0.025	0.023	0.919	0.358
Employee service	0.096	0.034	0.073	2.837	0.005
Retail operation	0.084	0.036	0.066	2.317	0.021
Retail services	-0.004	0.039	-0.002	-0.094	0.926
Store atmosphere	-0.049	0.043	-0.032	-1.134	0.257

R square value = 0.656 (F=156.346 and $p<0.01$)
Dependent Variable: Store satisfaction

atmosphere are insignificant to the clearance sales store satisfaction.

The result of the t-test confirms that, the estimated regression coefficients of merchandise, discount, employee service and retail operation such as 0.617, 0.255, 0.096 and 0.084 are highly significant at five percent level. As a result it is proved that higher level of merchandise, discount, employee service and retail operation will lead to higher clearance sales store satisfaction. Similarly price, promotion, retail services and store atmosphere have an insignificant effect on clearance sales store satisfaction.

6. CONCLUSION AND FUTURE AREAS OF RESEARCH

Shopping satisfaction is becoming increasingly important factor in modern retailing. The research reviewed in this paper has implications for both the measurement and the management of store satisfaction. With regard to implications for the management of retail events, this research suggests that, the retail mix dimensions are considered to be the most important one by the shoppers. The results suggest that retail strategy mix has the greatest bearing on shopper's overall satisfaction with the retail events.

The present study would be an exploratory one aiming to investigate the concept of retail event shopping satisfaction based on a sample of the Indian population. In this paper, we have developed a framework for analyzing the relationship among store attributes and shopping satisfaction. This paper divided dimension of store attributes component into eight variables merchandise, discount, employee service, retail operation, price, promotion, retail services and store atmosphere. These variables can effectively predict shopping satisfaction. Hence, manager of the retail outlets in Tamilnadu (India) should pay attention with these factors, and make good use of them. Finally our model at the strategic level allows the retail managers to understand the specific factors that significantly impact overall shopping satisfaction.

This model helps the managers to quantitatively assess the relative impact of merchandise, discount, employee service, retail operation, price, promotion, retail services and store atmosphere factors. Store attributes has become an integral part of the retailing. It is important for retailers to understand how customers evaluate this store attributes. Effective management of store attributes decision can be an excellent means of creating a competitive advantage. In this way, retail marketers and mangers will have a more complex view of the retail event shopping satisfaction and be better able to plan, allocate resources and sustain employees motivation for the retail business improvement.

Similarly discount may play several roles in the customer purchase decision process. The present study provides evidence of the contribution of discount to shopper's satisfaction. Thus, retailers need to be very careful about attempting to make the merchandise offered more appealing by lowering prices. They need to convince customers that a reduction in price is not accompanied by a reduction in the quality of merchandise. The promotional message should emphasis the benefits of the retail event purchase and educate customers to recognise its value. With this view, it is suggested that retailers should capture and communicate value to customers in their pricing strategy.

The causal model emerging through this research is developed with the objective of providing retail management with a framework to assist managers to understand retail event satisfaction. Our model provides the result that the store attributes which is the primary driver of the overall retail event satisfaction. We have quantified the component factors of a store attributes can help in raising the overall retail event shopping satisfaction. Our model establishes the factors which significantly impact the shopping satisfaction and gives direction to the satisfaction improvement strategy, helping managers to identify the key parts of their business processes. The model developed is general enough to be applied in any retail event in India. Attribute information was collected with a view to quantifying how it influenced overall retail event satisfaction. With this information, the retail manager could target particular facets of his retail business knowing that improving these attributes would have the most impact on shopper's overall satisfaction. The newly developed model and shopping satisfaction measurement instrument can be applied to the clothing and apparel retailing sector in India.

However, this study has few limitations that can be considered opportunities for both theoretical and empirical work. The present study was an exploratory one, with Aadi sale retail event from India. The samples of this study are taken from the southern India and the applicability of the results is limited. Shopping satisfaction determinants may vary among different customer segments. Treating the whole market as a homogenous segment would lead to market failure. Subsequent replication research is, therefore, needed to enhance the robustness of the relationships between the performances of retail strategy mix and retail event shopping satisfaction. That is, the further verification of model with other retail events like Great Singapore Sale festival is required to enhance the generalization of the study. Further study on the effect of different types of non store attributes such as complaints and waiting time on retail event shopping satisfaction is required. Similarly the study is conducted in the context of the clothing and apparel product. Future studies should incorporate additional products or multiple product categories to examine differences in consumer shopping segments between products.

REFERENCES

Aeron, H., Kumar, A., & Janakiraman, M. (2010). Application of data mining techniques for customer lifetime value parameters: A review. *International Journal of Business Information Systems*, *6*(4), 514–529. doi:10.1504/IJBIS.2010.035744

Andreu, L., Bigne, E., Chumpitaz, R., & Swaen, V. (2006). How does the perceived retail environment influence consumers' emotional experience? Evidence from two retail settings. *International Review of Retail, Distribution and Consumer Research*, *16*(5), 559–578. doi:10.1080/09593960600980097

Apte, C., Liu, B., Pednault, E. P. D., & Smyth, P. (2002). Business applications of data mining. *Communications of the ACM*, *45*(8), 49–53. doi:10.1145/545151.545178

Bharadwaj, V. T., Swaroop, G. M., & Vittal, I. (2005). *Winning the Indian consumer* (*Special Edition*, pp. 42–51). McKinsey Quarterly.

Burns, D. J., & Neisner, L. (2006). Customer satisfaction in a retail setting. *International Journal of Retail and Distribution Management*, *34*(1), 49–66. doi:10.1108/09590550610642819

Chang, C. H., & Tu, C. Y. (2005). Exploring store image, customer satisfaction and customer loyalty relationship: Evidence from Taiwanese hypermarket industry. *Journal of American Academy of Business*, *7*(2), 197–202.

Cheng, S., Dai, R., Xu, W., & Shi, Y. (2006). Research on data mining and knowledge management and its applications in China's economic development: significance and trend. *International Journal of Information Technology and Decision Making*, *5*(4), 585–596. doi:10.1142/S021962200600226X

Cooil, B., Keiningham, T. L., Aksoy, L., & Hsu, M. (2007). A longitudinal analysis of customer satisfaction and share of wallet: Investigating the moderating effect of customer characteristics. *Journal of Marketing*, *71*(1), 67–83. doi:10.1509/jmkg.71.1.67

Eroglu, S. A., Machleit, K., & Barr, T. F. (2005). Perceived retail crowding and shopping satisfaction: the role of shopping values. *Journal of Business Research*, *58*(8), 1146–1153. doi:10.1016/j.jbusres.2004.01.005

Fayyad, U., & Uthurusamy, R. (2002). Evolving data mining into solutions for insights. *Communications of the ACM*, *45*(8), 28–31. doi:10.1145/545151.545174

Ho, G. T. S., Lau, H. C. W., Ip, W. H., & Ning, A. (2004). An intelligent information infrastructure to support the streamlining of integrated logistics workflow. *Expert Systems: International Journal of Knowledge Engineering and Neural Networks*, *21*(3), 123–137. doi:10.1111/j.1468-0394.2004.00269.x

Hormozi, A. M., & Giles, S. (2004). Data mining: A competitive weapon for banking and retail industries. *Information Systems Management*, *1*, 62–71. doi:10.1201/1078/44118.21.2.20040301/80423.9

Jianan, W., & DeSarbo, W. S. (2005). Market segmentation for customer satisfaction studies via a new latent structure multidimensional scaling model. *Applied Stochastic Models in Business and Industry*, *21*(4/5), 303–309.

Jindal, T. (2008). Ride the tiger. *Financial Management*, *1*, 20–23.

Kijoo, K., & Kim, E. B. (2006). Suggestions to enhance the cyber store customers satisfaction. *Journal of American Academy of Business*, *9*(1), 233–240.

Kohavi, R., Rothleder, N. J., & Simoudis, E. (2002). Emerging trends in business analytics. *Communications of the ACM*, *45*(8), 45–48. doi:10.1145/545151.545177

Kumar, P., Varma, K. I., & Sureka, A. (2011). Fuzzy based clustering algorithm for privacy preserving data mining. *International Journal of Business Information Systems*, *7*(1), 27–40. doi:10.1504/IJBIS.2011.037295

Kuruvilla, S. J., & Ganguli, J. (2008). Mall development and operations: An Indian perspective. *Journal of Retail & Leisure Property*, *7*(3), 204–215. doi:10.1057/rlp.2008.14

Leela-Rani. (2008). Consumer reactions to retail out-of-stock: Replication into new contexts. *International Journal of Indian Culture and Business Management*, *1*(3), 319–334. doi:10.1504/IJICBM.2008.017788

Machleit, K. A., Eroglu, S. A., & Mantel, S. P. (2000). Perceived retail crowding and shopping satisfaction: What modifies this relationship? *Journal of Consumer Psychology*, *9*(1), 29–42. doi:10.1207/s15327663jcp0901_3

Martinez-Tur, V., Peiro, J. M., & Ramos, J. (2005). Linking situational constraints to customer satisfaction in a service environment. *Applied Psychology: An International Review*, *54*(1), 25–36. doi:10.1111/j.1464-0597.2005.00194.x

McDonald, G. M. (1991). The influence of supermarket attributes on perceived customer satisfaction: An East Asian study. *International Review of Retail, Distribution and Consumer Research*, *1*(3), 315–327. doi:10.1080/09593969100000031

Parikh, D. (2006). Measuring retail service quality: An empirical assessment of the instrument. *Vikalpa: The Journal for Decision Makers*, *31*(2), 45–55.

Rajagopal. (2008). Consumer response to seasonal clearance sales: Experimental analysis of consumer personality traits in self-service stores. *Global Business and Economics Review, 10*(1), 68–92.

Samli, A. C., Pohlen, T. L., & Bozovic, N. (2002). A review of data mining techniques as they apply to marketing: Generating strategic information to develop market segments. *The Marketing Review, 3*, 211–227. doi:10.1362/146934702763487270

Shalini, K. (2008). Knowledge management within information security: The case of Barings Bank. *International Journal of Business Information Systems, 3*(6), 652–667. doi:10.1504/IJBIS.2008.018996

Sharma, S. (2008). Principal component analysis (PCA) to rank countries on their readiness for e-tail. *Journal of Retail & Leisure Property, 7*(2), 87–94. doi:10.1057/rlp.2008.1

Sharma, S., Goyal, D. P., & Mittal, R. K. (2008). Data mining research for customer relationship management systems: a framework and analysis. *International Journal of Business Information Systems, 3*(5), 549–565. doi:10.1504/IJBIS.2008.018605

Shivani, K., & Usha, G. (2008). *Retail scene in India*. Chillibreeze Business Review, India: Chillibreeze Private Ltd.

Terblanche, N. S., & Boshoff, C. (2001). Measuring customer satisfaction with some of the controllable elements of the total retail experiences: An exploratory study. *South African Journal of Business Management, 32*(2), 35–41.

Terblanche, N. S., & Boshoff, C. (2006). A generic instrument to measure customer satisfaction with the controllable elements of the in-store shopping experience. *South African Journal of Business Management, 37*(3), 1–15.

Ting, S. C., & Chen, C. N. (2002). The asymmetrical and non-linear effects of store quality attributes on customer satisfaction. *Total Quality Management, 13*(4), 547–569. doi:10.1080/09544120220149331

Westbrook, R. A. (1981). Sources of consumer satisfaction with retail outlets. *Journal of Retailing, 57*(3), 68–85.

Zhu, D., Premkumar, G., Zhang, X., & Chu, C. (2001). Data mining for network intrusion detection: A comparison of alternative methods. *Decision Sciences, 32*(4), 635–660. doi:10.1111/j.1540-5915.2001.tb00975.x

Chapter 15
Innovation for E-Services Management

Kamaljeet Sandhu
University of New England, Australia

ABSTRACT

Over the last several years traditional services (face to face) have been transferred over to the electronic environment on the Web, also known as E-Services. There is very little knowledge to know how and why these services are used by consumers based on their knowledge and experience and motivation, ease of use, and usefulness of e-services, acceptance, and continued usage for e-services. This research explores the theoretical framework for developing e-services acceptance model (E-SAM).

1. INTRODUCTION

The Internet has created significant opportunities for organisations and their customers in terms of communication, acquisition of information, and conducting commercial and non-commercial e-Services activities (Rust and Lemon 2001). Though such opportunities are considered beneficial, little is understood of their effect on customer or user behaviour or acceptance. The rapidly growing number of new users of e-Services has led to the provision of many new possibilities and systems, implying numerous new considerations

DOI: 10.4018/978-1-4666-0948-8.ch015

when developing and designing those systems and services (D'Ambra and Rice 2001).

Studies of traditional services were focused on face-to-face interactions in various settings as a means of improving business efficiency or increasing customer satisfaction (Hoffman and Novak 1996. The development of e-Services adds a further dimension to business-customer interaction. As societies shift increasingly towards computer-mediated communication, it is important to investigate what influences customers' use of an e-Services system.

The interaction with e-Services is based on customer expectations that e-Services will meet their requirements (Zeithaml et al. 2000). A distinguishing feature of e-Services is direct customer interaction with websites compared to that in a traditional setting where customers are unable to directly access the systems providing the service and can select service options only indirectly via the trained operator, whereas in web- enabled e-Services system, customers are empowered to directly influence service choices. The websites form a platform for managing and delivering e-Services (van Riel et al. 2001; Xue et al. 2004).

Organizations engaged in e-businesses like banking, airlines, car rental, management consulting, music, software and educational institutions are increasingly opting for on-line services delivery to meet e-customer demand (Forrest and Mizerski 1996; Chea and Lou 2008; and Chellappan 2008). Today web-based e-services range from the electronic provision of traditional services (services with an "e" in front), such as investing and airline ticketing, intelligent interactivity in post-sales and pre-sales product support to online education course delivery (Ruyter et al 2001).

The developing web-based e-service domain seems limitless and expanding. From simple web-based e-service function to complex "service multiplier effect" (Aberdeen Group 1999) are being developed as the core function of web-based e-service. Any e-business creates a demand for pre-sales and after-sales service activities (Ruyter et al. 2001). Hewlett Packard, for instance, is rapidly transforming their after-sales service to web-based e-service business unit, providing users the chance to interact in real time.

In recent years, the Internet has been identified as the world's fastest growing marketplace with seemingly limitless opportunities for marketing products and services (Domains 1999). Web-based e-service delivery provides users with the opportunities of a virtual marketplace that are cost efficient, have 24/7 accessibility, lack geographic limitation, are interactive, and enable real time delivery of services.

As innovations in electronic service are rapidly emerging, it is yet unknown how the users are reacting and adjusting to this new web-based e-service function. Nevertheless, customer adoption and continuance are arguably a critical success factor in realizing the potential of web-based e-services and its future direction. From here onwards the terms users (referred in Information Systems literature), users and customers (referred in Services literature) will be used interchangeable and imply to have the same meaning, the theoretical understanding is borrowed from these two disciplines.

2. THEORETICAL PERSPECTIVES FOR THE INNOVATIVE E-SERVICES MODEL

Integrating Service and Information Systems literature in exploring the web-based e-service perspective (see Figure 1) will provide an *innovative* Knowledge of how users evaluate web-based e-services. An innovation is an idea, practice, or object that is perceived as new by an individual or other unit of adoption (Rogers 1983).

Figure 1. Web-based e-service perspective

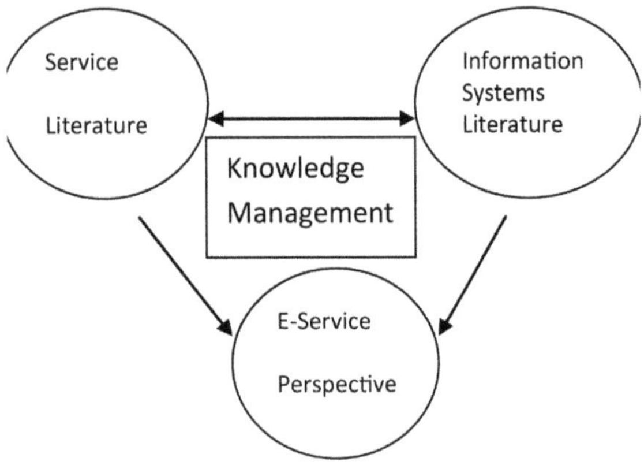

The two instruments of TAM have shown to have success in past IS studies; recent studies suggest it applies also to e-commerce and to adoption of the Internet technology (Gefen and Straub 2000). Jackson et al. (1997) used TAM to present a holistic framework and examine the various constructs that lead to behavioral intention to use an IS. TAM has its limitation of being employed beyond the workplace and the user task environment is not fully reflected (Moon and Kim 2001). Davis et al.'s (1992) measurement of perceived enjoyment does not reflect a comprehensive set of intrinsic motivation factors, such as perceived enjoyment or perceived fun, as a research construct needs further theoretical validation. Malhotra and Galleta (1999) pointed out that TAM is incomplete in one important respect: it does not account for social influence in the adoption and utilization of new information systems. Dishaw and Strong (1999) also suggest a weakness of TAM, in its lack of task focus. Davis (1989) himself argues that future technology acceptance research needs to address how other variables affect usefulness, ease of use, and user acceptance.

Adoption of web-based e-service by user may be treated as technology adoption. The Technology Acceptance Model (TAM) of Davis (1989) represents an important theoretical contribution toward understanding IS usage and IS acceptance behavior (Davis et al 1992; Robey 1979). Applying the TAM model to investigate the user requirements may provide insight into web-based e-service usefulness and user friendliness. TAM focuses on two such beliefs: perceived usefulness (PU) and perceived ease of use (PEOU). The former would enhance the user job performance, while the latter would be easy to use.

Important conclusions can be derived from prior studies using the TAM model when applying it to the web-based e-service user adoption. First, merely instrumental usefulness is rather an insufficient basis to develop widespread user adoption of web-based e-service. Second, the integration of users perception with usefulness and user friendliness may not explain the web-based e-service adoption and continuance factor holistically.

Considering user, technology and adoption in the user context provides a triangulation approach (see Figure 2). The triangulation approach takes into account the other variables, which may have an impact on the user context. Adoption models traditionally focus on "first purchase decision" (Mahajan and Muller 1990). These models provide understanding of the adoption process of separate user goods. However, web-based e-service user adoption is primarily related to real time intangible service delivery on the web, successively following to tangible products and services. The integration of this function into situation specific motivation, user experience and perception, usefulness and user friendliness provides an important contextual basis in understanding the user adoption, continuance or rejection process.

This exploration assumes that users of web-based e-services are already users of services in the traditional environment (offline). Understanding the traditional service complexities and transforming it to the online web-based e-service task is a challenge for both practitioners and research-

Figure 2. Suggested triangulation approach for understanding user perspective in web-based e-service

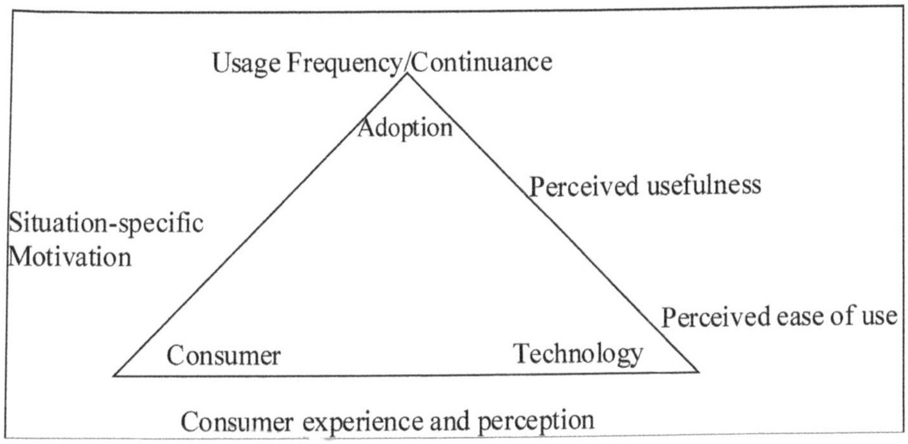

ers. The dimension and scale of such complexity in terms of technology and adoption further develops into user oriented situation task, which is centric to understanding the web-based e-service adoption and continuance pattern. Defining a web-based e-service task is not an easy and straightforward process. Rather developing an approach to studying the process on the basis of web-based e-service and user interaction is suggested. This paper specifically investigates issues related to web-based e-service user adoption and the process involving successive usage and continuation of web-based e-services. With technology constantly changing it is subsequently has an impact on the user's experience, usage and adoption behavior.

Unlike any other service, web-based e-service characteristics predominantly originate from the traditional offline environment involving human-to-human interaction (i.e., face-to-face interface). In the online environment this is differentiated by human-to-web interface. The user contextual factors influencing web-based e-service usage are considered to be the same whether online or offline. The information available to web-based e-service users is one of the determinants, which directs the user in achieving the desired objectives that form the purpose of using web-based e-service. This follows in discussion on users experience and perception in adopting web-based e-service task.

3. USER EXPERIENCE AND PERCEPTION WITH E-SERVICES

This exploration defines experience developed in the context of users activities and task conducted in an offline/online environment. Users engaged in web-based e-service activities tend to focus on prior perception and experience, especially from the offline environment.

Davidow and Uttal (1989) pointed: "service expectations are formed by many uncontrollable factors, from the experience of customers…to a customer's psychological state at the time of service delivery." Understanding users experience and perception solely on the basis of online experience or offline experience would tend to limit the research dimension; rather a combination approach is adopted.

Web-based e-services being relatively new and developing, the scope of users interpretation of web-based e-services is reflected on the basis of prior service experience. The impact of web-based e-service experience on first time users compared to the frequent users will vary, a user with no experience of web-based e-service can form high (or low) perception, especially via word of mouth communications. Such perceptions may behave differently from those developed via experience.

The level of experience gained by the user while conducting traditional service or web-based e-service provides an opportunity in retaining that experience to be applied in future similar situation. Such experience depends on previous interface involving combination of allied factors such as motivation, support, self-service, control, and usage frequency. The following discussion explores the role of these factors.

4. USER MOTIVATION

Intrinsic motivation in a task environment has also been associated with willingness to spend more time with the task, lower levels of anxiety, positive mood, and greater learning e.g. (Csikszentmihalyi 1988). The sequential process associated with learning followed by experience retention impacts the user in adopting motivational characteristics, which positively affect the web-based e-service task. Gattiker (1992) in a framework of training, suggested that individual motivation had an impact on substantive complexity. Based on intrinsic motivation research and user acceptance research, it can be expected that for a given objective level of effort, greater levels of intrinsic motivation during training had a favourable impact on perceptions of effort (perceived ease of use) (Venkatesh 1999).

Another element of motivation is willingness or readiness to act (MacInnis et al. 1991). Whether or not the users are dissatisfied with the offline service, not all users will equally willing or ready to adopt web-based e-service. The literature on innovation adoption suggests that innovators and early adopters are more willing to try new innovations than late adopters and laggards. Zaltman et al, (1985) studied attitudinal dimensions related to an innovation and the user willingness to consider its use. Mohr (1969) pointed out that willingness is an important precursor to actual adoption of the innovation. It is conclusive that the user in a state of willingness will opt to try the web-based e-service, but will continue its use is unknown. Although the willingness to use will depend on other factors such as its relative advantage to offline service, cost, risk, efficiency, compatibility, and complexity of the web-based e-service task.

Hoffman and Novak (1996) in their model of Network Navigation focus on extrinsic and intrinsic motivation characteristics, which impact users involvement and focused attention. The motivation characteristics impacts the activity task the user undertakes, it is unknown if the same motivational characteristics are retained on the return visits (continuance) to the website to use web-based e-service. This may also be true in a situation when the user may have a different set of motivational characteristics when visiting another website to use e-service. Prior research (Hoffman and Novak 1996; Csikszentmihalyi 1988; Csikszentmihalyi and LeFevre 1989; Abdelmessih 2000; and Ramaswami 2001) suggests that users involvement is characterized by situational involvement and experience. There are no substantial studies that suggest that users come with a set of motivational characteristics online and retain them until the task is completed. Due to the multiple visits made to the website and user getting accustomed to the mechanical process of conducting repeated web-based e-services task, it is of significance to know the state of motivation in user task interface.

Motivation can have a positive or negative effect on the users in an online environment, if a user had a positive experience shopping in an offline environment, the same positive belief will reflect on the willingness to using the online channel for web-based e-services and vice versa. But if a user of online web-based e-service had a negative experience, to know what caused the negative effect is low, compared to the offline environment where the human interaction is present. This has been reported in BCG Report (2000), for a small but significant number of users, a single bad experience can put an end to their online shopping careers. This leads in understanding the level of online support required by users in conducting the web-based e-service task.

The affect of motivation mechanisms on decision-making in online and offline environment involves the user in personalizing the web-based e-service needs. An important difference between online and offline markets is that for attributes for which information can be obtained in both media search costs are typically lower online than offline (Bakos 1997; Degeratu et al. 2000). The decision-making process the user undergoes is perceived from a similar prior situation. Web-based e-service information that is easier to search will be more "available" and hence, will have a larger influence on overall product evaluation (Kisielius and Sternthal 1984). Motivation in alliance with other situational specific personalization factors has a tendency to strongly influence users web-based e-service decision-making process.

The degree of motivation (intrinsic or extrinsic) with other situational specific personalization factors directs the user in achieving the task. Several studies have demonstrated that when information is presented in a suitable format (e.g., brand x attribute x matrix) as in Pcapod (Pcapod offers an online grocery subscription service in seven metropolitan areas), it facilitates both user information acquisition and comprehension (Degeratu et al 2000; Bettman and Kakkar 1977; and Russo et al 1986). Not many studies (Abdelmessih et al 2000; Velli 2000; and Degeratu et al 2000) investigated into users' behavior in understanding repeat online purchase and the users motivation behind it. BCG Report (2000) instead suggested online retailers to encourage users to share personal information and leverage this customer knowledge to make the experience more meaningful for the customers.

Creating a compelling reason for the user to make the first online purchase is one of the obstacles facing the researchers and practitioner. The study further suggests that to create a differentiated and low risk first purchase, engineer a flawless purchase experience, offer fast and reliable service, prove the integrity of online process, enable users to customize delivery options, and relieve anxiety over returns. Some of these factors, if not implemented in an online environment, tend to demotivate the user, and form poor or low expectation thus affecting experience (Johnson and Mathews 1997) which is similar to the reflection of prior offline experience, when the user didn't receive good service, goods were faulty, and the purchasing experience had a negative effect. This may discourage the users from acceptance and continuation of web-based e-services.

5. USER SUPPORT

The overall support strategy adopted by organizations offering web-based e-service is to allow support through telephone (call centers), frequently asked questions (FAQ) on websites, or through email support. The effect of support on users may form a positive/negative perception towards using web-based e-service. Researchers have consistently identified good support through well-experienced staff and effective communication with users as critical for the success of the business. In an online web-based e-service environment such an interaction is most wanted but appears to be absent.

Online/offline support has been one of the crucial decision making determinants in web-based e-service user adoption. Similar to the offline situation, users require a high level of support in user life cycle. The need for support seems more important in conducting web-based e-service task due to mediated interaction between the user and the web interface and absence of online human support. Not much is being done to integrate online support into the core functions of web-based e-services.

Zeithaml, Parasuraman, and Malhotra (2000) concluded that customers have no web-based e-service expectations, customers have been found to compare web-based e-service to competitor's services and to brick and mortar stores (Meuter et al 2000; Szymanski 2000). Thus users' tolerance level for web-based e-services, their immediate reactions to the service failure and their consecutive behavior, are intertwined and forms part of the experience and perception the user develops.

Meuter et al (2000) in their online study found that 80% of the customer complaints were made in person to the company, either by phone or by visiting a service facility. This suggests that when the user is confronted with a problematic web-based e-service experience, and to resolve the issue the user adopts the traditional approach of face-to-face interaction, rather than the online approach. When the service fails it has fallen outside the customer's zone of tolerance (Zeithaml et al. 1993). So far nothing is known about users tolerance levels of web-based e-services online, or the customers propensity to complain about online service failures (Riel et al 2001), and customers reaction to it.

6. USER CONTROL

The user has the potential to control the e-service interaction with the medium on a commercial website. They are in charge, choosing to progress, explore or exit the content of the interaction (Trevino and Webster 1992). Control is facilitated by the medium adapting to feedback from the individual, and also by providing explicit choices among alternatives (Webster et al 1993). Studies in user behavior suggest user require a higher degree of control on their activity (Hoffman and Novak 1996;Csikszentmihalyi 1988; and Ramaswami et al 2001).

The role of control in online user behavior is considered equally significant in understanding user web-based e-service adoption. Control in this exploration refers in the environmental and behavioral context of users of web-based e-service. user control of environment relates in terms of the flexibility and freedom provided in conducting the web-based e-service task. To retain interest in a web-based e-service, there should be enjoyment on the part of the user during the interaction with the site.

Environmental control has been considered as one of the main discriminator between the classes of on-line purchasers and non-purchasers, as the main factor restraining the adoption of on-line shopping (Velli et al 2000). users opting for online shopping experience higher control structures online and lesser flexibility compared to offline environment. In such a state the users draw a perception of their prior shopping experience offline and compare with the online experience. This usually is reflected in terms of 'what they can do offline' compared to 'what they cannot do online'. The ability to transfer the offline environmental characteristics to online is a task that involves considerable understanding of the web-based e-service user usage behavior in offline environment. In terms of user behavior this is reflected from the activities in traditional offline environment and provides useful information in determining the user activity and control characteristics.

The whole process tends to be reduced, removing the intricacies the user can encounter, and at the same time standardizing the web-based e-service across all domain and user developing a positive experience. It has been proposed that agents will likely develop from simple, understandable systems to more complex and intelligent systems as users' become accustomed to delegating activities and develop trust in the agent's abilities (Sproule and Archer 2000; Grosof 1997; and Etzioni 1997).

The development of intelligent agents guiding the user in conducting the task from start to completion tends to improve the user interface and reducing uncertainty and problematic experience, providing lesser control. An agent's ability to act on its own implies some sort of knowledge base and intelligence, but the level of intelligence may vary from the simple (e.g. instruction to run a procedure at a specific time) to the complex (e.g. flexible reasoning systems) (Sproule and Archer 2000). This has led to smart software's taking over the task and reducing users interactivity with the task and completion within a few ticks and clicks of a mouse (e.g., online banking, online bill payment).

Often the role of shop assistants is to resolve any user query in traditional offline environment. Aberg and Shahmehri (2000) in their study investigated into the role of human web assistants in electronic commerce. They designed and implemented a human web assistant system concentrating on three properties 1) human intelligence 2) individual user centered 3) user interface with different needs. There are few companies (e.g., liveperson.com, facetime.org) exploring the role of human assistance in websites. The development of a smart system able to interface human communication to machine understood communication would require the integration of users experience with the machine intelligence. Merging the two would be a difficult task, developments made would be considered useful.

7. USAGE FREQUENCY

Collecting and analyzing information on user movement frequency in web-based e-service usage on the World Wide Web is the core for understanding user behavior in an online environment. There exist vast amounts of information in the form of data, which is meaningless until it is formatted and processed to understand the user movement frequency (Lane and Koronios 2001). More recently several on-line tools like access log, agent log, error log, referrer log, cookies, user login ids, are available to capture and analyze user behavior and activity in web information systems and can reveal useful information in analyzing user movement frequency There are number of studies that have assessed the suitability of these tools in the development of web information systems, e.g. (Bauer and Chong 1999; Bertot and McClure 1997 and Wu et al 1998). These tools provide researchers with knowledge about the user requirements and may be integrated to the websites. Even with the availability of such tools, web-based e-service systems pose challenges regarding the capture of user requirements.

An alternative rationale Gelderman (1998) states that users are able to assess the value of the IS and will use if they conclude that the benefits (rewards) will outweigh the costs (efforts) (Robey 1979; Gelderman 1998; and Markus and Robey 1983). Both rationales assume that more usage is better, which is not necessarily the case. This is not true for web information systems, where users may engage for considerable period of time leading to high usage, without any specific purpose (such as surfing the Internet for fun).

User web-based e-service usage frequency is another determinant in understanding web-based e-service continuance after successful adoption. In order to fully understand web-based e-service usage frequency as a success measure it is suggested here to reflect on IS usage studies (see Figure 3). The debate on IS usage as a success measure is ongoing. Gelderman (1998), argues that a rational for the application of IS usage as a success measure is the idea that it does not contribute to performance if it is not used (and will contribute to performance when it is).

Gelderman (1998) argues that it is unclear what exactly is the amount usage of an IS and subjective measurement of usage maybe influenced by social desirability and usage measurement may suffer from time-dependent noise. In terms of web-based e-service usage this may be related to more usage the better. The application of usage as successful web-based e-service adoption and continuance determiner provides a basis in understanding successful and unsuccessful user visits for conducting the web-based e-service task. Though the number of visits to e-service websites cannot solely provide complete information about the success of web-based e-service adoption and continuance.

Figure 3. Conceptual framework for web-based e-services adoption model (E-SAM)

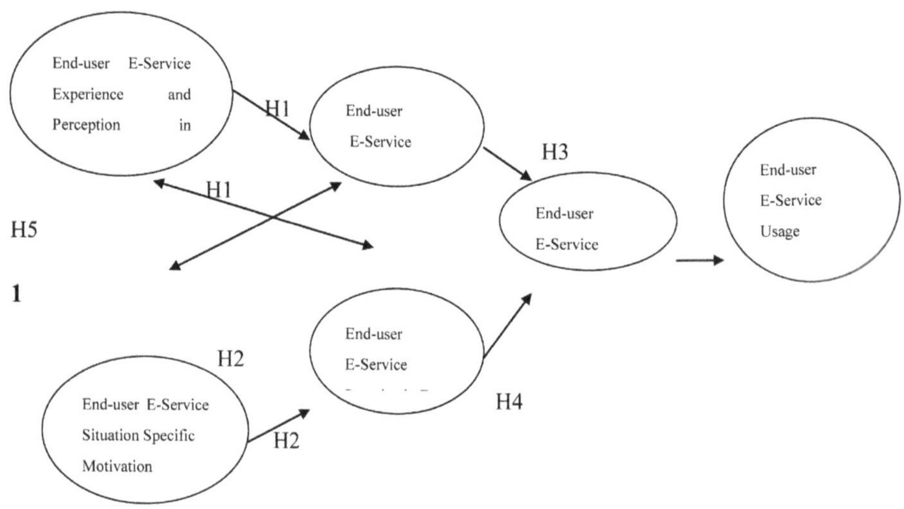

Lane and Koronios (2001) investigated user requirements in business-to-user web information systems. Business-to-user web information systems are IS based on web technology that supports user interaction such as on-line shopping through integration with databases and transaction processing systems (Isakowitz et al 1998). The development of effective mass information systems such as web information systems is critical to the success of web based electronic commerce (Lane and Koronios 2001; and Hansen 1995). Capturing user requirements is particularly important in the development of web information systems where user acceptance is often critical to the success of a web information system (Lane and Koronios 2001; Hansen 1995; and Bauer and Chong 1999). It is unknown which web-based e-service features user (individual and group) often use and why, and the user movement frequency from one section to another which is further complicated by user diversity, first time, second time, or repeat visits to the website, and differentiation between satisfied and dissatisfied users.

The model complements Davis's (1989) main characteristics (perceived usefulness and perceived ease of use) with significant contexts and factors. Whether the user adoption decision for web-based e-services emanates from: users experience and perception, situation specific motivation, or acceptance and continuance contexts in usage frequency needs investigation.

8. CONCLUSION

The earlier studies (Zeithaml 1993) investigated the adoption of web-based e-services in different contexts, but not provide insight into acceptance and continuance of web-based e-service by users. Though a user may use web-based e-service for the first time, its continuous usage lays the success. Understanding and developing users continuous usage behavior in web-based e-services has illustrated the same perspective and provided similar insights into what determines IS acceptance and continuance. This study will concentrate on those factors and at the same time reveal its core relationship to web-based e-service user behavior.

In line with the preceding discussion it is suggested that web-based e-service user adoption takes into account the individual user, technology, and adoption in the user context. Though prior studies even adopted the general technology user models such as the TAM, which is of significance, they do not take into account the user context issues on a commercial situation basis. To study the web-based e-service user adoption from a user perspective centered context and combining it with adoption and acceptance models would enhance the understanding. To explore the context further, issues related to situation specific personalization of individual users in motivation, support, control, self-service and usage frequency in online and offline environment may be used to produce evaluation guidelines that would facilitate the adoption and continuation process.

From the preceding discussion it has been clear that web-based e-services user adoption is not a simple and straightforward process. Rapid development in web-based e-service technology delivery is gradually shaping the user uptake and usage of this new innovation. The level of interaction in traditional services to web-based e-services and simultaneous use of both has laid a new set of implications for the organizations, government, users, practitioners, and researchers.

REFERENCES

Abdelmessih, N., Yolles, E., Grevler, C., Kuo, L., Sterling, K., & Davidson, K. (2000). *Winning of the online user: Insights into online user behavior*. The Boston Consulting Group.

Aber, J., & Shahmehri, N. (2000). The role of human web assistants in e-commerce: An analysis and a usability study. *Internet Research: Electronic Networking Applications and Policy*, *10*(2), 114–125. doi:10.1108/10662240010322902

Aberdeen Group. (1999). *Web-based e-service: Using the Internet to manage customers.* Retrieved from http://www.servicesoft.com/presskit-whitepaper.html

Bakos, J. Y. (1997). Reducing buyer search costs: Implications for electronic marketplaces. *Management Science*, *43*, 1676–1692. doi:10.1287/mnsc.43.12.1676

Bauer, C., & Chong, S. (1999). Electronic markets development: Using marketing research to determine user requirements. In *Global Networked Organizations: Proceedings of 12th BLED Electronic Commerce Conference*, Bled, Slovenia, (pp. 408-23).

Bertot, J., & McClure, C. R. (1997). Web usage statistics: measurement issues and analytical techniques. *Government Information Quarterly*, *14*(4), 373–395. doi:10.1016/S0740-624X(97)90034-4

Bettman, J. R., & Kakkar, P. (1977). Effects of information presentation format on user information acquisition strategies. *Journal of User Research*, *3*, 233–240.

Chea, S., & Lou, M. (2008). Post-adoption behaviors of e-service customers: The interplay of cognition and emotion. *International Journal of Electronic Commerce*, *12*(3), 29–56. doi:10.2753/JEC1086-4415120303

Chellappan, C. (2008). *E-services: The need for higher levels of trust by populace*. Chennai, India: Anna University.

Csikszentmihalyi, M. (1988). The future of flow. In Csikszentmihalyi, M., & Selega Csikszentmihalyi, I. (Eds.), *Optimal experience: Psychological studies of flow in consciousness*. Cambridge, UK: Cambridge University Press.

Csikszentmihalyi, M., & LeFevre, J. (1989). Optimal experience in work and leisure. *Journal of Personality and Social Psychology*, *56*(5), 815–822. doi:10.1037/0022-3514.56.5.815

Davidow, W. H., & Uttal, B. (1989). Service companies: Focus or falter. *Harvard Business Review*, (4): 17–34.

Davis, F. D. (1989). Perceived usefulness, perceived ease of use, and user acceptance of IT. *Management Information Systems Quarterly*, *13*(2), 319–340. doi:10.2307/249008

Davis, F. D., Bagozzi, R. P., & Warshaw, P. R. (1992). Extrinsic and intrinsic motivation to use computers in the workplace. *Journal of Applied Social Psychology*, *22*(14), 1111–1132. doi:10.1111/j.1559-1816.1992.tb00945.x

Degeratu, A. M., Rangaswamy, A., & Wu, J. (2000). *User choice behavior in online and traditional supermarkets: The effects of brand name, price, and other search attributes* (pp. 1-45). Working Paper. The Smeal College of Business, Penn State University; and A.B. Freeman School of Business, Tulane University.

Dishaw, M. T., & Strong, D. M. (1999). Extending the technology acceptance model with task-technology fit constructs. *Information & Management*, *36*, 9–21. doi:10.1016/S0378-7206(98)00101-3

Domains, C. (1999). Business on the Internet. Retrieved from http://www.cleverdomains.com/business.htm

Etzioni, O. (1997). Moving up the information food chain. *AI Magazine*, 11–18.

Forrest, E., & Mizerski, R. (1996). *Interactive marketing, the future present*. Chicago, IL: American Marketing Association.

Gattiker, U. E. (1992). Computer skills acquisition: A review and future directions for research. *Journal of Management*, *18*(3), 547–574. doi:10.1177/014920639201800307

Gefen, D., & Straub, D. (2000). The relative importance of perceived ease of use in IS adoption: A study of e-commerce adoption. *Journal of the Association for IS*, *1*, 1–20.

Gelderman, M. (1998). The relation between user satisfaction, usage of information systems and performance. *Information & Management*, *34*, 11–18. doi:10.1016/S0378-7206(98)00044-5

Grosof, B. N. (1997). *Building commercial agents: An IBM research perspective (invited talk)*. Exhibition on Practical Applications on Intelligent Agents and Multi-Agent Technology (PAAM 97). Retrieved from http://www.research.ibm.com/igents/paps/rc20305.pdf

Hansen, H. R. (1995). Conceptual framework and guidelines for the implementation of mass information systems. *Information & Management*, *28*(2), 125–142. doi:10.1016/0378-7206(95)94021-4

Hoffman, D. L., & Novak, T. P. (1996). Marketing in hypermedia computer-mediated environments: Conceptual foundations. *JMR, Journal of Marketing Research*, *60*(7), 50–68.

Isakowitz, T., Bieber, M., & Vitali, F. (1998). Web information systems. *Communications of the ACM*, *41*(7), 78–80. doi:10.1145/278476.278490

Jackson, C. M., Chow, C., & Leitch, R. A. (1997). Toward an understanding of the behavioral intention to use an information system. *Decision Sciences*, *28*(2), 357–390. doi:10.1111/j.1540-5915.1997.tb01315.x

Johnson, C., & Mathews, B. P. (1997). The influence of experience on service expectations. *International Journal of Service Industry Management*, *8*(4), 290–305. doi:10.1108/09564239710174381

Kisielius, J., & Sternthal, B. (1984). Detecting and explaining vividness effects in attitudinal judgments. *JMR, Journal of Marketing Research*, *21*, 54–64. doi:10.2307/3151792

Lane, M. S., & Koronios, A. (2001). A balanced approach to capturing user requirements in business-to-user web information systems. *Australian Journal of Information Systems*, *9*(1), 61–69.

MacInnis, D. J., Moorman, C., & Jaworski, B. J. (1991). Enhancing and measuring users' motivation, opportunity, and ability to process brand information from ads. *Journal of Marketing*, *55*(4), 32–53. doi:10.2307/1251955

Mahajan, V., & Muller, E. (1990). New product diffusion models in marketing: A review and directions for research. *JMR, Journal of Marketing Research*, *54*(1), 1–27. doi:10.2307/1252170

Malhotra, Y., & Galletta, D. F. (1999). Extending the technology acceptance model for social influence: theoretical bases and empirical validation. In *Proceedings of the 32nd ICSS*, 1999.

Markus, L. M., & Robey, D. (1983). The organizational validity of management information systems. *Human Relations*, *36*(3), 203–225. doi:10.1177/001872678303600301

Meuter, M. L., Ostrom, A. L., Roundtree, R. I., & Bitner, M. J. (2000). Self-service technologies: Understanding customer satisfaction with technology-based service encounters. *Journal of Marketing*, *64*, 50–64. doi:10.1509/jmkg.64.3.50.18024

Mohr, L. (1969). Determinants of innovations in organizations. *American Policy Science Review*, *63*, 111–126. doi:10.2307/1954288

Moon, J., & Kim, Y. (2001). Extending the TAM for a world-wide-web context. *Information & Management*, *38*, 217–230. doi:10.1016/S0378-7206(00)00061-6

Ramaswami, S. N., Strader, T. J., & Brett, K. (2001). Determinants of on-line channel use for purchasing financial products. *International Journal of E-Communications*, *5*(2), 95–118.

Riel, A. C. R., Liljander, V., & Jurriens, P. (2001). Exploring user evaluations of web-based e-services: A portal site. *International Journal of Service Industry Management*, *12*(4), 359–377. doi:10.1108/09564230110405280

Robey, D. (1979). User attitudes and management information system use. *Academy of Management Journal*, *22*(3), 527–538. doi:10.2307/255742

Rogers, E. (1983). *Diffusion of innovation* (2nd ed.).

Russo, J. E., Staelin, R., Nolan, C. A., Russel, G. J., & Metcalf, B. L. (1986). Nutrition information in the supermarket. *Journal of User Research*, *13*(June), 48–70.

Ruyter, K. D., Wetzels, M., & Kleijnen, M. (2001). Customer adoption of web-based e-service: An experimental study. *International Journal of Service Industry Management*, *12*(2), 184–207. doi:10.1108/09564230110387542

Sproule, S., & Archer, N. (2000). A buyer behavior framework for the development and design of software agents in e-commerce. *Internet Research: Electronic Networking Applications and Policy*, *10*(5), 396–405. doi:10.1108/10662240010349408

Szymanski, D. M., & Hise, R. T. (2000). E-satisfaction: An initial examination. *Journal of Retailing*, *76*(3), 309–322. doi:10.1016/S0022-4359(00)00035-X

Trevino, L. K., & Webster, J. (1992). Flow in computer-mediated communication. *Communication Research*, *19*(5), 539–573. doi:10.1177/009365092019005001

Velli, A., Lisboa, P. J. G., & Meehan, K. (2000). Quantitative characterization and prediction of on-line purchasing behavior: A latent variable approach. *International Journal of Electronic Commerce*, *4*(4), 83–104.

Venkatesh, V. (1999). Creation of favorable user perceptions: Exploring the role of intrinsic motivation. *Management Information Systems Quarterly*, *23*(2), 239–260. doi:10.2307/249753

Webster, J., Trevino, L. K., & Ryan, L. (1993). The dimensionality and correlates of flow in human-computer interactions. *Computers in Human Behavior*, *9*, 411–426. doi:10.1016/0747-5632(93)90032-N

Wu, K. L., Yu, P. S., & Ballman, A. (1998). Speed tracer: A Web usage mining and analysis tool. *IBM Systems Journal*, *37*(1), 89–106. doi:10.1147/sj.371.0089

Zaltman, G., Duncan, R., & Holbeck, J. (1985). *Innovations and organizations*. Malabar, FL: Robert E. Krieger.

Zeithaml, V. A., Berry, L., & Parasuraman, A. (1993). The nature and determinants of customer expectations of service. *Journal of the Academy of Marketing Science*, *21*(1), 1–12. doi:10.1177/0092070393211001

Zeithaml, V. A., Parasuraman, A., & Malhotra, A. (2000). *A conceptual framework for understanding e-service quality: Implications for future research and managerial practice*. Working Paper. Report No. 00-115.

Chapter 16
A Multi-Agent Knowledge Management System for Reactive and Proactive Knowledge Supply

Carlos M. Toledo
Institute of Development and Design, National Council of Scientific and Technological Research, Argentina

Omar Chiotti
Institute of Development and Design, National Council of Scientific and Technological Research, Argentina

María R. Galli
Institute of Development and Design, National Council of Scientific and Technological Research, Argentina

ABSTRACT

This chapter presents an agent-based architecture for integrating organizational knowledge repositories and business processes orchestrated by a workflow management system. This architecture proactively provides relevant knowledge to workflow tasks considering their context, and stores the information generated by its execution for future requirements. It describes components of the architecture, models a multi-agent system that enables the integration, presents a strategy to annotate and retrieval knowledge of non-structured information sources, and defines a new workflow pattern to be used in knowledge intensive tasks in order to make possible the knowledge provision. This architecture allows workers to count, in a proactive way, with all necessary information for the task executions without suspending their activities to retrieve information scattered in the organization. It reduces the wasted time in manual knowledge searches included in mostly knowledge management approaches.

DOI: 10.4018/978-1-4666-0948-8.ch016

INTRODUCTION

Knowledge is currently recognized as a valuable asset for organizations. It is considered a capital that has an economic value for an organization; a strategic resource used to increase productivity and offer stability in dynamic competitive environments (Ermine, 2000). In this new paradigm, in which physical capital and work are no longer the only fundamental basis for successful management, Knowledge Management (KM) has captured the attention of organizations as one of the most promising ways to reach success in this information era (Malone, 2003). Companies are beginning to understand the importance of knowledge in the organization as a resource which enables them to gain a sustainable competitive advantage (Bolloju et al.,2002).

In the pursuit of strategic competitiveness, great KM effort has dealt with capturing, codifying, storing, and disseminating knowledge in the organization (Lai, 2007). However, most of these efforts have been carried out in an isolated manner, without linking the organizational knowledge with organizational business processes. Nowadays, organizations coordinate their activities through business processes. To accomplish the tasks involved in a business process, workers can need information that is scattered along the organization.

This need for information should be considered in a contextualized way and be suitably delivered by the organizational KM infrastructure. Business Process Management (BPM) and KM are closely interrelated and are both essential elements of an organization. Therefore, this interrelation must be addressed in the development of a system architecture for KM.

Traditionally, KM approaches focused on providing information in a reactive way (Ale, 2009). When a worker needs information while executing a task, the worker must do an explicit search in an organizational knowledge repository with the aim of finding relevant information to continue the task execution. Once a task has been executed, the information generated as a result of its execution should be stored in a suitable way for future requirements. This paradigm is adequate in organizational areas in which the executed processes are unstructured, dynamic, unpredictable, and constantly changing without a fixed model that guides the control flow among their activities and workers. However, in areas where workers execute tasks belonging to a structured business process, information needs should be satisfied in a proactive way, allowing workers continue task execution while collecting all the necessary information from the organizational knowledge repository.

Workers will not do extra work to support a KM system unless it contributes to improve their jobs. In this case, organizational activities structured through a business process and automated by a Workflow Management System (WfMS) (Hollingsworth, 2005) should be considered as an opportunity to provide a KM infrastructure in order to bring the right knowledge to the right people in the right form and at the right time. WfMS should be considered a trigger of KM-support activities and a distributor of organizational knowledge that provides workers with necessary information to make better judgments and decisions.

In this new vision, process-based KM emerges as a potential challenge to support business processes with manual or semi-automatic tasks that need knowledge for their execution and, as a result, can produce new knowledge. Tasks with these needs are called Knowledge Intensive Tasks (KIT) and workflows composed of KITs are called knowledge intensive workflows (Sarnikar & Deokar, 2010). Process-based KM takes advantage of the task context provided by the workflow to deliver task-relevant knowledge. Organizations often execute activities with both types of information needs (reactive and proactive); thus, the KM architecture should support both needs (Jung et al., 2007).

In this chapter, we propose an agent-based architecture for an integration of business processes orchestrated by a WfMS with the organizational knowledge repository administered by ontology-driven KM systems. This architecture proactively provides relevant knowledge to tasks, considering their context and stores relevant knowledge in a proper way for future requirements. In case of necessity of more information, also the architecture reactively brings knowledge through natural language queries. Conventional workflows are extended with KM-support automatic tasks that are responsible for retrieving knowledge and storing results.

STATE OF THE ART

Since the beginning of the systematic management of knowledge, many efforts have dealt with the process-based KM in order to integrate the advantages of the both paradigms. Papavassiliou et al. (2002) propose a framework for weakly-structured and knowledge-intensive business processes. This approach is composed by a workflow meta-model which explicitly consider KM tasks and knowledge objects in business processes, and a business process modelling tool that enables the modelling of weakly-structured business process. Knowledge-intensive business processes generally contain document-centred activities and require workers' decisions based on their experiences. Weakly-structures business processes are composed by several steps in which are involved different peoples, roles, and organisational areas. The proposed workflow meta-model is an extension of reference model proposed by Workflow Management Coalition (Hollingsworth, 2005). The meta-model distinguishes two type of task: normal tasks (related with the work structure) and KM task (such as knowledge storage, knowledge distribution, knowledge generation, and knowledge application). This extended meta-model captures the knowledge perspective which describes the content of knowledge object by reference to ontological concepts. By means of this extension KM tasks are integrated in workflow model. However, these approach does not provide the services for proactive knowledge supply, it does not even present an explicit integration with organisational KM system.

Abecker et al. (2000) present two project for KM and BPM integration: VisualOffice and KnowMore projects. VisualOffice employs workflow-context data to integrate paper-based information in workflows. VisualOffice uses context information, a scanned document analysis, and information understanding system to provide kwnowledge to workflow worker. Relevant information of workflow instances are collected in order to use this information for document retrieval. KnowMore project is focused on the support of people who work on KITs by automatic delivery of relevant and context-sensitive information. KnowMore recommends relevant information to workflow workers and keeps track of workflows and record the results of task executions together with relevant context data. These solutions do not consider open environment, in which the knowledge domains are not known in advance.

Jung et al. (2007) define an architecture for integrating BPM and KM based on their lifecycle requirements. This approach tries to consolidate KM and BPM lifecycle extending these ones by means of process knowledge. Process knowledge contains three types of knowledge to support process-related activities: *process template knowledge* which contains the information collected during process creation, modelling, and evolution; *process instance knowledge* composed of information collected during and after the process enactment phase; and *process-related knowledge* which can be used by the activity performed when a business process is executed. These three types of knowledge support knowledge-intensive activities. Based on defined activities of the architecture, a framework is implemented following the proposed architecture.

Han et al. (2009) propose a framework for process-centred knowledge model, develop an enterprise ontology for context richness that links enterprise concepts for future knowledge retrieval, and also, they implement a KM system that support the framework. They consider the business process as knowledge itself in the proposed knowledge model, and the base for creating and using enterprise knowledge. The proposal is intended to provide knowledge enriched by the context for correct task executions. The model classify the knowledge objects in: process knowledge and task support knowledge. Process knowledge provides guidelines and tools for task execution, and the task support knowledge (such as document, business rules, expert consulting, and on-line forum) enables to make better decision during the process execution. The enterprise ontology has the main concepts of a process-centred enterprise (process, customer, product, participant, resource, supplier, and part). The related concepts are connected through the enterprise ontology allowing for the retrieval of a set of related documents instead of isolated information. When data is created it is registered in the ontology, thus, workers can retrieve relevant knowledge objects by means the interrelationships provided by the enterprise ontology. This proposal does not provide knowledge in a proactive way, it only makes relationships among concepts.

Most of these approaches deal with explicit modelling of context information in knowledge-intensive workflows, and its use for better retrieval and knowledge storage. But these proposals do not consider characteristics such as proactive information delivery and integration of business process with the current organizational knowledge repository. Also, they do not consider the fact that organizations are composed by areas with different needs for information (reactive and proactive) depending on the task execution structure implemented by the organizational area. For these reason, we consider necessary a novel architecture that includes these characteristics. In the next section, we propose this architecture which uses software agents facilitate their development and provide flexibility.

AN AGENT-BASED ARCHITECTURE

The proposed architecture consists of two components: the organizational knowledge repository and knowledge intensive workflows (Figure 1).

In the organizational knowledge repository component, the organization is considered as an interrelated groups of functional units, areas or departments formally defined in the organizational structure, or informal groups or practice communities. Each of these units is considered an organizational knowledge domain which executes activities and processes that produce and consume information. These activities and processes are often unstructured, dynamic, unpredictable, and constantly changing; and they are not included in a workflow. Due to this dynamism, the need for information is satisfied in a reactive way, generally by conventional information systems or natural language queries, through knowledge domain KM systems. KM systems are responsible for providing information to their own knowledge domain, to other knowledge domains, and, in the case of this architecture, to knowledge intensive workflows as well. The set of knowledge domains constitutes the organizational knowledge repository, i.e. the organizational memory (Kühn et al.,1997).

In the knowledge intensive workflows component, a set of business processes automated in a workflow is composed of one or more KITs that need and/or produce enterprise valuable knowledge as a result of their execution. For each KIT, the KM architecture proactively provides relevant information for its execution, considering the KIT context (worker profile, worker role profile, task specification, and workflow instance information) and workers' behavior in previous executions. Also, it stores relevant information produced as

Figure 1. Business process management and knowledge management integration architecture

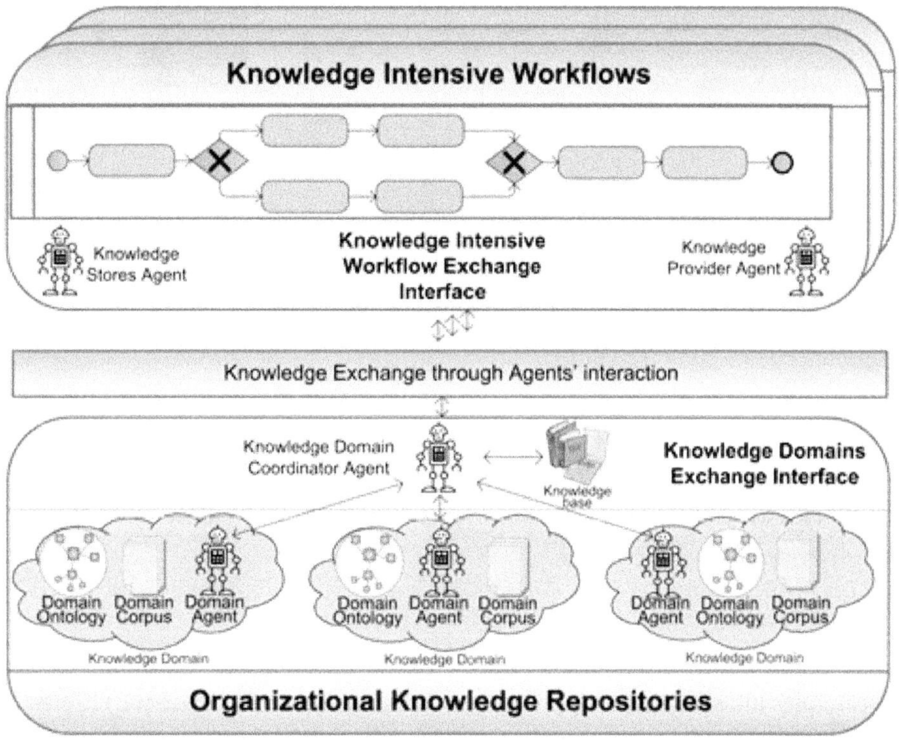

a result of their execution in a suitable knowledge domain. Unlike organization functional units, which execute their processes in an unstructured way, knowledge intensive workflows execute their tasks in a structured process orchestrated by a WfMS.

In this KM architecture, each knowledge intensive workflow can "belong to" or "be linked to" an organizational knowledge domain. Knowledge intensive workflows are not considered as a knowledge domain per se, i.e. they do not manage their own knowledge. They achieve their knowledge storage and retrieval by means of its interaction with organizational knowledge domains, in which KM systems are executed. Such knowledge generated by unstructured tasks performed in a knowledge domain, as knowledge generated in a knowledge intensive workflow are stored in the organization knowledge repository, under a distributed organizational memory paradigm (Souza, 2006). This restriction facilitates the integration and administration activities.

With the aim of exchanging knowledge between the two components, and proactively and reactively delivering knowledge, the architecture implements four software agents. These agents enable the integration between knowledge intensive workflows and KM systems executed in knowledge domains by means of suitable interaction protocols. Through interaction protocols, agents exchange the necessary information and data control to satisfy the workflow workers' need for information. The remainder of this chapter describes each component.

Organizational Knowledge Repository

Organizations are composed of several functional units (areas, departments, groups, practice communities, etc.) considered as knowledge domains.

Figure 2. KM system: conceptual architecture

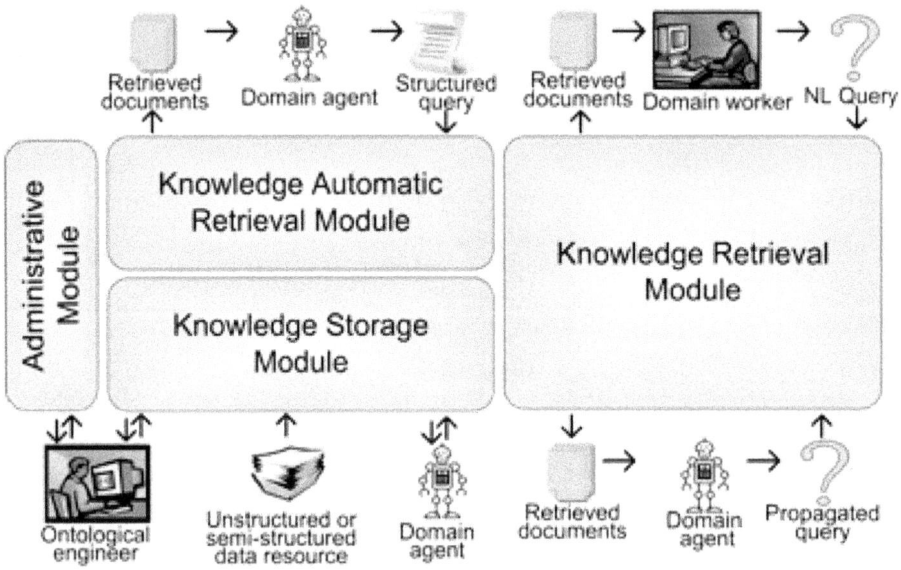

Each knowledge domain fulfills autonomy and coordination principles allowing a KM approach based on a distributed architecture. Autonomy capabilities enable each domain to manage the local information, providing the possibility of choosing more appropriate perspectives, mechanisms and politics (e.g. security politics, domain ontology) to denote the local knowledge. On the other hand, coordination capabilities enable the exchange information with other knowledge domains and sharing knowledge between organizational units (Bonifacio et al., 2002).

Each knowledge domain implements its own ontology-driven KM system (Figure 2). This KM system is part of a distributed organizational memory (Souza, 2006; Ale, 2009) and uses an ontology approach to annotate and retrieve information based on a strategy that processes users' natural language queries. These approaches enables the supply of concept-based contents rather than key-word based contents. Domain ontologies aim at capturing domain knowledge, providing a compromised understanding of a domain, and allowing integration between different formats of knowledge and information sources (e.g. text documents, databases, etc.) (Fensel, 2003).

Each KM system is composed of four modules: knowledge storage module, knowledge automatic retrieval module, knowledge retrieval module, and administrative module (Figure 2). The knowledge storage module is responsible for retrieving knowledge from heterogeneous information sources (text documents, memorandum, spreadsheets, graphs, databases, etc.) with natural language content, and its representation in a suitable form.

Knowledge acquisition and representation are crucial for organizational memory implementation. In an ideal case, an organizational memory would be self-adaptive and self-organized, collecting relevant knowledge during the operations of usual businesses. Although this would diminish acquisition costs, it is not always possible and often requires some type of manual intervention (Ale et al., 2008a).

In this strategy, the ontological engineer performs this intervention and has the following three responsibilities: first, developing the initial domain ontologies and updating it (Toledo et al., 2010a; Toledo et al., 2010b); second, deciding which are the more-representative domain concepts for each information source (document descriptors) in the annotation strategy; and third, watching over information security by means of an appropriate selection of information access permissions. The information author presents the access permission of the information, and during the annotation process the ontological engineer ensures that the knowledge domain preserves it.

The document annotation strategy implemented in knowledge storage module is based on domain ontologies and derives from the strategy proposed by Ale et al. (Ale et al., 2008a; Ale et al., 2008b). In the implemented strategy (Figure 3), each unstructured information source with content expressed in natural language goes through a tagging process or POSTagging (Part-Of-Speech Tagging) (Felman et al., 2007). A label with its syntactic nature (adjective, noun, verb, conjunction, determiner, etc.) is assigned to each element (words and symbols) in the document. Once the tagging process is finished, the lemma for each element is obtained and, based on a linguistic pattern, Document Concepts (DC) are selected. A DC derives from the following linguistic pattern: *DC – Noun+ | (Adjetive+Noun+)*[1]

Using the selected DC of the tagged text, a searching process of exact occurrences begins. In this process, each DC is compared with the concepts of the domain ontology that represent the knowledge in the domain. If matches are found, that DC is marked as a candidate document descriptor and it is linked to the corresponding ontological concept. If there is no match, such DC is added to an unlinked DC list for further treatment.

With the unlinked DC list, a process of semantic expansion begins, which extends the document representation. For each unlinked DC, a set of synonyms of its last noun (head noun) is searched in WordNet lexical database. These synonymous are replaced in the DC pattern and obtained DCs are compared with the ontological concepts. If a match between an obtained DC and an ontological concept is found, such DC is chosen as a candidate document descriptor and the original DC is eliminated from the unlinked DC list.

Then, for each DC that remains in the unlinked DC list, hyperonyms of its last noun are obtained in the WordNet and replaced in original DC and, again matches between obtained DCs and ontological concepts are searched.

Finally, if no coincidence can be found, the DCs included in the unlinked DC list are discarded. The ontological engineer should then choose document descriptors from candidate document descriptors obtained in the previous process, and stores them

Figure 3. Document annotation strategy

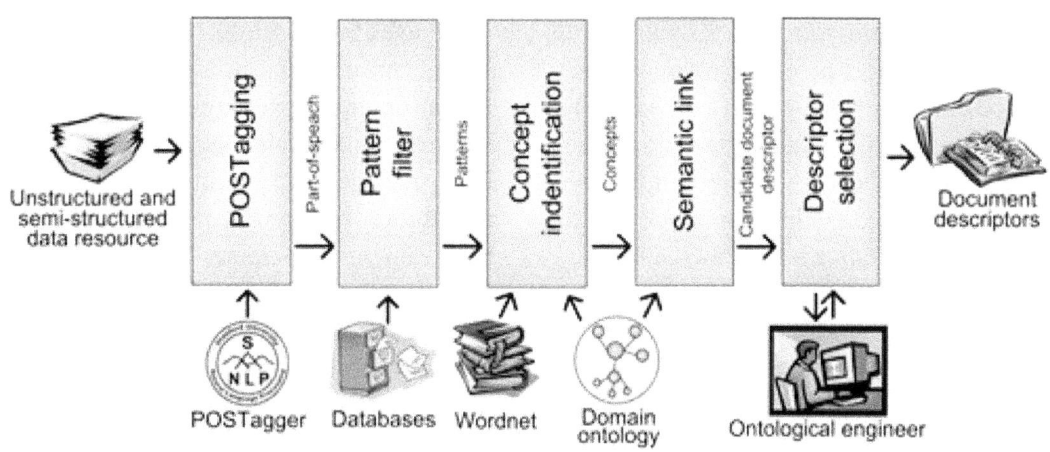

as document descriptors for later searches. These searches can be performed by means of natural language queries through the knowledge retrieval module, or structured queries through the knowledge automatic retrieval module.

The information retrieval strategy used in the knowledge retrieval module (Figure 3) was developed for Onto-DOM KM system (Ale et al., 2008b). When a user makes a query in natural language, the system transforms this query by eliminating natural language ambiguity and then, it acquires the most representative domain concepts. This process is carried out by using the domain ontology, and it aims at finding a similarity between query concepts (query concepts are obtained using the same linguistic pattern used by document concepts) and the ontological concepts.

Since natural language queries have a few words, the strategy increases those concepts by using WordNet lexical database and some heuristic rules like wh-words that give an idea of the type of answer expected by users (when: time, where: location, who: person, etc). Finally, retrieved documents are sorted by relevance taking in account the amount of found coincidences between query concepts and documents descriptors. In the documents with the same amount of concept coincidences, they are sorted by the frequency of appearance of each concept.

The knowledge automatic retrieval module is responsible for the automatic information retrieval by the domain agent. This module retrieves information through structured queries instead of natural language queries processed by knowledge retrieval module. Structured queries are made from the worker profile information, the worker role profile information, the KIT specification, and the workflow instance information. The implemented strategy aims at providing information, in a proactive way, to workers that execute workflow tasks. This information supply is accomplished through interactions among knowledge provider agent, the knowledge coordinator agent, and the domain agent (Section Knowledge Management Software Agents).

Maintenance activities are performed by means of the administrative module. In this module, the ontological engineer creates and updates the domain ontology, creates and modifies domain workers, sets and modifies the document access permissions, deletes document annotations, and modifies the domain workers' security credentials. Moreover, this module is responsible for domain workers' authentication, whereas workflow workers' authentication is performed by the knowledge coordinator agent.

The proposed strategies of annotation and retrieval are just recommendations, they can be replaced with others; even, each knowledge domain can implement its own strategy. This capability is achieved because the architecture is developed under a distributed organizational memory paradigm and autonomy and coordination principles, (Souza, 2006; Ale, 2009). In the same way, each knowledge domain creates and maintains its own domain ontology, as long as the implemented strategies enable domain interaction and allow information sharing with other domains and knowledge intensive workflows.

Knowledge Intensive Workflows

The other component is integrated by one or more knowledge intensive workflows. A workflow deals with the automation of a business process to achieve a business goal (Weske, 2007). The enactment of business processes involve knowledge and information exchange among participants, according to a defined set of rules. A WfMS defines, manages, and executes structured business processes (workflows) arranging task executions by means of a computer representation of the workflow logic (Hollingsworth, 2005). WfMS is the place where business processes are defined and daily executed; therefore, this feature makes it an ideal tool for the automatically spreading

Figure 4. KIT specification

```
<?xml version="1.0" encoding='iso-8859-1' standalone="yes" ?>
<kit>
<kitId> </kitId>
<kitName> </kitName>
<workflowId> </workflowId>

<informationNeeds>
      <requiredDocument>
            <document> </document>
            <domain> </domain>
      <\requiredDocument>
      <interestConcepts>
            <concept> </concept>
            <concept> </concept>
      <\interestConcepts>
      <preferredDomain>
            <domain> </domain>
            <domain> </domain>
      <\preferredDomain>
      </informationNeeds>
      <informationStorage>
            <defaultDomainStore domain="">
            <privateInformationStoreIn domain="">
            <storeByConcepts>
                  <concept> <\concept>
                  <domain> <\domain>
            <\storeByConcepts>
            <storeByWorker>
                  <worker> <\worker>
                  <domain> <\domain>
            <\storeByWorker>
      <\informationStorage>
</kit>
```

and capturing the knowledge throughout the organization.

Some complex business processes rely on intensive information needs, such as design process, government tenders, decision making, etc., in which workers would like WfMS to automatically and proactively offer the relevant knowledge (Lai et al., 2002).When a worker selects an item for its execution from a work list, the system should make relevant information available for executing the selected task. It allows workers to automatically count on relevant information, avoiding the waste of time in information searches. The system provides users with information based on the following criteria:

- Information created for this task in previously workflow enactments
- Information created for previously executed tasks
- Information prefixed in the KIT specification
- Information obtained through concepts of interest prefixed in the KIT specification

If these information, automatically provided by the KM architecture to KIT worker, is not enough to complete the task execution; KIT workers can make explicit searches. They are similar to searches conduced by knowledge domain workers and are made through natural language queries. They are responded for knowledge retrieval module of each knowledge domain. The knowledge coordinator agent's knowledge base is fed with information about these additional searches for future automatic recommendations of relevant information for workers of this KIT.

Figure 5. Knowledge intensive task wrapper

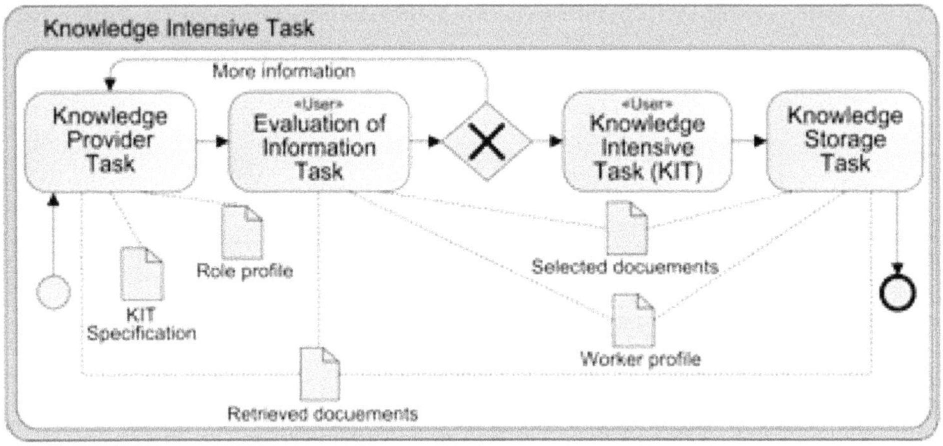

In order to satisfy the information offer criteria, the architecture has two information supply approaches: one of them is static and associates configuration data to each KIT by means of an eXtensible Markup Language (XML) data object (so-called KIT specification, Figure 4), where static information needs are preset. The second approach is implemented by means of machine learning techniques, in which the knowledge coordinator agent stores additional information requests made by workers and statistical data on the use of the information (which documents are retrieved when executing a query, which documents are consulted, how many times they have been consulted, who creates a document, and in which workflow it was created). This information is used to automatically offer relevant information in future executions of the same task.

Once the execution of a task is finished, the information produced during the task execution should be stored. To store this information, there are several options:

- Creating a specific knowledge domain to support a specific knowledge intensive workflow
- Linking a knowledge intensive workflow with an existing knowledge domain
- Linking a knowledge intensive workflow with several existing knowledge domains

According to these options, each KIT is independently configured with several parameters that allow specifying the storage of its results. Each KIT can define its storage in the following way: all results of a task execution are stored in a specific domain; results of a task execution that contain a specific concept are stored in a prefixed domain; documents with a specific security level are stored in a specific domain; documents created by a specific worker are stored in a specific domain; or any possible combination. The domain knowledge coordinator agent stores each result in one or more knowledge domains (Section Agents' behavior) taking in account these parameters. The stored information is administered with strategies (annotation, re-annotation, and retrieval strategy) and security policies implemented in the chosen domain and under the control of the ontological engineer of this domain.

Both information retrieval parameters and information storage parameters are configured in each KIT specification. KIT specification is a XML data object associated with each KIT that saves relevant information. A KIT specification has three parts to save these parameters: the first part is general task information. It includes a KIT identification, a workflow identification, and the KIT name. The second part has static information needs for the KIT execution. The third part configures the information storage criteria.

The general information part is used to identify unambiguously each task execution. The information needs part saves parameters that are necessary to satisfy information needed by workers, such as prefixed documents, information with specific key concepts, domains of preference. A specific document from a knowledge domain can be specified to be retrieved by means of *<requieredDocument>* tag. Key concepts can be defined through *<interestConcepts>* tag. These concepts are then used by domain agents to search information that contain them. Also, a KIT can specify which domains are preferred as knowledge providers by means of *<preferredDomain>* tag. These preferences not only allow retrieving information but also establish an importance order in the displayed information for workers

The information storage part saves the criteria of information storage. The *<defaultDomainStore domain="">* tag specifies a default domain to store the documents. The *<privateInformationStoreIn domain="">* tag sets up the domain where private information must be stored. The *<storeByConcepts>* tag defines that all documents with a specific concept should be stored in a specific domain. The *<storeByWorker>* tag presets that all documents created by a specific worker must be stored in a specific domain. The order of appearance of tags in each part of the KIT specification shows the application precedence of the criteria.

In addition to KIT specifications, information about worker profile and worker role profile is saved. This information is used to identify a particular worker and provide more accurate information. Also, this information is used to allow workers to access to information taking into account its security permissions.

We propose to extend conventional workflows with KM-support automatic tasks (knowledge provider task and knowledge storage task) and KM-support data (KIT specification, worker profile information, and worker role profile) to support context-aware knowledge delivery and storage. For each KIT, additional KM-support tasks and KM-support data are added. These additional KM- support elements aim to provide all the required mechanisms to provide workers with the right knowledge in the right form and at the right time for the KIT execution to worker. For organization purposes, each KIT with their additional KM-support elements are wrapped in a sub-process (Figure 5).

The KIT wrapper is a generic and recurring construct used in knowledge intensive workflows that are to be integrated with the KM system. The KIT wrapper is used as a workflow pattern (Russell et al., 2006) that should be employed for each workflow KIT. When a knowledge intensive workflow is being designed, each KIT should be replaced with the KIT wrapper construct. It enables the integration of the workflow with the organizational knowledge repository, through the proposed KM architecture, in a transparent way.

KNOWLEDGE MANAGEMENT SOFTWARE AGENTS

In order to exchange information and control data among workflows and knowledge domain, four software agents are necessary: domain agent and knowledge coordinator agent are executed in the organizational knowledge repository, and knowledge provider agent and knowledge storage agent are executed in each workflow KIT. A domain agent is executed in each knowledge domain and it is responsible for domain coordination, safeguarding correct information access, watching over information security of its own domain, and interacting with knowledge coordinator agent.

This interaction is necessary to satisfy information requests coming from the WfMS or other knowledge domains. The domain agent is the interface that allows the domain to exchange information with the outside. This exchange is made by means of structured queries when the communication is the KM system and WfMS, or natural language queries when the communication is among KM systems.

Knowledge coordinator agent is responsible for receiving information requests from KITs executed in knowledge intensive workflows and information requests from knowledge domains. KITs information needs can be formulated through a structured query (in the case of proactive information provision, without worker intervention) or through a natural language query (when a worker needs additional information and thus he makes a natural language query).

On the other hand, information requests from other knowledge domains are always formulated in a natural language; these queries are called propagated queries because we say when an user does not receive a suitable answer by its domain, it propagates this query to other domain with the aim of getting better answers. A propagated query enables a domain worker to ask for information stored in another knowledge domain, allowing information exchange between knowledge domains. The knowledge coordinator agent is also responsible for authenticating workflow workers before fulfilling any information requirement.

An instance of the knowledge provider agent is executed in each knowledge provider task. A knowledge provider task is an additional KM-support task added to a KIT (Figure 6). This agent is responsible for retrieving information related with the associated KIT. For this purpose, the agent starts a communication process with knowledge coordinator agent. The information recovery process takes into account data related with the worker profile and selects the KIT for its execution, the worker role profile, and the KIT specification to retrieve adequate information.

Finally, an instance of the knowledge storage agent is executed in each workflow knowledge storage task. This agent is responsible for collecting results generated by task execution. Then, it establishes a communication process with the knowledge coordinator agent with the aim of storing results in a suitable knowledge domain.

To determine the domain in which results will be stored, the knowledge coordinator agent takes into account preset parameters of the KIT specification. The following section describes the agents' behavior and their interrelation through interaction protocols.

Agents' Behavior

In order to describe the interaction among agents, we use AUML 2 (Huget et al., 2006). A successful integration largely depends on the agent interaction and their capabilities to provide the necessary information. Figure 6 depicts agents' interaction.

When a worker starts the execution of a KIT by selecting an item from the work list, the system run the KM-support task wrapped the KIT wrapper (Figure 6). The first task of the KIT wrapper to be executed is the knowledge provider task that contains an instance of the knowledge provider agent. This agent establishes a communication protocol with the knowledge coordinator agent providing the KM-support data (worker profile, worker role profile, and KIT specification). The knowledge coordinator agent authenticates the worker in the system and, based on the KM-support data, retrieves information from knowledge domain based on the following strategy:

First, the knowledge coordinator agent asks to the domain agent for the documents preset by means of <requiredDocument> tag in the KIT specification. The retrieved documents are sorted by order of appearance of <requiredDocument> tags in the KIT specification.

Second, the knowledge coordinator agent retrieves information with similar semantics to that of prefixed information documents. For this

Figure 6. Knowledge supply interaction protocol

propose, each domain agent selects similar information using the k-nearest neighbour method in the following way: nouns of prefixed documents are obtained and compares these nouns with nouns of other information sources stored in the domain. This comparison is performed by means of the cosine similarity function calculated between binary vector spaces of the information source, (Felman et al., 2008). The vector space is generated according to the presence or absence of a concept.

Third, the knowledge coordinator agent requests information that contain interest concepts preset in <interestConcepts> tags of the KIT specification. Each knowledge domain carries out a search, which is similar that of retrieval strategy (Ale et al., 2008a; Ale et al., 2008b). This search retrieves information that contain interest concepts or their synonyms.

Fourth, the knowledge coordinator agent asks its knowledge base and creates a ranking of information documents according to reading frequency and retrieves these best-ranking documents. This ranks first the *k* documents that have been-most frequently read by that worker in the current task, followed by *k* documents that have been most frequently read by any worker in the current task, and finally, the *k* documents that have been most frequently read by any worker in any task of the current workflow.

Finally, the knowledge coordinator agent informs of the information documents previously created by the worker and the documents previously created in the current workflow.

Once the knowledge coordinator agent informs the retrieved information, the knowledge provider agent displays it to the worker. The worker can select information document to read and/or perform additional searches by means of natural language queries. When a user selects a information document to be read, a new communication protocol is established for providing the content of the selected documents.

On another hand, when a worker carries out a search for additional information, the knowledge provider agent propagates this query to knowledge coordinator agent, which is responsible for requesting its execution in each knowledge domain.

DISCUSSION AND FUTURE WORK

We have presented an agent-based architecture for integrating business processes with the organizational knowledge repository. This architecture is intended to deliver knowledge in a proactive and reactive way, decreasing the time wasted in information searches and suitable document storage.

In this chapter, we laid the foundations for a software architecture for the knowledge and process integration. In future contributions, components of the architecture will be designed and implemented in JaCaMo framework[2]. JaCaMo is the platform for multi-agent programming that combines three independent existing MAS technologies: Jason (Bordini et al., 2007), CArtAgO (Ricci et al., 2010), and Moise (Hubner et al., 2007)

REFERENCES

Abecker, A., Bernardi, A., Maus, H., Sintek, M., & Wenzel, C. (2000). Information supply for business processes: coupling workflow with document analysis and information retrieval. *Knowledge-Based Systems*, *13*(5), 271–284. doi:10.1016/S0950-7051(00)00087-3

Ale, M. (2009). *An organizational knowledge management conceptual model PhD in Information Systems*. National Technological University.

Ale, M., Chiotti, O., & Galli, M. R. (2008b). Enterprise knowledge management for emergent organizations: An ontology-driven approach. knowledge management strategies. In Lytras, M. D., Russ, M., Maier, R., & Naeve, A. (Eds.), *A handbook of applied technologies* (pp. 218–249). Hershey, PA: IGI Global. doi:10.4018/978-1-59904-603-7.ch008

Ale, M., Gerarduzzi, C., Chiotti, O., & Galli, M. R. (2008a). Organizational knowledge sources integration through an ontology-based approach: The Onto-DOM architecture. In Lytras, M. D., Carroll, J. M., Damiani, E., & Tennyson, R. D. (Eds.), *World Summit On the Knowledge Society, LNCS 5288* (pp. 441–450). Springer. doi:10.1007/978-3-540-87781-3_48

Bolloju, N., Khalifa, M., & Turban, E. (2002). Integrating knowledge management into enterprise environments for the next generation decision support. *Decision Support Systems, 33*(2), 163–176. doi:10.1016/S0167-9236(01)00142-7

Bonifacio, M., Bouquet, P., & Traverso, P. (2002). Enabling distributed knowledge management: Managerial and technological implications. *Novatica and Informatik/Informatique, 3*(1).

Bordini, R. H., Hübner, J., & Wooldridge, M. (2007). *Programming multi-agent systems in AgentSpeak using Jason*. England: Wiley. doi:10.1002/9780470061848

Dustdar, S. (2005). Reconciling knowledge management and workflow management systems: The activity-based knowledge management approach. *Journal of Universal Computer Science, 11*(4), 589–604.

Ermine, J. (2000). Challenges and approaches for knowledge management in companies. In *Proceedings of Workshop in Knowledge Management: Theory and Applications*, France.

Feldman, R., & Sanger, J. (2007). *The text mining handbook: Advanced approaches in analyzing unstructured data*. USA: Cambridge University Press.

Fensel, D. A. (2003). *Ontologies: A silver bullet for knowledge management and electronic commerce* (2nd ed.). Springer.

Han, K. H., & Park, J. W. (2009). Process-centred knowledge model and enterprise ontology for the development of knowledge management system. *Expert Systems with Applications, 36*(4), 7441–7447. doi:10.1016/j.eswa.2008.09.031

Hollingsworth, D. (2005). *The workflow reference model*. Workflow Management Coalition, Tech. Rep. TC00-1003.

Hübner, J., Sichman, J., & Boissier, O. (2007). Developing organised multiagent systems using the Moise+ model: programming issues at the system and agent levels. *International Journal of Agent-Oriented Software Engineering, 1*(3/4), 370–395. doi:10.1504/IJAOSE.2007.016266

Huget, M., & Odell, J. (2004). Representing agent interaction protocols with agent UML. In *Proceedings of the 3rd International Joint Conference on Autonomous Agents and Multiagent Systems*, Vol. 3, (pp. 1244–1245). IEEE Computer Society.

Jung, J., Choi, I., & Song, M. (2007). An integration architecture for knowledge management systems and business process management systems. *Computers in Industry, 58*(1), 21–34. doi:10.1016/j.compind.2006.03.001

Kühn, O., & Abecker, A. (1997). Corporate memories for knowledge management in industrial practice: Prospects and challenges. *Journal of Universal Computer Science, 3*(8), 929–954.

Lai, J., & Fan, Y. (2002). Workflow and knowledge management: Approaching an integration. In Han, Y., Tai, S., & Wikarski, D. (Eds.), *LNCS 2480* (pp. 16–29). Springer. doi:10.1007/3-540-45785-2_2

Lai, L. F. (2007). A knowledge engineering approach to knowledge management. *Information Sciences*, *177*(19), 4072–4094. doi:10.1016/j.ins.2007.02.028

Malone, D. (2003). Knowledge management: A model for organizational learning. *International Journal of Accounting Information Systems*, *3*(2), 111–123. doi:10.1016/S1467-0895(02)00039-8

Papavassiliou, G., Mentzas, G., & Abecker, A. (2002). Integrating knowledge modelling in business process management. In *Proceedings of X European Conference on Information Systems.*

Ricci, A. Piunti, & M., Viroli, M. (2010). Environment programming in multi-agent systems: An artifact-based perspective. *Autonomous Agents and Multi-agent Systems*, (pp. 1-35).

Russell, N., Hofstede, A., & Mulyar, N. (2006). *Workflow control-flow patterns: A revised view.*

Sarnikar, S., & Deokar, A. (2010). Knowledge management systems for knowledge-intensive processes: Design approach and an illustrative example. In *Proceedings of Hawaii International Conference on System Sciences*, (pp. 1–10).

Souza, R. (2006). *Agent-oriented constructivist knowledge management*. Ph.D. dissertation, University of Twente, Enschede.

Toledo, C. M., Ale, M., Chiotti, O., & Galli, M. R. (2010a). *An agent-based architecture for ontology-driven knowledge management*. The Fifth International Conference on Knowledge, Information and Creativity Support Systems, Thailand.

Toledo, C. M., Ale, M., Chiotti, O., & Galli, M. R. (2010b). *An agent-based ontology evolution strategy for ontology-driven knowledge management systems. XXXVI Latin American Informatics Conferences*. Paraguay: CLEI.

Weske, M. (2007). *Business process management: Concepts, languages, architectures*. New York, NY: Springer-Verlag.

ENDNOTES

1. Plus (+) sign represents one o more times
2. Available at http://jacamo.sourceforge.net/

Chapter 17
Framework of Knowledge and Intelligence Base:
From Intelligence to Service

Marc Rabaey
University of Hasselt and Belgian Ministry of Defense, Belgium

Roger Mercken
University of Hasselt, Belgium

ABSTRACT

This chapter introduces the concept of the "Intelligence Base," developed in a study on the information requirement of the management of an (military) organization. The purpose of the study was to conceive, for each level of an organization, an appropriate Decision Support System (DSS) and/or Knowledge and Information System. All systems would eventually have been integrated in an overall Enterprise Architecture (EA). By discussing the OODA-cycle of John Boyd and the Naturalistic Decision Making (NDM) the authors show that the concept of Intelligence Base can be a DSS for very demanding environments. Related topics are knowledge, culture, and real options (business example). The proposed framework is based on Service-Oriented Architecture (SOA) and Cloud Computing, which will determine the configuration of the Information Technology (IT) systems.

INTRODUCTION FROM INTELLIGENCE TO SERVICE

Already in 1998 the society was a knowledge society (Davenport et al., 1998; Drucker, 1998; Neef, 1998). The evolution of Information Technology increased the growth of this society (Rabaey, 2011). The result is that service industry boomed (more than 50% of the 2011 US DOD budget are service contracts). This is only possible by the creativity in the organizations (profit and non-profit).

Another characteristic is the mass customization of the products in general, and services in particular. This demands an enormous flexibility in adapting processes to these requirements. The allocation of resources needs constantly to be

DOI: 10.4018/978-1-4666-0948-8.ch017

changed so that the capacity can be configured to satisfy the constant change in the market and the individualization of the customers. Not only the business processes and the related capabilities need fast adapting but also the strategies like the grand, business and operational strategies. In se strategy is the result of the balance between the resources and the objectives of an organization (Bernard, 1976).

If an organization is not capable of adapting quickly to its environment, chances are high that it will not survive. Since the pace of changes is continuously increasing, organizations don't have much time to think about "the" best solution, rather they will be satisfied with the choice of a best "acceptable" solution at that particular moment.

Another consequence of this accelerating pace of change is that the organization has to continuously monitor its productivity and the changes in the environment. In other words, the organization needs a constant stream of intelligence, which is not the same as information as we will show.

Parallels between warfare and the market of the knowledge economy are easily drawn. That's why we will start in the next section with the discussion of the importance of intelligence in a military environment. Intelligence cannot only be used to support the decision making of an organization but it also creates at the same time knowledge. Knowledge and intelligence are combined in a generic framework of "Intelligence base." This intelligence base will be the engine to facilitate the production of intelligence so that an organization can make faster and better decisions.

The following section will discuss more in depth decision support by the intelligence base. Two decision making approaches related to military decision making are put in the spotlight. The first is the Observe-Orient-Decide-Act (OODA-loop) of Colonel John Boyd. Especially the "Orient" phase will receive the most attention (Osinga, 2007), because it brings culture, structure, knowledge and related issues together which basically determine the way an organization observes (gets information), analyzes and decides.

The second decision making approach is Naturalistic Decision Making (NDM) which does not focus on decision models but focuses on the experience of the decision maker, the complexity of the task, and the environmental constraints (Rosen et al., 2008). However we will first start with the Babylonian confusion of tongues on risk and uncertainty, because in the assessments of unknown facts it is essential to know what can be measured (based on objective statistical data) and what can not be measured (subjective appreciation of a chance (probability) that something can happen), they cannot be mixed as homogeneous factors or chances.

The use of Intelligence Base for these two non-classical decision making approaches will be shown. Real Option Valuation (ROV) will serve as a business example. Real option is the right but not the obligation to act (invest, disinvest, postpone, start, delay, restart, stop projects). Although ROV is a very useful investment evaluation technique because it offers flexibility to management to decide and to tackle the risks, ROV can be complex and the follow up of these real options is quite intensive (especially the American type of options). We believe the use of an Intelligence Base can solve the majority of these problems.

Both knowledge management (KM) and Intelligence Base (tightly linked to each other) have to find a place in the overall architecture of an organization. In this context Enterprise Architecture (EA) is proposed as the appropriate framework. Since knowledge is obviously important in a knowledge economy, an additional knowledge layer will be introduced. Certainly now the use of (services in) Cloud Computing is increasing and Information Technology (IT) will become a "utility (commodity) [so] competitive/collaborative advantage will become almost fully dependent from the capability of producing intelligence for decision-making and knowledge management (in systems, processes and human resources)" (Rabaey, 2011).

We are also presenting some further directions of research (fuzzy sets, chaos theory, naturalistic decision making) where the proposed Intelligence Base will need to be extended with more knowledge tools to better support decisions in investments and allocation of resources in an organization.

ACOS EVAL

In 2002 the Belgian Defense was reorganized. The Assistant Chief of Staff Evaluation (ACOS Eval) was a new staff department responsible for the evaluation of the functioning of the Belgian Defense. Its main missions were to measure the performance of the other departments and to help them improve their functioning. A set of management tools was selected and introduced in the other departments: Balanced Scorecard (BSC), Self-assessment (European Foundation for Quality Management (EFQM)), Business Process Management (BPM)).

To support the functioning of ACOS Eval, the Chief Information Officer (CIO of ACOS Eval) conceived the Evaluation Information System (EIS) ([1]). Figure 1 depicts EIS which has three main components:

- Management Intelligence
- Business Management tools (as mentioned above) in the portal
- Social Network Portal for knowledge sharing and homologation of systems

The clients are the Chief of Defense (CHOD), other departments and the lower level management for their decision making and functioning.

The sources of the EIS are:

- External information sources (open source, NATO, EU, etc.)
- Internal information systems of the Belgian Defense with above a business intelligence layer.

The Management Intelligence provided management with intelligence and/or knowledge to improve decision making and functioning of their departments.

In se intelligence has two outputs, one is for decision making and the other is to create knowledge. In the next section, we will discuss intelligence.

INTELLIGENCE

Art of War

In a political-strategic context intelligence is the product resulting from the collection, evaluation, analysis, integration, and interpretation of all available information, that concerns one or more aspects of foreign nations or of areas of foreign operations, and that is immediately or potentially significant to military planning and operations (DSS, 2005).

Put into the economical and social context, intelligence is the product resulting from the collection, evaluation, analysis, integration, and interpretation of all available information (internal and external), that concerns one or more aspects of the agents on the market and/or social environment, and that is immediately or potentially significant to the business planning and the use of resources (like investments).

It is not a surprise that collecting intelligence is the only rule linked to the first principle of the Art of War. To Bernard (1976), there are three principles of the Art of War:

- Balance between Goals and Means;
- Liberty of Action;
- Economy of Forces.

Figure 1. ACOS Eval information system – concept

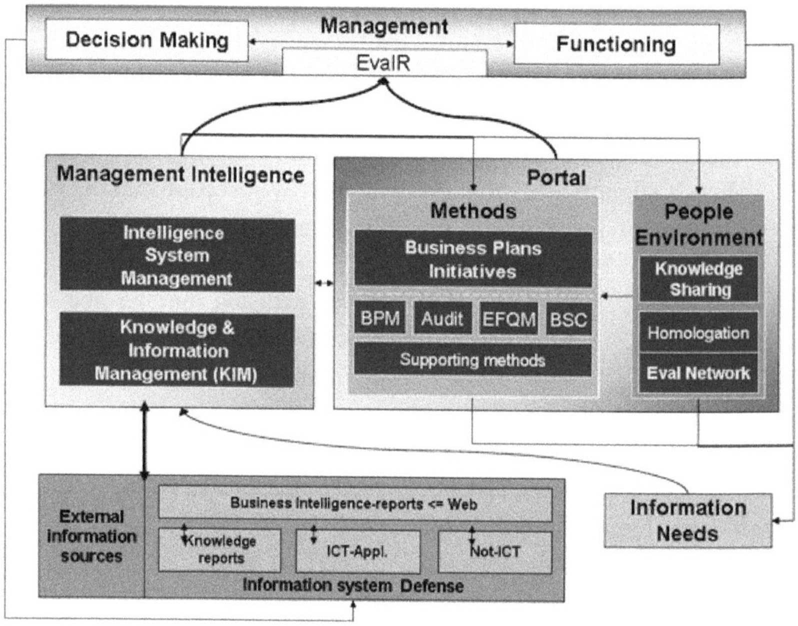

Regarding the military (Liddell Hart, 1991), (Bernard, 1976), grand strategy is the art to combine resources of an organization to attain its objectives. This is determined by the first principle of the Art of War, being the balance between objectives and resources. If a company uses too many resources to attain the objectives, then it is not efficient. If too few resources are used, then the company will not be effective and it will not attain its objectives

The collection of intelligence will inform the leaders on the environment, the resources and the feasibility of the goals. This collection is performed by the intelligence cycle process. However not only intelligence is obtained for the decision making process, also knowledge can be created with this process. This is not surprising because knowledge is also used to make decisions (Courtney, 2001) (see below).

Starting from a military environment we will show the importance of intelligence for an organization. Intelligence is used to reduce the uncertainty of the organization to enable it to make better decisions. This is only one aspect. Intelligence is also used to increase the knowledge asset of an organization and to improve it (adjust it).

To this end a concept of an Intelligence Base (IntB) has been developed (Rabaey et al., 2005). The Intelligence Base will support the classical Intelligence-cycle and it enriches the concrete knowledge of an organization and it determines the knowledge gap (what the organization does not know and is aware of). The whole system of detecting the unknown is very strategic to an organization. If its competitor/enemy knows what the organization does not know, then the competitor/enemy can have an advantage.

Intelligence Cycle and Process

As defined above, intelligence is the product resulting from the collection, evaluation, analysis, integration, and interpretation of all available information (internal and external), that concerns one or more aspects of the agents on the market and/or social environment, and that is immediately or potentially significant to the business planning and the use of resources. This intelligence is managed in the so-called intelligence cycle.

The essence of intelligence is the cycle of questioning and receiving answers, but this is not only the essence, it is also the driving force. Organizational issues (of intelligence) are secondary regarding this cycle.

The manager of the intelligence-cycle manages the memory (where all approved information is stored), the network (to get the desired answers) and the analysis capability. The latter analyses all incoming information and processes it into intelligence that will be stored into the memory, which is the knowledge-base.

The intelligence manager has the following resources in the so-called intelligence cycle: the memory (where all acquired information is stored), the network (of sensors) and the analysis capability. The latter analyses all incoming information and processes it into intelligence that will be stored into the memory. In the scheme of Besson et al. (2003) (Figure 2, top right) the 'unknown' actively drives the intelligence cycle. However the network is the system composed of sensors that collect the information internally and externally to fill the gap..

The most difficult task is to formulate and translate the question into a clear language, which would then lead the organization to the pertinent and relevant information. In other words, it conveys knowledge about opportunities and threats, which the organization ignores (Besson, 2003, p. 22).

Larry Kahaner (1997) sees the intelligence cycle as a process instead of a function (top left Figure 2). "Therefore it should appear in all aspects of your business as one seamless, continuous activity not relegated to one area, division or unit" (Kahaner 1997, p23). This process has four steps (Kahaner, 1997, p43):

- Planning & Direction;
- Collection;
- Analysis;
- Dissemination.

The step "Planning & Direction" starts with a clear understanding of the user's needs and includes his time constraints. Once well understood, further intelligence actions are planned. The "Collection" involves obtaining raw information that can be turned into usable intelligence for the decision making of an organization. "Analysis" is the process of taking information and integrating it with other information so that intelligence is created. "Dissemination" is distribution of the intelligence towards the client and other organizations that may also be concerned by this intelligence.

Figure 2 (bottom) combines the two perceptions. The intelligence manager plans and directs the intelligence efforts. In the case the intelligence is not in the system, information is collected from the network and once received analyzed and integrated into new intelligence, which is then disseminated to the clients and to the memory (See also Figure 3: Intelligence for Decision Maker and Knowledge Management).

Knowledge Base

Guida et al. (1994) define a knowledge-based system (KBS) as a software system capable of supporting the explicit representation of knowledge in some specific competence domain and of exploiting it through appropriate reasoning mechanisms in order to provide high-level problem-solving performance. The knowledge base stores available knowledge concerning the domain at hand, represented in an appropriate explicit form and ready to be used by the reasoning mechanism.

Is intelligence also knowledge? For Peter Drucker (1998) knowledge is information effective in action, so information focuses on results.

Figure 2. Intelligence cycle & process

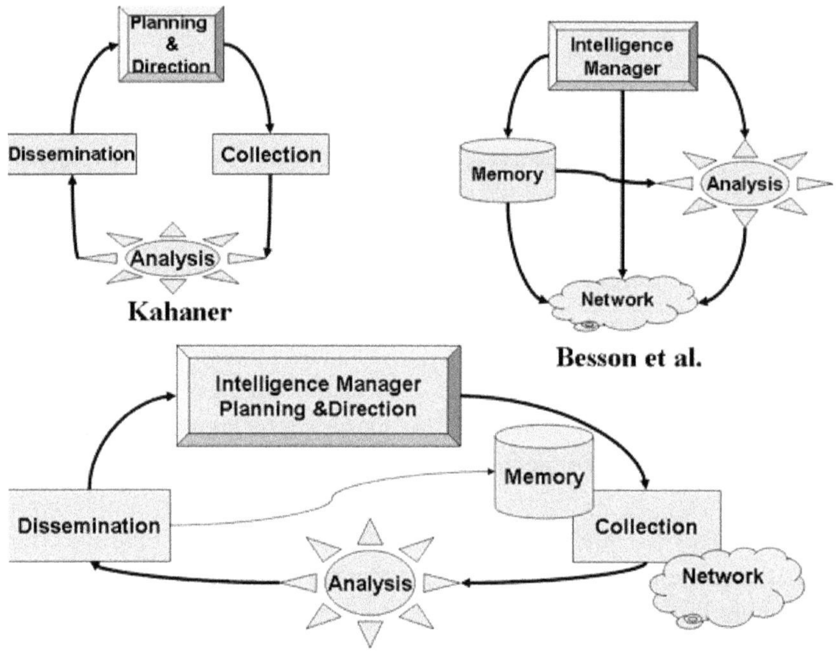

Figure 3. Intelligence for decision maker and knowledge management

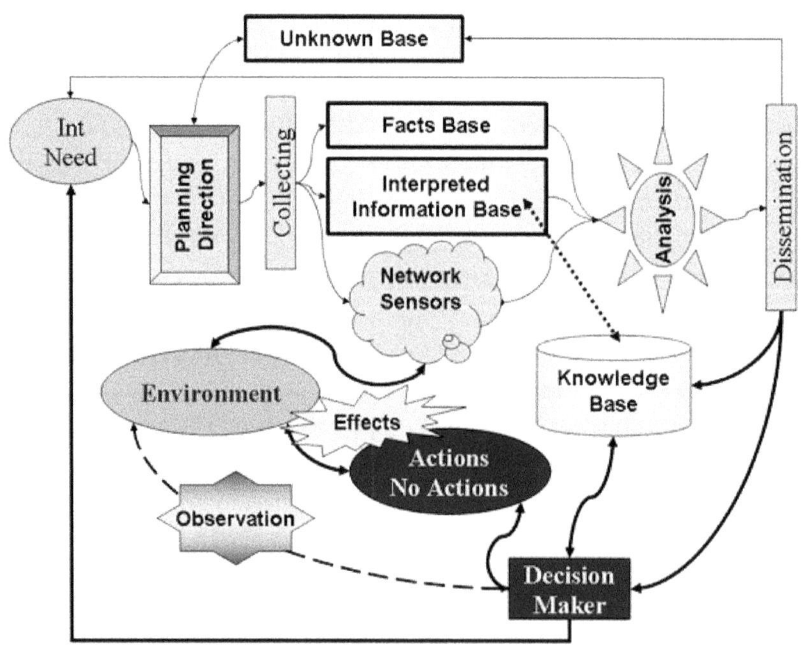

Sanchez et al. (1997) define knowledge as the set of beliefs held by an individual about causal relationships among phenomena. Causal relationships in this definition are cause and effect relationships between imaginable events or actions and likely consequences of those events or actions. Organizational knowledge is then defined as the shared set of beliefs about causal relationships held by individuals within a group. The link between belief and knowledge is that a belief is knowledge if the belief is true, and if the believer has a justification (reasonable and necessarily plausible evidence) for believing it is true. A false belief is not considered to be knowledge, even if it is sincere (Wikipedia Epistemology, n.d.).

Therefore, both terms (intelligence and knowledge) are supporting the decision-making process and these terms are sometimes interchanged (see (Kahaner, 1997, p.21) or confused with information. It is however clear that interpreted and integrated information becomes intelligence, which enables a person to make a decision using the inference rules of the concerned knowledge domain.

Yet knowledge evolves, facts stay. Therefore, an organization should store the facts (information) in a "Facts Base" for later re-interpreting the same facts but with other knowledge. But what is information? So far, we believe the most complete definition is coming from the US OMB Circular A-130 (White House, n.d.): Information is "Any communication or representation of knowledge, such as facts, data, or opinions in any medium or form, including textual, numerical, graphic, cartographic, narrative, or audio-visual forms."

This definition reflects the new era of IT: not only data is being seen as information, but also all other media that can deliver support in the decision process. This doesn't only imply that a decision-maker receives a lot more information than classical data, it also implies that the instruments to treat all kind of sources of intelligence have become more complex.

Technologies such as multimedia stores and document management systems have been added to the classical database systems. These technologies together form the knowledge base system of an organization; provided they are integrated into the IT systems (see below).

Besides tracking the intelligence, an organization should place the intelligence on a dedicated storage "Interpreted Information Base" to assess the quality of intelligence (Besson, 2001). In the same logic as intelligence assessment, the decision making process can be assessed (Yates, 2003) and thus the knowledge. Sanchez et al. defines three types of knowledge: factual knowledge (entities, relationships), inferential knowledge (reasoning functions) and strategic knowledge (problem-solving strategies) (Sanchez et al., 2000).

Later in the chapter, the decision cycle of John Boyd will be discussed: OODA: Observe – Orient – Decide – Act. The way information is collected is also in function of how an organization thinks (culture, belief system, knowledge), so how and why information is collected should as well be assessed to determine if the organization does not have structural or cultural blind spots in observing and interpreting the environment.

Unknown Base

If an organization knows what it knows, then it knows what it does not know and would like to know. The Unknown Base supports the management of the unknown. The whole system of detecting, managing and collecting the unknown is very strategic for an organization. If its competitor/enemy knows what the organization does not know, then the competitor/enemy can take advantage of this. Security is of the utmost importance.

The Unknown Base supports the management of the unknown. The whole system of detecting, managing and collecting the unknown is very strategic for an organization, as mentioned above. The management and the storages of the unknown, the facts and intelligence, and the supporting Intelligence Information system form together the "Intelligence Base" (Rabaey et al, 2005) (IntB) (see figure below) (adapted from Rabaey (2011)).

Rabaey et al. (2005) defined the knowledge base as the combination of "Facts Base" and "Interpreted Information Base" but it conflicts with the definition of Guida et al. (1994) or Wikipedia KB. (n.d.). Therefore in the figure "Intelligence for Decision Maker and Knowledge Management" the "Knowledge Base" is indicated as the "Interpreted Information Base." The facts base is storing the raw data. Its main purposes are to keep track how and where the raw data has been found and to enable later interpretation with other inferences rules or knowledge (see above).

Conceptual View Intelligence Base

The decision-maker can receive the intelligence in two ways (pull and push). Firstly, if the organization (decision maker, DM) does not dispose of all the elements or knowledge to make its decision, it will express an intelligence need (pull). The second way is the transmission of newly detected facts by the sensors to the intelligence unit to be interpreted and integrated. The intelligence will be brought to the attention of the unit(s) who can use this intelligence (push). The former is called "Information Pull," the latter "Information Push."

So, information pull is when the organization does not find the necessary intelligence (in the Intelligence Base or outside of it). It will then express its needs to the "Planning & Direction." The latter will then define the needed intelligence actions. The needed intelligence may not be in the Intelligence Base in which case the network has to be instructed (pull). The planning of the dynamic search-path is established (Besson et al., 2001) and the plan of action is managed in the Unknown Base.

The resulting information (if any) is then analyzed. Additional information may be required if there is not enough information to be integrated into intelligence. Once the intelligence is acquired, then it will be disseminated to the intelligence client. The information and intelligence are stored respectively in the Facts Base and the Interpreted Information Base, and the Unknown Base is updated.

In the case of "Information Push" the sensors are injecting information in the network (push). The transmitted information is then analyzed. If the information can be integrated, then the resulting intelligence is pushed to the units concerned in the organizations. The information and intelligence (if any) are stored respectively in the Facts Base and the Interpreted Information Base.

If the organization esteems that it has enough elements and knowledge to decide then it will give orders to act (or not act) and the sensors will detect the effects of the actions (or non-actions) of the organization on the environment. As such, the intelligence cycle acts also as a feedback system.

Multiple Layers

An organization consists of different elements, which can be organized in a hierarchal or in a more linear structure. Since intelligence production is a process, this process should be implemented in every organizational element, but should be interconnected. This interconnection can be configured as a hub (centralized) or as a network (decentralized) or as a combination hub-network, in which case all intelligence is centralized and only the (relevant) intelligence for an element stored in the intelligence base of that element (own intelligence and other relevant intelligence coming from other elements).

Strategic Investment

The exhibit above shows how in a hierarchical organization the higher levels can request intelligence from the lower levels (top-down) and how the lower levels can bring (pull or push) intelligence to higher levels (bottom-up). Of course, higher levels can also push intelligence.

The bidirectional push/pull system was chosen in the case of ACOS Eval.

Figure 5 shows a hybrid configuration of an Intelligence Base in a context of the allocation of resources (investments, leasing, etc.) in an organization (Rabaey, 2011). Strategy is the balance between means and goals. At the highest possible level it is the Grand Strategy. Derived from it are the resources and business strategy. The most probable way of interacting and creating intelligence is that of figure "Multiple layers of Intelligence process / Base."

Resources and business strategy are both joined together in the Interdisciplinary Forum (IF) where at the operational level resources are being allocated in business processes to obtain their goals (balance means and goals). Certainly in the domain of the resources strategy the topology will be more of a networked collection of intelligence bases in different (knowledge) domains. IF on the other hand will need –as the name already indicates- an interdisciplinary knowledge base. The intelligence requests will be cross-domain and for efficiency reasons it should hold all existing knowledge (centralized). In this case the analysis and integration function should certainly be composed of different kinds of knowledge workers (Figure 4).

Once the decisions are made, the resources and business strategy will be informed, so that they eventually can adjust their planning and operations. In this context we will discuss the OODA-cycle of John Boyd (OODA = Observe, Orient, Decide, Act) in the next section.

DECISION SUPPORT

Observe – Orient – Decide – Act (OODA)

Intelligence isn't just for the purpose of having intelligence. Besides creating knowledge, the intelligence process delivers information for the decision processes of the organization. Those decisions lead to actions which will be executed.

John Boyd and his OODA-cycle and philosophy are not common knowledge in the Belgian Defense, because Defense works with the Plan-Do-Check-Act (PDCA)-cycle of Deming, like most of the Belgian federal services. The fact that Boyd's theory is based amongst other theories on non-linearity, chaos theory and organic systems, makes his theory less accessible to the world of linear thinking managers and leaders. Still, it was during the research of the new concept of Evaluation Information System (EIS) and Intelligence Base in 2005, that the CIO came in contact with the work of John Boyd and quickly recognized the usefulness and richness of his work. Since then, the OODA-Cycle (Observe-Orient-Decide-Act) of John Boyd has influenced the work in an important way (in both the academic and military arenas) ([2]).

At first sight, the OODA-cycle looks very simple (Top part Figure 5). We first 'observe' our environment, then we think about what we can do and build a list of alternatives ('orient'). Out of this list, we 'decide' which alternative will be executed in the last phase of the loop ('act'). And then the cycle starts all over again. However Boyd also has an extended figure where the "Orient" phase is especially important and consists of:

- Cultural Traditions
- Genetic Heritage
- Previous Experiences
- Analysis & Synthesis
- New Information

Translated to an organization we have the following elements

- Cultural Traditions: Culture and Values
- Genetic Heritage: Organizational Structure
- Previous Experiences: Knowledge
- Analysis & Synthesis
- New Information

Figure 4. Multiple layers of Intelligence process / base

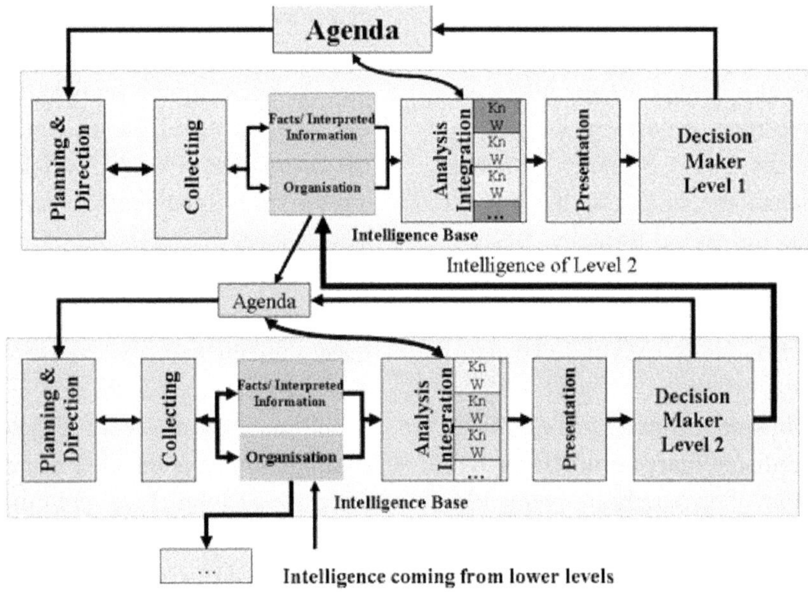

Figure 5. Intelligence base and investment forum

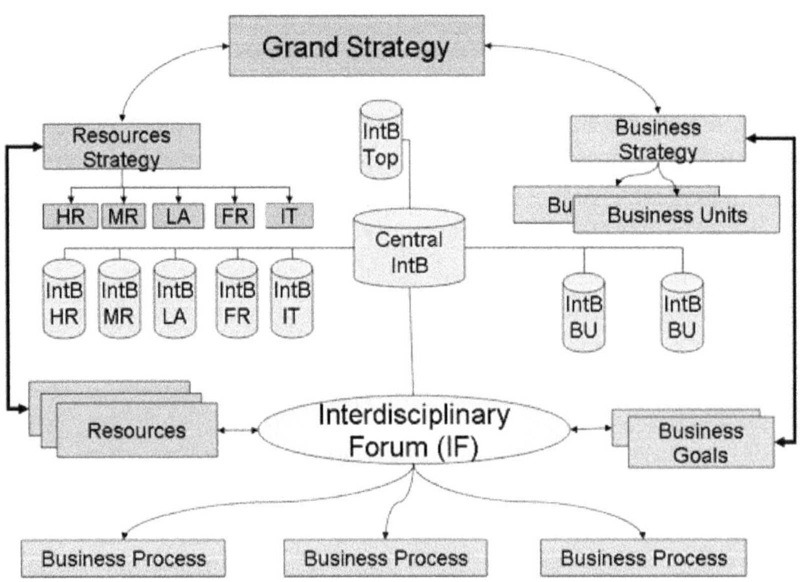

Figure 6. Simple OODA-cycle and elements from individual « orient »

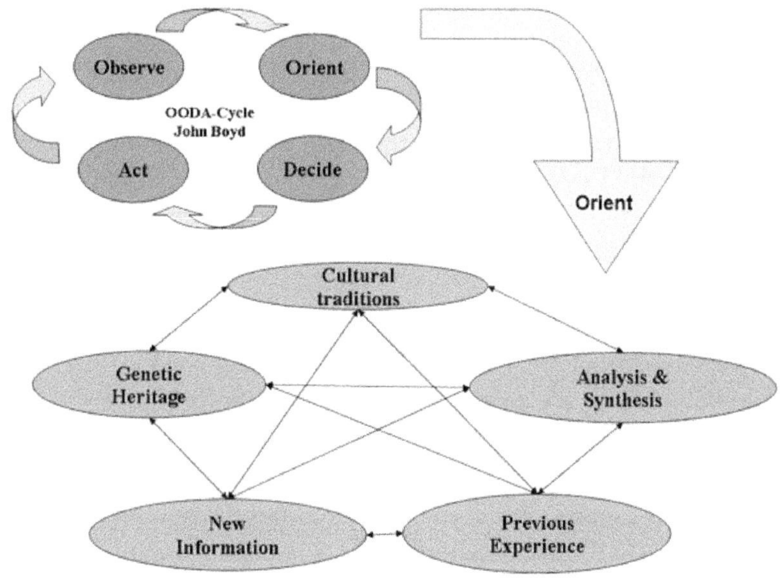

Knowledge (Management), Belief, and Culture

The "Previous Experience" of the individual is translated into knowledge. Experience can have as consequence that one person "knows that" something is or that one person "knows how" to do something. "Knowledge-that" is taken to be an attitude towards a proposition which is true (Wikipedia Epistemology, n.d.) and proposition itself predicates a property to some entity (Dienes et al., 1999) and therefore is a relation between a thinker and a true proposition, while "Knowledge-how" is an ability (Stanley et al., 2001) to solve problems or attain goals (act/react) in the environment.

Davenport et al. (1998, p. 5) define knowledge as "a fluid mix of framed experience, values, contextual information, and expert insight that provides a framework for evaluating and incorporating new experiences and information. It originates and is applied in the minds of knowers. In organizations, it often becomes embedded not only in documents or repositories but also in organizational routines, processes, practices, and norms." Except for the structure, this definition is a description of John Boyd's Orientation phase, which is logical because knowledge is produced and used in cognitive processes (Wikipedia Knowledge, n.d.).

"Knowledge can be developed in two different ways: through purchase or internal development." (Roos et al., 1997, p. 16). Although at first glance Intelligence Base is more focused on internal development, it also is a tool to make the implicit knowledge inside people's heads explicit. Examples of tools are Knowledge Transfer (KT) (Stevens et al., 2010) and Junior-Senior transfer (KM-Huis, 2011).

Culture has different meanings (Wikipedia Culture, n.d.) and is in one way or another related to knowledge:

- An integrated pattern of human knowledge, belief, and behavior that depends upon the capacity for symbolic thought and social learning;

- The set of shared attitudes, values, goals, and practices that characterizes an institution, organization or group.

The former interpretation implies that (objective) knowledge (intersection of believes and truth) moves to a belief system where values are added to the knowledge (Rabaey, forthcoming) and becomes a subjective matter, which determines the behavior ((re)acting in the environment).

"Cultural traditions" of the individual OODA-cycle are reflected in culture of an organization (latter interpretation). Culture is a very important factor because of the way values (anchored in a belief system) are being used in the preparation of decisions, and even in the acquisition and use of (management) techniques in the organization (see above, (Simion et al. 200)).

So, when translating to an organization, cultural traditions are extended with "values," and implicitly the belief systems of the members of the organization (Sharp et al., 2009). If new information is coming into the Orient-phase which provokes a conflict about the belief system, then it may be possible that the people concerned are rejecting the new information (Galileo). Therefore, the people of the organization must be open-minded and their thinking must never submit itself neither to a dogma, nor anything else but the observed facts. Management should first handle culture before implementing a (formal) knowledge management (Simion et al., 2000; Davenport et al. 1998; Zhu et al., 2010).

Structure

The "Genetic Heritage" is translated into "Structure" which influences a lot the acceptance of Knowledge Management (KM). KM in an organization comprises a range of strategies and methods to identify, create, represent, distribute, and enable adoption of insights and experiences (Wikipedia KM, n.d.) for the employees in order to exploit new markets or create innovative new products or services (Neef, 1998). Guptara (1999, p. 26) states that the "formal structure of most companies prevents KM from operating. Most companies are organized by function, region, division or business unit, each complete with its own recruitment, induction, and reward systems based on its 'own' bottom line." One example is a matrix structured organization which by definition is intensively focused on co-ordination, that it becomes slow to respond to the market and suffers from another "barrier": time. Because they don't have enough time to focus on KM, it is seen as an additional task (burden) instead of a resource. A second example is a functional division organization. A division is quasi independent so that other divisions are more seen as a competitor than as a collaborator. In this case, sharing knowledge is out of order (another barrier to KM: knowledge is power).

As the interdependency is shown in the OODA, the structure is of course linked to the organizational culture. "A collaborative culture must be nurtured, if it is not the KM initiative will never get off the ground." (Guptara, 1999, p. 27) or what Shaikh (2011) in her study defines as a constructive culture.

OODA and Intelligence Base

The Orient-phase in the OODA-cycle is very important (Osinga, 2005, 2007). Through the implicit guidance and control, it determines how an organization is observing its environment. Blind spots can be created due to the culture and/or knowledge of the organization. That is why the facts base should not only keep the information as observed but also the metadata like the reason it has been collected, how (push, pull), by who and if it has been reported more than once.

The knowledge and 'analysis and syntheses' are supported by the intelligence base, as well as the observation phase (network of sensors). The culture in contrast as such is not captured in the intelligence base because it represents the soul of an organization. It is only when there is a mentality of self-assessment that with self-assessment tools as Common Assessment Framework (CAF) observation are made and therefore new information created. The self-assessment and self-awareness are points that are important to the next topic "Naturalistic Decision Making."

NATURALISTIC DECISION MAKING (NDM)

Risk and Uncertainty

Literature on behavioral economics (Ariely, 2009; Montier, 2010), intuitive management (Burke et al., 1999), psychology (Libet, 2011; Pucket et al., 2011), naturalistic decision-making (NDM) (Brooks, 2007; Berryman, 2007; Shattuck et al., 2006) proves that decision-making is not always rational. A lot has to do with how people and their brains are coping with uncertainty and risk.

In an economical context (see also (Rabaey, 2011)), rationality has more to do with the ratio of benefits to costs instead of the philosophical meaning of reasoning (Wikipedia Rationality, n.d.). Related to the investments and/or resource allocation issues, is risk management. Risk management is the identification, assessment, and prioritization of risks (based on uncertainties) followed by coordinated and economical application of resources to minimize, monitor, and control the probability and/or impact of unfortunate events or to maximize the realization of opportunities (Wikipedia RM, n.d.).

But "Risk" and "Uncertainty" are interchanged in literature because of the fact that the outcome is the same (expected values) (Aven, 2010, p.55), but semantically they are very different in the approach regarding decision-making. Organizations have to make important decisions without complete information in a complex and fast changing environment. Uncertainty is a state in which the outcomes are unknown and perhaps unknowable, the more distant in time (future), the greater the uncertainty (Funston, 2010, p. xxiii). The decision horizon is farther at the strategic level than at the operational or tactical levels of the organization. For most of the organizations in this ever faster changing environment, the time line at the strategic level is from the present until the long term (at least a year), while the operational level is from now until short term (couple of weeks or months at most).

The most significant characteristic of risk is that it is an unknown factor that will have an unpleasant consequence for the person or the organization when it would happen (Mun, 2010; Wikipedia Risk, n.d.). Risk can be a measurable unknown based on previously collected statistical (objective) analyses on the issue or it is a non-measurable factor. However based on experiences (so subjective) one can estimate what the chances are that it will be produced or not. So it is better to talk about measurable unknown and immeasurable unknown where by definition the former can be assessed with objective statistical data (chances), while the latter is based on subjective experiences or reasoning (chances). So both are expressed in "chances," but the underlying base is significantly different, what should be remembered in the creation and dissemination of intelligence. Both can be further divided into known-unknown (one is aware of the existence) and unknown-unknown (non-awareness).

Regarding measurable risk, the organization will collect better statistical data, and of course it will look for better methods to avoid or reduce the risks. Fulton et al. (2010, p. xxiii) write that the risk intelligent enterprise recognizes that risk intelligence and risk management are not ends in themselves but a means toward the ends of creating and preserving value and surviving and thriving in uncertainty (non-measurable unknown).

Characteristics NDM

The need for information to produce intelligence comes from the fact that the actual reality is ever changing at an increasing pace, therefore "[p] ossessing the right information at the right time is obviously key to making good decisions." (Rosen et al., 2008). In the literature on decision making in crisis situations (like for firemen and military), we have retained the Naturalistic Decision Making (NDM). NDM studies how people are making decisions and are performing cognitively complex functions in crisis or demanding situations which are formed by constraints of (lack of) time and (lack of) information (Bryant, n.d). A typical environment consists of unstructured, real-world problems with complex and multiple signs and symptoms, often interacting without cause/effect relationships or interdependent (with cause/effect). The situation is dynamic and almost always dangerous and/or distracting. The features of NDM can be described as follows (Klein et al., 1999; Rosen et al., 2008; Shattuck et al., 2006):

- Ill-defined goals and ill-structured tasks;
- Uncertainty, ambiguity, and missing data;
- Dynamic and continually changing conditions;
- Action-feedback loops (real-time reactions to changed conditions);
- Time stress;
- High stakes;
- Multiple players;
- Organizational goals and norms;
- Experienced decision makers.

To resolve this, NDM in contrast to formal-empiricist decision making approach and rationalist approach, is not based on formal, normative models. The latter approaches fail to account for the experience of the decision maker, the complexity of the task, and the environmental constraints (Rosen et al., 2008), a such NDM is conform the OODA-approach. However NDM makes difference between a novice decision maker and an expert. A novice decision maker will act differently than an expert. The former will choose from among a set of options (comparison), while an expert will more decide from memory (experiences). "However, the biggest difference between experts and novices, especially in terms of NDM, is their ability to assess and evaluate the situation, rather than their ability to generate and choose among options." (Simpson, 2001, p.15). So, like OODA, NDM stresses the importance of situational awareness and therefore situational assessment (Shattuck et al., 2006; Polič, 2009). OODA (at the organizational level) could certainly use the intelligence base to tackle fast evolving and complex situations, but can the Intelligence Base philosophy similarly be used for NDM?

Intelligence Base and NDM

The Intelligence Base is certainly suited for the conventional decision making characterized by deductive, logical thinking, analysis of probabilities and statistical methods. In the naturalistic setting, the decision maker will have to use intuition, mental simulation, metaphor and storytelling. Regarding the mental simulation, in the section on "knowledge base," knowledge also could be defined as a set of beliefs held by an individual about causal relationships among phenomena (based on Sanchez et al. (2000). In the case of an expert, this set of beliefs will substantially be bigger than for the novice. Moreover the expert will recognize quicker the cues to determine the right cause and effect relationships. But NDM is not specifically focused on individual decision makers alone, on the contrary (Rosen et al., 2008) decision makers do not operate in isolation. As we have seen in the cascaded form of the intelligence base (Figure 4), teams of knowledge workers (experts) perform distributed decision making tasks, where the complexity of the problem or environment makes that a multidisciplinary approach is needed (Figure 5: Intelligence Base and Investment Forum)

In the context of intelligence base we will focus more on the behavior of an organization than on the behavior of individuals' (firemen, military, etc.). An organization need to be aware of its environment (situational awareness (SA)), which is done by the sensors of the Intelligence Base (Observe in OODA). Three levels of SA exist (Greitzer et al., 2009; Polič, 2009), but in accordance to fuzzy sets (further research) we add another level (0 of non-awareness):

- **Level 0:** Non-awareness of the situation;
- **Level 1:** Perceiving critical factors in the environment;
- **Level 2:** Understanding what those factors mean, particularly when integrated together in relation to the person's (organizational) goals.
- **Level 3:** Understanding what will happen in the near future.

Level 1 feeds forward to the orient phase of the OODA cycle (Figure 7: Extended form of OODA-cycle) and from level 2 we are in the Observe Orient cycle and in the cycle Planning/ Direction – Collecting – Analysis of IntB.

But in the case of a crisis (unexpected market penetration, new product, disaster due to nature, etc) decisions may have to be made based on lack of intelligence. For all models of NDM following characteristics are in common (Bryant, n.d.):

- Decisions are made by holistic evaluation of potential courses of action (COAs) rather than by feature-by-feature comparison of alternatives. Typically, the decision maker sequentially generates and evaluates potential COAs against some criterion of acceptability;
- Decisions are recognition-based in that decision makers rely on recognition of the situation and pattern matching of COAs rather than an exhaustive generation and comparison of alternatives, so the decision maker is falling back on his "experiences" (OODA);
- Decision makers adopt a satisfying criterion rather than search for an optimal solution.

Indeed, real world problems often demand rapid responses and in the case they don't have enough intelligence, then the decision makers may have to accept a merely workable solution without considering whether a better solution exists or not. When the decision maker is unable to recognize a given situation, then he will trigger the intelligence process to collect more information or to resolve the ambiguous situation through diagnostic processes such as story building (Bryant, n.d.) or developing scenario's (candidate CoA's).

With the story building, the decision maker creates a detailed hypothesis (see hypothesis in "Decision" phase in Figure 7) or story that could explain the situation. Through simulation (mental or computer aided), the decision maker can analyze the situation to form expectations about future events (SA – level 3) and test the working hypothesis. If there are too many inconsistencies between the hypothesis and the situation, the decision maker must revise his or her hypothesis.

Cognitive Business Intelligence is a new upcoming service that companies as IBM are providing. A more conceptual approach is given by Niu et al. (2007) with their CBIS (Cognitive Business Intelligence System), which can be implemented in the Intelligence Base philosophy.

Thus because of the similarities between NDM and OODA, which the Intelligence Base can support, the integration of knowledge and intelligence (decision making) and the possibilities of Information Technology today, we can state that the Intelligence Base also can support NDM.

Figure 7. Extended form of OODA-cycle

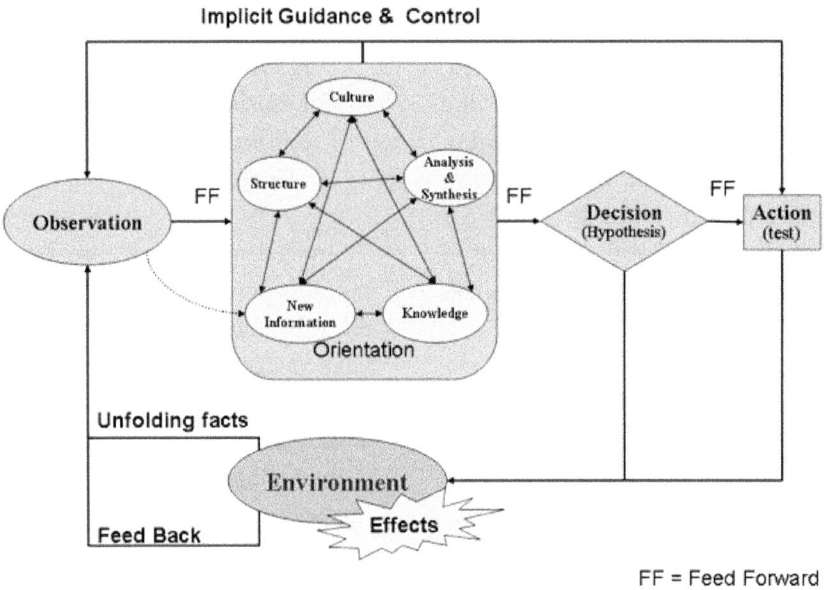

Emergent Strategies

For some kinds of decisions, the goal and the set of options evolve together. Over a period of time, the iterative process (cycles) can be depicted as in Figure 8. Small iterations (OODA) will adapt the plan to take into account the reactions of the other parties (interpreting the actions and effects of all the parties. The result is an emergent strategy (Rabaey, 1997). As a consequence of the small iterations, the emergences, and the complexity of the system itself and its environment, no plan survives the initial stages of a campaign (military, nor business).

The dynamic of the system is driven by the OODA-cycle. Authors as Yim et al. (2004) are proposing "knowledge-why" (reasoning) to bring dynamic and create interaction between "knowledge-that" and "knowledge-how," however reasoning does not interact with the environment, that's why John Boyd proposed "observe."

At the moment of Situation S-1 the commander and his/her staff establish a strategy on the supposition that the next situation will be S (big OODA-cycle). However during the COA they also need to perform OODA-cycle (based on a continuous collection of intelligence) and instead of situation S, they come into situation S' (etc.). Although unity of command (one leader) exists, there is an interaction of the commander with his staff and the depending units, so a higher "organ"(ization) is created (with culture, knowledge, etc.). NDM suggests also that experts and novices are collaborating close together.

Watts (2004, p.85) in his work on Clausewitzian friction and future wars confirms this by suggesting that evolutionary biology might offer an exemplar for an overarching theory of war than quantitative or hard sciences such as physics. "Behind that suggestion lays the suspicion that the parallels between the various levels of war and the hierarchy of biological organisms may be more than superficial. A key concept of evolutionary biology is emergence, meaning 'that in a structured system, new properties emerge at higher levels of integration which could not have been predicted

Figure 8. OODA and emergent strategies

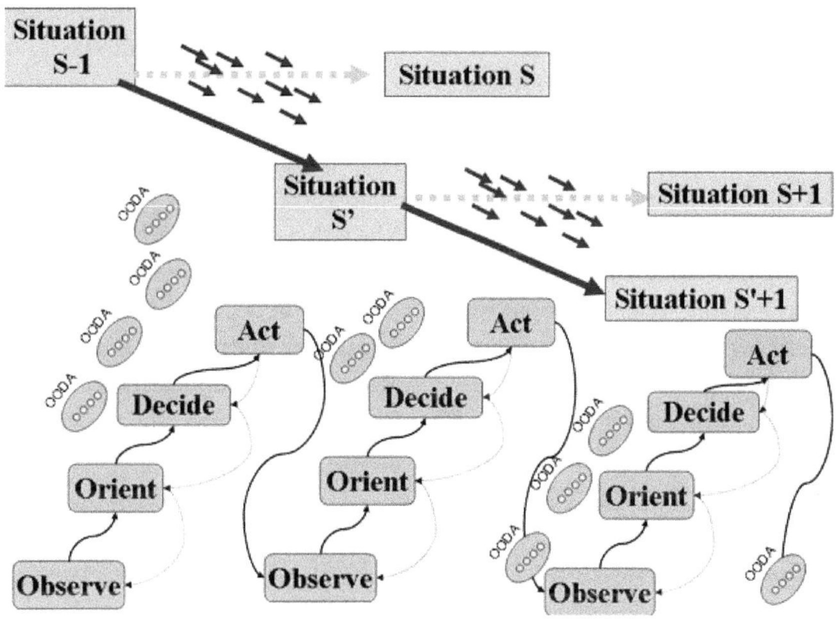

from knowledge of the lower-level components.' Emergence... is one of the two major pillars in the explanatory framework of modern biology, the other being the concept of genetic programs that evolve through natural selection. Emergence is also the fundamental concept of the relatively new field of artificial life. Typical experiments in this field involve setting up artificial worlds or environments inside a computer. These worlds generally contain 'agents, an environment, and rules that define and govern agent-agent, agent-environment, and environment-environment interactions.'... [E]mergence refers to 'the appearance of higher-level properties and behaviors' possessed by the 'whole' rather than by any of its individual parts, the point being that 'an air molecule is not a tornado and a neuron is not conscious'."

Earlier in this chapter, we have discussed the OODA-loop of John Boyd. One element of Orient is the genetic heritage that corresponds with the genetic programs pillar. Another element is what we call knowledge (originally Boyd called this passed experience, so in a way keeping history and the lessons learned from it), this knowledge is contained in the different domains of a staff (business and resources), but it is only by bringing them together that the organization can bring its consciousness to a higher level, and therefore can be open for emergencies."

In NDM the knowledge or the lack of this knowledge has the greatest influence on the decision strategy selection and the success of the chosen strategies. Moreover the ability to exercise this knowledge is equally important. "These two characteristics of the decision maker display the importance of experience and expertise to intuitive decision making process." (Simpson, 2001, p. 16). Not all experience and expertise can be transferred from humans to the Intelligence Base, but lessons learned or reports on experiences can be stored into it. The advantages are on the one hand that education and/or training (basis for the novices, advanced for the experts) can be developed and on the other hand processes, projects and procedures can be based on it.

Real Option Valuation (ROV)

Shattuck et al. (2006) point out that traditional models of cognitive processing and decision making often include modules which represent sensory input, different types of memory, encoding, response selection and execution, and attention (OODA-cycle of John Boyd), which are tested in laboratory environment for which no experience is necessary. Although necessary, this type of research neglects the types of cognitive activities that experienced people use in contexts with which they are familiar. This level of analysis is called 'macrocognition' and it includes the following as macrocognitive activities: decision making, uncertainty (see also Lipshitz, 2000, p. 17) management, mental simulation, sense making, situation awareness, attention management, problem detection, planning, and option generation.

In this context Real Option Valuation (ROV) is discussed as an example of a business situation of an organization. ROV is based on the theory of financial options and therefore they have common elements. In order to make decisions (delay, stop, start up, continue), management is waiting to collect more information, or is waiting for a better environment (market situation, political situation and so on) to make transactions with the underlying assets. In the case of financial options the underlying assets are financial products like stocks, while for real options the underlying assets can be projects like research and development, mining gold, oil exploitation and so on.

An option gives the holder the right to do something in the future, without the obligation to do it (Mercken, 2010; Mercken et al., 2010). For that right the option holder has to pay a price (money) to obtain the option. This is called the option premium. If events are unfolding in favor of the option holder, then he/she will exercise the option, while in the other case he/she will do nothing, what means that the loss is limited to the amount of the option premium. This option gives the decision maker the "flexibility" to decide later -after gaining more intelligence and/or waiting for better conditions- what to do.

The main difference between financial and real options beside the underlying assets, is the way the decision makers determine their values. The value of a real option is directly related to the value of the associated project and it requires a "subjective" assessment. The value of a financial option depends on the "market" value of the particular asset and on the contractual rights that buyers and sellers agreed to when they transferred the risk associated with the market asset (Barnett et al., 2008).

The different types of real options are (Copeland et al., 1998):

- **Invest-grow class**
- **Scale-Up:** Early entrants can scale up later through cost-effective sequential investments as market grows
- **Switch-Up:** Speedy commitment to first generation of product or technology gives company preferential position to switch to next generation
- **Scope-Up:** Investments in proprietary assets in one industry enable company to enter another industry cost-effectively.
- **Defer/Learn class**
- **Study/Start:** Delay investment until more information or skill is acquired
- **Disinvest/Shrink**
- **Scale-Down:** Shrink or shut down a project part way through if new information changes the expected payoffs
- **Switch-Down:** Switch to more cost-effective and flexible assets as new information is obtained
- **Scope-Down:** Limit the scope of (or abandon) operations when there is no further potential in a business opportunity

Compound real options are a combination of two or more real options of the 7-S framework.

When (inter)actions with the other players in the market are taking into account then we call them option games. They are real options placed into a strategic game-theoretic context (Fereira, 2009; Rabaey, 2011).

As we have already mentioned if an organization wants to gain competitive or collaborative advantage, it has to screen permanently its environment and its own functioning. Weeds (2006) points out that to use real options, the real options valuation (ROV) requires a detailed analysis of the full range of possible developments in the future and the probability of success of each one, not just the expected or average outcome. Furthermore, implementation of ROV requires managers to monitor the business environment to assess what should be done with the options. This is certainly the case with American options where the option can be taken at any time before the end of the contract (like the European option). But if they cannot bring up the effort to do so, then they are unlikely to achieves the values calculated using ROV. This and the complexity of ROV make it difficult to implement ROV.

The attentive reader will certainly remark that the effort to monitor the environment of the organization for strategic reasons, can also be used to collect information to implement and maintain the ROV and even more when both are combined in the option games. That's why the Intelligence Base is proposed, and since it is a generic system, every organization should instantiate it in function of its culture and capabilities. So by having an Intelligence Base for the strategic interactions with the environment, an organization can create intelligence for its strategic and operational evaluation of the environment and at the same time the intelligence base may deliver the necessary elements for the ROV. Therefore one of the reasons that ROV is hard to use (permanent seeking for intelligence) does not stand anymore.

KNOWLEDGE MANAGEMENT AND ENTERPRISE ARCHITECTURE

The purpose is to provide systems (be they automated or not) with knowledge so that processes (management, core business, corporate support) can function optimally.

Therefore we are proposing to introduce the knowledge architecture into the concept of Enterprise Architecture (EA). We will discuss the influence of this integration upon the other architecture layers (Business, Information, Application and Infrastructure).

It is important for KM that it is integrated in EA, because it will then be a part of the structure, processes and systems of the organization. If the organization wants to keep the classical structure of EA, then KM should be integrated into another layer. Since the combination with intelligence, KM can in that case be integrated into the information architecture.

With our proposal, a big advantage for KM is that it can use the same system as the function of strategic planning of the organization (top and business management), thus KM is not being perceived as another "separate" project.

Lots of different interpretations of the term Enterprise Architecture (EA) exist (Rabaey et al., 2007). Some hold lists of technological choices that an organization should make concerning infrastructure and application design. Others put these technological decisions into sets of guidelines to information architecture and business architecture.

The interdisciplinary forum (IF) has been proposed as a holistic framework for investments based on the right balance of goals and means. Therefore EA should be put in a broader context than merely infrastructure architecture and application architecture, because applications are built to support business processes and operate on information gathered through these business processes. Hence, architecture only concerned with infrastructure and application design is insufficient to support a business. The architecture of a building is based on the function that this building will have (store, house, manufacturing, etc.). So an Enterprise Architecture should consider the business and its dynamics so that it can take precautions for changing business requirements or the reuse of certain artifacts in other business domains.

The Enterprise Architecture Research Forum (EARF, n.d.) defines Enterprise Architecture as "the continuous practice of describing the essential elements of a socio-technical organization, their relationships to each other and to the environment, in order to understand complexity and manage change." Therefore Enterprise Architecture should consist of following levels:

- Business Architecture: Is about the description of the business processes as viewed from a business perspective. It should focus on the strategic environment and the business processes, which should attain the objectives.
- Knowledge Architecture: Brings the asset of knowledge in chart.
- Information Architecture: Describes the information the business is dependent on. This description must pay attention to where information enters the business processes, how this information enters the process, electronically or by other means, who is the owner of the information, and by whom it is to be used.
- Application Architecture: Is about how to implement the applications or IT systems in all of its aspects (programming, development environment, quality book of software, etc.).
- Infrastructure Architecture: Deals with guidelines concerning hardware platforms, network infrastructure, operating systems.

The knowledge architecture is an extra level we are proposing to be inserted into EA. If Cloud Computing will come up to the expectations of the market then IT will become a utility (commodity) and competitive/collaborative advantage will become almost fully dependent from the capability of producing intelligence for decision-making and knowledge management (in systems, processes and human resources). So the differentiation will be made on the level of knowledge assets and therefore knowledge has to be addressed in a specific architecture. That is why we are proposing this extra level.

Goal of EA

A well-developed and maintained Enterprise Architecture enables the organization to respond quickly and adequately to changes inside the organization and in the environment in which the organization operates. In combination with the strategic interaction analysis (game theory) it serves as a base to create scenarios and to assess the impact of the changes on each of the EA-layers. These scenarios are the input of the investment process (interdisciplinary forum, see above).

Therefore one of the goals of EA is to assess, plan and implement changes in the organization so that they can respond with more agile responsiveness of the organization and this in an efficient (cost- and resources based) and effective (strategic and operational objectives) way, and thus improve respectively the overall performance and output (good and/or services).

Stages

Ross (2003) defines four stages:

- Application Silo Stage
- Technology Standardization Stage
- Data Rationalization Stage
- Modular Architecture

Application Silo Stage is about the archipelago of isolated applications, most of them implemented in different technologies. Technology Standardization Stage is the first step towards an Enterprise Architecture in which technology gets standardized and often centralization is put in place. The deployment of resources shifts from application development into the development of a shared infrastructure. This phase is further often characterized by the introduction of business intelligence and a first attempt to manage business processes.

Data Rationalization Stage consists of process and data standardization. The deployment of resources shifts from application development into data management and infrastructure development. The involvement of senior business managers becomes institutionalized by a common forum of IT and business managers. In this phase we see a shift of data ownership from IT towards the business.

A Modular Architecture characterized by enterprise wide global standards with loosely coupled applications, information and technology components to preserve the global standards while enabling local differences through modules extending the core processes.

Business Process Embedded Information System (BPEIS)

Rabaey et al. (2006, 2007) have added a fifth stage: business process embedded information systems. At that moment Grid Computing and Enterprise Application Integration (EAI) were known, but not yet Cloud Computing (as a reality). Cloud computing in combination with Service Oriented Architecture (SOA) makes BPEIS technically possible.

Due to the ever faster changing environment of an organization and increasing interactions with it, a global and central "steering" becomes quite impossible, if the organization aims to have a flexible and rapid response. So the organization delegates to the business units and their processes. Therefore the Information Technology (IT) must be federated to obtain the necessary autonomy for the IT-applications. That is why the authors are proposing to embed information systems into business processes. In the context of cloud computing BPEIS can be considered as Business Process as a Service (BPaaS), which is a standardized and platform independent begin-to-end automated business process (in the Cloud).

All aspects of the information system can be federated without losing the consistency of the information system of the highest governmental level. However before going to the fifth stage, an organization and its departments have to perform a knowledge and information model as described above. Knowledge becomes a belief system and merging or separating processes (or structures) should be assessed to determine if the cultures of the different parties fit the new organization. Thus at the same time, the structure of the organization and its departments has to be defined, and the business processes have to be modeled in the Business Process Management tool, which is obviously managed at the business level of EA.

Once the business model, knowledge model and the conceptual information model are defined, then they need to be merged into a global model (information, knowledge mapping and business processes), where the departments should manage their own (embedded) information system. But as already mentioned, it has to start with a conceptual information model to solve the problems of information management. Following, the knowledge model should test the cultural compatibilities of the applications with the business.

Since the environment of the organization is permanently changing and thus the organization also, the information system of the organization has to be adapted to the new situation. This will reflect the most at the knowledge infrastructure, because information systems in the Cloud will become commodity.

So, if a business process could be fully automated and it holds itself the information, then a consistent part of the producible and needed information will be embedded in the business process, in accordance with the culture.

The concept of embedding is not new, Object-Oriented programming (OOP) keeps methods and data private in objects. Those objects are interfacing with their environment through public functions and data. A step further is the Service Oriented Architecture (SOA) where services are delivered through the contract of the web services, next to Software as a Service (SaaS) and BPaaS.

A characteristic of Cloud Computing is "you pay as you use" IT-resources. This is an interesting solution for situations that call for temporary IT-resources such as those required for a study or a knowledge creation process. The organization may have temporary needs for extra storage or servers in the Cloud. SaaS can be used to increase ad hoc the analysis capability of the organization. So, besides the advantage of increasing the server capacity, the organization can use analysis software without having to buy it.

Bus-Structure

A process consists of a logical set of activities organized to attain one or more goals. These activities can be clustered in sub-processes, which can be considered as services for the main process. The communication in these sub-processes (services) is hidden from the main process; however, the communication between these sub-processes is not.

This configuration can be represented as a communication-bus which connects all services (sub-processes). These services communicate with each other via an interface to the communication-bus (see figure below).

Regarding the Intelligence Process, the services are those sub-processes described above (Planning & Direction, Collection, Analysis, Dissemination, Network management) and the components of the Intelligence Base (Fact Base, Interpreted Information Base, Network of sensors and Unknown Base).

A special Management module manages the intelligence bus. Its responsibility is the good functioning of the Intelligence bus (like security, availability, interconnectivity). Additional services can be plugged into the bus, as long as they respect the rules of interfacing with the Intelligence bus.

Multi-Level and Collaboration

An intelligence bus should be capable of communicating with other intelligence busses (See also Figure 4: Multiple layers of Intelligence process / Base) and even with other systems. In that way, pulling and pushing information or intelligence can be done throughout the whole organization and even outside the organization with trusted, auditable relations and connections.

Nowadays technically all this is feasible; however competition between intelligence services (national and international) makes it difficult to implement such interconnectivity. "No rivalries are more intense than those between intelligence services working, by different means, on the same side." (Keegan, 2003, p.385). Likely, this will be the greatest challenge instead of the technical issues.

Figure 9 represents a multi-level organization where each level disposes of its own Intelligence Base. In function of the command structure and connections, the capabilities and resources will be organized and deployed.

FUTURE RESEARCH DIRECTIONS: FUZZY CHAOS

Fuzzy Sets and Chaos Theory

James (1996) shows how Chaos Theory systems can be detected and controlled in general, and in the military world in particular. "That is, my experience with Chaos gave me very specific behaviors to expect, in addition to obvious suggestions of ways to control the dynamics. Moreover, I had some idea of the kinds of dynamics to expect without knowing anything about the internal workings of

Figure 9. Intelligence base bus structure

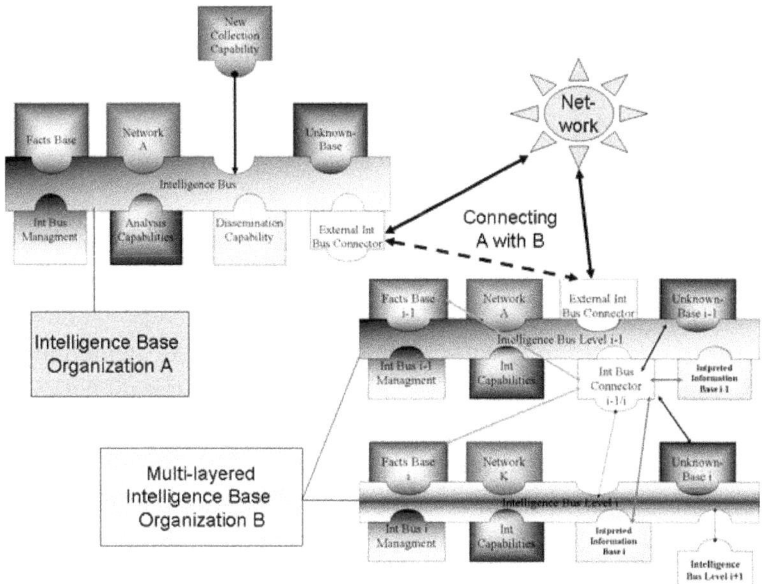

the system! This universality of chaotic dynamics underscores the power of understanding the basic results of Chaos theory. Certainly, not every system in the world is capable of generating Chaos, but in many systems we can control and analyze a system with no need for a model." (James, 1996, p.21). So one can find key parameters that describe in a way the behavior of a system, and key control parameters to manipulate the system to have some desired behavior.

Naturalistic Decision Making (NDM) does not use formal, normative models like formal-empiricist decision making approach and rationalist approach. NDM takes into account the experience of the decision maker, the complexity of the task, and the environmental constraints (Rosen et al., 2008) so the experts (and novices) can use NDM to support decision making for issues where chaotic systems are involved.

Amongst other authors, Lu et al. (2007), Zandi et al. (2010) propose the theory of fuzzy sets to capture the expert opinions and transform them suited for (fuzzy) numerical calculations. So we will combine Chaos theory, fuzzy sets theory and NDM to better support investment and resource allocations decisions.

For instance, the classical techniques of real options are very complex because of the correlations between decision variables and the amount of (historical) data to support the ROV. Fuzzy sets haven been proposed in this domain with Fuzzy ROV as result (Wikipedia Fuzzy Pay-Off Method for Real Option Valuation, n.d.; Collan, 2008; Collan et al., 2009). In interdisciplinary forum (IF), fuzzy ROV should be introduced, not to replace the classical ROV, but to complement it. Thus IF can extend its arsenal of financial investment techniques to handle investment issues where not much data is available and where a priori there does not seem to be clear (cor)relations amongst the decision variables. And as already mentioned, fuzzy sets have the advantage that numerical assessments of experts can be combined taking into account the level of expertise of the experts.

After the research on the link between NDM and Chaos theory and Fuzzy Sets, we will do research on the link NDM/fuzzy sets with Complex Adaptive Systems (economical, military) and with non-linear systems (military).

Knowledge Warehouse

To support the framework mentioned in previous point (chaos, fuzzy sets, NDM), the IntB will need to be extended with more knowledge tools because experts/novices in NDM are using knowledge and expertise from other experts. More than ever before, the need to make expertise and knowledge explicit will be crucial.

Besides rendering the knowledge explicit (storing), the retrieval of the right information, intelligence or knowledge in the mass of knowledge store will be as much important. Due to the different natures (physical and logical) of information (p.e. data, images, sound) and the ever increasing amount of information, the instruments of the decision makers and intelligence personnel have became more complex. Therefore, new technologies, such as intelligent agents, have to be examined to help reduce this complexity. By far, the biggest challenge in this research will be the integration of the knowledge and intelligence in to our framework. In this framework, we will develop the concept of a Knowledge Warehouse, wherein these intelligent agents can be used to collect and create intelligence, and/or contains knowledge which they combine with other intelligent agents and humans to solve problems or unfold new knowledge.

An IT architecture based on SOA and Cloud Computing should be conceived to build a Knowledge warehouse. Especially with Cloud Computing, Software as a Service (SaaS) and Business Process as a Service (BPaaS) are very promising because their solutions will deliver service to the end-users. As such, besides the creation of intelligence and knowledge, the Knowledge warehouse is the meta-knowledge of the supported processes and systems producing services (and/or goods).

Knowledge Value Added (KVA)

The main problem for non-profit organizations is the lack of revenues, which exist for profit organizations. The fact that most investment techniques are using revenues causes problems for non-profit organizations to apply these techniques properly.

Knowledge Value Added (KVA) replaces monetary output units (revenues) by knowledge value output units. The internal resources are contributing relatively to this output and therefore their performance and added value can be determined in the non-monetary output units.

KVA is also related to Real Options Valuation (ROV). It provides a framework for the analytical analysis of organizational knowledge assets. KVA will measure the value of knowledge embedded in an organization's core processes, employees, and IT investments. This measure is quantified in a return-on-knowledge (ROK) ratio, which can be used to identify how much value knowledge assets provide within each core business process.

This technique has been successfully used in the US DOD, profit and non-profit organizations. With Monte Carlo simulations the volatility of the real options can be calculated. The further research is to examine if this technique KVA along with ROV can be integrated into or with the intelligence base.

Another research is to investigate if there is a link between KVA and EA, more precisely the knowledge architecture.

CONCLUSION

Nowadays the socio-economical context of the market is demanding a lot of creativity, flexibility and agility from the organizations. Services need to be quickly created and brought to the market, but the possible advantage is only for a short period, due to the fact that competition can also quickly bring similar services to the market.

Because similar stress exists in the military environment, we have shown that -based on the principles of the Art of War- an organization should constantly monitor its environment (internal and external) and that it needs process-capacity to analyze and integrate the collected information into intelligence, and finally bring the intelligence to the clients.

We have proposed the Intelligence Base (IntB) (slightly adapted from (Rabaey et al., 2005)) to support the intelligence process, but this capability should be available in the whole organization, and not be limited to one part of the organization (like top management). The IntB is composed of:

- A "Facts Base" to store the information
- An "Interpreted Information Base," the knowledge base
- An "Unknown Base" to manage the unknown, which the organisation would like to have information about
- A network of sensors to push and pull information

The OODA-cycle (Observe-Orient-Decide-Act) and the Naturalistic DM are non-classical decision making models, and are more adapted to handle the increasing pressure organizations have in the actual knowledge (service) economy. The concept of Intelligence Base can support those two decision making approaches. Further, as a business example we looked at Real Option Valuation (ROV) and due to the fact that most of the "relevant" information was already collected for the different strategic levels, the IntB can equally support ROV. So, one of the reasons that ROV is hard to use (permanent seeking for intelligence) does not stand anymore.

Knowledge management (KM) and IntB are tightly linked to each other and therefore they should have a common place in the overall architecture of an organization. In this context Enterprise Architecture (EA) has been proposed as a framework. However in the original configuration of EA there was not an explicit place for knowledge, but since knowledge is obviously important in a knowledge economy an additional "knowledge layer" has been introduced. Rabaey (2011) amongst other authors states that since the use of (services in) Cloud Computing is increasing, IT will become a utility (commodity) and competitive and/or collaborative advantages will become almost fully dependent on the capability of producing intelligence for decision-making and knowledge management (in systems, processes and human resources). The proposed architecture for IntB is by consequence one of Service Oriented Architecture and Cloud Computing, which guarantees flexibility and interoperability.

As a final point, we can conclude that the philosophy of IntB helps organizations to have a blueprint of a strategic and operational IT-system that provides the organizations with knowledge and intelligence to arm them against the threats in this continuously changing environment. In function of their means, goals and components in the "Orient" phase of OODA, they can instantiate the right configuration for their IntB.

REFERENCES

Ariely, D. (2009). *Predictably irrational*. London, UK: Harper Collins Publishers.

Aven, T. (2010). *Misconceptions of risk*. Chichester, UK: John Wiley & Sons. doi:10.1002/9780470686539

Barnett, M., & Dunbar, R. (2008). Making sense of real options reasoning: An engine of choice that backfires. In Hodgkinson, G., & Starbuck, W. (Eds.), *The Oxford handbook of organizational decision making* (pp. 383–399). Oxford, UK: Oxford University Press. doi:10.1093/oxfordhb/9780199290468.003.0020

Bernard, H. (1976). *Totale Oorlog en Revolutionaire Oorlog* (*Vol. I*). Brussels, Belgium: Royal Military Academy.

Berryman, J. M. (2007). Judgments during information seeking: a naturalistic approach to understanding of enough information. *Journal of Information Science*, *20*(10), 1–11.

Besson, B., & Possin, J.-C. (2001). *Du renseignement à l'intelligence économique, Cybercriminalité, contrefaçon, veilles stratégiqus; détecter les menaces et les opportunités pour l'entreprise*. Paris, France: Dunod.

Besson, B., & Possin, J.-C. (2003). *L'Audit d'Intelligence Economique*. Paris, France: Dunod.

Brooks, B. (2007). The pulley model: a descriptive model of risky decision-making. *Safety Science Monitor, 11*(1), 1–14.

Bryant, D. (n.d.). *Making naturalistic decision making "fast and frugal."* Toronto, Canada. *Defence Research Development Canada.*

Burke, L. A., & Miller, M. K. (1999). Taking the mystery out of intuitive decision making. *The Academy of Management Executive, 13*(4), 91–99. doi:10.5465/AME.1999.2570557

Collan, M. (2008). *A new method for real option valuation using fuzzy numbers*. (Research Paper). Turku, Finland: Institute for Advanced Management Systems Research. Retrieved April 12, 2011, from http://ideas.repec.org/p/amr/wpaper/466.html

Collan, M., Fullér, R., & Mezei, J. (2009). A fuzzy pay-off method for real option valuation. *Journal of Applied Mathematics and Decision Sciences, 1*, 1–14. doi:10.1155/2009/238196

Copeland, T., & Keenan, P. (1998). How much is flexibility worth? *The McKinsey Quarterly*, (2): 38–49.

Courtney, J. F. (2001). Decision making and knowledge management in inquiring organizations: toward a new decision-making paradigm for DSS. *Decision Support Systems, 31*, 17–38. doi:10.1016/S0167-9236(00)00117-2

Davenport, T., & Prusak, L. (1998). *Working knowledge: How organizations manage what they know*. Boston, MA: Harvard Business School Press.

Dienes, Z., & Perner, J. (1999). A theory of implicit and explicit knowledge. *The Behavioral and Brain Sciences, 22*, 735–808. doi:10.1017/S0140525X99002186

Drucker, P. (1998). From capitalism to knowledge society. In Drucker, P. (Ed.), *Post-capitalist society* (pp. 19–47). New York, NY: Harper Collins.

DSS. (2005). *Defense security service* (DSS). Retrieved February 11, 2005 from http://www.dss.mil/isec/appendixc.htm

EARF. (n.d.). *Completed projects.* Retrieved April 11, 2001, from http://earf.meraka.org.za/earfhome/our-projects-1/completed-projects/

Fereira, N., Kar, J., & Trigeorgis, L. (2009). Option games: The key to competing in capital-intensive industries. *Harvard Business Review*, (March): 2009.

Funston, F., & Wagner, S. (2010). *Surviving and thriving in uncertainty: Creating the risk intelligent enterprise*. Hoboken, NJ: John Wiley & Sons.

Greitzer, F., Podmore, R., Robinson, M., & Ey, P. (2009). Naturalistic decision making for power system operators. *Proceedings of NDM9, the 9th International Conference on Naturalistic Decision Making*, London, June 2009.

Guida, G., & Tasso, C. (1994). *Design and development of knowledge-based systems: From life cycle to development methodology*. Chichester, UK: John Wiley & Sons.

Guptara, P. (1999). Why knowledge management fails. *Knowledge Management Review, 9*(July/August), 26–29.

James, G. E. (1996). *Chaos theory: The essentials for military applications*. Newport, RI: Naval War College.

Kahaner, L. (1997). *Competitive intelligence: How to gather, analyse and use information to move your business to the top*. New York, NY: Simon and Schuster.

Keegan, J. (2003). *Intelligence in war: Knowledge of the enemy from Napoleon to Al-Qaeda*. New York, NY: Knopf.

Klein, G., & Klinger, D. (1991). Naturalistic decision making. *Human Systems IAC Gateway*, *2*(1), 16–19.

KM-Huis. (2011). Retrieved April 17, 2011, from http://www.fedweb.belgium.be/nl/over_de_organisatie/kennismanagement/

Libet, B. (2011). Do We Have Free Will? In Sinnott-Armstrong, W., & Nadel, L. (Eds.), *Conscious Will and Responsibility* (pp. 1–10). Oxford: Oxford Press.

Liddle Hart, B. (1991). *Strategy*. New York: Prager.

Lipshitz, R., Klein, G., Orasanu, J., & Salas, E. (2000). *Taking Stock of Naturalistic Decision Making. Haifa*. University of Haifa.

Lu, J., Zhang, G., & Ruan, D. (2007). *Multi-objective group decision making: Methods, software and applications with fuzzy set techniques*. London, UK: Imperial College Press.

Mercken, R. (2010). *De investeringsbeslissing: Een beleidsgerichtee analyse*. Antwerpen, The Netherlands: Garant. (In Dutch)

Mercken, R., Leoni, P., Houben, G., & Motmans, L. (2010). Strategic investment decision-making: Communicating the true meaning of the real options framework to the board. *Argumenta Oecomica*, *2*(25), 137–162.

Montier, J. (2010). *The little book of behavioral investing*. Hoboken, NJ: John Wiley & Sons.

Mun, J. (2010). *Modeling risk, + DVD: Applying Monte Carlo simulation, real options analysis, forecasting, and optimization techniques*. Hoboken, NJ: John Wiley & Sons.

Neef, D. (1998). The knowledge economy: An introduction. In Neef, D. (Ed.), *The knowledge economy* (pp. 1–14). Woburn, MA: Butterworth-Heinemann.

Niu, L., Lu, J., Chew, E., & Zhang, G. (2007). *An exploratory cognitive business intelligence system*. IEEE/WIC/ACM International Conference on Web Intelligence. DOI 10.1109/WI.2007.21

Osinga, F. (2005). *Science, strategy and war: The strategic theory of John Boyd*. Delft, The Netherlands: Eburon Academic Publishers.

Osinga, F. (2007). *Science, strategy and war: The strategic theory of John Boyd*. London, UK: Routledge.

Polič, M. (2009). Decision making: Between rationality and reality. *Interdisciplinary Description of Complex Systems*, *7*(2), 78–89.

Pucket, S., & Purdy, S. C. (2011). Are voluntary movements initiated preconsciously? The relationships between readiness potentials, urges, and decisions. In Sinnott-Armstrong, W., & Nadel, L. (Eds.), *Conscious will and responsibility* (pp. 1–10). Oxford, UK: Oxford Press. doi:10.1093/acprof:oso/9780195381641.003.0005

Rabaey, M. (1997). *Militaire Strategie en Informatietechnologie (paper)*. Brussel, Belgium: Vrije Universiteit Brussel. (in Dutch)

Rabaey, M. (2011). *Game theoretic real option approach of the procurement of Department of Defense: Competition or collaboration*. Paper presented at the 8th Annual Acquisition Research Symposium (May 10-12, 2011). Montery CA, USA.

Rabaey, M. (2012). A public economics approach to enabling enterprise architecture with the government cloud in Belgium. In Saha, P. (Ed.), *Enterprise architecture for connected e-government: Practices and innovations*. Hershey, PA: IGI Global.

Rabaey, M., Leclercq, J.-M., Vandijck, E., Hoffman, G., & Timmerman, M. (2005). *Intelligence base: Strategic instrument of an organization.* Paper presented at the meeting of NATO IST-055 Specialist Meeting). The Hague, Netherlands.

Rabaey, M., Tromp, H., & Vandenborre, K. (2007). Holistic approach to align ICT capabilities with business integration. In Cunha, M., Cortes, B., & Putnik, G. (Eds.), *Adaptive technologies and business integration: Social, managerial, and organizational dimensions* (pp. 160–173). Hershey, PA: Idea Group Publishing. doi:10.4018/978-1-59904-048-6.ch008

Rabaey, M., Vandenborre, K., Vandijck, E., Tromp, H., & Timmerman, M. (2006, May). *Business process embedded information systems - For flexibility and adaptability*. Paper presented at 8th International Conference on Enterprise Information Systems: Databases and Information Systems Integration, Paphos, Cyprus.

Roos, J., Roos, G., Dragonetti, N., & Edvinsson, L. (1997). *Intellectual capital: Navigating the new business landscape*. Houndmills, UK: MacMillan Press.

Rosen, M., Salas, E., Lyons, R., & Fiore, S. (2008). Expertise and naturalistic decision making in organizations: Mechanisms of effective decision making. In Hodgkinson, G., & Starbuck, W. (Eds.), *The Oxford handbook of organizational decision making* (pp. 211–230). Oxford, UK: Oxford University Press. doi:10.1093/oxfordhb/9780199290468.003.0011

Sanchez, R., & Heene, A. (1997). A competence perspective on strategic learning and knowledge management. In Sanchez, R., & Heene, A. (Eds.), *Strategic learning and knowledge management* (pp. 3–18). Chichester, UK: John Wiley & Sons. doi:10.1016/B978-0-7506-7223-8.50004-6

Shaikh, S. (2011). The study on the relationship between organisational culture and knowledge management. *Journal of Money. Investment and Banking, 19*, 21–28.

Sharp, A., & Mcdermott, P. (2009). *Workflow modeling: Tools for process improvement and applications development*. Norwood, NJ: Artech House.

Shattuck, L. G., & Miller, N. L. (2006). Naturalistic decision making in complex systems: A dynamic model of situated cognition combining technological and human agents. *Organizational Behavior: Special Issue on Naturalistic Decision Making in Organizations, 27*(7), 989–1009.

Simion, C., & Radu, V. (2009). Relationship between organisation culture and knowledge management in SME's. *Review of International Comparative Management, 10*(4), 781–790.

Simpson, P. (2001). *Naturalistic decision making in aviation environments. Fisherman's Bend.* Australia: DSTO Aeronautical and Maritime Research Laboratory.

Stanley, J., & Williamson, T. (2001). Knowing how. *The Journal of Philosophy, 98*(8), 411–444. doi:10.2307/2678403

Stevens, R., Millage, J., & Clark, S. (2010). Waves of knowledge management: The flow between explicit and tacit knowledge. *American Journal of Economics and Business Administration, 2*(1), 129–135. doi:10.3844/ajebasp.2010.129.135

Watts, B. (2004). *Clausewitz friction and future war*. Washington, DC: Institute for National Strategic Studies.

Weeds, H. (2006). *Applying option games: When should real options valuation be used?* (paper). Colchester, UK: University of Essex. Retrieved April 10, 2011, from http://privatewww.essex.ac.uk/~hfweeds/

Whitehouse. (n.d.). *Office of e-government & information technology*. Retrieved March 26, 2011, from http://www.whitehouse.gov/omb/e-gov/

Wikipedia. (n.d.). *Culture*. Retrieved May 24, 2011, from http://en.wikipedia.org/wiki/Culture

Wikipedia. (n.d.). *Epistemology*. Retrieved May 24, 2011, from http://en.wikipedia.org/wiki/Epistemology

Wikipedia. (n.d.). *Fuzzy pay-off method for real option valuation*. Retrieved April 10, 2011, from http://en.wikipedia.org/wiki/Fuzzy_Pay-Off_Method_for_Real_Option_Valuation

Wikipedia. (n.d.). *Knowledge*. Retrieved May 24, 2011, from http://en.wikipedia.org/wiki/Knowledge

Wikipedia. (n.d.). *Knowledge base*. Retrieved May 24, 2011, from http://en.wikipedia.org/wiki/Knowledge_base

Wikipedia. (n.d.). *Knowledge management*. Retrieved May 24, 2011, from http://en.wikipedia.org/wiki/Knowledge_management

Wikipedia. (n.d.). *Rationality*. Retrieved March 24, 2011, from http://en.wikipedia.org/wiki/Rationality

Wikipedia. (n.d.). *Risk*. Retrieved April 12, 2011, from http://en.wikipedia.org/wiki/Risk

Wikipedia. (n.d.). *Risk management*. Retrieved April 12, 2011, from http://en.wikipedia.org/wiki/Risk_management

Yates, J. F. (2003). *Decision management: How to assure better decision in your company*. San Francisco, CA: Jossey-Bass.

Yima, N., Kima, S., Kimb, H., & Kwahk, K. (2004). Knowledge based decision making on higher level strategic concerns. *Expert Systems with Applications*, *27*, 143–158. doi:10.1016/j.eswa.2003.12.019

Zandi, F., & Tavana, M. (2010). A hybrid fuzzy real option analysis and group ordinal approach for knowledge management strategy assessment. *Knowledge Management Research & Practice*, *8*, 216–228. doi:10.1057/kmrp.2010.12

Zhu, V., & Sun, L. (2010). The interactive relationship between corporate cultures, leadership style and knowledge management. *International Journal of Asian Business and Information Management*, *1*(3), 54–68. doi:10.4018/jabim.2010070105

ENDNOTES

1 For political reasons the concept of ACOS Eval has been changed into an Internal Audit Department in 2007. Therefore the EIS has never been fully developed.

2 However we will not extensively discuss the theory of John Boyd. We refer to the excellent works of Frank Osinga: (Osinga, 2005, 2007), who in extenso has discussed John Boyd's theory.

Chapter 18
Enhancing Information Retrieval Capabilities of Knowledge Management Systems

Dinesh Rathi
University of Alberta, Canada

Shannon Lucky
University of Alberta, Canada

Ali Shiri
University of Alberta, Canada

ABSTRACT

User support services face complex problems in the efficient and satisfactory delivery of services to users. Knowledge management (KM) principles can be effectively implemented within this organizational context to support efficient and effective problem solving to improve service delivery to the users. A KM system with good information retrieval capabilities is critical in empowering front line employees to utilize organizational knowledge repositories for better service delivery. The purpose of this chapter is to present different aspects of the major information retrieval techniques that can be used in a user services environment and to propose new models to enhance retrieval capabilities of KM systems. The authors discuss the basic elements that make up an information retrieval system including metadata, controlled, and uncontrolled vocabularies. The authors also propose three experimental search interfaces for enhancing information retrieval capabilities of a KM system. The first uses a thesaurus for enhanced retrieval features through better query formulation and browsing of search results; the second uses the tag cloud concept to present thesaurus terms; and the third combines the structure of a controlled vocabulary with the flexibility of a folksonomy and tag cloud, thus incorporating the beneficial aspects of both uncontrolled and controlled vocabularies to support retrieval within a heterogeneous corporate environment.

DOI: 10.4018/978-1-4666-0948-8.ch018

INTRODUCTION

Users require support from their service providers for multiple reasons such as assistance in purchasing and support for resolving problems. Organizations typically aim to provide quick and efficient service to their customers/users, however organizations are facing increasing pressures such as large numbers of (problem resolution) calls, high employee turnover, escalation in employee training costs, (Chan, et al., 2000) and ineffective and inefficient re-use of the knowledge base, created from previously resolved cases, to provide solutions to their customers. Organizations are working to overcome some of these challenges by encouraging customer support staff to use the organizational knowledge resources for better service to the customers as well as by empowering the customer with appropriate self help options. In both scenarios, it is important that the customer support staff and the customers are able to efficiently and effectively use the knowledge base for problem solving. However the challenge in using an organizational knowledge base is the retrieval of relevant information when required by both the customer and the support staff. This chapter focuses on the importance of organizing and retrieving information within the context of knowledge management (KM) practices and elaborates on the use of different tools and strategies to aid in the organization and retrieval of information from knowledge repositories by users of information technology help support services with a focus on the emerging phenomenon of social tagging and tag clouds.

In this chapter we will first provide an overview of the importance of user services (or help desk support services) and discuss the problems facing user support services, and how the principles of knowledge management can be implemented within these contexts to support efficient problem solving. The next section will describe the importance of information retrieval in a KM system as this is the critical feature that extracts relevant information from organizational knowledge repositories for the user to support their work-flow. The chapter then describes metadata, controlled, and uncontrolled vocabularies as methods of information organization that support retrieval in KM systems and discuss the benefits and problems inherent in each approach. Throughout this chapter three experimental search interfaces are discussed that have the potential to enhance information retrieval capabilities in a KM system. The first two are discussed briefly in the controlled vocabulary section and the third is presented in detail in the uncontrolled vocabulary section along with a discussion of social tagging and folksonomy.

AN OVERVIEW OF USER SERVICES

Providing appropriate service to customers or users (the terms are used interchangeably in this chapter) is an important component of any business and the majority of organizations strive to provide excellent service to their customers. The role of the user services or help desk (the terms will be used interchangeable in this chapter) is to provide support and help to users by providing information about the operation of products as well as resolving problems encountered by the user (Göker & Roth-Berghofer, 1999) in the continuous operations of the product (i.e., providing support for problem resolution). Marcella and Middleton (1996) define the help desk as "an accessible service point" (p. 4) that gives solutions on request to solve users' or help seekers' problems. Support services can be broadly classified into two types: *internal support systems* (i.e., providing support to the users within an organization) and *external support systems* (i.e., providing support to external customers) (Gonzalez, et al., 2005) depending upon the type of customer they support. There are a number of channels (e.g., telephone based support services, email-based help desk system, etc.) called "touch points" for the customer to interact with service providers (Anton, 2000) and seek help from experts to solve their problems. The telephone-based support system has been the dominant method of communication in the past, but with the advent of the Internet and development of email-based technology, email-based help support systems are of growing importance (Nenkova & Bagga, 2003).

Problem resolution encompasses many different types of tasks such as providing information, replacement, servicing, repairs, warranty claims, technical training, and assistance (Sawy & Bowles, 2004; White & Jagielska, 2004). The concept of providing support to users was started by the Singer Sewing Machine Company way back in the 1850s (Lele & Seth, 1987 as referred in Sawy & Bowles, 2004) and since that time there has been continuous expansion of user support systems, encompassing practically all types of commercial establishments and extending into the educational domain as well. Help desk support systems in the information technology (IT) domain, for example, provide solutions to problems related to IT products and services. They serve as the contact point for users seeking help from experts to solve their problems related to software, hardware, logging problems, installation problems, update problems, etc. (Gonzalez, et al., 2005; Kriegsman & Barletta, 1993).

In today's world IT is crucial for the smooth, efficient, and effective functioning of an organization. We have seen a wide adoption of IT into organizations and there has been a dramatic increase in the diversity of the IT tools used. For example the user service desk in an educational institute is required to provide technology support to its members (i.e., staff, faculty, and students) for smooth functioning of the institute. The support for user services is required in every area of operation of an educational institute such as the classroom, software access, emails, course registration, etc. (Greer et al., 1998) and there has been a proliferation in the adoption and use of IT in educational institutes as a direct result. For example, a survey was conducted for different types of operating system installed on the Idaho State University campus. "*The options were Windows 9.x, NT. Mac 7.x, 8.x, 9.x, UNIX and LINUX, and mainframe. Every campus had Windows 9.x, 97% has at least one version of Mac OS, 89% has LINUX/UNIX, and 66% had mainframes. 43% reported having all eight operating systems on campus with another 23% having 7 of the 8 OS*" (Prescott, et al., 2001, p. 135). This diversity of operating systems creates a complex information and technology support environment for help desk workers to function in. It requires a great deal of information to be available at all times to resolve a myriad of potential problems.

Similarly, at the University of Illinois at Urbana-Champaign (UIUC), Campus Information Technologies and Educational Services (CITES) (www.cites.uiuc.edu) is the central service organization and provides service for over 70 domains (e.g., networking, email, courseware, webhosting, telephone services, etc.) [as listed on the "Index of All Services" page of the website, www.cites.uiuc.edu]. We can clearly see that the role of the help desk is expanding in step with the growing number of hardware and software technologies in use. In addition, the help desk units are facing numerous challenges such as high employee turnover, escalation of employee training costs, diversity in call types, and increasing call volume (Yang, et al, 1997; Chan, et al., 2000; Nenkova & Bagga, 2003; Gonzalez, et al., 2005). For example, the CITES help desk assists approximately 5,000 customers a month (as cited on www.cites.uiuc.edu on June 10, 2011). Similarly, Delic and Dayal (2000) note that "*one analyst usually covers 200-300 desktops, handles daily 20-30 phone calls, whose duration is typically 20 minutes and whose average cost is around $50*"(p. 7-3). Although these numbers may be contextually specific to this study, these figures do provide some insight into the often demanding job of help desk support service workers.

User services, even with constrained resources, aim to provide excellent service to their users by being efficient and effective in their problem resolution process. According to Göker and Roth-Berghofer (1999), help desk services are expected to resolve problems immediately and the staff must have expertise in resolving all types of issues. User services aim to achieve this by implementing different strategies such as adopting an organizational structure that meets the organization's overall service needs, directing problems to domain experts, and developing a knowledge base so that repeat problems can be resolved in the minimum time required. Related to the organizational structure of the help desk, many help desks have a two or three tier structure (Delic & Dayal, 2000; Halverson, et al. 2004). For example, Oregon State University (OSU) has a two tier structure; the central information technology (IT) organization and individual colleges/departments' help desks (Sinnett & Barr, 2004). This type of structure helps in solving the majority of problems locally within the school, sometime escalating a few problems to the central unit when required. Sawy and Bowles (1997) and Martin and Dean (1995) presented a three tier help desk structure. Sawy and Bowles (1997) in their study found that 67% of problems are resolved at level 1, 26% are resolved at level 2, and the remaining 7% are escalated further, while, Martin and Dean (1995) noted that 70% of user problems are resolved on the front-line, 20% are directed to the second line of support and the remaining 10% require further investigation (potentially by the experts).

Customer service and support models strive to provide quick and helpful service but can struggle with many common limitations such as restrictions on personnel resources, imperfect technology, usability issues, and access to required and relevant information. Knowledge management principles, originally developed to address the need to manage organizational knowledge within corporate environments, could be very beneficial in bringing the kinds of organizational success experienced by corporations that have implemented them to front line customer service workers and to the customers themselves. The comfort level of the general public with technical resources and online tools has grown exponentially in recent years and users are capable of (if not expecting) to take more control over their customer service experience. Knowledge management tools and principles could encourage knowledge sharing to support problem solving on the customer's end as well.

KNOWLEDGE MANAGEMENT AND USER SERVICES

Knowledge is a valuable resource for organizations and Johannessen, et al. (2001) note that knowledge as a resource will have a greater impact on organizational success than physical capital in the future. There are two kinds of knowledge; tacit knowledge and explicit knowledge (Polanyi, 1966 as cited in Nonaka, 1994) and knowledge management's (KM) goal is to help transform tacit knowledge into explicit knowledge and vice-versa (Cook & Brown, 1999; Nonaka, 1994). Therefore KM is defined as an organized and systematic approach to identify, create, capture, store, organize, retrieve, and disseminate knowledge within an organization (Benbya et al., 2004; Courtney, 2001; Darroch, 2003; Seaman, et al., 2003; Schultze & Stabell, 2004; Delic & Dayal, 2000). Similarly, Owen (1999) notes that KM aims to identify and analyze knowledge related work and develop procedures and systems to generate, store, distribute, and support the use of knowledge within an organization. These processes in turn aim to improve organizational efficiency by making resources available to users in a timely manner (Offsey, 1997). KM systems will help organizations in the utilization of knowledge for problem solving, dynamic learning, strategic planning, and decision making processes, thereby increasing firms' intelligence and flexibility (www.iknow.com). As Gupta et al.

(2000) argue, KM is becoming an important factor in organizations' performance and it is expected to provide some competitive advantage to those who utilize these principles.

A large number of organizations use KM systems to support the work of user services and make help desk operations more efficient. The average help desk supports a wide range of activities (e.g., information inquiries, application of usable problems, and others as identified in the User Service section of this chapter) and these activities require knowledge creation, sharing, and reuse (Delic & Dayal, 2000; O'Leary, 2002). According to these authors, the help desk's work is generally "supported by a problem-solving knowledge base" (p. 7-4) which consist of documents related to past problems and their related solution. Similarly Babilon (1998) presented the case of NCR Corporation in which the author noted that their knowledge management system archived work documents related to organizational processes for the help desk and other groups in the organization. In addition the NCR Corporation adopted the use of the Lotus Notes application to increase efficiency at the help desk because this application connects different knowledge repositories. In the literature a number of studies have been conducted to develop efficient and effective knowledge management systems so that user service teams can resolve repeat or similar problem in the shortest possible time by accessing previously solved cases or problems, using the solutions included in closed cases to resolve the problem at hand.

The predominant models of KM systems within the help desk domain are based on Frequently Asked Questions (FAQs), Case-Based Reasoning (CBR) and Rule-Based KM Systems. In FAQ-based KM systems (Halverson, et al., 2004) users can view the most commonly occurring problems and use them to troubleshoot before forwarding their problem to the help desk staff. In CBR systems similar cases (i.e., cases similar to the problem at hand) are retrieved (Becerra-Fernandez & Aha, 1999) and the knowledge embedded in past resolved cases is applied to solve the problem at hand. In the process the embedded knowledge is revised and updated. This process leads to the incremental addition of knowledge to the past solved cases in the system. Göker and Roth-Berghofer (1999), presented a case for creating a knowledge base or repository based on the CBR approach. Their rationale for proposing a shared knowledge base for the help desk is to assist staff who have varying levels of expertise to use this system to access the expertise and experience of others to solve user problems and reduce waiting (problem solving) time. This view is echoed by Gormly (2003) who argues that help desk personnel should have the skills needed to resolve the problem at the first point of contact which will potentially reduce time spent on problem resolution and minimize problem escalation to higher levels. Several researchers noted that CBR systems provide important contextual support to problem resolution (Watson & Marir, 1994; Choy et al., 2002; Chan et. al., 2000; Kriegsman & Barletta, 1993; Simoudis, 1992; Becerra-Fernandez & Aha, 1999). In addition, CBR systems are more intuitive and contain contextual knowledge that make them more popular with users when compared to "the distillated knowledge associated with rule-based system(s)" (Watson & Marir, 1994) which is question-answer based and can have use restrictions due to the limitation of rules. There are challenges inherent in rule-based systems as they require regular updates to the knowledge domain to generate new rules to accommodate new types of cases. These updates are often difficult and costly to generate and maintain (Liu & Yan, 1997; Kriegsman & Barletta, 1993).

It is important for organizations to have well-developed KM systems which can deliver and manage knowledge construction and aid in its dissemination. The abundance and overwhelming nature of knowledge in most contemporary workplaces requires methods of storing, cataloguing, searching, retrieving, and distributing relevant information efficiently and reliably to the end user.

INFORMATION RETRIEVAL AND KNOWLEDGE MANAGEMENT

Much of the KM literature discusses a multistage model that focuses on the capture, formalization, organization, storage, retrieval, and application of knowledge (Despres & Chauvel 1999; Eric, 2005). As the amount and complexity of information within an organization grows, more efficient systems are needed to be able to make these knowledge resources useable by filtering out irrelevant information, locating desired resources, aiding knowledge discovery, and helping users do their work in a productive and efficient manner. One of the challenges in the adoption and use of KM is the retrieval of relevant information efficiently and effectively (Moussavi, 1999; Offsey, 1999; Fischer & Ostwald, 2001; Stanoevska, et al., 1998). Information retrieval is dependent on how the documents within a KM system are organized or classified (Stanoevska, et al., 1998) and what information management strategies are used to aid retrieval of the information and knowledge from the KM system.

Moussavi (1999) notes that retrieval is a key feature of KM systems and only relevant documents (or cases) should be retrieved for a given query because retrieval is an important element in knowledge creation and dissemination and supports the process of internalization of knowledge (Stanoevska, et al., 1998). The prompt retrieval of user relevant documents will help in quick internalization; otherwise non-relevant document retrieval is likely to lead to information overload (Stanoevska, et al., 1998). Fischer and Ostwald (2001) argue for the incorporation of retrieval tools and technologies (Eric, 2005; Lindvall, et al., 2003; Stanoevska, et al., 1998) that can handle complex information use environments in user services. Moussavi (1999) further argues that with time, the size of knowledge bases will increase which will further impact the retrieval of relevant documents as greater numbers of documents will be retrieved in each search and the user will have to do multiple searches to find the information they are seeking. Offsey (1999), for example, suggests that the users of KM systems now want retrieval functionalities that can handle complex searches coupled with ease of use. Fischer and Ostwald (2001) suggest a few necessary features in retrieval functions including: the ability to search using natural language, support for the use of Boolean logic in search, support for thesaurus use, support for searching different media and format types (e.g., word document, video file, audio file etc.), ability to use different metadata elements as access point (i.e., other than traditional elements like author, title, subject, etc.), and finally and very interestingly, the support for searching concepts like the "Similar" function found in Google search (www.google.com).

Most discussions of enterprise knowledge management (KM) identify a non-linear five step process similar to Despres and Chauvel's (1999) knowledge management taxonomy: acquiring/capturing/creating, packaging/codifying/storing, applying/sharing/transferring, scanning/mapping, and reusing/innovating/transforming. There is no perfect, one-size KM solution for all organizations and each group must tailor their technology choices to their individual needs. The creation and implementation of a metadata system requires effort for the document creator and/or the skills and knowledge of a cataloguer (i.e., an expert) (Rowley, 1995 as cited in Golder & Huberman, 2006). Capturing and cataloguing information within an organization is not solely sufficient to create a successful KM system but the information must be effectively searchable and retrievable. Traditional database or document repository taxonomies are not always well suited to the flexibility demanded by contemporary knowledge workers. Also, repository taxonomies may not support quick and easy retrieval of documents from the KM system when the information worker and user services division are facing numerous challenges. For example, high call volumes exert pressure on information workers in user services to solve problems efficiently, quickly, and effectively so that they can take care of the next call. Hence, the workers require quick and easy ways of retrieving information from the KM system. User services often experience high staff turn-over and the high costs of training employees can be detrimental to organizations over time. In addition, user services personnel will often have varying degrees of expertise among the team members (i.e., novice vs. expert). The experts might be able to use the technical taxonomy with ease as compared to the front line novice staff. This type of heterogeneous work environment requires a KM system that can be used by both novices as well as experts. This means that workplace systems that are easy to learn, intuitive, and fit in with the way employees are used to manipulating information online are more likely to be adopted into regular practice and therefore more likely to be productive additions to their workflow. Users will not benefit from the system if it is complicated, difficult to learn, or ill suited to the way they want to work (Grudin, 2006).

Library and information science (LIS) and computer science researchers have long been at the forefront of research into information storage and retrieval systems. For example, the work done by Chris Buckley, Gerard Salton, James Allan, Amit Singhal, Nicholas J. Belkin, Ricardo Baeza-Yates, Berthier Ribeiro-Neto, Robert R. Korfhage and the famous ranking algorithm work of Google co-founders Sergey Brin and Lawrence Page in the area of information retrieval have all contributed to contemporary systems for information organization and retrieval. There are different approaches that have been developed and used in retrieving user relevant documents in the LIS and computer science domains. For example, describing documents (e.g., creating metadata) to aid retrieval and provide multiple access points thorough which to search a collection of documents, thereby forming the backbone of any knowledge repository and retrieval resource. Successful KM systems must include one or more strategies to aid in the organization and retrieval of information from the system. These include the creation of metadata for documents connected with controlled vocabularies and uncontrolled vocabularies to aid in retrieval. Social tagging and folksonomies can play an integral role in this process by using a bottom-up approach uncommon to the traditional top-down KM approach of classification and categorization (Hammond et al., 2005). Tagging systems are often much larger and more populist than keyword systems because all users (not only authors of documents) can annotate objects in the collection (Heymann & Garcia-Molina 2006, p. 2). Employing social tagging and folksonomies allows users to annotate information both on the World Wide Web and intranets. Researchers who have studied social tagging suggest that folksonomies can significantly aid in retrieval of documents from knowledge repositories (Trant, 2008).

In the following section we will provide a quick overview of different approaches and methods that may be used in the retrieval of documents from KM systems. The focus of our discussion will be on the role of social tagging and folksonomies in supporting the retrieval of documents from KM systems. We will also discuss three different experimental search interfaces that use thesauri, tag clouds, and folksonomies to enhance the retrieval capabilities of KM systems.

METADATA STANDARDS

Metadata, commonly defined as data about data (Garshol, 2004; Nadkarni, 2011; http://dublincore.org/metadata-basics/; Dempsey & Heery, 1998), plays a key role in information retrieval. In content management and knowledge management systems metadata is more specifically used to describe documents and can be defined as "information about a document, an image, a reusable content module, and so on" (Garshol, 2004, p. 2.1). These types of document description creates access points to the content of documents and provides multiple ways to search a collection including elements such as author, title, subject, etc (Bulterman, 2004; Lassila, 1998; Dempsey & Heery, 1998; Loffler, 2000). For example, metadata helps case based reasoning KM systems by organizing cases using subject keywords that describe which issues each case addresses (Stanoevska, 1998). Dublin Core is one of the most widely used metadata standards (Garshol, 2004; Loffler, 2000) and has been implemented across a wide variety of information organizations and management projects. An example of this system in use is the U.S. National Library of Medicine (NLM) which has developed a metadata schema based on Dublin Core (for more details, visit http://www.nlm.nih.gov/tsd/cataloging/metafilenew.html) and according to Guinchard's (2002) survey, many libraries and other institutions utilize Dublin Core metadata as part of their organizational strategy. The Dublin Core metadata standard is designed to be flexible, extensible, and able to be applied to a wide variety of domains to support the ability to integrate and search across multiple collections (Dempsey & Heery, 1998; Guinchard, 2002).

Dublin Core is essentially a framework that provides a set of fifteen possible descriptive elements [original thirteen elements, (http://lcweb2.loc.gov/ammem/award/docs/dublin-examples.html)] that can be used to define a document (Dempsey & Heery, 1998). These elements are; contributor, coverage, creator, date, description, format, identifier, language, publisher, relation, rights, source, subject, title, and type (for more details, visit http://dublincore.org/documents/dces/). Dublin Core rules define the fifteen properties that may be used but do not specify exactly how each property may be represented in terms of which words, languages, and syntax can be used. For example the NLM metadata schema, which is available at http://www.nlm.nih.gov/tsd/cataloging/metafilenew.html, is customized to the National Library of Medicine's specific requirements. Authors or cataloguers can choose to apply the entire set or a subset of the descriptive elements to their documents (depending on suitability to the collection and need) and can define acceptable content for the element fields which allows flexibility as well as the benefits of using a metadata standard (Dekkers, 2001; Guinchard, 2002).

Garshol (2004) describes the role of metadata as finding aid as a crucial task and poses the question *"what kind of information about the objects would help the user the most?"* to those designing knowledge repositories (2004, sec 2.2). Descriptive metadata (NISO, 2004; Taylor & Joudrey, 1999) (metadata that describes aspects of the document such as author, title, publisher, date, etc.) can help users find information or documents they already know are contained in the collection. If a user wishes to find information about a specific topic or searches for answers to a particular question, descriptive metadata can also be useful. Descriptive metadata provides information about the intellectual content of a document (Taylor & Joudrey, 1999) and in Dublin Core generally falls under the elements for description and subject. Description is "an abstract, a table of contents, a graphical representation, or a free-text account of the resource" (http://dublincore.org/documents/dces/) and subject is typically "represented using keywords, key phrases, or classification codes" (http://dublincore.org/documents/dces/). These key words can either be drawn from a defined and closed set of options or controlled vocabulary, or they can be created free-form by the author or users of the document using an uncontrolled vocabulary (http://dublincore.org/documents/usageguide/).

CONTROLLED VOCABULARY

Controlled vocabularies are subject based classification systems consisting of a defined set of terms (Taylor & Joudrey, 1999; Prieto-Díaz, 1991; Lee-Smeltzer, 2000). They employ a finite set of tags or index terms for information retrieval and these tags are generally created by information authority figures within the organization. In the library and information science world a common example of controlled vocabularies are subject heading lists (Plaunt & Norgard, 1998) such as the Library of Congress Subject Headings which consists of an authoritative list of terms that can be used to describe materials catalogued by libraries using this system (Chaplan, 1995; Golub, 2006). Thesaurus, taxonomies and ontologies are other examples of controlled vocabularies. In controlled vocabularies, like subject heading lists, generally no outside subject terms are allowed and often proper hierarchical (Lee-Smeltzer, 2000) descriptions are required. If the system is well understood and implemented it can be a powerful resource in aiding retrieval of documents by providing the user with metadata that is hierarchically organized and applied consistently to the collection (Taylor & Joudrey, 1999; Lee-Smeltzer, 2000). Consistency achieved through standardized terminology is important in this type of information retrieval because it ensures that all documents added to a KM repository are adequately and accurately catalogued and thus retrievable. The use of a controlled vocabulary avoids the problems inherent in the use of multiple different tags that mean the same thing, the use of deprecated or meaningless terms, inconsistent terms, and the avoidance of misspellings or alternate spellings that can negatively impact search results (Taylor & Joudrey, 1999; Lee-Smeltzer, 2000). While controlled vocabularies can be powerful retrieval tools, this extensibility is predicated on the knowledge of the user and their ability to develop appropriate search queries and the skills to browse and navigate through the system using the controlled vocabulary (Soergel, 1997). If users do not understand the terminology used to create tags or keywords or do not know the exact terminology or spelling used they may find it difficult to locate relevant information despite its existence in the repository. These are some of the challenges of using controlled vocabularies for information retrieval (Taylor & Joudrey, 1999).

Thesauri are a "collection of concepts or words arranged according to sense; also a dictionary of synonyms and antonyms" (Oxford English Dictionary as cited by Gilchrist, 2003; Aitchison & Clarke, 2004). Thesauri are controlled vocabularies, but they utilize hierarchical linkages to broader terms, narrower terms, related terms and equivalency relationships to locate related information (Garshol 2004; Taylor & Joudrey, 1999; Kwon et al., 1994; Aitchison & Clarke, 2004). The Library of Congress Subject Headings is a type of thesaurus for information organization but there are minor differences between them. According to Taylor and Joudery (1999), subject heading lists are created primarily by the library community and thesauri by the indexing community. Another difference between thesauri and subject heading lists is that subject heading lists are created using a pre-coordinate approach where the relationships between the facets of a subject terms are set beforehand. Thesauri, in contrast, follow a post-coordinate approach where the thesaurus terms can be combined at the retrieval stage. In addition thesauri may be in multiple languages. Thesauri allow for more detailed searching than simpler fixed-languages for subject descriptions but have certain limitations and might not be as flexible as open vocabularies (Vanopstal et al., 2011).

Taxonomies are controlled vocabularies that consist of classification systems that can be broken down into sub-classifications that can be quite domain specific (Vanopstal et al., 2011; Garshol 2004; Gilchrist, 2003; Aitchison and Clarke, 2004). These closed vocabularies start at a high level (the most general) and can be drilled down to be very specific. This method inherits the benefits of controlled vocabularies and also allows for very precise description of domain specific topics (Vanopstal et al., 2011; Gilchrist, 2003). For an example see the UNESCO Thesaurus and Art & Architecture Thesaurus (Aitchison & Clarke, 2004). Unfortunately taxonomies are also vulnerable to the same weaknesses that require users to understand, remember, and perfectly use the set vocabulary to describe and search for documents.

Ontology describes a subject and is defined as "a formal, explicit specification of a shared conceptualization" (Gilchrist, 2003, p. 13). It is "a model for describing the world that consists of a set of types, properties, and relationship types" (Garshol 2004, p. 384). An example of an ontology is 'Wordnet' which is considered to be one of the oldest ontologies on record (Fellbaum, 1998 as cited in Gilchrist, 2003). Ontologies based systems of knowledge organization describe an information resource using common vocabulary, terminology, and concepts (Gruber, 1993; Uschold & Gruninger, 2004; Stojanovic et al., 2002a). Ontologies tend to build up organically around communities of practice and specialized groups, and are domain specific (Gilchrist, 2003; Chowdhury & Chowdhury, 2004). The benefit of ontologies is that they are an open classification systems which are built up by the practitioners within a community but at the same time may be a challenge for non-community members who may have difficulty fully understanding its meaning. For example specialists in information architecture have an ontology belonging to that specific intellectual community and it is likely that the particular terms and the way they are used makes sense to those working within the community but is unlikely to make much sense to someone from another discipline or a novice (e.g., the new employee in the first tier of user services). According to researchers, KM is one of the focus areas of research in the use of ontologies (Gilchrist, 2003; Maedche et al., 2003; Abecker et al., 1998) and ways to manage the evolution of ontologies within KM practices (Stojanovic et al., 2002a; Stojanovic et al., 2002b).

It can be difficult to train a large group of employees to use controlled vocabularies to describe (or tag) work added to knowledge repositories considering there will be costs associated with the training of employees, high call volume (thus no or limited time for user service's employees to attend training), and more importantly there is high turnover of employees in user support services (issues related to user support services are discussed in the section - "An Overview of User Services). In the absence of appropriate training and other challenges experienced by user support services, the use of controlled vocabulary tags to search KM systems for needed information by the users (e.g., the new employees or the employees in the first tier of user services) would be challenging. This leaves KM tools that rely on strict or complex controlled vocabulary systems for knowledge organization and retrieval vulnerable to misuse or, perhaps even worse, being ignored by users. Some of these drawbacks can be addressed through the use of new forms of search interfaces to help users harness the organizational power of controlled vocabularies.

Search tools are important because they are the interface that allows users to search, browse, and retrieve information. Digital search systems are increasingly incorporating thesauri into their search functions to support search term selection, query formulation, and expansion (Soergel, 1997). Research addressing the use of controlled vocabularies' role in search term formulation point to the need to develop "intelligent" system functionality that help align the vocabulary of the searcher with that of the thesaurus (Fidel, 1991) or any other controlled vocabulary. The application of thesauri to search features is by no means consistent across interfaces and can appear as part of the main search, as an advanced feature, or not at all. For users more familiar with free text search boxes (like the Google search engine) the use of thesauri can be challenging or confusing. Numerous thesauri have been incorporated into new information environments such as digital libraries, portals, subject gateways and repositories, and open archives. In order to support the use of thesauri for information retrieval a system prototype with enhanced features is proposed for KM systems which will provide seamless access to thesauri with the goal of supporting user directed query formulation and expansion processes, aiding the retrieval of relevant documents. The two following examples are drawn from a major project developed exploring thesaurus-enhanced visual interfaces for digital libraries at the School of Library and Information Studies and Humanities Computing program at the University of Alberta (Shiri et al., 2006, 2011; Ruecker et al., 2010).

Searchling (Figure 1) is designed to support searching in a collection by using a thesaurus for enhanced retrieval features through better query formulation and browsing. The proposed system uses a bilingual thesaurus and has the capability to support searching of multilingual documents. The user interface of this system takes advantage of the Government of Canada Core Subject Thesaurus, a faceted bilingual thesaurus in English and French. The primary design aim for this version of the prototype is to provide the user with three active spaces within the interface: query space for forming a search statement, thesaurus space for browsing and navigating the thesaurus terminology, and document space for viewing the documents themselves. Searchling users are able to browse the thesaurus terms at a high level or they can drill down into the hierarchy to access more specific terms. They can search within the thesaurus to locate useful terms and the broader, narrower, or related terms associated with their search. This system functionality will help users to visualize and understand the search terms available to them through the thesaurus and allows them to navigate these options to formulate the most relevant query to using Boolean operators (right side of the screen), thus finding the relevant document to meet their information need to solve the problem at hand. As a tool, Searchling aims to address some of the difficulties inherent in using controlled vocabularies by aiding users in navigating the available terminology through this powerful visual interface and enhanced system features. It reduces the need to memorize which terms are used in a particular collection. The proposed prototype has the ability to assist in searching the same collection using multiple languages if an organization uses and include documents in more than one language.

The second version of the experimental thesaurus (Figure 2) based interface employs the visual element of the tag cloud, a graphical representation of weighted text data typically used to display keywords or tags (Sinclair, 2008; Panke & Gaiser, 2009). Tags are generally single words that describe the document or object they are attached to and in a tag cloud the importance, relevance, or predominance of each tag is represented by the font size, colour, and placement on the screen. This visual design tool is useful for quickly displaying all the tag options available to a user and to give some understanding of the makeup of the document collection. In this prototype the thesaurus terms are represented as a tag cloud where the size of the text represents the number of matches while proximity and opacity represent the scope and accuracy of the results. Related terms in the thesaurus are shown as shaded and displayed as smaller but related word clouds. More specific terms (narrower terms) are in regular type and are aligned with the main search term which appears largest and in the middle. More general terms (broader terms) use lighter type and form a separate word cloud about the main term. Synonyms are displayed in light italics and form another separate word cloud underneath the main term. Choosing a different language in the interface will rearrange the terms to show the French versions available in the thesaurus. A slider to facilitate zooming in and out of the tag clouds has been added in order to accommodate situations where there are a large number of term relationships to a particular search.

This proposed prototype that could be included in KM systems would encourage users to actively interact with the thesaurus and the system features to gain a more complete perspective of the information collection they are searching and terms that will allow them to retrieve relevant document from the KM system. The aim of con-

Figure 1. Searching thesaurus-enhanced visual interface

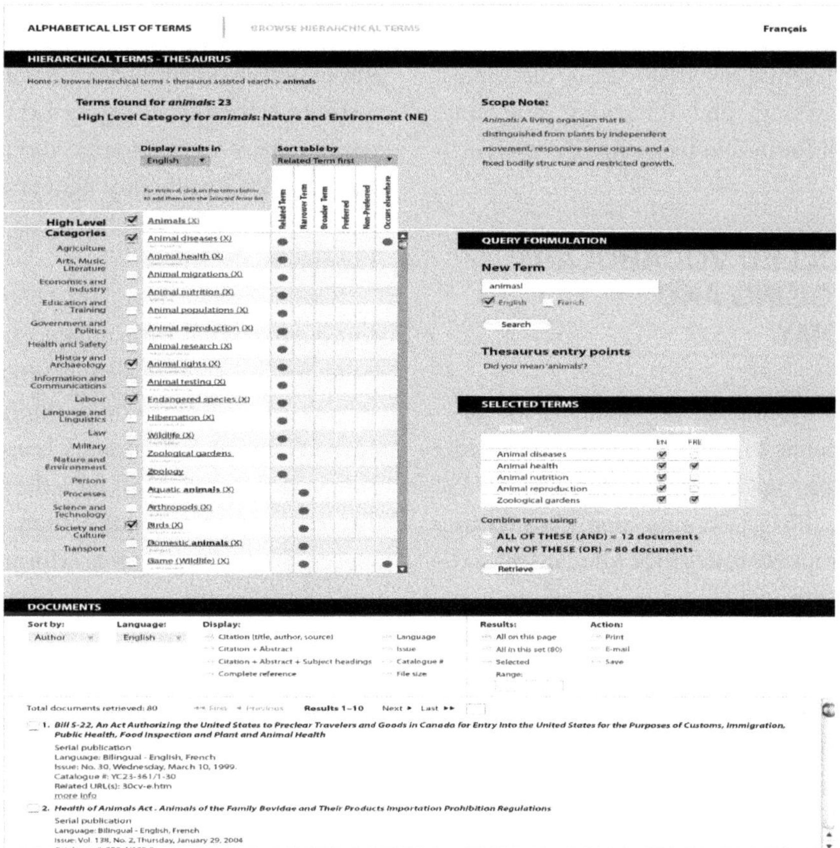

Figure 2. Thesaurus cloud visual user interface

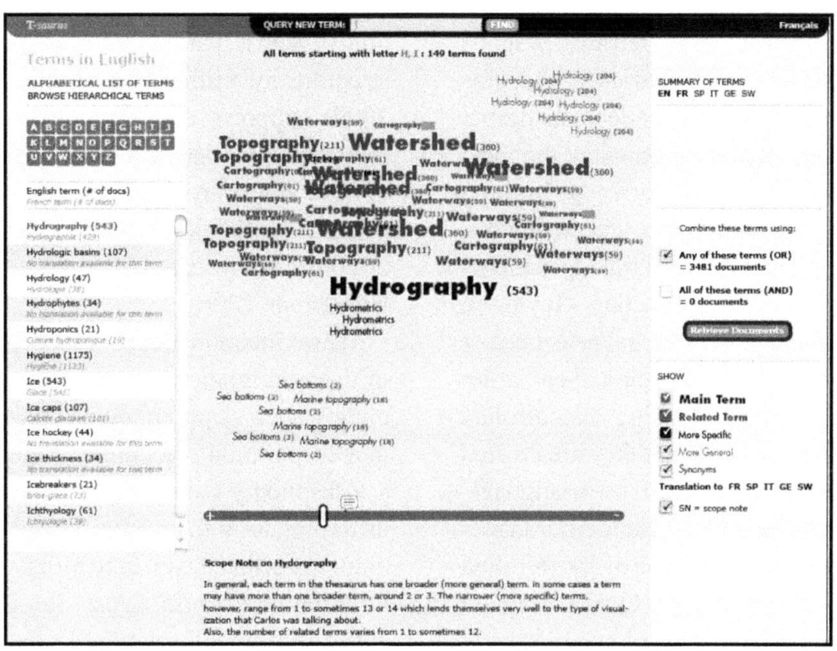

sidering this prototype for KM applications was to make use of the power of the semantic hierarchical structure found in thesauri and current visualization techniques that could facilitate searching, browsing, and retrieving relevant documents or information from the KM system.

UNCONTROLLED VOCABULARY: SOCIAL TAGGING AND FOLKSONOMY

Uncontrolled vocabularies are methods for describing documents that do not rely on a closed list of terminology options (Frakes & Pole, 1994; Lucredio et al., 2004). Users may apply any terms they deem appropriate to describe a document and searchers can formulate queries using their own vocabulary. This is an interesting method of cataloguing documents because it has the flexibility to capture subtle difference in meaning apparent in language use and can easily adjust to the addition of new terms, the discarding of outdated ones, and the shifting of meaning or use of terms over time. They can also be very adaptive to specific domain needs, a quality important in adapting knowledge management technologies to individual corporate environments. The problem for retrieval systems that use uncontrolled vocabularies is that this kind of categorization is dependent on proper execution by users including choosing the most relevant tags, spelling them correctly, limiting the use of synonyms, homonyms, and metonyms, and reusing relevant tags to build up patterns of documents within the collection (Taylor & Joudrey, 1999; Zhou et al., 2007). Perfect use of these systems is hard to define and even harder to enforce. The benefit of using uncontrolled vocabularies for retrieval is that they are created by the document users in their own language. Therefore it is important to include affordances in KM system that support the use of uncontrolled vocabularies by allowing users to add or assign new tags to information resources and to browse existing, thereby supporting the retrieval of resources using the user generated descriptive tags. These affordances are likely to help both novice and expert users to retrieve document from KM systems. A popular emerging form of uncontrolled vocabulary is social tagging and folksonomy, the uncontrolled vocabulary generated by groups of users or the crowd (Chi & Mytkowicz, 2007; Thomas et al., 2009).

Social tagging is quickly becoming the predominant method for using uncontrolled vocabularies for information organization and retrieval in Web 2.0 and many other digital systems. The open vocabulary of ontology is used in social tagging systems, but in this case the tags are defined directly by the users rather than an authoritative source. Social tagging aids information seekers in two ways. Firstly it supports known item searching by allowing users to browse through their collections of documents or to perform a search to find information using "the same or similar, terminology" (Sun, 2008 p. 120). Secondly social bookmarking enables exploratory search to help answer less structured questions where the user may be more interested in gathering information than completing a particular well defined task (Millen et al. 2007, 2). The strength of a social tagging system is that it helps in creating navigational structure for information resources (Goh et al., 2009), supports serendipitous discovery through browsing, (Mathes, 2004) and removes the need to have an expert or authority to develop appropriate classification schema based on taxonomy or controlled vocabulary approaches (Golder & Huberman, 2006).

The collection of tags created by a community of users in relation to a common body of information such as photographs on Flickr or reports in a corporation's document repository is called a folksonomy (Smith, 2004; Sun, 2008). What differentiates a folksonomy from a taxonomy or ontology is that it is created by users rather than an information authority figure (Sun, 2008; Goh et al., 2009) and that folksonomy is a flat organizational structure. As Mathes (2004) describes, "there is no hierarchy, and no directly specified parent- or sibling relationships between these terms" (p. 4). However in these systems tags can be algorithmically clustered into groups of related tags based on shared or common URLs. Folksonomies are not pre-defined and are composed uniquely of the collection of terms that a user groups applies to documents in the form of tags (Sun, 2008; Golder & Huberman, 2006).

Social tagging is highly responsive to the community of users who contribute to the categorization of information resources (Sun, 2008). They find information organized in this way intuitive to search because they can see their world view reflected in the way the metadata (tags) describes it (Peters & Stock, 2007). Adding to the complexity of creating an information retrieval system for a large, diverse organization, all members are unlikely to share the same vocabulary pertaining to their work, but they do need to access the same information (Weinberger, 2005). By using social tagging in combination with more controlled searching systems document repositories become more open to creative searching and more reflective of the culture of the organization.

Social or collaborative tagging systems allow users to annotate and categorize information in a manner most appropriate and meaningful to them (Thomas et al., 2009), independent of metadata structures created by formal cataloguers. For example, Kipp (2008) in her research found that the user uses "toread" tag quite often to mark a information resource related to time, task, or project. In its most basic form social tagging allows any kind of metadata to be associated with any digital object with no mediation or restrictions. Information categorized by users through personal tagging is meant to be shared; supporting the discovery of what others are interested in, what they are working on, and what their area of expertise might be (Hotho, et al. 2006; Matusiak, 2006). Social tagging systems create affordances for browsing and discovery that lead to the organic development of a folksonomy of common tags within a group of related users (Mathes, 2004). Users can see the descriptions that others have defined and may choose to also use these tags (Kang & Fu, 2010), or they may create new tags they find more relevant. This can lead to a proliferation of descriptive terms, but this open structure of folksonomy can also be one of its main strengths. The social network of information sharing and the innovation and knowledge discovery it fosters thrive on a common but rarely concise folksonomy. The tags themselves become valuable user created content that describe both details and the totality of a document collection. As Clay Shirky notes in his online writing about social tagging, "*you can extract a surprising amount of value from big messy data sets*" (2005). This is one of the many strengths of social tagging systems which we will explore in more depth in the following section.

Advantages of Social Tagging

Evident from the incredible popularity of online social tagging systems like Flickr and Delicious, people willingly use social tagging technologies recreationally as well as for organizational tasks as identified by Golder and Huberman (2006) such as using tags to identify a document, its type (e.g., book, news, etc.) and its quality, and to organize and develop categories of objects. The social network created by enterprise folksonomies also benefits users in multiple ways. Users benefit by being pointed to relevant information that others have serendipitously discovered (Toms, 2000) and by gaining an understanding of information that is being sought by their co-workers (Millen et al. 2007, p. 2). Giving users the ability to view information and tags created by others fosters an understanding of who within an organization is interested in which topics, indicating who may be an expert in that area (Hotho, et al. 2006; Matusiak, 2006). For example, if a particular user has tagged many articles about Java programming, it is more likely that they are knowledgeable in this area and would be a good resource for someone searching for this type of information. Mathes (2004) identifies serendipitous discovery through browsing as a strength of social tagging system. He asserts that folksonomies work because of their low barriers to entry for users; the systems are light weight, easy to learn, and similar to other Web 2.0 technologies (Barsky & Purdon, 2006) that many people use causally on the World Wide Web. Social tagging systems also have a tight feedback loop because the ability to share tags, comment on other's contributions, and interact with other users is instant (Mathes, 2004). Users are constantly benefiting from the system while they are feeding back into it. This keeps the folksonomy current and relevant to the needs of the user group that supports it.

Social information systems are organic in nature and constantly evolve to continue meeting the changing needs of their community (Ding et al., 2009). This flexibility is one of the most integral and unique aspects of social tagging (Bowler et al, 2011). The larger you scale folksonomic systems (i.e., increase user participation) and push their fluidity and flexibility the better the systems meet the needs of users as it would potentially contribute to better organization of the resources (Ding et al., 2009; Hong et al., 2008). Adapting to this kind of growth is incredibly difficult for traditional classification systems and the expense of maintaining a cataloguing system under pressure to constantly grow and adapt is untenable (Shirky, 2005). The lightweight software required for a social tagging system combined with the growing importance of user created content makes the development of an enterprise folksonomy attractive (Sinclair & Cardew-Hall, 2008). It often does not require a large financial investment and the folksonomy is designed by the employees to meet their particular needs, applied specifically to the knowledge resources of that group. Social tagging software has the potential to exist as a tool that can be sold and implemented 'out-of-the-box' because it is customized by the users as they use it. In this way social tagging software is unlike most other KM technologies which can be complex, expensive, and require staff to be trained to be able to use it (Alvi & Leidner, 1999). Folksonomies grow organically out of the information activities already common to a community and do not require extensive training and memorization, which is commonly the case with popular social media tools.

Shirky (2005) makes the compelling argument that allowing users to enter their own descriptive tags adds a nuanced layer of meaning that is often lost in strictly controlled taxonomies. This problem arises because cataloguers assume their classification terms should dominate. They underestimate the difficulty of understanding what users are thinking and they overestimate the degree to which users will agree (either with one another or with the taxonomy creators) about the best way to categorize information (Shirky, 2005). As an example, the real difference between people who say that they are interested in movies and those that love films can be vast and the specific words that people use to describe their interests or their documents are laden with extra meaning. This meaning is often lost when users are forced to choose from a limited set of descriptors that do not necessarily express what they really want to say.

Accommodating the realities of working with a wide variety of people possessing a wide variety of skills is a major strength of social tagging systems. In customer service environments help desk personnel are usually organized into multiple tiers of expertise (Delic & Dayal, 2000; Halverson, et al. 2004). Front line staff that handle the majority of customer interactions are far more likely to have less specialized training and to experience higher staff turn-over rates than upper level staff and management. These novice front line workers will have very different requirements for information retrieval than those who have been with the company for a long time and are experts in the domain. According to a study done by Kang and Fu (2010) "experts relied more on their own domain knowledge to generate search queries, while novices were influenced more by social cues in the social tagging system" (p. 329). The authors also noted that "experts are more likely to agree with each other than novices in tag choices" (p. 331). Thus, front line staff (so-called novice in comparison to expert users in the upper levels of the staffing structure) are less likely to require, and therefore to gain, an understanding of domain specific terminology.

The issues common in user support services (e.g., high call volumes, etc.) along with the high cost of training staff exert demands on organizational resources, therefore having a KM system with enhanced information retrieval feature (such as support for uncontrolled vocabulary) in place that does not require hours of specialized training in order to use could be a great benefit both financially and culturally. In traditional closed taxonomic (or controlled vocabulary based) cataloguing systems users are required to either learn a pre-defined set of tags or descriptions by rote or to look up the reference in a document every time they are needed or seek expert help (e.g., reference librarian) or get training on the use of the system (Kipp, 2010). This is an unsustainable system. People are not likely to spend the resources necessary to train themselves or learn a complicated information system perfectly even though the training might be beneficial to the users (Fenton, 2010). This is likely to result in imperfect use of the taxonomy or worse, users neglecting to categorize their documents at all. This undermines the intent of a strictly defined tag set to make the location of all information transparent. When things are not labelled or are named incorrectly they become invisible within a document collection similar to the invisible web i.e., "the part of the web that cannot be indexed by search engine" (Arroyo, 2004). Folksonomies are far more likely to be used by employees because they can choose to define the tags most relevant to their experience and to use words common to their professional vocabulary. These systems benefit the corporate environment most when co-workers share a common terminology. Folksonomies generated by social tagging systems are a less authoritative classification system than traditional top-down taxonomies (Hammond et al., 2005), but they are much more likely to reflect the actual information activities of employees by being current, inclusive, extensible, and self-moderating in addition to promoting information resource discovery (Mcgregor & McCulloch, 2006) and engendering a sense of community and responsibility. This is beneficial in an organization because it welcomes a variety of perspectives and allows novel and interesting ideas to spread even if they are not part of the predefined description of the information resources of the group.

Disadvantages of Social Tagging

One of the largest drawbacks to relying on social tagging and folksonomy is that they are vulnerable to many of the same frailties inherent in human activity, namely inconsistency. The most common complaint about folksonomy is that it cannot be a useful way to search a collection of information because people are very inconsistent in the words they use to describe things and individuals can have highly varied understandings of the same materials (Thomas et al., 2010; Mcgregor & McCulloch, 2006). The danger is that a collection will become heavily tagged but that few of the tags will duplicate in a meaningful way and the ability to identify popular items will be lost. Interestingly this hypothesis has not played out in public social tagging systems like Flickr. Likewise in a corporate KM example, Millen et al.'s (2007) study of IBM's use of Dogear concludes that over time "there is a gradual decline in new tags as end-users enter more bookmarks," indicating a considerable amount of tag re-use (p. 6). These trends seem to indicate that users are likely to use a common set of tags and to reuse tags created by others when they are appropriate. Tagging systems are self moderating and tend towards a stabilized vocabulary. This is not a hypothesis that has been heavily studied and it remains to be seen if this tendency toward tag set stability is consistent across contexts.

A corporate folksonomy is most efficient when it operates on a large corpus (Shirky, 2005). Smaller entities and groups may not possess the number of active contributors necessary to support this type of system. Social tagging systems draw their strength from the ability of users to browse large numbers of tags added by others and to see collections of popular, recent, and related items. If there are a small number of people using the system the reward for users is likely to be diminished because the social aspects of it are weakened (Millen, 2006). This increases the chance that the system will be disused and ultimately abandoned. Additionally enterprises cannot entrust all of their information and resources to external classification software; they likely will need to invest resources in purchasing or designing their own secure, closed system (Grudin, 2006).

Other arguments against social tagging are that there are no controls for synonymy, polysemy, or homonymy (Grudin, 2006; Mcgregor & McCulloch, 2006) which can lead to tag duplication and inaccurate descriptions. There is also a lack of precision and hierarchy inherent in these systems which can be seen to limit the value of a folksonomy as an indexing language and retrieval tool (Merholz, 2005). In this regard a well defined taxonomy is much more efficiently designed to avoid the linguistic pitfalls common to folksonomies already mentioned.

Lastly there is the opinion that the relevance of folksonomies are vulnerable to those trying to game of the system. Lee (2006) posits that tagging behaviours change when users are made aware of the social network they are participating in. This perceived social surveillance is likely to affect the way that users tag information, particularly if this system is being used within a community they want to remain a part of. In her study Lee (2006) found that users with more social data exposed (such as real name, email address, etc.) were more apt to annotate their bookmarks with care. The awareness that others were using the tags they created led users to be more conscientious in their participation in the social tagging system. This openness stands to benefit users of an enterprise social tagging system by promoting the conscientious creation of quality metadata.

In the following section we will discuss how these information retrieval principles were applied to the real-world example of IBM's use of the KM tool Dogear, a large corporate KM project that successfully employed folksonomic tagging to aid document discovery. We will also elaborate on the potential of folksonomic tagging for information retrieval by proposing alternate versions of an experimental interface employing social tagging, thesaurus, and tag clouds to meet the needs of a heterogeneous group of knowledge workers.

Role of Social Tagging and Folksonomy in KM: An Example of IBM and Dogear

Millen et al. (2007) conducted a quantitative and qualitative case study of the use of the social tagging system Dogear (http://domino.watson.ibm.com/comm/wwwr_thinkresearch.nsf/pages/20060627_dogear.html) within IBM, a large corporate entity. Dogear is a social bookmarking system specifically designed for use in large organizations. The researchers used event logs and in-depth interviews to gain an understanding of how the social bookmarking tool is used within this group for information rediscovery and to explore resources held within a corporate knowledge repository. To target this technology to a corporate environment the designers removed the ability to use pseudonyms when generating tags (Millen et al 2007), instead requiring that users employ their real names that match a defined corporate directory. This use of real names allows users to look-up additional information in related corporate databases such as personnel lists. Additionally, it enables communication through all other corporate collaboration tools that use real name identities such as office email and chat services. The use of real names as identifying profiles is important with an enterprise model for social tagging because it promotes responsible use of the system and the ability of users to be recognized for their contribution to the information community (Lee, 2006).

In the case study of Dogear the users all worked at IBM and were distributed across eight major organizations and geographical areas (Millen et al. 2007, p. 7). The research analysis identified three different types of social tagging related search: community browsing of bookmarks created by the group, personal search of one's own bookmarks, and explicit search of tags using a traditional search box. The popularity of browsing indicated that users are most curious about what other employees are bookmarking and tagging, and use this information to seek documents and sites relevant to their own work. One interesting finding was that some employees browsed link lists to discover the topics that interested thought leaders within the organization (Millen et al. 2007, p. 11). The research also indicated that employees browsed links to become familiar with other people in the organization and to keep up to date with what resources others who had similar tasks to complete were consulting. Personal bookmark list browsing was found to be the least common use of Dogear at IBM, an interesting finding considering that this technology grew out of traditional bookmarking for exclusively personal use with no ability to browse outside of one's own local source list. Perhaps the most convincing finding from this study to recommend the use of social tagging is that end-users indicated that a document's "inclusion in the Dogear collection mean[s] that the search ha[s] been actively pre-filtered by a community of interested or trusted IBM colleagues." (Millen et al. 2007, p. 14). Information that had been tagged in Dogear was found to be relevant to others in the user community and often popular items revealed by a tag search in Dogear were not found when conducting a standard enterprise search (Mukherjee & Mao, 2004 as cited in Millen et al. 2007). Dogear was used successfully within the IBM community as an knowledge retrieval and sharing system but it did not entirely replace other more formal methods of categorization and searching the vast knowledge repositories the company retains. The intellectual value of these repositories are crucial to the functioning of the company and are too important to rely on social tagging alone to ensure they are able to be found by users. This type of situation necessitates the implementation of the strengths of both authoritative closed vocabularies and dynamic folksonomies through a new type of hybrid search interface for corporate knowledge repositories.

A Hybrid Search Interface Prototype

We have discussed the benefits and drawbacks to both controlled vocabularies such as thesauri and uncontrolled vocabularies manifested as folksonomies created through social tagging systems. Both systems have their advantages for knowledge management information retrieval systems and each is likely to be of more benefit to particular user groups and users at different training levels. To take advantage of the opportunities a social tagging system would provide for information retrieval in a heterogeneous organizational environment (as most large corporations and their help desks are) we propose a prototype which is a modified version of the tag cloud interface for thesaurus based retrieval discussed earlier in the *Controlled Vocabulary* section (Figure 2). In this modified prototype (Figure 3), users adding documents to the system or browsing for information could tag documents themselves with a series of terms of their own choosing with the option of using popular tags already in use in the collection if they so choose. In this modified prototype, documents stored in the KM system could also

Figure 3. Hybrid social tagging and thesaurus search interface

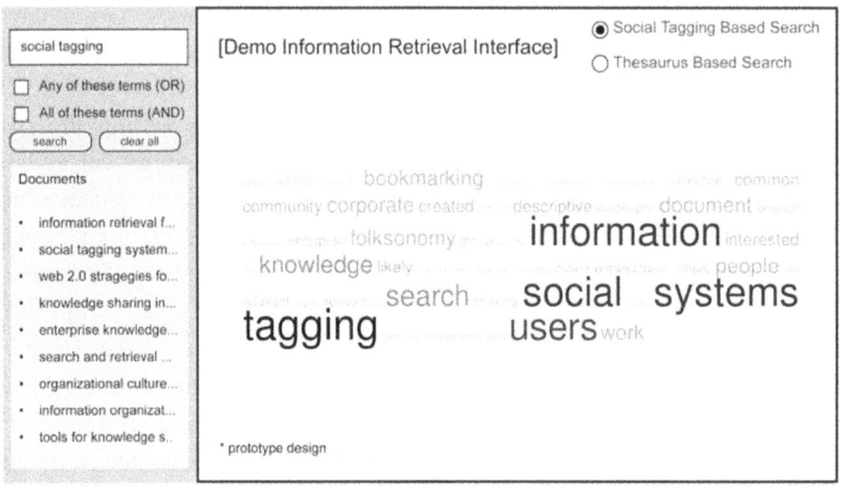

be searched by using traditional closed vocabulary thesaurus. This double pronged approach to document description is mirrored in the search interface that allows users to toggle between results from the thesaurus based search and folksonomic search to compare and expand their search result options without having to reformulate or refine their search terms. This creates one interface that can be used by both experts in the thesaurus mode and novices in the folksonomy mode to retrieve relevant information from the KM system. The proposed prototype will also support users in becoming more familiar with the thesaurus terms and bridging gaps between the two metadata systems that could potentially help users transition from novice to expert users of the KM system.

In the retrieval process a user would enter a desired search term. The result displayed in the interface would be a tag cloud with their search term in the middle surrounded by related tags that may be attached to documents that are also tagged with the search term (similar to the interface in Figure 2). The size of the terms in the word cloud represent the number of documents tagged with that term. By clicking on an individual tag in the cloud, the user would be presented with a list of relevant document in the left panel. The folksonomy based search interface is similar to the tag cloud thesaurus example but is quite different in one important aspect. Folksonomic description of documents is in the language of the user and therefore there are likely to be many examples of different spellings of the same word and use of synonyms in the collection. Additionally the organisational structure of a folksonomy is completely flat and does not have affordances for related, broader, or narrower term relationships. The tag cloud format is important in this interface not because it shows which relationships are present in the metadata (as in the thesaurus based example), but because it shows an overview of documents and subject headings that are related to your search, but does not (and cannot) define specifically why.

This interface strikes a balance between the lightweight and flexible infrastructure used to create the folksonomy and tag documents in a collection and the more powerful and orderly retrieval systems common to closed vocabularies like thesauri that have relationships between terms and documents hard coded into their systems. Both systems of information organization for KM document repositories have their own unique strong points and a truly flexible, extensible, and robust system that will meet the needs of employees with different levels of experience and different problem solving needs should incorporate the strengths of both.

CONCLUSION

KM systems to support information retrieval and discovery for knowledge workers in the context of user services stand to benefit from the integration of bottom-up folksonomies with more traditional enterprise searching techniques to take advantage of established and authoritative retrieval methods (Golub et al., 2009; Hammond et al., 2005) as well as the tacit and contextual knowledge of the user community. This combination could give users an extra layer of metadata information as resources that are returned by enterprise searching can be considered to have high authority while sources returned by searching the enterprise's folksonomy are likely to be more current, trendy, or innovative. Using the combined approach demonstrated in the Figure 3 experimental interface search results would be more complete; one would have the authority and reliability of traditional search along with the flexibility and chance of information discovery through the use of the folksonomy.

The key to making folksonomies useful for searching within an organizational knowledge environment is to strike a balance between controlling the creation of tags to limit inconsistencies and human error while also allowing the free expression of ideas and opinions. This combination makes systems like Flickr successful and self perpetuating in recreational online environments. Trant (2008) makes a strong argument for a hybrid approach that would bridge natural language processing, folksonomy, and controlled vocabularies with the semantic web (p. 23). These combinations require more exploration and the development of prototypes, but they posit an intriguing multi-faceted search technique that combines benefits of both a top-down and bottom-up approach to searching a common knowledge repository.

The future of folksonomies and social tagging systems appears to be secure on the World Wide Web. Social tagging has become an integral part of many of the most popular web 2.0 social networking sites and has expanded to become a system for personalized annotation of websites and collections of digital documents. The willingness of diverse populations to adopt this technology and use it to annotate and organize their personal digital information is a strong endorsement for the ease of use and individual benefits of the system. This stands to benefit KM practice within enterprise structures because users are already familiar with how the technology works, what it can be used for, and are amenable to adopting and adapting it to suit their specific needs. It is an economical solution for organizations because the users create the folksonomy as they integrate the system with their digital documents, helping avoid some of the high costs associated with training new staff in high turn-over organizations or hiring an information expert. It also requires little maintenance and is less likely than rigid taxonomies to become outdated or obsolete over time because it will evolve and adapt with the organization and the information needs of its users. Folksonomy based document description and retrieval systems address many of the flaws inherent in traditional enterprise cataloguing structures but are not without their own weaknesses. The proposed experimental interface combining both controlled and uncontrolled vocabularies to support the needs of different user groups will provide an excellent compliment to the more traditional and strictly defined systems currently common in digital repositories and corporate information structures.

REFERENCES

Aitchison, J., & Clarke, S. D. (2004). The thesaurus: A historical viewpoint, with a look to the future. *Cataloging & Classification Quarterly*, *37*(3/4), 5–21. doi:10.1300/J104v37n03_02

Alavi, M., & Leidner, D. E. (1999). Knowledge management systems: Issues, challenges, and benefits. *Communication of AIS, 1*.

Albecker, A., Bernardi, A., Hinckelmann, K., Kuhn, O., & Sintech, M. (1998). Towards a technology for organizational memories. *IEEE Intelligent Systems, 13*(3), 40–48. doi:10.1109/5254.683209

Anton, J. (2000). The past, present and future of customer access centers. *International Journal of Service Industry Management, 11*(2), 120–130. doi:10.1108/09564230010323534

Arroyo, N. (2004). *What is the invisible web? A crawler perspective*. AoIR-ASIST 2004 Workshop on Web Science Research Methods, Brighton (UK).

Babilon, M. (1998). The evolution of knowledge management with NCR corporation. In *Proceedings of the 16th Annual International Conference on Computer Documentation* (SIGDOC '98), (pp. 1–4).

Barsky, E., & Purdon, M. (2006). Introducing Web 2.0: Social networking and social bookmarking for health librarians. *Journal of the Canadian Health Libraries Association, 27*, 65–67. doi:10.5596/c06-024

Becerra-Fernandez, I., & Aha, D. W. (1999). Case-based problem solving for knowledge management systems. *Proceedings of the Twelfth International FLAIRS Conference*.

Benbya H., Passiante G., and Belbaly N. (2004) Corporate portal: a Tool for Knowledge Management Synchronization. *International Journal of Information Management, 24*(3), 201–220

Bowler, L., Koshman, S., Oh, J. S., He, D., Callery, B. G., Bowker, G., & Cox, R. J. (2011). Issues in user-centered design in LIS. *Library Trends, 59*(4), 721–752. doi:10.1353/lib.2011.0013

Bulterman, D. C. A. (2004). Is it time for a moratorium on metadata? *IEEE MultiMedia, 11*(4), 10–17. doi:10.1109/MMUL.2004.29

Chan, C. W., Chen, L. L., & Geng, L. (2000). Knowledge engineering for an intelligent case-based system for help desk operations. *Expert Systems with Applications, 18*(2), 125–132. doi:10.1016/S0957-4174(99)00058-5

Chaplan, M. A. (1995). Mapping "laborline thesaurus" terms to Library of Congress subject headings: Implications for vocabulary switching. *The Library Quarterly, 65*(1), 39–61. doi:10.1086/602752

Chi, E., & Mytkowicz, T. (2007). Understanding navigability of social tagging systems. *Proceeding of SIGCHI'07*. Retrieved July 25, 2001, from http://danm.ucsc.edu/~dustin/library/social_tagging.pdf

Chowdhury, S., & Chowdhury, G. (2004). *Using DDC to create a visual knowledge map as an aid to online information retrieval*. ISKO8: Knowledge Organization and the Global Information Society. Retrieved July 25, 2011 from http://strathprints.strath.ac.uk /2624/1/strathprints002624.pdf

Choy, K. L., Lee, W. B., & Lo, V. (2002). Development of a case based intelligent customer – Supplier relationship management system. *Expert Systems with Applications, 23*(3), 281–297. doi:10.1016/S0957-4174(02)00048-9

Cook, S. D. N., & Brown, J. S. (1999). Bridging epistemologies: The generative dance between organizational knowledge and organizational knowing. *Organization Science, 10*(4), 381–400. doi:10.1287/orsc.10.4.381

Courtney, J. F. (2001). Decision making and knowledge management in inquiring organizations: Toward a new decision-making paradigm for DSS. *Decision Support Systems, 31*(1), 17–38. doi:10.1016/S0167-9236(00)00117-2

Darroch, J. (2003). Developing a measure of knowledge management behaviors and practices. *Journal of Knowledge Management*, *7*(5), 41–54. doi:10.1108/13673270310505377

Dekkers, M. (2001). Application profiles, or how to mix and match metadata schemas. *Cultivate Interactive, 3*. Retrieved from http://www.cultivate-int.org/issue3/schemas/

Delic, K. A., & Dayal, U. (2000). Knowledge management in the service and support business. In U. Reimer (Ed.), *Third International Conference on Practical Aspects of Knowledge Management* (PAKM2000).

Dempsey, L., & Heery, R. (1998). Metadata: A current view of practice and issues. *The Journal of Documentation*, *54*(2), 145–172. doi:10.1108/EUM0000000007164

Despres, C., & Chauvel, D. (1999). Knowledge management(s). *Journal of Knowledge Management*, *3*(2), 110–123. doi:10.1108/13673279910275567

Ding, Y., Jacob, E. K., Zhang, Z., Foo, S., Yan, E., George, N. L., & Guo, L. (2009). Perspectives on social tagging. *Journal of the American Society for Information Science and Technology*, *60*(12), 2388–2401. doi:10.1002/asi.21190

Eric, T. (2005). The role of IT in KM: Where are we now and where are we heading? *Journal of Knowledge Management*, *9*(1), 3–6. doi:10.1108/13673270510584198

Fenton, C. (2010). Use of controlled vocabulary and thesauri in UK online finding aids. *Journal of the Society of Archivists*, *31*(2), 187–205. doi:10.1080/00379816.2010.506792

Fidel, R. (1991). Searcher's selection of search keys: I. The selection routine. *Journal of the American Society for Information Science American Society for Information Science*, *42*(7), 490–500. doi:10.1002/(SICI)1097-4571(199108)42:7<490::AID-ASI4>3.0.CO;2-V

Fischer, G., & Otswald, J. (2001). Knowledge management: Problems, promises, realities, and challenges. *Intelligent Systems, IEEE*, *16*(1), 60–72. doi:10.1109/5254.912386

Frakes, W. B., & Pole, T. P. (1994). An empirical study of representation methods for reusable software components. *IEEE Transactions on Software Engineering*, *20*(8), 617–630. doi:10.1109/32.310671

Garshol, L. M. (2004). Metadata? Thesauri? Taxonomies? Topic maps! Making sense of it all. *Journal of Information Science*, *30*(4), 378–391. doi:10.1177/0165551504045856

Gilchrist, A. (2003). Thesauri, taxonomies and ontologies – An etymological note. *The Journal of Documentation*, *59*(1), 7–18. doi:10.1108/00220410310457984

Goh, D. H., Chua, A., Lee, C. S., & Razikin, K. (2009). Resource discovery through social tagging: A classification and content analytic approach. *Online Information Review*, *33*(3), 568–583. doi:10.1108/14684520910969961

Göker, M., & Roth-Berghofer, T. (1999). Development and utilization of a case-based help-desk support system in a corporate environment. In Althoff, K.-D., Bergmann, R., & Branting, L. K. (Eds.), *ICCBR-99* (*Vol. 1650*, pp. 132–146). Lecture Notes in Computer Science. doi:10.1007/3-540-48508-2_10

Golder, S. A., & Huberman, B. A. (2006). Usage patterns of collaborative tagging systems. *Journal of Information Science*, *32*(2), 198–208. doi:10.1177/0165551506062337

Golub, K. (2006). Automated subject classification of textual web pages, based on a controlled vocabulary: Challenges and recommendations. *New Review of Hypermedia and Multimedia*, *12*(1), 11–27. doi:10.1080/13614560600774313

Golub, K., Moon, J., Tudhope, D., Jones, C., Matthews, B., Puzo, D. B., & Lykke Nielsen, M. (2009). EnTag: Enhancing social tagging for discovery. *Proceedings of the 9th ACM/IEEE-CS Joint Conference on Digital Libraries (JCDL '09)*. Retrieved July 30, 2011, from http://www.ukoln.ac.uk/projects/enhanced-tagging/dissemination/entag-jcdl09.pdf

Gonzalez, L. M., Giachetti, R. E., & Ramirez, G. (2005). Knowledge management-centric help desk: Specification and performance evaluation. *Decision Support Systems*, *40*, 389–405. doi:10.1016/j.dss.2004.04.013

Gormly, J. (2003) Rapid Help Desk Revitalization, User Services Conference, In *Proceedings of the 31st Annual ACM SIGUCCS Conference on User services*, San Antonio, TX, 159-162.

Greer, J., McCalla, G., Cooke, J., Collins, J., Kumar, V., Bishop, A., & Vassileva, J. (1998). The intelligent helpdesk: Supporting peer-help in a university course. In Goettl, B. P., Halff, H. M., Redfield, C. L., & Shute, V. J. (Eds.), *Intelligent Tutoring Systems* (*Vol. 1452*, pp. 494–503). Lecture Notes in Computer Science Berlin, Germany: Springer-Verlag. doi:10.1007/3-540-68716-5_55

Gruber, T. (1993). A translation approach to portable ontology specifications. *Knowledge Acquisition*, *5*, 199–220. doi:10.1006/knac.1993.1008

Grudin, J. (2006). Enterprise knowledge management and emerging technologies. *Proceedings of the 39th Annual Hawaii International Conference on System Sciences* (HICSS '06). Retrieved March 16, 2010, from http://research.microsoft.com/ enus/um/people/jgrudin/publications/orgse/GrudinHCIC.pdf

Guinchard, C. (2002). Dublin Core use in libraries: A survey. *OCLC Systems & Services*, *18*(1), 40–50. doi:10.1108/10650750210418190

Gupta, B., Iyer, L. S., & Aronson, J. E. (2000). Knowledge management: Practices and challenges. *Industrial Management & Data Systems*, *100*(1), 17–21. doi:10.1108/02635570010273018

Halverson, C. A., Erickson, T., & Ackerman, M. S. (2004). Behind the help desk: Evolution of a knowledge management system in a large organization. *Proceedings of the 2004 ACM Conference on Computer Supported Cooperative Work (CSCW '04)*, *6*(3), 304 – 313.

Hammond, T., Hannay, T., Lund, B., & Scott, J. (2005). Social bookmarking tools (I). *D-Lib Magazine*, *11*(4), 1–21. doi:10.1045/april2005-hammond

Heymann, P., & Garcia-Molina, H. (2006). *Collaborative creation of communal hierarchical taxonomies in social tagging systems*. InfoLab Technical Report 2006-10. Retrieved March 10, 2010 from http://ilpubs.stanford.edu:8090/775/1/2006-10.pdf

Hong, L., Chi, E. H., Budiu, R., Pirolli, P., & Nelson, L. (2008). SparTag.Us: A low cost tagging system for foraging of web content. *Proceedings of the Working Conference on Advanced Visual Interfaces (AVI '08)*, (pp. 65-72).

Hotho, A., Jaschke, R., Schmitz, C., & Stumme, G. (2006). Information retrieval in folksonomies: Search and ranking. *The Semantic Web: Research and Applications*. *Lecture Notes in Computer Science*, *4011*, 411–426. doi:10.1007/11762256_31

Johannessen, J., Olaisen, J., & Olsen, B. (2001). Mismanagement of tacit knowledge: The importance of tacit knowledge, the danger of information technology and what to do about it. *International Journal of Information Management*, *21*, 3–20. doi:10.1016/S0268-4012(00)00047-5

Kang, R., & Fu, W. (2010). Exploratory information search by domain experts and novices. *Proceedings of the 15th International Conference on Intelligent User Interfaces (IUI '10)*, (pp. 329–332).

Kipp, M. E. I. (2008). @toread and cool: Subjective, affective and associative factors in tagging. *Proceedings of the 36th Annual Conference of the Canadian Association for Information Science (CAIS)*. Retrieved July 25, 2011, from www.cais-acsi.ca/proceedings/2008/kipp_2008.pdf

Kipp, M. E. I. (2010). User, author and professional indexing in context: An exploration of tagging practices on CiteULike / Le contexte de l'indexation des usagers, des créateurs et des professionnels: une exploration des pratiques d'étiquetage social sur CiteULike. *Canadian Journal of Information and Library Science*, *35*(1), 17–48.

Kriegsman, M., & Barletta, R. (1993). Building a case-based help desk application. *IEEE Expert*, *8*(6), 18–26. doi:10.1109/64.248349

Kwon, O., Kim, M., & Choi, K. (1994). Query expansion using domain-adapted, weighted thesaurus in an extended Boolean Model. In N. R. Adam, B. K. Bhargava, & Y. Yesha (Eds.), *Proceedings of the Third International Conference on Information and Knowledge Management* (CIKM '94), (pp. 140–146).

Lassila, O. (1998). Web metadata: A matter of semantics. *Internet Computing, IEEE*, *2*(4), 30–37. doi:10.1109/4236.707688

Lee, K. J. (2006). What goes around comes around: An analysis of Del.icio.us as social space. *Proceedings of the 2006 20th anniversary conference on Computer Supported Cooperative Work* (CSCW '06), (pp. 191-194).

Lee-Smeltzer, K.-H. (2000). Finding the needle: Controlled vocabularies, resource discovery, and Dublin Core. *Library Collections, Acquisitions & Technical Services*, *24*(2), 205–215. doi:10.1016/S1464-9055(00)00131-7

Lindvall, M., Rus, I., & Sinha, S. S. (2003). Technology support for knowledge management. In Henninger, S., & Maurer, F. (Eds.), *Advances in Learning Software Organizations* (*Vol. 2640*, pp. 94–103). Lecture Notes in Computer Science Berlin, Germany: Springer-Verlag. doi:10.1007/978-3-540-40052-3_9

Liu, Z., & Yan, F. (1997). Fuzzy neural network in case-based diagnostic system. *IEEE Transactions on Fuzzy Systems*, *5*(2), 209–222. doi:10.1109/91.580796

Loffler, J. (2000). Content-based retrieval of 3D models in distributed web databases by visual shape information. *Proceedings of the IEEE International Conference on Information Visualization*, (pp. 82 – 87).

Lucredio, D., Prado, A. F., & de Almeida, E. S. (2004). A survey on software components search and retrieval. *Proceedings of the 30th Euromicro Conference*, (pp. 152–159).

Macgregor, G., & McCulloch, E. (2006). Collaborative tagging as a knowledge organisation and resource discovery tool. *Library Review*, *55*(5), 291–300. doi:10.1108/00242530610667558

Maedche, A., Motik, B., Stojanovic, L., Studer, R., & Volz, R. (2003). Ontologies for enterprise knowledge management. *IEEE Intelligent Systems*, *18*(2), 26–33. doi:10.1109/MIS.2003.1193654

Marcella, R., & Middleton, I. (1996). The role of the help desk in the strategic management of information systems. *OCLC Systems & Services*, *12*(4), 4–19. doi:10.1108/10650759610153993

Martin, A., & Dean, V. (1995). Back to the future – A management perspective on distributed support, realizing the potential of information resource: information, technology and services. *Proceeding of the 1995 CAUSE Annual Conference*, (pp. 4.3.1–4.3.9).

Mathes, A. (2004). *Folksonomies - Cooperative classification and communication through shared metadata*. Retrieved June 10, 2011, from http://www.adammathes.com/academic/computer-mediated-communication/folksonomies.html

Matusiak, K. (2006). Towards user-centered indexing in digital image collections. *International Digital Library Perspectives*, *22*(4), 283–298.

Merholz, P. (2005). *Clay Shirky's viewpoints are overrated*. peterme.com Retrieved June 10, 2011 from http://www.peterme.com/archives/000558.html

Millen, D. R., Yang, M., Whittaker, S., & Feinberg, J. (2007). Social bookmarking and exploratory search. *ECSCW'07: Proceedings of the Tenth European Conference on Computer Supported Co-operative Work.* Retrieved March 14, 2010, from http://www.ecscw.org/2007/02%20paper%20108%20Millen%20et%20al.pdf.

Moussavi, M. (1999). *A case-based approach to knowledge management*. AAAI Technical Report WS-99-10. Retrieved from June 10, 2011 from https://www.aaai.org/Papers/Workshops/1999/WS-99-10/WS99-10-015.pdf

Mukherjee, R., & Mao, J. (2004). Enterprise search: Tough stuff. *Queue*, *2*(2), 36–46. doi:10.1145/988392.988406

Nadkarni, P. M. (2011). *What is metadata? Metadata-driven Software Systems in Biomedicine, Health Informatics* (pp. 1–16). London, UK: Springer. doi:10.1007/978-0-85729-510-1_1

National Information Standards Organization. (2004). *Understanding metadata*. Retrieved June 10, 2011, from http://www.niso.org/publications/press/UnderstandingMetadata.pdf

Nenkova, A., & Bagga, A. (2003). Email classification for contact centers. *Proceedings of the 2003 ACM Symposium on Applied Computing*, (pp. 789–792).

Nonaka, I. (1994). A dynamic theory of organizational knowledge creation. *Organization Science*, *5*(1), 14–37. doi:10.1287/orsc.5.1.14

O'Leary, D. E. (2002). Knowledge management across the enterprise resource planning systems life cycle. *International Journal of Accounting Information Systems*, *3*(2), 99–110. doi:10.1016/S1467-0895(02)00038-6

Offsey, S. (1997). Knowledge management: Linking people to knowledge for bottom line results. *Journal of Knowledge Management*, *1*(2), 113–122. doi:10.1108/EUM0000000004586

Owen, M. J. (1999). Knowledge management and the information professional. *Information Services & Use*, *19*, 7–16.

Panke, S., & Gaiser, B. (2009). With my head up in the clouds: Using social tagging to organize knowledge. *Journal of Business and Technical Communication*, *23*(3), 318–349. doi:10.1177/1050651909333275

Peters, I., & Stock, W. G. (2007). Folksonomy and information retrieval. *Proceedings of the American Society of Information Science and Technology*, *44*(1), 1–28. doi:10.1002/meet.1450440226

Plaunt, C., & Norgard, B. (1998). An association based method for automatic indexing with a controlled vocabulary. *Journal of the American Society for Information Science American Society for Information Science*, *49*(10), 888–902.

Prescott, J., Kilty, T., Franklin, G., Cleary, A., Lovgren, T., & Mai, A. (2001). Evolution of three help desks. *Proceedings of the 29th Annual ACM SIGUCCS Conference on User Services (SIGUCCS '01),* (pp. 135-141).

Prieto-Díaz, R. (1991). Implementing faceted classification for software reuse. *Communications of the ACM*, *34*(5), 88–97. doi:10.1145/103167.103176

Ruecker, S., Shiri, A., Fiorentino, C., Bouchard, M., Stafford, A., & Bieber, M. (2010). Exploratory search interfaces for the UNESCO multilingual digital library: Combining visualization and semantics. *Proceedings of the 2010 Chicago Colloquium on Digital Humanities and Computer Science*, Evanston, Illinois, USA.

Sawy, O. A., & Bowles, G. (2004). Redesigning the customer support process for the electronic economy: Insight from storage dimensions. *Management Information Systems Quarterly*, *21*(4), 457–483. doi:10.2307/249723

Schultze, U., & Stabell, C. (2004). Knowing what you don't know? Discourses and contradictions in knowledge management research. *Journal of Management Studies*, *41*, 549–573. doi:10.1111/j.1467-6486.2004.00444.x

Seaman, C. B., Mendonca, M. G., Basili, V. R., & Kim, Y. M. (2003). User interface evaluation and empirically-based evolution of a prototype experience management tool. *IEEE Transactions on Software Engineering*, *29*(9), 838–850. doi:10.1109/TSE.2003.1232288

Shiri, A., Ruecker, S., Anvik, K., & Rossello, X. (2006). Thesaurus-enhanced visual interfaces for multilingual information retrieval. *Proceedings of the American Society for Information Science and Technology (ASIS&T) Annual Conference*, Austin, Texas, USA.

Shiri, A., Ruecker, S., Bouchard, M., Stafford, A., Mehta, P., Anvik, K., & Rossello, X. (2011). User evaluation of searchling: A visual interface for bilingual digital libraries. *The Electronic Library*, *29*(1), 71–89. doi:10.1108/02640471111111442

Shirky, C. (2005). *Ontology is overrated: Categories, links and tags*. Clay Shirky's Writings about the Internet. Retrieved March 16, 2010, from http://www.shirky.com/writings/ontology_overrated.html

Simoudis, E. (1992). Using case-based retrieval for customer technical support. *IEEE Expert*, *7*(5), 7–12. doi:10.1109/64.163667

Sinclair, J., & Cardew-Hall, M. (2008). The folksonomy tag cloud: When is it useful? *Journal of Information Science*, *34*(1), 15–29. doi:10.1177/0165551506078083

Sinnett, C. J., & Barr, T. (2004). OSU helpdesk: A cost-effective helpdesk solution for everyone. *Proceedings of the 32nd Annual ACM SIGUCCS Conference on User Services*, (pp. 209–216).

Smith, G. (2004). *Atomiq: Folksonomy: Social classification*. Retrieved June 10, 2011, from http://atomiq.org/archives/2004/08/folksonomy_social_classification.html

Soergel, D. (1997). *Multilingual thesauri in cross-language text and speech retrieval*. AAAI Symposium on Cross-Language Text and Speech Retrieval.

Stanoevska, K., Hombrecher, A., Handschuh, S., & Schmid, B. (1998). Efficient information retrieval: Tools for knowledge management. *Proceedings of the Second International Conference on Practical Aspects of Knowledge Management* (PAKM98). Retrieved June 10, 2011 from http://www.netacademy.org

Stojanovic, L., Maedche, A., Motik, B., & Stojanovic, N. (2002b). User-driven ontology evolution management. In Gómez-Pérez, A., & Benjamins, V. (Eds.), *Knowledge Engineering and Knowledge Management: Ontologies and the Semantic Web* (*Vol. 2473*, pp. 133–140). Lecture Notes in Computer Science. doi:10.1007/3-540-45810-7_27

Stojanovic, L., Stojanovic, N., & Handschuh, S. (2002a). Evolution of the metadata in the ontology-based knowledge management systems. *Proceedings of Experience Management*. Retrieved July 25, 2011, from http://projekte.l3s.uni-hannover.de/pub/nj_bscw.cgi/d17469/Stojanovic_et_al-Evolution.pdf

Sun, B. D. (2008). Folksonomy and health information access: How can social bookmarking assist seekers of online medical information? *Journal of Hospital Librarianship*, *8*(1), 119–126. doi:10.1080/15323260801943570

Taylor, A. G., & Joudrey, D. N. (1999). *The organization of information*. Westport, CT: Libraries Unlimited.

Thomas, M., Caudle, D. M., & Schmitz, C. (2010). Trashy tags: Problematic tags in library thing. *New Library World*, *111*(5/6), 223–235. doi:10.1108/03074801011044098

Thomas, M., Caudle, D. M., & Schmitz, C. M. (2009). To tag or not to tag? *Library Hi Tech*, *27*(3), 411–434. doi:10.1108/07378830910988540

Toms, E. G. (2000). Serendipitous information retrieval. *Proceedings of the First DELOS Network of Excellence Workshop on Information Seeking, Searching and Querying in Digital Libraries*, (pp. 17-20). Retrieved July 25, 2001, from http://www.ercim.eu/publication/ws-proceedings/DelNoe01/3_Toms.pdf

Trant, J. (2008). Studying social tagging and folksonomy: A review and framework. *Journal of Digital Information: Special Issue on Digital Libraries and User Generated Content*. Retrieved March 10, 2010, from http://journals.tdl.org/jodi/article/view/269

Vanopstal, K., Stichele, R. V., Laureys, G. & Buysschaert, J. (2011) Vocabularies and Retrieval Tools in Biomedicine: Disentangling the Terminological Knot. *Journal of Medical Systems*, *35*(4), 527 – 543.

Uschold, M., & Gruninger, M. (2004). Ontologies and semantics for seamless connectivity. *SIGMOD Record*, *33*(4), 58–64. doi:10.1145/1041410.1041420

Watson, I., & Marir, F. (1994). Case-based reasoning: A review. *The Knowledge Engineering Review*, *9*(4), 327–354. doi:10.1017/S0269888900007098

Weinberger, D. (2005). *Tagging and why it matters*. Retrieved June 10, 2011, from http://cyber.law.harvard.edu/sites/cyber.law.harvard.edu/files/07WhyTagging Matters.pdf

White, S., & Jagielska, I. (2004). Investigation into the application of data mining techniques to classification of call centre data, decision support in an uncertain and complex world. *The IFIP TC8/WG8.3 International Conference*, (pp. 793–802). Retrieved June 10, 2011, from http://dsslab.sims.monash.edu.au/dss2004/proceedings/pdf/78_White_Jagielska.pdf

Yang, Q., Kim, E., & Racine, K. (1997). Case advisor: Supporting interactive problem solving and case based maintenance for help desk applications. *Proceedings of the IJCAI'97 Workshop on Practical Use of CBR*, Nogoya, Japan, August 1997, (pp. 32–44). Retrieved June 10, 2011, from http://www.cs.ust.hk/~qyang/Papers/pubs/ijcai97ws.pdf

Zhou, M., Bao, S., Wu, X., & Yu, Y. (2007). An unsupervised model for exploring hierarchical semantics from social annotations. In Aberer, K. (Eds.), *The Semantic Web* (*Vol. 4825*, pp. 680–693). Lecture Notes in Computer Science. doi:10.1007/978-3-540-76298-0_49

Chapter 19
Knowledge Management in Educational Games

Miroslav Minović
University of Belgrade, Serbia

Miloš Milovanović
University of Belgrade, Serbia

Dušan Starčević
University of Belgrade, Serbia

ABSTRACT

Use of educational games during teaching process does not represent a new topic. However, the question "How to address the knowledge in educational games?" is still open. The purpose of this chapter is to propose a model that will attempt to establish the balance between knowledge integration into game on one side, and its reusability on other. The model driven approach presented in this chapter relies on the use of Learning Objects (LO) as constructing pieces of knowledge resources, which are specialized for educational game design purpose. Presented models contribute to methodology of educational games development in a way that they embrace principles of learning and knowledge management early in design process. The authors demonstrate applicability of their models in design case study, where they developed educational game editor where the educator can easily define new educational game utilizing existing knowledge, assessment, and multimedia from repository.

INTRODUCTION

There is a promising role of digital games in education process. Traditional forms of teaching and passing knowledge lose their strength daily, due to development of technology and different motivational factors for the upcoming generations.

DOI: 10.4018/978-1-4666-0948-8.ch019

Digital game-based learning is a novel approach applying at universities' courses and lifelong learning. In search for new role of universities in changing context of education, gaming is becoming a new form of interactive content, worth of exploration (Pivec, 2007). Features of games that could be applied to address the increasing demand for high quality education are already identified as (Federation of American Scientists, 2006): clear goals, lessons that can be practiced repeatedly until mastered, monitoring learner progress and adjusting instruction to learner level of mastery, closing the gap between what is learned and its use, motivation that encourages time on task, personalization of learning, and infinite patience.

Use of educational games during teaching process does not represent a new topic. Since the need for new forms of education has been recognized by the researchers in this area, new problem arose. The main issue in this area of research is "How to address the knowledge in educational games?" At this moment, development of educational games includes knowledge integration during game development process. This approach establishes strong coupling of game context and integrated knowledge which further disables reuse of that particular knowledge. In order to increase knowledge reuse, there is a need for a certain level of separation from the game. That extraction, on the other hand, can lead to poor integration with game context, which disrupts the flow of the game. Finding the right balance is essential regarding this matter.

Finding the right way to model the knowledge for use in educational games presents an important issue. Video games teach players certain skills and knowledge (De Aguilera & Mendiz, 2003; Estallo, 1995). The problem arises when there is a need to teach specific matter such as subject curriculum at universities etc. Integrating that kind of knowledge, while still making game interesting and playable presents a big challenge. The purpose of this chapter is to propose a model that will attempt to establish the balance between knowledge integration on one side, and its reusability on other. Our model driven approach is relying on use of Learning Objects (LO) as constructing pieces of knowledge resources which are specialized for educational game design purpose. Learning objects represent a small, reusable pieces of content relevant for learning (for example, an online exercise; a coherent set of introductory readings on a specific topic; or an assessment test) (Jovanović et al., 2007). Reusability of LO represents using LO in different courses, by different teachers and learners (Gašević et al., 2004). In this case LOs can be reused in different educational games as well as other eLearning forms, online classes, tests etc.

The chapter is structured as follows. In part 2, we give a brief discussion about this area of research and survey of research result regarding this matter. Next, we give a description of the proposed approach inspired by model-driven development that represents a basis of this work. Detailed description of our metamodel is a subject of part 4 of this chapter. An example of application of the described metamodel, is described in part 5. Part 6 gives a conclusion and issues in respect to our future work.

Games in Education

The essence of e-learning lies in knowledge management (Ronchetti & Saini, 2004; Kostas, Psarras & Papastefanatos, 2002). The ever-increasing importance of knowledge in our contemporary society calls for a shift in thinking about innovation in e-learning.

In the context of e-learning, ontologies serve as a means of achieving semantic precision between a domain of learning material and the learner's prior knowledge and learning goals (Kickmeier-Rust & Albert, 2008). Ontologies bridge the semantic gap between humans and machines and, consequently, they facilitate the establishment of the semantic web and build the basis for the exchange and re-use of contents that reaches across people and applications (Antoniou & van Harmelen, 2004).

It is important to be able to separate content from expression within a LO in order to be able to clearly distinguish two important types of questions: those dealing with the meaning that has to be conveyed by the LO, and those dealing with how meaning is to be expressed (Brajnik, 2007).

On the other side, main purpose of educational games is to teach and pass knowledge. That is why a majority of educational games is focused mainly on knowledge. Different skills and knowledge can be taught differently. Some games are using well-known, popular environment and set of rules, adapted for purposes of education - for example, the educational game based on "Who wants to be a millionaire?" quiz (Reinhardt & Cook, 2006). It uses all elements of the TV show, but questions are chosen by the teacher.

Some games are developed with certain subject matter in mind, like games for teaching electromagnetism called Supercharged! (Squire, 2004) or a fantasy adventure game for teaching the basic concepts of programming (Moser, 1997). In some cases, the modification of popular games (game modding) was used for teaching computer science, mathematics, physics and aesthetics (El-Nasr & Smith, 2006). Game design can be used to achieve similar goals - developing problem solving skills and teamwork (Steiner, Kaplan & Moulthrop, 2006).

Regardless of the rapid growth of this research field, knowledge modeling for the purpose of educational games is still in its initial phases. While there are many examples of practical work in knowledge modeling and knowledge management, there is very little practical work done in the field of knowledge modeling and integration with educational games. While there are numerous efforts that games can be applied to learning, relatively few attempts can be found where principles of learning and knowledge management were explicitly followed a priori in design (Kickmeier-Rust & Albert, 2008). Cognitive modeling and assessment tools have to be incorporated in to educational games, giving insight into learning outcomes and enabling their evaluation. The challenge with these games is also that they are very costly to develop, as they must compete with commercial video games in terms of quality of graphics, challenges, and game play (Federation of American Scientists, 2006).

PROPOSED APPROACH

Our approach is inspired by the model-driven development, where software development's primary focus and products are models rather than computer programs. In this way, it is possible to use concepts that are much less bound to underlying technology and are much closer to the problem domain (Selic., 2003).

Table 1 gives an overview of educational game development through MDA levels. It uses a platform-independent base model (PIM), and one or more platform-specific models (PSM), each describing how the base model is implemented on a different platform (Bezivin, 2001). In this way, the PIM is unaffected by the specifics of different implementation technologies, and it is not necessary to repeat the process of modeling an application or content each time a new technology or presentation format comes along. The views on game content from different levels of abstraction can be derived by *model transformations*. In MDA, platform-independent models are initially expressed in a platform independent modeling language, and are later translated to platform-specific models by mapping the PIMs to some implementation platform using formal rules. The transformation of the content models can be specified by a set of rules defined in terms of the corresponding higher level metamodels. The transformation engine itself may be built on any suitable technology such as XSLT tools. Our approach is based on standard technologies such as the Unified Modeling Language (UML) and XML, which are familiar to many software practitioners and are well supported by tools. Therefore, it is not necessary to develop complex solutions from scratch, and it is possible to reuse existing model-driven solutions and experiences from other domains. In our work we rely on existing UML modeling tools, XML parsers and software

Table 1. Mapping educational games concepts to the OMG's MDA levels

OMG MDA Level	Educational Game Metamodeling Architecture	Description
M3 – Meta-metamodel	The Meta Object Facilities (MOF)	The MOF is an OMG standard that defines a common, abstract language for the specification of metamodels. MOF is a meta-metamodel – the model of the metamodel
M2 – Meta models	The Educational Game Metamodel (EGM)	The Educational Game Metamodel provides a common and standardized language about phenomena from various domains relevant to the design of educative games. It is called a metamodel as it is the abstraction of platform specific models, sometimes also called an ontology.
M1 – Models	Platform-specific Shemas (XHTML, SAPI, SWIXml Schemas...)	Platform specific models of educational game content.
M0 – Objects, data	Content data (XHTML, SAPI, SWIXml files...)	Instances of platform specific models.

frameworks, developing only code that extends, customizes, and connects those components according to common and standardized language defined in the Educational Game Metamodel.

EDUCATIONAL GAME METAMODEL

Defining educational game models requires a vocabulary of modeling primitives. Therefore, our metamodel describes basic educational game concepts. Figure 1 shows a simplified educational game metamodel.

The metamodel's main concept is *EduGameElement* which is used as a basis for defining other concepts of educational game. *EduGameKnowledge* defines educational content that aims to convey to players in learning process. There is a need for expertise in science area for managing complexities of the underlying knowledge. Educational content needs some form of presentation to the user, therefore we introduce concept of *EduGameEngine*. It describes the mechanism used to present knowledge, which, for example, might be the learning tool to generate and answer questions that guide learner through the exploration and discovery of the required science area. *GameInteraction* concept describes communication between player and game. This concept describes interaction at high level of abstraction regardless of specific manifestations. In broad outline, interaction is established using multiple channels of communications, and concept is derived from our existing metamodel of multimodal human-computer interaction (Obrenovic & Starcevic, 2004). The overall goal is to convey knowledge in interactions rather than static data. *EduGameLevel* comprises previous modeling primitives in order to provide inherent mechanism for game progress as well as creating a sense of achievement. It also allows creating games at multiple scales of knowledge and skills.

Knowledge Metamodel for Educational Game

In this chapter, we will focus on knowledge modeling for educational games. Further development of knowledge metamodel for educational game should provide a good basis for modeling domain knowledge and integration with the game. Model should enable manageable learning path, through the game, as well as knowledge reusability. In addition, model must provide the ability of knowledge assessment and integrating that assessment with the game.

In order to structure domain knowledge, we introduce basic metamodel shown on the Figure 2. *EduGameKnowledge* consists of *EduGame KnowledgeCategory*, which defines hierarchy

Figure 1. Educational game basic concepts

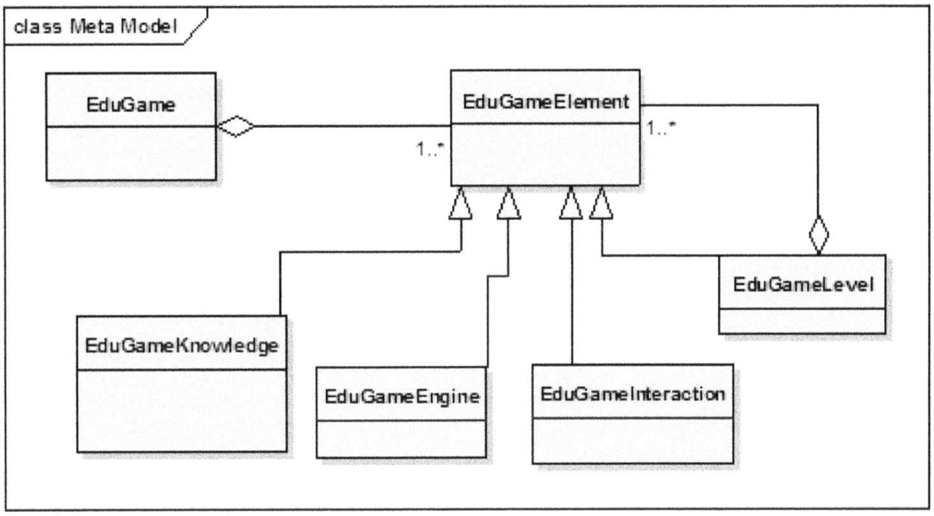

of knowledge, and contains zero or more domain models.

Domain model represents a specific knowledge area and consists of Domain Concepts, which are self-related. Domain Concept represents a specific unit of knowledge that constitutes a building block of mentioned knowledge area. Relation between Domain Concepts has two important aspects. If concept relates to other concept, than correlation attribute will have value between zero and one (one for exactly the same concept and zero for non-related concepts). Second important relation is prerequisite, which signifies concepts that must be adopted before related concept.

We define *EduGameLO* (Educational Game Learning Object) and *EduGameAO* (Educational Game Assesment Object) to introduce a relation between game and knowledge. One *EduGameLO/ EduGameAO* is related with one or more Domain Concepts. Finally, *EduGame Scene* consists of zero or more *EduGameLO* and zero or more *EduGameAO*. Inspiration for using the name *Scene* came from the field of movies. As in movies, scene represents an integral set of constituting parts that are presented to the viewers as a whole. In educational games domain, scene represents a composition of learning materials and assessments, that have a specific educational purpose, but its presentation depends on many different factors. Adequate interaction with learner required from us to develop another part of our framework, targeting Game Interaction (Minović et al., 2009), presented further in next section.

Major benefit of our metamodel is that construction of educational games is driven by "learning scenario", which actually defines domain concepts and learning path that learner should adopt. Less experienced educator can construct educational game, simply relying on domain model developed by experts in specific knowledge area, utilizing already established relations between concepts for given domain model.

On the other side, established relation enables us to create transformations on lower MDA levels, in order to automatically generate *EduGame Scene*. Educator can define "learning scenario" (or use existing one from repository), and educational game will be generated (by use of game template from repository). *EduGame Engine* can generate adequate *EduGame Scene*, by choosing Learning and Assesment Objects, and pass it to *EduGameInteraction* for presentation to learner.

Next model (Figure 2) gives in more detail specification of Learning and Assessment Ob-

Figure 2. Educational game knowledge metamodel

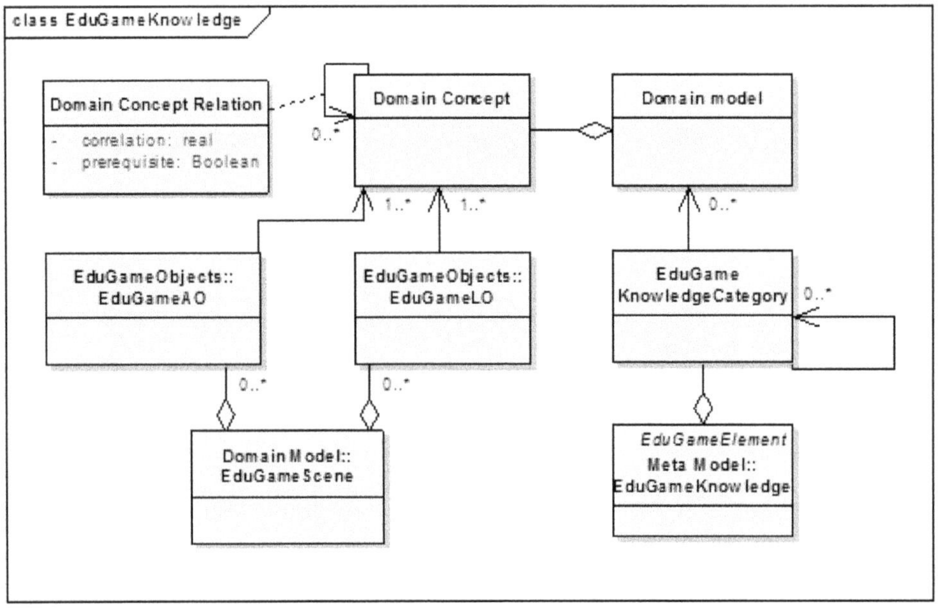

jects. Although learning and assessment is often overlapping, in our model we distinguish between Learning Object and Assessment Object. In this way, we can achieve separated management of learning and assessment paths, as well as easier manipulation by computers. Specific nature of educational games leads us to separation of LO and AO. In order to keep learners motivation high, game should provide a sense of achievement. Learner should be provided with a challenge adequate to his current knowledge state, which is established by use of AOs. Game platforms enable implementation of assessment objects which are different than in classical eLearning (for example mini-game inside the game which will verify acquired knowledge or skills). Finally, for learner this separation does not have to be so clear, since advanced educational games should mix these two concepts and blur the separation line between them. Further, *EduGameLO* can be Simple or Complex type. Simple LO can be: *TextEduGameLO, PictureEduGameLO, VideoEduGameLO* or *AudioEduGameLO*. *ComplexEduGameLO* represents any combination of Simple Learning Objects as well as combination with other Complex Learning Objects. *EduGameAO* has same specialization, as *Simple* and *Complex EduGameAO*.

We decided to continue specializing simple AO (Figure 3.) into *Question, Simulation, Puzzle* and *Mini-game*. *Question* covers all standard question types for knowledge assessment (like multiple-choice or free-text question). *Simulation* represents a specific kind of assessment, where learner has some kind of mini-model for manipulation and has to use it in order to solve a given problem. *Simulation* is particularly convenient for skill assessment. *Puzzle* refers to a group of tasks described as logical assignments or logical hurdles. *Mini-game* is assessment object in a form of a game. Important characteristic of every assessment object is to provide *EvaluationPoints* value (for example, at implementation level this can be valued between 0 and 100) in order to enable verification of knowledge. *Complex EduGameAO* can be aggregation of Simple EduGameAO (mini-game for example).

Interaction Metamodel For Educational Game

Interaction between player and game is realized using multiple channels of communication. In order to describe relevant concepts of communication between player and game, we propose metamodel as depicted by Figure 4.

Main concept in metamodel of communication between player and game is GameModality. It is defined as a form of interaction between player and game, which engages human capabilities to produce some effects on users (see Figure 5). Presented concept of GameModality is derived from existing metamodel of multimodal human-computer interaction (Obrenovic & Starcevic, 2004). Multimodal interaction can be established between multiple players (GamePlayer) and multiple game platforms (GamePlatform). GameContext defines set of conditions and facts that are pertinent to specific situation, and can affect interaction between player and game. GameContext is additionally classified into:

- **Physical context:** Defines environment conditions such as kind of space in which interaction is established, temperature value, luminance level, noise, humidity
- **Situational context:** Defines current situation in environment from the point of view of the task that user has to accomplish
- **Common knowledge:** Represents a set of facts that are understood by humans and computer
- **Social context :** Defines social environment of the interaction

Each modality engages human capabilities, producing some effect on the user. Effects are classified into four main categories (Obrenovic & Starcevic, 2004):

- Sensory effects describe the human sensory apparatus's processing of stimuli;
- Perceptual effects result from the human perceptual system's analysis of sensor data;
- Motor effects describe human mechanical actions, such as head movement or pressure;
- Cognitive effects occur at higher levels of human information processing and include memory, attention, and curiosity. In the design of educational games, these are the kcy assct.

Figure 3. Educational game learning object and assessment object metamodel

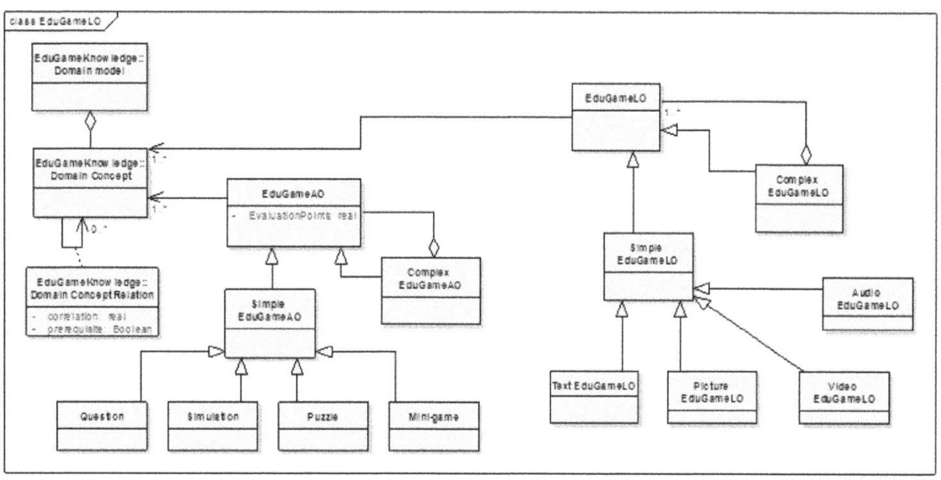

Figure 4. Basic concepts of communication between player and game

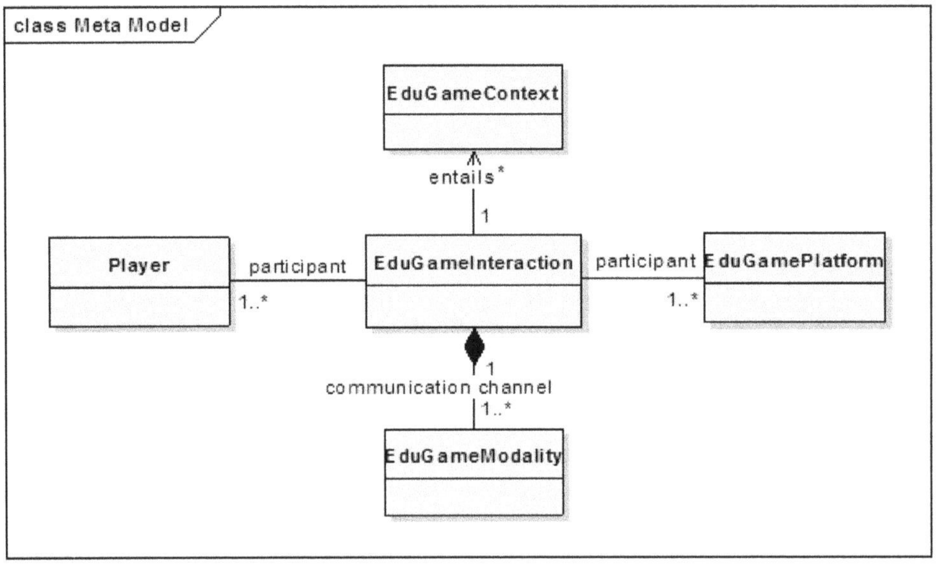

Figure 5. Detailed concepts of communication between player and game

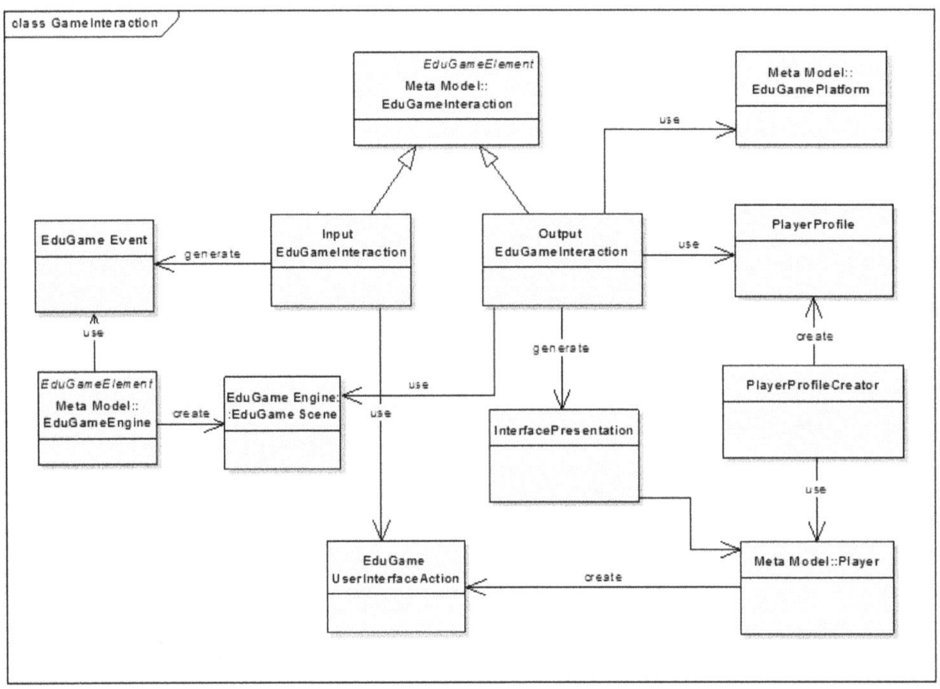

In this way, user interface can be described in terms of messages (effects) that designer sends to the user. Effects are interconnected. For example, all perceptual effects results from sensory effects. These relationships enable designers predicting the result of using some effects.

When we analyzed Game Interaction in more details, we found that EduGameInteraction could be specialized into Input and Output EduGameInteraction, representing user input and game interface output communication. EduGameEngine creates EduGame Scene, abstract concept which defines all elements of one scene in educational game, but without any user interface elements. Then, Output EduGameInteraction produces concrete InterfacePresentation based on given EduGame Scene and concrete EduGamePlatform. InterfacePresentation can be adjusted depending on PlayerProfile, created by PlayerProfileCreator. PlayerProfile is determined at the beginning of the game and can be dynamically adjusted during the game, depending on Player actions. For determining initial profile we can use psychological tests or try to capture it automatically, if possible, by analyzing Players actions produced at training game level. Since we are modeling educational games, we are mostly interested in finding out player's cognitive style and motivational state, in order to adapt educational content and game interface.

Input EduGameInteraction generates EduGame Event based on EduGame UserInterfaceAction created by Player. UserInterfaceAction represents low level actions performed by Player, such as mouse movement, or keyboard key press, if standard keyboard/mouse/screen interface is in use. EduGameInteraction handles such actions, trying to detect changes that significantly influence EduGame. When important action is detected, EduGame Event is raised, such as question answered or puzzle solved, and is being sent to EduGameEngine for further processing. EduGameEngine produces new EduGame Scene which triggers Output EduGameInteraction.

Clear separation between EduGameEngine and EduGameInteraction was our main aim. EduGameEngine represents educational game logic, while EduGameInteraction represents interaction with player. In this way we enabled game designer and educator separation of roles. Another benefit is reusable game interaction. To clarify, by applying this we gain the ability to keep game interaction while modifying just educational content. Such educational game can be applied to many different domains, without additional programming and user interface design. This brings a major contribution to educational game development.

In order to appropriately capture players profile proper classification is in order.

Game Player Profiles Metamodel

We have classified players/learners according to multiple intelligence theory (Howard, 2000). The eight intelligences are as follows and illustrated in Figure 6 (Armstrong, 2000):

- **Linguistic:** Think in words
- **Logical/Mathematical:** Think by reasoning
- **Spatial:** Think in images and pictures
- **Bodily/Kinesthetic:** Think through somatic sensations
- **Musical:** Think via rhythms and melodies
- **Interpersonal:** Think by bouncing ideas off other people
- **Intrapersonal:** Think in relation to their needs, feelings, and goals
- **Naturalist:** Think through nature and natural forms

The fact that some people impose multiple types of intelligences justifies introduction of *Complex* type. Gardner states that most schools focus on the linguistic and logical/mathematical intelligences. In this way individuals who show gifts in the other intelligences: the artists, architects, musicians, naturalists, designers, dancers,

Figure 6. Proposed player classification

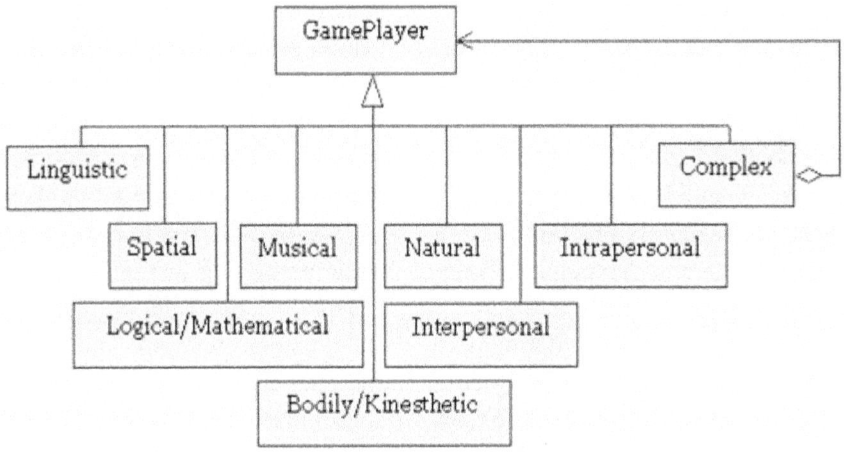

therapists, entrepreneurs are learning-confined by traditional educational process. Unfortunately, many children who have these gifts do not receive much reinforcement for them in school. McCue (McCue, 2005) describes how computer games can provide a multiintelligence approach to learning by exemplifying particular intelligences. In our approach we are reusing multiple intelligence concepts in order to (1) comprise users with diverse learning preferences inherently predefined by particular intelligences (2) identify the dominant content of learning interface according to intelligence type as (Armstrong, 2000): words (linguistic intelligence), numbers or logic (logical-mathematical intelligence), pictures (spatial intelligence), music (musical intelligence), self-reflection (intrapersonal intelligence), a physical experience (bodily-kinesthetic intelligence), a social experience (interpersonal intelligence), an experience in the natural world (naturalist experience).

In next section we will present our design case study, where we developed educational game editor as a proof of concept, based on our metamodels.

DESIGN CASE STUDY

We have applied our approach in designing pilot project educational game editor, where educator can easily define new educational game, utilizing existing knowledge, assessment and multimedia from repository (see Figure 7). For now, we provided support for adventure game type. For this specific game type, we use a 2D game environment.

The main idea is that learner has to solve all given quests inside adventure game world. In order to complete the quest, player (learner) must pass all assessment objects successfully. First, educator defines a map, which presents a game world environment. Upon that, he defines game regions and relations among them, and proceeds with detail definition of each region, where he can use existing learning objects or create new one for specific domain concept. Assessment objects can belong to a region, too. Also every *region* contains Non Playing Characters (NPC) that act as enemies, partners and support characters to provide challenges, offer assistance and

Figure 7. Graphical editor for educational games definition

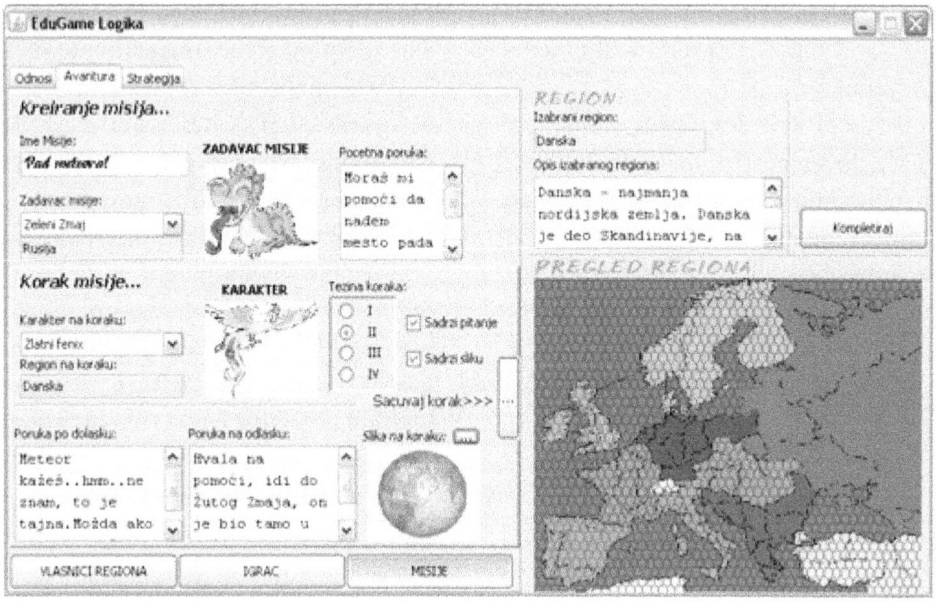

Figure 8. Web client game interface

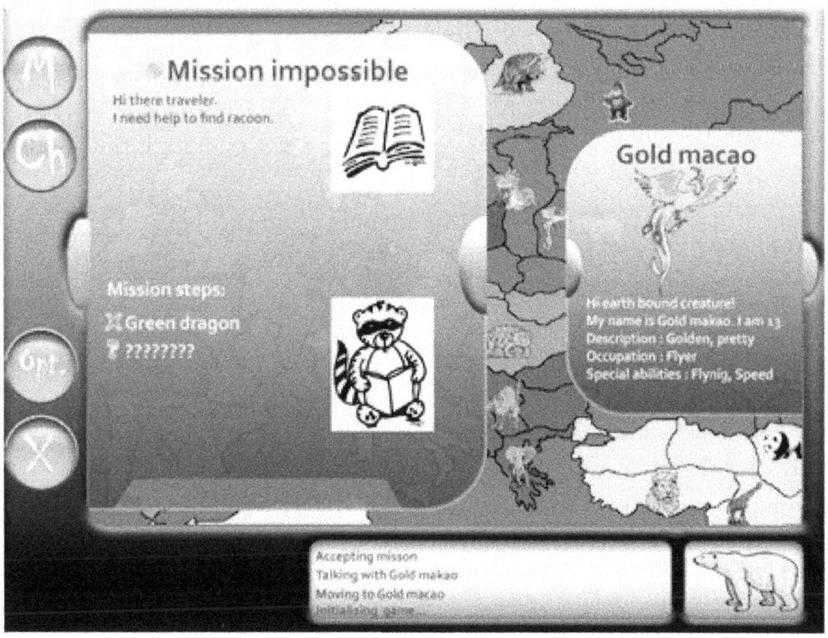

support the storyline. After the creation of regions, we can make different avatars, assign them different abilities, and make quests and assignments for future players.

The result of the process described is a uniquely structured XML document (Minović et al., 2008), which EduGameEngine uses for interpretation and presentation to learner.

Figure 8 shows how user see interpreted adventure game, implemented as Java Applet. By advancing through the game, and by solving the quests, the player gains knowledge and learns new concepts.

CONCLUSION

This chapter describes our research in knowledge modeling for educational games. Extending our previous work on Educational Game Metamodel (Jovanovic et al., 2008), this article provides further details of this approach and introduces a knowledge metamodel that enriches learning by creating platform for seamless integration between knowledge and game.

Presented models contribute to methodology of educational games development in a way that they embrace principles of learning and knowledge management early in design process. Together with metamodels for game interaction (Obrenovic & Starcevic, 2004), this presents a step toward a unified framework for development of educational games.

We also presented an approach to modeling educational games user interface that incorporates principles of motivation theory as well as multimodal human-computer interaction. The overall challenge is to increase player's motivation for studying. Proposed modeling framework is aimed to design user interfaces that motivate users with diverse learning abilities and preferences to get actually involved in learning process. This is achieved by identifying game player profiles according to player learning abilities and preferences and adopting game interaction to player profile.

We demonstrated applicability of our models in design case study, where we developed educational game editor where educator can easily define new educational game utilizing existing knowledge, assessment and multimedia from repository.

Further development will be focused on implementing XSLT transformations in order to automate Learning Scene generation. The main idea is that educator defines "learning scenario" with concepts that learner should adopt during the game, and game engine will perform the rest of the job, e.g. select adequate LOs and AOs, produce Learning Scene and present it to the learner.

REFERENCES

Antoniou, G., & van Harmelen, F. (2004). Web ontology language: OWL. In Staab, S., & Studer, R. (Eds.), *Handbook on ontologies* (pp. 67–92). Springer-Verlag.

Armstrong, T. (2000). *Multiple intelligences.* Retrieved from _Ref187139058lwww.thomasarmstrong.com/multiple_intelligences.htm

Bezivin, J. (2001). From object composition to model transformation with the MDA. *Proceedings of TOOLS.* Santa Barbara, CA: IEEE CS Press.

Brajnik, G. (2007). Modeling content and expression of learning objects in multimodal learning management systems. In *Proceedings of Universal Access in Human-Computer Interaction. Applications and Services* (pp. 501–510). Berlin, Germany: Springer-Verlag. doi:10.1007/978-3-540-73283-9_56

De Aguilera, M., & Mendiz, A. (2003). Video games and education. *Computers in Entertainment, 1*(1).

El-Nasr, M., & Smith, B. (2006). Learning through game modding. *ACM Computers in Entertainment, 4*(1).

Estallo, J. A. (1995). *Los videojugos. Juicios e prejuicios*. Barcelona, Spain: Planeta.

Federation of American Scientists. (2006). *R&D challenges in games for learning*. (Tech. Rep., Washington D.C., _Ref187133137). Retrieved from www.fas.org/learningfederation

Gašević, D., Jovanović, J., & Devedžić, V. (2004). Enhancing learning object content on the Semantic Web. *Proceedings of the IEEE International Conference on Advanced Learning Technologies ICALT'04*, Joensuu, Finland.

Howard, G. (2000). *Intelligence reframed: Multiple intelligences for the 21st century.*

Jovanović, J., Gašević, D., Brooks, C., Devedžić, V., Hatala, M., Eap, T., & Richards, G. (2007). Using Semantic Web technologies to analyze learning content. *IEEE Internet Computing, 11*(5), 45–53. doi:10.1109/MIC.2007.116

Jovanovic, M., Starcevic, D., Stavljanin, V., & Minovic, M. (2008). Lecture Notes in Computer Science: *Vol. 5288. Educational games design issues: Motivation and multimodal interaction* (pp. 215–224). Berlin, Germany: Springer-Verlag.

Kickmeier-Rust, M., & Albert, D. (2008). *The ELEKTRA ontology model: A learner-centered approach to resource description. Advances in Web Based Learning – ICWL 2007* (pp. 78–89). Berlin, Germany: Springer-Verlag.

Kostas, M., Psarras, J., & Papastefanatos, S. (2002). Knowledge and information management in elearning environments: The user agent architecture. *Information Management & Computer Security, 10*(4), 165–170. doi:10.1108/09685220210436958

McCue, P. (2005). The crucial role of animated children educational games. *Proceedings of International Conference on Computer Graphics and Interactive Techniques,* Los Angeles, California.

Minović, M., Milovanović, M., Jovanović, M., & Starčević, D. (2009). Model driven development of user interfaces for educational games. In *Proceedings of Human System Interaction Conference HSI09,* Catania, Italy.

Minović, M., Milovanović, M., Lazović, M., & Starčević, D. (2008). XML application for educative games. *Proceedings of European Conference on Games Based Learning ECGBL 08*, Barcelona, Spain.

Moser, R. (1997). A fantasy adventure game as a learning environment: Why learning to program is so difficult and what can be done about. *Proceedings of the ITiCSE '97*, Uppsala, Sweden.

Obrenovic, Z., & Starcevic, D. (2004). Modeling multimodal human-computer interaction. *IEEE Computer, 37*(9), 65–72. doi:10.1109/MC.2004.139

Pivec, M. (2007). Editorial: Play and learn: Potentials of game-based learning. *British Journal of Educational Technology, 38*(3), 387–393. doi:10.1111/j.1467-8535.2007.00722.x

Reinhardt, G., & Cook, L. (2006). Is this a game or a learning moment? *Decision Sciences Journal of Innovative Education, 4*(2), 301–304. doi:10.1111/j.1540-4609.2006.00119.x

Ronchetti, M., & Saini, P. (2004). Knowledge management in an e-learning system. In *Proceedings of the 4th IEEE International Conference on Advanced Learning Technologies ICALT'04*, Joensuu, Finland, (pp. 365–369).

Selic, B. (2003). The pragmatics of model-driven development. *IEEE Software, 20*(5), 19–25. doi:10.1109/MS.2003.1231146

Squire, K. B. (2004). Electromagnetism supercharged! Learning physics with digital simulation games, *Proceedings of the 2004 International Conference of the Learning Sciences,* Santa Monica.

Steiner, B., Kaplan, N., & Moulthrop, S. (2006). When play works: Turning game-playing into learning. *Proceedings of IDC '06*, Tampere, Finland.

Compilation of References

Abdelmessih, N., Yolles, E., Grevler, C., Kuo, L., Sterling, K., & Davidson, K. (2000). *Winning of the online user: Insights into online user behavior*. The Boston Consulting Group.

Abecker, A., Bernardi, A., Maus, H., Sintek, M., & Wenzel, C. (2000). Information supply for business processes: coupling workflow with document analysis and information retrieval. *Knowledge-Based Systems*, *13*(5), 271–284. doi:10.1016/S0950-7051(00)00087-3

Aberdeen Group. (1999). *Web-based e-service: Using the Internet to manage customers*. Retrieved from http://www.servicesoft.com/presskit-whitepaper.html

Aber, J., & Shahmehri, N. (2000). The role of human web assistants in e-commerce: An analysis and a usability study. *Internet Research: Electronic Networking Applications and Policy*, *10*(2), 114–125. doi:10.1108/10662240010322902

Adam, E. E. (1992). Quality improvement as an operations strategy. *Industrial Management & Data Systems*, *4*, 3–12. doi:10.1108/02635579210012223

Aeron, H., Kumar, A., & Janakiraman, M. (2010). Application of data mining techniques for customer lifetime value parameters: A review. *International Journal of Business Information Systems*, *6*(4), 514–529. doi:10.1504/IJBIS.2010.035744

Aitchison, J., & Clarke, S. D. (2004). The thesaurus: A historical viewpoint, with a look to the future. *Cataloging & Classification Quarterly*, *37*(3/4), 5–21. doi:10.1300/J104v37n03_02

Alavi, M., & Leidner, D. E. (1999). Knowledge management systems: Issues, challenges, and benefits. *Communication of AIS, 1*.

Alavi, M., & Leidner, D. (2001). Knowledge management and knowledge management systems: Conceptual foundations and research issues. *Management Information Systems Quarterly*, *25*(1), 107–136. doi:10.2307/3250961

Albecker, A., Bernardi, A., Hinckelmann, K., Kuhn, O., & Sintech, M. (1998). Towards a technology for organizational memories. *IEEE Intelligent Systems*, *13*(3), 40–48. doi:10.1109/5254.683209

Alderson, W. (1957). *Marketing behavior and executive action: A functionalist approach to marketing theory*. Homewood, IL: Richard D. Irwin, Inc.

Ale, M. (2009). *An organizational knowledge management conceptual model PhD in Information Systems*. National Technological University.

Ale, M., Chiotti, O., & Galli, M. R. (2008b). Enterprise knowledge management for emergent organizations: An ontology-driven approach. knowledge management strategies. In Lytras, M. D., Russ, M., Maier, R., & Naeve, A. (Eds.), *A handbook of applied technologies* (pp. 218–249). Hershey, PA: IGI Global. doi:10.4018/978-1-59904-603-7.ch008

Ale, M., Gerarduzzi, C., Chiotti, O., & Galli, M. R. (2008a). Organizational knowledge sources integration through an ontology-based approach: The Onto-DOM architecture. In Lytras, M. D., Carroll, J. M., Damiani, E., & Tennyson, R. D. (Eds.), *World Summit On the Knowledge Society, LNCS 5288* (pp. 441–450). Springer. doi:10.1007/978-3-540-87781-3_48

Andreu, L., Bigne, E., Chumpitaz, R., & Swaen, V. (2006). How does the perceived retail environment influence consumers' emotional experience? Evidence from two retail settings. *International Review of Retail, Distribution and Consumer Research, 16*(5), 559–578. doi:10.1080/09593960600980097

Antoniou, G., & van Harmelen, F. (2004). Web ontology language: OWL. In Staab, S., & Studer, R. (Eds.), *Handbook on ontologies* (pp. 67–92). Springer-Verlag.

Anton, J. (1997). *Call center management by numbers*. Purdue University Press/Call Center Press.

Anton, J. (2000). The past, present and future of customer access centers. *International Journal of Service Industry Management, 11*(2), 120–130. doi:10.1108/09564230010323534

Apte, C., Liu, B., Pednault, E. P. D., & Smyth, P. (2002). Business applications of data mining. *Communications of the ACM, 45*(8), 49–53. doi:10.1145/545151.545178

Arakji, R. Y., & Lang, K. R. (2007). Digital consumer networks and producer–consumer collaboration: Innovation and product development in the video game industry. *Journal of Management Information Systems, 24*(2), 195–219. doi:10.2753/MIS0742-1222240208

Archibugi, D., & Michie, J. (1997). *Innovation policy in a global economy*. Cambridge, UK: Cambridge University Press.

Argote, L., & Ingram, P. (2000). Knowledge transfer: A basis for competitive advantage in firms. *Organizational Behavior and Human Decision Processes, 82*(1), 150–169. doi:10.1006/obhd.2000.2893

Ariely, D. (2009). *Predictably irrational*. London, UK: Harper Collins Publishers.

Armstrong, T. (2000). *Multiple intelligences*. Retrieved from _Ref187139058 1www.thomasarmstrong.com/multiple_intelligences.htm

Arroyo, N. (2004). *What is the invisible web? A crawler perspective*. AoIR-ASIST 2004 Workshop on Web Science Research Methods, Brighton (UK).

Audretsch, D. B. (1995). *Innovation and industry evolution*. Cambridge, MA: MIT Press.

Audretsch, D. B., Carree, M. A., van Stel, A. J., & Thurik, A. R. (2002). Impeded industrial restructuring: The growth penalty. *Kyklos, 55*(1), 81–98. doi:10.1111/1467-6435.00178

Ausubel, D. P. (1960). The use of advance organizers in the learning and retention of meaningful verbal material. *Journal of Educational Psychology, 51*(5), 267–272. doi:10.1037/h0046669

Autry, C. W., Griffis, S. E., Goldsby, T. J., & Bobbitt, L. M. (2005). Warehouse management systems: An initial assessment, empirical analysis, and research agenda. *Journal of Business Logistics, 26*(2), 165–183. doi:10.1002/j.2158-1592.2005.tb00210.x

Aven, T. (2010). *Misconceptions of risk*. Chichester, UK: John Wiley & Sons. doi:10.1002/9780470686539

Babin, B. J., & Griffin, M. (1998). The nature of satisfaction: An updated examination and analysis. *Journal of Business Research, 41*, 127–136. doi:10.1016/S0148-2963(97)00001-5

Bakos, J. Y. (1997). Reducing buyer search costs: Implications for electronic marketplaces. *Management Science, 43*, 1676–1692. doi:10.1287/mnsc.43.12.1676

Barnett, M., & Dunbar, R. (2008). Making sense of real options reasoning: An engine of choice that backfires. In Hodgkinson, G., & Starbuck, W. (Eds.), *The Oxford handbook of organizational decision making* (pp. 383–399). Oxford, UK: Oxford University Press. doi:10.1093/oxfordhb/9780199290468.003.0020

Barney, J. (1991). Firm resources and sustained competitive advantage. *Journal of Management, 17*(1), 99–120. doi:10.1177/014920639101700108

Barsky, E., & Purdon, M. (2006). Introducing Web 2.0: Social networking and social bookmarking for health librarians. *Journal of the Canadian Health Libraries Association, 27*, 65–67. doi:10.5596/c06-024

Bates, D. W. (2003). Policy and the future of adverse event detection using information technology. *Journal of the American Medical Informatics Association, 10*(2).

Bates, D. W., Cullen, D. J., & Laird, N. (1995). Incidence of adverse drug events and potential adverse drug events. Implications for prevention. ADE Prevention Study Group. *Journal of the American Medical Association*, *274*(1), 29–34. doi:10.1001/jama.1995.03530010043033

Bauer, C., & Chong, S. (1999). Electronic markets development: Using marketing research to determine user requirements. In *Global Networked Organizations: Proceedings of 12th BLED Electronic Commerce Conference*, Bled, Slovenia, (pp. 408-23).

Baxter, G. J., Connolly, T. M., & Stansfield, M. (2009). How can organisations learn: An information systems development perspective. *Learning Inquiry*, *3*(1), 25–46. doi:10.1007/s11519-009-0038-8

Bayer, F., & Maier, R. (2006, September). *Knowledge risks in inter-organizational knowledge transfer.* Paper presented at the the 6th International Conference on Knowledge Management, Austria.

Beal, R. M., & Lockamy, A. III. (1999). Quality differentiation for competitive advantage: A contingency approach. *European Journal of Innovation Management*, *2*(2), 71–81. doi:10.1108/14601069910269781

Beatty, K., & Nunan, D. (2004). Computer-mediated collaborative learning. *System*, *32*, 165–183. doi:10.1016/j.system.2003.11.006

Becerra-Fernandez, I., & Aha, D. W. (1999). Case-based problem solving for knowledge management systems. *Proceedings of the Twelfth International FLAIRS Conference*.

Becerra-Fernandez, I., Gonzalez, A., & Shabherwal, R. (2004). *Knowledge management and KM software packages*. New Jersey: Prentice Hall.

Beeby, M., & Booth, C. (2000). Networks and inter-organizational learning: A critical review. *The Learning Organization*, *7*(2), 75–88. doi:10.1108/09696470010316260

Behrend, F. (2006). Collaborate today, compete tomorrow. *Knowledge Management Review*, *6*(5), 24–27.

Bennigton, L., Cummane, J., & Con, P. (2000). Customer satisfaction and call centers: An Australian study. *International Journal of Service*, *11*(2).

Bereiter, C. (2002). *Education and mind in the knowledge age*. Mahwah, NJ: Lawrence Erlbaum Associates.

Bernard, H. (1976). *Totale Oorlog en Revolutionaire Oorlog* (*Vol. I*). Brussels, Belgium: Royal Military Academy.

Berryman, J. M. (2007). Judgments during information seeking: a naturalistic approach to understanding of enough information. *Journal of Information Science*, *20*(10), 1–11.

Berthon, P., & Davies, T. (1999). Going with the flow: Websites and customer involvement. *Internet Research: Electronic Networking Applications and Policy*, *9*(2), 109–116. doi:10.1108/10662249910264873

Berthon, P., Pitt, L., & Watson, R. T. (1996). The World Wide Web as an advertising medium: Toward an understanding of conversion efficiency. *Journal of Advertising Research*, *36*, 43–45.

Bertot, J., & McClure, C. R. (1997). Web usage statistics: measurement issues and analytical techniques. *Government Information Quarterly*, *14*(4), 373–395. doi:10.1016/S0740-624X(97)90034-4

Besson, B., & Possin, J.-C. (2001). *Du renseignement à l'intelligence économique, Cybercriminalité, contrefaçon, veilles stratégiqus; détecter les menaces et les opportunités pour l'entreprise*. Paris, France: Dunod.

Besson, B., & Possin, J.-C. (2003). *L'Audit d'Intelligence Economique*. Paris, France: Dunod.

Bettman, J. R., & Kakkar, P. (1977). Effects of information presentation format on user information acquisition strategies. *Journal of User Research*, *3*, 233–240.

Bezivin, J. (2001). From object composition to model transformation with the MDA. *Proceedings of TOOLS*. Santa Barbara, CA: IEEE CS Press.

Bharadwaj, V. T., Swaroop, G. M., & Vittal, I. (2005). *Winning the Indian consumer* (*Special Edition*, pp. 42–51). McKinsey Quarterly.

Bierema, L., & Eraut, M. (2004). Workplace-focused learning: Perspective on continuing professional education and human resource development. *Advances in Developing Human Resources*, *6*(1), 52–58. doi:10.1177/1523422303260859

Billett, S. (2001). Learning through work: workplace affordances and individual engagement. *Journal of Workplace Learning, 13*(5), 209–214. doi:10.1108/EUM0000000005548

Billett, S. (2004). Workplace participatory practices. Conceptualising workplaces as learning environments. *Journal of Workplace Learning, 16*(6), 312–324. doi:10.1108/13665620410550295

Bitner, M. J., Booms, B. H., & Tetreault, M. S. (1990). The service encounter: Diagnosing favorable and unfavorable incidents. *Journal of Marketing, 54*, 71–84. doi:10.2307/1252174

Bitner, M. J., & Hubbert, A. R. (1994). Encounter satisfaction versus overall satisfaction versus service quality: The consumer's voice. In Rust, R. T., & Oliver, R. L. (Eds.), *Service quality: New directions in theory and practice*. Thousand Oaks, CA: Sage.

Blackman, D., & Kennedy, M. (2009). Knowledge management and effective university governance. *Journal of Knowledge Management, 13*(6), 547–563. doi:10.1108/13673270910997187

Blaikie, N. (2000). *Designing social research: The logic of anticipation*. Cambridge, UK: Polity Press.

Bock, F. (1999). The intelligent approach to knowledge management: Viewing KM in terms of content, culture, process, and infrastructure. *Knowledge Management Review, 7*, 22–25.

Boghossian, P. (2006). Behaviorism, constructivism, and socratic pedagogy. *Educational Philosophy and Theory, 38*(6), 713–722. doi:10.1111/j.1469-5812.2006.00226.x

Bolloju, N., Khalifa, M., & Turban, E. (2002). Integrating knowledge management into enterprise environments for the next generation decision support. *Decision Support Systems, 33*(2), 163–176. doi:10.1016/S0167-9236(01)00142-7

Bonanno, G., & Haworth, B. (1998). Intensity of competition and the choice between product and process innovation. *International Journal of Industrial Organization, 16*(4), 495–510. doi:10.1016/S0167-7187(97)00003-9

Bonifacio, M., Bouquet, P., & Traverso, P. (2002). Enabling distributed knowledge management: Managerial and technological implications. *Novatica and Informatik/Informatique, 3*(1).

Boone, J. (2001). Intensity of competition and the incentive to innovate. *International Journal of Industrial Organization, 19*, 705–726. doi:10.1016/S0167-7187(00)00090-4

Bordini, R. H., Hübner, J., & Wooldridge, M. (2007). *Programming multi-agent systems in AgentSpeak using Jason*. England: Wiley. doi:10.1002/9780470061848

Bouty, I., & Gomez, M.-L. (2010). Dishing up individual and collective dimensions in organizational knowing. *Management Learning, 41*(5), 545–559. doi:10.1177/1350507610377584

Bowerman, B. L., & O'Connell, R. T. (1990). *Linear statistical models: An applied approach*. Belmont, CA: Duxbury.

Bowler, L., Koshman, S., Oh, J. S., He, D., Callery, B. G., Bowker, G., & Cox, R. J. (2011). Issues in user-centered design in LIS. *Library Trends, 59*(4), 721–752. doi:10.1353/lib.2011.0013

Boyatzis, R. E. (1998). *Transforming qualitative information: Thematic analysis and code development*. London, UK: Sage.

Brajnik, G. (2007). Modeling content and expression of learning objects in multimodal learning management systems. In *Proceedings of Universal Access in Human-Computer Interaction. Applications and Services* (pp. 501–510). Berlin, Germany: Springer-Verlag. doi:10.1007/978-3-540-73283-9_56

Brooks, B. (2007). The pulley model: a descriptive model of risky decision-making. *Safety Science Monitor, 11*(1), 1–14.

Brown, L., Gans, N., Mandelbaum, A., Sakov, A., Shen, H., Zeltyn, S., & Zhao, L. (2002) *Statistical analysis of a telephone call center: A queuing-science perspective*. The Wharton School, The Wharton Financial Institutions Center. Retrieved December 3, 2006, from http://knowledge.wharton.upenn.edu /papers/1117.pdf

Brown, T. (2009). *Change by design: How design thinking transforms organizations and inspires innovation*. New York, NY: HarperBusiness.

Brüggen, A., Vergauwen, P., & Dao, M. (2009). Determinants of intellectual capital disclosure: Evidence from Australia. *Management Decision*, *47*(2), 233–245. doi:10.1108/00251740910938894

Bruner, J. (1986). *Actual minds, possible words*. Cambridge, MA: Harvard University Press.

Brush, C. G. (1992). Research of women business owners: Past trends, a new perspective and future directions. *Entrepreneur Theory and Practice*, *16*(4), 5–30.

Bryant, D. (n.d.). *Making naturalistic decision making "fast and frugal."* Toronto, Canada. *Defence Research Development Canada.*

Bulterman, D. C. A. (2004). Is it time for a moratorium on metadata? *IEEE MultiMedia*, *11*(4), 10–17. doi:10.1109/MMUL.2004.29

Burger-Helmchen, T. (2009). Capabilities is small high-tech firms: A case of plural-entrepreneurship. *Journal of Small Business and Enterprise Development*, *16*(3), 391–405. doi:10.1108/14626000910977125

Burke, L. A., & Miller, M. K. (1999). Taking the mystery out of intuitive decision making. *The Academy of Management Executive*, *13*(4), 91–99. doi:10.5465/AME.1999.2570557

Burns, D. J., & Neisner, L. (2006). Customer satisfaction in a retail setting. *International Journal of Retail and Distribution Management*, *34*(1), 49–66. doi:10.1108/09590550610642819

Burrows, B. A. (2004, November, 10). A little less swagger at Cisco. *Business Week*. Retrived from http://www.businessweek.com/technology/content/nov2004/tc20041110_9788_tc024.htm

Cainelli, G., Evangelista, R., & Savona, M. (2006). Innovation and economic performance in services. *Cambridge Journal of Economics*, *30*, 435–458. doi:10.1093/cje/bei067

Carlsson, S. (2003). Strategic knowledge managing within the context of networks. In *Handbook on knowledge management: Knowledge matters*. New York, NY: Springer-Verlag.

Carlucci, D., Marr, B., & Schiuma, G. (2004). The knowledge value chain – How intellectual capital impacts business performance. *International Journal of Technology Management*, *27*(6/7), 575–590. doi:10.1504/IJTM.2004.004903

Carrol, W. R., & Wagar, T. H. (2010). Is there a relationship between information technology adoption and human resource management? *Journal of Small Business and Enterprise Development*, *17*(2), 218–229. doi:10.1108/14626001011041229

Chait, L. P. (1999). Creating a successful knowledge management system. *The Journal of Business Strategy*, *20*(2), 23–26. doi:10.1108/eb039991

Chan, C. W., Chen, L. L., & Geng, L. (2000). Knowledge engineering for an intelligent case-based system for help desk operations. *Expert Systems with Applications*, *18*(2), 125–132. doi:10.1016/S0957-4174(99)00058-5

Chang, C. H., & Tu, C. Y. (2005). Exploring store image, customer satisfaction and customer loyalty relationship: Evidence from Taiwanese hypermarket industry. *Journal of American Academy of Business*, *7*(2), 197–202.

Chaplan, M. A. (1995). Mapping "laborline thesaurus" terms to Library of Congress subject headings: Implications for vocabulary switching. *The Library Quarterly*, *65*(1), 39–61. doi:10.1086/602752

Chea, S., & Lou, M. (2008). Post-adoption behaviors of e-service customers: The interplay of cognition and emotion. *International Journal of Electronic Commerce*, *12*(3), 29–56. doi:10.2753/JEC1086-4415120303

Cheetham, G., & Chivers, G. (2001a). Part I – How professionals learn – The theory! *Journal of European Industrial Training*, *25*(5), 250–269.

Cheetham, G., & Chivers, G. (2001b). Part II – How professionals learn – the practice! What the empirical research found. *Journal of European Industrial Training*, *25*(5), 270–292.

Chellappan, C. (2008). *E-services: The need for higher levels of trust by populace*. Chennai, India: Anna University.

Chen, X. K. (2004). The evolution of Chinese commerce revolution: Format innovation, in chain store. *Conference Proceedings: Shanghai Chain Association 10th Anniversary*, (pp. 17-27). Shanghai, China (In Chinese).

Cheng, S., Dai, R., Xu, W., & Shi, Y. (2006). Research on data mining and knowledge management and its applications in China's economic development: significance and trend. *International Journal of Information Technology and Decision Making*, *5*(4), 585–596. doi:10.1142/S021962200600226X

Chi, E., & Mytkowicz, T. (2007). Understanding navigability of social tagging systems. *Proceeding of SIGCHI'07*. Retrieved July 25, 2001, from http://danm.ucsc.edu/~dustin/library/social_tagging.pdf

Chowdhury, S., & Chowdhury, G. (2004). *Using DDC to create a visual knowledge map as an aid to online information retrieval*. ISKO8: Knowledge Organization and the Global Information Society. Retrieved July 25, 2011 from http://strathprints.strath.ac.uk /2624/1/strathprints002624.pdf

Choy, K. L., Lee, W. B., & Lo, V. (2002). Development of a case based intelligent customer – Supplier relationship management system. *Expert Systems with Applications*, *23*(3), 281–297. doi:10.1016/S0957-4174(02)00048-9

Chui, M., Miller, A., & Roberts, R. (2009). Six ways to make Web 2.0 work. *The McKinsey Quarterly*, February.

Clark, J. M. (1961). *Competition as a dynamic process*. Washington, DC: Brookings Institution.

Cleveland, B., & Mayben, J. (1997). *Call center management on fast forward*. Annapolis, MD: Call Center Press.

COBIT. (2001). *IT governance institute*. Retrieved from http://www.ITgovernance.org

Colla, E., & Dupuis, M. (2002). Research and managerial issues on global retail competition: Carrefour/Wal-Mart. *International Journal of Retail & Distribution Management*, *30*(2/3), 103–111. doi:10.1108/09590550210418128

Collan, M. (2008). *A new method for real option valuation using fuzzy numbers*. (Research Paper). Turku, Finland: Institute for Advanced Management Systems Research. Retrieved April 12, 2011, from http://ideas.repec.org/p/amr/wpaper/466.html

Collan, M., Fullér, R., & Mezei, J. (2009). A fuzzy pay-off method for real option valuation. *Journal of Applied Mathematics and Decision Sciences*, *1*, 1–14. doi:10.1155/2009/238196

Collin, K., & Tynjälä, P. (2003). Integrating theory and practice? Employees' and students' experiences of learning at work. *Journal of Workplace Learning*, *15*(7/8), 338–344. doi:10.1108/13665620310504828

Collins-Dodd, C., & Lindley, T. (2003). Store brands and retail differentiation: The influence of store image and store brand attitude on store own brand perceptions. *Journal of Retailing and Consumer Services*, *10*(6), 345–352. doi:10.1016/S0969-6989(02)00054-1

Communication from the Commission of February 5, 2003. (2003). *The role of the universities in the Europe of knowledge COM(2003) 58 final. The role of universities in the Europe of knowledge.*

Cooil, B., Keiningham, T. L., Aksoy, L., & Hsu, M. (2007). A longitudinal analysis of customer satisfaction and share of wallet: Investigating the moderating effect of customer characteristics. *Journal of Marketing*, *71*(1), 67–83. doi:10.1509/jmkg.71.1.67

Cook, S. D. N., & Brown, J. S. (1999). Bridging epistemologies: The generative dance between organizational knowledge and organizational knowing. *Organization Science*, *10*(4), 381–400. doi:10.1287/orsc.10.4.381

Cooper, S. (2009, June). Making sense of Web 2.0. *Small Business Edge*. Retrieved from http://www.smallbusinessedge.com/article/Technology/Making_Sense_of_Web_2.0_

Cooper, D. (2003). Findings from the competition commission's inquiry into supermarkets. *Journal of Agricultural Economics*, *54*(1), 127–143. doi:10.1111/j.1477-9552.2003.tb00054.x

Copeland, T., & Keenan, P. (1998). How much is flexibility worth? *The McKinsey Quarterly*, (2): 38–49.

Corstjens, M., & Lal, R. (2000). Building store loyalty through store brands. *JMR, Journal of Marketing Research*, *37*, 281–291. doi:10.1509/jmkr.37.3.281.18781

Courtney, J. F. (2001). Decision making and knowledge management in inquiring organizations: Toward a new decision-making paradigm for DSS. *Decision Support Systems*, *31*(1), 17–38. doi:10.1016/S0167-9236(00)00117-2

Creswell, J. W. (1994). *Research design: Qualitative & quantitative approaches*. London, UK: Sage.

Cronin, J. J., & Taylor, S. A. (1992). Measuring service quality: A reexamination and extension. *Journal of Marketing, 56*, 55–68. doi:10.2307/1252296

Crook, R. T., Ketchen, D. J., Combs, J. G., & Todd, S. Y. (2008). Strategic resources and performance: A meta-analysis. *Strategic Management Journal, 29*, 1141–1154. doi:10.1002/smj.703

Csikszentmihalyi, M. (1975). *Beyond boredom and anxiety*. San Francisco, CA: Jossey-Bass.

Csikszentmihalyi, M. (1988). The future of flow. In Csikszentmihalyi, M., & Selega Csikszentmihalyi, I. (Eds.), *Optimal experience: Psychological studies of flow in consciousness*. Cambridge, UK: Cambridge University Press.

Csikszentmihalyi, M., & LeFevre, J. (1989). Optimal experience in work and leisure. *Journal of Personality and Social Psychology, 56*(5), 815–822. doi:10.1037/0022-3514.56.5.815

Dahlander, L., & Gann, D. M. (2010). How open is innovation? *Research Policy, 39*, 699–709. doi:10.1016/j.respol.2010.01.013

D'Ambra, J., & Rice, R. E. (2001). Emerging factors in user evaluation of the world wide web. *Information & Management, 38*, 373–384. doi:10.1016/S0378-7206(00)00077-X

Darroch, J. (2003). Developing a measure of knowledge management behaviors and practices. *Journal of Knowledge Management, 7*(5), 41–54. doi:10.1108/13673270310505377

Das, T. K., & Teng, B. S. (1999). Managing risks in strategic alliances. *The Academy of Management 13*(4).

Das, T. K., & Teng, B. (2001). Trust, control, and risk in strategic alliances: An integrated framework. *Organization Studies, 22*(2), 251–284. doi:10.1177/0170840601222004

Davenport, H. T., & Prusak, L. (2000). *Working knowledge: How organizations manage what they know*. Boston, MA: Harvard Business School Press.

Davenport, T., & Prusak, L. (1998). *Working knowledge: How organizations manage what they know*. Boston, MA: Harvard Business School Press.

Davidow, W. H., & Uttal, B. (1989). Service companies: Focus or falter. *Harvard Business Review*, (4): 17–34.

Davis, F. D. (1989). Perceived usefulness, perceived ease of use, and user acceptance of information technology. *Management Information Systems Quarterly, 13*(2), 319–340. doi:10.2307/249008

Davis, F. D. (1993). User acceptance of information technology: Systems characteristics, user perceptions and behavioral impacts. *International Journal of Man-Machine Studies, 38*(3), 475–487. doi:10.1006/imms.1993.1022

Davis, F. D., Bagozzi, R. P., & Warshaw, P. R. (1989). User acceptance of computer technology: A comparison of two theoretical models. *Management Science, 34*(8), 982–1002. doi:10.1287/mnsc.35.8.982

Davis, F. D., Bagozzi, R. P., & Warshaw, P. R. (1992). Extrinsic and intrinsic motivation to use computers in the workplace. *Journal of Applied Social Psychology, 22*(14), 1111–1132. doi:10.1111/j.1559-1816.1992.tb00945.x

Dawson, J. (2001). Is there a new commerce in Europe? *International Review of Retail, Distribution and Consumer Research, 11*(3), 287–299.

Dawson, K. (1999a). *The call center handbook: The complete guide to starting, running and improving your call center*. Gilroy, CA: Telecom Books.

Dawson, K. (1999b). *The call center savvy: How to position your call center for the business challenges*. Gilroy, CA: Telecom Books.

De Aguilera, M., & Mendiz, A. (2003). Video games and education. *Computers in Entertainment, 1*(1).

De Long, D. W., & Fahey, L. (2000). Diagnosing cultural barriers to knowledge management. *The Academy of Management Executive, 14*(4), 113–127. doi:10.5465/AME.2000.3979820

De Wulf, K., Odekerken-Schroder, G., Goedertier, F., & Van Ossel, G. (2005). Consumer perceptions of store brands versus national brands. *Journal of Consumer Marketing, 22*(4), 223–232. doi:10.1108/07363760510605335

Dean, A. M. (2002). Service quality in call centres: Implications for customer loyalty. *Managing Service Quality, 12*(6). doi:10.1108/09604520210451894

Degeratu, A. M., Rangaswamy, A., & Wu, J. (2000). *User choice behavior in online and traditional supermarkets: The effects of brand name, price, and other search attributes* (pp. 1-45). Working Paper. The Smeal College of Business, Penn State University; and A.B. Freeman School of Business, Tulane University.

Dekkers, M. (2001). Application profiles, or how to mix and match metadata schemas. *Cultivate Interactive, 3*. Retrieved from http://www.cultivate-int.org/issue3/schemas/

Delanty, G. (1997). *Social science, beyond constructivism and realism*. Suffolk, UK: St. Edmundsbury Press Ltd.

Delic, K. A., & Dayal, U. (2000). Knowledge management in the service and support business. In U. Reimer (Ed.), *Third International Conference on Practical Aspects of Knowledge Management* (PAKM2000).

Dempsey, L., & Heery, R. (1998). Metadata: A current view of practice and issues. *The Journal of Documentation, 54*(2), 145–172. doi:10.1108/EUM0000000007164

Dempster, A. P. (1968). A generalization of the Baysian inference. *Journal of the Royal Statistical Society. Series A (General)*, *30*, 205–447.

Despres, C., & Chauvel, D. (1999). Knowledge management(s). *Journal of Knowledge Management, 3*(2), 110–123. doi:10.1108/13673279910275567

DeVellis, R. F. (1991). Applied Social Research Methods Series: *Vol. 26. Scale development: Theory and application*. Newbury Park, CA: Sage.

Devlin, D., Birtwistle, G., & Macedo, N. (2003). Food retail positioning strategy: a means-end chain analysis. *British Food Journal, 105*(9), 653–670. doi:10.1108/00070700310497372

DiCecio, R., Engemann, K., Owyang, M. T., & Wheeler, C. H. (2008). Changing trends in the labor force: A survey. *Federal Reserve Bank of St. Louis Review, 90*(1), 47–62.

Dickinson, J. G. (2000). FDA seeks to double effort on confusing drug names. *Dickinson 's FDA Review, 7*(3), 13-4.

Dienes, Z., & Perner, J. (1999). A theory of implicit and explicit knowledge. *The Behavioral and Brain Sciences, 22*, 735–808. doi:10.1017/S0140525X99002186

Ding, Y., Jacob, E. K., Zhang, Z., Foo, S., Yan, E., George, N. L., & Guo, L. (2009). Perspectives on social tagging. *Journal of the American Society for Information Science and Technology, 60*(12), 2388–2401. doi:10.1002/asi.21190

Dishaw, M. T., & Strong, D. M. (1999). Extending the technology acceptance model with task-technology fit constructs. *Information & Management, 36*, 9–21. doi:10.1016/S0378-7206(98)00101-3

Domains, C. (1999). Business on the Internet. Retrieved from http://www.cleverdomains.com/business.htm

Draper, N. R., & Smith, H. (1981). *Applied regression analysis* (2nd ed.). New York, NY: Wiley.

Driver, M. (2010). Learning as lack: Individual learning it organizations as an empowering encounter with failed imaginary constructions of the self. *Management Learning, 41*(5), 561–574. doi:10.1177/1350507610374427

Drucker, P. (1998). From capitalism to knowledge society. In Drucker, P. (Ed.), *Post-capitalist society* (pp. 19–47). New York, NY: Harper Collins.

Drucker, P. F. (1988). The coming of the new organization. *Harvard Business Review, 66*(1), 45–53.

Drucker, P. F. (1999). Knowledge worker productivity: The biggest challenge. *California Management Review, 41*(2), 79–94.

DSS. (2005). *Defense security service* (DSS). Retrieved February 11, 2005 from http://www.dss.mil/isec/appendixc.htm

Duan, Y., Edwards, J. S., & Xu, M. X. (2005). Web-based expert systems: Benefits and challenges. *Information & Management, 42*(6), 799–811. doi:10.1016/j.im.2004.08.005

Dubois, D., & Prade, H. (1980). *Fuzzy sets and systems: Theory and applications*. Academic Press.

Dubois, D., & Prade, H. (1991). Fuzzy sets in approximate reasoning II (Logical approaches). *Fuzzy Sets and Systems, 40*, 203–244. doi:10.1016/0165-0114(91)90051-Q

Dubois, D., & Prade, H. (2000). *Fundamentals of fuzzy sets*. Kluwer Academic.

Durkin, J. (1994). *Expert systems: Design and development*. Maxwell Macmillan.

Dustdar, S. (2005). Reconciling knowledge management and workflow management systems: The activity-based knowledge management approach. *Journal of Universal Computer Science*, *11*(4), 589–604.

Dymock, D., & Gerber, R. (2002). Unintegrated training? Exploring links between off- and on-the-job learning. *Education + Training, 44*(1), 23-30.

Dynes, S., Brechbühl, H., & Johnson, E. (2005). (2005). *Information security in the extended enterprise: Some initial results from a field study of an industrial firm.* Paper presented at the Workshop on the Economics of Information Security WEIS05, Boston, MA.

Dynes, S., Kolbe, L., & Schierholz, R. (2007, August). *Information security in the extended enterprise: A research agenda.* Paper presented at the the 13th Americas Conference on Information Systems AMCIS07, Denver, Colorado.

EARF. (n.d.). *Completed projects.* Retrieved April 11, 2001, from http://earf.meraka.org.za/earfhome/our-projects-1/completed-projects/

Edwards, J. (2007). Knowledge management in the energy sector: Review and future directions. *International Journal of Energy Sector Management, 2*(2), 197–217. doi:10.1108/17506220810883216

Ellis, M. S., & Rumizen, M. (2002). The evolution of KM at Buckman Laboratories: How its KM program has developed with the new leadership. *Knowledge Management Review*, *5*(1), 12–15.

El-Nasr, M., & Smith, B. (2006). Learning through game modding. *ACM Computers in Entertainment, 4*(1).

Engeström, Y., Engeström, R., & Kärkkäinen, M. (1995). Polycontextuality and boundary crossing in expert cognition: Learning and problem solving in complex work activities. *Learning and Instruction*, *5*, 319–336. doi:10.1016/0959-4752(95)00021-6

Eraut, M. (2004). Informal learning in the workplace. *Studies in Continuing Education*, *26*(2), 247–273. doi:10.1080/158037042000225245

Eric, T. (2005). The role of IT in KM: Where are we now and where are we heading? *Journal of Knowledge Management*, *9*(1), 3–6. doi:10.1108/13673270510584198

Ermine, J. (2000). Challenges and approaches for knowledge management in companies. In *Proceedings of Workshop in Knowledge Management: Theory and Applications*, France.

Eroglu, S. A., Machleit, K., & Barr, T. F. (2005). Perceived retail crowding and shopping satisfaction: the role of shopping values. *Journal of Business Research*, *58*(8), 1146–1153. doi:10.1016/j.jbusres.2004.01.005

Ertmer, P. A., & Newby, T. J. (1993). Behaviorism, cognitivism, constructivism: Comparing critical features from an instructional design perspective. *Performance Improvement Quarterly*, *6*(4), 50–70. doi:10.1111/j.1937-8327.1993.tb00605.x

Estallo, J. A. (1995). *Los videojugos. Juicios e prejuicios*. Barcelona, Spain: Planeta.

Etkind, J., Bennaceur, K., Dmec, M., & Luppens, C. (2003). Knowledge portals support widely distributed oil fields projects. *Proceedings of IEEE International Professional Communication Conference IEEE*, Orlando, FL, (pp. 189-200).

Etzioni, O. (1997). Moving up the information food chain. *AI Magazine*, ▪▪▪, 11–18.

European Commission. (2002b). *Innovation tomorrow: Innovation policy and the regulatory framework: Making innovation an integral part of the broader structural agenda.* Louis Lengrand & Associés, Innovation Papers, No: 28, Luxembourg.

European Commission. (2005). *Special Eurobarometer*.

Evensen, A., Harker, P. T., & Frei, F. X. (1999). *Effective call center management: Evidence from Financial Services*. The Wharton School, The Wharton Financial Institutions Center. Retrieved December 3, 2008, from http://knowledge.wharton.upenn.edu /papers/50.pdf

Fanning, E. (2007, March 19). Editor's note: Security for Web 2.0. *Computer World*. Retrieved from http://www.computerworld.com/s/article/283283/Security_for_Web_2.0

Farahmand, F., Navathe, S., Sharp, G., & Enslow, P. (2003, September). *Managing vulnerabilities of information systems to security incidents.* Paper presented at the the 5th International Conference on Electronic Commerce, Pittsburgh, Pennsylvania

Farahmand, F., Sharp, G., & Enslow, P. (2005). A management perspective on security threats to information systems. *Information Technology Management*, *6*, 203–225. doi:10.1007/s10799-005-5880-5

Fayyad, U., & Uthurusamy, R. (2002). Evolving data mining into solutions for insights. *Communications of the ACM*, *45*(8), 28–31. doi:10.1145/545151.545174

Federation of American Scientists. (2006). *R&D challenges in games for learning*. (Tech. Rep., Washington D.C., _Ref187133137). Retrieved from www.fas.org/learningfederation

Feinberg, R. A., Hokama, L., Rajesh, K., & Kim, I. (2002). Operational determinants of caller satisfaction in the banking/financial services call center. *International Journal of Bank Marketing*, *20*(4). doi:10.1108/02652320210432954

Feinberg, R. A., Kim, I., Hokama, L., Ruyter, K., & Keen, C. (2000). Operational determinants of caller satisfaction in the call center. *International Journal of Service Industry Management*, *11*(2). doi:10.1108/09564230010323633

Feldman, R., & Sanger, J. (2007). *The text mining handbook: Advanced approaches in analyzing unstructured data*. USA: Cambridge University Press.

Fensel, D. A. (2003). *Ontologies: A silver bullet for knowledge management and electronic commerce* (2nd ed.). Springer.

Fenton, C. (2010). Use of controlled vocabulary and thesauri in UK online finding aids. *Journal of the Society of Archivists*, *31*(2), 187–205. doi:10.1080/00379816.2010.506792

Fereira, N., Kar, J., & Trigeorgis, L. (2009). Option games: The key to competing in capital-intensive industries. *Harvard Business Review*, (March): 2009.

Fidel, R. (1991). Searcher's selection of search keys: I. The selection routine. *Journal of the American Society for Information Science American Society for Information Science*, *42*(7), 490–500. doi:10.1002/(SICI)1097-4571(199108)42:7<490::AID-ASI4>3.0.CO;2-V

Field, A. (2005). *Discovering statistics using SPSS for Windows*. London, UK: Sage.

Fischer, G., & Otswald, J. (2001). Knowledge management: Problems, promises, realities, and challenges. *Intelligent Systems, IEEE*, *16*(1), 60–72. doi:10.1109/5254.912386

Fornell, C. A. (1992). National customer satisfaction barometer: The Swedish experience. *Journal of Marketing*, *56*, 6–21. doi:10.2307/1252129

Forrest, E., & Mizerski, R. (1996). *Interactive marketing, the future present*. Chicago, IL: American Marketing Association.

Foulkes, V. S. (1994). How consumers predict service quality: What do they expect? In Oliver, R. L. (Ed.), *Service quality, New directions in theory and practice*. Beverly Hills, CA: Sage Publication.

Foxon, T. J., Gross, R., Chase, A., Howes, J., Arnall, A., & Anderson, D. (2005). UK innovation systems for new and renewable energy technologies: drivers, barriers and systems failures. *Energy Policy*, *33*, 2123–2137. doi:10.1016/j.enpol.2004.04.011

Frakes, W. B., & Pole, T. P. (1994). An empirical study of representation methods for reusable software components. *IEEE Transactions on Software Engineering*, *20*(8), 617–630. doi:10.1109/32.310671

Franco, M., & Haase, H. (2009). Entrepreneurship: An organizational learning approach. *Journal of Small Business and Enterprise Development*, *16*(4), 628–641. doi:10.1108/14626000911000965

Freeze, R., & Kulkarni, U. (2005, January 3-6). *Knowledge management capability assessment: Validating a knowledge assets measurement instrument.* Paper presented at the the 38th Hawaii International Conference on Systems Sciences, Waikoloa, Hawaii

Funston, F., & Wagner, S. (2010). *Surviving and thriving in uncertainty: Creating the risk intelligent enterprise*. Hoboken, NJ: John Wiley & Sons.

Gable, R. A. (1993). *Inbound call centers: Design, implementation and management*. Boston, MA: Artech House.

Garcia-Crespo, A., Ruiz-Mezcua, B., López-Cuadrado, J. L., & González-Carrasco, I. (2011). Semantic model for knowledge representation in e-business. *Knowledge-BasedSystems*, *24*(2). doi:10.1016/j.knosys.2010.09.006

Garshol, L. M. (2004). Metadata? Thesauri? Taxonomies? Topic maps! Making sense of it all. *Journal of Information Science*, *30*(4), 378–391. doi:10.1177/0165551504045856

Gašević, D., Jovanović, J., & Devedžić, V. (2004). Enhancing learning object content on the Semantic Web. *Proceedings of the IEEE International Conference on Advanced Learning Technologies ICALT'04*, Joensuu, Finland.

Gatignon, H., & Soberman, D. (2000). Competitive response and market evolution. In Weitz, B., & Wensley, R. (Eds.), *Handbook of marketing* (pp. 126–147). London, UK: Sage.

Gattiker, U. E. (1992). Computer skills acquisition: A review and future directions for research. *Journal of Management*, *18*(3), 547–574. doi:10.1177/014920639201800307

Gefen, D., & Straub, D. (2000). The relative importance of perceived ease of use in IS adoption: A study of e-commerce adoption. *Journal of the Association for IS*, *1*, 1–20.

Gelderman, M. (1998). The relation between user satisfaction, usage of information systems and performance. *Information & Management*, *34*, 11–18. doi:10.1016/S0378-7206(98)00044-5

Ghauri, P., & Gronhaug, K. (2002). *Research methods in business studies. A practical guide*. Harlow, UK: Pearson Education Limited.

Gherardi, S. (2001). From organizational learning to practice-based knowing. *Human Relations*, *54*(1), 131–139. doi:10.1177/0018726701541016

Giese, J. L., & Cote, J. A. (2000). Defining consumer satisfaction. *Academy of Marketing Science Review*, *1*. Retrieved December 20, 2008, from http://www.amsreview.org /articles/giese01-2000.pdf

Gilchrist, A. (2003). Thesauri, taxonomies and ontologies – An etymological note. *The Journal of Documentation*, *59*(1), 7–18. doi:10.1108/00220410310457984

Gilmore, A. (2001). Call centre management: Is service quality a priority? *Managing Service Quality*, *11*(3). doi:10.1108/09604520110391315

Glasersfeld von, E. (1989). Cognition, construction of knowledge, and teaching. *Synthese*, *80*(1), 121–140. doi:10.1007/BF00869951

Glasersfeld von. E. (1995). *Radical constructivism. A way of knowing and learning*. London, UK: The Falmer Press.

Goh, D. H., Chua, A., Lee, C. S., & Razikin, K. (2009). Resource discovery through social tagging: A classification and content analytic approach. *Online Information Review*, *33*(3), 568–583. doi:10.1108/14684520910969961

Göker, M., & Roth-Berghofer, T. (1999). Development and utilization of a case-based help-desk support system in a corporate environment. In Althoff, K.-D., Bergmann, R., & Branting, L. K. (Eds.), *ICCBR-99* (*Vol. 1650*, pp. 132–146). Lecture Notes in Computer Science. doi:10.1007/3-540-48508-2_10

Golder, S. A., & Huberman, B. A. (2006). Usage patterns of collaborative tagging systems. *Journal of Information Science*, *32*(2), 198–208. doi:10.1177/0165551506062337

Goldman, A. (2000). Supermarkets in China: The case of Shanghai. *International Review of Retail, Distribution and Consumer Research*, *10*(1), 1–21. doi:10.1080/095939600342370

Golub, K., Moon, J., Tudhope, D., Jones, C., Matthews, B., Puzo, D. B., & Lykke Nielsen, M. (2009). EnTag: Enhancing social tagging for discovery. *Proceedings of the 9th ACM/IEEE-CS Joint Conference on Digital Libraries (JCDL '09)*. Retrieved July 30, 2011, from http://www.ukoln.ac.uk/projects/enhanced-tagging/dissemination/entag-jcdl09.pdf

Golub, K. (2006). Automated subject classification of textual web pages, based on a controlled vocabulary: Challenges and recommendations. *New Review of Hypermedia and Multimedia*, *12*(1), 11–27. doi:10.1080/13614560600774313

Gómez, A., Juristo, N., Montes, C., & Pazos, J. (1997). *Ingeniería del conocimiento*. Centro de Estudios Ramón Areces.

Gonzalez, L. M., Giachetti, R. E., & Ramirez, G. (2005). Knowledge management-centric help desk: Specification and performance evaluation. *Decision Support Systems*, *40*, 389–405. doi:10.1016/j.dss.2004.04.013

Goto, S. (2007). The bounds of classical risk management and the importance of a behavioral approach. *Risk Management & Insurance Review*, *10*(2). doi:10.1111/j.1540-6296.2007.00118.x

Graeff, C. L. (1980). Some methodological issues concerning comparative hospital studies. *Academy of Management Review*, *5*, 539–548.

Greer, J., McCalla, G., Cooke, J., Collins, J., Kumar, V., Bishop, A., & Vassileva, J. (1998). The intelligent helpdesk: Supporting peer-help in a university course. In Goettl, B. P., Halff, H. M., Redfield, C. L., & Shute, V. J. (Eds.), *Intelligent Tutoring Systems* (*Vol. 1452*, pp. 494–503). Lecture Notes in Computer Science Berlin, Germany: Springer-Verlag. doi:10.1007/3-540-68716-5_55

Greitzer, F., Podmore, R., Robinson, M., & Ey, P. (2009). Naturalistic decision making for power system operators. *Proceedings of NDM9, the 9th International Conference on Naturalistic Decision Making*, London, June 2009.

Grimm, C. (2001). Creating balanced measures in a multichannel world. *Call Center Management Review*, *3*, 9–11.

Grönroos, C. (1984). A service quality model and its marketing implications. *European Journal of Marketing*, *18*(4), 36–44. doi:10.1108/EUM0000000004784

Grosof, B. N. (1997). *Building commercial agents: An IBM research perspective (invited talk).* Exhibition on Practical Applications on Intelligent Agents and Multi-Agent Technology (PAAM 97). Retrieved from http://www.research.ibm.com/igents/paps/rc20305.pdf

Gruber, T. (1993). A translation approach to portable ontology specifications. *Knowledge Acquisition*, *5*, 199–220. doi:10.1006/knac.1993.1008

Grudin, J. (2006). Enterprise knowledge management and emerging technologies. *Proceedings of the 39th Annual Hawaii International Conference on System Sciences* (HICSS '06). Retrieved March 16, 2010, from http://research.microsoft.com/ enus/um/people/jgrudin/publications/org-se/GrudinHCIC.pdf

Guida, G., & Tasso, C. (1994). *Design and development of knowledge-based systems: From life cycle to development methodology*. Chichester, UK: John Wiley & Sons.

Guinchard, C. (2002). Dublin Core use in libraries: A survey. *OCLC Systems & Services*, *18*(1), 40–50. doi:10.1108/10650750210418190

Gupta, B., Iyer, L. S., & Aronson, J. E. (2000). Knowledge management: Practices and challenges. *Industrial Management & Data Systems*, *100*(1), 17–21. doi:10.1108/02635570010273018

Guptara, P. (1999). Why knowledge management fails. *Knowledge Management Review*, *9*(July/August), 26–29.

Guthrie, J., Petty, R., & Ricceri, F. (2006). The voluntary reporting of intellectual capital. Comparing evidence from Hong Kong and Australia. *Journal of Intellectual Capital*, *7*(2), 254–271. doi:10.1108/14691930610661890

Hackett, B. (2000). *Beyond knowledge management: New ways to work and learn*. New York, NY: The Conference Board.

Hájek, P., & Godó, L. (1997). Deductive systems of fuzzy logic. In *Fuzzy Structures Current Trends*.

Halstead, D., Hartman, D., & Schmidt, S. L. (1994). Multisource effects on the satisfaction formation process. *Journal of the Academy of Marketing Science*, *22*, 114–129. doi:10.1177/0092070394222002

Halverson, C. A., Erickson, T., & Ackerman, M. S. (2004). Behind the help desk: Evolution of a knowledge management system in a large organization. *Proceedings of the 2004 ACM Conference on Computer Supported Cooperative Work (CSCW '04)*, *6*(3), 304 – 313.

Hamm, S. (2006, October 23). IBM Takes on Amazon. *Business Week*. Retrieved from http://www.businessweek.com/technology/content/oct2006/tc20061023_158174.htm?chan=top+news_top+news+index_businessweek+exclusives, Hargadon, A., & Sutton, R. (2000). Building innovation factory. *Harvard Business Review*, 157-166.

Hammond, T., Hannay, T., Lund, B., & Scott, J. (2005). Social bookmarking tools (I). *D-Lib Magazine*, *11*(4), 1–21. doi:10.1045/april2005-hammond

Han, K. H., & Park, J. W. (2009). Process-centred knowledge model and enterprise ontology for the development of knowledge management system. *Expert Systems with Applications*, *36*(4), 7441–7447. doi:10.1016/j.eswa.2008.09.031

Hansen, H. R. (1995). Conceptual framework and guidelines for the implementation of mass information systems. *Information & Management*, *28*(2), 125–142. doi:10.1016/0378-7206(95)94021-4

Hargadon, A., & Sutton, R. I. (1997). Technology brokering and innovation in a product development firm. *Administrative Science Quarterly*, *42*, 716–749. doi:10.2307/2393655

Hargadon, A., & Sutton, R. I. (2000). Building an innovation factory. *Harvard Business Review*, (3): 157–166.

Hasher, L., & Zacks, R. T. (1984). Automatic processing of fundamental information: The case of frequency of occurrence. *The American Psychologist*, *39*, 1372–1388. doi:10.1037/0003-066X.39.12.1372

Health Promotion Board. (2004). *Report of the National Nutrition Survey 2004*. Singapore: Health Promotion Board.

Helms, M. M., Dibrell, C., & Wright, P. (1997). Competitive strategies and business performance: Evidence from the adhesives and sealants industry. *Management Decision*, *35*(9), 689–703. doi:10.1108/00251749710186531

Herbst, M. (2009, January 9). Satyam's U.S clients face tough choices. *Business Week*. Retrieved from http://www.businessweek.com/bwdaily/dnflash/content/jan2009/db2009019_127597.htm?chan=technology_technology%20index%20page_computers

Hertog, J. F. D., & Huizenga, E. (2000). *The knowledge enterprise: Implementation of intelligent business strategies*. London, UK: Imperial College Press.

Heymann, P., & Garcia-Molina, H. (2006). *Collaborative creation of communal hierarchical taxonomies in social tagging systems.* InfoLab Technical Report 2006-10. Retrieved March 10, 2010 from http://ilpubs.stanford.edu:8090/775/1/2006-10.pdf

Hill, P. (1999). Tangibles, intangibles and services: A new taxonomy for the classification of output. *The Canadian Journal of Economics. Revue Canadienne d'Economique*, *32*, 426–446. doi:10.2307/136430

Hipp, C., & Grupp, H. (2005). Innovation in service sector: The demand for service-specific measurement concepts and typologies. *Research Policy*, *34*, 517–535. doi:10.1016/j.respol.2005.03.002

Hlavacka, S., Bacharova, L., Rusnakova, V., & Wagner, R. (2001). Performance implications of porter's generic strategies in Slovak hospital. *Journal of Management in Medicine*, *15*(1), 33–66. doi:10.1108/02689230110386489

Hoffman, D. L., & Novak, T. P. (1996). Marketing in hypermedia computer-mediated environments: Conceptual foundations. *JMR, Journal of Marketing Research*, *60*(7), 50–68.

Ho, G. T. S., Lau, H. C. W., Ip, W. H., & Ning, A. (2004). An intelligent information infrastructure to support the streamlining of integrated logistics workflow. *Expert Systems: International Journal of Knowledge Engineering and Neural Networks*, *21*(3), 123–137. doi:10.1111/j.1468-0394.2004.00269.x

Höhle, U., & Rodabaugh, S. E. (1999). *Mathematics of fuzzy sets: Logic, topology, and measure theory*. Kluwer Academic.

Hollingsworth, D. (2005). *The workflow reference model*. Workflow Management Coalition, Tech. Rep. TC00-1003.

Holmes, T. J., & Schmitz, J. A. Jr. (1990). A theory of entrepreneurship and its application to the study of business transfers. *The Journal of Political Economy*, *98*(4), 265–294. doi:10.1086/261678

Hommen, L., & Doloreux, D. (2004). Bring back labour in: A 'new' point of departure for the regional innovation approach. In Flensburg, P., Hörte, S. A., & Karlsson, K. (Eds.), *Knowledge spillovers and knowledge management in industrial clusters and industrial networks*. London, UK: Edward Elgar Publisher.

Hong, L., Chi, E. H., Budiu, R., Pirolli, P., & Nelson, L. (2008). SparTag.Us: A low cost tagging system for foraging of web content. *Proceedings of the Working Conference on Advanced Visual Interfaces (AVI '08)*, (pp. 65-72).

Hormozi, A. M., & Giles, S. (2004). Data mining: A competitive weapon for banking and retail industries. *Information Systems Management*, *1*, 62–71. doi:10.1201/1078/44118.21.2.20040301/80423.9

Hotho, A., Jaschke, R., Schmitz, C., & Stumme, G. (2006). Information retrieval in folksonomies: Search and ranking. *The Semantic Web: Research and Applications. Lecture Notes in Computer Science*, *4011*, 411–426. doi:10.1007/11762256_31

Howard, G. (2000). *Intelligence reframed: Multiple intelligences for the 21st century.*

Howard, J. A., & Sheth, J. N. (1969). *The theory of buyer behavior*. New York, NY: John Wiley and Sons.

Hübner, J., Sichman, J., & Boissier, O. (2007). Developing organised multiagent systems using the Moise+ model: programming issues at the system and agent levels. *International Journal of Agent-Oriented Software Engineering*, *1*(3/4), 370–395. doi:10.1504/IJAOSE.2007.016266

Huget, M., & Odell, J. (2004). Representing agent interaction protocols with agent UML. In *Proceedings of the 3rd International Joint Conference on Autonomous Agents and Multiagent Systems*, Vol. 3, (pp. 1244–1245). IEEE Computer Society.

Hunt, S. D. (2000). *A general theory of competition: Resources, competence, productivity, economic growth.* London, UK: Sage.

Hunt, S. D. (2002). Marketing and a general theory of competition. *Journal of Marketing Management*, *18*(1/2), 239–247. doi:10.1362/0267257022775909

Hunt, S. D., & Derozier, C. (2004). The normative imperatives of business and marketing strategy: grounding strategy in resource advantage theory. *Journal of Business and Industrial Marketing*, *19*(1), 5–22. doi:10.1108/08858620410516709

Hu, Y. L., & Xiao, X. L. (2003). *Supermarket marketing.* China: Business Administration Publication. (In Chinese)

IFC and World Bank. (2009). *Doing business 2010.* London, UK: Palgrave Macmillan.

Information Technology Infrastructure Library ITIL. (2001). *The office of governement commerce.* Retrieved from http://www.itil-officialsite.com

Institute of Medicine. (1999). *To err is human: Building a safer health system*. Washington, DC: National Academy Press.

Institute of Medicine. (2001). *Crossing the quality chasm: A New health system for the 21st century*. Washington, DC: National Academy Press.

Isakowitz, T., Bieber, M., & Vitali, F. (1998). Web information systems. *Communications of the ACM*, *41*(7), 78–80. doi:10.1145/278476.278490

Jackson, C. M., Chow, C., & Leitch, R. A. (1997). Toward an understanding of the behavioral intention to use an information system. *Decision Sciences*, *28*(2), 357–390. doi:10.1111/j.1540-5915.1997.tb01315.x

James, G. E. (1996). *Chaos theory: The essentials for military applications*. Newport, RI: Naval War College.

Jarvis, P. (2009). Learning to be a person in society. Learning to be me. In Illeris, K. (Ed.), *Contemporary theories of learning. Learning theorists...in their own words* (pp. 21–34). New York, NY: Routledge.

JCAHO. (2006). *Reporting of medical/health care errors: A policy statement*. Joint Commission on Accreditation of Healthcare Organizations.

Jianan, W., & DeSarbo, W. S. (2005). Market segmentation for customer satisfaction studies via a new latent structure multidimensional scaling model. *Applied Stochastic Models in Business and Industry*, *21*(4/5), 303–309.

Jindal, T. (2008). Ride the tiger. *Financial Management*, *1*, 20–23.

Johannessen, J., Olaisen, J., & Olsen, B. (2001). Mismanagement of tacit knowledge: The importance of tacit knowledge, the danger of information technology and what to do about it. *International Journal of Information Management*, *21*, 3–20. doi:10.1016/S0268-4012(00)00047-5

Johansson, U., Koga, C., Skoog, M., & Henningsson, J. (2006). The Japanese Government's intellectual capital reporting guideline. What are the challenges for firms and capital markets agents? *Journal of Intellectual Capital*, *7*(4), 474–491. doi:10.1108/14691930610709121

Johnson, E., & Dynes, S. (2007, June 7-8). *Inadvertent disclosure: Information leaks in the extended enterprise.* Paper presented at the the 6th Workshop on the Economics of Information Security, Pittsburgh, PA.

Johnson, C., & Mathews, B. P. (1997). The influence of experience on service expectations. *International Journal of Service Industry Management, 8*(4), 290–305. doi:10.1108/09564239710174381

Johnston, R. (1995). The determinants of service quality: Satisfiers and dissatisfiers. *International Journal of Service Industry Management, 6*(4), 53–71. doi:10.1108/09564239510101536

Jorgenson, D. W., Goettle, R. J., Ho, M., Slesnick, D. T., & Wilcoxen, P. J. (2008). U.S. labor supply and demand in the long run. *Journal of Policy Modeling, 30*(4), 603–618. doi:10.1016/j.jpolmod.2008.04.008

Jovanović, J., Gašević, D., Brooks, C., Devedžić, V., Hatala, M., Eap, T., & Richards, G. (2007). Using Semantic Web technologies to analyze learning content. *IEEE Internet Computing, 11*(5), 45–53. doi:10.1109/MIC.2007.116

Jovanovic, M., Starcevic, D., Stavljanin, V., & Minovic, M. (2008). Lecture Notes in Computer Science: *Vol. 5288. Educational games design issues: Motivation and multimodal interaction* (pp. 215–224). Berlin, Germany: Springer-Verlag.

Jung, J., Choi, I., & Song, M. (2007). An integration architecture for knowledge management systems and business process management systems. *Computers in Industry, 58*(1), 21–34. doi:10.1016/j.compind.2006.03.001

Kahaner, L. (1997). *Competitive intelligence: How to gather, analyse and use information to move your business to the top.* New York, NY: Simon and Schuster.

Kang, R., & Fu, W. (2010). Exploratory information search by domain experts and novices. *Proceedings of the 15th International Conference on Intelligent User Interfaces (IUI '10)*, (pp. 329–332).

Karahanna, E., Straub, D. W., & Chervany, N. L. (1999). Information technology adoption across time: A cross sectional comparison of pre-adoption and post-adoption beliefs. *Management Information Systems Quarterly, 23*(2), 183–213. doi:10.2307/249751

Kaufmann, A., & Gupta, M. M. (1985). *Introduction to fuzzy arithmetic.* V.N. Reinhold.

Keegan, J. (2003). *Intelligence in war: Knowledge of the enemy from Napoleon to Al-Qaeda.* New York, NY: Knopf.

Kelliher, F., & Rainl, L. (2009). A resource-based view of micro-firms management practice. *Journal of Small Business and Enterprise Development, 16*(3), 521–532. doi:10.1108/14626000910977206

Kenteris, M., Gavalas, D., & Economou, D. (2009). An innovative mobile electronic tourist guide application. *Personal and Ubiquitous Computing, 13*(2), 103–118. doi:10.1007/s00779-007-0191-y

Kickmeier-Rust, M., & Albert, D. (2008). *The ELEKTRA ontology model: A learner-centered approach to resource description. Advances in Web Based Learning – ICWL 2007* (pp. 78–89). Berlin, Germany: Springer-Verlag.

Kijoo, K., & Kim, E. B. (2006). Suggestions to enhance the cyber store customers satisfaction. *Journal of American Academy of Business, 9*(1), 233–240.

Kim, L. (1997). *Imitation to innovation: The dynamics of Korean technological learning.* Boston, MA: Harvard Business School Press.

Kipp, M. E. I. (2008). @toread and cool: Subjective, affective and associative factors in tagging. *Proceedings of the 36th Annual Conference of the Canadian Association for Information Science (CAIS).* Retrieved July 25, 2011, from www.cais-acsi.ca/proceedings/2008/kipp_2008.pdf

Kipp, M. E. I. (2010). User, author and professional indexing in context: An exploration of tagging practices on CiteULike / Le contexte de l'indexation des usagers, des créateurs et des professionnels: une exploration des pratiques d'étiquetage social sur CiteULike. *Canadian Journal of Information and Library Science, 35*(1), 17–48.

Kisielius, J., & Sternthal, B. (1984). Detecting and explaining vividness effects in attitudinal judgments. *JMR, Journal of Marketing Research, 21*, 54–64. doi:10.2307/3151792

Klein, G., & Klinger, D. (1991). Naturalistic decision making. *Human Systems IAC Gateway, 2*(1), 16–19.

KM-Huis. (2011). Retrieved April 17, 2011, from http://www.fedweb.belgium.be/nl/over_de_organisatie/kennismanagement/

Kohavi, R., Rothleder, N. J., & Simoudis, E. (2002). Emerging trends in business analytics. *Communications of the ACM*, *45*(8), 45–48. doi:10.1145/545151.545177

Kolb, D. A. (1984). *Experiential learning. Experience as the source of learning and development*. New Jersey: Prentice-Hall P T R.

Korres, G. (2011). *A Handbook of innovation economics*. New York, NY: Nova Publishers.

Kostas, M., Psarras, J., & Papastefanatos, S. (2002). Knowledge and information management in elearning environments: The user agent architecture. *Information Management & Computer Security*, *10*(4), 165–170. doi:10.1108/09685220210436958

Kotler, P., & Keller, K. L. (2004). *Marketing management* (12th ed.). Upper Saddle River, NJ: Prentice-Hall.

Krieg, R. (2004). Impact of structured product definition on market success. *International Journal of Quality & Reliability Management*, *21*(9), 991–1002. doi:10.1108/02656710410561808

Kriegsman, M., & Barletta, R. (1993). Building a case-based help desk application. *IEEE Expert*, *8*(6), 18–26. doi:10.1109/64.248349

Krogh, G. V., Ichijo, K., & Nonaka, I. (2000). *Enabling knowledge creation: How to unlock the mystery of tacit knowledge and release the power of innovation*. New York, NY: Oxford University Press.

Kühn, O., & Abecker, A. (1997). Corporate memories for knowledge management in industrial practice: Prospects and challenges. *Journal of Universal Computer Science*, *3*(8), 929–954.

Kumar, P., Varma, K. I., & Sureka, A. (2011). Fuzzy based clustering algorithm for privacy preserving data mining. *International Journal of Business Information Systems*, *7*(1), 27–40. doi:10.1504/IJBIS.2011.037295

Kuruvilla, S. J., & Ganguli, J. (2008). Mall development and operations: An Indian perspective. *Journal of Retail & Leisure Property*, *7*(3), 204–215. doi:10.1057/rlp.2008.14

Kwon, O., Kim, M., & Choi, K. (1994). Query expansion using domain-adapted, weighted thesaurus in an extended Boolean Model. In N. R. Adam, B. K. Bhargava, & Y. Yesha (Eds.), *Proceedings of the Third International Conference on Information and Knowledge Management* (CIKM '94), (pp. 140–146).

Lai, J., & Fan, Y. (2002). Workflow and knowledge management: Approaching an integration. In Han, Y., Tai, S., & Wikarski, D. (Eds.), *LNCS 2480* (pp. 16–29). Springer. doi:10.1007/3-540-45785-2_2

Lai, L. F. (2007). A knowledge engineering approach to knowledge management. *Information Sciences*, *177*(19), 4072–4094. doi:10.1016/j.ins.2007.02.028

Lane, M. S., & Koronios, A. (2001). A balanced approach to capturing user requirements in business-to-user web information systems. *Australian Journal of Information Systems*, *9*(1), 61–69.

Lassila, O. (1998). Web metadata: A matter of semantics. *Internet Computing, IEEE*, *2*(4), 30–37. doi:10.1109/4236.707688

Lazarou, J., Pomeranz, B. H., & Corey, P. N. (1998). Incidence of adverse drug reactions in hospitalized patients: A meta-analysis of prospective studies. *Journal of the American Medical Association*, *279*(15), 1200–1205. doi:10.1001/jama.279.15.1200

Leape, L. L. (1993). Preventing medical injury. *Quality Review Bulletin*, *19*(5), 144–149.

Lee, K. J. (2006). What goes around comes around: An analysis of Del.icio.us as social space. *Proceedings of the 2006 20th anniversary conference on Computer Supported Cooperative Work* (CSCW '06), (pp. 191-194).

Lee, C. C. (1990). Fuzzy logic in control systems: Fuzzy logic controller-parts 1 and 2. *IEEE Transactions on Systems, Man, and Cybernetics*, *20*(2), 404–435. doi:10.1109/21.52551

Leela-Rani. (2008). Consumer reactions to retail out-of-stock: Replication into new contexts. *International Journal of Indian Culture and Business Management*, *1*(3), 319–334. doi:10.1504/IJICBM.2008.017788

Lee-Smeltzer, K.-H. (2000). Finding the needle: Controlled vocabularies, resource discovery, and Dublin Core. *Library Collections, Acquisitions & Technical Services*, *24*(2), 205–215. doi:10.1016/S1464-9055(00)00131-7

Lehtinen, J. R. (1983). *Customer oriented service system*. Service Management Institute Working Paper, Helsinki, Finland.

Leitner, K.-H. (2005). Managing and reporting intangible assets in research technology organisations. *R & D Management*, *35*(2), 125–136. doi:10.1111/j.1467-9310.2005.00378.x

Leslie, B. H., Koshmal Aring, M., & Brand, B. (1998). Informal learning: The new frontier of employee & organizational development. *Economic Development Review (Schiller Park, Ill.)*, *15*(4), 12–18.

Levy, M., & Powell, P. (2003). SMEs, co-opetition and knowledge sharing: The role of information systems. *European Journal of Information Systems*, *12*, 3–17. doi:10.1057/palgrave.ejis.3000439

Liao, S. H. (2005). Expert system methodologies and applications - a decade review from 1995 to 2004. *Expert Systems with Applications*, *28*, 93–103. doi:10.1016/j.eswa.2004.08.003

Libet, B. (2011). Do We Have Free Will? In Sinnott-Armstrong, W., & Nadel, L. (Eds.), *Conscious Will and Responsibility* (pp. 1–10). Oxford: Oxford Press.

Liddle Hart, B. (1991). *Strategy*. New York: Prager.

Lindvall, M., Rus, I., & Sinha, S. S. (2003). Technology support for knowledge management. In Henninger, S., & Maurer, F. (Eds.), *Advances in Learning Software Organizations* (*Vol. 2640*, pp. 94–103). Lecture Notes in Computer Science Berlin, Germany: Springer-Verlag. doi:10.1007/978-3-540-40052-3_9

Lipshitz, R., Klein, G., Orasanu, J., & Salas, E. (2000). *Taking Stock of Naturalistic Decision Making. Haifa*. University of Haifa.

Liu, Z., & Yan, F. (1997). Fuzzy neural network in case-based diagnostic system. *IEEE Transactions on Fuzzy Systems*, *5*(2), 209–222. doi:10.1109/91.580796

Loffler, J. (2000). Content-based retrieval of 3D models in distributed web databases by visual shape information. *Proceedings of the IEEE International Conference on Information Visualization*, (pp. 82 – 87).

Lowson, R. H. (2003). The nature of an operations strategy: Combining strategic decisions from the resource-based and market-driven viewpoints. *Management Decision*, *41*(6), 538–549. doi:10.1108/00251740310485181

Lucredio, D., Prado, A. F., & de Almeida, E. S. (2004). A survey on software components search and retrieval. *Proceedings of the 30th Euromicro Conference*, (pp. 152-159).

Lu, J., Zhang, G., & Ruan, D. (2007). *Multi-objective group decision making: Methods, software and applications with fuzzy set techniques*. London, UK: Imperial College Press.

Lundstrom, A., & Stevenson, L. (2001). *Entrepreneurship policy for the future*. Stockholm, Sweden: Swedish Foundation for Small Business Research.

Macgregor, G., & McCulloch, E. (2006). Collaborative tagging as a knowledge organisation and resource discovery tool. *Library Review*, *55*(5), 291–300. doi:10.1108/00242530610667558

Machleit, K. A., Eroglu, S. A., & Mantel, S. P. (2000). Perceived retail crowding and shopping satisfaction: What modifies this relationship? *Journal of Consumer Psychology*, *9*(1), 29–42. doi:10.1207/s15327663jcp0901_3

MacInnis, D. J., Moorman, C., & Jaworski, B. J. (1991). Enhancing and measuring users' motivation, opportunity, and ability to process brand information from ads. *Journal of Marketing*, *55*(4), 32–53. doi:10.2307/1251955

Maedche, A., Motik, B., Stojanovic, L., Studer, R., & Volz, R. (2003). Ontologies for enterprise knowledge management. *IEEE Intelligent Systems*, *18*(2), 26–33. doi:10.1109/MIS.2003.1193654

Mahajan, V., & Muller, E. (1990). New product diffusion models in marketing: A review and directions for research. *JMR, Journal of Marketing Research*, *54*(1), 1–27. doi:10.2307/1252170

Malerba, F. (Ed.). (2004). *Sectoral systems of innovation*. Cambridge, UK: Cambridge University Press. doi:10.1017/CBO9780511493270

Malhotra, Y., & Galletta, D. F. (1999). Extending the technology acceptance model for social influence: theoretical bases and empirical validation. In *Proceedings of the 32nd ICSS*, 1999.

Malhotra, N. (2001). *Pesquisa acadêmica de marketing: Uma orientação aplicada*. Porto Alegre, Brazil: Bookman.

Malone, D. (2003). Knowledge management: A model for organizational learning. *International Journal of Accounting Information Systems*, *3*(2), 111–123. doi:10.1016/S1467-0895(02)00039-8

Mandelbaum, A., Koole, G., & Gans, N. (2003). *Call centers: Tutorial, review, and research prospects*. Retrieved December 4, 2008, from http://iew3.technion.ac.il /serveng/ References/CCReview.pdf

Marcella, R., & Middleton, I. (1996). The role of the help desk in the strategic management of information systems. *OCLC Systems & Services*, *12*(4), 4–19. doi:10.1108/10650759610153993

Maria, B. (1998). The evolution of knowledge management with NCR corporation. *Proceedings of the 16th Annual International Conference on Computer Documentation* (SIGDOC '98), (pp. 1–4).

Markus, L. M., & Robey, D. (1983). The organizational validity of management information systems. *Human Relations*, *36*(3), 203–225. doi:10.1177/001872678303600301

Marshall, R. S., Nguyen, T., & Bryant, S. E. (2005). A dynamic model for trust development and knowledge sharing in strategic alliances. *Journal of General Management*, *31*(1), 41–57.

Martin, A., & Dean, V. (1995). Back to the future – A management perspective on distributed support, realizing the potential of information resource: information, technology and services. *Proceeding of the 1995 CAUSE Annual Conference*, (pp. 4.3.1–4.3.9).

Martinez-Tur, V., Peiro, J. M., & Ramos, J. (2005). Linking situational constraints to customer satisfaction in a service environment. *Applied Psychology: An International Review*, *54*(1), 25–36. doi:10.1111/j.1464-0597.2005.00194.x

Martin, J. (1990). Breaking up the mono-method monopolies in organizational analysis. In Hassard, J., & Pym, D. (Eds.), *The theory and philosophy of organizations: Critical issues and new perspectives*. London, UK: Routledge.

Martin, M. P. (1991). *Analysis and design of business information systems*. New York, NY: Macmillan Publishing Company.

Masso, J., & Vahter, P. (2011). The link between innovation and productivity in Estonia's service sectors. *University of Tartu - Faculty of Economics & Business Administration Working Paper Series, 80*, 3-34.

Mathes, A. (2004). *Folksonomies - Cooperative classification and communication through shared metadata*. Retrieved June 10, 2011, from http://www.adammathes.com/academic/computer-mediated-communication/folksonomies.html

Matter Neto, J. A. (2002). *Metodologia cientifica na era da informática*. São Paulo, Brazil: Saraiva.

Matusiak, K. (2006). Towards user-centered indexing in digital image collections. *International Digital Library Perspectives*, *22*(4), 283–298.

McCue, P. (2005). The crucial role of animated children educational games. *Proceedings of International Conference on Computer Graphics and Interactive Techniques,* Los Angeles, California.

McDonald, G. M. (1991). The influence of supermarket attributes on perceived customer satisfaction: An East Asian study. *International Review of Retail, Distribution and Consumer Research*, *1*(3), 315–327. doi:10.1080/09593969100000031

McFadzean, E. (2001). Supporting virtual learning groups. Part 1: A pedagogical perspective. *Team Performance Management*, *7*(3/4), 53–62. doi:10.1108/13527590110395658

Mcgrath, R. G., Tsai, M. H., Venkataraman, S., & Macmillan, I. C. (1996). Innovation, competitive advantage and rent: A model and test. *Management Science*, *42*, 389–403. doi:10.1287/mnsc.42.3.389

Medcof, J. W. (1997). Why too many alliances end in divorce. *Long Range Planning*, *30*(5). doi:10.1016/S0024-6301(97)00050-2

Mehra, A. (1996). Resource and market based determinants of performance in the U.S. banking industry. *Strategic Management Journal, 3*, 307–322. doi:10.1002/(SICI)1097-0266(199604)17:4<307::AID-SMJ820>3.0.CO;2-2

Menard, S. W. (1995). *Applied logistic regression analysis* (2nd ed.). Thousand Oaks, CA: Sage.

Mentzas, G., Apostolou, D., Kafentzis, K., & Georgolios, P. (2006). Inter-organizational networks for knowledge sharing and trading. *Information Technology Management, 7*(4), 259–276. doi:10.1007/s10799-006-0276-8

Mercken, R., Leoni, P., Houben, G., & Motmans, L. (2010). Strategic investment decision-making: Communicating the true meaning of the real options framework to the board. *Argumenta Oecomica, 2*(25), 137–162.

Merholz, P. (2005). *Clay Shirky's viewpoints are overrated.* peterme.com Retrieved June 10, 2011 from http://www.peterme.com/archives/000558.html

Metaxiotis, K. S., Askounis, D., & Psarras, J. (2002). Expert systems in production planning and scheduling: a state-of-the-art survey. *Journal of Intelligent Manufacturing, 13*, 253–260. doi:10.1023/A:1016064126976

Meuter, M. L., Ostrom, A. L., Roundtree, R. I., & Bitner, M. J. (2000). Self-service technologies: Understanding customer satisfaction with technology-based service encounters. *Journal of Marketing, 64*, 50–64. doi:10.1509/jmkg.64.3.50.18024

Miciak, A., & Desmarais, M. (2001). Benchmarking service quality performance at business-to-business and business-to-consumer call centers. *Journal of Business and Industrial Marketing, 16*(5). doi:10.1108/08858620110400205

Miettinen, R. (2000). The concept of experiential learning and John Dewey's theory of reflective thought and action. *International Journal of Lifelong Education, 19*(1), 54–72. doi:10.1080/026013700293458

Millen, D. R., Yang, M., Whittaker, S., & Feinberg, J. (2007). Social bookmarking and exploratory search. *ECSCW'07: Proceedings of the Tenth European Conference on Computer Supported Cooperative Work.* Retrieved March 14, 2010, from http://www.ecscw.org/2007/02%20paper%20108%20Millen%20et%20al.pdf.

Minović, M., Milovanović, M., Jovanović, M., & Starčević, D. (2009). Model driven development of user interfaces for educational games. In *Proceedings of Human System Interaction Conference HSI09,* Catania, Italy.

Minović, M., Milovanović, M., Lazović, M., & Starčević, D. (2008). XML application for educative games. *Proceedings of European Conference on Games Based Learning ECGBL 08*, Barcelona, Spain.

Mohr, L. (1969). Determinants of innovations in organizations. *American Policy Science Review, 63*, 111–126. doi:10.2307/1954288

Montier, J. (2010). *The little book of behavioral investing.* Hoboken, NJ: John Wiley & Sons.

Moon, J., & Kim, Y. (2001). Extending the TAM for a world-wide-web context. *Information & Management, 38*, 217–230. doi:10.1016/S0378-7206(00)00061-6

Morra, L., & Friedlander, A. C. (1999). *Case study evaluations.* Working Paper Series. OED (Operations Evaluation Department), World Bank, n. 2.

Moser, R. (1997). A fantasy adventure game as a learning environment: Why learning to program is so difficult and what can be done about. *Proceedings of the ITiCSE '97*, Uppsala, Sweden.

Moussavi, M. (1999). *A case-based approach to knowledge management.* AAAI Technical Report WS-99-10. Retrieved from June 10, 2011 from https://www.aaai.org/Papers/Workshops/1999/WS-99-10/WS99-10-015.pdf

Mukherjee, R., & Mao, J. (2004). Enterprise search: Tough stuff. *Queue, 2*(2), 36–46. doi:10.1145/988392.988406

Mun, J. (2010). *Modeling risk, + DVD: Applying Monte Carlo simulation, real options analysis, forecasting, and optimization techniques.* Hoboken, NJ: John Wiley & Sons.

Musolesi, A., & Huiban, J. P. (2010). Innovation and productivity in knowledge intensive business services. *Journal of Productivity Analysis, 34*, 63–81. doi:10.1007/s11123-009-0163-5

Myers, R. H. (1990). *Classical and modern regression with applications.* Boston, MA: Duxbury.

Nadkarni, P. M. (2011). *What is metadata? Metadata-driven Software Systems in Biomedicine, Health Informatics* (pp. 1–16). London, UK: Springer. doi:10.1007/978-0-85729-510-1_1

National Information Standards Organization. (2004). *Understanding metadata*. Retrieved June 10, 2011, from http://www.niso.org/publications/press/Understanding-Metadata.pdf

Neef, D. (1998). The knowledge economy: An introduction. In Neef, D. (Ed.), *The knowledge economy* (pp. 1–14). Woburn, MA: Butterworth-Heinemann.

Nelson, H. R. (1997). Virtual seminars. *Computers & Geosciences*, *23*(5), 601–606. doi:10.1016/S0098-3004(97)00029-0

Nenkova, A., & Bagga, A. (2003). Email classification for contact centers. *Proceedings of the 2003 ACM Symposium on Applied Computing*, (pp. 789–792).

Neo, B. S., & Chen, G. (2007). *Dynamic governance: Embedding culture, capabilities and change in Singapore*. Singapore: World Scientific Publishing. doi:10.1142/9789812771919

Nilsson, J., & Eriksson, K. (2008). The role of the Individual – A key to learning in preparedness organizations. *Journal of Contingencies and Crisis Management*, *16*(3), 135–142. doi:10.1111/j.1468-5973.2008.00542.x

Niosi, J. (2010). Rethinking science, technology and innovation (STI) institutions in developing countries. *Innovation: Management. Policy & Practice*, *12*(3), 250–268. doi:10.5172/impp.12.3.250

Nissen, M. E. (2005). Experimental assessment of an innovation knowledge system for decision support. *Business Process Management Journal*, *11*(5), 444–475. doi:10.1108/14637150510619821

Niu, L., Lu, J., Chew, E., & Zhang, G. (2007). *An exploratory cognitive business intelligence system*. IEEE/WIC/ACM International Conference on Web Intelligence. DOI 10.1109/WI.2007.21

Nonaka, I. (1991). The knowledge creating company. *Harvard Business Review*, *69*(November–December), 96–104.

Nonaka, I. (1994). A dynamic theory of organizational knowledge creation. *Organization Science*, *5*(1), 14–37. doi:10.1287/orsc.5.1.14

Nonaka, I., & Konno, N. (1998). The concept of 'ba': Building a foundation for knowledge creation. *California Management Review*, *40*(3), 1–15.

Nonaka, I., & Takeuchi, H. (1995). *The knowledge-creating company: How Japanese companies create the dynamics of innovation*. New York, NY: Oxford University Press.

NQF. (2007). *Serious reportable events in healthcare—2006 update*. ISBN 1-933875-08-9

Null, G., et al. (2007). *Death by medicine*. Life Extension Foundation, 2007.

Nurminen, J. K., Karonen, O., & Hatonen, K. (2003). What makes expert systems survive over 10 years - Empirical evaluation of several engineering applications. *Expert Systems with Applications*, *43*, 199–211. doi:10.1016/S0957-4174(02)00149-5

Obrenovic, Z., & Starcevic, D. (2004). Modeling multimodal human-computer interaction. *IEEE Computer*, *37*(9), 65–72. doi:10.1109/MC.2004.139

Observatory of the European University. (2006). *Methodological guide*. Final Report of the Observatory of the European University, PRIME Project. Retrieved from www.prime-noe.org

OECD. (2009). *Innovation in firms. A microeconomic perspective*. Paris, France: OECD.

OECD. (2010). *Patent database*. Paris, France: OECD.

Ofek, E., & Sarvary, M. (2001). Leveraging the customer base: creating competitive advantage through knowledge management. *Management Science*, *47*(11), 1441–1456. doi:10.1287/mnsc.47.11.1441.10249

Offsey, S. (1997). Knowledge management: Linking people to knowledge for bottom line results. *Journal of Knowledge Management*, *1*(2), 113–122. doi:10.1108/EUM0000000004586

O'Leary, D. E. (2002). Knowledge management across the enterprise resource planning systems life cycle. *International Journal of Accounting Information Systems*, *3*(2), 99–110. doi:10.1016/S1467-0895(02)00038-6

Oliver, R. L. (1992). An investigation of the attribute basis of emotion and related affects in consumption: Suggestions for a stage-specific satisfaction framework. In Sherry, J. F., & Sternthal, B. (Eds.), *Advances in consumer research* (pp. 237–244). Ann Arbor, MI: Association for Consumer Research.

Oliver, R. L. (1993). *Service quality, new directions in theory and practice*. Beverly Hills, CA: Sage Publication.

Oliver, R. L. A. (1980). Cognitive model of the antecedents and consequences of satisfaction decisions. *JMR, Journal of Marketing Research*, *17*, 460–469. doi:10.2307/3150499

Ong, P (2010). *Role of PS21 and leadership in supporting public service productivity*. Opening address by Mr Peter Ong, Head of Singapore Civil Service at the PS21 ExCEL Convention forum and award ceremony, 2 November.

Ordóñez de Pablos, P. (2004). A guideline for building an intellectual capital statement: The 3R model. *International Journal of Learning and Intellectual Capital*, *1*(1), 3–18. doi:10.1504/IJLIC.2004.004420

Ordóñez de Pablos, P. (2005). Intellectual capital reports in India: Lessons from a case study. *Journal of Intellectual Capital*, *6*(1), 141–149. doi:10.1108/14691930510574717

Osinga, F. (2005). *Science, strategy and war: The strategic theory of John Boyd*. Delft, The Netherlands: Eburon Academic Publishers.

Osinga, F. (2007). *Science, strategy and war: The strategic theory of John Boyd*. London, UK: Routledge.

Owen, M. J. (1999). Knowledge management and the information professional. *Information Services & Use*, *19*, 7–16.

Panke, S., & Gaiser, B. (2009). With my head up in the clouds: Using social tagging to organize knowledge. *Journal of Business and Technical Communication*, *23*(3), 318–349. doi:10.1177/1050651909333275

Panteli, N., & Sockalingam, S. (2005). Trust and conflict within virtual inter-organizational alliances: A framework for facilitating knowledge sharing. *Decision Support Systems*, *39*(4), 599–617. doi:10.1016/j.dss.2004.03.003

Papavassiliou, G., Mentzas, G., & Abecker, A. (2002). Integrating knowledge modelling in business process management. In *Proceedings of X European Conference on Information Systems.*

Pappu, R., Quester, P., & Cooksey, R. (2006). Consumer-based brand equity and country-of-origin relationships: Some empirical evidence. *European Journal of Marketing*, *15*(5/6), 696–717. doi:10.1108/03090560610657903

Parasuraman, A. (2002). Service quality and productivity: A synergistic perspective. *Managing Service Quality*, *12*(1). doi:10.1108/096045202104

Parasuraman, A., Zeithaml, V., & Berry, L. (1985). A conceptual model of service quality and its implications for future research. *Journal of Marketing*, 49.

Parasuraman, A., Zeithaml, V., & Berry, L. (1988). SERVQUAL: A multiple item scale for measuring customer perceptions of service quality. *Journal of Retailing*, *64*(1), 1988.

Pardo, A. T., Cresswell, A., & Zhang, T. F. (2007). Knowledge sharing in cross boundary information system development in the public sector. *Information Technology Management*, *7*, 293–313. doi:10.1007/s10799-006-0278-6

Parikh, D. (2006). Measuring retail service quality: An empirical assessment of the instrument. *Vikalpa: The Journal for Decision Makers*, *31*(2), 45–55.

Passemard, D., & Kleiner, B. H. (2000). Competitive advantage in global industries. *Management Research News*, *23*(7/8), 111–117. doi:10.1108/01409170010782307

Patterson, P. G. (1993). Expectations and product performance as determinants of satisfaction for a high-involvement purchase. *Psychology and Marketing*, *10*(5), 449–465. doi:10.1002/mar.4220100507

Peteraf, M. A., & Barney, J. B. (2003). Unravelling the resource-based tangle. *Managerial & Decision. Economics*, *24*, 309–323.

Peters, I., & Stock, W. G. (2007). Folksonomy and information retrieval. *Proceedings of the American Society of Information Science and Technology*, *44*(1), 1–28. doi:10.1002/meet.1450440226

Pham, D., & Pham, P. (1999). Artificial intelligence in engineering. *International Journal of Machine Tools & Manufacture*, *39*, 937–949. doi:10.1016/S0890-6955(98)00076-5

Piaget, J. (1978). *The development of thought. Equilibration of cognitive structures*. Oxford, UK: Basil Blackwell.

Piaget, J. (2000). Commentary on Vygotsky's criticisms on language and thought of the child and Judgement and reasoning in the child. *New Ideas in Psychology*, *18*(2-3), 241–259. doi:10.1016/S0732-118X(00)00012-X

Pivec, M. (2007). Editorial: Play and learn: Potentials of game-based learning. *British Journal of Educational Technology*, *38*(3), 387–393. doi:10.1111/j.1467-8535.2007.00722.x

Plaunt, C., & Norgard, B. (1998). An association based method for automatic indexing with a controlled vocabulary. *Journal of the American Society for Information Science American Society for Information Science*, *49*(10), 888–902.

Polič, M. (2009). Decision making: Between rationality and reality. *Interdisciplinary Description of Complex Systems*, *7*(2), 78–89.

Porac, J. F., Thomas, H., & Baden Fuller, C. (1989). Competitive groups as cognitive communities: The case of Scottish knitwear manufacturers. *Journal of Management Studies*, *26*(4), 397–416. doi:10.1111/j.1467-6486.1989.tb00736.x

Porac, J. F., Thomas, H., Wilson, F., Paton, D., & Kanfer, A. (1995). Rivalry and the industry model of Scottish knitwear producers. *Administrative Science Quarterly*, *40*(2), 203–227. doi:10.2307/2393636

Porter, M. E. (1980). *Competitive strategy: Techniques for analyzing industries and competitors*. New York, NY: The Free Press.

Porter, M. E. (1985). *Competitive advantage: Creating and sustaining superior performance*. New York, NY: The Free Press.

Powers, T. L., & Hahn, W. (2004). Critical competitive methods, generic strategies, and firm performance. *International Journal of Bank Marketing*, *22*(1), 43–64. doi:10.1108/02652320410514924

Prescott, J., Kilty, T., Franklin, G., Cleary, A., Lovgren, T., & Mai, A. (2001). Evolution of three help desks. *Proceedings of the 29th Annual ACM SIGUCCS Conference on User Services (SIGUCCS '01),* (pp. 135-141).

Prieto-Díaz, R. (1991). Implementing faceted classification for software reuse. *Communications of the ACM*, *34*(5), 88–97. doi:10.1145/103167.103176

Probasco, M. (2009, July 20). *Workers flood blogs with company secrets*. Retrieved from http://www.newser.com/story/64791/workers-flood-blogs-with-company-secrets.html

Pucket, S., & Purdy, S. C. (2011). Are voluntary movements initiated preconsciously? The relationships between readiness potentials, urges, and decisions. In Sinnott-Armstrong, W., & Nadel, L. (Eds.), *Conscious will and responsibility* (pp. 1–10). Oxford, UK: Oxford Press. doi:10.1093/acprof:oso/9780195381641.003.0005

Qiang, G., & Harris, R. P. (1990). Retailing reform and trends in China. *International Journal of Retail and Distribution Management*, *18*(5), 31–39.

Quality Interagency Coordination Task Force (QuIC). (2000). *Report to the President, doing what counts for patient safety: Federal actions to reduce medical errors and their impact* Retrieved September 7, 2003, from http://www.quic.gov /report/mederr4.htm#evidence

Rabaey, M. (2011). *Game theoretic real option approach of the procurement of Department of Defense: Competition or collaboration*. Paper presented at the 8th Annual Acquisition Research Symposium (May 10-12, 2011). Montery CA, USA.

Rabaey, M., Leclercq, J.-M., Vandijck, E., Hoffman, G., & Timmerman, M. (2005). *Intelligence base: Strategic instrument of an organization*. Paper presented at the meeting of NATO IST-055 Specialist Meeting). The Hague, Netherlands.

Rabaey, M., Vandenborre, K., Vandijck, E., Tromp, H., & Timmerman, M. (2006, May). *Business process embedded information systems - For flexibility and adaptability*. Paper presented at 8th International Conference on Enterprise Information Systems: Databases and Information Systems Integration, Paphos, Cyprus.

Rabaey, M. (1997). *Militaire Strategie en Informatietechnologie (paper)*. Brussel, Belgium: Vrije Universiteit Brussel. (in Dutch)

Rabaey, M. (2012). A public economics approach to enabling enterprise architecture with the government cloud in Belgium. In Saha, P. (Ed.), *Enterprise architecture for connected e-government: Practices and innovations*. Hershey, PA: IGI Global.

Rabaey, M., Tromp, H., & Vandenborre, K. (2007). Holistic approach to align ICT capabilities with business integration. In Cunha, M., Cortes, B., & Putnik, G. (Eds.), *Adaptive technologies and business integration: Social, managerial, and organizational dimensions* (pp. 160–173). Hershey, PA: Idea Group Publishing. doi:10.4018/978-1-59904-048-6.ch008

Rajagopal. (2008). Consumer response to seasonal clearance sales: Experimental analysis of consumer personality traits in self-service stores. *Global Business and Economics Review*, *10*(1), 68 92.

Ramaswami, S. N., Strader, T. J., & Brett, K. (2001). Determinants of on-line channel use for purchasing financial products. *International Journal of E-Communications*, *5*(2), 95–118.

Rastogi, P. N. (2000). Knowledge management and intellectual capital: the new virtuous reality of competitiveness. *Human Systems Management*, *19*(4), 39–49.

Reagans, R., Argote, L., & Brooks, D. (2005). Individual experience and experience working together: Predicting learning rates from knowing who knows what and knowing how to work together. *Management Science*, *51*(6), 869–881. doi:10.1287/mnsc.1050.0366

Rees, J., Bandyopadhyay, S., & Spafford, E. (2003). PFIRES: A policy framework for information security. *Communications of the ACM*, *46*(7). doi:10.1145/792704.792706

Reinhardt, G., & Cook, L. (2006). Is this a game or a learning moment? *Decision Sciences Journal of Innovative Education*, *4*(2), 301–304. doi:10.1111/j.1540-4609.2006.00119.x

Report from the Commission to the Council on the Council Resolution of 23 November 2007. (October 2008). *On modernising universities for Europe's competitiveness in a global knowledge economy.*

Rethlefsen, M. L. (2007). Tags help make libraries Del.icio.us: Social bookmarking and tagging boost participation. *The entity from which ERIC acquires the content, including journal, organization, and conference names, or by means of online submission from the author. Library Journal*, *15*(September '07), 26–28.

Reynolds, P. D., Hay, M., Bygrave, W. M., Camp, S. M., & Autio, E. (2000). *Global entrepreneurship monitor*. Kansas City, MO: Kaufman Center for Entrepreneurial Leadership.

Ribiere, V., & Sitar, A. (2003). Critical role of leadership in nurturing knowledge supporting culture. *Knowledge Management Research and Practice*, *1*(1), 39–48. doi:10.1057/palgrave.kmrp.8500004

Ricci, A. Piunti, & M., Viroli, M. (2010). Environment programming in multi-agent systems: An artifact-based perspective. *Autonomous Agents and Multi-agent Systems*, (pp. 1-35).

Riel, A. C. R., Liljander, V., & Jurriens, P. (2001). Exploring consumer evaluations of e-services: A portal site. *International Journal of Service Industry Management*, *12*(4), 359–377. doi:10.1108/09564230110405280

Robey, D. (1979). User attitudes and management information system use. *Academy of Management Journal*, *22*(3), 527–538. doi:10.2307/255742

Rogers, E. (1983). *Diffusion of innovation* (2nd ed.).

Ronchetti, M., & Saini, P. (2004). Knowledge management in an e-learning system. In *Proceedings of the 4th IEEE International Conference on Advanced Learning Technologies ICALT'04*, Joensuu, Finland, (pp. 365–369).

Roos, J., Roos, G., Dragonetti, N., & Edvinsson, L. (1997). *Intellectual capital: Navigating the new business landscape*. Houndmills, UK: MacMillan Press.

Rosati, M. (2001). *Motivating call center agents with goals and measurements*. Credit & Collections World. Retrieved December 29, 2008, from http://www.collectionsworld.com /10papr01.htm

Rosen, M., Salas, E., Lyons, R., & Fiore, S. (2008). Expertise and naturalistic decision making in organizations: Mechanisms of effective decision making. In Hodgkinson, G., & Starbuck, W. (Eds.), *The Oxford handbook of organizational decision making* (pp. 211–230). Oxford, UK: Oxford University Press. doi:10.1093/oxfordhb/9780199290468.003.0011

Rowley, J. (2001). Knowledge management in pursuit of learning: The learning with knowledge cycle. *Journal of Information Science*, *27*(4), 227–237. doi:10.1177/016555150102700406

Rozich, J. D., Haraden, C. R., & Resar, R. K. (2003). Adverse drug event trigger tool: A practical methodology for measuring medication related harm. *Quality & Safety in Health Care*, *12*, 194–200. doi:10.1136/qhc.12.3.194

Ruecker, S., Shiri, A., Fiorentino, C., Bouchard, M., Stafford, A., & Bieber, M. (2010). Exploratory search interfaces for the UNESCO multilingual digital library: Combining visualization and semantics. *Proceedings of the 2010 Chicago Colloquium on Digital Humanities and Computer Science*, Evanston, Illinois, USA.

Russell, N., Hofstede, A., & Mulyar, N. (2006). *Workflow control-flow patterns: A revised view*.

Russo, J. E., Staelin, R., Nolan, C. A., Russel, G. J., & Metcalf, B. L. (1986). Nutrition information in the supermarket. *Journal of User Research*, *13*(June), 48–70.

Ruyter, K. D., Wetzels, M., & Kleijnen, M. (2001). Customer adoption of web-based e-service: An experimental study. *International Journal of Service Industry Management*, *12*(2), 184–207. doi:10.1108/09564230110387542

Saaty, T. (2008). Decision making with the analytic hierarchy process. *International Journal of Services Sciences*, *1*(1), 83–89. doi:10.1504/IJSSCI.2008.017590

Samli, A. C., Pohlen, T. L., & Bozovic, N. (2002). A review of data mining techniques as they apply to marketing: Generating strategic information to develop market segments. *The Marketing Review*, *3*, 211–227. doi:10.1362/146934702763487270

Sanchez, R., & Heene, A. (1997). A competence perspective on strategic learning and knowledge management. In Sanchez, R., & Heene, A. (Eds.), *Strategic learning and knowledge management* (pp. 3–18). Chichester, UK: John Wiley & Sons. doi:10.1016/B978-0-7506-7223-8.50004-6

Sandhu, K., & Corbitt, B. (2002). *Exploring an understanding of electronic service end-user adoption*. The International Federation for Information Processing, WG8.6, Sydney.

Sarnikar, S., & Deokar, A. (2010). Knowledge management systems for knowledge-intensive processes: Design approach and an illustrative example. In *Proceedings of Hawaii International Conference on System Sciences*, (pp. 1–10).

Sauter, E. (1999). The risks and opportunities of learning on the job. *European Journal of Vocational Training*, *17*(2), 14–24.

Sawy, O. A., & Bowles, G. (2004). Redesigning the customer support process for the electronic economy: Insight from storage dimensions. *Management Information Systems Quarterly*, *21*(4), 457–483. doi:10.2307/249723

Schein, E. H. (1996). Three cultures of management: The key to organizational learning. *Sloan Management Review*, *38*(1), 9–20.

Schein, E. H. (1999). *The corporate culture survival guide*. San Francisco, CA: Jossey-Bass.

Schiaffino, S., & Amandi, A. (2009). Building an expert travel agent as a software agent. *Expert Systems with Applications*, *36*(2), 1291–1299. doi:10.1016/j.eswa.2007.11.032

Schiuma, G., Lerro, A., & Sanitate, D. (2008). Intellectual capital dimensions of Ducati's turnaround – Exploring knowledge assets grounding a change management program. *International Journal of Innovation Management*, *12*(2), 161–193. doi:10.1142/S1363919608001935

Schlaak, B., Dynes, S., Kolbe, L., & Schierholz, R. (2008, August 14-17). *Managing of information systems risks in extended enterprises-The case of outsourcing*. Paper presented at the the 14th Americas Conference on Information Systems, Toronto, Canada.

Schultze, U., & Stabell, C. (2004). Knowing what you don't know? Discourses and contradictions in knowledge management research. *Journal of Management Studies*, *41*, 549–573. doi:10.1111/j.1467-6486.2004.00444.x

Seaman, C. B., Mendonca, M. G., Basili, V. R., & Kim, Y. M. (2003). User interface evaluation and empirically-based evolution of a prototype experience management tool. *IEEE Transactions on Software Engineering*, *29*(9), 838–850. doi:10.1109/TSE.2003.1232288

Selic, B. (2003). The pragmatics of model-driven development. *IEEE Software*, *20*(5), 19–25. doi:10.1109/MS.2003.1231146

Shafer, G. (1976). *A mathematical theory of evidence*. Princeton, NJ: Princeton University Press.

Shaikh, S. (2011). The study on the relationship between organisational culture and knowledge management. *Journal of Money. Investment and Banking*, *19*, 21–28.

Shalini, K. (2008). Knowledge management within information security: The case of Barings Bank. *International Journal of Business Information Systems*, *3*(6), 652–667. doi:10.1504/IJBIS.2008.018996

Sharma, S. (2008). Principal component analysis (PCA) to rank countries on their readiness for e-tail. *Journal of Retail & Leisure Property*, *7*(2), 87–94. doi:10.1057/rlp.2008.1

Sharma, S., Goyal, D. P., & Mittal, R. K. (2008). Data mining research for customer relationship management systems: a framework and analysis. *International Journal of Business Information Systems*, *3*(5), 549–565. doi:10.1504/IJBIS.2008.018605

Sharp, A., & Mcdermott, P. (2009). *Workflow modeling: Tools for process improvement and applications development*. Norwood, NJ: Artech House.

Shattuck, L. G., & Miller, N. L. (2006). Naturalistic decision making in complex systems: A dynamic model of situated cognition combining technological and human agents. *Organizational Behavior: Special Issue on Naturalistic Decision Making in Organizations*, *27*(7), 989–1009.

Shiri, A., Ruecker, S., Anvik, K., & Rossello, X. (2006). Thesaurus-enhanced visual interfaces for multilingual information retrieval. *Proceedings of the American Society for Information Science and Technology (ASIS&T) Annual Conference*, Austin, Texas, USA.

Shiri, A., Ruecker, S., Bouchard, M., Stafford, A., Mehta, P., Anvik, K., & Rossello, X. (2011). User evaluation of searchling: A visual interface for bilingual digital libraries. *The Electronic Library*, *29*(1), 71–89. doi:10.1108/02640471111111442

Shirky, C. (2005). *Ontology is overrated: Categories, links and tags*. Clay Shirky's Writings about the Internet. Retrieved March 16, 2010, from http://www.shirky.com/writings/ontology_overrated.html

Shivani, K., & Usha, G. (2008). *Retail scene in India*. Chillibreeze Business Review, India: Chillibreeze Private Ltd.

Short, J. (2009, June). Risks in a web 2.0 world. *Risk Management*. Retrieved from http://www.rmmagazine.com/MGTemplate.cfm?Section=RMMagazine&NavMenuID=128&template=/Magazine/DisplayMagazines.cfm&IssueID=328&AID=3760&Volume=55&ShowArticle=1

Simion, C., & Radu, V. (2009). Relationship between organisation culture and knowledge management in SME's. *Review of International Comparative Management*, *10*(4), 781–790.

Simoudis, E. (1992). Using case-based retrieval for customer technical support. *IEEE Expert*, *7*(5), 7–12. doi:10.1109/64.163667

Simpson, P. (2001). *Naturalistic decision making in aviation environments. Fisherman's Bend.* Australia: DSTO Aeronautical and Maritime Research Laboratory.

Sinclair, J., & Cardew-Hall, M. (2008). The folksonomy tag cloud: When is it useful? *Journal of Information Science*, *34*(1), 15–29. doi:10.1177/0165551506078083

Sinnett, C. J., & Barr, T. (2004). OSU helpdesk: A cost-effective helpdesk solution for everyone. *Proceedings of the 32nd Annual ACM SIGUCCS Conference on User Services*, (pp. 209–216).

Smith, G. (2004). *Atomiq: Folksonomy: Social classification*. Retrieved June 10, 2011, from http://atomiq.org/archives/2004/08/folksonomy_social_classification.html

Smith, R. G., & Farquhar, A. (2000). The road ahead for knowledge management - An AI perspective. *AI Magazine, 21*(4), 17–40.

Soergel, D. (1997). *Multilingual thesauri in cross-language text and speech retrieval*. AAAI Symposium on Cross-Language Text and Speech Retrieval.

Song, J., Almeida, P., & Wu, G. (2003). Learning by hiring: When is mobility more likely to facilitate interfirm knowledge transfer? *Management Science, 49*(4), 351–365. doi:10.1287/mnsc.49.4.351.14429

Souza, R. (2006). *Agent-oriented constructivist knowledge management*. Ph.D. dissertation, University of Twente, Enschede.

Sparrow, L. B. (1991). Managing the telephone enquiry bureau at British Gas West Midlands. In Littlechild, S. C., & Shutler, M. F. (Eds.), *Operations research in management* (pp. 167–173). London, UK: Prentice Hall International.

Spender, J.-C. (2006a). Method, philosophy and empirics in KM and IC. *Journal of Intellectual Capital, 7*(1), 12–28. doi:10.1108/14691930610639741

Spender, J.-C. (2006b). Getting value from knowledge management. *The TQM Magazine, 18*(3), 238–254. doi:10.1108/09544780610659970

Spring, T. (2008, May 23). Work for a big company? Odds are good your boss is reading your e-mail: Study. *PC World*. Retrieved from http://blogs.pcworld.com/staffblog/archives/007005.html

Sproule, S., & Archer, N. (2000). A buyer behavior framework for the development and design of software agents in e-commerce. *Internet Research: Electronic Networking Applications and Policy, 10*(5), 396–405. doi:10.1108/10662240010349408

Squire, K. B. (2004). Electromagnetism supercharged! Learning physics with digital simulation games, *Proceedings of the 2004 International Conference of the Learning Sciences,* Santa Monica.

Stanley, J., & Williamson, T. (2001). Knowing how. *The Journal of Philosophy, 98*(8), 411–444. doi:10.2307/2678403

Stanoevska, K., Hombrecher, A., Handschuh, S., & Schmid, B. (1998). Efficient information retrieval: Tools for knowledge management. *Proceedings of the Second International Conference on Practical Aspects of Knowledge Management* (PAKM98). Retrieved June 10, 2011 from http://www.netacademy.org

Steiner, B., Kaplan, N., & Moulthrop, S. (2006). When play works: Turning game-playing into learning. *Proceedings of IDC '06*, Tampere, Finland.

Stevens, L. (1985). *Artificial intelligence. The search for the perfect machine*. Hayden Book Company.

Stevens, R., Millage, J., & Clark, S. (2010). Waves of knowledge management: The flow between explicit and tacit knowledge. *American Journal of Economics and Business Administration, 2*(1), 129–135. doi:10.3844/ajebasp.2010.129.135

Stewart, T. A. (2001). *The wealth of knowledge*. London, UK: Nicholas Brealy Publishing.

Stojanovic, L., Stojanovic, N., & Handschuh, S. (2002a). Evolution of the metadata in the ontology-based knowledge management systems. *Proceedings of Experience Management*. Retrieved July 25, 2011, from http://projekte.l3s.uni-hannover.de/pub/nj_bscw.cgi/d17469/Stojanovic_et_al-Evolution.pdf

Stojanovic, L., Maedche, A., Motik, B., & Stojanovic, N. (2002b). User-driven ontology evolution management. In Gómez-Pérez, A., & Benjamins, V. (Eds.), *Knowledge Engineering and Knowledge Management: Ontologies and the Semantic Web* (*Vol. 2473*, pp. 133–140). Lecture Notes in Computer Science. doi:10.1007/3-540-45810-7_27

Stoneburner, G., Goguen, A., & Feringa, A. (2001). *Risk management guide for information technology systems: Recommendations of the National Institute of Standards and Technology*. NIST.

Strauss, A., & Corbin, J. (1990). *Basics of qualitative research: Grounded theory procedures and techniques*. Newbury Park, CA: Sage.

Sugiyama, S. (1994a). *Semantic and logic theories in neuron networks*. IEEE International Conference on system, Man and Cybernetics.

Sugiyama, S. (2001b). *Reflex transformation of consciousness*: *Toward a science of consciousness*.

Sugiyama, S. (2002c). *Basic model for muscle control in primitive neural sets with reflection*. First World Congress on Biomimetics. CDROM version.

Sugiyama, S. (2004e). *Augmented agent for multi-purposes*. World Congress Biomimetics, Artificial Muscles & Nano-Bio 2004.

Sugiyama, S. (2005g). Multiple layer control method. In J. A. Meech & Y. Yoshiyuki Kawazoe (Eds.), *Intelligence in a Small Materials World: Selected Papers from LPMM-2003*, (pp. 286-298). ISBN1932078193

Sugiyama, S. (2006h). *Tele diagnostic by Web*. SPIE2006 Medical Imaging, CA.

Sugiyama, S. (2008i). *Fundamental behaviour in communication method*. IEEE/INFORMS International Conference on Service Operations and Logistics, and Informatics (IEEE/SOLI'2008).

Sugiyama, S. (2009k). *Feature extraction in system*. INFORMS International Conference on Service Science (ICSS'2009). Hong Kong.

Sugiyama, S. (Ed.). Imai, S., Kobayashi, T., Takeuchi, A., Hirayu, H., Miwa, S. (2002d). *Investigational research report: Studies on next generation industry and company system*. Tokai Techno Highland.

Sugiyama, S. (2004f). *Agent talk in neural networks*. ANNIE.

Sugiyama, S. (2008j). *Ubiquitous framework in service science. The 2008 Logic and Science of Service*. The New Wealth and Wellbeing of Nations.

Sugiyama, S., & Burgess, L. (2011). Advanced design approaches to emerging software system: Principles, methodology, and tools. In Liu, X., & Li, Y. (Eds.), *Principle for engineering service based system by swirl computing*. Hershey, PA: IGI Global.

Sun, B. D. (2008). Folksonomy and health information access: How can social bookmarking assist seekers of online medical information? *Journal of Hospital Librarianship*, *8*(1), 119–126. doi:10.1080/15323260801943570

Sun, L., Srivastava, R., & Mock, T. (2006). An information systems security risk assessment model under the Dempster-Shafer theory of belief functions. *Journal of Management Information Systems*, *22*(4), 109–142. doi:10.2753/MIS0742-1222220405

Sutherland, P. (1999). The application of Piagetian and Neo-Piagetian ideas to further and higher education. *International Journal of Lifelong Education*, *18*(4), 286–294. doi:10.1080/026013799293702

Sutton, S., Hampton, C., Khazanchi, D., & Arnold, V. (2008). Risk analysis in extended enterprise environments: Identification of critical risk factors in B2B e-Commerce relationships. *Journal of the Association for Information Systems*, *9*(3/4).

Szymanski, D. M., & Hise, R. T. (2000). E-satisfaction: An initial examination. *Journal of Retailing*, *76*(3), 309–322. doi:10.1016/S0022-4359(00)00035-X

Taylor, A. G., & Joudrey, D. N. (1999). *The organization of information*. Westport, CT: Libraries Unlimited.

Terblanche, N. S., & Boshoff, C. (2001). Measuring customer satisfaction with some of the controllable elements of the total retail experiences: An exploratory study. *South African Journal of Business Management*, *32*(2), 35–41.

Terblanche, N. S., & Boshoff, C. (2006). A generic instrument to measure customer satisfaction with the controllable elements of the in-store shopping experience. *South African Journal of Business Management*, *37*(3), 1–15.

The OCTAVE Approach. (2003). *CERT Coordination Center*. Retrieved from http://www.cert.org/

Thomas, E. J., & Petersen, L. A. (2003). Measuring errors and adverse events in health care. *Journal of General Internal Medicine*, *18*(1), 61–67. doi:10.1046/j.1525-1497.2003.20147.x

Thomas, E. J., Studdert, D. M., & Runciman, W. B. (2000). A comparison of iatrogenic injury hospital characteristics. *International Journal for Quality in Health Care*, *12*, 371–378. doi:10.1093/intqhc/12.5.371

Thomas, M., Caudle, D. M., & Schmitz, C. (2010). Trashy tags: Problematic tags in library thing. *New Library World*, *111*(5/6), 223–235. doi:10.1108/03074801011044098

Thomas, M., Caudle, D. M., & Schmitz, C. M. (2009). To tag or not to tag? *Library Hi Tech*, *27*(3), 411–434. doi:10.1108/07378830910988540

Ting, S. C., & Chen, C. N. (2002). The asymmetrical and non-linear effects of store quality attributes on customer satisfaction. *Total Quality Management*, *13*(4), 547–569. doi:10.1080/0954412022014933l

Toledo, C. M., Ale, M., Chiotti, O., & Galli, M. R. (2010a). *An agent-based architecture for ontology-driven knowledge management*. The Fifth International Conference on Knowledge, Information and Creativity Support Systems, Thailand.

Toledo, C. M., Ale, M., Chiotti, O., & Galli, M. R. (2010b). *An agent-based ontology evolution strategy for ontology-driven knowledge management systems. XXXVI Latin American Informatics Conferences*. Paraguay: CLEI.

Toms, E. G. (2000). Serendipitous information retrieval. *Proceedings of the First DELOS Network of Excellence Workshop on Information Seeking, Searching and Querying in Digital Libraries,* (pp. 17-20). Retrieved July 25, 2001, from http://www.ercim.eu/publication/ws-proceedings/DelNoe01/3_Toms.pdf

Trant, J. (2008). Studying social tagging and folksonomy: A review and framework. *Journal of Digital Information: Special Issue on Digital Libraries and User Generated Content.* Retrieved March 10, 2010, from http://journals.tdl.org/jodi/article/view/269

Trevino, L. K., & Webster, J. (1992). Flow in computer-mediated communication. *Communication Research*, *19*(5), 539–573. doi:10.1177/009365092019005001

Uschold, M., & Gruninger, M. (2004). Ontologies and semantics for seamless connectivity. *SIGMOD Record*, *33*(4), 58–64. doi:10.1145/1041410.1041420

Uusitalo, U. (2004). Competitive reactions to market entry: The case of the Finnish grocery retailing industry. *British Food Journal*, *106*(9), 663–672. doi:10.1108/00070700410558193

Uzzi, B., & Lancaster, R. (2003). The role of relationships in interfirm knowledge transfer and learning: The case of corporate debt markets. *Management Science*, *49*(4), 383–399. doi:10.1287/mnsc.49.4.383.14427

Vandenbergh, C., De Keyser, V., Vlerick, P., & D'Hoore, W. (2004). *Organizational changes, employee stress, and customer satisfaction: Emergence of the flexihealth concept*. Brussels: Belgian Science Policy.

Velli, A., Lisboa, P. J. G., & Meehan, K. (2000). Quantitative characterization and prediction of on-line purchasing behavior: A latent variable approach. *International Journal of Electronic Commerce*, *4*(4), 83–104.

Venkatesh, V. (1999). Creation of favorable user perceptions: Exploring the role of intrinsic motivation. *Management Information Systems Quarterly*, *23*(2), 239–260. doi:10.2307/249753

Vermunt, J. D. (1998). The regulation of constructive learning process. *The British Journal of Educational Psychology*, *68*, 149–171. doi:10.1111/j.2044-8279.1998.tb01281.x

Vieira, M. M. F., & Zouain, D. M. (2004). *Pesquisa qualitativa em administração*. Rio de Janeiro, Brazil: Editora FGV.

Vincent, C., Stanhope, N., & Crowley-Murphy, M. (1999). Reasons for not reporting adverse incidents: An empirical study. *Journal of Evaluation in Clinical Practice*, *5*(1), 13–21. doi:10.1046/j.1365-2753.1999.00147.x

Vince, R. (1998). Behind and beyond Kolb's learning cycle. *Journal of Management Education*, *22*(3), 304–319. doi:10.1177/105256299802200304

Visser, M. (2007). Deutero-learning in organizations: A review and a reformulation. *Academy of Management Review*, *32*(2), 659–667. doi:10.5465/AMR.2007.24351883

Vozikis, A., & Riga, M. (2008). M.E.R.I.S: Information system for the identification, collection, analysis and reporting of medical errors. *2nd International Scientific Conference e R A-2 Proceedings,* (pp. 423-437).

Vozikis, A. (2009). Information management of medical errors in Greece: The MERIS proposal. *International Journal of Information Management*, *29*, 15–26. doi:10.1016/j.ijinfomgt.2008.04.012

Vygotsky, L. S. (1979). Mind in society. In Cole, M., John-Steiner, V., Scribner, S., & Souberman, E. (Eds.), *The development of higher psychological processes*. Cambridge, MA: Harvard University Press.

Wald, H., & Shojania, K. G. (2001). Incident reporting. In Shojania, K. G., Duncan, B. W., & McDonald, K. M. (Eds.), *Making health care safer: A critical analysis of patient safety practices*. Rockville, MD: Agency for Healthcare Research and Quality.

Watson, I., & Marir, F. (1994). Case-based reasoning: A review. *The Knowledge Engineering Review*, *9*(4), 327–354. doi:10.1017/S0269888900007098

Watts, B. (2004). *Clausewitz friction and future war*. Washington, DC: Institute for National Strategic Studies.

Webster, J., Trevino, L. K., & Ryan, L. (1993). The dimensionality and correlates of flow in human-computer interactions. *Computers in Human Behavior*, *9*, 411–426. doi:10.1016/0747-5632(93)90032-N

Weeds, H. (2006). *Applying option games: When should real options valuation be used?* (paper). Colchester, UK: University of Essex. Retrieved April 10, 2011, from http://privatewww.essex.ac.uk/~hfweeds/

Weinberger, D. (2005). *Tagging and why it matters*. Retrieved June 10, 2011, from http://cyber.law.harvard.edu/sites/cyber.law.harvard.edu/files/07WhyTagging Matters.pdf

Weir, M., Huggins, R., Schiuma, G., Lerro, A., & Prokop, D. (2009). Managing knowledge assets in renewable energy industry: Defining a research agenda for Scotland's SMEs. *Proceedings of the 5th EIASM Workshop on Visualing, Measuring and Managing and Intangibles and Intellectual Capital*, 7-8 October, Dresden, Germany.

Wernerfelt, B. (1984). A resource-based view of the firm. *Strategic Management Journal*, *5*(2), 171–180. doi:10.1002/smj.4250050207

Weske, M. (2007). *Business process management: Concepts, languages, architectures*. New York, NY: Springer-Verlag.

Westbrook, R. A. (1981). Sources of consumer satisfaction with retail outlets. *Journal of Retailing*, *57*(3), 68–85.

Westbrook, R. A. (1987). Product/consumption-based affective responses and postpurchase processes. *JMR, Journal of Marketing Research*, *24*, 258–270. doi:10.2307/3151636

White, S., & Jagielska, I. (2004). Investigation into the application of data mining techniques to classification of call centre data, decision support in an uncertain and complex world. *The IFIP TC8/WG8.3 International Conference*, (pp. 793–802). Retrieved June 10, 2011, from http://dsslab.sims.monash.edu.au/dss2004/proceedings/pdf/78_White_Jagielska.pdf

Whitehouse. (n.d.). *Office of e-government & information technology*. Retrieved March 26, 2011, from http://www.whitehouse.gov/omb/e-gov/

Wikipedia. (n.d.). *Culture*. Retrieved May 24, 2011, from http://en.wikipedia.org/wiki/Culture

Wikipedia. (n.d.). *Epistemology*. Retrieved May 24, 2011, from http://en.wikipedia.org/wiki/Epistemology

Wikipedia. (n.d.). *Fuzzy pay-off method for real option valuation*. Retrieved April 10, 2011, from http://en.wikipedia.org/wiki/Fuzzy_Pay-Off_Method_for_Real_Option_Valuation

Wikipedia. (n.d.). *Knowledge base*. Retrieved May 24, 2011, from http://en.wikipedia.org/wiki/Knowledge_base

Wikipedia. (n.d.). *Knowledge management*. Retrieved May 24, 2011, from http://en.wikipedia.org/wiki/Knowledge_management

Wikipedia. (n.d.). *Knowledge*. Retrieved May 24, 2011, from http://en.wikipedia.org/wiki/Knowledge

Wikipedia. (n.d.). *Rationality*. Retrieved March 24, 2011, from http://en.wikipedia.org/wiki/Rationality

Wikipedia. (n.d.). *Risk management*. Retrieved April 12, 2011, from http://en.wikipedia.org/wiki/Risk_management

Wikipedia. (n.d.). *Risk*. Retrieved April 12, 2011, from http://en.wikipedia.org/wiki/Risk

Wilcox King, A., & Zeithaml, C. P. (2003). Measuring organizational knowledge: A conceptual and methodological framework. *Strategic Management Journal*, *24*, 763–772. doi:10.1002/smj.333

Wilkesmann, U., & Würmseer, G. (2007). Wissensmanagement an Universitäten. *Hochschulmanagement*, *1*, 1–6.

World Bank. (2008) *Entrepreneurship database*. WBGES08, Washington DC.

World Health Organization. (1984). *Publication DEM/NC/84.153(E), June 1984.*

Wu, K. L., Yu, P. S., & Ballman, A. (1998). Speed tracer: A Web usage mining and analysis tool. *IBM Systems Journal, 37*(1), 89–106. doi:10.1147/sj.371.0089

Xiang, Z., Kim, S. E., Hu, C., & Fesenmaier, D. R. (2007). Language representation of restaurants: Implications for developing online recommender systems. *Hospital Management, 26*(4), 1005–1018. doi:10.1016/j.ijhm.2006.12.007

Yang, Q., Kim, E., & Racine, K. (1997). Case advisor: Supporting interactive problem solving and case based maintenance for help desk applications. *Proceedings of the IJCAI'97 Workshop on Practical Use of CBR*, Nogoya, Japan, August 1997, (pp. 32–44). Retrieved June 10, 2011, from http://www.cs.ust.hk/~qyang/Papers/pubs/ijcai97 ws.pdf

Yates, J. F. (2003). *Decision management: How to assure better decision in your company*. San Francisco, CA: Jossey-Bass.

Yeo, R. K. (2005). Revisiting the roots of learning organization. *The Learning Organization, 12*(4), 368–382. doi:10.1108/09696470510599145

Yima, N., Kima, S., Kimb, H., & Kwahk, K. (2004). Knowledge based decision making on higher level strategic concerns. *Expert Systems with Applications, 27*, 143–158. doi:10.1016/j.eswa.2003.12.019

Yin, R. K. (1994). *Case study research: Design and methods* (2nd ed.). Sage Publications.

Yiu, H. L. (2003). The check point of retailers' own brand development. [In Chinese]. *Journal of Xinjiang, 11*(1), 24–26.

Yi, Y. (1990). A critical review of consumer satisfaction. In Zeithaml, V. A. (Ed.), *Review of marketing* (pp. 68–123). Chicago, IL: American Marketing Association.

Yuan, W. H. (2000). Commercial Chain management and analysis of its issues. [In Chinese]. *Financial and Trade Research, 3*, 29–30.

Yu, S. H., & Li, C. F. (1995). The status and suggestions of Shanghai supermarket development. [In Chinese]. *Market Modernization, 5*, 20–23.

Zadeh, L. A. (1965). Fuzzy sets. *IEEE Information & Control, 8*, 338–353. doi:10.1016/S0019-9958(65)90241-X

Zadeh, L. A. (1988). Fuzzy logic. *Computer, 1*(4), 83–93. doi:10.1109/2.53

Zadeh, L. A. (1989). Knowledge representation in fuzzy logic. *IEEE Transactions on Knowledge and Data Engineering, 1*, 89–100. doi:10.1109/69.43406

Zaltman, G., Duncan, R., & Holbeck, J. (1985). *Innovations and organizations*. Malabar, FL: Robert E. Krieger.

Zandi, F., & Tavana, M. (2010). A hybrid fuzzy real option analysis and group ordinal approach for knowledge management strategy assessment. *Knowledge Management Research & Practice, 8*, 216–228. doi:10.1057/kmrp.2010.12

Zeithaml, V. A., Parasuraman, A., & Malhotra, A. (2000). *A conceptual framework for understanding e-service quality: Implications for future research and managerial practice*. Marketing Science Institute, Working paper, Report no: 00-115.

Zeithaml, V. A., Berry, L., & Parasuraman, A. (1993). The nature and determinants of customer expectations of service. *Journal of the Academy of Marketing Science, 21*(1), 1–12. doi:10.1177/0092070393211001

Zemke, R., & Connellan, T. (2001). *E-service: 24 ways to keep your customers when the competition is just a click away*. American Management Association.

Zhang, C., & Li, S. (2006). Secure information sharing in internet-based supply chain management systems. *Journal of Computer Information Systems, 46*(4), 18–24.

Zhou, M., Bao, S., Wu, X., & Yu, Y. (2007). An unsupervised model for exploring hierarchical semantics from social annotations. In Aberer, K. (Eds.), *The Semantic Web* (*Vol. 4825*, pp. 680–693). Lecture Notes in Computer Science. doi:10.1007/978-3-540-76298-0_49

Zhu, D., Premkumar, G., Zhang, X., & Chu, C. (2001). Data mining for network intrusion detection: A comparison of alternative methods. *Decision Sciences*, *32*(4), 635–660. doi:10.1111/j.1540-5915.2001.tb00975.x

Zhu, V., & Sun, L. (2010). The interactive relationship between corporate cultures, leadership style and knowledge management. *International Journal of Asian Business and Information Management*, *1*(3), 54–68. doi:10.4018/jabim.2010070105

About the Contributors

Patricia Ordóñez de Pablos is Professor in the Department of Business Administration in the Faculty of Economics of the University of Oviedo, Spain. She received her PhD from The University of Oviedo (Best PhD Award, 2001) and completed her education in the London School of Economics (UK) (International Business Strategy, Econometrics). Her teaching and research interests focus on the areas of strategic management, knowledge management, intellectual capital, human resources management, and Asia. She serves as Editor in Chief of the *International Journal of Asian Business and Information Management,* Associate Editor of *Behaviour and Information Technology,* and Executive Editor of the *International Journal of Learning and Intellectual.* From 2008-2010, she served as Editor in Chief of *International Journal of Chinese Culture and Management.*

Miltiadis D. Lytras is Lecturer at the American College of Greece. His research focuses on Semantic Web, knowledge management and e-learning, with many publications in these areas. He has co-edited / co-edits, 25 special issues in international journals (e.g. *IEEE Transaction on Knowledge and Data Engineering, IEEE Internet Computing, IEEE Transactions on Education, Computers in Human Behavior, Interactive Learning Environments, Journal of Knowledge Management, Journal of Computer Assisted Learning*, etc.).

* * *

Ruba Aljafari is a Graduate Student at the University of Nebraska at Omaha, where she is working on a degree in Management Information Systems. She holds a Bachelor's degree in Management Information Systems and a Master's degree in International Business/Economics. Her research is based on three main streams, decision support systems and knowledge management, risk assessment, and collaboration science.

Vozikis Athanassios is a Lecturer at the Department of Economics of the University of Piraeus. He holds a M.Sc. in Health Informatics from Kapodistriako University of Athens and a Ph.D. in Health Economics and Information Systems from the University of Piraeus. He has participated in several research projects related to the analysis–development and implementation of information systems, business re-engineering processes in the health care sector, as well as in various other sectors in public and private organizations. His research interests are in the field of health economics, quality of healthcare, environmental health, E.R.P. systems, health information systems, and digital economy.

Omar Chiotti is a Professor of Information Systems Engineering at National Technological University since 1988. He received a PhD from National University of Litoral in 1989. He has been working for the Argentina's National Council of Scientific Research (CONICET) as a researcher since 1992. Currently, he is director of Research Center in Information System Engineering. His current research interests include knowledge management, ontologies, Semantic Web, and multi-agent systems.

Ricardo Colomo-Palacios is an Associate Professor at the Computer Science Department of the Universidad Carlos III de Madrid. His research interests include applied research in Information Systems, Software Project Management, People in Software Projects and Social and Semantic Web. He received his PhD in Computer Science from the Universidad Politécnica of Madrid (2005). He also holds a MBA from the Instituto de Empresa (2002). He has been working as software engineer, project manager, and software engineering consultant in several companies including Spanish IT leader INDRA. He is also an Editorial Board Member and Associate Editor for several international journals and conferences and Editor in Chief of *International Journal of Human Capital and Information Technology Professionals.*

Andrés Cosmen is Chairman of ALSA CHINA since 2005.Prior to joining ALSA CHINA he was an executive director at COFINEX S.A. in Madrid. For the years 2000-2006 he was Chairman of the Spanish chapter of the China-Spain Business Council. He has a Master in Finance (Instituto de Empresa Business School, Spain) and a Diploma in International Management (INSEAD, Fontainebleau, France). Since 1987, he has lived in Hong Kong where ALSA CHINA headquarters are located and travels frequently to mainland China to oversee the business operations.

María R. Galli is a Professor of Information Systems Engineering at National Technological University since 1988. She received a PhD from National University of Litoral in 1989. She has been working for the Argentina's National Council of Scientific Research (CONICET) as a researcher since 1992. Currently, she is directory member of Research Center in Information System Engineering. Her current research interests include knowledge management, ontologies, Semantic Web, and multi-agent systems.

Angel García-Crespo is the Head of the SofLab Group at the Computer Science Department in the Universidad Carlos III de Madrid and the Head of the Institute for promotion of Innovation Pedro Juan de Lastanosa. He holds a PhD in Industrial Engineering from the Universidad Politécnica de Madrid (Award from the Instituto J.A. Artigas to the best thesis) and received an Executive MBA from the Instituto de Empresa. Professor García-Crespo has led and actively contributed to large European Projects of the FP V and VI, and also in many business cooperations. He is the author of more than a hundred publications in conferences, journals, and books, both Spanish and international.

Israel Gonzalez-Carrasco is an Assistant Professor in the Computer Science Department of Universidad Carlos III of Madrid. He holds his PhD degree in Computer Science by this University. He is co-author of several papers in international journals and conferences and his main lines of research are neural networks, expert systems, and software engineering. He is involved in international projects and he is also an Editorial Board and Review Board Member for several international journals.

M. Hemalatha completed her Doctorate in the field of Retail Clearance Sales from National Institute of Technology, Trichy, India. She has completed M.B.A., Marketing and Systems from Bharathidasan University, India. Currently she is working as an Associate Professor in M.A.M. College of Engineering, India. She worked as a Business Consultant in Pearl Feasibility studies and Consultancy, Dubai, U.A.E. for a period of 5 years in the area of Business plan formulation and Marketing research and she also worked as a Business Analyst in a finance Company, India. She has presented papers in 12 international conferences and has published 15 articles in the international and national journals. Her area of interest includes retailing, shopping behaviour, and data analytics.

Robert Huggins is a Professor of Management and Policy and Director of the Centre for International Competitiveness at the Cardiff School of Management, University of Wales Institute, Cardiff. Robert is the co-founder of the /World Knowledge Competitiveness Index/, and is the founder on the European Competitiveness Index/ and the /UK Competitiveness Index/. His key areas of research include the study of competitiveness, business networks, knowledge-based economic development and entrepreneurship. He is an economic development specialist of international standing, and acts as a policy advisor and consultant to a range of organizations, and is committed to furthering research that informs corporate strategy and public policy, especially practical actions aimed at improving the competitiveness of small businesses and the regions in which they are located. Professor Huggins has published extensively and his most recent book is "Competition, Competitive Advantage, and Clusters: The Ideas of Michael Porter" (Oxford University Press, 2011) co-edited with Hiro Izushi. He is an Honorary Senior Research Fellow at the Management School, University of Sheffield."

Luiz Antonio Joia is an Associate Professor and Principal of the *e:lab* – Research Laboratory on e-Government and e-Business at the Brazilian School of Public and Business Administration of Getulio Vargas Foundation. He is also an Adjunct Professor at Rio de Janeiro State University. He holds a B.Sc. in Civil Engineering from the Military Institute of Engineering, Brazil, an M.Sc. in Civil Engineering, and a D.Sc. in Production Engineering from the Federal University of Rio de Janeiro. He also holds an M.Sc. in Management Studies from the Oxford University, U.K. He was a World Bank consultant in Educational Technology and is an invited member of the Technical Board of the Working Group WG 8.5 (Informatics in the Public Administration) of the IFIP (International Federation for Information Processing). His research interests lie on IT for development, e-government, e-business, strategic use of IT, and actor-network theory.

Aino Kianto is a Professor of Knowledge Management in the School of Business at Lappeenranta University of Technology, Finland. Her teaching and research focus on knowledge management, intellectual capital, creativity, innovation, and organizational renewal. She has authored and co-authored several academic articles, papers, books, and book chapters related to knowledge management, intellectual capital, and innovation.

George M. Korres holds a Doctorate in Economic Sciences (Economics of Innovation) from University of London (QMW) and an M.Sc from Essex University. He is currently a visiting fellow at the University of Newcastle, Centre of Urban and Regional Development Studies (CURDS) and an Associate Professor at the University of the Aegean, Department of Geography. Over the last 12 years, during both his academic and professional career, he has gained an in depth experience in the fields of economics, business, and politics in the area of European economics and innovation systems. His main areas of interest and specialisation include: European integration, social policy and social inclusion, economic and innovation policies, EU enlargement, and the Euro-Mediterranean partnership. He has collaborated with many European universities, institutions, NGOs, as well as academia.

Antonio Lerro is a Research Fellow at University of Basilicata, Italy, where he joined the Centre for Value Management. Antonio held his degree in Economics at University of Rome "Tor Vergata" and Ph.D. at University of San Marino. He also joined Cranfield School of Management, UK, and Centre for International Competitiveness at University of Wales Institute Cardiff (UWIC), UK, as visiting research fellow. His research is focused on the management and the measurement of the Intellectual Capital, innovation and change management, clusters, regional development, and regional innovation systems. He is a regular speaker at national and international conferences and author of over 20 academic and practitioner papers.

Jose Luis Lopez-Cuadrado is Assistant Professor in the Computer Science Department at the Universidad Carlos III of Madrid. He holds his PhD degree in Computer Science by this University. His research is focused on Web based expert systems applications, neural networks, software engineering, and processes improvement. Also he is co-author of several contributions published in international congresses and journals.

Shannon Lucky is a current graduate student at the University of Alberta in the joint Library and Information Studies and Humanities Computing MA program. She has earned undergraduate degrees in both History from the University of Saskatchewan and Photography from Concordia University in Montreal, QC. She has been involved in several SSHRC funded large collaborative research including INKE and GRAND-NCE as a Research Assistant and has presented at multiple national conferences in Canada. Originally from Saskatoon, SK her research interests led her to the University of Alberta where she pursues her work in information organization, digital humanities projects, including gaming for learning, and digital solutions for knowledge management issues in complex organizational structures.

Roger Mercken is full Professor of Auditing and Strategic Information Management, Hasselt University, Belgium. He teaches courses on accounting, auditing, capital budgeting, and information systems and author of papers and books on those subjects. He holds the degrees of Master of Applied Economics, Master of Business Administration, and a PhD in Applied Economics and Business Information Systems (K.U. Leuven, Belgium).

Sari Metso is a postgraduate student of Knowledge Management in the School of Business at Lappeenranta University of Technology, Finland. Her research focus is on knowledge management and professional skills learning. She has several years of experience developing and planning vocational education.

Miloš Milovanović is a Teaching Assistant at the University of Belgrade, School of Business Administration. He is also member of Laboratory for Multimedia Communications. Recently he acquired a masters degree in Information Technologies and became a PhD student in the same area. His research interests include game-based learning, distributed informational systems, and multimedia.

Pak Tee Ng is Associate Dean of Leadership Learning and an Associate Professor at the National Institute of Education (NIE), Nanyang Technological University (NTU), Singapore. He teaches in the programmes for school leaders (Principal-ship and Head-of-Department-ship) and postgraduate programmes for research candidates (Master, EdD, and PhD). Dr. Ng is currently an Editor/Editorial Board Member of several international refereed journals. He was recently a Visiting Fellow at Cambridge University, UK and a Visiting Scholar at Boston College, USA.

Alexandre Ferreira Oliveira is a researcher at the *e:lab* – Research Laboratory on e-Government and e-Business - Brazilian School of Public and Business Administration of Getulio Vargas Foundation. He is also a Professor at Federal Center of Technological Education Foundation (FUNCEFET) and an invited Professor at the executive education programs at Getulio Vargas Foundation. He has held executive positions at the telecommunication industry in Brazil. He holds a B.Sc. in Electronic Engineering at the Federal University of Rio de Janeiro and an MBA at the Brazilian School of Public and Business Administration of Getulio Vargas Foundation. His research interests lie on CRM, e-business, strategic use of IT, and logistics.

Daniel Prokop is a Research Associate in the Centre for International Competitiveness at the Cardiff School of Management, University of Wales Institute, Cardiff. He has worked on projects studying the innovation practices of the UK firms, the impact of university knowledge on the regional competitiveness. He is currently studying for a PhD on academic spin-out companies.

Marc Rabaey is senior officer in the Belgian Ministry of Defense (MOD) where he fulfilled different functions: IT-manager Medical Service, CIO of the Assistant Chief of Staff Evaluation, and Technical Director Royal Military Academy. He is now System Manager Education of MOD. His main projects were the migration of the applications of the Belgian Medical Service from Mainframe to Client/Server architecture and the conceptualization of the IS Evaluation MOD. His current project is the implementation of an Education IS Management in MOD. He holds the degrees of Commercial Engineer (IT) and Master in Social and Military Science. Currently, he has a PhD Applied Economics in progress.

Dinesh Rathi is Assistant Professor in the School of Library and Information Studies at the University of Alberta. His research interests are in the area of knowledge management, social media, e-marketing, human computer interaction, text mining, email-based customer support, and help desk systems. Dinesh has an MS in Finance and a Ph.D. from the University of Illinois at Urbana-Champaign, Illinois, USA. Dinesh also has a Post Graduate Diploma in Business Administration (PGDBA) with a major in Marketing and International Business and an undergraduate degree in Mechanical Engineering.

Belen Ruiz-Mezcua holds a PhD in Physics by the ETSI Telecommunications of the Politécnica University of Madrid. She is currently a Professor in the Information Technology Department of the Carlos III University of Madrid and Technical Director of the Spanish Center for Subtitled and Audio-description (CESYA) under the Royal Patronage on Disability. She is co-author of several papers in lectures and congress. She is Deputy Vice-Chancellor for Scientific Technological Park.

Miroslav Minović is Assistant Professor of Informational Technology at University of Belgrade, School of Business Administration. He is also active member of Laboratory for Multimedia Communications. His research interests include human-computer interaction as well as the development of advanced user interfaces in education and games. Minovic received his PhD in Informational Technology from University of Belgrade in 2010.

Kamaljeet Sandhu is a Senior Lecturer of Accounting and Information Systems at the School of Business, Economics and Public Policy of the University of New England. He earned his Ph.D. in Information Systems from Deakin University, Melbourne. His teaching and research expertise are in electronic services and services management at universities, corporate governance, accounting information systems, management accounting, asset management, and e-learning.

Surendra Sarnikar is an Assistant Professor in Information Systems at the College of Business and Information Systems, Dakota State University. He holds a Bachelor's degree in Engineering from Osmania University, India, and a PhD in Management Information Systems from the University of Arizona. He teaches design research and knowledge management at the Dakota State University and has published several conference and journal publications in the area of knowledge management systems, information retrieval, and healthcare information systems.

Giovanni Schiuma is a Professor at the University of Basilicata, Italy, where he coordinates as Scientific Director the Centre for Value Management. Giovanni is a Visiting Professor at Cambridge University, UK, a Visiting Fellow at the Cranfield School of Management, UK, and an Adjunct Professor at Tampere University of Technology, Finland. Giovanni's research, teaching, and consulting focus on linking knowledge assets and organization behaviour to performance management and organization value creation. Giovanni is Co-Editor in Chief of the internationally recognised *Measuring Business Excellence* (Emerald publisher). His primary research interests focus around the following areas: knowledge asset & intellectual capital management, performance management systems, innovation and change management, organizational behaviour, organizational learning, industrial district, and local development.

Hak Seng is the CEO of the Singapore Health Promotion Board (HPB) where he oversees national health promotion and prevention policies to tackle challenges such as obesity and promote mental well-being. He is leading the effort to create a ground-up health movement, enhancing HPB's capabilities in engaging the 3Ps (People, Public and Private sectors). Hak Seng holds a Master of Business Studies (MBS, 1st Class Hons) from Massey University and a Master of Science in Management of Technology (MOT) from Massachusetts Institute of Technology. He has also attended the Advanced Management Program at Harvard Business School.

Ali Shiri is an Associate Professor in the School of Library and Information Studies at the University of Alberta, Edmonton, Canada. Before Joining the University of Alberta, Ali has worked as Senior Researcher in the Centre for Digital Library Research at the University of Strathclyde in Glasgow, and has been project officer for the development of the NHS Glasgow Health Information Gateway. Ali's research areas include: User search and interaction behavior, digital library user interfaces, user-centred search term selection and query expansion, knowledge organization systems in digital libraries, institutional repositories, and subject gateways and social tagging trends and interfaces.

Wei Song received her PhD in Management from the University of Edinburgh, UK. She has had a solid international experience, including teaching at a range of universities and working at a major US corporation. She is a regular visiting Professor at Chinese institutions while holding an Assistant Professor post at Thompson Rivers University, BC Canada. Her research interests are in the areas of innovation in retail strategy, the U.K. own brand strategic model in emerging markets, Chinese consumer buying behavior and social marketing. She conducts research and publishes the papers regularly. In a consultation capacity, Dr. Song serves as a senior academic advisor for both US and Chinese educational firms.

Dušan Starčević is a full Professor at the School of Business Administration, University of Belgrade, and a visiting Professor at the university's School of Electrical Engineering. He is also vice-dean for Scientific Research at the School of Business Administration. His main research interests include distributed information systems, multimedia, and computer graphics. He received a PhD in Information Systems from the University of Belgrade.

Shigeki Sugiyama has been working on various fields from industrial engineering, control, AI, neural networking, virtual reality, e-learning, embedded technology, computer, to consciousness studies for more than 30 years and has presented more than 70 papers. Sugiyama put much attention on Service Science, especially on a network behavior in a scalable situation. He touched upon setting up a science park project about the matters of IT during 1994 – 1999 and has done some cooperative research works with Universities in US and in Europe about IT.

Carlos M. Toledo is a PhD student in Information System Engineering at National Technological University and a PhD fellow of National Council of Scientific Research (CONICET). Currently, he is an assistant professor of Information Systems Engineering at National Technological University. He has been working at INGAR since 2009. His current research interests include knowledge management, ontologies, multi-agent systems, and model-driven development.

Maria Weir has played a key role as a member of the senior management team at the Intellectual Assets Centre in Scotland. Maria specializes in working within a number of sectors as an intangible asset expert. She has developed and run the extremely successful *Love me Tender* programme which takes an innovative approach to the management and exploitation of intangible assets within the tendering and supply chain process. She also provides specialist support to SMEs, the public sector and Charities/ Third Sector organizations particularly helping Social Enterprises to transform their business models to develop new approaches to making profits and has an extensive track record of academic research internationally. Maria also acts as a specialist advisor to government.

Index

E

F

G

H

I

www.ingramcontent.com/pod-product-compliance
Ingram Content Group UK Ltd.
Pitfield, Milton Keynes, MK11 3LW, UK
UKHW050951290926
15470UKWH00005B/1765

9 781466 609488